CARDIAC CRITICAL CARE NURSING

Edited by

Leslie S. Kern, RN, MN, CCRN
UCLA Medical Center
School of Nursing
Los Angeles, California

Aspen Series in Critical Care Nursing,
Kathleen Dracup, Series Editor

AN ASPEN PUBLICATION®
Aspen Publishers, Inc.
Rockville, Maryland
Royal Tunbridge Wells
1988

Library of Congress Cataloging-in-Publication Data

Cardiac critical care nursing.

"An Aspen publication."
Includes bibliographies and index.
1. Cardiovascular disease nursing. 2. Intensive
care nursing. I. Kern, Leslie S. [DNLM: 1. Critical
Care—nurses' instruction. 2. Heart Diseases—nursing.
3. Nursing Assessment. WY 152.5 C26717]
RC674.C28   1988   610.73'691   87-24125

The authors have made every effort to ensure the accuracy of the information herein,
particularly with regard to drug selection and dose. However, appropriate information sources should be consulted, especially for new or unfamiliar drugs or procedures. It is the responsibility of every practitioner to evaluate the appropriateness of
a particular opinion in the context of actual clinical situations and with due consideration to new developments. Authors, editors, and the publisher cannot be held responsible for any typographical or other errors found in this book.

Editorial Services: Carolyn Ormes

Library of Congress Catalog Card Number: 87-24125
ISBN: 0-87189-880-2

Printed in the United States of America

1 2 3 4 5

To the cardiac critical care nurse:
past, present, and future.

Contents

Contributors

Laura J. Burke, RN, MSN
Cardiovascular Clinical Nurse
  Specialist
St. Luke's Hospital
Milwaukee, WI

Suzanne Clark, RN, MSN, MA
Consultant in Nursing in Private
  Practice
Cardiovascular and Mental Health
Los Angeles, CA

Brigid Doyle, RN, MS
Clinical Nurse Specialist, Cardiology
UCSF Medical Center
San Francisco, CA

Diane Dressler, RN, MSN, CCRN
Clinical Cardiac Transplant
  Coordinator
Midwest Heart Surgery Institute, Ltd.
Milwaukee, WI

Polly E. Gardner, RN, MN
Critical Care Clinical Nurse
  Specialist
Evergreen Hospital
  and
Clinical Instructor
Department of Physiological Nursing

University of Washington
Seattle, WA

Anna Gawlinski, RN, MSN, CCRN
Cardiovascular Clinical Nurse
  Specialist
UCLA Medical Center
Assistant Clinical Professor
UCLA School of Nursing
Los Angeles, CA

Gemma Kennedy, RN, MSN
Instructor of Medicine
Clinical Instructor of Nursing
University of Texas Health Science
  Center
San Antonio, TX

Debra Laurent-Bopp, RN, MN
Cardiovascular Clinical Nurse
  Specialist
Clinical Assistant Professor
Department of Physiological Nursing
University of Washington
Seattle, WA

Linda J. Lewicki, RN, MSN
Clinical Chairman, Surgical Nursing
Cleveland Clinic Foundation
Cleveland, OH

Carolyn Murdaugh, RN, PhD, CCRN
Associate Professor
College of Nursing
University of Arizona
Tucson, AZ

Susan O'Brien Norris, RN, MS, CCRN
Cardiac-Surgical Clinical Nurse
  Specialist
St. Luke's Samaritan Health Care,
  Inc.
Milwaukee, WI

Susan Quaal, RN, MS, CVS, CCRN
Cardiovascular Clinical Specialist
VA Hospital Medical Center

Adjunct Associate Clinical Professor
  and Doctoral Student
University of Utah Medical Center
Salt Lake City, UT

Barbara Riegel, RN, MN, CS
Doctoral Student, University of
  California, Los Angeles
Cardiovascular Clinical Nurse
  Specialist in Private Practice
Formerly, Lecturer, San Diego State
  University
San Diego, CA

Patricia Hooper Wolff, RN, MSN, CCRN
Cardiovascular Clinical Nurse
  Specialist
Memorial Hospital Heart Institute
South Bend, IN

Foreword

Very few of us survived our nursing education without one or more somnolence-inducing lectures on "the art and science of nursing." Often these lectures appeared at the beginning of the nursing curriculum. Usually we greeted them with thinly-veiled impatience, since we were all eager to get on with the business of learning how to care for acutely ill patients. We had no patience for such ethereal topics.

After spending twenty years in nursing, with most of these years spent caring for patients with cardiovascular disease, I now appreciate the wisdom expressed in those introductory lectures. Nursing is both science and art. Nurses are most effective when their practice reflects the confluence of both.

The science required to treat patients with cardiovascular disease is reflected most dramatically in the critical care environment. Here nurses and physicians have learned to use all the products of scientific discovery to ward off death and to limit disability. Nurses have become experts in using intraaortic balloon pumps, temporary pacemakers, computerized monitoring, and a pharmacological arsenal to treat people in physiological crisis. In their clinical practice, they have often achieved the impossible. They have helped to prolong life and to add to its abundance. Moreover, nurses have become adept at using the scientific process in caring for patients with cardiac disorders.

But what about the art? I believe that this aspect of our practice is exemplified in a well-known story in Buddhism, which tells of a woman named Kisa Gotami who approached the Buddha when her only son, at the age of two, died suddenly. Half-crazed by sorrow, she refused to take her son's body for cremation. Instead, she was convinced that the Buddha, known for his sympathy and holiness, could bring her son back to life. He told her that he could do this only after she had brought to him mustard seeds gathered from a house that had known no sorrow. Seeking such seeds, Kisa Gotami went from house to house. At each home, she found that the inhabitants were willing to give her mustard seeds, but that they had indeed experienced sorrow. Brought to her senses by the futility of her search, the mother returned to the Buddha. "Now I know what you were trying to teach me," she said. With that, she lifted up the body of her dead son and carried him to the funeral pyre to be burned.

Cardiovascular nursing requires a blend of many traditions—the skepticism and aggression of Western science and the gentle acceptance of Eastern philosophy. I think that this is what is meant by the blending of art and science in nursing. Nurses, in some instances, can prevent catastrophic illness and prolong life. But they also must help patients and their families accept the consequences of cardiac disease with serenity when no other course is possible.

Cardiac Critical Care Nursing reflects both the art and science of our nursing specialty. The distinguished contributing authors discuss the major scientific developments in cardiovascular medicine and surgery. For example, recent advances in echocardiography and radionuclear imaging—diagnostic tests that we have come to rely on for both initial diagnosis and evaluation of therapy—are graphically described. In sifting through the results of multiple diagnostic studies, we need to know how to tell the chaff from the wheat. Physical findings, as described in the first chapter, provide an important framework for interpreting other diagnostic data.

The authors have summarized the latest medical and nursing approaches to optimize the supply-demand ratio in patients with coronary atherosclerosis, for example, coronary thrombolysis, percutaneous coronary transluminal angioplasty, and pain management techniques. The latest approaches to the pharmacological, mechanical, and surgical support of the failing heart are described, along with the special nursing needs of patients recovering from one or more of the recently developed procedures. The latest research related to clinical nursing practice in cardiac intensive care is summarized and critiqued.

Nurses bring a unique perspective to the diagnosis and treatment of cardiac disease. We are concerned particularly with the ability of the patient and family to cope with a high-risk, chronic disease. We also are concerned with the effect of the disease on the patient's other physiological processes, functional status, and quality of life. We are in the process of developing labels for these targets of our concern in the form of nursing diagnoses. The editor and authors are to be commended for incorporating this framework in their discussion.

But what about the art? Often, as cardiac critical care nurses, we find ourselves dealing with patients and families in areas where science is sorely absent. It may be that researchers have yet to provide the data to guide our practice or that the techniques that have evolved from scientific efforts are insufficient. Then nurses must rely on their professional intuitions to facilitate the responses of patients and their families. The discussions by the various authors consistently reflect this aspect of practice. There are many difficult issues seen in cardiac critical care, such as anticipatory grief, ethical issues related to life support, and the optimism surrounding transplant. The authors treat them with sensitivity and insight.

This text is the first in a series on various aspects of critical care nursing. It has set a fine tradition for those that follow.

Kathleen Dracup, RN, DNSc, FAAN
Series Editor
Associate Professor
School of Nursing
University of California, Los Angeles

Preface

Nursing is in a period of transformation: reshaping its current structure into a different value system. While nursing is evolving, medical advances continue; and so, the challenge for nurses is to keep abreast of these advances while integrating a new structure. *Cardiac Critical Care Nursing* attempts to do both.

The contributors met the challenge of weaving current medical knowledge and techniques into nursing's evolving structure. Medical and surgical developments in the treatment of heart disease at the advanced level are addressed in detail. The pathophysiology and rationale for treatment modalities are described. More importantly, the nursing implications, including nursing diagnoses, are incorporated, highlighting nursing's unique and important role in the care of the cardiac critically ill patient.

We hope that this book will prove useful not only to the experienced cardiac care clinician, but will be valuable to the nurse educator, the clinical nursing specialist, and others who wish to update their knowledge and skills in cardiac critical care nursing.

Leslie S. Kern, RN, MN, CCRN
Editor

Acknowledgments

The contributors and I wish to thank several individuals whose input and support were of great value in developing this book. A special thanks to Bill Burgower, Carolyn Ormes, and Betty Bruner from Aspen Publishers, Inc., for their guidance and support throughout the production process. Thank you to the following distinguished clinicians who reviewed specific chapters: Christine Breu, Mary Canobbio, Suzette Cardin, Suzanne Clark, Stephen T. Denker, Kathleen Dracup, Belinda T. Flores, Kathleen L. Grady, Peter Guzy, James Jengo, Miguel San Marco, Markus Schwaiger, Jan Tillisch, Cathy Ward, Lynn Warner-Stevenson, Dan Wohlgelernter, and Susan L. Woods. Phyllis Faschingbauer's assistance in typing parts of the manuscript is appreciated.

I would like to acknowledge my husband, Aaron, the person to whom I am most indebted. His patience and support with all my professional endeavors has been nothing less than astonishing. I appreciate very much the many hours he spent occupying our daughter Rachel while I worked.

Leslie S. Kern

Chapter 1

Clinical Cardiac Assessment

Gemma Kennedy, RN, MSN

The nursing assessment is essential to the role of the cardiac critical care nurse. The ability to perform an advanced physical assessment and make critical decisions about patient care distinguishes the expert practitioner from the novice. The physical assessment provides not only crucial information about the patient's condition and response to therapy but serves as the foundation for the nursing data base and the formation of nursing diagnoses (Figure 1-1).[1-3] A complete physical assessment of cardiovascular patients should be performed upon their arrival to the critical care unit and repeated at least every 4 hours.[4]

This chapter focuses on the physical assessment of the cardiovascular patient, reviews the pathophysiology associated with specific physical findings, and gives examples of how this assessment leads to the development of nursing diagnoses (Exhibit 1-1). Psychosocial data, laboratory tests, and diagnostic test results are also an important part of a holistic nursing data base and are covered in detail in Chapters 2 and 8 and throughout other chapters. Other books and articles are available that provide more detail on the physical examination for specific cardiac disorders, such as congenital abnormalities, not addressed here.[5-7]

GENERAL APPEARANCE

The physical assessment begins with the examination of the patient's general appearance. Distinctive physical appearance can predict specific coexisting cardiac diseases.[8] Observation may be done during the initial contact with the patient and while taking the patient's history.[9,10] The general build and appearance of the patient, as well as skin color, presence of shortness of breath, position, and verbal responses are assessed.

Patients with chronic congestive heart failure are often thin, malnourished, and cachectic, indicating a long chronic disease process. Jaundice, anasarca, and ascites are late and ominous signs of severe heart failure that are produced

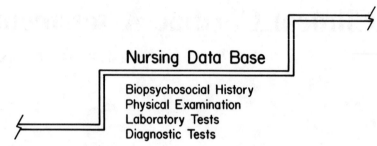

Figure 1-1 The nursing data base.

by prolonged passive congestion of the liver. Pitting edema and engorged neck veins accompany fluid retention because of cardiac decompensation.

Patients with pulmonary congestion often appear restless, have rapid shallow breathing, and prefer the upright position to increase their lung capacity. In pericarditis secondary to acute myocardial infarction (AMI), patients also prefer the upright position, which decreases inspirational pain.

Mental confusion, memory loss, altered affect, and slowed verbal responses may be signs of decreased cerebral perfusion, suggesting a low cardiac output in patients with AMI.

The diagnosis of coronary artery disease can be suspected when minor details, such as an ear lobe crease or raised yellow, painless, lipid-filled plaques of xanthelasma around the eyes, are present.

INTEGUMENTARY SYSTEM

Compromised circulation to the integumentary system is evaluated by the color, texture, turgor, and temperature of the skin. The nail beds, conjuctivae mucosa, and mucous membranes are in general the best areas to observe color imparted by the blood because the blood vessels are near the surface. With adequate tissue perfusion, the skin is normal in color, nail beds are rosy in color,

Exhibit 1-1 Nursing Diagnoses Related to Complications of the Cardiovascular Patient

> Cardiac output, alteration in, decreased
> Breathing pattern, ineffective
> Fluid volume, alteration in, excess
> Gas exchanged, impaired
> Nutrition, alteration in, less than body requirements
> Tissue perfusion, alteration in
> Comfort, alteration in

and mucous membranes are usually pink and moist. Cold, pale, moist extremities occur in any condition related to decreased blood flow to an area. Pale skin (pallor) also occurs in anemia and is best seen in conjunctivae mucous membranes, nail beds, and palms.

Cyanosis is a bluish discoloration of the skin and the mucous membrane attributable to an increased amount of deoxygenated hemoglobin. Central cyanosis is attributable to decreased oxygenation of the arterial blood in the lungs. Peripheral cyanosis is attributable to a marked desaturation of hemoglobin at the tissue level caused by a slowing in the circulation.

Central cyanosis is manifested in blue-tinged conjunctivae and mucous membranes of the mouth and tongue.[11–13] When central cyanosis is present in AMI, it may indicate impaired pulmonary function or shunting of blood right-to-left as found in ventricular septal rupture or congenital heart conditions.

Peripheral cyanosis produces a bluish discoloration of nail beds, nose, lips, ear lobes, and toes. It occurs in severe heart failure when arterial blood flow to the peripheral vessels is decreased by severe peripheral vasoconstriction secondary to a low cardiac output and/or decreased oxygen content of the venous blood as a result of increased oxygen extraction by the tissues.[14–16] When peripheral cyanosis is localized in an extremity, arterial or venous obstruction should be suspected.[17]

Skin temperature is evaluated with attention to symmetric temperature of the body parts. Temperature decreases in any situation in which blood flow to the dermis is decreased. Skin temperature is lowered with shock, local peripheral vascular disease, coarctation of the aorta, and congestive heart failure.

EXTREMITIES

Extremities should be examined for the skin changes described above, clubbing, and edema. Clubbing of the fingers and toes is a sign of chronic oxygen deficiency and is frequently found in patients with advanced cor pulmonale, arteriovenous shunts, and certain pulmonary diseases.[18] It may also appear within a few weeks of infective endocarditis development. Clubbing enlarges the distal phalanges and changes the angle between the skin and nail base.[19] In clubbing, the angle increases from normal (160°) to greater than 180°, and the base of the nail becomes spongy.

Edema is a visible increase of interstitial fluid. The location of edema helps determine its underlying cause.[20] Bilateral edema of the legs that increases in the evening is seen in heart failure and in chronic venous insufficiency. Abdominal and leg edema is generally found in patients with heart failure and cirrhosis of the liver. Edema found in only one extremity may be attributable to venous thrombosis or a lymphatic blockage of the extremity.

VENOUS AND ARTERIAL PULSATIONS

Venous Pulsations

Observation of the internal and external venous pulsations are used to assess circulatory blood volume, right heart function, and central venous pressure. Numerous clues about the patient's cardiac disease and/or arrhythmias can be obtained from these pulsations. Estimation of jugular venous pressure (JVP) is best seen in the right internal jugular vein.

To find the optimum viewing point of the JVP, the patient should be placed in the supine position. Then, the head of the bed should be raised until the top of the oscillating column of blood in the internal jugular vein is seen.[21] Normally, the oscillation of the JVP is seen when patients are at 30°, but if patients have an elevated venous pressure, the head of the bed may need to be elevated to 90°. Shining a beam of light across the internal jugular vein will aid in seeing the neck vein pulsations.[22] The height of the column is established by drawing an imaginary horizontal line from the column to the sternal angle. Regardless of body position, the center of the right atrium lies 5 cm below the sternal angle. In the average patient, the vertical distance from the top of the venous oscillating column to the level of the sternal angle is usually 3 cm. Normal JVP is 3 cm + 5 cm, or 8 cm (see Figure 1-2).

Increases in JVP are caused by conditions that lead to right ventricular (RV) failure such as right ventricular MI, tricuspid regurgitation, tricuspid stenosis, pulmonary hypertension, increased left ventricular end-diastolic pressure (LVEDP), increased blood volume, cardiac tamponade, and constrictive pericarditis.[23,24] JVP may also be elevated in AMI patients because of the compensatory mechanisms of increased sympathetic tone.

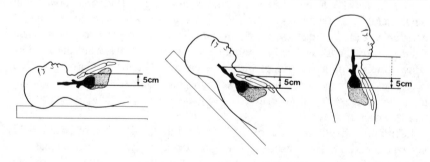

Figure 1-2 The mean jugular venous pressure is measured as the vertical distance above the sternal angle. The latter is 5 cm above the mid-right atrium. *Source*: Reprinted from *The Heart*, 6th ed., by J.W. Hurst and C.W. Rackely (Eds.), p. 147, with permission of McGraw-Hill Book Company, © 1986.

Table 1-1 Differentiation of the Carotid Arterial Pulse from the Internal Jugular Pulse

	Carotid Pulse	*Internal Jugular Pulse*
Respiratory effect	No effect	Decrease with inspiration
Venous compression	No change	Pulse eliminated
Quality	1 positive component	3 positive components
Posture	No change	Prominent in supine position Decreased in upright position

Frequently, the internal jugular pulsations are confused with those of the carotid artery. They can be differentiated by respiratory effects, venous compression, quality, and position[25,26] (see Table 1-1).

In normal inspiration, the JVP decreases as pressure falls in the thoracic cavity and increases with expiration. No effect with respiration is noted with the carotid arterial pulse. A positive Kussmaul's sign (a failure of the JVP to decline on inspiration) is seen in patients with RV infarction, severe heart failure, and constrictive pericarditis. When light pressure is placed over the vein, just at the sternal end of the clavicle, pulsations are eliminated. Greater pressure is needed to eliminate carotid pulsations. Carotid arterial pulses are generally unaffected by changes in posture, whereas venous pulses are more prominent in the supine position and less prominent in the sitting position.

The pulsations of the jugular vein consist of three positive waves, *a*, *c*, and *v*, and two descents, *x* and *y*[27,28] (see Figure 1-3). Frequently it is difficult to see all the waves of the JVP, but usually one can see two prominent waves (*a* and *v*) during the cardiac cycle. The dominant wave, the presystolic *a* wave, is generated by right atrial contraction and can be seen before feeling the carotid pulse or hearing the first heart sound. The *c* wave is not generally visible in the

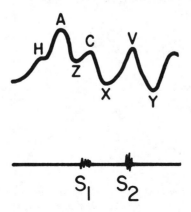

Figure 1-3 The normal jugular venous pulse (JVP). S_1 and S_2 = first and second heart sounds.

neck. It is caused by the closure of the tricuspid valve and occurs about the time of the carotid pulse. The *v* wave is caused by filling of the right atrium by systemic venous return (SVR). At the peak of the *v* wave, the tricuspid valve opens, allowing the right atrium to empty into the RV. It occurs after the second heart sound and is seen after palpation of the carotid pulse. The *x* descent follows the *c* wave and occurs before the second heart sound. The *x* descent is caused by a decline in pressure after atrial systole. The *y* descent follows the *v* wave and occurs after the second heart sound. The *y* descent is produced by the opening of the tricuspid valve. When the valve opens, the RV is filled by the right atrium, causing a decrease in right atrial pressure and in blood in the jugular vein. If diastole is long, a small positive wave, the *h* wave, may occur just before the next *a* wave. Usually the three positive and two negative waves can be seen when the heart rate is below 90 beats per minute with a normal PR interval. Fusion of waves occurs with faster heart rates.

Large *a* waves (Cannon waves) are produced when the right atrium contracts against an increased resistance or when dysrhythmias cause the right atrium to contract when the tricuspid valve is closed.[29-31] Cannon waves are caused by (1) increased ventricular stiffness (severe pulmonary hypertension, pulmonic stenosis, pulmonary emboli, RV infarction, or RV failure); (2) tricuspid stenosis; and (3) cardiac dysrhythmias (complete heart block, ventricular tachycardia, premature ventricular contractions). In dysrhythmias that lack atrial contraction, such as atrial fibrillation, the *a* wave is not present (see Figure 1-4).

Augmented *v* waves are seen in patients with tricuspid regurgitation[32-34] (see Figure 1-4). In patients with atrial fibrillation and tricuspid regurgitation there may be only one visible wave in the jugular venous pulse. The most common cause of tricuspid regurgitation is RV enlargement secondary to RV infarction

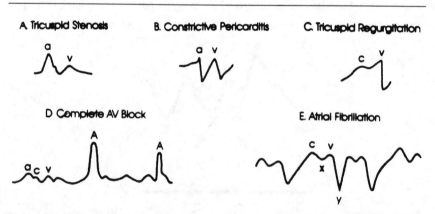

Figure 1-4 Abnormal jugular venous pulse waveforms frequently seen in patients with cardiac disease and/or arrhythmias. *Source:* Reprinted from *Harrison's Principles of Internal Medicine*, 11th ed., by E. Braunwald (Ed.), p. 867, with permission of McGraw-Hill Book Company, © 1986.

and/or left ventricular (LV) failure. In RV enlargement, the orifice of the valve is stretched as the chamber enlarges. It is also seen in intraventricular septal rupture.[35] The *v* wave is normally lower in amplitude than the *a* wave; however, atrial septal defect causes an elevation in left atrial pressure that is transmitted to the right atrium so the *a* and *v* waves are often equal. This equalization may also be seen in patients with constrictive pericarditis (see Figure 1-4).

The pulmonary artery wedge pressure (PAWP) parallels that of the left atrial pressure, and it is similar to the right atrial pressure except the *v* instead of the *a* wave is dominant. The *c* wave again is not commonly seen in patients with normal heart function. Normally, the right atrial pressure (RAP) does reflect the approximate level of the left atrial pressure as reflected by the PAWP (RAP + 7 = PAWP).[36] PAWP is increased in LV failure, mitral stenosis, and mitral regurgitation. In patients with AMI, it is the most critical hemodynamic measurement assessing the patient's clinical status. When there is a normal PAWP, but an increase in the RAP, it indicates impaired RV performance, as seen in pulmonary emboli, primary lung disease, and right ventricular MI.[37]

Arterial Pulsations

Examination of the arterial pulses gives information about the cardiovascular system such as arterial wall structure, magnitude of cardiac output, the state of the aortic valve, and evidence of heart failure.[38] All major pulses, i.e., carotid, brachial, radial, ulnar, femoral, popliteal, posterior tibial, and dorsalis pedis, need to be assessed for amplitude, contour, equality, rate, and rhythm. The carotid pulse is the best to use in assessing abnormal changes, but the brachial pulse may be used if an artifact from radiating murmurs obscures carotid findings. To examine the carotid artery, the forefinger or thumb should be placed lightly over the artery without turning the patient's head.

The normal carotid arterial pulse starts with a rapid smooth upstroke in ventricular systole, felt after the first heart sound. The pulse reaches a peak or plateau that is round and smooth followed by aortic valve closure, represented by the dicrotic notch, and then pressure decreases as seen in the descending limb, which is less steep than the ascending limb. Although the dicrotic notch is seen on arterial tracings, it is not palpable, although one can sense a change as downslope begins. Figure 1-5 shows a normal arterial pulse tracing and where it occurs in relation to the electrocardiogram (ECG) and phonocardiogram, along with arterial pulse tracings frequently seen in the critical care setting.

Hypokinetic, or weak, pulse is slow to rise and has a sustained plateau and slower descending slope.[39,40] It is seen in patients with hypovolemia, physical obstruction to outflow (aortic stenosis), and decreased cardiac output attributable to left ventricular dysfunction as seen in MI and cardiomyopathy.[41,42] A hyperkinetic or large bounding pulse usually indicates rapid ejection of blood from

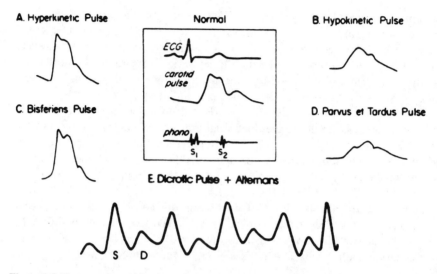

Figure 1-5 The normal carotid pulse and abnormal pulses frequently seen in patients with cardiac disease. ECG = electrocardiogram; Phono = phonocardiogram; S_1 and S_2 = first and second heart sounds; S = systolic; D = diastolic. *Source*: Adapted from *The Heart*, 6th ed., by J.W. Hurst and C. Rackely (Eds.), p. 144, with permission of McGraw-Hill Book Company, © 1986.

the LV caused by an increased volume of blood. It is seen in patients with a high cardiac output (exercise or disease) or with increased sympathetic nervous system activity (pain, anxiety, fever).[43,44]

Pulsus alternans is one of the most frequently overlooked signs of decreased LV function.[45] Palpation reveals an alternating weak pulse with a strong pulse despite a regular heart rhythm. It is appreciated more by palpating a distal artery such as the radial or brachial, since they have a slightly wider pulse pressure than the carotid.[46] Patients are instructed to hold their breath in midexpiration to eliminate artifacts of respiration that may cause false findings or obscure recognition.[47] Pulsus alternans is often associated with a third heart sound and can be confirmed by using a sphygmomanometer. The mechanism of this finding is controversial, but it is thought to be caused by a variation in LV end-diastolic volume that alternates the force of contraction.[48]

Pulsus bisferiens (from Latin "twice beating") is found in patients with aortic stenosis and aortic regurgitation and is characterized by two peaks (two positive waves). It may also occur in conditions with rapid ejection of an increase in stroke volume from the LV (exercise, fever). The first peak, or percussion wave, is caused by the pulse pressure, and the second peak, called a tidal wave, is caused by reverberations from the peripheral circulation. If palpable, it is best felt in the carotid artery. It can always be seen in arterial tracings.[49,50]

Pulsus paradoxus is defined as a marked decrease in pulse amplitude during normal quiet inspiration or a decrease in systolic arterial pressure by more than 10 mmHg (normal is 3 to 10 mmHg). This finding may be palpated, but cuff sphygmomanometer during normal respirations is the best method to detect pulsus paradoxus.[51] The cuff is inflated approximately 20 mmHg above the systolic blood pressure. The cuff is slowly deflated by 1 to 2 mmHg/sec until the Korotkoff's sounds appear only during expiration. Then, the cuff is deflated until sounds are heard equally during both inspiration and expiration. The difference between these sounds determines the degree of pulsus paradoxus.

Pulsus paradoxus is common with cardiac tamponade but infrequent with constrictive pericarditis.[52–54] In patients with hypotension, these changes may be hard to hear. Pulsus paradoxus may be heard in patients with acute or chronic respiratory distress, hypovolemic shock, or massive pulmonary emboli, as well as in intubated patients undergoing positive pressure ventilation.

A dicrotic pulse (from Greek "double beating") is found in patients with cardiomyopathy attributable to decreased stroke volume and increased peripheral resistance or with cardiac tamponade during inspiration. It may also be seen in patients with aortic regurgitation or who are febrile.[55] It is perceived as a double arterial impulse with one peak in systole and the second in diastole, the latter because of palpable dicrotic wave after the second heart sound.[56,57]

Parvus et tardus pulse is a small pulse with a delayed systolic peak and is frequently found in patients with moderate or severe aortic stenosis. The elderly patient with aortic stenosis may have a normal pulse because of the decreased distensibility of large arteries, which alters the arterial pulse.[58]

Auscultation of the carotid arteries occurs after palpation. The bell of the stethoscope is placed over the skin of the carotid artery, and patients are asked to hold their breath. No sound should be heard if there is normal unobstructed blood flow. A bruit or blowing sound is heard with obstruction. A palpable thrill may also accompany a bruit.[59,60] The presence or absence of a bruit does not correlate with the severity of carotid disease.

Arterial blood pressure has an important role in the evaluation of the cardiovascular system. Besides detecting the pressure of hypertension or hypotension, it may provide clues to other conditions or abnormalities of the circulation.[61] To obtain an accurate blood pressure measurement, the guidelines provided by the American Heart Association[62] need to be strictly followed. Improper cuff size and technique can greatly alter findings. The normal ranges for measurements in adults over 45 years of age are approximately 110 to 140 mmHg systolic and 65 to 95 mmHg diastolic. Findings above and below these ranges may be normal in certain patients, and the findings of hypertension and hypotension depend on other clinical findings. In the critical care setting, blood pressure should initially be taken in both arms while the patient is in the supine position. Peak systolic pressure is greater during expiration than inspiration by as much as 10 mmHg.

A greater difference is seen in patients with cardiac tamponade (pulsus paradoxus).

The pulse pressure, the difference between systolic and diastolic values (mmHg), needs to be determined in every patient. The normal pulse pressure is 30 to 40 mmHg. Pulse pressure is increased with increased stroke volume and decreased peripheral resistance, as when patients are given intravenous (IV) inotropic drugs or afterload reduction with dobutamine and nitroprusside. Pulse pressure may also be increased in patients with complete heart block, marked sinus bradycardia, aortic regurgitation, atherosclerosis, aging, and hypertension.[63] Decreased pulse pressure is caused by increased peripheral resistance, decreased stroke volume, or decreased intravascular volume, and is seen in patients with heart failure, cardiogenic shock, or hypovolemia, with peripheral vasoconstrictive drug use, and in mechanical abnormalities caused by aortic valve obstruction, mitral valve obstruction, or regurgitation.[64]

CARDIAC ASSESSMENT

Inspection and Palpation

Inspection and palpation are an integral part of the physical examination of the precordium. Both are best done with the patient lying in the supine position. Dyspneic patients who cannot lie flat may have a 45° elevation of the head and chest without altering the movements of the chest wall.[65] The chest should be inspected from the side, at a right angle and downward over the areas where significant vibrations are usually detected. Inspection is often useful since some cardiac motion is so subtle or of such low amplitude that it is easily missed by palpation but is visible to the eye. Inward movements are better seen than felt. Palpation should be done from the right side of the patient. Examiners need to decide which part of their hand is the most sensitive for detecting precordial motion and thrills. Remember, varying the pressure of the hand or fingers is very helpful in achieving maximal tactile sensitivity. Turning the patient 45° to 60° on the left side will result in a palpable apical impulse in most patients. This left lateral decubitus position can be used to assess the quality of an impulse but not the location. Palpating the chest wall helps the auscultator by giving tactile clues to underlying cardiac disease as well as confirming auscultatory findings. When palpating impulses, several factors need to be considered: (1) amplitude; (2) duration of the impulse; (3) direction of the impulse; (4) location; (5) distribution, if impulse is diffuse or localized; and (6) timing of the impulse in relation to the cardiac cycle. Simultaneous auscultation and/or palpation of the carotid artery may be necessary to identify systole accurately for timing of the impulses. Figure 1-6 shows the major areas where abnormal movements are detected.

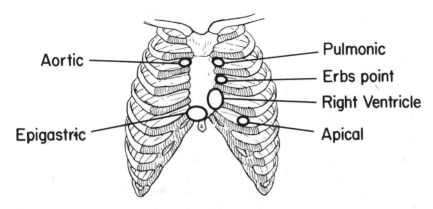

Figure 1-6 Areas for myocardial inspection and palpation.

In a majority of patients, the apical impulse will be the same as the point of maximal impulse (PMI), but in some patients a more prominent precordial pulsation elsewhere on the chest will actually be the area of maximal impulse.

Normal Apical Impulse

The normal apical LV impulse is usually located at or in the left midclavicular line in the fifth intercostal space, but may be located medial or lateral to the midclavicular line.[66] The normal impulse is localized and is <3 cm (no larger than a quarter) in diameter and is usually felt in only one intercostal space. It is an early systolic outward movement produced by isovolemic contraction of the LV and occurs after the first heart sound, before the upstroke of the carotid pulse.[67,68] The duration of this impulse is brief (≤ 0.08 seconds), and the amplitude is a nonforceful tapping. Rolling patients on their left side may help locate the impulse.

Left Ventricular Enlargement

LV hypertrophy has an abnormal forceful thrust, sustained duration, and an outward movement.[69,70] Impulses in patients with LV pressure loads without ventricular dilatation, such as with aortic stenosis and hypertension, are more localized, sustained, and forceful throughout systole and usually are not particularly displaced and may even be located in the midclavicular line. Thrust is felt using the palm or heel of the hand.[71] When ventricular dilatation occurs as a condition such as aortic regurgitation, mitral regurgitation, and chronic congestive heart failure, it produces a diffuse impulse that has sustained thrusting force and may be displaced laterally. When the diameter of the impulse is >3 cm, it is a specific and sensitive indicator of an enlarged LV attributable to increased LV and diastolic volume.[72]

Right Ventricular Enlargement

The outward systolic lift of RV hypertrophy is a diffuse impulse over the left parasternal area extending from the fourth to the fifth interspace at the left sternal border.[73] An outward movement of the sternum may also occur. It is a diffuse, brisk, outward, early systolic movement. This lift is assessed by using the palm or heel of the hand placed slightly on the above area. The impulse may move the examiner's hand anteriorly. This lift is frequently seen in patients with chronic lung disease or with RV enlargement attributable to congestive heart failure, RV infarction, intraventricular rupture, or tricuspid or pulmonary valve dysfunction.

Myocardial Infarction

After MI, areas of the myocardium may not contract normally (aneurysm) and may balloon out during systole. This ballooning is called *bulging* and frequently occurs in the midprecordial or apical area. Bulges are usually sustained throughout systole and may be difficult to distinguish from LV enlargement.[74,75] Palpation may be the only way to assess this by physical examination.

Thrills, Pulsations, and Vibrations

Any loud murmur (grade 3–6/6) can produce vibrations that can be palpable. These vibrations are called *thrills* and have been described as being similar to a cat purring.[76,77] Tricuspid regurgitation can cause a palpable thrill in the anterior precordium. Tricuspid regurgitation is frequently caused by RV enlargement and can also be secondary to interventricular rupture.[78] A thrill located in the apical area is caused by mitral regurgitation. Mitral regurgitation is frequently seen in patients with LV enlargement, which causes stretching of the valve orifice, and/ or with rupture of the papillary muscle secondary to MI.[79,80] In severe mitral regurgitation, there is an enlarged left atrium that causes the heart to thrust anteriorly, resulting in a palpable impulse in the left parasternal area. The impulse is in late systole coinciding in time with the peak of the *v* wave in the left atrial pulse and differs from the lift of RV hypertrophy that occurs in early systole.[81,82] Mitral and tricuspid thrills can be enhanced with the patient in the left lateral decubitus position. Since thrills are sometimes difficult to palpate because of their high frequency, the ball of the hand is placed across one area through a number of cardiac cycles.[83] Pericardial friction rubs can be felt in the anterior pericardium and give a rubbing sensation.[84]

Pulmonary artery pulsations, thrills, and vibrations may be felt in the second or third left intercostal spaces near the sternum. The most common findings are thrills of pulmonic stenosis or vibrations caused by accentuated pulmonic valve closure (P_2) from increased pulmonary artery pressure secondary to LV failure, mitral stenosis, pulmonary disease, or primary pulmonary hypertension.[85]

Thrills found in the aortic area, the second right intercostal space near the sternum, are usually caused by aortic stenosis. Pulsations in this area are also caused by aortic aneurysms, which may be felt in the sternoclavicular area. Vibrations of accentuated closure of the aortic valve (A_2) caused by hypertension can also be felt.

Auscultation

Auscultation of the heart provides a means for clinically evaluating the mechanical and hemodynamic changes of the heart. After inspection and palpation, auscultation of heart sounds should be done over the five major areas seen in Figure 1-7: the aortic, pulmonic, tricuspid, and mitral valve areas and Erb's point. It is helpful to palpate and auscultate in the same systemic order: Identify the first and second heart sounds starting at the aortic or pulmonic areas where the second heart sound (S_2) is the loudest, then inch down to the left lower sternal border where the first heart sound (S_1) is as loud or louder than the second sound. Use the second sound as a guide to time other sounds. In patients with MI, auscultation of the heart should be performed every 4 to 8 hours to check for gallops, murmurs (especially systolic), changes in intensity of the first heart sound, paradoxical splitting of the second heart sound, and rubs.[86]

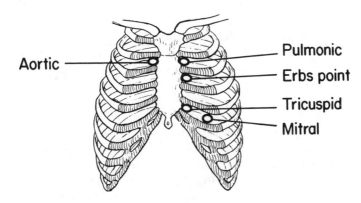

Figure 1-7 Area for auscultation.

Normal Heart Sounds

The first heart sound is caused by the closing of the mitral and tricuspid valves. The first sound is usually softer or of lower pitch than the second sound and is best heard at the lower left sternal border. This sound occurs at the time of onset or shortly after the onset of pressure rises in the ventricles, which exceed atrial pressures, closing both valves. The first heart sound marks the onset of ventricular systole and occurs right after the onset of the QRS complex on the ECG.[87] Physiologically, LV contraction occurs slightly before RV contraction, causing splitting of the first sound. Clinically, this sound is not appreciated since the mitral closure is louder than the tricuspid, drowning it out unless other factors intervene. In right bundle branch block, systole of the RV is delayed, and the closure of the tricuspid valve may be sufficiently late to be easily recognized. However, a split S_1 is frequently confused with an S_4 or an early systolic click.

Accentuation of the first heart sound is heard because of hyperdynamic activity of the heart (exercise, hyperthyroidism), a short PR interval, and in mitral stenosis. The louder sound is attributable to ventricular systole occurring when the mitral valve is still open and then slams shut. Decreased intensity is frequently associated with MI and is also found with a prolonged PR interval, mitral regurgitation, and congestive heart failure. The first heart sound varies in intensity with complete heart block where atria and ventricles are beating independently and in atrial fibrillation. In these conditions, the mitral valve is in various positions before being shut, and its sound varies in loudness.

The second heart sound is primarily caused by the closure of the aortic and pulmonic valves. It is heard at the end of ventricular systole. Normal splitting can be heard in the pulmonic area and is accentuated by inspiration and narrows on expiration.[88,89] Splitting is caused by the longer systolic ejection time of the RV. This is attributable to inspiration-induced venous filling and characteristics of the pulmonary tree causing the pulmonic sound to occur later than the aortic. During expiration, this disparity becomes less pronounced or nonexistent.

Paradoxical or reverse splitting occurs when there is a wider split on expiration than on inspiration.[90] This is found in conditions in which the RV empties before the left, causing the pulmonic valve to close first. This can occur when left ventricular performance is severely depressed during MI, myocardial ischemia, and congestive heart failure. Other conditions that delay aortic closure by overloading the ventricle include aortic stenosis, aortic regurgitation, and severe hypertension.[91] Also, the conduction abnormalities caused by left bundle branch block or an RV pacemaker can cause paradoxical splitting. Surprisingly, the most common cause of a paradoxically split second sound in MI patients is usually left bundle branch block and not LV failure.[92]

Conditions that cause persistent splitting of the second heart sound during both inspiration and expiration are caused by either a delayed pulmonary component (P_2) or an early aortic component (A_2). A delayed P_2 is seen when there is a delay in RV activation as found in right bundle branch block or with an LV pacemaker.[93]

Gallops, Murmurs, and Rubs

LV diastolic gallop sounds, third heart sound (S₃), and fourth heart sound (S₄) are frequently found in patients with transient myocardial ischemia and MI. The third heart sound is produced during the rapid filling phase of ventricular diastole when blood flows from the atrium into a noncompliant ventricle. The fourth heart sound occurs as blood enters the ventricles at the end of ventricular diastole and is associated with atrial systole (sometimes called an atrial gallop). Both sounds are heard best with the patient in the left lateral decubitus position with the bell of the stethoscope over the apical impulse.[94,95] At times, it may be heard over the lower left sternal border and apex when the patient is recumbent.[96] Having the patient cough several times causes a transient rise in pulmonary venous pressure and a slight increase in heart rate, which may bring out faint third or fourth heart sounds.[97] In patients with emphysema or increased chest diameter, the gallop sounds may be dampened; in such cases, auscultation over the xiphoid process or just under the rib cage can be done. Decreased compliance of the RV may cause right-sided third and fourth heart sounds, which are heard along the left sternal border and are loudest on inspiration.[98] Left third heart gallops are louder on expiration.

A physiologic third heart sound is a normal finding frequently heard in children and young adults until the age of 30 to 35. When it is heard in adults over 40 years, it is a sign of a decrease in LV compliance, regardless of the cause.[99] The third heart sound may be the first sign and only clinical sign of a failing heart and is usually one of the earliest signs of LV failure in AMI patients.[100] It is found in atrioventricular valve incompetence and accompanies certain complications of MI such as ventricular septal rupture and ruptured papillary muscles.[101] The nurse's skill in detecting a third heart sound may contribute greatly to early identification of these complications.

The fourth heart sound is one of the first signs of mechanical dysfunctions in AMI and is heard in 98% of these patients if they are in sinus rhythm.[102] It is also frequently heard in patients with angina pectoris. A left- or right-sided fourth heart sound occurs with other myocardial conditions that alter ventricular compliance and increase end-diastolic pressure such as ventricular hypertrophy, severe aortic or pulmonic stenosis, and pulmonary emboli.[103,104] An atrial gallop sound does not always imply cardiac failure, but can be seen in anemia and severe hyperthyroidism, which increase blood volume to the heart, or with age because of a stiffened ventricle.[105]

Murmurs reflect the movement of blood as it accelerates and decelerates at high flow rates through normal or abnormal valves. They are labeled according to their time of occurrence in systole or diastole (see Figure 1-8).

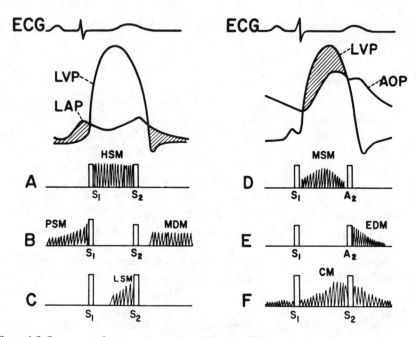

Figure 1-8 Occurrence of murmurs in systole and diastole. ECG = electrocardiogram; LAP = left atrial pressure; LVP = left ventricular pressure; HSM = holosystolic murmur; PSM = presystolic murmur; MDS = mid-diastolic murmur; MSM = midsystolic murmur; EDM = early diastolic murmur; LSM = late systolic murmur; and CM = continuous murmur. *Source*: Reprinted from *Harrison's Principles of Internal Medicine*, 11th ed., by E. Braunwald (Ed.), p. 869, with permission of McGraw-Hill Book Company, © 1986.

Systolic murmurs (see Table 1-2) are usually caused by tricuspid and mitral regurgitation or aortic and pulmonic stenosis. A systolic murmur of mitral regurgitation in patients with AMI usually results from papillary muscle dysfunction (PMD).[106] PMD is caused by ischemic damage to the papillary muscles as well as by stretching of the mitral orifice because of ventricular dilatation secondary to LV failure. It develops over the first few days of infarction, and serial auscultation will reveal at least temporary mitral regurgitation in almost one half the patients. It is a high-pitched, holosystolic murmur best heard at the apex. It is usually louder on expiration than inspiration (Figure 1-9). It rarely is loud enough to have a thrill.[107] The character of the murmur may vary according to the extent of ischemic involvement of the muscles. In PMD, the PAWP is usually normal, and there are no physical signs of pulmonary edema.[108]

A rare complication of AMI is papillary muscle rupture (PMR). Death occurs rapidly as the entire muscle ruptures, but survival is possible if a single head of the muscle ruptures. Patients present with the onset of a new systolic murmur and acute pulmonary edema. This murmur is heard best at the apex and may

Table 1-2 Systolic Murmurs

Type of Murmur	Area	Quality	Cause
Early to Holosystolic	Apex	High pitched Musical	Mitral regurgitation (papillary muscle rupture)
Early to Holosystolic	Apex	High pitched Soft, blowing	Mitral regurgitation attributable to papillary muscle dysfunction
Holosystolic	LSB 4–5 ICS apex	Loud, harsh	Ventricular septal rupture
Early to Holosystolic	LSB 4–5 ICS	Blowing ↑ Inspiration ↓ Expiration	Tricuspid regurgitation (pulmonary hypertension, right ventricular failure)
Midsystolic	RSB 2 ICS	Harsh Diamond-shaped Crescendo/ decrescendo	Aortic stenosis (calcification)
Midsystolic	LSB 2 ICS	Harsh Crescendo/ decrescendo ↑ Inspiration Ejection click	Pulmonary stenosis (congenital abnormalities)

Abbreviations: LBS = left sternal border; ICS = intercostal space; RSB = right sternal border.

radiate to the axilla (see Table 1-2). It is also heard along the left sternal border and in the aortic area. PMR is a high-pitched holosystolic murmur that can be musical in quality and is always accompanied by a third heart sound. The patient may experience severe LV failure and pulmonary edema because of the inability of the mitral valve to close. Pulmonary congestion develops with audible bi-basalar rales. PAWP is increased and a large regurgitant *v* wave may be seen in the wedge pressure tracings and may be reflected in pulmonary artery tracings.[109,110]

Ventricular septal rupture (VSR) presents as a loud, harsh, holosystolic murmur heard to the right of the sternum and at the apex. It is frequently associated with a third heart sound. Rupture of the interventricular septum causing an opening from the LV to the RV during systole causes a parasternal lift of the right ventricle, a palpable systolic thrill, and may increase JVP. Symptoms of RV failure are usual but develop over time. The right atrial tracing may show an increase in pressure and *a*-wave amplitude. The only way to differentiate a VSR from a PMR is through right-heart catheterization: VSR is characterized by an oxygen step-up from the right atrium to the pulmonary artery. PMR shows no step-up and will have large *v* waves. VSR is amenable to medical or surgical therapy and is an important complication to recognize early in the course of AMI before the development of irreversible heart failure.[111–113]

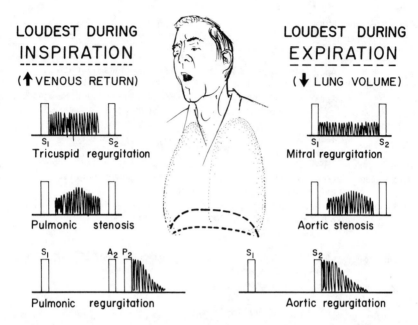

Figure 1-9 Respiratory variation of murmurs. *Source*: Reprinted from "A Systematic Approach to the Bedside Differentiation of Cardiac Murmurs and Abnormal Sounds" by R.A. O'Rourke and M.H. Crawford in *Current Problems in Cardiology*, Vol. 1, No. 11, p. 15, with permission of Year Book Medical Publishers, Inc., © February 1977.

Tricuspid regurgitation is frequently caused by RV dilatation and failure, which stretches the tricuspid annulus. It is seen frequently in patients with chronic heart failure and any conditions that produce LV failure, RV failure, and pulmonary hypertension. The murmur is heard at the fourth and fifth intercostal spaces along the left sternal border. It is a blowing pansystolic murmur that increases during inspiration and decreases during expiration (Carvallo's sign) (see Figure 1-9). The regurgitant flow of blood from the ventricle into the atrium during systole can lead to increased right atrial and jugular venous pressure, and may cause symptoms of systemic congestion (peripheral edema, ascites).[114,115]

Murmurs of aortic stenosis are best heard at the second intercostal space (aortic region) along the right sternal border and may radiate widely.[116,117] The murmur occurs right before the second heart sound and is a harsh, diamond-shaped crescendo/decrescendo murmur. The most common cause of aortic stenosis seen in the critical care area is degenerative calcification of a previously normal valve. The LV usually compensates for a stenotic valve, so severe aortic stenosis can exist for years without the LV failing from the increased pressure. Once the LV fails, then symptoms of right- and left-sided heart failure occur. A systolic thrill is felt at the base of the heart, and when patients are in the left lateral decubitus position a double apical impulse may be palpated.[118] A third heart sound can occur, and a fourth heart sound may indicate LV hypertrophy.[119,120]

Abnormalities of the pulmonary valve are rare and are usually caused by congenital abnormalities. The classic physical finding in pulmonic stenosis is a systolic thrill in the second intercostal space along the left sternal border. The murmur is a harsh, diamond-shaped murmur that occurs in systole. It is loudest during inspiration; a systolic ejection click is usually present. The first heart sound is normal, and the second heart sound is usually split.[121]

Diastolic murmurs are infrequently heard in the critical care setting. These murmurs are caused by mitral and tricuspid stenosis and aortic and pulmonary regurgitation.[122] Table 1-3 gives the physical findings of these murmurs. Mitral stenosis is usually found in patients with a history of rheumatic fever, thrombus formation, bacterial vegetation, and calcium accumulation. Mitral stenosis increases left atrial pressure, which is reflected in increased pulmonary artery pressures. Symptoms develop over long periods of time, and patients may remain asymptomatic. Tricuspid stenosis is an uncommon valvular lesion and is rarely seen in the critical care setting.[123,124]

Aortic regurgitation can be caused by congenital abnormalities, infective endocarditis, rheumatoid arthritis, hypertension, and a dissecting aortic aneurysm. There is a gradual increase in LV pressure over the years, and in general the patient remains asymptomatic because of the compensatory ability of the LV. The murmur of aortic regurgitation is a blowing, high-pitched, crescendo, diastolic murmur heard at the second right intercostal space and radiates to the left

Table 1-3 Diastolic Murmurs

Type of Murmur	Area	Quality	Causes
Mid-diastolic	Apex	Faint	Mitral stenosis (thrombus, rheumatic fever)
Mid-diastolic	LSB 4th ICS	Rumbling Increase on inspiration	Tricuspid stenosis (congenital)
Holodiastolic ending pre-S_1	LSB 3 + 4th ICS	Faint, blowing High pitched Decrescendo	Aortic regurgitation (hypertension, endocarditis, aneurysm)
Early or holodiastolic	LSB 2 ICS	Blowing High pitched Decrescendo	Pulmonary regurgitation (pulmonary hypertension)

sternal border. It is loudest during expiration (see Figure 1-9). An Austin Flint murmur, a rumbling diastolic murmur at the apex, may also be heard.[125,126]

Pulmonary regurgitation is the most frequent abnormality of the pulmonary valve and is frequently caused by pulmonary hypertension. This murmur is a decrescendo diastolic sound best heard at the third or fifth intercostal space at the left sternal border and may be difficult to distinguish from the murmur of aortic regurgitation.[127] It appears to be louder during inspiration than expiration (see Figure 1-9). Pulmonary regurgitation may lead to RV failure over time. Once this occurs, a palpable RV lift may be present.

Pericarditis is a common finding in patients with MI. Pericardial friction rubs occur in 7% to 42% of these patients in the early course of their MI.[128] They may also be heard in 40% to 50% of patients with cardiac tamponade.[129] A rub occurs with the movements of the heart in atrial systole, ventricular diastole, and ventricular systole. Only one or two components may be present. The loudest and longest component is heard in systole, and the two softer components in diastole. Rubs are best heard along the left sternal border with the patient sitting upright or leaning forward, and are accentuated during inspiration. Rubs may vary with position and number of components but can be distinguished from murmurs by their high-pitched scratchy sound. If a rub persists longer than 3 days, it may be a poor prognostic sign indicating further extension of MI.[130] Table 1-4 reviews some of the major complications accompanying AMI.

RESPIRATORY ASSESSMENT

Components of respiratory system assessment in patients with cardiovascular disease include inspection, palpation, percussion, and auscultation of the thorax.

Inspection

Invaluable information is obtained by the inspection process. This process covers observing the shape and symmetry of the chest and respiratory movements. In general, changes in chest wall shape are attributable to lung disease. Chronic obstructive pulmonary disease increases the diameter of anteroposterior chest wall diameter, intercostal space bulging, and hypertrophy of the neck muscle.

In normal respiratory movement, the inspiration phase is shorter than expiration since expiration is a passive process. The inspiration/expiration ratio is 1:2. If muscles are used during expiration, it indicates forced expiration. This may be an early sign of respiratory distress in congestive heart failure.[131] When pulmonary capillary wedge pressure is greater than 22 mmHg, there is a shift of fluids from the vascular compartments into the interstitial spaces, causing interstitial edema. This edema reduces lung compliance and increases the work

Table 1-4 Complications of Acute Myocardial Infarction: Physical, Hemodynamic, and Clinical Findings

Complication	Murmurs and Rales	Gallops	Palpation	Hemodynamics	Clinical Impression
Ventricular septal defect	Pansystolic	S₃	Thrill	O₂ step-up from RA to PA	Left and right ventricular failure
Papillary muscle rupture	Early/pansystolic	S₃	Rare	Large *v* waves in PAWP tracing	Pulmonary edema
Papillary muscle dysfunction	Systolic variable	No	No	Increased PAWP	None to moderate left ventricular failure
Cardiac tamponade	Pericardial friction rub	S₃	Rub	↑ RA equalization of RA, RVED, PAWP prominent *y* descent	Increased JVP Pulsus paradoxus
Pulmonary emboli/ infarction	Pleural friction rub	No/right S₃	No	↑ RVP	Dyspnea Increased temperature and pulse Pleuritic pain Hemoptysis

Abbreviations: RAP = right atrial pressure; RVP = right ventricular pressure; RVED = right ventricular end-diastolic pressure; PAWP = pulmonary artery wedge pressure.

of breathing. In patients with chronic obstructive pulmonary disease, the respiratory phase may be prolonged and the rib cage lifted by the accessory neck muscles. These muscles may also be used in patients who are acutely short of breath, and lack of muscle hypertrophy helps to differ these patients from those with lung disease.[132]

A rapid respiratory rate (tachypnea) may be an early sign of heart failure. When an increase in rate is seen with sudden unexplained dyspnea, it may be a sign of pulmonary emboli and/or pulmonary infarction.[133] Shallow respirations are seen in patients with pericarditis and pulmonary infarction attributable to pleuritic pain that increases with normal or deep respirations. Cheyne-Stokes respirations are frequently seen in elderly patients and in patients with severe congestive heart failure. It is characterized by a cycle of shallow respirations that increase in rate and depth followed by a decrease in rate and depth and then periods of apnea. The cycle recurs with an abrupt start of respirations. The mechanism of Cheyne-Stokes respirations seems to be a prolongation of circulation from the lungs to the respiratory centers of the brain. This delay interferes with the normal feedback mechanisms of the respiratory system.[134] It is caused by a prolonged circulation time or a dysfunction of the normal feedback control or rate and depth or respirations.[135]

Palpation

Palpation is used to confirm findings noted on inspection, such as symmetry and muscles used for respiration, to evaluate vibrations, and to locate areas of tenderness. Vibrations are usually caused by turbulence associated with rales and may confirm their presence. Increases in tactile or vocal fremitus may be caused by interstitial edema, atelectasis, pneumonia, or any condition that causes intrapulmonary consolidation. Remember, the more solid the tissue, the better sound travels through it.[136] A decrease in fremitus is found when fluid or air is in the extrapulmonary spaces and is heard in emphysema, pleural effusions, and pneumothorax. The placement of the trachea should also be palpated. Acute deviations are found with pneumothorax.

Areas of tenderness indicate that pericarditis or pleuritis may be present. This technique is useful to help determine the source of chest pain since localization of pain is infrequently seen in angina pectoris, MI, and pulmonary emboli.[137,138]

Percussion

Percussion is useful in assessing respiratory function and in localizing lung abnormalities. It helps identify whether the underlying tissues are air filled, fluid filled, or solid. Normal air-filled lungs are resonant. Hyper-resonance is heard when there are large amounts of air in the lungs, as in emphysema. Tympany is normally found over the stomach and bowel and results from air enclosed in a chamber. This sound should never be heard over the normal chest. When it is present, pneumothorax and tension pneumothorax may be the cause. Dullness occurs when solid or liquid replaces some of the normal air in the lungs. The greater the amount of solid or liquid, the duller the percussion. Dullness is found in pneumonia, pulmonary fibrosis, tumors, pleural effusion, atelectasis, and in AMI patients and is associated with pulmonary edema, enlarged heart or liver, and pericardial effusion.[139–141]

Auscultation

Auscultation of the lungs is the most widely used respiratory assessment in the critical care area. Auscultation requires assessment of the anterior, lateral, and posterior chest walls. Since lung sounds are high pitched, the diaphragm is used. Auscultation should be done simultaneously from side to side. The nurse auscultates the chest, noting the presence of normal breath sounds and adventitious or extra breath sounds.[142] Breath sounds are produced in the alveoli and larger bronchial tubes. Bronchial sounds are tubular or hollow sounding with a prolonged expiration and are best heard over the trachea. The alveolar sounds have a soft and breezy quality and a longer inspiration than expiration. These are called *vesicular sounds* and are heard over major lung fields.

When there is decreased LV performance, left atrial pressure increases and is transmitted to the pulmonary capillaries, which eventually results in transudation of fluid into the alveoli.[143] Alveolar fluid produces audible pulmonary rales. Rales are fine, crackling, crepitent sounds with a moist, dry quality, are best heard at the end of inspiration, and do not clear with cough. Medium-to-coarse, moist rales develop when fluids are in large airways. Rales are not specific for LV failure and can be attributable to primary lung disease. Differentiation often presents a diagnostic problem in MI patients. Rales attributable to lung disease can be differentiated from those attributable to LV dysfunction by their failure to migrate to the most dependent part of the lungs when body position is changed. When examining patients, position them on their side for approximately 30 minutes, and then ascultate the lung field. Rales attributable to heart failure will be most prominent over the posterior lung field on the side upon which the patient has been lying.[144] Audible bibasalar rales always develop with ventricular septal rupture and are the most frequent finding accompanying the holosystolic murmur. In papillary muscle rupture, one sees acute onset of pulmonary edema and a murmur. In the presence of papillary muscle dysfunction, pulmonary edema is unusual. In papillary muscle dysfunction, the pulmonary capillary wedge pressure may be normal or slightly normal, but in papillary muscle rupture, giant *v* waves can be seen in the pulmonary capillary wedge tracing.[145]

Continuous, high-pitched musical sounds are called *wheezes*. They are caused by movement of air through narrow bronchial tubes. Wheezes occur in congestive heart failure because of the congestion and narrowing of respiratory bronchials and are heard first on expiration. On inspiration, bronchials expand but go back to a narrow state on expiration.[146] Wheezes can be heard throughout inspiration and expiration when severe obstruction occurs. Wheezes usually accompany moderately dense rales in congestive heart failure.

Rhonchi, which are related to wheezes, occur because of movement of air through fluid-filled narrowed air passages. Rhonchi have a coarse, rumbling, or snoring sound (sonorous rhonchi), mingled with cracklinglike wheezes. Rhonchi are first heard on expiration, then early inspiration, whereas end expiration remains clear.[147,148]

Pulmonary emboli usually present as a sudden, unexplained dyspnea. They are frequently accompanied by pleuritic pain, cough, and hemoptysis and can be also associated with a rise in temperature and pulse rate.[149] Pulmonary infarction, as a result of emboli, is more common with AMI. Also, indwelling right heart catheters may occlude pulmonary arteries, causing pulmonary infarction to be a source of thrombi. A pleural friction rub may be heard with pulmonary infarction. It can be distinguished from a pericardial rub by location, its augmentation by breathing, and a lack of relation to various components of the cardiac cycle.[150] Although the arterial PO_2 is usually depressed in pulmonary emboli, this finding is of little value in AMI and may be decreased for a variety of reasons including LV failure and sedation.[151]

In acute pulmonary edema, coarse bubbling rales and wheezes are heard over both lung fields. Unilateral rales in this condition are rare, but when they occur they are over the right lung. If audible only in the left, an acute pulmonary embolus may be present.[152]

Occasionally, physical findings may be misleading. In patients who receive diuretics the difference in hemodynamic evaluations is reflected by a rapid reduction of pulmonary capillary wedge pressure toward normal. However, the patient may still have persistent rales. There is a phase lag of as much as 48 hours between hemodynamic stabilization and resolution of abnormal physical and x-ray findings.[153] Patients with chronic obstructive pulmonary disease are often mistaken as having pulmonary congestion because of the presence of dyspnea and rales. Yet hemodynamic findings are usually within normal range, indicating the patient's physical signs are extracardiac. In patients with chronic compensated heart failure, selected peripheral vasoconstriction can mask a low cardiac output, and thickening of the pulmonary vascular walls can occur, allowing the lung to tolerate a substantial elevation in pulmonary capillary wedge pressure without signs of clinical congestion. Thus, a disparity between clinical and hemodynamic evaluation secondary to such compensatory mechanisms can occur.[154]

NURSING DIAGNOSIS

The detection and prevention of complications in patients with AMI depend on the prompt recognition of their accompanying physical findings. The physical examination is not only important in establishing a medical diagnosis but is an essential component in the nursing diagnosis. Table 1-5 lists some of the physical findings frequently seen in patients with cardiovascular disease and their accompanying nursing diagnosis. A care plan for a patient with anterior MI who is suspected of having a pulmonary embolus is given in Table 1-6.

Table 1-5 Examples of Physical Findings Accompanying Nursing Diagnoses and Etiologies

Physical Findings	Nursing Diagnosis	Medical Etiology
Peripheral cyanosis	Tissue perfusion, alteration in: peripheral	Vasoconstriction Low cardiac output secondary to AMI
Clubbing	Gas exchange, impaired: actual	Decreased lung perfusion secondary to advanced cor pulmonale
Increased jugular venous pressure	Cardiac output, alteration in: decreased	RVF secondary to LVF
Cannon *a* waves	Cardiac output, alteration in: decreased	Decreased contractility and/or dysrhythmias to AMI
Hypokinetic pulse	Fluid volume deficit: actual	Hypovolemia secondary to nausea and vomiting
Pulsus alternans	Cardiac output, alteration in: decreased	Decreased contractility secondary to AMI
Hypotension	Fluid volume deficit: actual	Hypovolemia secondary to vigorous diuresis
S_3	Cardiac output, alteration in: decreased	LVF secondary to AMI
Holosystolic murmur	Cardiac output, alteration in: decreased	Papillary muscle dysfunction secondary to AMI
Tachypnea	Gas exchange, impaired: actual	Decreased perfusion to the lung secondary to AMI
Cheyne-Stokes respiration	Gas exchange, impaired: actual	Decreased perfusion to the lung secondary to chronic CHF

Abbreviations: RVF = right ventricular failure; LVF = left ventricular failure; AMI = acute myocardial infarction; CHF = congestive heart failure.

Table 1-6 Care Plan for a Patient Suspected of Having a Pulmonary Embolus

Assessment	Nursing Diagnosis	Expected Outcomes
1. Assess for changes in lung function: 　a. tachypnea 　b. tachycardia 　c. diaphoresis 　d. restlessness 　e. increase in rate and depth of breathing 　f. increase in accessory muscle use 　g. diminished chest expansion 　h. sudden dyspnea 　i. rales and decreases breath sounds 　j. pleural fraction rub	Gas exchange, impaired: decreased Medical etiology: pulmonary embolus causing a decrease in lung tissue perfusion	To maintain optimal gas exchange
2. Assess for elevated temperature		
3. Assess for hemodynamic changes (elevated PAEDP and normal PAWP)		
4. Assess for characteristics of pain		
5. Assess for right ventricular heart failure 　a. S_2 splitting 　b. loud pulmonic component of S_2 　c. S_3, S_4 right-sided 　d. increased jugular venous pressure 　e. positive hepatojugular reflex 　f. pedal edema	Cardiac output, alteration in: decreased Medical etiology: pulmonary hypertension causing right ventricular heart failure and left ventricular heart failure secondary to right-sided heart failure and acute myocardial infarction	To maintain an optimal cardiac output
6. Assess for left ventricular heart failure 　a. hypotension 　b. pulsus alternans 　c. S_3, S_4 　d. rales and wheezes 　e. dyspnea 　f. cough 　g. tachycardia		

Abbreviations: PAEDP = pulmonary artery end diastolic pressure; PAWP = pulmonary artery wedge pressure.

NOTES

1. American Association of Critical Care Nurses, *Standards for Nursing Care of the Critically Ill* (Reston, Va.: Reston Publishing Co., Inc., 1981).

2. American Nurses' Association Division on Medical-Surgical Nursing Practice and American Heart Association Council on Cardiovascular Nursing, *Standards of Cardiovascular Nursing Practice* (Kansas City: American Nurses' Association, 1981).

3. C.E. Guzzetta and B.M. Dossey, eds., *Cardiovascular Nursing: Bodymind Tapestry* (St. Louis: The C.V. Mosby Co., 1984), pp. 78–97, 490–497, 526–529.

4. C.R. Michaelson, *Congestive Heart Failure* (St. Louis: The C.V. Mosby Co., 1983), pp. 123–178.

5. B. Bates, *A Guide to Physical Assessment*, 3rd ed. (New York: J.B. Lippincott Co., 1979).

6. J.W. Hurst, ed., *The Heart*, 5th ed. (New York: McGraw Hill Book Co., 1982), pp. 147–215, 228–282.

7. P. Vaughan, "Bedside Assessment of the Myocardial Infarction Patient," *Critical Care Nursing* 4 (1984): 60.

8. J.K. Perloff, "Physical Examination of the Cardiovascular System," in Jay Stein, ed., *Internal Medicine* (Boston: Little, Brown and Co., 1983), pp. 424–434.

9. Ibid.

10. E. Braunwald, "The Physical Examination," in E. Braunwald, ed., *Heart Diseases: A Textbook of Cardiovascular Medicine* (Philadelphia: W.B. Saunders Co., 1980), pp. 13–38.

11. Ibid.

12. Vaughan, "Bedside Assessment."

13. Hurst, *Heart*.

14. Ibid.

15. Vaughan, "Bedside Assessment."

16. Braunwald, "Physical Examination."

17. Hurst, *Heart*.

18. Braunwald, "Physical Examination."

19. Vaughan, "Bedside Assessment."

20. Perloff, "Cardiovascular System."

21. Michaelson, *Heart Failure*.

22. Hurst, *Heart*.

23. M.H. Crawford and R.A. O'Rourke, "The Bedside Diagnosis of the Complications of Myocardial Infarction," in R.S. Elliot, ed., *Cardiac Emergencies* (Mt. Kisco, N.Y.: Futura Publishing Co., Inc., 1982), pp. 63–76.

24. Vaughan, "Bedside Assessment."

25. Ibid.

26. Braunwald, "Physical Examination."

27. Vaughan, "Bedside Assessment."

28. Michaelson, *Heart Failure*.

29. Ibid.

30. Vaughan, "Bedside Assessment."

31. Braunwald, "Physical Examination."

32. Ibid.

33. Vaughan, "Bedside Assessment."

34. Michaelson, *Heart Failure.*

35. Crawford and O'Rourke, "Bedside Diagnosis."

36. J.S. Forrester, et al., "Medical Therapy of Acute Myocardial Infarction by Application of Hemodynamic Subsets," *New England Journal of Medicine*, 295 (1976): 1356, 1404.

37. Crawford and O'Rourke, "Bedside Diagnosis."

38. Hurst, *Heart.*

39. Ibid.

40. Michaelson, *Heart Failure.*

41. Ibid.

42. Hurst, *Heart.*

43. Ibid.

44. Michaelson, *Heart Failure.*

45. Crawford and O'Rourke, "Bedside Diagnosis."

46. Hurst, *Heart.*

47. Crawford and O'Rourke, "Bedside Diagnosis."

48. Ibid.

49. Hurst, *Heart.*

50. Michaelson, *Heart Failure.*

51. Ibid.

52. Ibid.

53. Hurst, *Heart.*

54. Crawford and O'Rourke, "Bedside Diagnosis."

55. Michaelson, *Heart Failure.*

56. Ibid.

57. Hurst, *Heart.*

58. Ibid.

59. Michaelson, *Heart Failure.*

60. Hurst, *Heart.*

61. Ibid.

62. W.M. Kierkendall, et al., "AHA Committee Report: Recommendations of Human Blood Pressure Determination by Sphygmomanometers," *Circulation* 62 (1980): 1146A.

63. Hurst, *Heart.*

64. Ibid.

65. Ibid.

66. S.D. Eilen, M.H. Crawford, and R.A. O'Rourke, "Accuracy of Precordial Palpation for Detecting Increased Left Ventricular Volume," *Annals of Internal Medicine* 99 (1983): 628.

67. Ibid.

68. Hurst, *Heart.*

69. Ibid.

70. Vaughan, "Bedside Assessment."

71. Hurst, *Heart.*

72. Eilen, Crawford, and O'Rourke, "Precordial Palpation."

73. Hurst, *Heart.*
74. Ibid.
75. Crawford and O'Rourke, "Bedside Diagnosis."
76. Hurst, *Heart.*
77. Vaughan, "Bedside Assessment."
78. Crawford and O'Rourke, "Bedside Diagnosis."
79. Ibid.
80. Vaughan, "Bedside Assessment."
81. Crawford and O'Rourke, "Bedside Diagnosis."
82. Hurst, *Heart.*
83. Ibid.
84. Crawford and O'Rourke, "Bedside Diagnosis."
85. Hurst, *Heart.*
86. Vaughan, "Bedside Assessment."
87. Ibid.
88. Ibid.
89. Hurst, *Heart.*
90. Crawford and O'Rourke, "Bedside Diagnosis."
91. Michaelson, *Heart Failure.*
92. Crawford and O'Rourke, "Bedside Diagnosis."
93. Hurst, *Heart.*
94. Ibid.
95. Vaughan, "Bedside Assessment."
96. Hurst, *Heart.*
97. Ibid.
98. Michaelson, *Heart Failure.*
99. Hurst, *Heart.*
100. Crawford and O'Rourke, "Bedside Diagnosis."
101. Ibid.
102. Ibid.
103. Hurst, *Heart.*
104. Crawford and O'Rourke, "Bedside Diagnosis."
105. Ibid.
106. Ibid.
107. Ibid.
108. Ibid.
109. Ibid.
110. Vaughan, "Bedside Assessment."
111. Ibid.
112. Hurst, *Heart.*
113. Crawford and O'Rourke, "Bedside Diagnosis."
114. Michaelson, *Heart Failure.*
115. Hurst, *Heart.*

116. Ibid.
117. Michaelson, *Heart Failure*.
118. Ibid.
119. Ibid.
120. Hurst, *Heart*.
121. Ibid.
122. Michaelson, *Heart Failure*.
123. Ibid.
124. Hurst, *Heart*.
125. Ibid.
126. Michaelson, *Heart Failure*.
127. Ibid.
128. Crawford and O'Rourke, "Bedside Diagnosis."
129. Michaelson, *Heart Failure*.
130. Crawford and O'Rourke, "Bedside Diagnosis."
131. Michaelson, *Heart Failure*.
132. Ibid.
133. Crawford and O'Rourke, "Bedside Diagnosis."
134. Braunwald, "Physical Examination."
135. Ibid.
136. Michaelson, *Heart Failure*.
137. Ibid.
138. Vaughan, "Bedside Assessment."
139. Michaelson, *Heart Failure*.
140. Hurst, *Heart*.
141. Vaughan, "Bedside Assessment."
142. Ibid.
143. Crawford and O'Rourke, "Bedside Diagnosis."
144. Ibid.
145. Ibid.
146. Michaelson, *Heart Failure*.
147. Ibid.
148. Vaughan, "Bedside Assessment."
149. Crawford and O'Rourke, "Bedside Diagnosis."
150. Ibid.
151. Ibid.
152. Braunwald, "Physical Examination."
153. Forrester et al., "Medical Therapy."
154. Ibid.

REFERENCES

Carpenito, L.J. *Nursing Diagnosis Application to Clinical Practice*. Philadelphia: J.B. Lippincott Co., 1983.

McCarthy, E. "Hemodynamic Effects and Clinical Assessment of Dysrhythmias." *Critical Care Quarterly* 4(1981):9–15.

Michaelson, C. "Bedside Assessment and Diagnosis of Acute Left Ventricular Failure." *Critical Care Quarterly* 4(1981):1–11.

O'Rourke, R.A. "The Physical Examination of the Arteries and Veins." In *The Heart*, 6th ed., edited by J.W. Hurst. New York: McGraw Hill Book Co., 1986, pp. 143–149.

O'Rourke, R.A., and Braunwald, E. "Physical Examination of the Heart." In *Harrison's Principles of Internal Medicine*, 11th ed. New York: McGraw Hill Book Co., 1986, pp. 865–870.

O'Rourke, R.A., and Crawford, M.H. "Physical Findings in Heart Failure and Their Physiologic Basis." In *Congestive Heart Failure*, edited by D.T. Mason. New York: Medical Books, 1976, pp. 183–190.

O'Rourke, R.A., and Crawford, M.H. "A Systematic Approach to the Bedside Differentiation of Cardiac Murmurs and Abnormal Sounds." *Current Problems in Cardiology* 1(1977):15.

Papenhausen, J.L. "Data-based Criteria for Cardiovascular Nursing Intervention." *Critical Care Quarterly* 4(1981):1–7.

Partridge, S.A. "Cardiac Auscultation." *Dimensions of Critical Care Nursing* 1(1982):152–156.

Chapter 2

New Diagnostic Techniques

Anna Gawlinski, RN, MSN, CCRN

In the past decade, a proliferation of noninvasive imaging techniques useful in the diagnosis of acquired and congenital cardiac disease has emerged. These techniques have become an important part of the routine care of cardiac patients. In this chapter we consider new diagnostic techniques in the evaluation of cardiac disease and myocardial perfusion. These tests include echocardiography, exercise myocardial perfusion imaging with thallium, myocardial infarct imaging with pyrophosphate, and radionuclide ventriculography. In addition, some of the newer technologies available, i.e., positron emission tomography (PET), magnetic resonance imaging (MRI), and computer-assisted tomography (CT) are discussed in relation to the future of imaging. This chapter presents a simplified approach to this information, discusses these noninvasive tests in general, and provides specific examples of their use in various cardiac disease processes.

ECHOCARDIOGRAPHY

Refinements in noninvasive imaging techniques have led to the evolution of echocardiography. During the 1970s, the M-mode echo technique was the only ultrasound method used for evaluating left ventricular (LV) function. Although this modality was extremely useful, several limitations became apparent, including the lack of spatial resolution and the inability to examine large areas of the ventricular myocardium. Consequently, the two-dimensional (2-D) echo has become the mainstay of ultrasound imaging. Today, the combination of M-mode and 2-D echo continues to provide the best supportive information. The strength of the M-mode is that it allows more precise measurements of wall thickness and valvular motion. The strengths of 2-D echo are in terms of location and spatial orientation.[1]

Procedure

A transducer containing a piezoelectric crystal is placed on the chest. The crystal generates a high frequency sound beam; the sound waves can be directed at various structures in the heart. The transducer converts mechanical energy to electrical energy and the reverse: electrical energy to mechanical energy. Therefore, the transducer can both send and receive sound waves. The transducer sends out sound waves for a very short time interval. It then converts to a listening mode to record the sound "echoes" that return when reflected off of cardiac structures. The echoes are recorded on video tape along with an electrocardiograph (ECG) so that there can be a reference to the cardiac cycle. Structures can be viewed from different angles simply by changing the position of the transducer. Cavities filled with fluid do not reflect the waves and are represented on the graphic record as empty areas. It is possible to observe the valvular motion in both systole and diastole.[2]

Modes

The most common is the M-mode or motion echocardiogram. This allows the physician to assess the motion of various cardiac structures as they change shape and positions relative to the transducer position during the cardiac cycle. Measurements and excursions can be obtained of structures that reflect the ultrasound beam. Structures with broad surfaces perpendicular to the echo beam reflect well. The characteristic patterns of movement of these structures allow their anatomical identification. The anterior leaflet of the mitral valve is a strong echo reflector. Many other structures can be identified by their relation to the mitral valve.[3]

The M-mode is unable to depict the entire chamber of the heart or valve structure as a whole. This information must be obtained by a composite of many views, or important areas can be missed.

The 2-D echocardiogram permits even more analysis of the cardiac structures by portraying the echoes as a planar image instead of the unidimensional time-motion display that lacks spatial orientation. Qualitative estimation of segmental wall motion abnormalities is better obtained by the 2-D echocardiogram; its advantages include determinations of anatomic information, mitral valve orifice size, valvular vegetations, mitral valve prolapse, and loculated pericardial effusions.[4]

Echocardiograms can also be used to detect and assess pericardial effusion, atrial tumors, and thrombi. This technique is very useful for visualizing not only the walls of the heart but both normal tissue and prosthetic valve structure and function.

Echocardiography has major advantages. It can be performed at the bedside and can be repeated many times. There is no radiation or known biologic hazard. It is an ideal method for assessing segmental wall function since 2-D echo can visualize multiple planes of the heart. It is, however, somewhat less satisfactory for visualizing global function. Multiple views are necessary to assess overall ventricular function or ejection fraction.[5] Wall motion may not always be accurate since the endocardium is not always well visualized. Other disadvantages include difficulty in visualizing a portion or all of the heart.

In recent years there has been much interest in the use of Doppler techniques in combination with echo that additionally measure blood flow velocity in the great vessels and heart valves. Many of the new echocardiographic instruments are also equipped with a Doppler mode for measuring blood flow velocity. When a sound wave is reflected by a moving target (e.g., blood cells), a frequency, or Doppler, shift occurs that is proportional to the velocity of the target. The pulsed-Doppler mode is derived by electronically creating a region of interest called *the sample volume*. The velocity of blood flow in the sample volume can be calculated. This technique is an important complement to echocardiographic imaging by allowing evaluation of normal and abnormal flow. Measurements of blood velocities can be combined with echocardiographic imaging to quantitate flow through the cardiac chambers and great vessels.[6]

With only intermittent sampling, the pulsed-Doppler echo is limited to quantifying only high-velocity jets, such as those observed with stenotic valvular lesions. A newer instrument with continuous-wave Doppler allows identification of all velocities encountered by the sound beam. It can quantify a broader range of velocities noninvasively.[7] A Doppler echo is, therefore, valuable in valvular disease for the demonstration of regurgitant lesions and the quantification of stenotic lesions. Doppler techniques have become a part of the routine echo examination in many institutions.

Doppler Color Flow Mapping (CFM)

Doppler CFM is the newest modality for cardiac imaging. CFM is a type of pulsed-wave (PW) Doppler. In conventional pulse wave, a sample volume is positioned in a 2-D image to collect Doppler-shifted information from a small discrete area. In contrast, the CFM instrument automatically gathers Doppler-shifted information from multiple sample volumes along each 2-D scan line. Mean velocities are calculated from the Doppler shifts and color coded for direction and velocity. The resulting colors are superimposed in real time upon the 2-D image of the flow area. The result is a "noninvasive angiogram" that is a 2-D image of cardiac anatomy with a color representation of blood as it flows through the anatomy. Because CFM is a combination of Doppler flow information and 2-D imaging, it shortens the cardiac ultrasound examination time. It offers real-time imaging of cardiovascular blood flow and faster mapping of the extent of regurgitant lesions.[8]

CFM is easily incorporated into the routine cardiac ultrasound examination. M-mode and 2-D data are obtained in the usual way. Then, instead of beginning the usual PW Doppler examination, color is turned on, and the CFM information is overlaid upon the 2-D image. The cardiac chambers and inflow and outflow tracts are viewed using an imaging technique that is essentially the same as the technique used for 2-D imaging. When abnormal flows such as shunt flows or regurgitant/stenotic jets are detected, their spatial extents and directions are displayed immediately in the flow map. Color representation of blood flow is seen on the 2-D image. The colors are coded according to the direction and velocity of flow relative to the transducer position. Once abnormal blood flows are evident, their velocities are determined by sampling the identified flow disturbance areas with conventional PW Doppler. Thus, CFM eliminates the time-consuming task of identifying the areas of abnormal flow, and diminishes the possibility of missing flow abnormalities.[9]

Indications for Echocardiography

Coronary Artery Disease (CAD)

In CAD patients, it is important to estimate overall LV function. The echocardiographic detection of CAD is dependent on detection of abnormal regional wall motion in areas perfused by narrowed or occluded coronary arteries. The presence of wall motion abnormalities at rest and with exercise may have a major role in prognosis and therapy of the CAD patient. In addition to wall motion, it is useful to know whether ischemia manifested by decreased regional wall motion develops during exercise.

Echocardiography is useful for detailing regional wall motion abnormalities of the ventricle. Areas of asynergy may be detected as abnormal, and the overall size of the LV and left atrium can be estimated. Although quantification of overall ejection fraction may be performed, this is not usually done because of the time-consuming image analysis.[10]

Echocardiography currently provides no information about perfusion defects. Patients with symptoms suggestive of CAD can be evaluated by combining stress testing with echocardiography. This would aid in identifying exercise-induced abnormal wall motion. It can be difficult to obtain adequate echocardiographic images during exercise, and, therefore, exercise echocardiography is not the technique of choice for exercise LV performance studies. Although echo provides important information about CAD patients, radionuclear techniques are superior in this setting.

Acute Myocardial Infarction (AMI)

In patients with acute myocardial infarction (AMI), information about regional wall motion and overall ventricular function is needed. Studies have shown that both the ejection fraction and the wall motion index were predictive of acute and long-term prognosis post MI. Echocardiography is becoming increasingly useful in the localization and evaluation of the severity of LV involvement in AMI. In addition, it is important to detect LV thrombi in these patients since they may warrant anticoagulation therapy. Some AMI patients may develop complications including hypotension, decreased cardiac output, and a new murmur. Doppler echo is used to localize the origin of a new murmur. In addition, it can distinguish the difference in the etiology of the murmur, i.e., attributable to mitral regurgitation or to a ventricular septal defect.[11]

Echocardiography may aid in evaluating the AMI patient. Some MI patients may have left bundle branch block or other abnormalities that can mask the ECG diagnosis of infarction. Patients with MI may have nondiagnostic enzyme levels or may be seen several days after the acute event. Detection of an area with abnormal regional wall motion is helpful in the determination of the diagnosis in these patients. Echocardiography may also be useful in detecting right ventricular (RV) infarction complicating the AMI patient. The echo can show RV dilation and abnormal RV function noninvasively.[12]

Echocardiography currently remains the procedure of choice for detection of an LV thrombus. In clinical practice, a thrombus is identified as an echo-dense mass in an area of akinesis or dyskinesis that usually involves the apex. Echocardiography is perhaps the most useful noninvasive technique in AMI because of the information it can supply concerning mitral regurgitation and LV thrombi.[13]

Congestive Cardiomyopathy

In congestive cardiomyopathy it is important to assess overall LV function (ejection fraction) as well as the relative sizes of the various chambers of the heart. Echocardiography provides visualization of both chambers of the heart and great vessels and can provide most of the information necessary in congestive cardiomyopathy. The test is an excellent technique for assessing overall LV function. M-mode echocardiograms will record dilatation of the LV with decreased wall motion and normal wall thickness. Abnormalities of valvular and aortic root motion that reflect hemodynamic disturbances can also be seen.[14] Varying degrees of left atrial, right atrial, and RV enlargement are present. 2-D echocardiography better shows the abnormalities of the right chambers; it also shows that LV function is globally rather than segmentally depressed. This distinguishes cardiomyopathy from ischemic heart disease.[15]

An elevated LV end-diastolic pressure (LVEDP) is suggested by the presence of a notch on the a-to-e slope of the mitral valve. Doppler echo yields information about valvular regurgitation and stenosis, and therefore aids in detecting these valvular lesions and in determining an etiology for the congestive cardiomyopathy. The major problem with echo in these patients is its difficulty in providing an accurate and quantitative value for ejection fraction.

The presence of an LV or atrial thrombus will influence the need for anticoagulation therapy. Information about valvular regurgitation may be helpful in determining the etiology of cardiomyopathy and the degree of failure.

Hypertrophic Cardiomyopathy

Hypertrophic cardiomyopathy may be difficult to diagnose, especially when it is nonobstructive. Asymmetric hypertrophy is the hallmark of definitive diagnosis. There may be LV outflow obstruction at rest or in response to exercise. The prime M-mode echocardiographic markers of this disorder have been evidence of asymmetric septal hypertrophy, and in the presence of LV outflow obstruction, systolic anterior motion of the mitral valve and systolic notching of the aortic valve.[16] If the diagnosis of hypertrophic cardiomyopathy is made, it is important to determine whether there is obstruction to LV outflow.

Doppler echo may aid in detecting mitral regurgitation. Consequently, echo is the major technique for the diagnosis of hypertrophic cardiomyopathy and its significance.

Pericardial Effusion

In patients with suspected pericardial effusion, noninvasive imaging should detect the effusion, estimate the amount of effusion, show abnormalities of the pericardium and fluid, and give some indication of the hemodynamic consequences of such effusions.[17]

Echo has become the procedure of choice for the diagnosis, semiquantification, and assessment of the hemodynamic significance of pericardial effusion. With M-mode and 2-D techniques, the test is extremely sensitive for small pericardial effusions. In many disease states, small effusions with no clinical significance may be found. Echo allows a semiquantitative measurement of small, moderate, or large effusions.[18]

Localized effusions may also be detected by this technique. Sometimes an examination of the pericardium for implants or increased thickness, and the clear space containing the fluid for masses, can yield information about the etiology of the effusion. Although cardiac tamponade is primarily a clinical diagnosis, some echo criteria are usually present when tamponade occurs. These include systolic expiratory collapse of the RV. In extreme cases of pericardial effusion, it is sometimes possible to see echo correlations to the electrical alternans.

Echocardiography has provided a method to diagnose and follow pericardial effusions noninvasively. This is one of the most important uses of echo since no other technique is so sensitive. However, high-quality results must be obtained in the combined use of the M-mode and 2-D echo so an accurate diagnosis can be made.

Valvular Heart Disease

Noninvasive imaging can have a very important role in diagnosing and planning therapy for the patient with valvular heart disease. It is important to ascertain cardiac chamber sizes and function to determine the effects of valvular disease on ventricular function at rest and with exercise. This will aid in the proper timing of surgical intervention. In multiple lesions and murmurs that cannot be adequately assessed on physical examination, various noninvasive imaging techniques may be useful for determining the degree of stenosis or insufficiency of each of the cardiac valves, determining the presence or absence of pulmonary hypertension, and quantitating such measurements.

Echocardiography is useful in patients with valvular heart disease. As in other disorders, echo may determine the size of all the heart chambers and measure left and right ventricular function. As stated previously, the major limitation is the method for quantitative measurements of LV function such as ejection fraction. The technique is laborious and cannot be performed on all patients.[19]

Echocardiography is an excellent tool for observing valve morphology. For example, in patients with aortic stenosis it is often possible to see calcification in the valve with restricted motion; in mitral stenosis, doming of the anterior leaflet and thickening of the mitral valve may be observed. However, in most regurgitant lesions, no specific abnormalities are seen directly in the valve other than a flail mitral leaflet secondary to ruptured chordae.[20]

The combination of M-mode and 2-D echo with Doppler echo in the past several years has given additional information in using echo in valvular disease. Doppler techniques seem to be very sensitive for valvular regurgitation. This is helpful for the full assessment of a patient with multiple murmurs. The quantification of regurgitant lesions is a problem with conventional methods. Currently, severity may be assessed noninvasively by the timing and the spatial extent of the regurgitation. In stenotic lesions of the valve, measurements of maximum velocities and other variables have proved quite useful in assessing the gradients across these valves. However, with the introduction of CFM, the noninvasive quantification of valvular lesions may no longer be difficult in the future. Continued clinical experience with this technique will provide us with valuable information concerning its ability to estimate the approximate severity of the lesions.[21]

Overall, echo is an excellent technique for diagnosis and quantification of valvular disease. However, the combination of nuclear studies and echo are important in determining the response of the patient to exercise. This ability is imperative because exercise variables are used in the assessment of optimal timing of surgery in asymptomatic or mildly symptomatic valvular heart disease. Thus both techniques are necessary in the full evaluation of these patients.

Mitral Valve Prolapse

The diagnosis of mitral valve prolapse, a common "abnormality" of the heart, should be properly made. There is some dispute about the diagnostic criteria and therapeutic implications, including infective endocarditis prophylaxis. Echocardiography is useful to document mitral valve prolapse. Echo will reveal abnormal posterior motion of the mitral valve during systole and may indicate left atrial size. Doppler echo may determine whether mitral regurgitation is present.[22]

Echocardiography is the most useful imaging technique available for the diagnosis of mitral valve prolapse. However, there is no set standard for the diagnosis of this syndrome. Most physicians have seen patients with definite clicks and symptoms in whom the echo has been negative. Thus the clinician must rely predominantly on the history and physical examination.

Nursing Considerations

Knowledge Deficit: Echocardiogram

The patient should verbalize an understanding of the purpose of the test, the technique, and post-test care.

1. Assess the patient's understanding of the disease process and the purpose of the test.
2. Explain in simple and clear terms the purpose: to evaluate the motion of the various structures in the heart, and the size and shape of the heart.
3. Inform the patient of the name of the person performing the test, the location, and any equipment used during the test.
4. Inform the patient that lights will be dim so that information can be seen on the screen.
5. Assure the patient that the procedure is painless.
6. Explain that a dime-shaped transducer will be placed over the chest, and that conductive jelly will be applied. Some pressure will be applied to keep the transducer in contact with the skin. The transducer will be angled to visualize different parts of the heart and structure in the heart.
7. Instruct the patient to lie still during the test and to follow any instructions as to position, holding one's breath, or breathing in and out.
8. Answer any questions the patient may have in a simple and clear manner. Assist the patient in formulating any questions appropriate for the physician and have the patient write them down.

THALLIUM IMAGING

Thallium-201 is the commonly used radionuclide tracer to determine perfusion of the myocardium. Thallium is a small atom basically the size of a potassium atom. It is a potassium analog, which means it is in the same group of ions as potassium on the periodic chart. It behaves physiologically like potassium in the body. It is actively transported and concentrated in healthy muscle cells like potassium. It is not concentrated in ischemic myocardial tissue, scar or necrotic tissue, or bone. Its half-life is 72 hours, and it is excreted through the kidneys. Thallium is considered a low-energy isotope.[23] Thallium scanning can be done at rest and as an exercise test. The test is most useful as an exercise study. When thallium is injected, its uptake by the myocardium is directly flow related. That is, the amount of flow at the time of injection will dictate the distribution of the isotope.

Procedure

If the procedure is to be done at rest, the patient will be taken to the nuclear medicine department and given 2 mCi of thallium-201 into an intravenous (IV) catheter. The scintillation camera (radioactive scanner) is placed over the patient's chest. Imaging begins within 10 minutes. Thallium is largely extracted by the cells during the initial pass through the circulation. The usual views are anterior and 45° and 70° left anterior oblique (LAO). The computer-generated images show a doughnut-shaped myocardium. The center of the doughnut is the ventricular cavity, which does not show up well because it is fluid filled.

If the test is done in conjunction with exercise, patients exercise on a treadmill with a standard Bruce protocol until 1 minute before they feel they cannot continue. At maximum exercise, thallium is injected. An attempt is made to keep the patient exercising for 1 minute more to allow for clearance of the thallium from the circulating blood pool. Imaging is immediately begun, and should not begin any longer than 10 minutes after exercise has ceased. Exercise increases flow (thallium) in the normal vessel, but will not increase flow in vessels with limited flow. Any defect (cold spot) observed immediately after exercise can indicate myocardial ischemia or an old MI. To separate ischemic from infarcted tissue, there needs to be a repeat, resting study. This is called a *redistribution study* and is obtained approximately 4 hours later. If the area of abnormal perfusion remains, this will indicate an old infarct. If the area "fills in," there is evidence for ischemic myocardium.[24] Thus, redistribution indicates an ischemic episode during stress testing.

In administering this test, one must look at the myocardium in a number of views to see the entire myocardium. The most useful view is the LAO position. The area of the mitral valve does not concentrate thallium. The left lateral view is least useful. Although the RV wall picks up thallium similarly to the LV wall per cell, it is much thinner and stretched. Consequently, it does not image successfully. Since there can be a lot of subjectivity in reading the study, the test is considered 80% to 90% accurate for documenting CAD.[25,26] Computer techniques now available are nonsubjective; however problems still exist, such as poor inferior wall images and soft tissue attenuation.

Indications

Coronary Artery Disease

Thallium images can be used to establish the diagnosis of CAD. Since ECGs are not perfect diagnostic tests, and a patient's set of symptoms can be variable, it may be difficult to identify patients with CAD. A thallium stress test is helpful to clarify the meaning of the patient's signs and symptoms and to identify who does and does not have CAD. It can be used in patients who are asymptomatic with a positive stress test, have an equivocal ECG, or are symptomatic with a negative ECG.

Thallium imaging can be used to evaluate a patient with known CAD. If the clinician can make the diagnosis of CAD on the basis of history, thallium imaging is useful in determining the area at risk. It is useful to know which area is affected. A thallium study will aid in determining the viability of the myocardium. Most infarcts are not completely transmural; usually there is some viable tissue left in the risk area. A thallium stress test will aid in identifying regional ischemic tissue in an area of infarct.

Evaluation of Percutaneous Transluminal Angioplasty

Thallium imaging can be used to evaluate patients pre- and postangioplasty. Thallium studies can determine the functional significance of an equivocal lesion. They can also determine the effect of angioplasty on restoring regional perfusion to ischemic areas of the heart.

Evaluation of Coronary Artery Bypass Graft

Thallium studies can be used to determine the patency of grafts after coronary bypass surgery. A normal exercise and resting thallium scan is evidence for graft patency.

Nursing Considerations

Knowledge Deficit: Thallium Imaging Technique

The patient should be able to verbalize an understanding of the rationale for the test, the technique, and post-test care.

1. Assess the patient's understanding of the disease process and rationale for the test.
2. Instruct the patient as to the purpose of the test: to determine if any areas of the heart muscle are not receiving an adequate blood supply.

3. If an exercise thallium is scheduled, instruct the patient for the need to be NPO (for 3 hours before the test) and to eliminate alcohol, tobacco, and unprescribed medications for 24 hours before the test.
4. Inform the patient of the name of the person performing the test, the location of the test, and the equipment used.
5. Instruct the patient on the duration of the test, initially approximately 1.5 hours, and that an additional scan may be required 4 hours later.
6. Inform the patient that an IV line will be started and that a radioactive tracer will be injected to help see the perfusion of blood through the heart muscle.
7. Reassure the patient that the radioactive tracer presents no danger.
8. If the patient has a stress treadmill, instruct the patient on wearing walking shoes and to report any signs of fatigue, chest pain, or shortness of breath immediately.
9. Inform the patient that ECG electrodes will be in place during the testing period.
10. Encourage the patient to ask questions, and provide information in a simple and clear manner. If any questions are appropriate for the physician, assist the patient in formulating the questions and in writing them down.

MYOCARDIAL IMAGING

The radionuclide substance used in MI imaging is technetium-99m pyrophosphate. This test is used to detect recent MI and to determine its extent. Pyrophosphate was originally used for bone scanning since it is taken up by calcium. In the early 1970s it was shown to be taken up by infarcted myocardial tissue. With regional MI there is a large amount of free calcium in the necrotic cells. Necrosis of the cells causes high intracellular calcium levels as part of the inflammatory response. Pyrophosphate will bind to that calcium and reveal the area of necrosis. This is called a *hot spot*.[27] Normal myocardial tissue does not take up pyrophosphate.

Procedure

The patient receives an injection of approximately 15 mCi of technetium-99m pyrophosphate in a peripheral vein. After 1 to 4 hours, the patient is taken to the nuclear medicine department where the scan is performed. A standard scintigraphic camera measures the uptake in the bone and tissue. The camera is placed close to the chest, and the results are recorded on film. The areas that take up the substance appear as hot spots on the film, indicating the infarcted tissue, its location, and size. If the patient is very ill, the test may be done at the bedside. Personnel who are pregnant should not care for a patient who had this test done within the last 24 hours since minute amounts of radiation are given off by the patient.

The test is almost 100% accurate for diagnosing transmural infarctions if done 12 hours to 7 days after the infarction occurred. The optimum time for imaging is 48 to 72 hours after the infarction, although scans have been positive as early as 12 hours after the onset of symptoms. The scans revert to normal approximately 1 week after MI. Persistently positive images are associated with poor prognosis.[28]

For subendocardial infarction, the test is less accurate, 40% to 90% depending on the investigator. The test must be interpreted by a trained individual since many other disorders can give a hot spot in the area of the myocardium, e.g., pericarditis, fractured ribs, valve calcification, hypertension, and myocarditis with inflammation.

Indications

Acute Myocardial Infarction

Myocardial imaging with pyrophosphate is not frequently done since there are easier ways to diagnose an MI. However, there are times when it may be difficult to determine infarction with standard enzyme tests and ECG changes. Patients for whom pyrophosphate imaging may be useful include:

- the patient with left bundle branch block for whom the ECG may not be useful in diagnosing an MI
- the patient who develops unexplained heart failure whose ECG changes are not indicative of infarction
- the postoperative open-heart surgery patient who develops new ECG changes suggestive of AMI, and enzyme tests are nondiagnostic or confusing
- the patient with chest pain several days previously who comes to the hospital 4 days post-onset of chest pain; the enzyme peak has been missed.

Nursing Diagnosis and Interventions for a Knowledge Deficit Related to Myocardial Infarct Scanning Technique

The patient should verbalize an understanding of the purpose of the test, the technique, and post-test care.

1. Assess the patient's understanding of the disease process and the rationale for the test.

2. Instruct the patient on the purpose of the test: to help determine if any areas of the heart muscle are injured.
3. Inform the patient of the name of the person doing the test, the location where the test is performed, and any equipment used during the test.
4. Instruct the patient that an IV line will be started, and a radioactive tracer will be used to visualize any areas of muscle damage.
5. Reassure the patient of the safety in using a radioactive tracer.
6. Instruct the patient that the scanning procedure is painless and that multiple images of the heart will be taken during the test.
7. Instruct the patient to lie motionless during the test and to follow any directions to change position.
8. Inform the patient that an ECG will be placed on the chest during the procedure.
9. Answer any questions the patient may have in a simple and clear manner. If questions are appropriate for the physician, assist the patient in formulating the questions and have the patient write them down.

RADIONUCLIDE VENTRICULOGRAPHY

There are two types of radionuclide ventriculograms: the first pass study and the gated blood pool study. Radionuclide ventriculography evaluates regional and global ventricular performance. These techniques are extremely helpful in noninvasive diagnosis, prognosis, and evaluation of therapy.

Procedure

After IV injection of the isotope technetium-99m, a scintillation camera records the radioactivity emitted by the isotope in its initial pass through the left ventricle. This is called the *first pass imaging*. The ejection fraction is calculated by taking counts of radioactivity during end-diastole, minus counts during systole, divided by counts at end-diastole. Counts are higher in diastole because there is more blood, and hence more radioactivity in the ventricular chamber. When the blood is ejected during systole, the counts fall. With three to five cardiac cycles, a representative cycle is constructed by the computer. The portion of the isotope ejected during each heartbeat can then be calculated to determine the ejection fraction. The ejection fraction is the fraction of blood ejected compared with the volume in the ventricle at the beginning of diastole. This method is very accurate and compares well with the ejection fraction obtained by cardiac catheterization. It may even be more accurate since any abnormality in ventricular geometry is accounted for by this technique.[29] The presence and size of intracardiac shunts can also be determined.

Gated cardiac blood pool imaging, performed after first pass imaging or as a separate test, uses a signal from an ECG to trigger the computer. In multiple gated acquisition (MUGA) scanning, the camera records usually 16 frames (or 14 to 64 points) of a single cardiac cycle, yielding sequential images. These can be studied like motion picture films to evaluate regional wall motion and determine the ejection fraction and other indices of cardiac function. The ejection fraction is closely related to the ejection fraction obtained by contrast ventriculography.

In the stress MUGA test, the same test is performed at rest and during exercise to detect changes in ejection fraction and cardiac function. An exercise MUGA can be done to evaluate cardiac function during exercise. A bicycle table is provided for the patient. The patient is asked to exercise as the scintillation camera records gated images. The workload on the heart is increased during exercise. Sixteen pictures play in rapid sequence. The test determines regional wall motion and functional characteristics of the ventricle when put under stress.[30]

Normally, the ejection fraction is 50% to 75%. During exercise, ventricular volume should decrease, and the ejection fraction should increase 5% to 10%. If there is ischemia present, the ejection fraction will decrease. The test can also determine if the dysfunction is regional or global. Regional dysfunction suggests discrete CAD. Global dysfunction can suggest severe three-vessel disease, cardiomyopathy, or valvular disease.[31]

Indications

Coronary Artery Disease

Radionuclide ventriculography is a good technique to diagnose myocardial dysfunction associated with significant CAD. Normally, the ejection fraction will increase by at least 10% during maximum exercise. Patients with ischemic heart disease may show regional wall motion abnormalities and/or failure to increase the ejection fraction with exercise. This can be detected by exercise ventriculograms and, when used in conjunction with exercise stress testing, may be the most sensitive noninvasive indicator of significant CAD.[32]

Valvular Disease

Radionuclide ventriculography can be used to determine appropriate timing for valve surgery. If the ventricle is functioning well at rest and during exercise, it is more beneficial for the patient to keep the dysfunctional valve. If, however, the ventricular function begins to deteriorate, prosthetic valvular replacement is recommended while the myocardium is healthy. Consequently, the clinician can use this test to follow patients with valvular disease. When the ventricle is dilated and the ejection fraction falls during exercise, this indicates it is time for a valvular replacement.

Ventricular Aneurysm

Radionuclide ventriculography can tell the degree of LV dysfunction attributable to ventricular aneurysm. The test can identify areas of akinesis or dyskinesis.

Prognosis for Post-Myocardial Infarction

The extent of myocardial damage and its effect on global LV function is probably the most significant long-term predictor of risk in coronary heart disease. The size of the infarct and the degree of myocardium involved is a major determinant of the degree of LV dysfunction produced and the subsequent prognosis.

Studies determining the ejection fraction using radionuclide ventriculography showed that patients with initially low or deteriorating ejection fractions had a greater incidence of early mortality. Another study showed that a history of a previous MI and an ejection fraction of less than 40% was 100% sensitive in identifying subsequent mortality in a follow-up period of 30 months.[33,34]

Nursing Considerations

Knowledge Deficit: Radionuclide Ventriculography

The patient should be able to verbalize the rationale for the test, the technique, and post-test care.

1. Assess the patient's understanding of the disease process and the purpose of radionuclide ventriculography.
2. Instruct the patient in simple and clear terms as to the purpose of the test: to assess the heart's LV.
3. Inform the patient regarding the name of the individual performing the test and where the test will be performed.
4. Explain that an IV line is necessary, and that a radioactive tracer will be injected to follow the circulation through the heart.
5. Reassure the patient that the tracer will not present any danger.
6. Inform the patient that ECG electrodes will be positioned on the chest.
7. Explain that the actual imaging is painless, and that the patient should remain motionless unless requested to change position during imaging.
8. Encourage the patient's questions, and answer them in a simple and clear manner. If questions are appropriate for the physician, assist the patient in formulating them and writing them down.

USE OF NUCLEAR IMAGING TECHNIQUES IN CARDIAC DISEASE PROCESSES

Although these noninvasive imaging techniques are extremely helpful in cardiac evaluation, diagnosis, and prognosis, they all have limitations.

In this section the application of the nuclear imaging techniques is examined. These examples illustrate the relative roles of different imaging techniques.

Chronic Coronary Artery Disease

Radionuclide ventriculography studies are important for the study of CAD. The detection of a wall motion defect during exercise and the determination of an abnormal response to exercise are important aids in diagnosing CAD and its severity. Because of the ease in doing these studies with exercise, they remain the primary method for the determination of overall LV function.

Currently, thallium perfusion studies at rest and with exercise are the only clinical method for detecting reversible perfusion abnormalities as a sign of reversible ischemia induced by exercise. This may be extremely helpful in patients whose standard stress ECG is equivocal or cannot be interpreted because of medications, or whose resting ECG shows abnormalities such as left bundle branch block or LV hypertrophy.

Acute Myocardial Infarction

Radionuclear techniques provide information regarding the overall ventricular function and regional wall motion abnormalities. Although mitral regurgitation may be detected by a change in the regurgitant index on gated blood pool studies, this test is neither so sensitive nor specific as echo. However, radionuclide ventriculographic studies are a major asset in diagnosing RV infarction since they easily determine RV function.

Although perfusion defects may be detected in acute MI, there can be thallium resolution problems. The sensitivity of the test is not sufficient to suggest it as a routine technique. Infarct imaging with pyrophosphate may not detect small areas of infarction; its role arises only when other accepted methodologies (i.e., ECG and enzyme studies) do not give a complete picture.

In acute MI patients, the combination of echo and radionuclide ventriculographic studies gives information about overall ventricular function and regional wall motion abnormalities. However, echocardiography can also provide information concerning mitral regurgitation and LV thrombi.

Congestive Cardiomyopathy

Radionuclide ventriculography is useful in studying overall and regional LV function. However, the additional information provided by the echo makes it very useful. The disadvantage is the inability of the echo to provide a more accurate measurement of the ejection fraction.

Hypertrophic Cardiomyopathy

Although the abnormally thickened septum may be seen on a gated blood pool scan, only a small amount of additional information is offered by this test. In patients with chest pain, thallium perfusion studies may be valuable in excluding CAD. Standard stress testing may be totally inadequate because of LV hypertrophy. Strain patterns visualized and thallium perfusion studies may be helpful in the differential diagnosis of CAD. However, the major technique for the diagnosis of hypertrophic cardiomyopathy and its significance is the echo.

Pericardial Effusion

It is possible to see pericardial effusion as an increased separation of the radioactive indicator in the blood pool of the heart and liver; however, this technique is not sensitive and has little role in the routine evaluation of pericardial effusion. Echo remains the procedure of choice.

Valvular Heart Disease

Radionuclide ventriculography and first pass techniques assess overall LV function. In valvular disease patients, they are additionally beneficial since they may be performed during exercise to assess fully LV functional capacity. This finding may be essential to the timing of surgical intervention. A regurgitant index may be calculated to aid in the identification and semiquantification of the regurgitation; it is derived from the ratio of the stroke volumes of the ventricles determined by radionuclide ventriculography. Deviations from the normal ratio signify that one ventricle is pumping a larger stroke volume consequent to regurgitation when it is isolated to either side. Although valuable in research, the full clinical impact is not yet explored. Data from exercise tests are more readily available with radionuclide ventriculographic studies than with echo. This quality is important because of the growing interest in using exercise variables as a guide for determining surgical valvular replacement in an asymptomatic or mildly symptomatic patient. Thus, both techniques are necessary in the full evaluation of these patients. The combination of echo-Doppler studies can determine the gradient and severity of stenosis. These data aid in estimating the need for a more invasive test such as cardiac catheterization.

Mitral Valve Prolapse

Although nuclear techniques have been used in patients with mitral valve prolapse, the technique does not have a major role in this diagnosis. The best use of these tests is in a subgroup of patients whose differential diagnosis is either mitral valve prolapse or CAD. Thallium studies may be used in conjunction with stress testing in patients with suspected CAD. However, echo is still the most useful imaging technique for mitral valve prolapse without suspected CAD.

MODERN DIAGNOSTIC IMAGING TECHNIQUES

CT, NMR/MRI, and PET scanning are three imaging techniques that have greatly affected diagnosis of disease processes. Each imaging technique presents information in the form of a "tomogram," which is simply the Greek word for cross-sectional slice. CT has been in widespread clinical use for approximately a decade, and has firmly established the usefulness of modern imaging techniques by providing a wealth of information not previously available. During the last several years, NMR scanners have begun to appear in clinical settings and have already shown great potential. PET scanners have been used in clinical research for several years and have shown usefulness in evaluating myocardial metabolism.[35]

CT, NMR, and PET exploit different physical properties of the atoms and molecules making up the tissues of the human body. It is important to understand that the picture produced by each of these techniques represents a particular characteristic of the tissue density, water concentration, or metabolic rate. Each technique has its limitations and advantages. The three procedures differ also in the form of radiation employed. CT uses conventional x-rays that are emitted and recorded in a new and unique fashion. PET scanners measure radioactive particles that are introduced into the body by injection. In NMR, the response of tissues to a strong applied magnetic field is studied.[36]

Computerized Tomography

At present, it is unclear as to what role CT scans will have in the assessment of the cardiac patient. The CT scan is a map of the density of various tissues of the body. It is especially helpful in detailing information about the structure of soft tissue, such as brain tissue.

In CT, multiple narrow x-ray beams pass through the patient while detectors record the tissue attenuation of the x-ray beam. The number of x-rays received by the detector is compared with the number produced by the x-ray source to calculate the number of x-rays deleted from the beam by the tissues. The number of x-rays deleted from the beam is directly proportional to the amount of tissue in the path of the beam. A computer reconstructs this information as a three-dimensional image on an oscilloscope. This is then transferred to x-ray film. The amount of radiation the patient receives during a CT scan is actually no greater than the amount received in a series of skull x-ray studies.[37]

Data regarding various tissue densities do not always provide the information needed to diagnose the disease process. Use of IV contrast medium during CT scans can provide additional information. The contrast medium strongly absorbs x-rays. Consequently, the contrast CT scan shows a map of tissue density onto which is projected a map of the blood volume. This test is especially useful in diagnosing certain pathologies of the brain.[38]

Currently, the CT scan is used in cardiac evaluation in a limited number of cardiac disorders. This is attributable in part to several physiologic differences between heart and brain tissue. The heart is composed of homogenous muscle, which limits image resolutions. The capillaries of the heart act as leaky pipes that are large enough for contrast medium to diffuse through the capillary wall, which limits the use of a contrast CT.[39] In addition, the heart being a moving structure requires high-speed (millisecond) exposures and stop-motion images during many phases of the cardiac cycle. Consequently, conventional CT has not become a practical tool for cardiac imaging primarily because of the 2- to 5-second scan exposures. Despite these technical limitations, conventional CT has proved useful for several diagnostic applications including aortic aneurysms, congenital heart disease, coronary artery grafts, and cardiac tumors.

High-speed cardiac CT, a new imaging modality, was specifically designed to improve cardiac diagnosis. The scan for each image is only 50 msec. High-speed CT images the heart in real time. This allows a wide variety of cardiac disorders to be studied including:

- identification of patent coronary artery grafts
- localization and sizing of MI
- diagnosis and evaluation of aortic aneurysms and dissections
- evaluation of congenital heart disease
- cardiac quantitation (e.g., cardiac output, blood flow, etc.)
- evaluation of pericardial disease.[40]

Positron Emission Tomography

PET is a noninvasive technique that permits measurements of local tissue concentrations of radioactive tracers and the use of short-lived positron emitting isotopes that are tagged to metabolically active compounds.[41] PET is used to study myocardial metabolism in cardiovascular disease on the premise that metabolic abnormalities will reflect quantitatively the underlying pathologic condition.

In normal myocardial metabolism, the myocardial cells will preferentially metabolize free fatty acids in the presence of oxygen. If, theoretically, there are no free fatty acids present, or there are high concentrations of glucose, the normal cell can also metabolize glucose. If oxygen is not available to the cell, and the cell is ischemic, it cannot metabolize free fatty acids. In the anaerobic state, the ischemic cell can only metabolize glucose.

In the PET scan, two radioactive isotopes are used as tracers. Fluorodeoxyglucose (FDG) is used to measure glucose uptake in the ischemic cells. Ammonia (N13) is used to measure flow to the area. In normal myocardial tissue there is a match between flow (high N13 uptake) and glucose metabolism (high FDG uptake). In necrotic myocardial tissue there is also a match between flow (decreased N13 uptake) and glucose metabolism (no FDG uptake).[42]

A "mismatch" is shown by a decreased N13 uptake but a high FDG uptake. This indicates an area of ischemia (low flow with decreased N13), but metabolically active tissue (high FDG). This is extremely beneficial in distinguishing reversible from irreversible ischemic injury.

The ability of the PET scan to distinguish reversible from irreversible injury has important clinical applications in patients with CAD. Identification of zones with ischemic glucose use and evaluation of the natural history of these regions with PET in acute infarct patients might serve as a basis for performing and evaluating current therapeutic interventions.[43] In addition, the data from the PET scan may help in the decision whether to perform surgical coronary artery bypass depending on the reversibility of injured tissue.

Magnetic Resonance Imaging

MRI is a noninvasive technique for the visualization of the cardiovascular system. It uses magnetic fields and radiofrequency pulses to generate tomographic images of the body with high soft tissue contrast. When the perpendicular field is pulsed into the patient, the protons in both the blood and blood vessel walls are moved perpendicular to the external magnetic field. As blood and the vessel wall protons realign, they are moved downstream. Thus, there is a strong signal returned from the vessel wall and surrounding tissues and a reduced signal from the blood. Unlike x-ray films that perceive blood and surrounding tissue as having similar densities, MRI is uniquely capable of separating flowing blood from stationary tissue.[44]

There is currently too little clinical experience to predict the eventual role of MRI in cardiovascular diagnosis. However, because of its ability to distinguish stationary tissue from flowing blood, it provides for imaging of anatomic features without the use of radioisotopes. Consequently, it is useful in assessing congenital heart defects. The most promising aspect of MRI is the potential for evaluating metabolic activity of the myocardium through measuring chemical shifts. It may be able to measure tissue oxygen supply and demand noninvasively. MRI has been used to assess a variety of cardiovascular abnormalities including atherosclerosis, AMI, remote infarctions and their complications, and pericardial disorders.[45] As clinical research and development of the technique progresses, they are expected to advance the understanding and treatment of congenital and ischemic heart disease.

Nursing Implications

Modern imaging techniques such as CT, PET, and MRI may prove to have a vital role in the early diagnosis and effective management of cardiac disease.

The implications for critical care nurses are vast. Nurses must increase their awareness of these technologic advances and keep abreast of their clinical application in various cardiac diseases. Critical care nurses need to provide simple, clear explanations of these tests to patients and families. Nursing diagnoses appropriate for patients undergoing testing must be identified. These include: (1) knowledge deficit regarding noninvasive diagnostic tests, and (2) anxiety regarding uncertainty of findings from tests and subsequent diagnosis. Nurses also need to increase their awareness of the cost and the politics associated with advanced technology.

Nursing research must be conducted regarding the impact of technology on critically ill patients and their family. Finally, critical care nurses need to be involved in ethical decisions regarding who receives technology as resources become more scarce.

CONCLUSION

Cardiovascular diagnostics is a dynamic and rapidly growing area. The advances in diagnostic testing are extremely significant in contributing to patient care. They provide for thorough noninvasive assessment of cardiac disease and the response to therapy. Nursing has an important role in keeping current in these technologic advances since we are often faced with providing the patient with instructions, explanations, support, and reassurance.

NOTES

1. Miguel Quinones and Marian Limacher, "Echocardiography in Adult Heart Disease," *Baylor College of Medicine Cardiology Series* 7(1984):5.

2. Ursula K. Anderson, "Cardiovascular Laboratory Testing Procedures," in Cathie E. Guzzetta and Barbara Montgomery Dossey, eds., *Cardiovascular Nursing Bodymind Tapestry* (St. Louis: The C.V. Mosby Co., 1984), p. 219.

3. H. Feigenbaum, "Echocardiographic Measurements and Normal Values," in H. Feigenbaum, ed., *Echocardiography* (Philadelphia: Lea & Febiger, 1981), p. 549.

4. Quinones and Limacher, "Echocardiography."

5. R.L. Popp, "Echocardiographic Assessment of Cardiac Disease," *Circulation* 54 (1976):538.

6. Alan Pearlman, J. Geoffrey Stevenson, and Donald Baker, "Doppler Echocardiography: Applications, Limitations and Future Directions," *American Journal of Cardiology* 46 (1980):1256.

7. Morris Kotler, Anthony Goldman, and Wayne Parry, "Noninvasive Evaluation of Cardiac Valve Prosthesis," in Morris N. Kotler and Robert M. Syeiner, eds., *Cardiac Imaging: New Technologies and Clinical Applications* (Philadelphia: F.A. Davis Co., 1986), p. 181.

8. D.F. Switzer and N.C. Nanda, "Color Doppler Evaluation of Valvular Regurgitation," *Echocardiography*, November, 1985, pp. 533–543.

9. B.C. Corya et al., "Anterior Left Ventricular Wall Echoes in Coronary Artery Disease," *American Journal of Cardiology* 34(1974):652.

10. J.V. Nixon, C.N. Brown, and T.C. Smitherman, "Identification of Transient and Persistent Segmental Wall Motion Abnormalities in Patients with Unstable Angina by Two-dimensional Echocardiography," *Circulation* 47(1973):997.

11. R.F. Kerber and F.M. Abboud, "Echocardiographic Detection of Regional Myocardial Infarction," *Circulation* 47(1973):997.

12. R.S. Horowitz et al., "Immediate Diagnosis of Acute Myocardial Infarction by Two-dimensional Echocardiography," *Circulation* 65(1982):323.

13. R.S. Gibson et al., "Value of Early Two-dimensional Echocardiography in Patients with Acute Myocardial Infarction," *American Journal of Cardiology* 49(1982):1110.

14. A.S. Abbasi et al., "Ultrasound in the Diagnosis of Primary Congestive Cardiomyopathy," *Chest* 63(1973):937.

15. A.E. Weyman, *Cross-sectional Echocardiography* (Philadelphia: Lea & Febiger, 1982), pp. 326–330.

16. A.S. Abbasi et al., "Echocardiographic Diagnosis of Idiopathic Hypertrophic Cardiomyopathy without Outflow Obstruction," *Circulation* 46(1972):897.

17. L.E. Teicholz, "Echocardiographic Evaluation of Pericardial Diseases," *Progress in Cardiovascular Diseases* 21(1978):133.

18. H. Feigenbaum, J.A. Waldhausen, and C.P. Hyde, "Ultrasonic Diagnosis of Pericardial Effusion," *Journal of the American Medical Association* 191(1965):711.

19. Abdulmassih S. Iskandrian, A-Hamid Hakki, and Morris Kotler, "Value of Echocardiography and Nuclear Techniques in Assessment of Valvular Heart Lesions," in Morris N. Kotler and Robert M. Steiner, eds., *Cardiac Imaging: New Technologies and Clinical Applications* (Philadelphia: F.A. Davis Co., 1986), p. 181.

20. Gibson et al., "Two-dimensional Echocardiography."

21. W.J. Stewart, R.A. Levine, Joan Main, and Mary Etta King, "Initial Experience with Color Coded Doppler Flow Mapping," *Echocardiography*, November, 1985, pp. 511–521.

22. A.N. DeMaria et al., "The Variable Spectrum of Echocardiographic Manifestations of Mitral Valve Prolapse Syndrome," *Circulation* 50(1974):33.

23. Anderson, "Cardiovascular Laboratory Testing."

24. G. Zeluff, W. Cashion, and D. Jackson, "Evaluation of Coronary Arteries and the Myocardium by Radionuclide Imaging," *Heart and Lung* 9(1980):344.

25. Teicholz, "Echocardiographic Evaluation."

26. Feigenbaum, Waldhausen, and Hyde, "Ultrasonic Diagnosis."

27. Peter Mclaughlin et al., "Detection of Acute Myocardial Infarction by Technetium-99m Pyrophosphate," *American Journal of Cardiology* 35(1975):390.

28. M.J. Cowley et al., "Technetium-99m Stannous Pyrophosphate Myocardial Scintigraphy: Reliability and Limitations in Assessment of Acute Myocardial Infarction," *Circulation* 56(1977):192.

29. R. Sanderson, "Diagnostic Techniques," in R. Sanderson and C. Kurth, eds., *The Cardiac Patient: A Comprehensive Approach*, ed. 2 (Philadelphia: W.B. Saunders Co., 1983).

30. Zeluff, Cashion, and Jackson, "Evaluation of Coronary Arteries."

31. L.W. Klein and R.H. Helfart, "Value of Noninvasive Techniques Following Acute Myocardial Infarction," in Morris N. Kotler and Robert M. Syeiner, eds., *Cardiac Imaging: New Technologies and Clinical Applications* (Philadelphia: F.A. Davis Co., 1986), pp. 289–296.

32. Iskandrian, Hadikin, and Kotler, "Value of Echocardiography."

33. H.R. Schelbert et al., "Serial Measurements of Left Ventricular Ejection Fraction by Radionuclide Angiography Early and Late Post Myocardial Infarction," *American Journal of Cardiology* 38(1976):407.

34. G.J. Taylor et al., "Predictors of Clinical Cause, Coronary Anatomy, and Left Ventricular Function After Recovery from Post Myocardial Infarction," *Circulation* 62(1980):920.

35. A.H. Maurer, "Emission Tomography and Cardiac Nuclear Medicine," in Morris N. Kotler and Robert M. Syeiner, eds., *Cardiac Imaging: New Technologies and Clinical Application* (Philadelphia: F.A. Davis Co., 1986), p. 145.

36. W.H. Olderdorff, "NMR Imaging: Its Potential Clinical Impact," *Hospital Practice*, September, 1982, pp. 114–128.

37. G.N. Housfield, "Computerized Transverse Axial Scanning (Tomography). Part I: Description of System," *British Journal of Radiology* 46(1973):16.

38. Iskandrian, Hadikin, and Kotler, "Value of Echocardiography."

39. R. Moncada et al., "Diagnostic Role of Computerized Tomography in Pericardial Heart Disease: Congenital Defects, Thickening, Neoplasms and Effusions," *American Journal of Cardiology* 103(1982):263.

40. Donald Farmer et al., "High-Speed (CINE) Computed Tomography of the Heart," in Morris N. Kotler and Robert M. Syeiner, eds., *Cardiac Imaging: New Technologies and Clinical Applications* (Philadelphia: F.A. Davis Co., 1986), p. 345.

41. Markus Schwaiger and Heinrich Schelbert, *Assessment of Tissue Viability in Ischemic Heart Disease by Positron Emission Tomography,* (Chicago: Year Book Medical Publishers, Inc., 1986), p. 155.

42. Heinrich R. Schelbert, "Positron Emission Tomography: Assessment of Myocardial Blood Flow and Metabolism," *Circulation* 72(1985):122.

43. Burton E. Sobel, "Diagnostic Promise of Positron Tomography," *American Heart Journal* 103(1982):673.

44. Leon Kaufman et al., "The Potential Impact of Nuclear Magnetic Resonance Imaging on Cardiovascular Diagnosis," *Circulation* 67(1983):251.

45. Charles B. Higgins, Leon Kauffman, and Lawrence Crooks, "Magnetic Resonance Imaging of the Cardiovascular System," *Progress in Cardiology* 109(1985):136.

REFERENCES

Berger, H.J. "Nuclear Cardiology." *New England Journal of Medicine* 305(1981):799–865.

Burtow, R.D.; Strauss, W.; Singleton, R.; Pond, M.; Rehn, T.; Bailey, I.; Griffith, L.; Nickoloff, E.; and Bertram, P. "Analysis of Left Ventricular Function from Multiple Gated Acquisition Cardiac Blood Pool Imaging." *Circulation* 56(1977):1024–1028.

Chu, Alan; Murdock, Robert; and Cobb, Fredrick. "Relation Between Regional Distribution of Thallium-201 and Myocardial Blood Flow in Normal, Acutely Ischemic, and Infarcted Myocardium." *American Journal of Cardiology* 50(1982):1141–1144.

Cruz, Lillian, and Sahn, David. "Two Dimensional Echo Doppler for Non-Invasive Quantization of Cardiac Flow: A Status Report." *Modern Concepts of Cardiovascular Disease* 51(1982):123–128.

Leitl, George; Buchanan, Julia; and Wagner, Henry. "Monitoring Cardiac Function with Nuclear Techniques." *American Journal of Cardiology* 46(1980):1125–1132.

Nishimura, Rick; Miller, F.A.; Callahan, M.J.; Benassi, R.C.; Seward, J.B.; and Tajik, A.J. "Doppler Echocardiography: Theory, Instrumentation, Technique, and Application." *Mayo Clinic Proceedings* 60(1985):321–343.

Pandian, Natesa; Skorton, David; and Kerber, Richard. "Role of Echocardiography in Myocardial Ischemia and Infarction." *Modern Concepts of Cardiovascular Disease* 53(1984):19–23.

Parisi, Alfred; Tow, Donald; and Sasahara, Arthur. "Clinical Appraisal of Current Nuclear and Other Noninvasive Cardiac Diagnostic Techniques." *American Journal of Cardiology* 38(1976):722–729.

Pitt, Bertram, and Strauss, H. William. "Myocardial Perfusion Imaging and Gated Cardiac Blood Pool Scanning: Clinical Application." *American Journal of Cardiology* 38(1976):739–746.

Popp, Richard. "Echocardiographic Assessment of Cardiac Disease." *Circulation* 54(1976):538–552.

Rasmussen, Susan; Lovelace, E.; Knoebel, S.B.; Ransburg, R.; and Corya, B. "Echocardiographic Detection of Ischemic and Infarcted Myocardium." *Journal of the American College of Cardiology* 3(1984):733–743.

Spann, James. "Changing Concepts of Pathophysiology, Prognosis, and Therapy in Acute Myocardial Infarction." *American Journal of Medicine* 74(1983):877–886.

Strauss, W.H.; McKusick, K.A.; and Bingham, J.B. "Cardiac Nuclear Imaging: Principles, Instrumentation and Pitfalls." *American Journal of Cardiology* 46(1980):1109–1116.

Wagner, H.N. "Symposium on Advances in Cardiovascular Nuclear Medicine: Introduction." *American Journal of Cardiology* 38(1976):709–710.

Zaret, B.L., and Cohen, L.S. "Cardiovascular Nuclear Medicine." *Modern Concepts of Cardiovascular Disease* 46(1977):33–42.

BIBLIOGRAPHY

Barret, N., and Schwartz, M. "What Patients Really Want to Know." *American Journal of Nursing* 81(1982):1642–1644.

Becker, Lewis; Silverman, K.T.; and Bulkley, B.H. "Comparison of Early Thallium-201 Scinti-graphy and Gated Blood Pool Imaging for Predicting Mortality in Patients with Acute Myocardial Infarction." *Circulation* 67(1983):1272–1282.

Beller, G.A. "Radionuclide Techniques in the Evaluation of the Patient with Chest Pain." *Modern Concepts of Cardiovascular Disease* 50(1981):43–48.

Berger, H., and Zaret, B. "Nuclear Cardiology." *New England Journal of Medicine* 305(1982):305.

Coats, K. "Noninvasive Diagnostic Procedures." *American Journal of Nursing* 75(1977):1980.

Dunn, Richard; Uren, R.F.; Sadick, N.; Bautovich, G.; McLaughlin, M.B.; Hiroe, M.; and Kelly, D. "Comparison of Thallium-201 Scanning in Idiopathic Dilated Cardiomyopathy and Severe Coronary Artery Disease." *Circulation* 66(1982):804–810.

Goldman, Mark; Pohost, G.M.; Ingwall, J.S.; and Fossel, E.T. "Nuclear Magnetic Resonance Imaging: Potential Cardiac Applications." *Journal of Cardiology* 46(1980):1278–1283.

Horowitz, Michael; Schultz, C.S.; and Stinson, E.B. "Sensitivity and Specificity of Echocardi-ographic Diagnosis of Pericardial Effusion." *Circulation* 59(1974):239–246.

Mason, D.; Demaria, A.; and Berman, D. *Principles of Noninvasive Cardiac Imaging: Echo-cardiography and Nuclear Cardiology.* New York: LeJacq Publishing, Inc., 1980.

Nishimura, Rick; Tasick, J.; Miller, F.; and Seward, J.B. "Doppler Echocardiography in Valvular Heart Disease." *Learning Center Highlights* 1(1985):6–11.

Pagana, K.D., and Pagana, T.J. *Diagnostic Testing and Nursing Implications.* St. Louis: The C.V. Mosby Co., 1982.

Chapter 3

Acute Myocardial Infarction: Nursing Interventions to Optimize Oxygen Supply and Demand

Barbara Riegel, RN, MN, CS

Morbidity and mortality associated with acute myocardial infarction (AMI) are directly related to the amount of tissue necrosis. The larger the area of infarct, the less effective the heart is as a pump. Patients with decreased cardiac output from myocardial damage report a compromised ability to perform activities of daily living[1] and an impaired quality of life.[2] Those with extensive damage and severe heart failure (ejection fraction <30%) have a poor prognosis; approximately 50% die within 5 years.[3]

Acute coronary care has evolved to include limitation of infarct size. A decade ago, care of the AMI patient involved close observation to detect and treat cardiac arrhythmias early. Now, AMI patients are treated aggressively to optimize hemodynamics and improve the balance of oxygen supply and demand to the myocardium, thereby limiting MI size.

This chapter summarizes the theoretical framework, major nursing diagnoses, and interventions designed to limit infarct size, many of which are within nursing's practice realm. Nurses prescribe and restrict activity, allow visitors, monitor environmental stimuli, promote sleep, titrate intravenous (IV) medications, facilitate individual and family coping, and relieve pain. These decisions are based on an understanding of the need for increased oxygen supply and an assessment of the patient's ability to tolerate stimulation that may increase oxygen demand. This chapter reviews the literature on these and other interventions from the perspective of balancing myocardial oxygen supply and demand. Guidelines are given to assist critical care nurses to make research-based decisions about patient care that may affect infarct size.

THEORETICAL FRAMEWORK

Tissue Injury

MI implies irreversible tissue death from obstruction of the oxygen supply provided by one or more coronary arteries. The principal lesion is an atherosclerotic plaque or atheroma in the intima of the artery. The atheroma usually progresses at a variety of rates, leading to wall thickening and lumen narrowing. An acute coronary event is usually the result of a thrombin and platelet aggregate that forms at the narrowing of the lumen.[4,5]

AMI evolves over 3 to 4 hours (Figure 3-1).[6] Surrounding the injured tissue is a border zone of ischemic but salvageable myocardium. This border zone, termed *jeopardized myocardium*, is an area of cells receiving suboptimal flow.[7] Buda and colleagues[8] suggested that infarct extends during the first 10 days in 10% to 30% of patients. Intermittent chest pain may signal some loss of myocardium with each incident of discomfort, although those without continuing pain may still have a jeopardized zone.[9,10] Interventions to salvage the myocardium at risk should be implemented for all AMI patients in critical care units and intermediate units, and for whom AMI is the probable medical diagnosis.

Myocardial Oxygen Consumption

Injury to the border zone is potentially modifiable by various protective interventions to optimize the balance of myocardial oxygen supply and demand. A decrease in oxygen demand can effectively delay damage to jeopardized

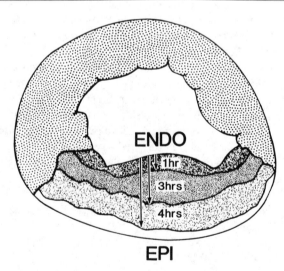

Figure 3-1 Myocardial infarction is a dynamic process that evolves over a 3- to 4-hour period. During that time, injury progresses from the endocardium to the epicardium. *Source*: Courtesy of Dr. William Ganz.

myocardium,[11] although interventions that increase oxygen supply most successfully limit infarct size.[12]

Energy expenditure of the heart can be estimated from its oxygen consumption. However, contraction of the cardiac muscle represents only part of the total energy used. The work of developing and maintaining the tension of contraction is significantly greater than the mechanical work performed by the heart in expelling blood from its chambers. Hence, the major determinant of oxygen usage, and therefore energy consumption, is wall tension. Wall tension is a function of preload and afterload. Preload is the force that stretches the fibers before the onset of contraction. Afterload refers to the stress and tension in the wall of the ventricle during systole. Heart rate and contractility, the force developed by cardiac muscle, also affect myocardial oxygen consumption ($M\dot{V}O_2$).

These determinants of energy consumption do not function in isolation. Homeostatic mechanisms maintain the balance of oxygen usage by increasing the oxygen supply or decreasing the demand by reflex change in one of the other variables. For example, a sudden rise in blood pressure stimulates the baroreceptors in the aortic arch and carotid sinuses, causing slowing of the heart rate and vasodilation. The body is often able to maintain $M\dot{V}O_2$ within a normal range by this reciprocal reflex activity.

Oxygen Supply and Demand

Reflex control of MVO_2 is important since myocardial oxygen supply is limited. Myocardial oxygen extraction from arterial blood is almost maximal under resting conditions, so increased extraction is not a potential method of augmenting supply.[13] In normally pliable coronary vessels, local tissue hypoxia causes coronary vasodilation, which increases coronary flow. However, in vessels with fixed stenoses, caliber increase is not possible. Aggressive interventions aimed at opening the coronary artery blockage, such as thrombolysis, percutaneous transluminal coronary angioplasty (PTCA), or emergency coronary revascularization, are necessary to increase oxygen supply. Supplemental oxygen therapy is only effective in increasing oxygen supply when arterial oxygen tension (PaO_2) declines below approximately 65 mmHg or 93% arterial oxygen saturation (SaO_2).[14] Myocardial oxygen demand is limited by decreasing wall tension, optimizing contractility, and decreasing heart rate.

Wall tension, a function of ventricular diameter, is influenced by preload and afterload. Preload is affected by venous return and ventricular compliance. The volume of blood in the left ventricle (LV) at the end of diastole (preload) stretches the myocardial fibers. Analysis of the Frank-Starling curve (Figure 3-2) reveals that as the fiber length increases, the effectiveness of contractility and cardiac output also increases, up to a point.[15] When an increase in preload and left ventricular end-diastolic filling pressure (LVEDP) exceeds the optimum level

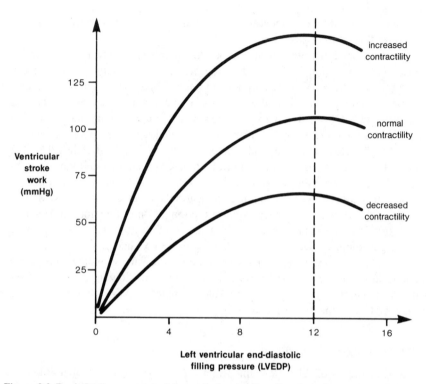

Figure 3-2 Frank-Starling curve. As left ventricular end-diastolic volume increases, so does ventricular stroke work, or contractility. When left ventricular end-diastolic filling pressure exceeds a maximal point, stroke work, contractility, and cardiac output diminish. *Source*: Reproduced by permission from "Review of Functional Cardiovascular Anatomy and Physiology" by K.M. Lewis, *Congestive Heart Failure* by C.R. Michaelson (Ed.), p. 30, St. Louis, © 1983, The C.V. Mosby Company.

(as seen on the curve), stroke volume no longer increases. Any increase in cardiac output is then accomplished by an increase in heart rate or contractility, and therefore the work of the heart.

Inadequate preload can also harm the infarcting heart by compromising cardiac output. This causes a reflex increase in heart rate, contractility, and the work of the heart. Preload, therefore, must be regulated to enhance contractility and cardiac output without increasing $M\dot{V}O_2$.

Preload is best monitored by the Swan-Ganz catheter. The pulmonary artery wedge pressure (PAWP) obtained with the balloon inflated reflects left atrial and LVEDP when the mitral valve is competent. The contractility and cardiac output of an infarcted LV are improved by the fiber stretch that occurs with a slightly elevated preload, so PAWP is kept at 16 to 18 mmHg, instead of 8 to 12 mmHg, in patients with cardiogenic shock.

Afterload refers to the stress and tension in the wall of the ventricle during systole. It is the force against which the LV must eject. The tension of afterload is the result of rising pressure as the LV forces blood out against resistance such as aortic stenosis or systemic hypertension. In the critical care unit, afterload is commonly estimated by computing systemic vascular resistance (SVR) using mean arterial pressure, right atrial pressure, and cardiac output. As vascular resistance or afterload decreases, ventricular ejection improves, a favorable response in patients with AMI.

Heart rate is another factor affecting $M\dot{V}O_2$. The normal adult heart rate varies between 60 to 100 beats per minute. A rate adequate to maintain blood pressure and organ perfusion is essential, but a pulse higher than necessary detrimentally increases $M\dot{V}O_2$ in the infarcted heart. Factors such as disease states, pharmacologic agents, and sympathetic stimulation because of stress raise the heart rate and may extend infarct size.

Contractility refers to the ability of the cardiac muscle fibers to shorten when electrically stimulated. In the failing heart, an increase in contractility increases wall tension but augments $M\dot{V}O_2$ only minimally. However, in the nonfailing heart, pharmacologic agents or sympathetic stimulation that increase the force of contraction actually increase the work of the heart. Conversely, negative inotropic agents such as beta-adrenergic blocking agents reduce $M\dot{V}O_2$.[16]

The theoretical framework of this chapter is summarized in Figure 3-3. Nurses who care for AMI patients routinely use the hemodynamic principles presented and a knowledge of factors that affect the delicate balance of myocardial oxygen supply and demand. This information assists the nurse in independent and collaborative decision making.

INTERVENTIONS TO OPTIMIZE OXYGEN SUPPLY AND DEMAND

Recent advances in the treatment of AMI have focused on methods to open an occluded coronary artery within the 3- to 4-hour time limit so that tissue injury is minimized. Many of the techniques to increase supply are within medicine's purview, and are therefore not the focus of this chapter, but are detailed elsewhere in this book. A summary of medical therapeutics designed to manipulate myocardial oxygen supply and demand is given in Table 3-1. A wide variety of interventions on both sides of the supply and demand equation are within nursing's realm of practice and are described in this section.

Pharmacologic Agents

One common role of critical care nurses is the administration of medications. Many familiar pharmacologic agents are administered to increase oxygen supply

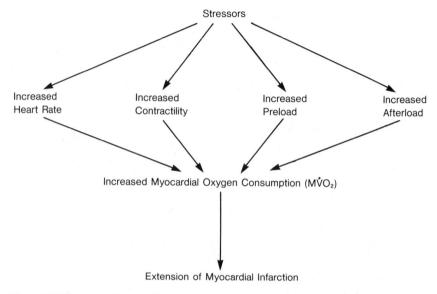

Figure 3-3 Theoretical framework on which this chapter is based. Physiologic and psychologic stressors increase heart rate, contractility, wall tension, and therefore myocardial oxygen consumption. In patients with acute myocardial infarction, jeopardized myocardium is at risk from anything that increases the work of the heart.

to or decrease the demand on jeopardized myocardium. This section discusses some of the medications administered to accomplish these goals using the hemodynamic principles previously presented.

Vasodilator Therapy

Physiologic effects of vasodilators are complex and not fully understood. The primary action of these drugs is afterload reduction attributable to dilation of the arterial (resistance) beds. Afterload reduction facilitates ventricular emptying and decreases the work of the heart. But, coronary perfusion occurs primarily during diastole, and decreased blood pressure may compromise coronary perfusion pressure. Severe hypotension limits blood flow through stenotic coronary vessels with a detrimental effect on jeopardized myocardium.[17] Some vasodilators also dilate the venous (capacitance) system, reducing preload, which may be associated with lower filling pressures, decreased cardiac output, and a compensatory increase in heart rate.

Nitroglycerin (NTG) is commonly used in acute coronary care. Low plasma concentrations of nitrates cause a decrease in preload because of venodilation with an increasing dose-response effect. Coronary vascular resistance is reduced at high nitrate plasma and tissue concentrations.[18] Nitroprusside (NTP) has greater

Table 3-1 Summary of Selected Interventions That Affect Myocardial Oxygen Supply and Demand

Interventions	Oxygen Supply	Oxygen Demand		
		Heart Rate	Contractility	Wall Tension
Thrombolysis	↑			
PTCA	↑			
Bypass surgery	↑			
Balloon pump	↑			↓
Oxygen therapy	↑	(↑)		(↑)
Arrhythmia control	↑	↓		
Pharmacologic agents				
Nitrates	↑	(↑)		↓
Calcium blockers	↑		↓	↓
Beta blockers		↓	↓	↓
Hyaluronidase	↑			
Vasodilators	↑	(↑)		↓
Nitroprusside-dopamine	↑		↑	↓
Dobutamine		(↑)	↑	
Amrinone			↑	
Angiotensin converting enzyme inhibitors		↓	↓	↓

Note: Potentially detrimental effects are in parentheses. See text for more detail.

arteriolar vasodilating effects than does NTG and therefore is associated with a higher incidence of reflex tachycardia and coronary hypoperfusion. For this reason, the use of NTP in limitation of infarct size is controversial.[19]

Vasodilator therapy must be carefully monitored using systemic arterial pressure, PAWP, and the cardiac output. The normal response to these drugs is a decrease in LV filling pressure and an increase in cardiac output. Hypotension and reflex tachycardia must be prevented. An increase in chest pain may indicate "coronary steal," a situation in which coronary blood flow is diverted from ischemic to normal myocardium.

Calcium Channel Blockers

Calcium channel blockers are effective in increasing myocardial oxygen supply and decreasing oxygen demand. The drugs in this class inhibit the flow of calcium ions across cellular membranes. The limited availability of intracellular calcium needed for cardiac contraction decreases the force of contraction, thereby reducing $M\dot{V}O_2$. Coronary vasodilation increases coronary blood flow and oxygen supply. Blockage of calcium influx in smooth muscles of resistance vessels causes peripheral vasodilation and thus a reduction in afterload. This effect is seen primarily with low-dose nifedipine and high-dose diltiazem. Verapamil, and to a lesser extent diltiazem, decreases the rate of sinoatrial node depolarization and atrioventricular conduction, resulting in a lower heart rate, which decreases oxygen demand. The slower pulse allows increased diastolic filling time, thereby improving coronary blood flow.

Monitoring the effectiveness of calcium channel blockers involves monitoring primarily blood pressure, SVR, heart rate, and cardiac output. All drugs in this class potentially cause hypotension and chest pain from coronary steal. Verapamil may accentuate heart failure. Bradycardia is most severe with verapamil, but is also associated with diltiazem. Nifedipine may cause reflex tachycardia and increased contractility with a detrimental effect on $M\dot{V}O_2$.[20] Nifedipine causes paradoxical coronary spasm in some patients.

Beta-Adrenergic Blockade

Use of this class of drugs is controversial in AMI. Myocardial oxygen demand is decreased by the negative inotropic and chronotropic effects produced by the blockade of cardiac beta-1 receptors. However, these same effects are potentially harmful to patients with the compromised LV function or bradycardia. Their use is therefore contraindicated in patients with heart failure, bradyarrhythmias, and atrioventricular block.

An important outgrowth of research on ways to limit infarct size has been the recognition that certain drugs are deleterious to an evolving infarction. Knowledge that tachycardia can extend infarct size has limited the once widespread use of drugs like atropine, isoproterenol, and other catecholamines. Epinephrine is a potential stimulant of myocardial contractility and is used only in emergency situations. Inotropic activity is also increased by cardiac glycosides usually at the cost of increased oxygen use.[21] The use of such agents in AMI is not so common as it once was. However, inotropic agents that facilitate ventricular emptying may decrease wall tension by lowering ventricular volume, thereby limiting $M\dot{V}O_2$. (See Chapter 4 for additional information.)

Supplemental Oxygen

Hypoxemia is a serious complication in the patient with AMI. Dilation of coronary arteries by pharmacologic agents will be inadequate if insufficient oxygen is carried in the blood to meet the oxygen demand. The administration of supplemental oxygen is an intervention commonly initiated under standing protocol or at the request of the nurse.[22] It is undoubtedly beneficial to restore arterial oxygen saturation to normal levels in hypoxemic individuals. However, augmentation of oxygen above full saturation has uncertain value. Research has shown potentially detrimental effects, including increased heart rate, SVR, and arterial pressure during high-flow oxygen therapy.[23]

In the clinical setting, oxygen therapy does not seem to be associated with major problems. In fact, anecdotal reports suggest relief of AMI pain with supplemental oxygen therapy. It has been suggested that the symptom relief may be attributable to increased coronary perfusion pressure because of elevated arterial pressure.[24] Oxygen-induced vasoconstriction of coronary arteries supplying nonischemic zones may also divert blood flow to the ischemic zone, termed *reverse coronary steal.*[25]

Cardiac Arrhythmias

Changes in cardiac rate and rhythm are common and potentially lethal in patients with AMI. The sequella of ventricular fibrillation, for instance, is well known. However, the effect of increased heart rate and ineffective cardiac rhythms on MI size is less well appreciated.

The lowest heart rate compatible with adequate cardiac output is ideal for the AMI patient. Cardiac rhythms that allow for an ''atrial kick'' or adequate ventricular filling augment cardiac output. Atrial fibrillation, for instance, because of the incoordination of atrial and ventricular contraction, usually results in poor atrial emptying and compromised cardiac output, especially at accelerated rates.[26]

Patients with changes in cardiac rhythm and rate must be monitored for the nursing diagnosis *decrease in cardiac output.* The defining characteristics of this diagnosis include[27]:

- variations in hemodynamic readings
- electrocardiographic (ECG) changes; arrhythmias
- fatigue
- jugular vein distention
- cyanosis; pallor of skin and mucous membranes
- oliguria; anuria
- decreased peripheral pulses
- cold, clammy skin
- rales
- dyspnea.

Rhythms such as supraventricular tachycardia, often thought of as uncomfortable but not life-threatening, should be reported immediately because of detrimental effects on $M\dot{V}O_2$. Conversely, a slow idioventricular rhythm with evidence of clear mentation and a urine output of at least 30 cc/hr does not indicate immediate use of antiarrhythmic agents.

The nurse must be particularly aware of the potential for a *decrease in cardiac output* secondary to reperfusion arrhythmias after thrombolytic therapy. Once an occluded coronary vessel is recanalized, arrhythmias are common and probably suggest restoration of antegrade flow. Accelerated idioventricular rhythm is most common, although sinus bradycardia and atrioventricular block with hypotension may occur when the vessels supplying the inferioposterior LV are opened.[28] After thrombolytic therapy, vital signs (VS) and cardiac rhythm are monitored frequently.

Physical Conditions

Awareness that an elevated heart rate increases $M\dot{V}O_2$ necessitates that nurses monitor for problems that may cause tachycardia. Conditions that must be reported, and treated expediently, include fever and anemia. Reflex tachycardia may result from hypotension, hypoxemia, pain, fear, anxiety, a deficit in fluid volume, and any decrease in cardiac output. *Alteration in fluid volume* can be monitored by daily weights if a pulmonary artery catheter is not in place. *Alteration in cardiac output* is suspected with hypotension and sudden arrhythmias that compromise cardiac filling.

Conditions that increase wall tension also warrant immediate treatment to limit infarct size. An acute increase in preload or diastolic overload is produced most commonly in AMI patients by mitral regurgitation from papillary muscle dysfunction. A murmur, especially a new holosystolic murmur, that is loudest at the cardiac apex, characteristic of mitral regurgitation, or usually associated with an S_4 should be reported immediately. Aortic insufficiency may cause a chronic increase in the amount of blood in the LV at the end of diastole (increased LVEDP). This chronic condition may be well tolerated, but it also may complicate the hemodynamic balance during AMI. A murmur that increases in loudness may indicate deteriorating hemodynamic status and should be reported immediately. Other physical signs to assess include jugular venous distension and evidence of congestive heart failure on chest x-ray films or lung auscultation.

Afterload is frequently elevated in acutely ill patients. A variety of endogenous and exogenous agents may elevate systemic vascular resistance (SVR), including epinephrine, caffeine, nicotine, hypothermia, and stress. As previously noted, supplemental oxygen therapy may increase SVR, and should be suspected if all other causes have been ruled out.

Activity Regulation

The nursing diagnosis *activity intolerance* is defined as a state in which the individual experiences an inability to endure or tolerate an increase in activity.[29] The defining characteristics of this diagnosis include[30]:

- verbal report of fatigue or weakness
- abnormal heart rate or blood pressure response to activity
- exertional discomfort of dyspnea
- ECG changes reflecting arrhythmias or ischemia.

Activity that is poorly tolerated may increase heart rate, blood pressure, and energy consumption—and therefore $M\dot{V}O_2$—in AMI patients with an acutely compromised oxygen supply. Activity that causes a demand greater than available supply may extend infarct size.

Until recently, activity was severely restricted in patients with AMI. Winslow[31] reminded us that until the early 1950s, patients were immobilized for 6 to 8 weeks based on a study showing that small infarcts healed in 5 weeks and large ones in 8.[32] Besides enforcing bed rest, nurses guarded patients against voluntary movements or effort. Patients were fed, shaved, and made to use the bedpan in the belief that exertion would cause cardiac rupture and death. Later data showed that cardiac rupture was related to systolic hypertension, not activities of daily living.[33]

Bed Rest

Bed rest causes a variety of physiologic alterations. Prolonged bed rest increases the resting heart rate up to 15 beats per minute, and accentuates the heart rate response to submaximal activity such as walking. Saltin et al.[34] showed a 27% increase in heart rate response to submaximal exercise testing after 20 days on bed rest compared with before bed rest. During the study, subjects moved freely in bed and were out of bed for 10 minutes daily for bathroom privileges, but no standing was allowed. Despite the pronounced increase in heart rate, cardiac output was significantly lower after bed rest as a result of a reduced ventricular filling, and consequently, stroke volume.

The normal distribution of blood changes during bedrest. In the supine position, 50% of the total blood volume is in the systemic veins, approximately 30% in the intrathoracic vessels, and less than 20% in the systemic arteries. Upon standing, approximately 500 ml of blood shifts from the intrathoracic cardiovascular compartments to the dependent parts of the body because of gravity and the imperfect circulatory adjustments to it.[35] Ventricular filling, or preload, is decreased because of plasma volume losses early in the bed rest period. Blood and plasma volume losses accentuate the supine shift in fluid from the lower to the upper half of the body. This fluid shift activates the body's compensatory mechanisms designed to buffer pressure and volume alterations, and may be more important in causing cardiovascular dysfunction after bed rest than is the physical inactivity.[36]

Orthostatic intolerance caused by bed rest accentuates tachycardia, narrows pulse pressure, and may cause syncope in response to the upright position. These physiologic effects are more pronounced the longer a patient is on bed rest, but occur after as few as 6 hours supine.[37] The response is more pronounced in the elderly and those taking drugs such as vasodilators. Winslow[38] suggested that supine exercise helps maintain exercise capacity, but is ineffective in preventing orthostatic intolerance and has unclear effects on plasma volume. However, the upright position may prevent the physiologic consequences of bed rest such as tachycardia, which may be detrimental to an evolving infarction.

Exercise Response

Activity for patients in the early stages of AMI has been liberalized in recent years to include discharge from the critical care unit to telemetry after only a few days, with ambulation allowed. With the onset of moderate or submaximal exercise, such as graded exercises, the resistance vessels supplying the active muscles dilate. Generalized sympathetic nervous activity occurs, causing an increase in heart rate, myocardial contractility, and peripheral resistance in non-active tissues. Norepinephrine is the predominant catecholamine released at these lower exercise levels.[39] Arterial pressure starts to rise with the onset of activity, and the increase in blood pressure parallels the severity of exertion. Systolic pressure increases more than diastolic pressure, probably because of an increase in stroke volume. Heart rate, contractility, and wall tension, the determinants of $M\dot{V}O_2$, all increase to a small degree in patients doing minimal exertion such as walking in the halls.

A variety of factors influence sympathoadrenal activity during exercise. Patients on diuretics may be dehydrated, a factor associated with higher levels of plasma norepinephrine and epinephrine, and less exercise tolerance.[40] Patients who have been on prolonged bed rest or who are receiving medications for afterload reduction may have an accentuated response to activity. Psychologic stress increases plasma catecholamine levels, even without exertion.[41] Patients with poor LV ejection fractions, such as those with congestive heart failure, have an elevated plasma norepinephrine response to exercise.[42] The normal sympathetic response to exercise is inhibited in patients taking beta-adrenergic blocking agents.[43]

The higher the metabolic level of activity (Figure 3-4), the higher the increase in oxygen demand. The additive effect of two or more metabolic demands at one time will probably decrease the patient's ability to perform. For instance, graded exercises should not be done by any patient immediately after incentive spirometry. The obese expend extra energy during any physical activity because of the cost of moving a large body mass.[44,45] Marmor et al.[46] reported that infarcts extended more frequently in obese patients. Activities for these patients should be carefully planned.

A rest period should follow each activity. Alteri[47] studied 10 male AMI patients to determine an adequate rest period after activities of daily living during the

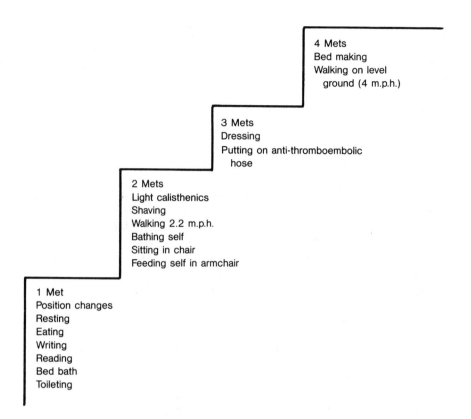

Figure 3-4 Energy cost (in mets*) of activity and exercise. Data on the metabolic cost of a variety of activities of daily living performed by hospitalized patients suggest that these activities are light or very light and are safe for most acute myocardial infarction patients.

*Note: 1 met = 3.5 cc O_2/kg body weight/min.

immediate post-MI period. Showering, stair climbing, and walking were evaluated using the pressure-rate product (PRP). The amount of time needed for return of the PRP to the resting baseline state for 90% of the sample was designated an adequate rest period for that activity. After showering, 90% of the sample returned to baseline within 30.5 minutes; after stair climbing within 7 minutes; and after walking within 10 minutes. Subjective reports did not coincide with objective data, however. All patients reported a readiness to continue activities without any rest period.

Although few clinical studies have been conducted with AMI patients, initial nursing implications can be drawn from this summary of factors affecting the exercise response. If AMI is an evolving process, rather than a static one, as the data suggest,[48,49] a gradual increase in activity in the acute stages of AMI is essential to limit infarct size. Assessment of the response to activity is essential and is easily done by calculation of the PRP. There is an excellent correlation between myocardial oxygen consumption and the product of heart rate and systolic blood pressure.[50]

The Borg category-ratio perceived exertion scale (Table 3-2) could also be used to evaluate response to activity. Noble and colleagues[51] found a correlation of 0.99 between the perceived exertion scale and measures of blood and muscle lactate in 10 physically active men. However, the correlation between heart rate and perceived exertion was poor, suggesting that the scale may be a better indicator of actual exertion than the PRP.

Whatever the method used to evaluate response to activity, exertion should be terminated for any of the following: (1) complaints of angina, (2) generalized fatigue, (3) shortness of breath, (4) dizziness or lightheadedness, (5) unsteady gait, (6) heart rate increase greater than 120 beats per minute, (7) ST segment depression greater than 1.5 mm, (8) a drop in systolic blood pressure below the resting level or its failure to rise, (9) significant arrhythmias such as premature ventricular beats in excess of 10 per minute, couplets, or R-on-T phenomenon.[52]

Research on Activity

Bathing. Johnston and associates[53] studied oxygen consumption and hemodynamic response to three types of bathing—basin, tub, and shower—in 12 stable patients 3 to 5 days after AMI. Heart rate response was determined by radial pulse palpation halfway through and at the completion of each bath, and is summarized in Table 3-3. The shower was associated with significantly more demand than either the tub or basin bath as measured by oxygen con-

---

Table 3-2 The Borg Perceived Exertion Scale

0	Nothing at all	
0.5	Very, very weak	(just noticeable)
1	Very weak	
2	Weak	(light)
3	Moderate	
4	Somewhat strong	
5	Strong	(heavy)
6		
7	Very strong	
8		
9		
10	Very, very strong	(almost max)
•	Maximal	

Source: Reprinted from, "A Category-Ratio Perceived Exertion Scale: Relationship to Blood and Muscle Lactates and Heart Rate" by B.J. Noble, *Medical Science Sports and Exercise*, Vol. 15, No. 6, pp. 523–528, with permission of American College of Sports Medicine, © 1983.

Table 3-3 Metabolic and Cardiac Work of Selected Activities in Patients

Bathing[1,2]	Ml/Kg/Min[1,2]	Mets[1,2]	After Bath PRP[1,2]	Mean Peak Heart Rate[2]	Range[2]
Basin	6–9	2–2.5	115–130	105	76–120
Tub	7–9	2–2.5	120–140	108	80–144
Shower	6.5–13	2–3.5	110–150	112	84–132

Toileting[3,4]	Ml/Kg/Min[3,4]	Mets[3,4]	Peak PRP[3,4]	Mean Peak Heart Rate[3,4]
Bedpan	4.4	1.5	110	89
Bedside commode	4.6	1.5	109	94
In-bed urinal	4.5	1.3	94	84
Standing urinal	4.7	1.4	102	91

[1]Barbara Johnston, Edward Watt, and Gerald Fletcher, "Oxygen Consumption and Hemodynamic and Electrocardiographic Response to Bathing in Recent Post-Myocardial Infarction Patients," *Heart and Lung* 10 (1981): 666.

[2]Elizabeth Hahn Winslow, Lynda Lane, and Andrew Gaffney, "Oxygen Uptake and Cardiovascular Responses in Control Adults and Acute Myocardial Infarction Patients During Bathing," *Nursing Research* 34, no. 3, (1985): 164.

[3]J.G. Benton, H. Brown, and H.A. Rusk, "Energy Expended by Patients on the Bedpan and Bedside Commode," *Journal of the American Medical Association* 144 (1950): 1443.

[4]Elizabeth Hahn Winslow, Lynda Lane, and Andrew Gaffney, "Oxygen Uptake and Cardiovascular Response in Patients and Normal Adults During In-Bed and Out-of-Bed Toileting," *Journal of Cardiac Rehabilitation* 4 (1984): 348.

Note: The author would like to acknowledge the assistance of Elizabeth Winslow in the preparation of this table.

sumption ($p < 0.01$) and PRP ($p < 0.05$), which may be attributed to the upright position and venous pooling. The authors concluded that caution was warranted with showers, but either basin or tub baths were safe for stable AMI patients.

Winslow and colleagues[54] studied oxygen uptake, cardiovascular responses, and subjective perception of exertion and preference in 22 control adult and 18 AMI patients during bathing. Cardiovascular response was monitored by continuous ECG through each bathing procedure. The data are summarized in Table 3-3 and show the physiologic cost of basin, tub, and shower bathing to be similar. Differences in physiologic responses to bathing seemed more a function of individual variability than bath type. It is important to note that cardiac patients showed significantly lower oxygen consumption during bathing than control subjects, interpreted as conservation of energy. The authors suggested that cardiac patients perceive bathing as light exertion and most can take a tub bath or shower earlier in hospitalization. However, more study is needed, as a few patients had high heart rate responses and PRPs.

Patients who continue to have bouts of chest pain, suggesting postinfarct ischemia or signs of decompensation because of heart failure, may need to delay a tub bath because of the isometric activity required to get in and out of a tub.

Isometric activity increases afterload by raising systolic and diastolic pressure. Continuing chest pain is also an indication to delay showering, as the data of Johnston and colleagues[55] showed an increase in PRP during showering, and Alteri[56] showed that the recovery time after this exertion was higher than with other activities. However, the data suggest that uncomplicated patients in the first few days after AMI may consider taking a bath or a sitting or standing shower so long as the water temperature is controlled at 96 to 98 degrees, a thermoneutral temperature with minimal heart rate and blood pressure effects.

A variety of factors should be evaluated when nurses are deciding what type of bath a patient may take. The physiologic responses to bathing are similar to those of exercise in general. Orthostatic intolerance may be accentuated by bed rest, vasodilators, fever, varicosities, a warm environment, and hot water temperature. Obesity and weakness may decrease activity tolerance. Drugs that limit cardiac output or affect contractility, such as beta-adrenergic blocking agents or calcium antagonists, may decrease the patient's ability to respond physiologically to exertion.[57] Patients allowed to take a tub bath should be evaluated for the ability to get into and out of a tub.

More research on patient response and tolerance to various bathing methods is needed before comprehensive guidelines for bath method selection can be developed. A decision tree to assist with this process is given in Figure 3-5, but further research is needed to validate the suggestions given. Delineation of the factors that predict the ability to tolerate types of bathing and the environmental variables that must be controlled is needed. In the meantime, careful individualized assessment can help nurses plan care that balances myocardial oxygen supply and demand.

Toileting. Benton and associates[58] studied the energy cost of two toileting methods in 15 cardiac and 13 noncardiac subjects during simulated defecation in the bedpan and bedside commode. Oxygen consumption was measured during toileting and during a recovery period after toileting. Blood pressure, heart rate, and ECG were recorded during and after each toileting method, but not reported because of the extreme variability. They found that the bedpan required 50% more energy above resting levels than did the commode (Table 3-3).

Winslow and colleagues[59] studied oxygen uptake, cardiovascular response, perceived exertion, and preference for in-bed and out-of-bed toileting in 16 acute post-MI patients, 27 medical inpatients, 16 cardiac outpatients, and 26 healthy volunteers. No physiologically important differences were found between in-bed and out-of-bed toileting in any group. Both required minimal energy expenditure and cardiac work over resting levels. Subjects reported that the commode was significantly easier to use than the bedpan ($p < 0.0005$) and clearly preferred. As in the bathing study, the researchers found that hospitalized patients used less energy than control subjects, perhaps because of slower, more deliberative movements. The authors suggested that patients should be allowed out of bed

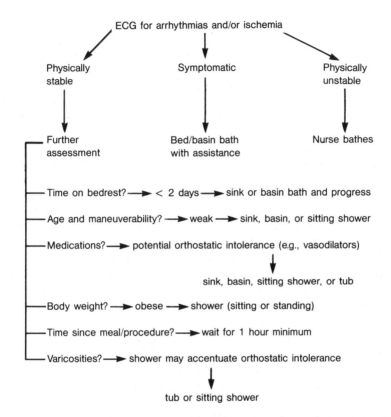

Figure 3-5 Decision tree for bathing. This decision tree can be used to evaluate patient variables known to affect activity response. This assessment facilitates prescription of an appropriate method of bathing.

Note: Response to bathing can be evaluated during the activity by leaving the monitoring unit on the patient and covering it with a rubber glove.

to use the commode if other factors such as low cardiac output syndrome do not contraindicate the activity.

The results of both studies on the physiologic cost of toileting agree that the metabolic work of in-bed and out-of-bed toileting are not significantly different. The bedside commode is certainly preferred to the bedpan, and both studies found use of the bedside commode to be a safe activity for AMI patients.

Evaluation of the research on bathing and toileting suggests that these activities may be better tolerated during illness than the research on normal subjects would predict. The concept of conservation of energy suggests that the ill human being apparently slows activity normally, in an attempt to heal, except when denial interferes with common sense.

Positioning and Transfer

Positioning patients is another common nursing intervention that should be based on the need to decrease oxygen demand in AMI. McCarthy[60] studied the metabolic cost of maintaining five fixed body positions—supine, prone, left and right lateral, and sitting—in five young women. Although the heart rate was higher in the sitting position, overall the metabolic cost of maintaining any one of the five positions did not significantly differ.

Jackson and Kinney[61] examined energy expenditure, heart rate, rhythm, and blood pressure in 50 normal women during transfer between a sequence of fixed positions—semi-Fowler's in bed with one pillow, dangling on the side of the bed, sitting in a wheelchair, semi-Fowler's in bed with one pillow, and flat on a stretcher with one pillow. They found that moving from the dangling position to the wheelchair expended less energy than moving from a semi-Fowler's position in the bed to the stretcher. Sitting in a wheelchair consumed less energy than lying on a stretcher. However, moving from a stretcher to a bed expended less energy than going from the wheelchair to the bed. Their results showed wide variability, for unclear reasons, limiting any implications for practice.

Quaglietti[62] studied the hemodynamic response of 12 uncomplicated AMI patients during transfer between a sequence of four positions—supine to 70° semi-Fowler's to dangle to chair—on the second day after AMI. Heart rate and systolic blood pressure were recorded 3 minutes after the position was assumed. There was no difference in the PRP in any of the four positions, suggesting that movement to these positions is a safe form of early activity for the uncomplicated AMI patient.

Geden[63] studied oxygen consumption, heart rate, respiratory rate, and blood pressure in 14 normal female subjects during five lifting techniques—mechanical lift, rocking axillary, self-lift, shoulder-assist, and straight-pull. Lifting via a mechanical lift device was the most taxing on the person being lifted, perhaps because of greater manipulation before the procedure or the subject's anxiety about being lifted with the device.

The data on positions and modes of transfer between positions suggest that moving patients from one position to another has a very low energy cost. The clinical relevance of any statistically significant differences is questionable. Research in this area is essential before any change in practice can be recommended, but at this time it seems that position changes are safe for all but the most unstable AMI patients.

Summary of Implications Related to Activity

The nursing research related to activity is in its infancy. Many of these studies are one of a kind, using small samples of normal subjects. Nursing implications cannot be drawn with confidence from this data base. However, some initial direction can be suggested with the caveat that further research is needed.

A general finding, supported by the physiology literature, is that a low met level activity does not seem to be detrimental to the AMI patient. In fact, the result of enforced bed rest is deconditioning, which causes a decrease in activity tolerance and other undesirable consequences.[64] Activities that expend minimal energy such as out-of-bed toileting can be used to counteract the physiologic effects of bed rest.[65] In this way, $M\dot{V}O_2$ can be minimized by judicious activity that prevents deconditioning. Progressive exercise that is monitored and supervised is beneficial in the early days after AMI. Exhibit 3-1 suggests guidelines for activity after AMI.

COPING ABILITY

Activity is not the only, or perhaps even the major, phenomenon that increases the work of the heart and threatens ischemic myocardium. During hospitalization, AMI patients often experience a magnified stress state, which may lead to decreased coping ability.[66] Ineffective coping occurs when the individual is

---

Exhibit 3-1 Nursing Care Plan for Activity after AMI

Nursing diagnosis: Activity intolerance
Etiology: Inadequate cardiac oxygen supply for myocardial demand
Manifestations: Verbal report of fatigue or weakness, abnormal heart rate or blood pressure response to activity, exertional discomfort or dyspnea, ECG changes reflecting arrhythmias or ischemia
Long-term goal: Patient can do activities of daily living with minimal symptoms by discharge.
Short-term objectives: Patient will be able to do the following with minimal symptoms: use bedside commode, feed self, assist with bath (1st day); sit in chair, bathe from sink or basin (2nd day); increase time in chair, discharge from CCU (3rd day); walk in halls, shower or tub bath (4th day).
Interventions:
- Assess physical stability (vital signs, physical examination, arrhythmias, ECG, chest x-ray films, subject reports)
- Assess influencing factors (medications, e.g., vasodilators, body weight, age, period on bed rest, meal and treatment times, varicosities, sleep)
- Assess patient preferences (rituals, motivation, energy)
- Decrease cardiac workload: provide adequate rest/sleep, teach to pace/space activities, avoid strenuous physical activity, plan progressive activities

Evaluate response to activity:
- Monitor response: vital signs, subjective response, ECG evidence of arrhythmias and/ or ischemia (cover unit with glove during shower)
- Alter activity according to response

unable to manage internal or environmental stressors sufficiently because of inadequate physical, psychologic, or behavioral resources.[67] (See also Chapter 8.) The defining characteristics of the nursing diagnosis *ineffective individual coping* include[68]:

- verbalization of inability to cope or inability to ask for help
- inability to meet role expectations
- alteration in social participation
- change in usual communication patterns
- inappropriate use of defense mechanisms
- inability to problem-solve
- inability to meet basic needs.

Factors Affecting Coping

According to Lazarus and colleagues,[69] the ability to cope with stress depends on the meaning of the stimulus and its relevance and significance for the individual. Three major influences combine to determine an individual's emotional response to a particular stimulus: cognitive appraisal of the situation, biologic and cultural determinants of emotion, and past history and psychologic structure.

Cognitive appraisal of situations is influenced by our development as a biologic species. For instance, the brain wave response to stimuli differs among individuals.[70] "Augmentors" show a magnified brain wave response to environmental stimuli; "reducers" have minimal brain wave responses to the same stimuli, and therefore can tolerate more stimulation in the environment. Further research may show that "augmentors" should be placed in quiet rooms to avoid sensory overload.

Cultural background affects coping ability. The response to pain, need for family support, and rituals of daily living all vary among cultures.[71] Staff acceptance of cultural variations may influence the patient's cognitive appraisal of stimuli and emotional response.

Finally, individual development and psychologic makeup affect emotional response and the ability to cope. Analysis of a situation is influenced by the individual's style of searching out, responding to, or selectively attending to stimuli. Individual responses to stimuli will always vary.

Emotions change with feedback and efforts to cope with the reaction such as reappraisals or direct actions. Reappraisals are cognitive re-evaluations of situations. For instance, an initial appraisal may be that a situation such as transfer out of the coronary care unit (CCU) is threatening. Reappraisal may convince the patient that transfer is benign. Defense mechanisms are types of reappraisals that involve conscious or unconscious distortions of reality that decrease the threat of a situation.

Direct actions, such as attack or avoidance, aim to alter the situation to reduce or eliminate the threat, and are accompanied by physiologic arousal. It is this state of physiologic arousal that is associated with an increase in the work of the heart and a potential extension of MI size.

Physiologic Response to Stress

The sympathetic nervous system response is a nonspecific, widespread, energy-consuming phenomenon produced by the outpouring of catecholamines. Physiologic arousal of the stress state occurs because of the release of norepinephrine from nerve endings. Epinephrine, the primary catecholamine released from the adrenal medullae, is responsible for maintaining long-lasting sympathetic arousal. Secretion of epinephrine at levels above threshold influences susceptible tissues even during minimal stress or light-to-moderate exercise.

Cardiovascular effects of epinephrine and norepinephrine include increased heart rate, contractility, stroke volume, and cardiac output. In large doses, catecholamines elevate arterial pressure; in small doses arterial pressure is reduced. Catecholamine secretion causes restlessness, anxiety, and increased oxygen consumption. Other effects include enhanced protein catabolism and increased insulin release, which increases the availability of energy for the "fight or flight" response. During the stress response, the majority of blood is shunted to those organs needing to function at a high level. Table 3-4 presents a summary of the physiologic stress response.[72]

In the normal cardiovascular system, sympathetic stimulation causes coronary vasoconstriction, but associated metabolic factors such as lactic acid, hydrogen and potassium ions, histamine, prostaglandins, and others cause vasodilation. The overall response therefore to stimulation of the sympathetic nerves is a marked increase in coronary blood flow.[73] This is a beneficial effect, but one that is offset by rate acceleration and more forceful systole. The marked increase in coronary blood flow supplies increased oxygen, which helps meet the demand of positive inotropic action and generalized vasoconstriction.

Almost the entire increase in $M\dot{V}O_2$ attributable to catecholamines comes from increased heart rate and contractility rather than a biochemical "oxygen-wasting" effect of catecholamines on myocardial metabolism, as previously thought.[74] In patients with atherosclerosis and limited oxygen supply, $M\dot{V}O_2$ can be minimized by limiting stressors that stimulate the stress response.

Some of the internal and environmental stressors that may compromise the ability to cope include sensory overload, sleep deprivation, alteration in comfort, and anxiety and fear. Patients who cannot cope effectively with the crisis of

Table 3-4 Autonomic Control of Various Tissues and Organs

Organ	Autonomic Control*	Neuroeffector Transmitter* S	Neuroeffector Transmitter* PS	Adrenergic Receptor	Sympathetic Effects†	Parasympathetic Effects†
Pupil	S, PS	NE	ACh	α	Dilatation	Constriction
Ciliary muscle	S, PS	NE	ACh	β	Relaxation	Contraction
Lacrimal gland	PS	—	—	—	—	Secretion
Heart	S, PS	NE	ACh	β	Rate ↑, force ↑, conduction velocity ↑	Rate ↓, conduction velocity →
Blood vessels						
Cerebral	S, PS	NE	ACh	α	Constriction (slight)	Dilatation (slight)
Coronary	S, PS	NE	—	α β	Constriction (slight)	Dilatation (slight)
Gut	S	NE	—	α β	Constriction	—
Renal	S	NE	—	α	Constriction	—
Skin	S	NE	—	α	Constriction	—
Skeletal muscle	S	NE and ACh	—	α β	Constriction, dilatation	—
Gut	S, PS	NE	ACh	α β	Motility ↓, secretion ↓, sphincter tone ↑, thick secretion	Motility ↑, secretion ↑, sphincter tone ↓, thin secretion
Salivary glands	S, PS	NE	ACh	α	Dilatation, secretion ↓	Constriction, secretion ↑
Bronchi	S, PS	NE	ACh	β		
Ureter	S, PS	NE	ACh	α	Increased tone and motility, detrusor relaxes, sphincter contracts	Increased tone and motility, detrusor contracts, sphincter relaxes
Bladder	S, PS	NE	ACh	α β		
Genitalia	S, PS	NE	ACh	α	Ejaculation	Erection
Sweat glands	S	ACh	—	—	Sweating ↑	—

*S = sympathetic; PS = parasympathetic; NE = norepinephrine; ACh = acetylcholine.
† ↑ = function is increased; ↓ = function is decreased.

Source: Reproduced with permission from G. Ross: *Essentials of Human Physiology*, 2nd edition, p. 112. Copyright © 1982 by Year Book Medical Publishers, Inc., Chicago.

hospitalization may have a physiologic stress response that may increase $M\dot{V}O_2$ and actually threaten jeopardized myocardium.

Sensory Overload

A common source of stress in any intensive care unit is sensory overload. Although a CCU is generally quieter than a large surgical intensive care unit, research suggests that patients are still exposed to levels of noise and stimulation that are detrimental to recovery.[75]

Sensory overload in the CCU is attributable to the amount and unfamiliarity of the environmental stimuli and the meaning attributed to it by the patient. Defining characteristics of the nursing diagnosis *sensory perceptual alteration* include:

- altered abstraction and conceptualization
- change in problem-solving abilities
- change in sensory acuity
- anxiety
- apathy
- restlessness
- irritability
- altered communication patterns.

Specific stimuli include lighting, crowding, unpleasant smells, painful touch, and noise from machinery, people, or the background environment.[76] Continuous lighting distorts the patient's sense of time and natural circadian rhythm. Many biologic functions have a rhythmic, diurnal pattern, including cortisol secretion, growth hormone, blood pressure, and body temperature.[77,78] Sensory overload that is continuous in nature may well disrupt not only the sleep cycle, but the biologic clock necessary for coping and healing. Crowding with strangers and unfamiliar mechanical devices are other sources of sensory overload in the CCU. Crowding threatens a loss of privacy, territoriality, and control over the environment.

Routine nursing care contributes to this invasion of privacy and loss of territory. Baxter[79] suggested that nursing interventions that are uncomfortable or painful may destroy trust between patients and staff. Thomas and colleagues[80] documented increased cardiac arrhythmias in CCU patients when the nurse simply entered the room to give medications. Interventions such as handholding[81] and backrubs are usually effective stress reducers, but may actually accentuate stress with sensory overload.

Noise is probably the most common cause of sensory overload in the CCU. Sounds contributing to noise pollution include mechanical equipment, alarms, movement of people and objects, telephones, computer printers, noise accompanying nursing care such as suctioning, coughing or moaning of patients, and staff talking and laughing. Sound levels of 35 to 40 dB—commonly found in a library—are recommended for sleep, but levels of 45 to 85 dB have been recorded in hospitals (Figure 3-6).[82]

Noise as low as 68 to 70 dB at 1,000 Hz (pitch) stimulates the pituitary-adrenal axis, causing the release of adrenocorticosteroids, epinephrine, and norepinephrine.[83] The body does not adapt physiologically to sustained noise. Noise that continues at 70 dB or greater continues to stimulate the adrenal-pituitary axis.

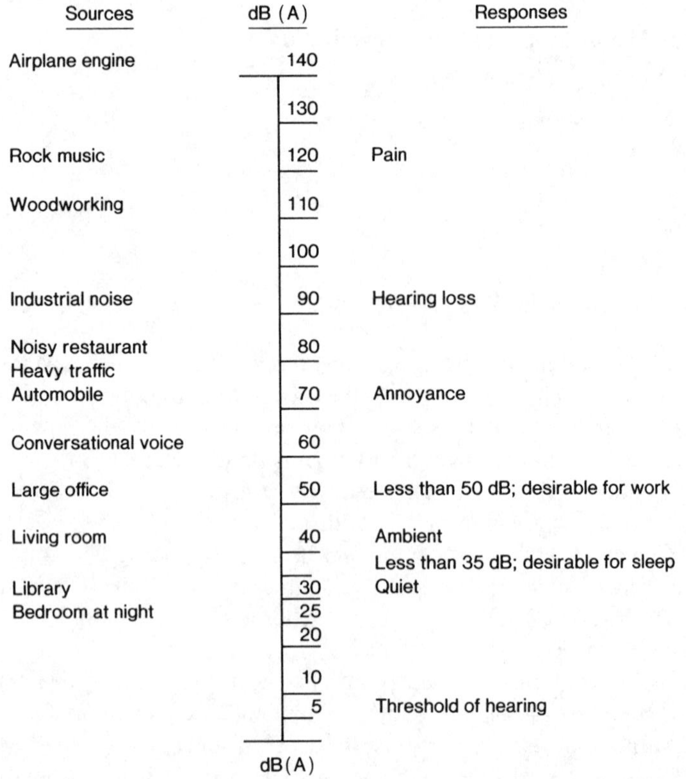

Sources	dB (A)	Responses
Airplane engine	140	
	130	
Rock music	120	Pain
Woodworking	110	
	100	
Industrial noise	90	Hearing loss
Noisy restaurant	80	
Heavy traffic		
Automobile	70	Annoyance
Conversational voice	60	
Large office	50	Less than 50 dB; desirable for work
Living room	40	Ambient
		Less than 35 dB; desirable for sleep
Library	30	Quiet
Bedroom at night	25	
	20	
	10	
	5	Threshold of hearing

dB(A)

Figure 3-6 Sources and responses to noise can be evaluated in an attempt to minimize noise disruptions and facilitate sleep. *Source*: Reprinted from *Critical Care Quarterly*, Vol. 6, No. 4, p. 70, Aspen Publishers, Inc., © 1984.

Marshall[84] studied patients' heart rate responses to noise levels in the CCU. A positive relation was found between mean pulse rates and acoustic stimuli. Conn[85] did a similar study and found a positive relation between ventricular arrhythmias and noise levels greater than 55 dB. Wessman[86] found that a general increase in noise level or abruptly loud noises in the CCU were related to increased episodes of ventricular arrhythmias after AMI.

Much of the sensory stimulation in the CCU can be minimized. The unit should be evaluated at various times of the day and night. Is the computer printing out laboratory values at 10 PM? Can the auditory component of the bedside monitor be turned off so that the pulse rate is not audible? Can a system of staff reminders be used to minimize talking and laughing during sleep times? Other suggestions given by Fabijan and Gosselin[87] included turning off lights at night, plugging the patient's ears with cotton, consolidating activities, and charting the amount of uninterrupted sleep per shift. Patients who have less sensory overload should cope more effectively with critical illness, manifest less physiologic stress, and lose less myocardium.

Sleep Deprivation

One factor complicating coping is a *disturbance in sleep pattern*, defined as a state in which the individual experiences a change in the quantity or quality of the rest pattern necessary for biologic and emotional needs.[88] The defining characteristics of this nursing diagnosis include[89]:

- verbal complaints of difficulty falling asleep
- not feeling well rested
- restlessness
- interrupted sleep
- expressionless face
- thick speech with mispronunciation and incorrect words
- changes in posture
- awakening earlier or later than desired.

Many factors contribute to a disturbance in this pattern including sensory overload, interruptions, the pain of AMI, and the situational anxiety of being hospitalized for a critical illness.

One sleep cycle is approximately 90 minutes, consisting of the rapid eye movement (REM) stage, and four non-REM (NREM) sleep stages.[90] The cycle is a continuous process that when interrupted must begin again.[91] Dreaming, previously thought to occur only during the REM stage, is now known to occur during all sleep cycles and even some waking states.[92] When deprived of sleep, individuals report behavioral, psychologic, and physiologic disturbances including poor memory, labile mood, nausea, slurred speech, irritability, tremors, poor activity tolerance, difficulty with motor skills, and decreased pain tolerance.

Sleep is essential for emotional coping and physical healing, and extra sleep is required during stressful times. Sleep is thought to be necessary for psychologic coping by providing an opportunity to clear irrelevant data from the brain's storage areas and by reinforcing data necessary for adaptation.[93] During sleep and dream deprivation, brain functioning deteriorates, perhaps because of difficulties integrating, storing, and relinquishing recent experiences. The fourth and deepest stage of sleep (NREM) is most essential for psychologic stability and is the first to rebound after sleep deprivation. It is also during stage four that the body produces substances such as antibodies that are necessary for healing.[94,95]

Woods[96] studied cardiac surgery patients and found that more than half reported poor sleep during hospitalization. Nursing interventions such as blood pressure monitoring and checking of IV flow rates were shown to contribute to sleep disturbances.

Sleep deprivation could delay healing of the damaged myocardium, accentuate the heart rate and blood pressure response to exertion, and increase the work of the heart by stimulating the stress response. Deep sleep is essential for coping and healing, therefore it should be a priority during hospitalization. Suggested interventions to promote sleep include pain relief, back rubs, sedative teas, "do not disturb" signs, minimization of environmental noise, mimicking the patient's usual sleep pattern, avoiding routine 5 AM weight-taking, and questioning doctor's orders for every-2-hour vital signs and other interruptions. Sleep medications should be used only when essential as they interfere with REM sleep. Research on the effect of sleep deprivation on $M\dot{V}O_2$ and patient responses is needed.

Alteration in Comfort

Pain is the predominant symptom of AMI. Severe pain causes an outpouring of endogenous catecholamines.[97] A significant increase in secreted and circulating epinephrine has been documented during coronary pain persisting approximately 3 hours. Metabolic alterations are even more pronounced during acute coronary pain that is accompanied by fear and anxiety.[98]

During AMI, pain is a protective device signaling the need to stop activity and seek medical attention. However, the sympathetic response from circulating catecholamines may be detrimental, perhaps to the point of destroying jeopardized myocardium. Catecholamines stimulate heart rate and contractility and cause systemic vasoconstriction, all of which increase myocardial oxygen demand. In the normal heart, coronary vasodilation associated with circulating catecholamines would balance increased demand. In stenotic vessels, this response is compromised, and oxygen demand may increase beyond the heart's ability to increase supply, thereby extending infarct size. In this manner, harm may come to infarcting myocardium because of the pain itself. Thus, it is suggested that two subsets of pain exist: protective and destructive. The pain of AMI can be destructive.[99]

Analgesic medications should be administered liberally in the acute stages of AMI.[100] Stress-reducing interventions such as education, relaxation techniques, and touch may be effective in decreasing the severity or frequency of the pain of AMI by limiting catecholamine outpouring, but have not been tested in the clinical setting. These interventions are not recommended as a replacement for analgesic relief of the pain of AMI.

Anxiety and Fear

Anxiety and fear both cause a state of subjective uneasiness and activate the autonomic nervous system. *Anxiety* occurs in response to a nonspecific threat; with *fear*, the threat can be identified.[101] The AMI patient probably experiences both anxiety and fear. Threats are easily identified—the reality of being hospitalized in a CCU, hearing that the heart muscle is damaged, and having one's activity, diet, and visiting privileges limited by someone else.

Anxiety also occurs in AMI patients because of the vague and sometimes intermittent realization that this is a transition stage in life. According to Pruett,[102] major life-cycle stressors of the adult aged 30 to 65 years are predominantly related to career and changes in the structure of the family unit. Patients in this age group may be worrying about the effects of this crisis on their ability to work, to have sex, or to maintain the family. A major stressor during the later phase of adulthood is coping with the variety of losses, including the loss of physical health. Coping with the possibility of imminent death is an issue with which any AMI patient is grappling.

Geertsen and colleagues[103] studied satisfaction with selected aspects of coronary care in 215 AMI patients from 11 hospitals. They suggested that nurses may not be effective in decreasing the psychologic trauma of admission to a CCU. Although the vast majority of patients were extremely satisfied with their care, 75 patients (35%) felt that staff needed to make more effort in helping them handle their emotional response. Specific requests of 23% of subjects were that staff be more friendly and make a greater effort to get to know their patients.

Expert knowledge and skill in psychologic counseling are not essential for compassionate care of the individual. Remembering that the environment is foreign to the patient will remind nurses to explain equipment, noises, routines, and procedures. Research on various interventions such as music therapy, relaxation training, and cognitive reappraisal has shown the effectiveness of these techniques.[104]

Realization that this physical crisis and hospitalization is but one small saga in the patient's life may encourage nurses to liberalize visiting hours so that the patient can be supported by loved ones. Stillwell[105] studied visiting needs of family members of critically ill patients and found that the family's need to see their relative frequently increased in importance as the perceived severity of the patient's condition increased. Clinical experience suggests that the need for patients to see their families is just as essential, although the data regarding the physiologic response to visiting are conflicting and need further study.[106,107] Recognition of the trauma patient's suffering and efforts to minimize it may decrease the physiologic stress response and potentially limit infarct size.

SUMMARY

The theoretical framework of myocardial oxygen supply and demand was presented because of the crucial need for nurses to understand the physiologic basis for care routinely given to AMI patients. Although interventions to limit myocardial oxygen demand alone will delay but not stop an infarct, decisions about factors that limit $M\dot{V}O_2$ are important in salvaging jeopardized myocardium before initiating interventions to augment supply.

A wide variety of physiologic and psychologic stimuli bombard the AMI patient. Many of these have a detrimental physiologic effect on the AMI patient by stimulating the normal response to exercise or the stress response. Activity intolerance is a common problem for AMI patients, but one that health care providers may be accentuating by limiting activity and enforcing bed rest. Encouraging activities of daily living such as bathing, toileting, and ambulation may minimize activity intolerance.

Ineffective coping is a potential problem because of the inherent stress of hospitalization and situational factors such as sleep deprivation, sensory overload, pain, anxiety, and fear that tax patients' resources. The stress of hospitalization may activate the stress response, thereby increasing $M\dot{V}O_2$ and potentially extending infarct size. Further research is needed to validate the interventions nurses use daily to enhance viability of myocardium.

NOTES

1. Burton Sobel et al., "Estimation of Infarct Size in Man and its Relation to Prognosis," *Circulation* 46(1972):640.

2. Thomas Rector and Jay Cohn, "Quality of Life and Congestive Heart Failure: Implications for Clinical Care," *Quality of Life and Cardiovascular Care* 1(1985):262.

3. Prediman Shah et al., "Left Ventricular Ejection Fraction Determined by Radionuclide Ventriculography in Early Stages of First Transmural Myocardial Infarction," *American Journal of Cardiology* 45(1980):542.

4. P. Rentrop et al., "Selective Intracoronary Thrombolysis in Acute Myocardial Infarction and Unstable Angina Pectoris," *Circulation* 63(1981):307.

5. James E. Muller, "Coronary Artery Thrombosis: Historical Aspects," *Journal of the American College of Cardiology* 1(1983):893.

6. S.R. Bergmann et al., "Temporal Dependence of Beneficial Effects of Coronary Thrombolysis Characterized by Positron Tomography," *American Journal of Medicine* 73(1982):573.

7. William E. Shell and Burton E. Sobel, "Deleterious Effects of Increased Heart Rate on Infarct Size in the Conscious Dog," *American Journal of Cardiology* 31(1973):474.

8. A.J. Buda et al., "Myocardial Infarct Extension: Prevalence, Clinical Significance, and Problems in Diagnosis," *American Heart Journal* 105(1983):744.

9. Ibid.

10. D.J. Fitzgerald et al., "Platelet Activation in Unstable Coronary Disease," *New England Journal of Medicine* 315(1986):983.

11. Robert Rude, James Muller, and Eugene Braunwald, "Efforts to Limit the Size of Myocardial Infarcts," *Annals of Internal Medicine* 95(1981):736.

12. Rolf Schroeder et al., "Follow-up after Coronary Arterial Reperfusion with Intravenous Streptokinase in Relation to Residual Myocardial Infarct Artery Narrowings," *American Journal of Cardiology* 55(1985):313.

13. Robert Berne and Matthew Levy, *Cardiovascular Physiology*, 5th ed. (St. Louis: The C.V. Mosby Co., 1986).

14. John B. West, *Respiratory Physiology: The Essentials*, 2nd ed. (Baltimore: The Williams & Wilkins Co., 1979), pp. 69–85.

15. Cydney Michaelson, ed., *Congestive Heart Failure* (St. Louis: The C.V. Mosby Co., 1983), pp. 1–500.

16. Ibid.

17. Schroeder et al., "Follow-up."

18. Keith Deans and Jeanette Hartshorn, "Cardiovascular Pharmacology: Nitrates in the Treatment of Coronary Artery Disease," *Journal of Cardiovascular Nursing* 1(1986):81.

19. Schroeder et al., "Follow-up."

20. Margaret A. Eberts, "Advances in the Pharmacologic Management of Angina Pectoris," *Journal of Cardiovascular Nursing* 1(1986):15.

21. Eugene Braunwald et al., *New Concepts in Ischemic Heart Disease: The Role of Coronary Artery Spasm* (New York: Pfizer Laboratories, 1979).

22. Christine Breu and Kathleen Dracup, "Survey of Critical Care Nursing Practice: Part III. Responsibilities of Intensive Care Unit Staff," *Heart and Lung* 11(1982):157.

23. J.M. Rawles and A.C.F. Kenmure, "Controlled Trial of Oxygen in Uncomplicated Myocardial Infarction," *British Medical Journal* 1(1976):1121.

24. A.C.F. Kenmure et al., "Circulatory and Metabolic Effects of Oxygen in Myocardial Infarction," *British Medical Journal* 4(1968):360.

25. Massimo Chiarello et al., " 'Reverse Coronary Steal' Induced by Coronary Vasoconstriction Following Coronary Artery Occlusion in Dogs," *Circulation* 56(1977):809.

26. Ronald W.F. Campbell, "Prophylactic Antiarrhythmic Therapy in Acute Myocardial Infarction," *American Journal of Cardiology* 54(1984):8E.

27. Mi Ja Kim, Gertrude K. McFarland, and Audrey M. McLane, *Pocket Guide to Nursing Diagnoses* (St. Louis: The C.V. Mosby Co., 1987).

28. Susan Quaal, "Thrombolytic Therapy: An Overview," *Journal of Cardiovascular Nursing* 1(1986):45.

29. Lynda J. Carpenito, ed., *Nursing Diagnosis: Application to Clinical Practice* (Philadelphia: J.B. Lippincott Co., 1983), pp. 1–535.

30. Kim, McFarland, and McLane, *Nursing Diagnoses*.

31. Elizabeth Hahn Winslow, "Cardiovascular Consequences of Bed Rest," *Heart and Lung* 14(1985):236.

32. G. Kenneth Mallory, Paul White, and Jorge Salcedo-Salgar, "The Speed of Healing of Myocardial Infarction: A Study of the Pathologic Anatomy in Seventy-Two Cases," *American Heart Journal* 18(1939):647.

33. D.J. Christensen et al., "Effect of Hypertension on Myocardial Rupture in Acute Myocardial Infarction: A Review of 72 Consecutive Cases," *Chest* 72(1977):618.

34. Bengt Saltin et al., "Response to Exercise after Bed Rest and after Training: A Longitudinal Study of Adaptive Changes in Oxygen Transport and Body Composition," *Circulation* 38, Suppl. 7 (1968):1.

35. O.H. Gaier and H.L. Thron, "Postural Changes in the Circulation," in W.F. Hamilton, ed., *Handbook of Physiology* (Washington: American Physiological Society, 1965), pp. 1025–1063.

36. Winslow, "Bed Rest."

37. Aram Chobanian et al., "The Metabolic and Hemodynamic Effects of Prolonged Bed Rest in Normal Subjects," *Circulation* 49(1974):551.

38. Winslow, "Bed Rest."

39. H. Galbo, J.J. Holst, and N.J. Christensen, "Glucagon and Plasma Catecholamine Responses to Graded and Prolonged Exercise in Man," *Journal of Applied Physiology* 38(1975):70.

40. Robert Fagard et al., "Effects of Angiotensin Antagonism at Rest and During Exercise in Sodium-Deplete Man," *Journal of Applied Physiology* 45(1978):403.

41. Joel E. Dimsdale and Jonathan Moss, "Plasma Catecholamines in Stress and Exercise," *Journal of the American Medical Association* 243(1980):340.

42. R.J. Vecht, G.W.S. Graham, and P.S. Sever, "Plasma Noradrenaline Concentrations during Isometric Exercise," *British Heart Journal* 40(1978):1216.

43. Berne and Levy, *Cardiovascular Physiology.*

44. Karen Segal and Bernard Gutin, "Exercise Efficiency in Lean and Obese Women," *Medical Science Sports and Exercise* 15(1983):106.

45. G.A. Bray et al., "Some Respiratory and Metabolic Effects of Exercise in Moderately Obese Men," *Metabolism* 26(1977):403.

46. A. Marmor, Burton E. Sobel, and E. Roberts, "Factors Presaging Early Recurrent Myocardial Infarction ('Extension')," *American Journal of Cardiology* 48(1981):603.

47. Catherine A. Alteri, "The Patient with Myocardial Infarction: Rest Prescriptions for Activities of Daily Living," *Heart and Lung* 13(1984):355.

48. Shell and Sobel, "Deleterious Effects."

49. Buda et al., "Myocardial Infarct."

50. F.L. Gobel et al., "The Rate-Pressure Product as an Index of Myocardial Oxygen Consumption during Exercise in Patients with Angina Pectoris," *Circulation* 57(1978):549.

51. Bruce J. Noble et al., "A Category-Ratio Perceived Exertion Scale: Relationship to Blood and Muscle Lactates and Heart Rate," *Medical Science Sports and Exercise* 15(1983):523.

52. Alteri, "Rest Prescriptions."

53. Barbara Johnston, Edward Watt, and Gerald Fletcher, "Oxygen Consumption and Hemodynamic and Electrocardiographic Response to Bathing in Recent Post-Myocardial Infarction Patients," *Heart and Lung* 10(1981):666.

54. Elizabeth Hahn Winslow, Lynda Lane, and Andrew Gaffney, "Oxygen Uptake and Cardiovascular Responses in Control Adults and Acute Myocardial Infarction Patients During Bathing," *Nursing Research* 34(1985):164.

55. Johnston, Watt, and Fletcher, "Oxygen Consumption."

56. Alteri, "Rest Prescriptions."

57. Winslow, Lane, and Gaffney, "Oxygen Uptake."

58. J.G. Benton, H. Brown, and H.A. Rusk, "Energy Expended by Patients on the Bedpan and Bedside Commode," *Journal of the American Medical Association* 144(1950):1443.

59. Elizabeth Hahn Winslow, Lynda Lane, and Andrew Gaffney, "Oxygen Uptake and Cardiovascular Response in Patients and Normal Adults During In-Bed and Out-of-Bed Toileting," *Journal of Cardiac Rehabilitation* 4(1984):348.

60. Rosemary McCarthy, "The Metabolic Cost of Maintaining Five Fixed Body Positions," *Nursing Research* 17(1968):539.

61. Bettie Jackson and Marguerite Kinney, "Energy Expenditure, Heart Rate, Rhythm and Blood Pressure in Normal Female Subjects Engaged in Common Hospitalized Patient Positions and Modes of Patient Transfer," *International Journal of Nursing Studies* 15(1978):115.

62. Susan E. Quaglietti, "The Effect of Selected Positions on Rate Pressure Products of the Postmyocardial Infarction Patient," unpublished masters thesis. University of California, San Francisco, 1986.

63. Elizabeth Geden, "Effects of Lifting Techniques on Energy Expenditure: A Preliminary Investigation," *Nursing Research* 31(1982):214.

64. Mallory, White, and Salcedo-Salgar, "Speed of Healing."

65. Winslow, Lane, and Gaffney, "Oxygen Uptake."

66. Helen Erickson and Mary Ann Swain, "A Model for Assessing Potential Adaptation to Stress," *Research in Nursing and Health* 5(1982):93.

67. Carpenito, *Nursing Diagnosis.*

68. Kim, McFarland, and McLane, *Nursing Diagnoses.*

69. Richard Lazarus, James Averill, and Edward Opton, "Towards a Cognitive Theory of Emotion," in M.B. Arnold, ed., *Feelings and Emotions: The Loyola Symposium* (New York: Academic Press, 1970), pp. 207–232.

70. Gordon Barnes, "Individual Differences in Perceptual Reactions: A Review of the Stimulus Intensity Modulation Individual Difference Dimension," *Canadian Psychological Review* 17(1976):77.

71. Modesta Orque, Bobbie Bloch, and Lidia Monrroy, *Ethnic Nursing Care: A Multicultural Approach* (St. Louis: The C.V. Mosby Co., 1983).

72. Gordon Ross, ed., *Essentials of Human Physiology*, 2nd ed. (Chicago: Year Book Medical Publishers, Inc., 1982), pp. 104–119.

73. Berne and Levy, *Cardiovascular Physiology.*

74. Eugene Braunwald, "Control of Myocardial Oxygen Consumption: Physiologic and Clinical Considerations," *American Journal of Cardiology* 27(1971):416.

75. Carol Baker, "Sensory Overload and Noise in the ICU: Sources of Environmental Stress," *Critical Care Quarterly* 6, no. 4 (1984):66.

76. Nancy Fugate Woods, "Noise Stimuli in the Acute Care Area," *Nursing Research* 23(1974):144.

77. Ibid.

78. Susan Leddy, "Sleep and Phase Shifting of Biological Rhythms," *International Journal of Nursing Studies* 14(1977):137.

79. Sam Baxter, "Psychological Problems of Intensive Care," *Nursing Times* 71(1975):63.

80. Sue Ann Thomas, James Lynch, and Mary E. Mills, "Psychosocial Influences on Heart Rhythm in the Coronary-Care Unit," *Heart and Lung* 4(1975):746.

81. Jacqueline Knable, "Handholding: One Means of Transcending Barriers of Communication," *Heart and Lung* 10(1981):1106.

82. Alvis Turner, Charles King, and John Craddock, "Measuring and Reducing Noise," *Hospitals* 49(1975):85.

83. Robert W. Cantrell, "Physiological Effects of Noise," *Otolaryngology Clinics of North America* 12(1979):537.

84. Louise Marshall, "Patient Reaction to Sound in an Intensive Coronary Care Unit," *Communicating Nursing Research* 5(1972):81.

85. V. Conn, "Patient Reactions to Noise in CCU," master's thesis. (Columbia, MO: University of Missouri, 1981).

86. J. Wessman, "Selected Prediction Variables Pertaining to Prevention of Myocardial Irritability Following Infarction and the Development of a Nursing Framework," doctoral dissertation. (Austin, TX: University of Texas at Austin, 1979).

87. Lucia Fabijan and Marie-Diane Gosselin, "How to Recognize Sleep Deprivation in Your ICU Patient and What to Do About It," *The Canadian Nurse*, April, 1982, pp. 21–23.

88. Carpenito, *Nursing Diagnosis*.

89. Kim, McFarland, and McLane, *Nursing Diagnoses*.

90. Judith A. Hemenway, "Sleep and the Cardiac Patient," *Heart and Lung* 9(1980):453.

91. Mary Chuman, "The Neurological Basis of Sleep," *Heart and Lung* 12(1983):177.

92. Gerald Vogel, "A Review of REM Sleep Deprivation," *Archives of General Psychiatry* 32(1975):749.

93. Kenneth Gaarder, "A Conceptual Model of Sleep," *Archives of General Psychiatry* 14(1966):253.

94. Hemenway, "Sleep and Cardiac Patient."

95. Chuman, "Neurological Basis of Sleep."

96. Nancy Fugate Woods, "Patterns of Sleep in Postcardiotomy Patients," *Nursing Research* 21(1972):347.

97. C.A. Carlsson and L. Pellettieri, "A Clinical View on Pain Physiology," *Acta Chirurgica Scandinavia* 148(1982):305.

98. T. Zaleska and L. Ceremuzynski, "Metabolic Alterations During and After Termination of Coronary Pain in Myocardial Infarction," *European Journal of Cardiology* 11(1980):201.

99. Barbara Riegel, "The Role of Nursing in Limiting Infarct Size," *Heart and Lung* 14(1985):247.

100. Ibid.

101. Kim, McFarland, and McLane, *Nursing Diagnoses*.

102. Harold Pruett, "Stressors in Middle Adulthood," *Family and Community Health* 2, no. 4 (1980):53.

103. Reed Geertsen, Marilyn Ford, and Hilmon Castle, "The Subjective Aspects of Coronary Care," *Nursing Research* 25(1976):211.

104. Gloria M. Bulechek and Joanne C. McCloskey, *Nursing Interventions: Treatments for Nursing Diagnoses* (Philadelphia: W.B. Saunders Co., 1985).

105. Susan B. Stillwell, "Importance of Visiting Needs as Perceived by Family Members of Patients in the Intensive Care Unit," *Heart and Lung* 13(1984):238.

106. Agnes J. Brown, "Effect of Family Visits on the Blood Pressure and Heart Rate of Patients in the Coronary-Care Unit," *Heart and Lung* 5(1976):291.

107. Barbara F. Fuller and Gale M. Foster, "The Effects of Family/Friend Visits vs. Staff Interaction on Stress/Arousal of Surgical Intensive Care Patients," *Heart and Lung* 11(1982):457.

Chapter 4

Recent Advances in the Treatment of Coronary Artery Disease

Linda J. Lewicki, RN, MSN

Cardiovascular disease continues to be our nation's number one health problem,[1] and since 1940 has been our leading cause of death. Medicine has attacked this disease with aggressive pharmacologic therapies, nonsurgical methods of revascularization, and surgical revascularization. This chapter highlights current medical interventions and their implications for nursing. Nursing diagnoses and their resultant actions and outcomes are addressed.

PERCUTANEOUS TRANSLUMINAL CORONARY ANGIOPLASTY (PTCA)

The method of nonsurgical dilatation of atherosclerotic lesions was first developed in 1964 by Dotter and Judkins[2] who, using coaxial dilating catheters, performed the procedure in the femoral artery. More than a decade elapsed before Gruentzig developed mechanical dilatation using a double-lumen catheter with a nonelastic inflatable balloon introduced through the skin. In 1977, Gruentzig[3] performed the first PTCA. Since then, the procedure has gained clinical and technical merit, offering an alternative to surgical intervention for specific coronary lesions.

Mechanism of Action

The precise mechanism by which the procedure dilates the arterial lumen is unknown. Dotter and Judkins[4] proposed that the lumen enlarged because of displacement or compression of the atherosclerotic material. Compressibility of the plaque is dependent on the stage of its development: the relation between the atheromatous deposition and associated fibrous proliferation.[5] The compression and displacement may cause two morphologic alterations in the vessel. Medial and adventitial stretching with associated endothelial desquamation has been observed[6]; and a localized coronary artery aneurysm results.[7,8] Overstretching can produce dissection, aneurysm, and vascular rupture.[9] The second morphologic alteration is a "controlled dissection."[10] Block et al.[11] were the first to note the disruption of the endothelial lining of the plaque so that an intimal or medial tear may occur. This splitting or tear can be noted by a hazy or fuzzy angiographic appearance of the atherosclerotic lesion postangioplasty, but is not an essential prerequisite for the long-term success of the procedure.[12] Atherosclerotic debris may be formed by the splitting, but clinical reports of emboli are rare.[13]

Technique

The procedure entails using two arterial catheters, an outer guiding catheter, and a double-lumen dilatation catheter. A guide wire of a diameter of 0.3 mm with torque control, a floppy atraumatic tip, and radiographic visibility allows for greater maneuverability.[14]

The femoral artery is generally used, although the brachial artery can be entered via an arteriotomy. The guiding catheter is advanced into the ostium of the coronary artery requiring dilatation. The dilatation catheter can inflate and also allows for pressure monitoring and injection of contrast medium. It is introduced with the guide wire inside, through the guiding catheter. Advancement of the catheter is enhanced by the guide wire and fluoroscopic guidance. Pressure is also monitored during positioning of the dilatation catheter for precautionary surveillance against occlusion of the coronary artery ostium and to measure the predilatation pressure gradient. The dilatation catheter is advanced to within a few centimeters of the guiding catheter tip. The guide wire is then advanced through the lesion in a position in the distal portion of the vessel (Figure 4-1). The dilatation catheter is advanced next over the wire and also through the lesion (Figure 4-2). The tip of the guiding catheter measures proximal coronary artery pressure. The dilatation catheter monitors distal coronary artery pressure. The distal pressure falls when the lesion is entered, reflecting the pressure gradient across the stenosis. The balloon of the dilatation catheter is inflated with a 50% saline and a 50% contrast medium solution. The optimum number of inflations, inflation time, inflation pressure, and size of balloon are relative to the coronary vessel undergoing angioplasty.[15]

The procedure is generally conducted in a catheterization laboratory. However, cardiac surgical facilities must be available onsite and at the time of the procedure. The adjunct use of drugs, vasodilators, and antiplatelet therapy during the procedure is determined by the physician.

The patient is awake during the procedure; therefore patient teaching before the procedure should include environmental information, data regarding sensations and stimulations occurring during the procedure, a review of cardiac struc-

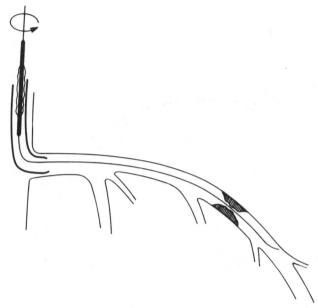

Figure 4-1 Placement and advancement of a guiding wire catheter and a balloon catheter. *Source*: Reprinted from *Acta Radiologica*, Vol. 26, No. 5, p. 499, with permission of Acta Radiologica, © 1985.

ture and function, and a description of the procedure. As emergency cardiac surgery is a potential outcome of the procedure, the patient should be provided a brief description of the operative and immediate postoperative period. The depth of the content is dependent on the patient's medical condition, anxiety level, ability to handle the material, and perhaps institutional guidelines or policy.

The patient is made as comfortable as possible on the procedure table. The patient may be asked to cough and assume different positions, or the table itself may change positions to facilitate the procedure. Fluoroscopy is used; therefore, lead aprons and covering are used.

Patient Selection

The ideal angioplasty candidate has single-vessel disease; lesions that are proximal, discrete, subtotal, relatively concentric, and noncalcified; and is a reasonable candidate for bypass surgery.[16] Retrospective analyses of patients undergoing PTCA showed that the percentage of patients who fulfill all these criteria is small, approximately 3.5%.[17] These original criteria proved very restrictive; technologic advances and experience with the procedure have broadened them (Exhibit 4-1).

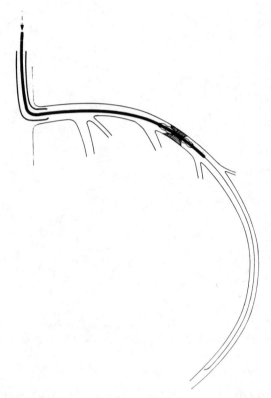

Figure 4-2 Satisfactory positioning of guide wire distal to the lesion and engagement of the balloon with the lesion. *Source*: Reprinted from *Acta Radiologica*, Vol. 26, No. 5, p. 499, with permission of Acta Radiologica, © 1985.

Several factors have been proven to minimize complications and maximize success rates.[18] A positive relation between patients with a short duration of angina and their suitability for and success of the angioplasty procedure has been noted.[19,20] This is attributable to the duration of symptoms, which is correlated with distensibility of the lesion. Ideally, the patient should have single-vessel disease; however, the performance of angioplasty for multivessel involvement is increasing. Tandem lesions, sequential stenoses in the same vessel, and stenosis of venous bypass grafts are also amenable to the procedure.[21] Intraoperative angioplasty as an adjunct to coronary bypass surgery has been reported when there were multiple lesions in a vessel requiring grafting.[22]

The advances in catheters and guide wires have made some distal lesions accessible for angioplasty, but certain anatomic features may prohibit the procedure. Left mainstem involvement is generally regarded as a contraindication because of the consequences of complications associated with the site.[23] Branch

Exhibit 4-1 Current Selection Criteria of Patients for PTCA

Clinical
    Myocardial ischemia
        Functional testing
        Angina testing
    Myocardial infarction

Angiographic
    Single-vessel disease
    Multivessel disease
        All stenoses suitable for intervention
        Some stenoses suitable for intervention
    Coronary arterial occlusions
        Acute, during myocardial infarction
        Chronic, less than 3 months' duration

Source: Reprinted from "Percutaneous Transluminal Coronary Angioplasty: Current Status and Future Trends" by D.R. Holmes, Jr. and R.E. Vlietstra in *Mayo Clinic Proceedings*, Vol. 61, pp. 865–876, with permission of Mayo Foundation, © 1986.

points are also assessed for extent of stenoses and vessel size. This assessment is done because branches may become occluded during the procedure. Small branches may not contraindicate the procedure. However, larger ones such as a diagonal branch of the left anterior descending may be contraindications because of the outcomes of a potential procedural occlusion of the branch. Meier et al.[24] noted that if a branch originates from within a plaque, there will be risk for iatrogenic occlusion. This risk lowers considerably if the branch is adjacent to the plaque. A combination of length and degree of eccentricity of a coronary artery stenosis increases the risk of the procedure.[25]

Results

The desired outcomes of PTCA are reduction in the degree of coronary artery narrowing as evidenced by angiographic findings (Figure 4-3), decreased pressure gradients measured across the narrowing, and relief of symptoms.[26] Hodgson and Williams[27] in clinical studies have shown that postdilatation pressure gradients can predict long-term success, and that pressure gradients should be reduced to less than 12 mmHg during angioplasty to maximize the likelihood of sustained favorable outcome.

Failure in the procedure reflects an inability to engage the ostium of the coronary artery, engage the artery ostium without obstructing blood flow around the tip of the guiding catheter, advance the guiding catheter into the stenotic artery, and dilate the lesion.[28]

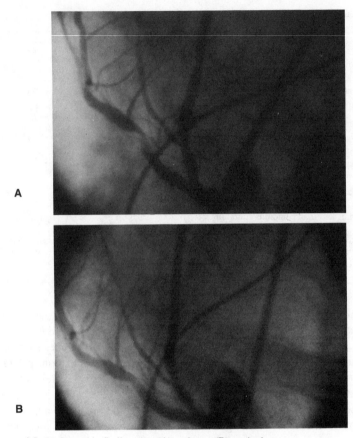

Figure 4-3 Angiographic findings pre (**A**) and post (**B**) angioplasty.

The National Heart, Lung and Blood Institute has maintained a registry of PTCA procedures and relevant data since 1977. Participation in the registry is voluntary. Numerous studies from the registry have appeared in print.[29-33] A portion of the data in the registry from which statistics are derived was collected before the evolution of catheter improvements, including the improved maneuverability. Detre et al.[34] reported on registry data collected from 105 centers, which combined, represent 3,079 procedures. The reported overall primary success rate was 61% with 6.6% requiring emergency surgery, a 0.9% mortality rate, and 5.5% occurrence of myocardial infarction (MI). Adverse success factors included patient age over 65 years, female gender, and multivessel disease. Since collection of this initial data and with a change in selection criteria to include high-risk candidates, i.e., multivessel disease, decreased left ventricular (LV) function, and acute infarction, complication rates have not increased. The incidence of infarction is less than 5%, and the frequency of mortality is from 1.0% to 1.5%.[35]

A prime factor of success seems to be the experience of the physician performing the procedure. For example, Cumberland[36] in summarizing the late Dr. Gruentzig's success figures revealed rates of 91% to 95%. Based on the PTCA registry data, an initial learning curve was thought to be approximately 100 cases.[37] At this point a success rate of 80% to 85% was achieved.

Holmes and Vlietstra[38] reporting on the 1979 to 1985 Mayo Clinic results showed that when defining successful dilation as more than a 40% increase in the luminal diameter of the stenotic vessel post-procedure, the success rates for single-vessel disease increased from 67% to 85%. For multivessel disease, the success rates increased from 69% to 87%.

The prognostic role of PTCA in defining completeness of revascularization is not yet proven.[39] The rate of restenosis after a successful angioplasty has been reported to be 25% to 35%.[40] The rate is dependent on the definition of restenosis. When restenosis occurs, it usually is evident within 6 to 8 months after the initial procedure.[41] Experimental models and studies have shown that platelet deposition has a major role in restenosis.[42] Results from the National Heart, Lung and Blood Institute registry[43] revealed that if repeat angioplasty is used for restenosis, an 85% rate for long-term success can be expected.

Complications

Complications of the procedure include spasm, occlusion, arrhythmias, and MI. Spasm can occur during and post-procedure. The administration of nitrates and calcium antagonists before, during, and after, including months after the attempted angioplasty, has abated this complication. However, there have been reported cases of refractory spasm.[44] Cragg and associates[45] showed that angioplasty causes a derangement of arachidonic acid metabolism at the site of the procedure; this results in a decrease in prostaglandins with a concomitant increase in hydroperoxy acid, a vasoconstrictor. This sets the stage for vasospasm. The administration of aspirin is potentially beneficial in two respects: an antithrombotic effect and an inhibitive effect on peroxidase production, which reduces hydroperoxy acid concentrations.[46]

Occlusion can occur abruptly at the site of the attempted angioplasty possibly from spasm, dissection, or thrombosis. Immediate surgical intervention is usually required.

Minor complications and their incidence match those of cardiac catheterization and include bradycardia, hypotension, hematoma, arterial thrombosis, and arrhythmias.[47]

Mortality statistics vary among institutions; the reported mean is approximately 1%. The risk of mortality is increased in women, individuals over 60 years of age, and those who have previously undergone bypass surgery.[48]

Nursing Considerations

Pre-PTCA

The major nursing action pre-PTCA is patient education. A teaching plan should be goal directed and individualized to patient needs. Therefore, the patient's pre-existing knowledge base should be assessed. Content is similar to the teaching plan for a patient undergoing a cardiac catheterization. The patient's knowledge and feelings regarding the previous catheterization should be explored. Pre-existing knowledge of the pathophysiology of the coronary artery disease (CAD) process and physician description of the procedure should be reinforced. Teaching content also includes visual, auditory, and tactile sensations the patient may experience during the procedure. As emergency cardiac surgery is a potential outcome, preparation for the event is also an element of the teaching plan.

Physical preparation for the procedure includes the performance of diagnostic tests including chest x-ray, electrocardiogram (ECG), cardiac enzymes, serum electrolytes, and coagulation survey. The patient is also typed and cross-matched should emergency surgery be required. Myocardial radionuclide imaging may be performed to establish baseline evidence of perfusion defects and/or exercise-induced LV dysfunction for postprocedure comparison. A record of the recent catheterization is also used for postprocedure comparison. The patient should be NPO the evening before the procedure. A betadine scrub of the groin, upper thigh, and lateral trunk is performed by the patient; the chest and legs are also scrubbed as preparation for potential open heart surgery.

The patient may be medicated with aspirin to decrease platelet adhesiveness. Heparin and dextran may also be administered to prevent thrombus formation. Calcium channel blocking agents may be given to prevent and/or reduce coronary artery spasm during the procedure.

Post-PTCA

The patient may return to a general cardiology unit or be admitted to an intensive care unit postprocedure. The patient is placed on bed rest with a pressure dressing and sandbags in place, ensuring pressure on the site and immobilization of the extremity. General comfort measures are employed during the period of immobilization, which generally lasts 8 hours. The head of the bed should not be raised higher than 15° during this period. Elevation beyond 15° may cause undue site stress and lead to disruption of the small clot at the procedure entry site.[49]

Care is directed at prevention, early assessment, and immediate intervention of the possible complications of the procedure: recurrent angina, dysrhythmias, thrombus formation, and bleeding. The potential nursing diagnoses include alterations in cardiac output, potential for injury, and alteration in fluid volume (Table 4-1).

In a review of 5,578 procedures performed at Emory University Hospital from 1980 to 1985, 215 patients (4%) experienced acute closure: sudden closure of the treated vessel with chest pain and/or ECG changes.[50] Two events that may precipitate acute closure were identified: systemic arterial hypotension and discontinuation of heparin. Nursing interventions that prevent hypotension, recognize it early, and deliver prompt intervention are warranted to prevent hypotension-induced acute closure. These findings should also alert the nurse to careful observation of patients after heparin discontinuation.

Discharge instruction involves the introduction or reintroduction of the patient to the cardiac rehabilitation process. There is emphasis on wellness, health behaviors, and reduction of risk factors. A teaching plan also includes the discharge medication schedule: a course of aspirin or warfarin therapy. Dosages, actions, side effects, and precautions of all medications are taught. Appointment schedules for repeat angiography, ECG, exercise testing, and thallium scan conclude the discharge plan.

LASER THERAPY

Laser usage has gained widespread application in many medical fields including opthalmology, dermatology, gynecology, and gastroenterology. Its suitability as a scalpel and coagulating instrument in these fields is documented. Lasers have also been used to repair small vessels because of their microcautery capabilities. Potential application of lasers in the treatment of atherosclerotic disease has been explored in the laboratory.

Instrumentation

A laser is light amplification by stimulated emission of radiation; it is a light energy. The laser generates photons or electromagnetic radiation that has three properties: monochromatic, coherent, and collimated. These properties allow the light waves to have a narrow band of wavelengths, to be coordinated in time and space, to travel parallel to each other in one direction, and to be packaged into a beam of enormous energy capacity. These properties and the ability to carry laser radiation by optical fibers make it suitable for medical application.

Table 4-1 Nursing Care Plan for the Post-PTCA Patient

Patient discharge criteria: Patient will exhibit an understanding of the results of the procedure, the medication protocol, and the rehabilitation program components by verbalizations and behaviors.

Nursing Diagnosis	Expected Outcomes	Nursing Orders
1. Potential for alteration in cardial output: decreased, related to complications of angioplasty: vessel occlusion, MI, and coronary spasm.	Patient will exhibit physiologic stability as evidenced by freedom from anginal pain, normal heart rate and rhythm, normal blood pressure, measured C.O. 4.0–6.0 L/min.	1. Complete an initial cardiovascular assessment: —Evaluate ECG. Note rate and rhythm. Compare with preprocedure rhythm. —Obtain blood pressure. 2. Follow established medical prophylactic thrombus prevention protocol: —Protocol dependent on physician and institution. May include dextran, daily oral anticoagulant, aspirin, warfarin. —Observe appropriate lab data: prothrombin time, partial thromboplastin time. —Protect patient from potential injury: oral care, shaving, brushing. 3. Observe continuous rhythm strip for evidence of myocardial ischemia. —Daily 12-lead ECG —Serum creatinine phosphokinase isoenzymes per protocol. 4. Review patient anginal history and symptoms, especially location, pattern, and relief methods. 5. Instruct patient to take one NTG sublingual at the occurrence of pain and to notify nursing staff immediately.

6. If anginal attack occurs:
   —Contact physician
   —Monitor response to NTG
   —Complete full cardiovascular assessment
   —STAT ECG.
7. Monitor vital signs for evidence of hypotension; ensure adequate volume replacement.

2. Potential for alteration in cardiac output: decreased, related to arrhythmias.

Patient will exhibit physiologic stability as evidenced by absence of arrhythmias or restoration of normal rhythm via antiarrhythmic therapy.

1. Monitor ECG rhythm continuously.
2. Maintain patent IV route.
3. Monitor electrolyte levels; K$^+$.
4. Observe for bradyarrhythmias during sheath removal.

3. Potential alteration in tissue perfusion: affected leg, related to presence of angioplasty sheath, thrombosis, or localized bleeding.

Patient will exhibit physiologic stability as evidenced by good vascular integrity: re-establishment of pretest pedal pulses, presence and volume; warm extremities; lack of numbness or tingling; absence of hematoma formation.

1. Immobilize affected extremity; use draw sheet folded over affected leg and under other leg at knee; tuck ends under mattress. Maintain immobilization according to protocol.
2. Maintain pressure dressing over femoral puncture site. Sandbags, 5–10 lb may also be used to immobilize extremity and to apply pressure.
3. Maintain head of bed no higher than 15°.
4. Monitor site for external or subcutaneous bleeding; observe for retroperitoneal ecchymosis and c/o back pain. Frequency of observations dependent on established observations dependent on established protocol:

continues

Table 4-1 continued

Nursing Diagnosis	Expected Outcomes	Nursing Orders

		—q30 minutes × 4 hours
		   —progress to q2 hour.
		5. Monitor vascular integrity:
		   —Pedal pulse, color, temperature, sensation, evidence of numbness/tingling
		   —Frequency of observations dependent on established protocol:
		     —q30 minutes × 4 hours
		     —progress to q2 hour.
		6. Instruct patient to notify nursing staff of feeling of warmth and wetness at femoral site and of tingling numbness in affected extremity.
		7. Provide comfort measures:
		   —Analgesia, sedation
		   —Passive range of motion exercises of unaffected extremity.
		8. If bleeding occurs:
		   —Apply immediate pressure to area
		   —Have another member of staff notify physician.

4. Alteration in fluid volume and electrolyte balance related to osmotic diuresis accompanying the use of contrast dye.	Patient will exhibit physiologic stability through evidence of adequate hydration and normal electrolyte values: K^+ = 3.8–5.0 mEq/L.	1. Maintain IV route. 2. Resume po intake when patient can tolerate. 3. Record intake and output. 4. Monitor serum K^+ levels. 5. Assess adequacy of fluid volume. After the discontinuation of the bed rest order, observe for signs of orthostatic hypotension.

5. Knowledge deficit: discharge instructions and coronary risk factors.	Patient will demonstrate knowledge of risk reduction behaviors and medication protocols.	1. Evaluate patient's readiness and potential for compliance (see Chapter 7). 2. Provide a conducive learning environment. 3. Involve appropriate team members: dietician, rehab team, pharmacist. 4. Topics to be covered: aspirin and dipyridamole, smoking cessation, low fat/low cholesterol diet, stress reduction and exercise plan (see Chapter 7). 5. Evaluate effectiveness of teaching plan.

There are three types of lasers: solid state, liquid, and gas. Each generates photons with wavelengths from a specific portion of the electromagnetic spectrum. Each wavelength is absorbed according to the properties of the tissue being irradiated.[51] For example, carbon dioxide laser light has an infrared wavelength that is readily absorbed by water, a major component of cells. The wavelengths of argon laser light are readily absorbed by red tissue and are therefore good photocoagulators.[52] The total amount of energy delivered is defined by the power multiplied by the duration of exposure. Power can be controlled by beam attenuation, and computerized shuttering can control exposure time.

Another laser variable is spot size. Spot size can be controlled by the catheter design. The fiber tip can be enclosed in an optical shield. Manipulation of the distance between the end of the fiber and the shield's surface controls spot size.

Effects

Gerrity and associates[53] documented three tissue responses to laser therapy: (1) tissue destruction, vaporization of the plaque; (2) secondary tissue responses in adjacent tissue attributable to the conduction of thermal energy, effects of the primary event on hormonal and neural controls, and secondary reactions to other cells; and (3) the healing of the lasered area.

Studies using swine and human cadaver coronary vessels showed that lasers can penetrate and affect vaporization of atherosclerotic plaques (Figure 4-4). The ability of a laser to penetrate a plaque depends on the absorptive characteristics of the plaque material, the beam focus, the power intensity, and the duration of exposure.[54]

The area and depth of penetration of the atherosclerotic plaque is inversely related to the density of the atherosclerotic tissue the laser must transverse.[55] Highly lipid-laden lesions are more easily transversed than hyalinized fibroused or calcified areas.[56]

In experiments with human cadaver coronary arteries, Lee and associates[57] effected a 35% increase in the luminal area of a stenotic vessel. They also noted the emission of gas during the vaporization process and remnants of charred material (Figure 4-4). The nature of the tissue undergoing irradiation determines the extent of debris left. Lipid tissue leaves no debris, and hyalinized or fibrous tissue leaves residual fragments. Lee et al. concluded in 1983 that additional basic research delineating power intensity, time exposure, the refinement of catheters, and methods to estimate plaque density should continue.

Several cases of human percutaneous laser angioplasty of peripheral arteries have been reported.[58–60] Successful laser angioplasty procedures have been performed in the popliteal and femoral arteries. Narrow recanalized channels and vessel perforation remain limitations to the procedure as described in these studies.

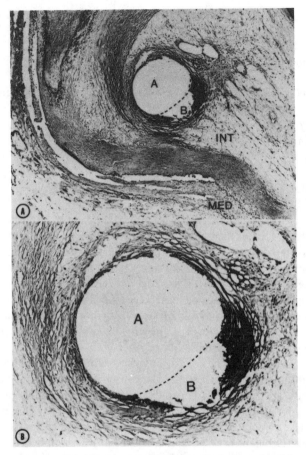

Figure 4-4 Cross-section with enlargement of human atherosclerotic epicardial coronary artery showing the original lumen (**A**) and expansion of the luminal area (**B**) of approximately 25% by phototherapy from a carbon dioxide laser. *Source*: Reprinted from *American Heart Journal*, Vol. 105, No. 6, p. 887, with permission of The C.V. Mosby Company, © 1983.

Livesay and associates[61] in a preliminary report of a study to determine the effectiveness of laser endarterectomy in 20 patients with diffuse coronary disease undergoing bypass revealed that in three patients with six distally stenosed coronary vessels, relief of the stenosis without perforation, deaths, or significant myocardial complications occurred. Postprocedure angiography at 1 week showed patency in five of the six treated vessels, with no residual stenosis. They concluded that their preliminary report and early experience may present laser angioplasty as a value for coronary revascularization, but called for further comprehensive clinical study. The preliminary data are encouraging, and in vivo animal and human studies continue to document recanalization with minimal vascular disruption, tissue charring, and debris.

The introduction of laser therapy to cardiovascular nursing will expand its repertoire and challenge its teaching, assessment, and interventional skills. It seems the care of the laser angioplasty patient will parallel that of the patient who has undergone a PTCA (Table 4-1), directing care at prevention, early assessment, immediate intervention of complications, and adequate discharge planning. Potential nursing diagnoses include alterations in cardiac output, potential for injury, and knowledge deficit.

THROMBOLYSIS AND THROMBOLYTIC THERAPY

The multiple interventions employed in the treatment of an acute myocardial infarction (AMI) have as their goal improvement in the myocardial oxygen supply and demand imbalance, thereby limiting the quality of myocardium that may undergo necrosis. Although these therapies retard the rate of necrosis, they do not ultimately affect the size of the MI.[62,63] The salvaging of the ischemic myocardium through reperfusion has been shown in experimental studies.[64] Pharmacologically mediated thrombolysis offers coronary artery reperfusion and is currently used quickly; with rapid hospital access it is considered a therapy to reduce the morbidity and mortality of AMI.

Past medical debate on the role of coronary thrombosis in AMI centered on the role of thrombosis as the result or the cause of the infarct. The presence of fresh coronary artery thrombi, generally at the site of an intimal tear near the atherosclerotic lesion, has been shown in the majority of patients with AMI.[65-68] The combined effects of platelet aggregation at the lesion site and the secondary turbulent flow proximal and distal to a high-degree lesion have been proposed as the mechanisms for thrombus formation.[69] Most authorities agree that a transmural MI is attributable to coronary thrombosis.

Laffel and Braunwald[70] concluded that the case for pursuing thrombolytic therapy rests on three principles: (1) the most common cause of transmural infarction is thrombotic occlusion of a coronary artery; (2) the experimental animal model reveals early reperfusion results in myocardial salvage and may enhance survival; and (3) in humans, similar reperfusion results have been documented via spontaneous and surgical models; however, spontaneous reperfusion is unpredictable and widespread surgical application is impractical.

The objective of thrombolytic therapy is to lyse the coronary thrombi and thereby improve myocardial oxygenation and coronary perfusion, limit the ischemic zone, improve LV function, reduce arrhythmias, improve morbidity, and decrease mortality.[71]

Despite the causative or initiating circumstances, thrombogenesis is completed when fibrinogen is converted into fibrin (Figure 4-5). Fibrin monomers poly-

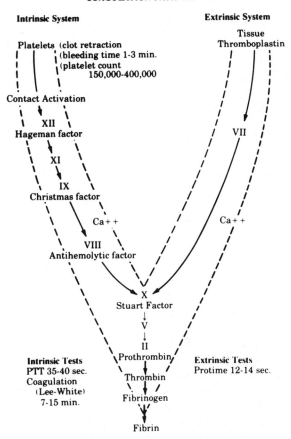

Figure 4-5 Coagulation pathway. *Source*: Reprinted from *Handbook of Health Assessment*, 2nd ed., by E. Rudy and V.R. Gray, p. 272, with permission of Appleton & Lange, © 1986.

merize into a meshwork that traps blood elements, and a thrombus is formed.[72] An endogenous thrombolytic system functions to lyse formed thrombi (Figure 4-6). The essential step in this system is the conversion of the inactive proenzyme synthesized in the liver, plasminogen, to the active nonspecific proteolytic enzyme plasmin. Plasmin can lyse fresh fibrin clots and digest clotting factors V, VIII, prothrombin, and fibrinogen.[73,74] Tissue plasminogen activators (t-Pa), which are serine proteases found in vascular endothelium, catalyze the conversion of plasminogen to plasmin. They bind to fibrin, and circulating plasminogen binds to this complex. Plasmin is then formed at the site, and thrombolysis ensues without the development of a systemic lytic state.[75]

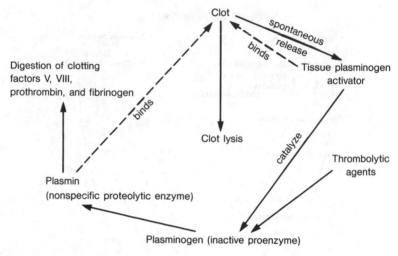

Figure 4-6 Clot lysis.

Patient Criteria

The patient selection criteria for thrombolysis include a recent onset of typical chest pain and ST segment elevations that persist despite sublingual nitroglycerin (NTG). The chest pain must be less than 6 hours old. The persistent ST segment is used as a criterion as it has a high predictive value for the development of a transmural MI.[76] Patients who have Q waves and ST elevations are often excluded, as they are considered to have had a completed or virtually completed infarction. Patients with nonspecific ST waves and ST depression with prolonged chest pain are also excluded, as their incidence of thrombi is low.[77] Contraindications to thrombolytic therapy include recent surgery, biopsies, or intra-arterial procedures; recent CPR; cerebrovascular disease, especially cerebrovascular accident (CVA) or aneurysm; current anticoagulation; and recent history of active bleeds.[78,79]

Thrombolytic Agents

Three exogenous activators of the fibrinolytic system, streptokinase, urokinase, and t-Pa, each offer benefits and risks. The ideal thrombolytic agent would be specific for the fibrin clot and not interfere with the systemic intrinsic fibrinolytic mechanism, lack antigenicity, have a short biologic half-life, and be convenient and inexpensive.[80]

Urokinase is produced by human renal tubular cells. It directly activates the fibrinolytic system, as it does not need to bind to produce the effect. Urokinase cost is approximately five times the cost of streptokinase.

Streptokinase is a filtrate of Group C beta hemolytic streptococcus and is therefore antigenic. Patients who have had streptococcal infections may have neutralizing antibodies against it.[81] It is also pyrogenic.

Since both urokinase and streptokinase have a poor specificity for thrombi, a large thrombolytic dose is required. This depletes the levels of circulating fibrinogen and creates a systemic thrombolytic state associated with bleeding complications.

Streptokinase can be administered via the intravenous (IV) or intracoronary route. Its infusion is generally preceded by the administration of corticosteroids and antihistamines as a precaution against immunologic reactions. The patient may also receive analgesia, lidocaine, and NTG. Intracoronary streptokinase is generally injected during angiography. Intracoronary NTG or nifedipine may be given to rule out spasm as the cause of obstruction.[82] A bolus dose of 10,000 to 30,000 U is administered, followed by a continuous infusion of 2,000 to 4,000 U/min. This infusion continues until results are achieved or a predetermined level of the drug has been infused, generally 150,000 to 500,000 U. Angiography is performed every 15 minutes during the infusion. Lysis usually occurs within 30 minutes after initiation of therapy requiring approximately 65,000 U.[83] The infusion is continued for 30 to 60 minutes after antegrade flow is established. The rethrombosis rate will be high if streptokinase is discontinued immediately after antegrade flow is established. Heparin is generally administered after the streptokinase infusion. A loading dose of 10,000 U is given, followed by a continuous infusion to maintain the partial thromboplastin time at twice control values. Anticoagulation is continued postprocedure. The IV infusion protocol delivers an infusion of 500,000 to 1,700,000 U in a 30- to 60-minute period.

The search for less expensive and more widely applicable thrombolytic agents is ongoing. Currently, much attention is centered on t-Pa. It is a normally occurring enzyme in humans that converts plasminogen to plasmin after binding to the fibrin clot. This specificity makes it advantageous over streptokinase. Pennica and associates[84] identified and cloned the gene that codes for human plaminogen activator. The product of this genetic recombinant technique is an S27-amino acid protein having the same fibrinolytic properties as human plasminogen activator. This protein, t-Pa, is nonantigenic and has a half-life of 5 to 8 minutes. Clinical trials are presently underway. One study showed successful thrombolysis within 90 minutes after administration of 0.50 to 0.75 mg/kg IV or intracoronary in 69% to 75% of patients.[85]

In 1985, the National Heart, Lung and Blood Institute established the Thrombolysis in Myocardial Infarction study group. This multicentered group is studying thrombolytic therapy in two phases: (1) assessment of effects of IV streptokinase and t-Pa in patients with AMI and angiographic findings of infarct-related total occlusion of the coronary artery, and (2) a placebo-controlled trial. Results of phase one revealed that of 290 treated patients in the randomized, double-blind study, t-Pa was almost twice as effective as IV streptokinase in opening occluded infarct-related coronary arteries.[86] IV streptokinase recanalization rates were half the rate that would be expected with intracoronary streptokinase recanalization. Study design may have had a part in the low rate. These findings are inconsistent with other trials: t-Pa led to similar recanalization rates as intracoronary streptokinase with the same or lower incidence of side effects and produced prompt recanalization in more than half the patients with total coronary occlusion.

Signs and symptoms of lysis include angiographic evidence, decreased chest pain, rapid resolution of ST segment abnormalities, and new onset arrhythmias. A rapid rise in serum creatinine kinase and creatinine kinase myocardial band (MB) is also noted. A peak occurs 8 to 15 hours after the onset of symptoms versus the normally observed peak 18 to 24 hours with conventional therapy.[87]

Efficacy of Treatment

The efficacy of intracoronary streptokinase to achieve reperfusion of the affected coronary vessel has been documented to be 75%.[88–91] Factors that influence this reperfusion rate include the vessel involved, the site of occlusion in the vessel, the presence or absence of collaterals, procedural variables of the time lapsed from initiation of therapy and onset of symptoms, the dose and length of treatment, and the position of the catheter in the vessel in relation to the occlusion.[92] IV infusion causes thrombolysis in approximately 50% of patients with AMI.[93] Although definitive measurement of infarct size is limited, empirical evidence provided during inspection and myocardial biopsies confirmed that necrosis is confined to the subendocardium.[94] This suggests that myocardium can be salvaged by streptokinase infusion. Assessment of the efficacy of this treatment in improving LV function is difficult. Spontaneous changes in LV function occur unpredictably after an MI. Changes in its contractile state are largely regional, not global, and compensatory hyperkinesis in noninfarct zones makes assessment of segmental wall motion difficult. The Health and Policy Committee of the American College of Physicians[95] in their 1985 report stated that further randomized studies must be undertaken. They noted that continued areas of investigation include whether the therapy can be delivered early enough to affect infarct size, preserve LV function, and reduce morbidity and mortality.

Complications

Complications associated with streptokinase infusion include myocardial and systemic hemorrhage and reperfusion arrhythmias. Hemorrhagic infarctions have occurred in both survivors and nonsurvivors of the therapy. Myocardial hemorrhage is confined to the area of myocellular necrosis; therefore it does not increase infarct size.[96] Other systemic hemorrhages, intracranial, retroperitoneal, mediastinal, and gastrointestinal, are rare. The incidence of hemorrhage requiring transfusion has been reported from 1.5% to 5%.[97,98] Other hemorrhagic complications are generally confined to hematoma formation at the site of arterial punctures and localized oozing at venipuncture sites, which resolve with pressure dressings. Hemorrhaging of other body systems is rare.

Reperfusion arrhythmias can occur in as many as 80% of patients receiving intracoronary streptokinase.[99] Arrhythmias may be a sign of successful reperfusion. An idioventricular rhythm and premature ventricular contractions are the most common arrhythmias. Reperfusion of the inferioposterior myocardium is associated with transient bradycardia, varying degrees of atrioventricular block, and hypotension.[100] This hypotensive bradycardiac response is caused by stimulation of the Bezold-Jarisch reflex;[101] atropine and fluid administration are sufficient treatment.

Nursing Care

The ideal candidate for thrombolysis is the patient with recent chest pain and a fresh AMI; therefore the same nursing diagnoses and plan of care for the MI patient follow. The nursing diagnoses may include alterations in cardiac output, alterations in tissue perfusion, alterations in comfort, and anxiety. Therefore, control of pain and anxiety and constant vigilance to arrhythmias, ECG, and other physiologic changes are essential. A patient history should be taken noting any recent surgeries, trauma, cerebrovascular problems, bleeding abnormalities, and anticoagulation therapy.

During treatment, pertinent diagnoses are potential for injury and alterations in cardiac output. If streptokinase is the agent of choice, signs of allergic and anaphylactic responses should be monitored.

Post-treatment diagnoses include potential for bleeding related to pharmacologic interference with the body's hemostatic mechanism, potential for altered cardiac output related to reperfusion arrhythmias, and reocclusion or reinfarction[102] (Table 4-2). If a femeral approach is used, the patient should be monitored for retroperitoneal ecchymosis and/or complaints of back pain. Both signs are indicative of blood in the abdominal cavity.[103] As the patient will continue on anticoagulants while hospitalized and posthospitalization, effective patient teaching on anticoagulation therapy must be employed. Observe for arrhythmias. Standard protocols for treatment should be used. Patient anxiety can be alleviated by reminding the patient that arrhythmias are an indication of success of the thrombolytic therapy.

Table 4-2 Nursing Care Plan for the Patient Undergoing Thrombolytic Therapy*

Patient discharge criteria: Patient will exhibit an understanding of the medical procedure and the subsequent rehabilitation program as evidenced by verbalizations and behaviors.

Nursing Diagnosis	Expected Outcomes	Nursing Orders
1. Potential for alteration in cardiac output: decreased, related to reperfusion arrhythmias.	Patient will exhibit physiologic stability as evidenced by a stable heart rate, arrhythmia free/controlled rhythm. Note: Arrhythmias may be a sign of successful reperfusion.	1. Complete an initial cardiovascular assessment and maintain a flow sheet: —Evaluate ECG. Note rate and rhythm. Compare with preprocedure rhythm. —Observe for transient bradycardia, atrioventricular blocks. —Obtain blood pressure; observe for hypotension. 2. Follow established medical protocol for bradycardias, blocks: —Protocol dependent on physician and institution. May include atropine. —Standby temporary pacer.
2. Potential for alteration in cardiac output: decreased, related to myocardial injury, secondary to reocclusion or reinfarction.	Patient will exhibit physiologic stability as evidenced by stable hemodynamic parameters: blood pressure, heart rate, normal ST segments, angina free.	1. Complete an initial and continued cardiac assessment: —Continuously evaluate ECG. Note rate, rhythm, and ST segment. —Observe for onset of chest pain. Notify physician immediately and obtain 12-lead ECG, blood pressure, and heart rate.
3. Potential for injury: myocardial and systemic hemorrhage related to use of thrombolytic agents.	Patient will exhibit physiologic stability as evidenced by hemodynamic stability and vascular integrity: absence of hematoma formation, flank ecchymosis, normal hematocrit, clotting results within desired range,	1. Compare pre- and post-therapy lab values of plasminogen, fibrinogen, prothrombin time (PT), partial thromboplastin time (PTT), and fibrin degradation products (FDP). Note effect of agents on coagulation tests.

normal blood pressure, normal heart rate and rhythm.

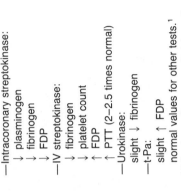

—Intracoronary streptokinase:
  → plasminogen
  → fibrinogen
  → FDP
—IV streptokinase:
  → fibrinogen
  → platelet count
  ← FDP
  ↑ PTT (2–2.5 times normal)
—Urokinase:
  slight ↓ fibrinogen
—t-Pa:
  slight ↑ FDP
  normal values for other tests.[1]

2. Maintain pressure over arterial puncture site. Observe for bleeding and hematoma formation at the site.

3. Continued assessment for overt/covert bleeding:
  —Skin: petechiae, bruising, discoloration
  —Retroperitoneal ecchymosis or c/o back pain
  —Guaiac checks on excretions.

4. Hemodynamically monitor for signs of hemorrhagic/hypovolemic shock: tachycardia, decreased blood pressure, decreased pulmonary artery wedge pressure, decreased right atrial pressure, decreased hematocrit, and decreased measured CO.

5. Assess readiness to learn for anticoagulant patient education. Topics to discuss:

continues

Table 4-2 continued

Nursing Diagnosis	Expected Outcomes	Nursing Orders
		signs of overt/covert bleeding to report, rationale for blood tests, precautions (i.e., wearing of gloves for gardening), what to do in case of major injury/accident.
4. Potential for injury: allergic and anaphylactic responses related to thrombolytic agents, particularly streptokinase.	Patient will exhibit physiologic stability for allergic responses; will be quickly assessed and treated leaving no sequelae.	1. Observe for allergic manifestations: fever, flushing, periorbital swelling, bronchospasm. Allergic reaction can develop several days postinfusion. 2. Prophylactic steroid administration if ordered.

*Note: The patient undergoing thrombolytic therapy has sustained an MI. The nursing care plan should address all nursing diagnoses pertinent to an MI patient. This nursing care plan focuses on diagnoses specific to thrombolytic therapy.
1. S. Quaal, "Thrombolytic Therapy: An Overview," *Journal of Cardiovascular Nursing* 1(1986):45.

BETA-ADRENERGIC BLOCKERS

Beta blockers can inhibit the response to adrenergic stimuli by competitively blocking adrenergic receptors. These drugs may selectively block beta-1 adrenergic receptors in the myocardium or both the myocardial beta-1 receptors and beta-2 receptors in the bronchial and vascular smooth muscle. The affinity to bind to the different beta receptors varies with each drug. Some drugs have an affinity for beta-1 receptors and are considered cardioselective because of the predominance of beta-1 receptors in the myocardium (Table 4-3). However, as dosages of the cardioselective drugs are increased, beta-2 receptors are generally also inhibited. Airway resistance increases. Therefore, patients receiving cardioselective beta blockers must be observed as patients receiving the other beta blockers for bronchospasm.

Competition at the beta-1 receptor site inhibits the binding of a catecholamine agonist, which, in turn, inhibits the stimulation of adenyl cyclase. The flow of calcium into the contractile apparatus is therefore decreased.[104] Myocardial contractility decreases. Myocardial oxygen consumption is reduced because of the combined negative inotropic effect of decreased heart rate. The blockade of circulating catecholamines decreases pacemaker automaticity and produces sinus slowing. Myocardial oxygen requirements are decreased for any given level of activity by a reduction in rate and automaticity (Exhibit 4-2).

The competition at beta-2 receptor sites results in unopposed alpha-receptor stimulation, resulting in enhanced transmembrane calcium influx and increased vascular smooth muscle tone, causing vasoconstriction.[105]

Table 4-3 Beta-Adrenergic Blockers: Pharmacologic Properties

	Cardio-selective	Membrane Stabilizing	Intrinsic Sympathomimetic Activity
Acebutolol	Yes	—	Yes
Alpenolol	No	Yes	Yes
Atenolol	Yes	No	No
Labetolol hydrochloride	No	Yes	Yes; some beta-2, little if any beta-1
Metoprolol tartate	Yes	No	No
Nadolol	No	No	No
Oxprenolol	No	Yes	Yes
Pindolol	No	Yes	Yes
Practolol	Yes	No	Yes
Propranolol	No	Yes; at blood concentration levels greater than required for blockade	No
Sotalol	No	No	No
Timolol maleate	No	No	No

Exhibit 4-2 Beta Blockers: Cardiovascular Effects

Decrease force of contraction at rest and exercise
Decrease heart rate
Decrease systemic arterial pressure
Decrease in rate of rise LV pressure
Increase ventricular volume
Increase LV end-diastolic pressure
Lengthen systolic ejection

Some beta blockers may cause receptor stimulation, referred to as intrinsic sympathomimetic activity (Table 4-3). When sympathetic tone is low, the mimetic effect is predominant, and the heart rate may increase slightly; conversely, when sympathetic tone is high, the beta-blocking effect is predominant, and the heart rate response is blunted.[106]

A membrane stabilizing effect is observed with some beta blockers. This property serves a potential role in arrhythmia control. Often, however, it is only observed at high concentrations, higher than those required for the blocking effect.

The FDA-approved beta blockers are listed in Table 4-4.

Clinical Uses

Angina Pectoris

Beta-adrenergic blockers are clinically effective in the treatment of angina; approximately 75% of patients have a favorable response.[107] The balance between myocardial oxygen delivery and demand is improved. A reduction in heart rate, contractility, and systemic arterial pressure at any given level of activity accounts for the reduced oxygen requirements. A decreased frequency of attacks along with a reduction in NTG dosage and increased exercise tolerance is observed.

Research on the use of beta blockers in chronic therapy for angina patients showed their ability to reduce mortality and coronary events.[108–115]

Myocardial Infarction

After coronary artery occlusion, raised levels of circulating catecholamines or enhanced sympathetic drive can increase both the severity of myocardial ischemia and the frequency of ventricular arrhythmias.[116,117] Beta blockers reduce the effects of catecholamines and therefore reduce factors that favor the occurrence of infarction such as tachycardia and increased contractility. Their reduction of systemic arterial pressure, heart rate, and myocardial contractility each decrease myocardial oxygen requirements.

Table 4-4 Beta-Adrenergic Blockers: Pharmacologic Effects

	Initial Dose (po unless otherwise indicated)	Maintenance Dose	Uses	Metabolism	Side Effects	Precautions	Contra-indications	Drug Interactions
Nadolol	40 mg daily, alone or combination with diuretic	Increased 40–80 mg daily at 2 to 14 day intervals. Usual maintenance dose: 80–320 mg	HTN	Renal	CV: bradycardia, peripheral vascular insufficiency CNS: dizziness, fatigue (2%) GI: nausea, diarrhea, vomiting, constipation (0.1–0.5%)	Inadequate cardiac function Hyperthyroidism Hypoglycemia General anesthesia Impaired renal and liver function	Bronchospastic disease Bronchial asthma Sinus bradycardia, heart block greater than first degree Cardiogenic shock Overt cardiac failure	Sympathomimetic drugs, antagonize Antimuscarinic drugs, counteract Diuretics and hypotensive drugs, additive effect Antiarrhythmic drugs, additive effect Neuromuscular blocking drugs, potentiate
	40 mg daily	Increased 40–80 mg daily at 3–7 day intervals	AP		Bronchospasm (0.1%)			
Timolol maleate	10 mg bid	Increased 20–40 mg daily given in 2 divided doses	HTN	Liver	CV: as with nadolol, hypotension (37%); arrhythmia, AV, & SA block (17%) CNS: as with nadolol (2–5%)	As with nadolol, myasthenia	As with nadolol, severe COPD	Cardiovascular drugs, potentiate Nonsteroidal anti-inflammatory drugs, antagonize

continues

Table 4-4 continued

	Initial Dose (po unless otherwise indicated)	Maintenance Dose	Uses	Metabolism	Side Effects	Precautions	Contra-indications	Drug Interactions
	Limited 1–4 wk after infarction	15–45 mg daily given in 3–4 divided doses	AP		GI: as with nadolol (1–5%) Rales, bronchospasm, dyspnea (0.6–2%)			
	Initiated 1–4 wk after infarction	10 mg twice daily	Long-term after AMI					
Propranolol HCl	Should be given before meals and at bedtime	Increased at 3 to 7 day intervals	HTN	Liver	CV: as with nadolol, fluid retention, pulmonary edema CNS: as with nadolol GI: as with nadolol Dermatologic: rashes, rare, hyperkeratosis	As with nadolol Patients receiving adrenergic augmenting psychotherapeutic drugs, monoamine oxidase inhibitors and for 2 weeks after withdrawal	As with nadolol	Psychotherapeutic drugs Sympathomimetic drugs, antagonize Antimuscarinic drugs, counteract Diuretics, additive effect Neuromuscular blocking drugs, potentiate Cimetidine, reduce clearance of drug
	40 mg bid conventional or 80 mg daily, extended release capsules	Usual maintenance dose: 160–480 mg daily, conventional 120–160 mg daily, extended release capsules						
	10–20 mg tid, qid-conventional	Increased at 3 to 7 day intervals	AP		Hematologic: traumatic eosinophilia Elevated BUN	Neuromuscular blocking drugs, potentiate		

80 mg once daily, extended release capsules	160–240 mg daily				Cimetidine, reduce clearance of drug
80-mg daily in divided doses, conventional or once daily, extended release capsules		MI			
Initiated 5 to 21 days after infarction	180–240 mg daily, conventional	MI			
Labetalol HCl: 100 mg bid, alone or in combination with a diuretic. Maximum affect seen within 1–4 hr	Increase every 2 to 3 days at 100 mg bid increments	HTN	Liver	CV: symptomatic hypotension, development exacerbation of CHF; CNS: as with nadolol (5%); GI: as with nadolol	Diuretics and hypotensive agents, additive effect; Halothane, synergistic hypotensive effect; Cimetidine, increases bioavailability; Glutethimide, decreases bioavailability

continues

Table 4-4 continued

Initial Dose (po unless otherwise indicated)	Maintenance Dose	Uses	Metabolism	Side Effects	Precautions	Contra-indications	Drug Interactions
IV slow, 20 mg	IV 40–80 mg at 10 min intervals	Hypotensive emergencies		Respiratory: dyspnea, wheezing, bronchospasm, nasal congestion			Nitroglycerin, antagonizes reflex tachycardia Tricyclic antidepressants, increased tremors
	po maintenance after IV, 200 mg initial, followed by 200–400 mg in 6–12 hr Increased at 1 day increments until desired outcome			GU: ejaculatory failure, impotence, difficult/painful micturition, acute urinary retention Derm: rashes Lupus-erythematosuslike illness			
Metoprolol 100 mg daily either in single or divided doses	Increased at weekly increments 50–100 mg bid or tid	HTN AP	Liver	CV: SOB, bradycardia, peripheral vascular responses, cold extremities CNS: as with nadolol Derm: pruritus, dry skin, alopecia	As with nadolol	As with nadolol AMI with HR less than 45	Cardiovascular drugs, potentiate Sympathomimetic drugs, antagonize Vasodilator (hydralazine), may cause pulmonary hypertension

Drug	Dosage	Dosage adjustment	Indication	Metabolism	Side Effects	Contraindications/Precautions		Drug Interactions
Pindolol	5 mg bid, alone or combination with a diuretic Hypotensive effect seen within 1 wk: maximum therapeutic effect may not be seen for 2 wk or longer	Increase 10 mg daily at 3–4 wk intervals Usual maintenance dose, 10–30 mg bid or tid	HTN	Liver	Hematologic: iosinophilia, agranulocytosis CV: as with nadolol (2%); peripheral edema (6–16%), dyspnea CNS: as with nadolol (15–19%) GI: as with nadolol (2–79%) Slight and persistent SGOT and SGPT concentrations Muscle and leg cramps (2–10%)	As with nadolol Diabetes mellitus	As with nadolol	Hypotensives, additive effect Digoxin, transient decrease in serum digoxin levels

Abbreviations: AV = atrioventricular; SA = sinoatrial; COPD = chronic obstructive pulmonary disease; HTN = hypertension; CHF = congestive heart failure; SOB = shortness of breath; AP = angina pectoris; AMI = acute MI; HR = heart rate; SGOT = serum glutamic-oxalacetic transaminase; SGPT = serum glutamic-pyruvic transaminase.

An antiarrhythmic effect, although not strong, is seen with beta blockers because of their effect on cellular electrical activity. Beta blockers may abolish sympathetic and catecholamine-induced arrhythmias.[118] This effect may assist in stabilizing electrical activity. The nurse should observe for the drug's effect on the patient's ECG activity.

An antihypertensive effect is also observed, but the precise mechanism has not been determined. It was proposed that the drugs block peripheral adrenergic receptors, decrease sympathetic outflow from the central nervous system (CNS), and/or suppress renin release.[119] Monitoring of blood pressure (BP), fluid balance, and urine output are necessary.

Beta blockers have also reduced abnormally increased platelet aggregability in patients with angina pectoris[120] and increased tissue oxygen delivery through alteration of hemoglobin-oxygen affinity.[121] These effects are beneficial in preventing infarction. The nurse should remember these effects when planning care to improve the balance between myocardial oxygen supply and demand.

Propranolol hydrochloride has two additional properties: a nonspecific platelet membrane effect that may affect platelet aggregation, and redistribution of 2,3-diphosphoglyceric acid in erythrocytes, which decreases the affinity of hemoglobin for oxygen.[122]

Beta blockers can alter the natural history of CAD postinfarction.[123] Successful prophylaxis against reinfarction, sudden death, and/or total mortality was shown in clinical trials.[124–136] These studies employed numerous beta blockers that were administered over varying periods of time. The most positive results were seen with propranolol and timolol. Baber et al.[137] failed to show beneficial results with propranolol; however, the prescribed dosage may have been too small to be of benefit.[138]

Based on clinical trials, it is reasonable to recommend routine treatment with an oral beta blocker for at least 1 year after infarction and possibly for 2 to 3 years.[139] Nursing should therefore include information on the drugs' continued use in any discharge teaching plan. Reinforcement that these medications are part of the patient's successful rehabilitative course is necessary.

Nursing Considerations

The drugs are contraindicated in severe congestive heart failure, bronchial asthma, disorders of atrioventricular and sinus node function, vasospastic angina, hypotension, and Raynaud's phenomenon.[140] Beta blockers must also be used with extreme care in patients with heart failure as the condition may worsen.

Several nursing diagnoses may be used with patients taking beta blockers.

Potential Alteration in Cardiac Output: Decreased

Patient discharge instructions are extremely important. The teaching plan should include the following information: (1) these drugs should never be abruptly discontinued as this may perpetuate heart failure and ischemia; (2) pulse taking; (3) improvement in condition as evidenced by reduced anginal attacks and NTG use at rest, and (4) exercise should not be translated into meaning that exercise levels can be increased without consultation with the cardiac rehabilitation team.

Potential for Impaired Gas Exchange

Beta blockers increase airway resistance and are contraindicated in patients with bronchospastic disease and bronchial asthma. A thorough patient history and respiratory assessment are essential. Low-dose beta-1 blockers, atenolol and metaprolol tartrate, have been successfully administered in patients with chronic obstructive pulmonary disease (COPD). Instruction on signs and symptoms of airway obstruction should, however, be reinforced.

Potential for Hypoglycemia

Certain beta blockers, nadolol and propranolol hydrochloride, inhibit the release of free fatty acids and insulin by adrenergic stimulation. Labetalol may increase plasma glucose concentrations. These drugs should be cautiously administered to Type I diabetic patients. Patient instruction on monitoring signs and symptoms of hypoglycemia should be done. Both atenolol and metaprolol tartrate are preferred beta blockers for a diabetic patient.

CALCIUM CHANNEL BLOCKERS

Calcium

Calcium has a critical role in cardiovascular physiology: the electrical activation of the cardiac cell, the coupling of the electrical event to the mechanical contraction, smooth muscle contraction in coronary and peripheral arteries, and intracellular energy storage and use.[141]

The movement of positively and negatively charged ions across the cell membrane creates the electrical activity of cardiac cells. An action potential curve is produced as ionic movement occurs during depolarization and repolarization (Figure 4-7). The action potential curve varies among types of cardiac cells because different currents predominate in the different areas of the heart.[142] The action potential from the atrial and ventricular tissue, intracardiac conduction tissue, and the distal region of the atrioventricular (AV) node depends on both the fast and slow inward calcium currents; pacemaker cells in the sinoatrial (SA) node and in the central and proximal regions of the AV node are stimulated by the slow inward calcium current. Therefore, depolarization (phase 0) is slowed (Figure 4-7).

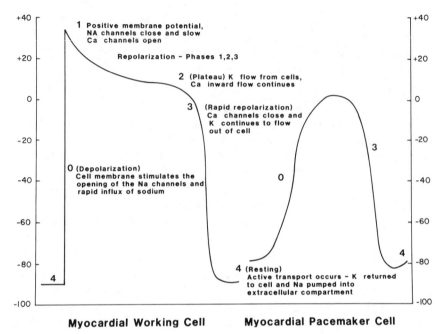

Figure 4-7 Action potential curves: myocardial pacemaker cell, myocardial working cell.

The linking of the electrical activation to mechanical activity is mediated by calcium. The interaction of the thin actin filaments and the thick myosin filaments causes muscle contraction. The force of a contraction is determined by the number of actin-myosin crossbridges. Actin in cardiac muscle is associated with tropomyosin, a regulatory protein. Tropomyosin, in turn, is linked to troponin. In the absence of calcium, tropomyosin-troponin inhibits the interaction of actin and myosin. As depolarization spreads throughout the heart, calcium enters the cell via slow channels. The influx of calcium stimulates the release of intracellular stores of calcium in the sarcoplasmic reticulum. Calcium binds to troponin-C. This binding results in a rearrangement of the tropomyosin-troponin complex, which allows actin and myosin to interact electrochemically, causing shortening of cardiac muscle and contraction.

The initiation of vascular smooth muscle contraction is also dependent on calcium. Intracellular calcium concentrations increase upon excitation, causing calcium to interact with one of the four binding sites of calmodulin. The calmodulin-calcium complex activates myosin light chain kinase, which phosphorylates the myosin light chain.[143] Actin and myosin interact, and contraction results. As calcium is removed from the cell, the myosin light chain kinase is inactivated, dephosphorylation occurs, the actin and myosin dissociate, and relaxation results. The amount of available intracellular calcium determines the amount of available myosin light chain kinase and therefore is key in determining the balance between vascular smooth muscle contraction and relaxation.

Calcium's role in intracellular energy storage and use is best illustrated by ischemia. In an ischemic state, intracellular calcium levels are increased, causing a decrease in mitochondrial production of adenosine triphosphate (ATP), loss of cell membrane integrity, and enhanced ATP breakdown. Cellular structure and function are jeopardized.

Action

By impeding calcium entry, the calcium blocking agents or the calcium antagonists influence all calcium-dependent processes. Three calcium antagonists are available: nifedipine, verapamil hydrochloride, and diltiazem hydrochloride. Each produces different actions (Table 4-5); their exact site and mechanism of action are unknown. They all block calcium passage across the cell membrane. Their specific actions are indicated for different clinical uses (Table 4-6).

The blockage of calcium influx across the cell membrane of the SA node depresses its automaticity and the rate of repolarization. A decrease in calcium influx across the AV node slows AV nodal conduction and prolongs AV refractoriness. Therefore, a *negative chronotropic* effect of a decreased heart rate and slowed AV conduction is appreciated. The latter is especially important in the treatment of supraventricular tachycardias.

Myocardial contraction is depressed through the calcium antagonists' disruption of actin-myosin interaction. This *negative inotropic* effect is appreciated when lowered myocardial oxygen needs and enhanced relaxation are required, such as with angina and hypertrophic cardiomyopathies respectively.

The calcium antagonists are *vasodilators*; nifedipine is the most potent vasodilator. It dilates arterioles and has little effect on veins. The vasodilation reduces systolic BP. A concomitant reflex increase in heart rate and cardiac output is seen; however the amount of myocardial oxygen consumption is unchanged because of the reduced afterload. The vascular smooth muscles of the

---

Table 4-5 Calcium Channel Blockers: Cardiovascular Effects

	Diltiazem HCl	Nifedipine	Verapamil HCl
HR, SA node conduction	Moderate ↓	Mild ↑ (reflex)	Moderate ↓
AV node conduction	Moderate ↓	None	Marked ↓
AV node contractility	Mild ↓	Mild ↑ ↓ (reflex)	Moderate ↓
Coronary vasodilatation	Marked ↑	Marked ↑	Moderate ↑
Peripheral vasodilatation	Mild ↑	Marked ↑	Mild ↑

Table 4-6 Calcium Channel Blockers: Pharmacologic Effects

| Drug | Dosage* | | Onset | Peak | Uses | Metabolism | Adverse Effects | Precautions | Contra-indications | Drug Interactions |
	Initial	Maintenance								
Nifedipine	10 mg tid Increased at 7 to 14 day intervals until optimal control maintained Single dose should not exceed 30 mg, daily dose should not exceed 180 mg	30–60 mg daily in 3 divided doses	20 min	1–2 hr	Prinzmetal variant or chronic stable angina pectoris	Liver	Vasodilation of vascular smooth muscle: dizziness, headache, flushing, lightheadedness (25%) Hypotension, weakness, palpitation, peripheral edema Nausea, heartburn, muscle cramps, nervousness and mood changes, dyspnea, cough, wheezing GI: diarrhea, constipation, cramps CNS: shakiness, difficulty with postural balance, blurred	BP monitoring for hypotension especially during initiation and dose adjustments CHF and aortic stenosis may precipitate heart failure	Known hypersensitivity	Beta blockers: may increase risk of hypotension, anginal exacerbation, CHF Fentanyl: hypotension, severe Digoxin: serum concentrations may increase Hypotensive drugs: may increase hypotensive episodes

Drug	Dose			Indications	Metabolism	Adverse Effects	Precautions	Contraindications	Drug Interactions
						vision, sleep disturbances			
Verapamil HCl	IV 5–10 mg; if no response IV 10 mg 30 min after initial dose 80 mg q6–8 hr 240–480 mg daily; usual 320–480 mg daily in 3–4 divided doses	2 hr	3 hr	Supraventricular tachycardias Prinzmetal variant or chronic stable angina pectoris	Liver	Effect on conduction system: bradycardia, first-second-third degree block (17%) Congestive heart failure (CHF), pulmonary edema (17%) Dizziness, symptomatic hypotension (4%) Constipation (7%) Nausea, headache, abdominal discomfort	BP monitoring as above Severe or moderately severe ventricular dysfunction may worsen or precipitate heart failure Hepatic or renal impairment, potential for overdosage	Severe LV dysfunction	Beta blockers: as above Digoxin: as above; serum concentration may increase 50–70% during first week of therapy Hypotensive drugs: additive effect or potentiate effect Antiarrhythmic drugs: quinidine; substantial hypotension
Diltiazem HCl	30 mg qid, before meals and at bedtime Increased at 1–2 day intervals until optimal control maintained Lowest level to maintain relief of symptoms	15 min	30 min	Prinzmetal variant or chronic stable angina pectoris	Liver	Effect on conduction system as with verapamil HCl (17%) Anoxia and nausea (3%)	BP monitoring as with verapamil HCl	Known hypersensitivity Sick sinus syndrome Second or third degree heart block Severe hypotension	Digoxin: serum concentrations may increase

*PO doses unless otherwise indicated.

coronary arteries are also affected by the calcium antagonists, causing dilatation and reduced coronary artery resistance. The effectiveness in producing vasodilation in the coronary arteries is three to ten times more than the myocardial contractile depressant effect.[144] Small doses can therefore be administered to affect coronary artery resistance without affecting contraction. Calcium antagonists are useful in the treatment of angina, can reverse or inhibit coronary artery spasm, and are useful in the treatment of variant angina.

A reversal of ischemia cellular changes is evidenced by calcium antagonists. Reduced calcium influx, increased myocardial blood flow through their dilatation properties, and afterload reduction all reduce myocardial oxygen consumption and pose implications for use in MI.

Clinical Uses

Angina

Calcium antagonists reduce myocardial oxygen demand through systemic arteriolar dilatation and increase oxygen delivery through coronary artery and arteriolar dilatation and platelet disaggregation. They have been effective in reducing the number of anginal attacks and in improving exercise intolerance. The calcium-influx blocking effect relieves or prevents coronary artery vasospasm. Through a reduction in afterload, myocardial oxygen consumption and secondary angina are reduced.

Breland and Boland,[145] summarizing numerous clinical trials, reported on efficacy rates for diltiazem, nifedipine, and verapamil of 90.8%, 94% and 85.7%, respectively. Calcium antagonists are effective for the treatment of rest angina, particularly with spasm.[146-149]

The calcium antagonists can be used as solo therapy for the treatment of angina or can be combined with nitrates and/or beta-adrenergic agents. They have especially been beneficial in combination with the beta-adrenergic agents, allowing for reduced dosage, reducing the side effects of the beta-adrenergic drugs. The calcium antagonists have also been appropriate for patients with chronic obstructive pulmonary disease and diabetes mellitus when beta-adrenergic blockers were contraindicated.

Myocardial Infarction

It has not been demonstrated in animal models or human studies that calcium antagonists can significantly reduce infarct size or complication mortality once the cell membrane is disrupted or the cardiac cell is dead.[150] As previously summarized, the effect on coronary artery resistance and flow and reduction in afterload are positive in ischemic states. Administration before or immediately after ischemic states can protect tissue by altering calcium influx, reducing early catecholamine release, and reducing ATP breakdown.[151]

Hypertension

The systemic arteriolar dilatation effect of the calcium antagonists has made them effective as solo or adjunct therapy for hypertension. Nifedipine is the noted calcium antagonist for this use.

Arrhythmias

The effect of the calcium antagonists on AV conduction has made them appropriate for treating re-entry ventricular tachycardias. Verapamil has the largest effect on AV conduction. The prolonged AV refractoriness it produces reduces the number of atrial impulses conducted to the ventricles. Verapamil has been effective both IV and orally in correcting supraventricular tachycardia.

Nursing Considerations

The side effects of the calcium antagonists (Table 4-6) are extensions of their pharmacologic activity. Numerous nursing diagnoses can be identified.

Potential for Alteration in Cardiac Output: Decreased

The most prominent side effect relates directly to their dilatation of regional vascular beds. Dizziness, lightheadedness, headaches, and hypotension can occur. The BP should be monitored during initiation of the drugs for severe hypotension responses. Bradycardia and AV blocks should also be monitored.

Knowledge Deficit

Patients taking verapamil or diltiazem should be instructed to take their pulse as a monitoring safeguard against conduction disturbances. Verapamil is contraindicated in patients with sick sinus syndrome and second- and third-degree heart block. Patients should also be taught the signs and symptoms of congestive heart failure as it is a side effect of the therapy. *Alteration in elimination constipation* is the leading side effect of verapamil administration; dietary supplements and/or over-the-counter laxatives may be necessary.

Potential for Injury: Drug Interactions

The calcium antagonists interact with several other drug types (Table 4-6). The most notable interaction occurs with digoxin, quinidine, and the beta-adrenergic blockers. Serum digoxin levels may increase when it is administered with a beta blocker and can increase 50% to 70% during the first week of verapamil therapy. The patient should be taught or reinforced about the signs and symptoms of digoxin toxicity. Quinidine levels have been altered; lower dosages should be used in combination with verapamil. Finally, the risk of hypotension, failure, and anginal exacerbation may all be increased with concurrent use of calcium and beta blockers.

NITRATES

Brunton[152] in 1857 was the first to use a nitrate in the form of amyl nitrate to treat angina. He used the drug operating under the premise that BP reduction would decrease myocardial oxygen demand and therefore relieve angina. More than a century has passed, and the organic nitrates have been the mainstay of therapy for angina pectoris. They are now available as sublingual, IV, transcutaneous, buccal, and oral spray preparations in short- and long-term acting forms (Table 4-7).

The nitrates affect vascular smooth muscle and are arteriolar and venous dilators. The dilatation of the venous capacitance vessels reduces preload. Accompanying decreases in both end-systolic and end-diastolic volumes and in wall tension further reduce myocardial oxygen demand. Afterload is also reduced through decreased peripheral arterial resistance. These effects are more pronounced when the patient is standing, when venous return is further reduced.[153]

NTG also has a direct effect on the coronary arteries. Vasodilation of native vessels and improved collateral flow have been noted.[154]

Nitrates, therefore, have a coronary vasculature effect and a systemic hemodynamic effect that enhance myocardial oxygen delivery and decrease myocardial oxygen demand. However, a reflux increase in heart rate and contractility with nitrates is noted.

Clinical Uses

Nitrates have been widely shown in clinical trials to prevent anginal attacks,[155–157] and controlled trials have shown its efficacy in treating unstable angina and in relieving exertional vasospasm.[158–160]

The development of tolerance to the antianginal and circulatory effects of nitrates during chronic therapy is controversial. Tolerance develops rapidly with respect to nitrate-induced headaches, and veno- and arterio-dilatation are attenuated by long-term therapy.[161] Controversy remains regarding tolerance development to the antianginal efficacy of long-acting nitrates when given over a long time period.[162,163]

Table 4-7 Nitrates: Pharmacologic Properties

Drug	Dosage	Long-term Prophylactic	Onset	Duration
Isosorbide dinitrate		Oral 10–20 mg tid or qid	1 hr	5–6 hr
Capsules, extended release		20 or 40 mg q6–12 hr or 80 mg q8–12 hr	30 min	6–8 hr
Tablets				
Chewable	2.5–10 mg at 5–10 min intervals; not to exceed 3 doses in 15–30 min		Within 3 min	0.5–2 hr
Extended release		20 or 40 mg q6–12 hr or 80 mg q8–12 hr	30 min	6–8 hr
Sublingual	2.5–10 mg at 5–10 min intervals; not to exceed 3 doses in 15–30 min		Within 3 min	2 hr
Nitroglycerin				
Sublingual	0.15–0.6 mg at 5 min intervals; no more than 3 doses in 15 min		Within 2 min	Up to 5 to 30 min
Topical ointment 2%, transdermal systems		3.5 in by 2.25 1 system/q24 hr	Within 30 min	3 hr
Lingual: aerosol (0.4 mg/metered spray)	1–2 sprays			
Oral: capsules and tablets, extended release		1.3–9 mg q8–12 hr		

Nitrate Preparations

Sublingual nitrates are standard for treating acute ischemic pain. They are rapidly absorbed and have an onset of action within 2 to 5 minutes, with maximal effect within 3 to 15 minutes. Duration of action is 20 to 30 minutes. Sublingual NTG is effective in the prevention of anginal pain before exertion,[164,165] but the duration of protection is probably not longer than 30 minutes.[166] Long-acting sublingual preparations are as effective as short-term sublingual preparations, but their duration of action is debatable.[167] Hairy areas, such as the chest, affect effectiveness. NTG paste or ointment should be covered by a piece of paper and/or plastic wrap to avoid loss of medication. The transdermal preparations rely on controlled transcutaneous absorption. Onset of action is observed in 30 minutes, with steady-state concentrations reached 2 hours after application and uniform concentration achieved for 24 hours.[168] The transdermal patches vary in size, type of adhesive, and degree of patient comfort. As with the ointment, hairy areas should be avoided.

IV administration provides immediate action. The rapid onset is matched by a very short half-life. Plasma concentrations fall rapidly after discontinuation. A continuous NTG infusion must be closely monitored because of hypotensive effects. Since NTG is absorbed by plastic, plastic IV bottles and tubing should be avoided.

Nursing Considerations

Side effects of nitrate therapy include headache and postural hypotension. The headache most commonly appears early in therapy and is described as throbbing. It can be responsive to dosage reduction or analgesics. Postural hypotension, dizziness, and flushing all result from the effect of venodilatation.

The nitrates are contraindicated in patients with glaucoma and severe anemia, and should be used with caution in patients with increased intracranial pressure.

SUMMARY

The medical treatment of coronary artery disease continues to evolve, with the goal of preservation of the myocardium. PTCA and IV thrombolytic agents are being used successfully to reopen stenotic vessels. Future lasers may dissolve plaque entirely. New generations of calcium channel blockers, beta blockers and nitrates are contributing to the preservation of myocardium by optimizing oxygen supply. The nurse's role in monitoring patient responses to these newer treatment modalities is crucial, requiring specialized knowledge and skills. It is hoped that this chapter has enhanced this vital nursing component.

NOTES

1. American Heart Association, *Heart Facts* (Dallas: American Heart Association, 1986).

2. C.T. Dotter and M.P. Judkins, "Transluminal Treatment of Atherosclerotic Obstruction: Description of a New Technique and a Preliminary Report on its Application," *Circulation* 30(1964):654.

3. A.R. Gruentzig, A. Senning, and W.E. Siegenthaler, "Nonoperative Dilatation of Coronary Artery Stenosis," *New England Journal of Medicine* 301(1979):61.

4. Dotter and Judkins, "Transluminal Treatment."

5. F.L. Shillinger, "Percutaneous Transluminal Coronary Angioplasty," *Heart and Lung* 12(1983):46.

6. G. Lee, R.M. Ikeda, and J.A. Joyce, "Evaluation of Transluminal Angioplasty of Chronic Coronary Artery Stenosis: Value and Limitations Assessed in Fresh Human Cadaver Hearts," *Circulation* 61(1980):77.

7. T.A. Sanborn, D.P. Faxon, and C. Haudenscheld, "The Mechanism of Transluminal Angioplasty: Evidence for Formation of Aneurysm in Experimental Atherosclerosis," *Circulation* 68(1983):1136.

8. J.A. Hall et al., "Coronary Arterial Aneurysm Formation after Balloon Angioplasty," *American Journal of Cardiology* 52(1983):261.

9. J.E. Saffetz, T.E. Rose, and W.C. Roberts, "Coronary Arterial Rupture During Coronary Angioplasty," *American Journal of Cardiology* 51(1983):902.

10. L.D. Hillis, "Southwestern Internal Medicine Conference: Percutaneous Transluminal Coronary Angioplasty," *American Journal of the Medical Sciences* 228(1984):92.

11. P.C. Block, K.L. Baughman, and R.C. Pasternak, "Transluminal Coronary Angioplasty: Correlation of Morphologic and Angiographic Findings in an Experimental Model," *American Journal of Cardiology* 51(1983):676.

12. J.M. Isner and D.M. Sallem, "The Persistent Enigma of Percutaneous Angioplasty," *International Journal of Cardiology* 6(1984):391.

13. P.C. Block et al., "Morphology after Transluminal Angioplasty in Human Beings," *New England Journal of Medicine* 305(1981):382.

14. D.C. Cumberland, "The Current Status of Percutaneous Coronary Angioplasty," *Acta Radiologica* 26(1985):497.

15. Ibid.

16. Hillis, "Southwestern Conference."

17. Gruentzig, Senning, and Siegenthaler, "Nonoperative Dilatation."

18. A.J. Greenspon and S. Goldberg, "What is the Role of Percutaneous Transluminal Coronary Angioplasty?" *Cardiovascular Clinics* 13(1983):265.

19. R.I. Hamby and S. Katz, "Percutaneous Transluminal Coronary Angioplasty: Its Potential Impact on Surgery for Coronary Artery Disease," *American Journal of Cardiology* 45(1980):1161.

20. D.R. Holmes, R.E. Vlietstra, and L.D. Fisher, "Follow-up of Patients from CASS Potentially Suitable for Percutaneous Transluminal Coronary Angioplasty," *American Heart Journal* 106(1983):981.

21. Cumberland, "Percutaneous Angioplasty."

22. R.S. Faro, J.A. Alexander, and R.L. Feldman, "Intraoperative Balloon Catheter Dilatation: University of Florida Experience," *American Heart Journal* 107(1984):84.

23. Cumberland, "Percutaneous Angioplasty."

24. B. Meier, A.R. Gruentzig, and S.B. King, "Risk of Side Branch Occlusion during Coronary Angioplasty," *American Journal of Cardiology* 53(1984):10.

25. B. Meier, A.R. Gruentzig, and J. Hollman, "Does Length of Eccentricity of Coronary Stenosis Influence the Outcome of Transluminal Dilatation? " *Circulation* 67(1983):487.

26. Shillinger, "Transluminal Angioplasty."

27. J.M. Hodgson and D.D. Williams, "The Transstenotic Pressure Gradient During Coronary Angioplasty Predicts Longterm Clinical Success," *Circulation* 72, Suppl. 3 (1985):371.

28. B.B. Ott, "Percutaneous Transluminal Coronary Angioplasty," *Heart and Lung* 11(1982):294.

29. G. Dorros, M. Cowley, and J. Simpson, "National Heart, Lung and Blood Institute Registry Report of Complications of Percutaneous Transluminal Coronary Angioplasty," *American Journal of Cardiology* 47(1981):396.

30. D.R. Holmes, R.E. Vlietstra, and H.C. Smith, "Restenosis after Percutaneous Transluminal Coronary Angioplasty: A Report from the PTCA Registry of the National Heart, Lung and Blood Institute," *American Journal of Cardiology* 53(1984):77.

31. K.M. Detre, R.K. Myler, and S.F. Kelsey, "Baseline Characteristics of Patients in the National Heart, Lung and Blood Institute Percutaneous Transluminal Coronary Angioplasty Registry," *American Journal of Cardiology* 54(1984):7C.

32. K.M. Kent, L.G. Bentiviglio, and P.C. Block, "Long-term Efficacy of Percutaneous Transluminal Coronary Angioplasty: Report from the Heart, Lung and Blood Institute PTCA Registry," *American Journal of Cardiology* 53(1984):27C.

33. G. Dorros, M.J. Cowley, and L. Janke, "In-Hospital Mortality Rate in the National Heart, Lung and Blood Institute Percutaneous Transluminal Coronary Angioplasty Registry," *American Journal of Cardiology* 33(1984):17C.

34. Detre, Myler, and Kelsey, "Baseline Characteristics."

35. Dorros, Cowley, and Janke, "In-Hospital Mortality."

36. Cumberland, "Percutaneous Angioplasty."

37. S.F. Kelsey et al., "Effect of Investigator Experience on Percutaneous Transluminal Coronary Angioplasty," *American Journal of Cardiology* 53(1984):56C.

38. D.R. Holmes and R.E. Vlietstra, "Percutaneous Transluminal Coronary Angioplasty: Current Status and Future Trends," *Mayo Clinic Proceedings* 61(1986):865.

39. Cumberland, "Percutaneous Angioplasty."

40. Holmes, Vlietstra, and Smith, "Restenosis."

41. Holmes and Vlietstra, "Transluminal Angioplasty."

42. Ibid.

43. Kent, Bentiviglio, and Block, "Long-term Efficacy."

44. J. Hollman, G.E. Austin, and A.R. Gruentzig, "Coronary Artery Spasm at the Site of Angioplasty in the First Two Months after Successful Percutaneous Transluminal Coronary Angioplasty," *Journal of American College of Cardiology* 2(1983):1039.

45. A. Cragg, S. Einzig, and W. Castaneda-Zuniga, "Vessel Wall Arachidonate Metabolism after Angioplasty: Possible Mediators of Postangioplasty Vasospasm," *American Journal of Cardiology* 51(1983):1441.

46. Hillis, "Southwestern Conference."

47. Greenspon and Goldberg, "Role of Angioplasty."

48. Dorros, Cowley, and Simpson, "Registry Report."

49. J.A. Purcell and P.A. Givvin, "Percutaneous Transluminal Coronary Angioplasty," *American Journal of Nursing* 81(1981):1620.

50. N. Hutchison et al., "Acute Closure Syndrome After Coronary Angioplasty: Nursing Perspectives," *Circulation* 74, Suppl. 2 (1986):292.

51. J. Fox, "Laser Coronary Angioplasty," *Journal of Cardiovascular Nursing* 1(1986):57.

52. Ibid.

53. R.B. Gerrity et al., "Arterial Response to Laser Operation for Removal of Atherosclerotic Plaques," *Journal of Thoracic and Cardiovascular Surgery* 85(1983):427.

54. G. Lee et al., "Current and Potential Uses of Lasers in the Treatment of Atherosclerotic Disease," *Chest* 84(1984):431.

55. G. Lee et al., "The Qualitative Effects of Laser Radiation on Human Arteriosclerotic Disease," *American Heart Journal* 105(1983):888.

56. Ibid.

57. Ibid.

58. G.S. Abela et al., Abstract, "Laser Recanalization of Peripheral Arteries in Man: A Preliminary Report," *Circulation* 72, Suppl. 3 (October 1985):111.

59. T.A. Sanborn et al., Abstract, "Human Percutaneous Laser Thermal Angioplasty," *Circulation* 72, Suppl. 3 (1985):111.

60. D.I. Taylor and D.C. Cumberland, Abstract, "Laser Assisted Balloon Angioplasty," *Circulation* 72, Suppl. 3 (1985):111.

61. J.J. Livesay et al., Abstract, "Preliminary Report on Laser Coronary Endarterectomy in Patients," *Circulation* 72, Suppl. 3 (1985):111.

62. W. Ganz, I. Geft, and M. Jamshid, "Nonsurgical Reperfusion in Evolving Myocardial Infarction," *Journal of American College of Cardiology* 1(1983):1247.

63. R.E. Rude, J.E. Muller, and E. Braunwald, "Efforts to Limit the Size of Myocardial Infarcts," *Annals of Internal Medicine* 95(1981):726.

64. W.R. Ginks et al., "Coronary Artery Perfusion: II. Reduction of Myocardial Infarct Size at One Week after the Coronary Occlusion," *Journal of Clinical Investigation* 51(1972):2717.

65. M.A. DeWood, J. Spores, and M.D. Notske, "Prevalence of Total Coronary Occlusion during the Early Hours of Transmural Myocardial Infarction," *New England Journal of Medicine* 303(1980):897.

66. W.C. Little, "Thrombolytic Therapy of Acute Myocardial Infarction," *Current Problems in Cardiology* 8(1983):1.

67. W.C. Roberts, "Coronary Thrombosis and Fatal Myocardial Ischemia," *Circulation* 49(1974):1.

68. H.J.C. Swan, "Thrombolysis in Acute Evolving Myocardial Infarction: A New Potential for Myocardial Infarction," *New England Journal of Medicine* 308(1983):1354.

69. G.A. Vetrovec, M.J. Cowley, and H. Overton, "Intracoronary Thrombus in Syndromes of Unstable Myocardial Ischemia," *American Heart Journal* 102(1981):1202.

70. G.L. Laffel and E. Braunwald, "Thrombolytic Therapy: A New Strategy for the Treatment of Acute Myocardial Infarction: First of Two Parts," *New England Journal of Medicine* 311(1983):710.

71. V.J. Marder, "Pharmacology of Thrombolytic Agents: Implications for Therapy of Coronary Artery Thrombosis," *Circulation* 68, Suppl. 1 (1983):2.

72. Laffel and Braunwald, "Thrombolytic Therapy, Part 1."

73. DeWood, Spores, and Notske, "Prevalence of Coronary Occlusion."

74. C.V.R.K. Sharma et al., "Thrombolytic Therapy," *New England Journal of Medicine* 306(1982):1268.

75. Laffel and Braunwald, "Thrombolytic Therapy, Part 1."

76. M.A. DeWood, J. Spores, and R.N. Notske, "Medical and Surgical Management of Myocardial Infarction," *American Journal of Cardiology* 44(1979):1356.

77. Laffel and Braunwald, "Thrombolytic Therapy, Part 1."

78. E. Strauss and E.B. Rudy, "Tissue-Plasminogen Activator: A New Drug in Reperfusion Therapy," *Critical Care Nurse* 6, no. 3(1986):30.

79. Health and Public Policy Committee, American College of Physicians, "Thrombolytis for Evolving Myocardial Infarction," *Annals of Internal Medicine* 103(1985):463.

80. Strauss and Rudy, "Tissue-Plasmogin Activator."

81. K.H. Cockins, A.C. Jain, and D.Z. Morgan, "A Review of Fibrinolytic Therapy in Acute Myocardial Infarction," *West Virginia Medical Journal* 81(1985):191.

82. Health and Public Policy Committee, "Thrombolytis."

83. Ibid.

84. D. Pennica, W.E. Holmes, and W.J. Kohr, "Cloning and Expression of Human Tissue-Type Plasminogen Activator in eDNA in *E. coli,*" *Nature* 30(1983):214.

85. D. Collen, E.J. Topal, and A.J. Tieferbrunn, "Coronary Thrombolysis with Recombinant Human Tissue-Type Plasminogen Activator: A Prospective, Randomized, Placebo-Controlled Trial," *Circulation* 70(1984):1012.

86. TIMI Group, "The Thrombolysis in Myocardial Infarction Trial," *New England Journal of Medicine* 312, no. 14(1985):932.

87. Laffel and Braunwald, "Thrombolytic Therapy, Part 1."

88. Ibid.

89. Health and Public Policy Committee, "Thrombolytis."

90. M.J. Cowley, "Methodologic Aspects of Intracoronary Thrombolysis: Drugs, Dosage and Duration," *Circulation* 68, Suppl. 1 (1983):90.

91. J.F. Spann and S. Sherry, "Coronary Thrombolysis for Evolving Myocardial Infarctions," *Drugs* 28(1984):463.

92. Health and Public Policy Committee, "Thrombolytis."

93. J. Weinstein, "Treatment of Myocardial Infarction with Intracoronary Streptokinase: Efficacy and Safety Data from 209 United States Cases in the Hoeschst-Roussel Registry," *American Heart Journal* 194(1982):894.

94. K.P. Rentrop, H. Blanke, and K.R. Karsch, "Effects of Nonsurgical Coronary Reperfusion on the Left Ventricle in Human Subjects compared with Conventional Treatment: Study of 18 Patients with Acute Myocardial Infarction Treated with Intracoronary Infusion of Streptokinase," *American Journal of Cardiology* 49(1983):1.

95. Health and Public Policy Committee, "Thrombolytis."

96. G.L. Laffel and E. Braunwald, "Thrombolytic Therapy: A New Strategy for the Treatment of Acute Myocardial Infarction: Second of Two Parts," *New England Journal of Medicine* 311(1984):770.

97. M.W. Matthews et al., "Incidence of Bleeding Complications Associated with Intracoronary Streptokinase Therapy for Acute Myocardial Infarction," *Circulation* 68, Suppl. 3 (1983):111.

98. D.T. Mason, "International Experiences with Percutaneous Transluminal Coronary Recanalization by Streptokinase Thrombolysis Reperfusion in Acute Myocardial Infarction: New, Safe, Landmark Therapeutic Approach Salvaging Ischemic Muscle and Improving Ventricular Function," *American Heart Journal* 102(1981):1126.

99. S. Goldbert, A.J. Greenspon, and P.L. Urban, "Reperfusion Arrhythmia: A Marker of Restoration of Antegrade Flow during Intracoronary Thrombolysis for Acute Myocardial Infarction," *American Heart Journal* 105(1983):26.

100. Laffel and Braunwald, "Thrombolytic Therapy, Part 2."

101. J.Y. Wei et al., "Cardiovascular Reflexes Stimulated by Reperfusion of Ischemic Myocardium in Acute Myocardial Infarction," *Circulation* 67(1983):796.

102. Strauss and Rudy, "Tissue-Plasmogin Activator."

103. Ibid.

104. A. Fleckenstein, "Specific Pharmacology of Calcium in Myocardium, Cardiac Pacemakers and Vascular Smooth Muscle," *Annual Review of Pharmacology and Toxicology* 17(1977):149.

105. C. Shub, R.E. Vlietstra, and M.D. McGoon, "Selection of Optimal Drug Therapy for the Patient with Angina Pectoris," *Mayo Clinic Proceedings* 60(1985):539.

106. Ibid.

107. Ibid.

108. G.J. Goldman and A.D. Pichard, "The Natural History of Coronary Artery Disease: Does Medical Therapy Improve the Prognosis? " *Progress in Cardiovascular Disease* 25(1983):513.

109. E.A. Amsterdam, R. Gorten, and S. Walfson, "Evaluation of Long-term Use of Propranolol in Angina Pectoris," *Journal of the American Medical Association* 21(1969):103.

110. E.A. Amsterdam, S. Walfson, and R. Gorten, "Effect of Therapy on Survival in Angina Pectoris," *Annals of Internal Medicine* 69(1968):1151.

111. H.J. Zeft, S. Patterson, and E.S. Orgain, "The Effect of Propranolol in the Long-term Treatment of Angina Pectoris," *Archives of Internal Medicine* 124(1969):578.

112. S.G. Warren, D.L. Brewer, and E.S. Orgain, "Long-term Propranolol Therapy for Angina Pectoris," *American Journal of Cardiology* 87(1976):420.

113. D.M.D. Lambert, "Beta Blockers and Life Expectancy in Ischemic Heart Disease," *Lancet* 1(1972):793.

114. D.M.D. Lambert, "Effect of Propranolol in Mortality in Patients with Angina," *Postgraduate Medicine* 52, Suppl. 4 (1976):57.

115. R.V. Davies et al., "Prospective Controlled Trial of Long-term Propranolol on Acute Coronary Events in Patients with Unstable Coronary Artery Disease," *Clinical Pharmacology Therapeutics* 17(1975):232.

116. S.F. Vanter et al., "Effects of Catecholamines, Exercise and Nitroglycerin on the Normal and Ischemic Myocardium in Conscious Dogs" *Journal of Clinical Investigation* 54(1974):563.

117. J. Han, "Mechanisms of Ventricular Arrhythmias Associated with Myocardial Infarction," *American Journal of Cardiology* 24(1969):800.

118. Goldman and Pichard, "Natural History."

119. G.K. McEvoy, *Drug Information 86* (Bethesda, Md.: American Society of Hospital Pharmacists, Inc., 1986).

120. W.H. Freshman et al., "Reversal of Abnormal Platelet Aggregability and Change in Exercise Tolerance of Patients with Angina Pectoris following Oral Propranolol: Part 1," *Circulation* 50(1974):887.

121. J.D. Schrumpf et al., "Altered Hemoglobin-Oxygen Affinity with Long-term Propranolol Therapy in Patients with Coronary Artery Disease," *American Journal of Cardiology* 40(1977):76.

122. McEvoy, *Drug Information*.

123. Goldman and Pichard, "Natural History."

124. C. Wilhelmsson et al., "Reduction of Sudden Deaths after Myocardial Infarction by Treatment with Alprenolol," *Lancet* 2(1974):1157.

125. G. Ahlmark and H. Saetre, "Long-term Treatment with Beta-Blockers after Myocardial Infarction," *European Journal of Clinical Pharmacology* 10(1976):77.

126. Multicentre International Study, "Improvement in Prognosis of Myocardial Infarction by Long-term Beta-Adrenoreceptor Blockade using Practolol," *British Medical Journal* 3(1975):435.

127. J.M. Barber et al., "Practolol in Acute Myocardial Infarction," *Acta Medica Scandinavica* 587(1976):213.

128. M.P. Anderson et al., "Effect of Aprenolol on Mortality Among Patients with Definite or Suspected Acute Myocardial Infarction: Preliminary Results," *Lancet* 2(1979):865.

129. N.S. Baber et al., "Multicentre Post-infarction Trial of Propranolol in 49 Hospitals in the United Kingdom, Italy and Yugoslavia," *British Heart Journal* 44(1980):96.

130. The Norwegian Multicenter Study Group, "Timolol-Induced Reduction in Mortality and Re-infarction in Patients Surviving Acute Myocardial Infarction," *New England Journal of Medicine* 304(1981):801.

131. A. Hjalmarson et al., "Effect on Mortality of Metoprolol in Acute Myocardial Infarction: A Double-Blind Randomized Trial," *Lancet* 2(1981):823.

132. Beta-Blocker Heart Attack Trial Research Group, "A Randomized Trial of Propranolol in Patients with Acute Myocardial Infarction: I. Mortality Results," *Journal of the American Medical Association* 247(1982):1707.

133. V. Hansteen et al., "One Year's Treatment with Propranolol after Myocardial Infarction: Preliminary Report of Norwegian Multi-centre Trial," *British Medical Journal* 284(1982):155.

134. D.G. Julian et al., "Controlled Trial of Sotalol for One Year after Myocardial Infarction," *Lancet* 1(1982):1142.

135. Australian and Swedish Pindolol Study Group, "The Effect of Pindolol on the Two Year Mortality after Complicated Myocardial Infarction," *European Heart Journal* 4(1983):367.

136. European Infarction Study Group, "European Infarction Study: A Secondary Beta-Blocker Prevention Trial after Myocardial Infarction," *Circulation* 68, Suppl. 3 (1983):294.

137. Baber et al., "Multicentre Trial of Propranolol."

138. Goldman and Pichard, "Natural History."

139. R.M. Norris, "Status of Beta Blocker Therapy in Acute Myocardial Infarction," *Methods and Findings in Experimental Clinical Pharmacology*, 4 no. 6, (1984):219.

140. W.H. Frishman, C.D. Furbert, and W.T. Friedewald, "Beta-Adrenergic Blockade for Survivors of Acute Myocardial Infarction," *New England Journal of Medicine* 310(1984):830.

141. V. Rice, "Calcium, the Heart and Calcium Antagonists," *Critical Care Nurse* 2(1982):30.

142. Ibid.

143. C.R. Conti et al., "Calcium Antagonists," *Cardiology* 72(1985):287.

144. P. Stone, "Calcium Channel Blocking Agents in the Treatment of Cardiovascular Disorders: Part II. Hemodynamic Effects and Clinical Applications," *Annals of Internal Medicine* 93(1980):883.

145. B.D. Breland and M.J. Boland, "Use of Calcium Channel Blocking Agents in Angina Pectoris," *Journal of the Mississippi Medical Association*, 25, no. 3 (March 1984):57.

146. J.F. Hansen and E. Sandoe, "Treatment of Prinzmetal's Angina Due to Coronary Artery Spasm Using Verapamil: Report of Three Cases," *European Journal of Cardiology* 7(1978):327.

147. J.E. Muller and S.J. Gunther, "Nifedipine Therapy for Prinzmetal's Angina," *Circulation* 52(1978):137.

148. B. Lown, ed., "Symposium on Nifedipine and Calcium Flux Inhibition in the Treatment of Coronary Artery Spasm and Myocardial Ischemia," *American Journal of Cardiology* 44(1979):780.

149. E. Antman et al., "Nifedipine Therapy for Coronary Artery Spasm: Experience in 127 Patients," *New England Journal of Medicine* 302(1980):1269.

150. P.G. Hugenholtz et al., "Why Calcium Antagonists are Most Useful before or during Early Myocardial Ischemia," *Practical Cardiology* 12, no. 4(April 1986):62.

151. Ibid.

152. T.L. Brunton, "Use of Nitrate of Amyl in Angina Pectoris," *Lancet* 2(1967):97.

153. Shub, Vlietstra, and McGoon, "Selection of Drug Therapy."

154. M.V. Cohen et al., "Effects of Nitroglycerin on Coronary Collaterals and Myocardial Contractility," *Journal of Clinical Investigation* 52(1973):2836.

155. N. Riechek et al., "Sustained Effects of Nitroglycerin Ointment in Patients with Angina Pectoris," *Circulation* 50(1974):348.

156. S.E. Epstein et al., "Angina Pectoris: Pathophysiology, Evaluation and Treatment," *Annals of Internal Medicine* 75(1971):263.

157. B. Christensson, T. Karlefors, and H. Wertling, "Hemodynamic Effects of Nitroglycerin in Patients with Coronary Heart Disease," *British Heart Journal* 27(1965):511.

158. P. Dauwe et al., "Intravenous Nitroglycerin in Refractory Unstable Angina," *American Journal of Cardiology* 43(1979):416.

159. G.D. Curfman et al., "Intravenous Nitroglycerin in the Treatment of Spontaneous Angina Pectoris: A Prospective Randomized Trial," *Circulation* 67(1983):176.

160. C.M. Fuller et al., "Exercise-Induced Coronary Artery Spasm: Angiographic Demonstration of Ischemia by Myocardial Scintigraphy and Results of Pharmacologic Intervention," *American Journal of Cardiology* 46(1980):500.

161. V. Thadani et al., "Oral Isosorbide Dinitrate in Angina Pectoris: Comparison of Duration of Action and Dose-Response Relation during Acute and Sustained Therapy," *American Journal of Cardiology* 49(1982):411.

162. S. Corwin and J.A. Reiffel, "Nitrate Therapy for Angina Pectoris: Current Concepts About Mechanism of Action and Evaluation of Currently Available Preparations," *Archives of Internal Medicine* 145(1985):538.

163. V. Thadani, "Nitrates for Angina Pectoris: A Critical Review of Therapeutic Efficacy and Tolerance," *Herz* 9(1984):123.

164. A.P. Claus et al., "Comparative Evaluation of Sublingual Long-acting Nitrates," *Circulation* 48(1973):519.

165. R.E. Goldstein et al., "Clinical and Circulatory Effects of Isosorbide Dinitrate: Comparison with Nitroglycerin," *Circulation* 43(1981):629.

166. Ibid.

167. Corwin and Reiffel, "Nitrate Therapy."

168. Ibid.

REFERENCES

Percutaneous Transluminal Coronary Angioplasty

Gruentzig, A.R. "Percutaneous Transluminal Coronary Angioplasty: Six years' experience." *American Heart Journal* 107(1984):818–819.

Hall, D., and Gruentzig, A.R. "Percutaneous Transluminal Coronary Angioplasty: Current Procedure and Future Direction." *American Journal of Roentgenology* 142(1980):13–16.

Herzel, H.O.; Eichhorn, M.D.; Kappenber, F.; Gander, M.P.; Schlump, M.; and Gruentzig, A.R. "Percutaneous Transluminal Coronary Angioplasty: Late Results of Five Years Following Intervention." *American Heart Journal* 109(1985):575–581.

Ischinger, T.; Gruentzig, A.R.; and Hollman, J. "Should Coronary Arteries with Less Than 60% Diameter Stenosis be Treated by Angioplasty?" *Circulation* 68(1983):148–154.

Silverton, N.P. "Current Place of Coronary Angioplasty." *British Medical Journal* 290(1985):954–956.

Laser

Abela, G.S.; Seeger, J.M.; Fenech, A.; Pepine, C.J.; and Conti, C.R. "Laser Recanalization of Peripheral Arteries in Man: A Preliminary Report." *Circulation* 72, Suppl. 3(1985):111.

Gerrity, R.G.; Loop, F.D.; Golding, L.A.R.; and Argenyi, A.B. "Arterial Response to Laser Operation for Removal of Atherosclerotic Plaques." *Journal of Thoracic and Cardiovascular Surgery* 85(1983):409–421.

Lee, G.; Ideda, R.M.; Chan, M.C.; Stobbe, D.; Kozena, J.; Jiang, M.C.; Reis, R.L.; and Mason, D.T. "Current and Potential Uses of Lasers in the Treatment of Atherosclerotic Disease." *Chest* 85(1984):429–434.

Lee, G.; Ideda, R.; Herman, I.; Devyer, R.M.; Bass, M.; Hussein, H.; Kozena, J.; and Mason, D.T. "The Qualitative Effects of Laser Irradiation on Human Arterosclerotic Disease." *American Heart Journal* 105(1983):885–889.

Livesay, J.J.; Leachman, D.R.; Hogan, P.J.; Cooper, J.R.; Sweeney, M.S.; Frazier, D.H.; and Cooley, D.A. "Preliminary Report on Laser Coronary Endarterectomy in Patients." *Circulation* 72, Suppl. 3 (1985):111–302.

Sanborn, T.A.; Cumberland, D.C.; Tayler, D.I.; and Ryan, T.J. "Human Percutaneous Laser Thermal Angioplasty." *Circulation* 72, Suppl. 3 (1985):111–302.

Taylor, D.I., and Cumberland, D.C. "Laser Assisted Balloon Angioplasty." *Circulation* 72, Suppl. 3 (1985):111–371.

Beta-Adrenergic Blockers

Boyle, D.M.; Barber, J.M.; McIlmoyle, E.L.; Salathia, K.S.; Evans, A.E.; Cran, G.; Elwood, H.H.; and Shanks, R.G. "Effects of Very Early Intervention and Metaprolol on Myocardial Infarct Size." *British Heart Journal* 49(1983):229–233.

Frishman, W.H.; Ruggio, J.; and Furgerg, C. "Use of Beta-Adrenergic Blocking Agents after Myocardial Infarction." *Postgraduate Medicine* 78(1985):49–53.

Herlitz, J.; Hjalmarson, A.; Waagstein, F.; Waldenstrom, A.; Wilhelmsson, C.; Vedin, A.; and Swedberg, K. "Effect of Metoprolol on the Severity of Acute Myocardial Infarction." *Australian and New Zealand Journal of Medicine* 13(1983):412.

Hjalmarson, A. "Early Intervention with a Beta-Blocking Drug after Acute Myocardial Infarction." *American Journal of Cardiology* 54(1984):118–138.

Jurgensen, S.J.; Fredericksen, J.; Hansen, V.A.; and Pedersen-Bjergaard, D. "Limitation of Myocardial Infarct Size in Patients less than 66 Years Treated with Alprenolol." *British Heart Journal* 45(1981):583–588.

Norris, R.M.; Sammel, N.L.; Clarke, E.D.; and Brandt, P.W.T. "Treatment of Acute Myocardial Infarction with Propranolol: Further Studies on Enzyme Appearance and Subsequent Left Ventricular Function in Treated and Control Patients with Developing Infarcts." *British Heart Journal* 43(1980):617–622.

Peter, T.; Norris, R.M.; Clarke, E.D.; Heng, M.K.; Singh, B.N.; Williams, B.; Howell, D.R.; and Amber, P.K. "Reduction of Enzyme Levels by Propranolol after Acute Myocardial Infarction." *Circulation* 57(1978):1091–1095.

Pratt, C., and Lichstein, E. "Ventricular Antiarrhythmic Effects of Beta-Adrenergic Blocking Drugs: A Review of Mechanisms and Clinical Studies." *Journal of Clinical Pharmacology* 22(1982):335–347.

Pratt, C.M.; Young, J.B.; and Roberts, R. "The Role of Beta-Blockers in the Treatment of Patients after Infarction." *Cardiology Clinics* 2(1984):13–20.

Thadani, V. "Assessment of Optimal Beta Blockade in Treatment of Patients with Angina Pectoris." *Acta Med Scand* Suppl. 694(1984):178–187.

Tin Eick, R.E.; Singer, D.H.; and Solbert, L.E. "Coronary Occlusion: Effect on Cellular Electrical Activity of the Heart." *Medical Clinics of North America* 60(1976):49–67.

Willerson, J.T., and Biya, M. "Short and Long-term Influence of Beta-Adrenergic Antagonists After Acute Myocardial Infarction." *American Journal of Cardiology* 54(1984):16E–20E.

Wit, A.L., and Friedman, P.L. "The Basis of Ventricular Arrhythmias Accompanying Myocardial Infarction: Alterations in Electrical Activity of Ventricular Muscle and Purkinje Fibers after Coronary Artery Occlusion." *Archives of Internal Medicine* 135(1975):459–472.

Yusuf, S.; Ransdale, D.; Peto, R.; Furse, L.; Bennett, D.; Bray, C.; and Sleight, P. "Early Intravenous Atenolol Treatment in Suspected Acute Myocardial Infarction." *Lancet* 2(1980):273–276.

Yusuf, S.; Ransdale, D.; Rossi, P.; Peto, R.; Pearson, M.; Sterry, H.; Furse, L.; Motivani, R.; Paris, S.; Gaay, R.; Bennett, D.; Bray, C.; and Sleight, P. "Reduction in Infarct Size, Morbidity and Short-term Mortality by Early Intravenous Beta-Blockage." *Journal of American College of Cardiology* 1(1983):676.

Calcium Antagonists

Andreasen, F.; Boye, E.; Christoffersen, E.; Dalsgaard, E.; Hennelberg, E.; Kallenbach, A.; Sadefoged, S.; Lillquist, K.; Mikkelson, E.; Nordero, E.; Olsen, J.; Pedersen, J.K.; Pedersen, V.; Bruum, P.G.; Schroll J.; Schultz, H.; and Seidelin, J. "Assessment of Verapamil in the Treatment of Angina Pectoris." *European Journal of Cardiology* 2(1975):443–452.

Antman, E.; Muller, J.; Goldberg, S.; MacAlpin, R.; Rubenfire, M.; Tabatznik, B.; Liang, G.S.; Heupler, F.; Achuff, S.; Reichek, N.; Geltman, E.; Kerin, N.Z.; Neff, R.K.; and Braunwald, E. "Nifedipine Therapy for Coronary Artery Spasm: Experience in 127 Patients." *New England Journal of Medicine* 302(1980):1269–1273.

Antman, E.; Stone, P.; Muller, J.; and Braunwald, E. "Calcium Channel Blocking Agents in the Treatment of CV Disorders: Part I. Basic and Clinical Electrophysiologic Effects." *Annals of Internal Medicine* 93(1980):875–885.

Atterhog, J.A.; Ekelund, L.G.; and Melin, A.J. "Effect of Nifedipine on Exercise Tolerance in Patients with Angina Pectoris." *European Journal of Cardiology* 8(1975):125–130.

Bourget, C. "Verapamil: A Calcium-Channel Blocker." *Dimensions of Critical Care Nursing* 1(1982):134–138.

Braun, L.T. "Calcium Channel Blockers for the Treatment of Coronary Artery Spasm: Rationale, Effects and Nursing Responsibilities." *Heart and Lung* 12(1983):226–232.

Breland, B.D., and Boland, M.J. "Use of Calcium Channel Blocking Agents in Angina Pectoris." *Journal of the Mississippi Medical Association* 25, no. 3(March 1984):57–62.

Faris, J.; Childress, R.; and Watanabe, A. "Effects of Nifedipine on Exercise Tolerance in Coronary Artery Disease." *American Journal of Cardiology* 45(1980):611.

Hansen, J.F., and Sandoe, E. "Treatment of Prinzmetal's Angina due to Coronary Artery Spasm using Verapamil: Report of Three Cases." *European Journal of Cardiology* 7(1978):327–335.

Hugenholtz, P.G.; Serruys, P.W.; Fleckenstein, A.; and Nayler, W. "Why Calcium Antagonists are Most Useful before or during Early Myocardial Ischemia." *Practical Cardiology* 12, no. 4(April 1986):62–72.

Kennedy, G.T. "Slow Channel Calcium Blockers in the Treatment of Chronic Stable Angina." *Cardiovascular Nursing* 20(January–February 1984):1–5.

Livesley, B.; Catley, P.; Campbell, R.C.; and Oram, S. "Double-blind Evaluation of Verapamil, Propranolol and Isosorbide Dinitrate Against Placebo in the Treatment of Angina Pectoris." *British Medical Journal* 850(1973):375–378.

Lown, B., ed. "Symposium on Nifedipine and Calcium Flux Inhibition in the Treatment of Coronary Artery Spasm and Myocardial Ischemia." *American Journal of Cardiology* 44(1979):780–782.

Muller, J.E., and Gunther, S.J. "Nifedipine Therapy for Prinzmetal's Angina." *Circulation* 52(1978):137–139.

Neumann, M., and Luisada, A.A. "Studies of Iproveratrial on Oral Administration in Double-blind Trials in Patients with Variant Angina." *American Journal of Medical Science* 251(1966):552–556.

Sandler, G.; Glayton, G.A.; and Thornicroft, S.G. "Clinical Evaluation of Verapamil in Angina Pectoris." *British Medical Journal* 3(1968):224–227.

Singh, B.N.; Nademanee, K.; and Baky, S.H. "Calcium Antagonist: Clinical Use in the Treatment of Arrhythmias." *Drugs* 25(1983):125–153.

Therous, P.; Taeymans, Y.; and Waters, D.D. "Calcium Antagonists: Clinical Use in the Treatment of Angina." *Drugs* 25(1983):178–195.

Zsoter, T.T., and Church, J.G. "Calcium Antagonists: Pharmacodynamic Effects and Mechanism of Action." *Drugs* 25(1983):93–112.

SUGGESTED READINGS

Allen, J.A., and Throm, L.A. "Percutaneous Transluminal Coronary Angioplasty: A New Alternative for Ischemic Heart Disease." *Critical Care Nurse* 2(January–February 1982):24–29.

Block, P.C. "Setting Parameters for Percutaneous Transluminal Coronary Angioplasty." *Cardiovascular Medicine* 10(1985):4–5.

Cimine, D.M., and Goldfarb, J. "Standard of Care for the Patient with Percutaneous Transluminal Coronary Angioplasty." *Critical Care Nurse* 3(1983):76–78.

Doran, K.A., and Hansen, C. "PTCA: Patient Education," *Dimensions of Critical Care Nursing* 2, no.1(January–February 1983):56–64.

Gershan, J.A., and Jiricka, M.K. "Percutaneous Transluminal Coronary Angioplasty: Implications for Nursing." *Focus on Critical Care* 11, no. 4(August 1984):28–35.

Partidge, S.A. "The Nurses Role in Percutaneous Transluminal Coronary Angioplasty." *Heart and Lung* 11(1982):505–511.

Chapter 5

Nursing Care of the Patient with Recurrent Ventricular Dysrhythmias

Laura J. Burke, RN, MSN
Susan O'Brien Norris, RN, MS, CCRN

Recurrent ventricular dysrhythmias are being detected and treated with greater frequency for three reasons. First, an increased number of patients with coronary artery disease (CAD) are being monitored for potential dysrhythmias as medical and surgical treatment options have increased their survival. Second, physicians recognize the lethality of certain recurrent ventricular dysrhythmias and better evaluate patients to identify and control their *causes* as well as the dysrhythmias themselves. Third, patients are better educated health care consumers and therefore are more willing to discuss seemingly "minor" symptoms such as dizziness or palpitations with their physicians. The combination of these factors has increased the number of recurrent ventricular dysrhythmia patients cared for by critical care nurses.

This chapter discusses the significance; diagnosis; and pharmacologic, surgical, and adjunctive therapies for recurrent ventricular dysrhythmias. Nursing diagnoses and interventions common to patients undergoing diagnosis and treatment are discussed in detail.

Recurrent ventricular dysrhythmias can occur in many forms: as premature ventricular contractions (PVC), and/or as ventricular tachydysrhythmias, including ventricular tachycardia (VT) and ventricular fibrillation (VF). These ventricular dysrhythmias can occur either in combination or alone.

PREMATURE VENTRICULAR CONTRACTIONS

PVCs are extremely common. They occur in 10% to 60% of healthy adults undergoing 24-hour ambulatory monitoring, in 10% to 60% of adults having an exercise stress test, and in almost all post-myocardial infarction (MI) patients.[1] The frequency of ectopy seems to increase with age.[2]

There have been attempts to categorize PVCs to identify more clearly when treatment is indicated. Lown's classification system has been widely used for more than a decade (Table 5-1).[3] Classes 3 through 5 were considered "advanced'' forms of ventricular ectopy, and treatment was recommended. However, this classification has been criticized as being based on unquantitated clinical observations derived from post-MI patients.[4]

An alternative classification system that differentiates PVC frequency and form was recently proposed by Myerburg et al. (Table 5-2).[5] This system defines ''advanced'' forms of ventricular ectopy as those in either Class III or IV in frequency or in Class C, D, or E in form. Use of the Myerburg scheme is becoming increasingly more common.[6]

Decisions to treat PVCs are based on a number of factors. In a review of research on the clinical significance of PVCs, Moss[7] concluded that frequent PVCs in apparently healthy individuals may indicate undetected CAD. He recommended that the patient receive further evaluation for organic heart disease before the PVCs are considered benign.

Kennedy et al.[8] longitudinally followed 69 subjects for 10 years who were accidentally or incidentally found to have frequent and complex PVCs for a mean of 6.5 years. The presence of frequent and complex PVCs in these apparently healthy people carried no increased risk for death or sudden death as compared with the normal U.S. population. Thus, simple, frequent, and complex PVCs in healthy individuals can be ignored. If the PVCs are felt by the patient as palpitations, the patient will often need reassurance about his or her benign prognosis.

Complex ventricular ectopy (Myerburg Classes III, IV, C, D, E), previous MI, and a left ventricular (LV) ejection fraction of less than 40% have all been found to be independent risk factors of sudden death in the presence of heart

---

Table 5-1 Lown-Wolf Grading Scale of Ventricular Ectopy

Grade	Observed
0	No ventricular ectopic beats
1	Occasional, isolated VPB
2	Frequent VPB (greater than 1/min or 30/hr)
3	Multiform VPB
4	Repetitive VPB
(a)	Couplets
(b)	Salvos
5	Early VPB

VPB = ventricular premature beat

Source: Reprinted from ''Approaches to Sudden Death from Coronary Heart Disease'' by B. Lown and M. Wolf in *Circulation*, Vol. 44, p. 137, by permission of the American Heart Association, Inc., © July 1971.

Table 5-2 Classification of Ventricular Arrhythmias Based on Frequency and Forms

Hierarchy of Frequencies	Hierarchy of Forms
CLASS 0—Nil	Class A—Uniform morphology, unifocal
CLASS I—Rare (<1 VPC/hr)	Class B—Multiform, multifocal
CLASS II—Infrequent (1 to 9 VPCs/hr)	Class C—Repetitive forms Couplets Salvos, repetitive responses (3–5 consecutive ventricular complexes)
CLASS III—Intermediate (10–29 VPCs/hr)	Class D—Nonsustained VT (>6 consecutive ventricular complexes to runs <30 sec)
CLASS IV—Frequent (>30 VPCs/hr)	Class E—Sustained VT (runs of ventricular complexes > 30 sec)

VPCs = ventricular premature complexes; VT = ventricular tachycardia.

Source: Reprinted from *American Journal of Cardiology*, Vol. 54, pp. 1355–1358, with permission of Technical Publishing Company, © 1984.

disease.[9] Data from the 26-year-old Framingham study showed that complex PVCs associated with sudden death occurred concurrently with electrocardiogram (ECG) signs of LV hypertrophy, intraventricular block, and nonspecific (ST-T) abnormalities. These authors recommended that complex PVCs be treated when found in the presence of ischemic heart disease.[10]

A number of factors may cause PVCs (Table 5-3). The factors may be cardiovascular, respiratory, neurologic, metabolic, or drug-related in origin.

VENTRICULAR TACHYDYSRHYTHMIAS

In the United States, ventricular tachydysrhythmias cause between 350,000 and 500,000 sudden cardiac deaths each year.[11–13] In a review of 72 sudden death patients who were wearing 24-hour ambulatory monitoring when they died, Panidis and Morganroth[14] found that 90% had VT, which then degenerated into VF in 83%. Other authors have reported similar findings.[15–17]

Wellens et al.[18] classified ventricular tachydysrhythmias according to their defining characteristics (Table 5-4). Monomorphic nonsustained VT in patients with apparently normal hearts is a benign condition, and patients have a normal

Table 5-3 Causes of Premature Ventricular Contractions

Cardiovascular	*Metabolic*
Atherosclerosis	Hypocalcemia
MI	Hypoglycemia
Coronary artery spasm	Hypokalemia
Cardiomyopathy	Pheochromocytoma
Mitral valve prolapse	Thyrotoxicosis
Hypertensive heart disease	*Neurologic*
Myocardial contusion	Acute anxiety attack
Anemia	Acute stress response
Acute myocarditis	
Ventricular aneurysm	*Respiratory-Induced Hypoxias*
Congenital heart disease	Asthma
Cardiac tumors (myxoma)	Bronchitis
	Chronic obstructive lung disease
Drug-Induced	Pulmonary edema
Antidysrhythmics	Adult respiratory distress syndrome
Cardiac glycosides	
Diuretics	
Phenothiazines	
Sympathomimetics	
Tricyclic antidepressants	
Adriamycin (antineoplastic)	

life expectancy. Patients with sustained VT or VF without an MI have an esti-mated risk of 20% to 50% for recurrent sudden death within the following year.[19] Therefore, these dysrhythmias must be treated aggressively.

Two main mechanisms can cause ventricular tachydysrhythmias: enhanced or abnormal automaticity and re-entry.[20,21] Several types of cardiac cells (sinoatrial, atrioventricular, Purkinje fibers) normally spontaneously depolarize to reach threshold. If one of these cells depolarizes at a more rapid rate, the cell has enhanced automaticity. If a cell that does not usually depolarize begins to do so, the cell has abnormal automaticity. In either case, this rapid rate of firing may cause the cell to assume a pacemaker function. Should this occur at a rapid and uncontrolled rate in the ventricle, VT or VF will result. Metabolic or patho-logic conditions in the heart may cause enhanced or abnormal automaticity.

Re-entry is a more common mechanism causing VT/VF (Figure 5-1). Re-entry occurs when one of two branches of a Purkinje fiber has a unidirectional block. An electrical impulse will travel with slow conduction down one branch; through the ventricular myocardium; back up the other conducting branch in a retrograde fashion; and re-enter the first branch again, which is ready to be activated again. Re-entrant cycles usually occur in border zones between normal myocardial tissue and scar tissue from an MI, ventricular aneurysm, cardio-myopathies, or surgery.

Table 5-4 Characteristics of Ventricular Tachydysrhythmias

Appearance	Defining Characteristics
Nonsustained monomorphic	6 beats to 29 sec duration Consistent beat-to-beat morphology Ventricular rate faster than 100 beats/min
Sustained monomorphic	>30 sec duration or requiring intervention for termination Consistent beat-to-beat morphology Ventricular rate faster than 100 beats/min
Nonsustained polymorphic	6 beats to 29 sec in duration Frequent changes in QRS morphology and/or axis that occur at least every 1 to 2 sec or every 6 beats Ventricular rate faster than 100 beats/min
Sustained polymorphic	>30 sec duration or requiring intervention for termination Frequent changes in QRS morphology and/or axis that occur at least every 1 to 2 sec or every 6 beats Ventricular rate faster than 100 beats/min

Ventricular tachydysrhythmias may have cardiac, neurologic, respiratory, metabolic, or drug-related origins (Table 5-5). One-third of all patients with sudden cardiac death have an acute MI. Of the two-thirds of patients who do not, 90% have severe CAD or cardiomyopathy. The remaining 10% of patients usually have a pre-excitation syndrome, metabolic abnormality, prolonged QT syndrome, or coronary artery spasm.[22]

Risk factors for sudden death have also been identified (Exhibit 5-1).[23] Figure 5-2 diagrams one hypothesis of how these risk factors can provoke VF and sudden cardiac death.

Kannel and McGee[24] noted that prospective studies indicated that the risk factors for sudden death are a subset of risk factors for CAD. They recommended reduction of the risk of coronary attacks, because the first prolonged attack of cardiac ischemia is fatal for 33% of the population. Specifically, smoking cessation, weight loss, and reduction of hypertension are essential.

NURSING IMPLICATIONS

Critical care nurses must be familiar with the predisposing causes as well as the characteristics of the patients' recurrent ventricular dysrhythmias in order to assess their patients' risk and to understand the rationale for therapies. They must also be knowledgeable about the strategies used to diagnose and treat

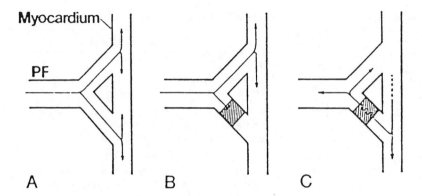

Figure 5-1 A terminal Purkinje fiber (PF) is depicted at its junction with ventricular myocardium. In A, conduction proceeds normally down both branches of the PF, activating the adjoining myocardium. In B, a diseased area is shown in the lower branch of the PF, which now displays unidirectional block; conduction proceeds normally down the upper branch, but not at all down the lower diseased branch. In C, showing events a few msec later in the same beat, the impulse has spread through myocardium back to the (as yet unactivated) distal end of the lower PF branch. This area is now able to conduct the impulse, although slowly. By the time the diseased area has been traversed, the remainder of the PF is ready to be activated again. Re-entry ensues, involving both branches and the adjoining myocardium. *Source*: Reprinted from *Hospital Formulary*, Vol. 19, p. 907, with permission of Modern Medicine Publications, Inc., © 1984.

ventricular dysrhythmias. This knowledge enables critical care nurses to monitor and treat patients with recurrent ventricular dysrhythmias effectively.

DIAGNOSIS OF RECURRENT VENTRICULAR DYSRHYTHMIAS

Recurrent, sustained ventricular dysrhythmias are evaluated by defining the cause of the dysrhythmia, when possible, as well as its characteristics. To define the cause, patient evaluation may include diagnostic tests such as nuclear imaging, echocardiogram (see Chapter 2), exercise stress testing, and cardiac catheterization. These tests are done to detect the degree and location of cardiac ischemia, structural and wall motion abnormalities, and/or the degree of cardiac functional capacity. Blood tests may be done to determine subtherapeutic or toxic levels of antidysrhythmics, electrolytes, and blood gases.

Diagnostic tests are also performed to identify characteristics of the ventricular dysrhythmias such as the 12-lead ECG, exercise test, and Holter monitoring. Transtelephonic ECG transmission with a retrospective recorder may be used to document difficult-to-detect ventricular dysrhythmias. However, the electrophys-

Table 5-5 Causes of Ventricular Tachydysrhythmias

Cardiovascular	*Metabolic*
Atherosclerosis	Hypocalcemia
MI	Hypoglycemia
Coronary artery spasm	Hypokalemia
Cardiomyopathy	Pheochromocytoma
Mitral valve prolapse	Hypothermia
Aortic stenosis	Acute or chronic alcoholism
Hypertensive heart disease	Thyrotoxicosis
Anemia	Alkalosis
Coronary artery spasm	
Acute pericardial tamponade	*Drug-Induced*
Cardiac tumors (myxoma)	Cardiac glycosides
Accessory atrioventricular conduction	Antidysrhythmics
syndrome	
Congenital prolonged QT-Syndrome (Jervell	*Respiratory-Induced Hypoxias*
and Lange-Nielsen syndrome, Romano-	Pulmonary hypertension
Ward syndrome)	Pulmonary embolism
Acute myocarditis	
Aortic or ventricular aneurysm	*Neurologic*
Congenital heart disease	Acute anxiety attacks
	Acute stress response
	Cerebral or subarachnoid hemorrhage

iologic study is the most accurate test to predict recurrence of recurrent, sustained ventricular dysrhythmias.[25] If a dysrhythmia is induced through programmed electrical stimulation techniques during electrophysiologic testing, it will then be possible to test the patient later to determine the effectiveness of pharmacologic or surgical interventions used to control the dysrhythmias. Definition of the cause and the characteristics through diagnostic testing enables the physician and critical care nurse to identify patients at risk for further dysrhythmias and provides direction for therapy (Figure 5-3).

The physician and nurse begin each patient evaluation for ventricular dysrhythmias with a history and physical. Most often, patients complain of palpitations and/or fainting, blackout, or cardiac arrest episodes. Asymptomatic patients may have had their dysrhythmias detected during telemetry monitoring.

Patients may have a history of myocardial ischemia, cardiomyopathy, mitral valve prolapse, or no significant cardiac disease (see Table 5-3 and Exhibit 5-1). Care is taken during the history to elicit prodromal factors, such as ingestion of cardiac stimulants, the effects of exertion, and the presence of recent myocardial damage or electrolyte imbalance. Patients with recurrent ventricular dysrhythmias may have been treated for the problem in the past. It is helpful for the nurse to determine which medications were taken, the dose, whether therapeutic levels were reached, and the effect (anti- or prorhythmic) the medications had on the

Exhibit 5-1 Risk Factors for Sudden Coronary Death

Occlusive coronary artery disease (with or without accompanying symptoms) especially when accompanied by:
  —History of VF without AMI
  —History of MI
  —LV dysfunction
  —High grade ventricular ectopy (Holter monitor)
  —Ventricular tachycardia inducible by programmed ventricular stimulation
  —LV aneurysm
  —Male sex
  —Cigarette smoking
  —Obesity

  Source: Reprinted from *Consultant*, Vol. 23, with permission of Cliggot Publishing Company, © April 1983.

dysrhythmia. The physical examination may reveal a range of patients from the physically fit to the critically ill.

With any of the diagnostic tests, patients often fear the unknown. Patient teaching should focus on the purpose of the test; whether or not food and/or fluids are restricted; duration of the test; whether or not the patient needs to give informed consent; what the patient will see, hear, and feel; and post-test care as described in Table 5-6.

NURSING CARE OF THE PATIENT DURING THE DIAGNOSTIC PHASE

Patients undergoing diagnostic evaluation of recurrent ventricular dysrhythmias face many stressors that can be managed with nursing strategies. Research has shown that patients with ventricular dysrhythmias undergo psychologic dysfunction. Haggerty and others[26] conducted serial psychiatric interviews with 33 patients who survived an episode of VT/VF during outpatient follow-up for treatment with amiodarone hydrochloride. Although the patients' dysrhythmias were successfully controlled, 58% experienced severe debilitative anxiety, and 21% experienced debilitating depression, despondency, and preoccupation with death. Anxiety symptoms tended to decrease in patients who were free of recurrent VT/VF for more than 1 year.

Summers and colleagues[27] surveyed clinical and personal background data and general psychologic status in 60 sudden death patients and 45 patients with serious ventricular dysrhythmias without prior cardiac arrest. The patients with sudden death had statistically significant reports of anxiety, inability to concen-

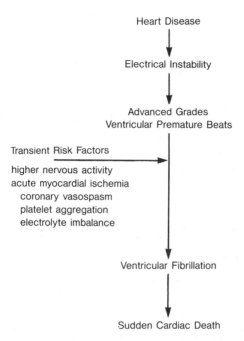

Figure 5-2 Hypothesis for the occurrence of sudden cardiac death. Heart disease leads to the development of myocardial electrical instability. Ventricular premature beats, especially repetitive forms, are the clinical markers for this instability. Transient risk factors, such as higher nervous activity, can alter the electrical properties of the heart, provoking ventricular fibrillation and sudden cardiac death. *Source*: Reprinted from *Cardiovascular Clinics*, Vol. 15, No. 3, p. 266, with permission of F.A. Davis Company, © 1985.

trate, feelings of dependence, and perceived change in life style than ventricular dysrhythmia patients. The patients with sudden death and ventricular dysrhythmias over a long period of time were more psychologically distressed than healthy individuals.

In both studies, the authors concluded that it is important to detect and treat emotional disabilities in patients with ventricular dysrhythmias. The nursing strategies to assist patients through the diagnostic phase of ventricular dysrhythmias as discussed below will help patients cope with physical and emotional concerns.

Activity Intolerance (Actual or Potential)

Rossi[28] found that 40% of patients who survived a sudden cardiac death experienced decreased activity tolerance. Patients usually complain of fatigue

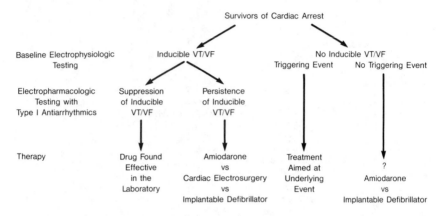

Figure 5-3 A flow diagram for the evaluation and management by electrophysiologic testing of survivors of cardiac arrest. VT = ventricular tachycardia; VF = ventricular fibrillation. *Source*: Adapted from *Cardiovascular Clinics*, Vol. 15, No. 3, p. 184, with permission of F.A. Davis Company, © 1985.

or weakness. Because ventricular dysrhythmias are usually associated with CAD, the activity intolerance is usually attributable to decreased cardiac output.

During the diagnostic phase, schedule the patient's activities and tests to allow for adequate rest periods. Provide assistance for bathing, feeding, and ambulation as needed. Provide more frequent, smaller meals if eating causes fatigue.

Anxiety/Fear

Patients may be anxious or fearful during the diagnostic phase for a number of reasons. Some may have recently survived a sudden death episode. Others are fearful that the dysrhythmia may escalate into death. Others are fearful of the imagined pain or discomfort associated with the diagnostic procedures or the anticipated discomfort associated with repeated defibrillations. Many are fearful that no treatment will control the dysrhythmia, and they often suspect there are only one or two treatment choices available. Others still are concerned about the effects of their illness on their future, family, and/or work life.

Determine the sources of the patient's fears. It is often helpful to initiate these discussions as "other patients have often commented that they are fearful during this time. How are you feeling?"

Problem-solving or education to address patient concerns often alleviates anxiety. Often, time, conclusion of the diagnostic phase, and development of a

Table 5-6 Patient Teaching for Diagnostic Tests for Recurrent Ventricular Dysrhythmias

Test	Purpose	Restrictions of Food/Fluids	Duration of Test	Informed Consent	What Patient Will See, Hear, Feel	Post-Test Care
Tests to define cardiac pathology leading to ventricular dysrhythmias						
Echocardiogram	Evaluate size, shape, motion, function of cardiac structures	None	15–30 min	No	1. Conductive jelly spread over chest area 2. Dime-sized transducer rubbed over chest area; may become uncomfortable 3. Room may be darkened 4. Patient may lie on left side 5. Breathe slowly, deeply, inhale certain medications	Skin washed
Technetium pyrophosphate (PYP Scan) (MI Scan)	Confirm recent MI Identify size and location of MI	None	40–60 min	No	Before scan, tracer material injected into a vein	No special care
Thallium scan At rest	Determine if certain areas of heart are receiving adequate blood supply	None	45 min	No	1. Before scan, tracer material injected into a vein	No special care

continues

Table 5-6 continued

Test	Purpose	Restrictions of Food/Fluids	Duration of Test	Informed Consent	What Patient Will See, Hear, Feel	Post-Test Care
					2. During scan, lies in bed while scintillation camera placed close to chest and multiple images taken	
With exercise		1. Before test, alcohol, tobacco, nonprescription medications restricted for 24 hr 2. Nothing by mouth for 24 hr 3. Diet restricted to clear liquids between two scans	45–90 min followed by resting scan hours later	Yes	1. Same as for exercise ECG and thallium scan with rest 2. During scan, lies in bed while scintillation camera placed close to chest and multiple images taken	No special care
Cardiac blood pool imaging Multiple gated acquisition scan (MUGA Scan)	Evaluate LV function Detect abnormal wall motion	None	1 hr	Yes	1. Twenty minutes before scan, blood sample taken and tagged with tracer material	No special care

Test	Purpose		Duration	Radioactive	Instructions	Care after
					2. Before scan, tagged blood reinjected into patient's vein 3. Patient attached to ECG leads and lies quietly in bed 4. Scintillation camera placed close to chest 5. Patient remains quiet and motionless unless otherwise directed	No special care
MUGA with exercise	Determine effects of exercise on heart	None	2 hr	Yes	Same as above. Will also pedal bicycle apparatus after resting scan and then be rescanned.	
MUGA with NTG	Determine effects of NTG on heart	None	2 hr	Yes	Same as resting MUGA. Will also take sublingual NTG and then be rescanned.	
First pass angiography	1. Evaluate heart muscle function 2. Detect abnormal wall motion or septal wall defects	None	15 min	No	Same as for thallium scan	

continues

Table 5-6 continued

Test	Purpose	Restrictions of Food/Fluids	Duration of Test	Informed Consent	What Patient Will See, Hear, Feel	Post-Test Care
First pass with exercise	3. Determine effects of exercise on heart	None	45 min	Yes	Same as above. Will also pedal bicycle apparatus after resting scan and then be rescanned.	
Cardiac catheterization	1. Record films of blood flow through coronary arteries 2. Determine blood flow and pressures in heart 3. Record films of valve and myocardium	Nothing by mouth for 6 hr before test	2 hr	Yes	1. Before going to cath lab, patient should go to bathroom, put on hospital gown. May receive preop med. 2. In cath lab, patient lies on table, camera close to chest 3. Patient IV started, draped with towels 4. Personnel wear sterile gowns, hats, masks, gloves	1. Monitor vital signs every 15 min for 1 hr, then every hour until stable. If unstable, monitor VS every 5 min and notify physician. 2. Bed rest for 8 hr for leg approach; 3 hr for arm approach 3. Patient not to bend extremities used

5. Room may be darkened
6. Procedure can be done through arm or groin
7. Insertion site cleaned, shaved, anesthetized
8. No pain when catheter moves through body
9. When contrast material injected, patient may feel hot, flushed, nauseated
10. Patient may be asked to cough, breathe deep
11. Med given if patient develops discomfort

4. Check for bleeding, arterial occlusion
5. Encourage patient to drink plenty of fluids
6. Check with physician about resuming precath med and diet

Tests to define characteristics of ventricular dysrhythmias

Resting ECG	Record electrical activity of heart at rest	None	15 min	No	1. Chest and legs exposed 2. Skin rubbed vigorously with alcohol	1. Electrodes removed 2. Conductive jelly washed off

continues

Table 5-6 continued

Test	Purpose	Restrictions of Food/Fluids	Duration of Test	Informed Consent	What Patient Will See, Hear, Feel	Post-Test Care
					3. Electrodes applied to arms, legs, chest 4. Conductive jelly put on skin under electrodes 5. No discomfort	
Exercise ECG	Record electrical activity of heart with exercise	Should not eat, drink alcohol or caffeinated beverages, smoke for 3 hr before test	Dependent on patient's performance	Yes	1. Patient should wear comfortable walking shoes, socks, lightweight pants or shorts, short-sleeved shirts 2. Chest area shaved, washed, electrodes placed 3. Patient walks on treadmill or rides bicycle 4. Test continues until heart rate reaches predetermined rate, ECG changes occur, symptoms appear	1. Patient assessed by cardiologist 2. Electrodes removed 3. Conductive jelly washed off 4. Should not shower for 1 hr

				5. Normal to feel sweaty, breathless, tired 6. Cardiologist present	
Ambulatory (Holter) monitoring	Record electrical activity of heart in response to normal daily activities	None	24 hr	1. Chest area shaved; electrodes applied 2. Electrodes attached to small tape recorder 3. Shoulder strap provided 4. Patient should do all normal daily activities and record in diary 5. Do not tub bathe or shower	No — Bring equipment and diary back to department
Transtelephonic ECG transmission	Periodic or sporadic: record electrical activity of heart in response to sporadic symptoms suggestive of dysrhythmias	None	5 min ECG as needed over several months	1. At regular intervals, or when experiencing symptoms suggestive of dysrhythmias, patient connects self to transtelephonic ECG transmitter, calls designated phone line.	Bring equipment back to department

continues

Table 5-6 continued

Test	Purpose	Restrictions of Food/Fluids	Duration of Test	Informed Consent	What Patient Will See, Hear, Feel	Post-Test Care
					2. Depending on type of recorder, patient transmits real time single lead ECG data or a delayed recording of ECG data stored when patient self-activated recorder at time of symptoms.	
Electrophysiology study	Evaluate abnormalities of heart rhythm	1. No food for 6 hr before procedure 2. Fluids not restricted	2–4 hr	Yes	1. Before going to cath lab, patient should go to the bathroom, put on hospital gown. May receive preop med. 2. In cath lab, patient lies on table 3. Patient monitored with ECG, has IV started, draped with sterile towels	1. Monitor vital signs every 15 min for 1 hr, then every hour until stable. If unstable, monitor VS every 5 min and notify physician. 2. Bed rest for 8 hr 3. Patient not to bend extremities used

4. Personnel wear sterile gowns, hats, masks, gloves
5. Room may be darkened
6. Procedure done through 1 or more sites
7. Insertion sites cleaned, shaven, anesthetized
8. No pain when catheters move through body
9. When heart is stimulated, patient may feel fluttering in chest. May need defibrillation/resuscitation.
10. Med given if patient develops discomfort

4. Check for bleeding, arterial occlusion
5. Check with physician about resuming precath meds and diet

Source: Adapted from "Patient Teaching in the Diagnosis of Heart Disease" by Laura J. Burke, with permission of St. Luke's Samaritan Health Care, Inc., Milwaukee, Wisconsin, © 1986.

treatment plan reduce anxiety. During diagnostic testing, encourage the patient to seek accurate information, correct misperceptions, and use available social supports such as family, spiritual advisors, health care professionals, and participation in support groups.

Diversional Activity Deficit

During the diagnostic phase, patients are hospitalized for invasive procedures, such as cardiac catheterization or electrophysiology studies. Post-test care may include bed rest for several hours to prevent bleeding at the surgical site. Patients may need activities that can divert them during this period, such as reading, watching television, listening to the radio, and sleeping. Also, during the diagnostic process, patients may have to remain hospitalized as they undergo a series of tests, perhaps each one daily (e.g., Holter monitoring, cardiac catheterization, electrophysiology studies).

Help the patient determine interests or activities that can be pursued while hospitalized. If the patient is usually active, perhaps participation in the in-hospital cardiac rehabilitation program will provide a monitored setting to continue an exercise program. Encourage the patient to continue to participate in home and work-related activities, if possible.

Knowledge Deficit

Rossi[29] identified knowledge deficit as the most common nursing diagnosis in 70% of 20 patients who were hospitalized after surviving an episode of sudden cardiac death. Initially, determine the patient/family's perceptions of the sequence of events that led up to and followed the dysrhythmia events. Often, patients assume that ventricular dysrhythmias are synonymous with AMI. Clarify any misperceptions.

Determine the patient and family's readiness to learn about the disease process and diagnostic plan. Some have such a high anxiety level that they have little desire to learn. Offer these people only information necessary to answer the few questions they ask.

Some patients and family members seek information to allay their anxiety. For these people, explain the normal functioning of the heart's conduction system. Relate the patient's symptoms of the dysrhythmia to the associated pathophysiology. Review each diagnostic test with the patient and family to determine any concerns. Ascertain that the patient is aware of the reason for the test, the associated sensory experiences, and post-test care (Table 5-6). Anxiety may be reduced by touring, or seeing a videotaped tour of the facility before the procedure.

After patients have received their test results, review their perception of the significance of the findings. Clarify any misperceptions. Continue to explain subsequent tests as they are ordered. Encourage the patient to set realistic short-term goals during this time, since a definite endpoint of diagnosis is not always predictable.

Sleep Pattern Disturbance

Rossi[30] found that 40% of patients hospitalized after surviving a sudden cardiac death experienced sleep disturbances. Patients usually complain of difficulty falling asleep, early awakening, interrupted sleep, and fatigue. Patients with recurrent ventricular dysrhythmias are at high risk of this problem because of fear associated with potential recurrence of sudden death.

Dlin and colleagues[31] found that fear of dying during sleep was a common misperception when 30 survivors of cardiac arrest were interviewed. The hospital environment must be structured to promote sleep. Patients need at least three 2-hour periods of uninterrupted sleep to promote a normal sleep pattern.

Discuss the patient's concerns about sleep. Correct any misperceptions. If monitored, reassure the patient that rhythm disturbances will be detected and treated even during sleep. Set realistic goals to increase total sleep time gradually.

Often these patients have nightmares about dying or resuscitation. Encourage the patient to discuss these fears. Have patients consciously talk about the worst dreams experienced, but then, have them imagine a successful ending to the dream (e.g., despite arrest, they are resuscitated, and treatment controls dysrhythmia).

Review the patient's medications since beta blockers and certain other antidysrhythmics can induce sleep disturbances. Adjust medications as appropriate. Schedule medication administration times to allow as much sleep time as possible.

These patients present unique physiologic and emotional problems that are intensified by the diagnostic process and hospital environment. Support and education provided by the nurse can help the patient deal with these problems.

PHARMACOLOGIC TREATMENT OF VENTRICULAR DYSRHYTHMIAS

Many antidysrhythmic drugs are available to treat recurrent ventricular dysrhythmias. These agents may suppress ventricular dysrhythmias by (1) altering the conductivity of myocardial tissue, (2) altering the refractoriness of myocardial tissue, and/or (3) increasing myocardial electrical stability. Antidysrhythmic drugs can be classified according to their effect on the cardiac muscle action potential.

Critical care nurses may see certain changes on the ECG as a result of these effects, which are described in Table 5-7.

Class I drugs act by depressing the fast inward sodium current, which lengthens the effective refractory period and delays spontaneous depolarization in the cardiac muscle. The effect on repolarization varies. This class of drugs is very effective in treating recurrent ventricular dysrhythmias by enhanced or abnormal automaticity or re-entry. Class I antidysrhythmic drugs have been arbitrarily subdivided into three groups based on the effects on depolarization and repolarization of the action potential.[32] Class IA drugs moderately depress phase 0 depolarization and moderately prolong repolarization. Class IB drugs have little effect on phase 0 depolarization and shorten repolarization. Class IC drugs strongly depress phase 0 depolarization and have little effect on repolarization.[26]

On the electrocardiogram, the critical care nurse will see varying responses due to drug effects of Class I agents. Class IA drugs will have some effect on prolonging the QRS interval, but will have greater effect on prolonging the QT interval. Class IB drugs will cause no change in either the QRS or QT interval. Class IC drugs prolong the QRS interval but have no effect on prolonging the QT interval. Overall, Class I drugs, singularly or in combination, are the initial drugs selected for treating recurrent, sustained ventricular tachycardias.

Class II drugs act by blocking sympathetic excitation at the beta-adrenergic receptor sites of the heart. Beta-blocking drugs have been reported to control or prevent the ventricular dysrhythmias associated with exercise or adrenergic stimulation.[33]

On the electrocardiogram, the critical care nurse will see no effects on the QRS or QT duration with Class II drugs. However, Class II drugs are not commonly used to treat recurrent, sustained ventricular dysrhythmias. Class II drugs are more commonly used to treat angina associated with ischemic myocardium.

Class III drugs act by lengthening the duration of the cardiac muscle cell action potential. This effect has had remarkable success in terminating resistant ventricular dysrhythmias. Amiodarone, in particular, is extremely effective in patients with recurrent, sustained VTs refractory to other drugs.[34]

Class IV drugs, the calcium channel blocking drugs, act to block selectively the slow calcium channels in the sinoatrial (SA) and atrioventricular (AV) node. They are rarely used to treat recurrent ventricular dysrhythmias.

Verapamil hydrochloride has been suggested in two isolated reports to be effective in treating recurrent VT in younger patients with good LV function and possibly no detectable structural heart disease.[35,36] Bepridil, a new investigational drug, is currently being tested for its effects on the treatment of VT.[37] However, Class IV drugs are more commonly used to treat angina from myocardial ischemia or supraventricular dysrhythmias.

Table 5-7 Classification of Antidysrhythmic Drugs Based on Electrophysiologic Properties

Class Name	Class	Drug	Action on Cardiac Action Potential	Action on ECG
Sodium channel blocking agents	IA	Quinidine Procainamide (Pronestyl) Disopyramide (Norpace) Propafenone (Rythmonorm)	Depress phase 4 (decrease automaticity) Moderately depress phase 0 (decrease conductivity) Moderately prolong phase 3 (prolong repolarization)	Little effect on QRS interval; marked prolongation of QT interval
	IB	Lidocaine (Xylocaine) Phenytoin (Dilantin) Tocainide (Tonocard) Mexiletine (Mexitil) Aprindine (Fibocil) Cibenzoline Moricizine (Ethmozine)	Depress phase 4 (depress automaticity) Has little effect on conductivity Decrease phase 2 of action potential (decrease refractoriness) Decrease phase 3 (shorten repolarization)	No effect on QRS or QT intervals
	IC	Flecainide (Tambocar) Encainide (Enkaid) Lorcainide	Markedly depress phase 0 of action potential (decrease conductivity) Has little effect on refractoriness Has little effect on repolarization	Prolongs QRS interval, no effect on QT interval
Beta-blocking agents	II	Propranolol (Inderal) Acebutolol (Sectral) Metoprolol Pindolol	Depress phase 4 (decreases automaticity) Decrease heart rate and myocardial contractility Blunt catecholamine effect	No effect on QRS or QT intervals
	III	Amiodarone (Cordarone) Bretylium (Bretylol) Sotalol	Prolong phase 3 of action potential (repolarization)	Mild prolongation of QRS interval, marked prolongation of QT interval
Slow calcium channel blocking agents	IV	Verapamil (Calan, Isoptin) Bepridil	Depress phase 4 Lengthen phases 1 and 2	No effect on QRS or QT intervals

NURSING CARE OF THE PATIENT RECEIVING
PHARMACOLOGIC ANTIDYSRHYTHMIC THERAPY

Nurses are responsible for knowing and monitoring for the drug action, route, dose, side effects, drug interactions, and nursing implications when administering pharmacologic agents. Table 5-8 describes these properties for some of the newer conventional and investigational antidysrhythmic drugs. Patients receiving pharmacologic antidysrhythmic therapy have many problems that can be treated with nursing interventions.

Potential for Decreased Cardiac Output

Many of the antidysrhythmic agents can exacerbate ventricular dysrhythmias, such as flecainide acetate, quinidine sulfate, and bepridil, and/or decrease myocardial contractility such as propranolol hydrochloride (Inderal). To assess cardiac function, obtain and record vital signs at least QID and look for changes such as bradycardia and hypotension. Obtain 12-lead ECGs as ordered, and monitor the PR interval, QRS width, QT interval, and observe for AV blocks and significant worsening of the dysrhythmias. Assess for subjective complaints of syncope and/or dizziness.

Knowledge Deficit

Adherence to the prescribed drug regimen is crucial for effective therapy to control dysrhythmias. A study of 98 outpatients receiving long-term antidysrhythmic drug therapy showed that 71% who stated they had taken their medication at the appropriate times had subtherapeutic serum drug levels. The authors felt this was because of noncompliance rather than inadequate dosage.[38]

Instruct patients and their families on the action, dose, and side effects of their medications. Design a dosing schedule tailored to the patient's life style. Help the patient establish a reminder system to remember to take medications. Suggest leaving small supplies of the medications in safe, common locations (work, home, purse) to improve access. Emphasize that patients should discuss with their physician if the dosage schedule is too frequent to fit their life style. Sometimes (but not always) the medication is available in long-acting forms. Also, emphasize that patients should notify the physician or nurse if they experience any side effects of the drugs. Often, the side effects can be reduced or eliminated by decreasing the dose without decreasing the effectiveness of the drug, or, other antidysrhythmic drugs from the same or other classes can be tried.

Table 5-8 Pharmacologic Properties of Newer Conventional and Investigational Antidysrhythmic Drugs

Name	Side Effects	Drug Interactions	Nursing Observations/ Interventions
Propafenone (Rhythmonorm)	CNS: paresthesias, blurred vision, dizziness, headache GI: vomiting, anorexia, nausea, constipation Cardiovascular: fatigue, AV block, sinus arrest, decreased myo. contractility Other: Bitter metallic taste; numb tongue, lips	—Addition of propafenone to a maintenance digoxin regimen will increase plasma digoxin concentrations. —Administration of propafenone with isosorbide dinitrate may increase dizziness. —When propafenone is added to amiodarone treatment, ventricular fibrillation or severe sinus slowing can occur.	Give with meals or snack to minimize the bitter taste and surface anesthetic effect.
Tocainide (Tonocard)	GI: nausea, vomiting, constipation, anorexia Neurologic: headache, tremors, blurred vision, anxiety, lightheadedness, paresthesias, hot flashes, twitching, diplopia, dizziness, memory loss, confusion Cardiovascular: shortness of breath, palpitations, sweating, increase in congestive heart failure, bradycardia Other: rash	—Use of tocainide with either digitalis or quinidine allows a decreased dosage of tocainide and therefore lowers the incidence of tocainide side effects. —Digoxin concentrations do not increase with concomitant tocainide use. —No adverse effects with warfarin.	1. Neurologic side effects are most often the first symptoms of tocainide toxicity. 2. Give tocainide with meals or snacks to minimize the appearance of side effects. 3. Changing the dose frequency from every 12 to every 8 hours may minimize the appearance of side effects.
Mexiletine (Mexitil®)	GI: vomiting, diarrhea, nausea, esophageal burning CNS: fine hand tremors, dizziness, blurred vision, diplopia,	—Clearance is reduced by propranolol and other beta blockers via reduction in liver blood flow.	1. Give oral doses after meals or with a snack to minimize the nausea and esophageal burning. *continues*

Table 5-8 continued

Name	Side Effects	Drug Interactions	Nursing Observations/ Interventions
	ataxia, nystagmus, drowsiness, confusion Cardiovascular: hypotension, bradycardia Other: insomnia, tinnitus, skin rash, thrombocytopenia		2. Check blood pressure and pulse carefully and frequently for first 48 hours when drug is first started. 3. Changing the dose frequency from every 12 to every 8 hours may minimize the appearance of side effects.
Aprindine (Fibocil®)	CNS: dizziness, ataxia, tremors, hallucinations, headache, cramps, dysphagia GI: nausea, vomiting, diarrhea Cardiovascular: fatigue, bradycardia, hypotension, AV block Other: agranulocytosis, cholestatic jaundice, urticaria, neutropenia, hepatitis	—Caution should be taken when administering with other anesthetic and CNS agents because of the danger of severe cerebral side effects. —Avoid concurrent administration of potassium and magnesium.	1. Monitor CBC weekly during 4th through 16th weeks of treatment to detect agranulocytosis or cholestatic jaundice. 2. Because of possible agranulocytosis, instruct the patient to notify M.D. if a sore throat, fever, oral ulcers, or pharyngitis develops. 3. Clinically, the antidysrhythmic effect may not occur for several days, even when it is given with a loading dose. 4. Because Aprindine has a narrow therapeutic/toxic margin, observe closely for side effects.

Drug	Side Effects	Drug Interactions	Comments
Cibenzoline	Dry mouth, urinary hesitancy, blurred vision Epigastric pain Hypotension, GI upset	Insufficient data	Insufficient data
Moricizine HCl (Ethmozine®)	GI: nausea, vomiting, abdominal pain CNS: dizziness, vertigo, blurred vision, headache Cardiovascular: mild hypotension	Insufficient data	Insufficient data
Flecainide (Tambocor®)	GI: nausea, constipation, abdominal pain, diarrhea CNS: dizziness, blurred vision, nervousness, headache, paresthesias, fatigue, tremors Cardiovascular: AV block and decreased myo. contractility Other: metallic taste	—May decrease myocardial contractility when given with beta blockers	1. May have a prorhythmic effect, monitor for aggravation of ventricular dysrhythmias. 2. Monitor patient for development of heart failure.
Encainide (Encaid)	GI: nausea CNS: headaches, weakness, dizziness, tremors, blurred vision, ataxia Other: metallic taste, leg cramps	—No adverse effects when used with digoxin, warfarin, beta blockers, calcium channel blockers —Cimetidine will increase plasma concentrations of encainide	May have a prorhythmic effect, monitor for aggravation of ventricular dysrhythmias.
Lorcainide	CNS: dizziness, tremors, blurred vision Cardiovascular: complete heart block Sleep: insomnia, nightmares, vivid dreams, increased perspiration	Insufficient data	Because sleep problems are common, encourage the patient to maintain use of a prescribed sedative at bedtime for the first 2 months to ensure compliance with Lorcainide therapy.

continues

Table 5-8 continued

Name	Side Effects	Drug Interactions	Nursing Observations/ Interventions
Acebutolol (Sectral)	Sinus bradycardia, AV block, depressed myocardial contractility	—Should not be taken with alpha stimulants (cold remedies, vasoconstrictive nasal sprays).	1. Instruct patient to never abruptly stop taking drug. 2. May mask symptoms of hypoglycemia, hyperthyroidism.
Amiodarone	GI: constipation, anorexia, nausea, abdominal pain, vomiting Other: insomnia, photosensitivity, reversible grey-blue skin discoloration, thyroid disorders, halovision, bilateral symmetrical corneal deposits Pulmonary: interstitial fibrosis, alveolitis Cardiovascular: symptomatic bradycardia, sinus arrest CNS: tremors, ataxia, impaired memory	—Suppression of ventricular dysrhythmias is enhanced when used with an antidysrhythmic from Class II. —Elevation of serum digoxin levels. —Potentiation of anticoagulant effects of warfarin.	1. Liver, lung, thyroid, neurologic function should be regularly assessed. 2. Monitor patient's serum digoxin, prothrombin time levels. 3. Instruct patient to use sunscreen, level 15, on areas of the skin exposed to the sun.
Bretylium Tosylate (Bretylol®)	GI: nausea, vomiting, diarrhea Cardiovascular: orthostatic hypotension, vertigo, syncope	—Aggravates arrhythmias associated with digitalis toxicity	Keep patient on bed rest to prevent falls during infusion.
Sotalol	Cardiovascular: hypotension, sinus bradycardia, AV block	—May precipitate Torsade de Pointes if given with drugs known to prolong QT interval, such as Class I antiarrhythmics, phenothiazines, tricyclic antidepressants	1. Monitor potassium levels to prevent hypokalemia. 2. Bradycardia may result in the patient's need of a pacemaker.

Verapamil	Cardiovascular: hypotension, AV block	—Should not be given with IV beta blockers —Do not give disopyramide within 48 hours before or 24 hours after Verapamil	Monitor for AV block, bradycardia when given.
Bepridil	GI: constipation, diarrhea, abdominal pain, anorexia CNS: headache, insomnia, dizziness, diplopia, drowsiness, dry mouth, tremors Cardiovascular: AV block	—May precipitate Torsade de Pointes if given with drugs known to prolong QT interval, such as Class I antiarrhythmics, phenothiazines, tricyclic antidepressants —May precipitate antidepressants.	1. May have a prorhythmic effect, monitor for aggravation of ventricular dysrhythmias. 2. Monitor potassium levels to prevent hypokalemia.

Above all, patients need reassurance that the drug regimen will be manageable and tolerable, and an effective regimen to control the dysrhythmias will continue to be sought.

Alteration in Thought Processes

Drugs from Class IB may cause confusion. This may be very distressful to both patients and their families. Often, decreasing the dosage or stopping the drug will alleviate this problem. In the meantime, reassurance that the effect is temporary is helpful. Also, maintain patient safety during this time through re-orientation methods (clocks, calendars, signs), restraints (family, siderails, posey), and assistance with ambulation.

Alteration in Sensory Perception (Visual, Auditory, Kinesthetic, Gustatory, Tactile, Olfactory)

All Class I drugs can cause some forms of visual, kinesthetic, and/or tactile alterations. These are usually described as blurred vision, diplopia, ataxia, tremors, and paresthesias. Mexiletine can also cause ringing in the ears. Encainide, flecainide, and propafenone can cause a metallic taste. Propafenone can also cause numb tongue and lips. Also, amiodarone (a Class III drug) can cause halovision around objects. All of these side effects are attributable to the action of the drugs on the central nervous system.

Usually, decreasing the dose or stopping the drug will decrease the severity or eliminate the side effects. Again, maintain patient safety. Consider having patients use a walker or other assistance for ambulation if sensory impairments affect their balance. Suggest that the patient avoid driving or working with machinery while sensorily impaired.

Sexual Dysfunction

Flecainide and the noncardioselective beta blockers can cause impotence. Usually, changing the medication to another drug allows the patient to return to normal sexual function.

Bowel Elimination (Constipation or Diarrhea)

All Class I drugs except lorcainide cause nausea, vomiting and anorexia, constipation, and/or diarrhea. Amiodarone (a Class III drug) also commonly causes constipation. These effects can be quite problematic for the patient, who may even choose to forego therapy rather than tolerate the effects. Often, decreasing the dosage will alleviate the effects, as may giving the medication with food, milk, or an antacid. Monitor the patient's elimination carefully. Encourage consumption of high-fiber foods. Use stool softeners, laxatives, enemas, or antidiarrheal agents as needed. Bretylium tosylate and sotalol (Class III drugs) have very little reported gastrointestinal (GI) effect.

Impaired Gas Exchange

Amiodarone can cause amiodarone-induced pulmonary toxicity as manifested by pulmonary fibrosis, fibrosing alveolitis, interstitial fibrosis, pneumonitis, and/ or interstitial pneumonitis. When symptomatic, patients usually report exertional dyspnea, nonproductive cough, and weight loss, and have rales or decreased breath sounds. Occasionally, patients have a low-grade fever, but no sweats or chills, and associated muscle weakness. Rarely, they may report pleuritic pain and have a pleuritic friction rub.

Usually, amiodarone-induced pulmonary toxicity is dose related, and the respiratory problems may be dissipated by stopping the drug and possibly treating the patient with steroids. Patients may not be monitored by ECG while their antidysrhythmic therapies are adjusted since the effects of amiodarone may last several weeks after the drug is stopped, because of its long half-life. Anxiety during respiratory distress is high, but working with patients to concentrate on use of controlled breathing patterns may help them regain control over their respiratory rates.

Altered Sleep Patterns

Lorcainide and amiodarone can disrupt sleep patterns. Lorcainide usually causes more interrupted sleep. Amiodarone causes sleeplessness in 28% of patients.[39] These disappear when the dosage of the drug is reduced. Also, suggest that the patient promote sleep by avoiding caffeinated beverages, exercising regularly, and avoiding daytime naps.

Patients receiving antidysrhythmic drug therapy face many problems while control of their dysrhythmias is sought. Knowledge of drug effects and side effects can help the critical care nurse detect potential problems and offer nursing interventions to make the treatment plan tolerable to the patient.

SURGICAL INTERVENTIONS IN THE TREATMENT OF VENTRICULAR DYSRHYTHMIAS

Surgical intervention is used to remove or destroy the focus of malignant ventricular dysrhythmias. Re-entry is the most common cause of ventricular dysrhythmias. Surgical intervention, intended to excise the focus or interrupt re-entrant conduction, is used to abolish or increase drug manageability.[40] Current methods of surgical treatment include encircling endocardial ventriculotomy (EEV), endocardial resection, and cryoablation. These procedures may be used alone or in combination. Laser photoablation and transvenous catheter electrical ablation are new therapeutic modalities under investigation.

Various indirect and direct surgical techniques have been employed to eliminate ventricular dysrhythmias. Examples of indirect methods include coronary artery bypass grafting and LV aneurysectomy. Initially, it was thought that these therapies would eliminate the myocardial ischemia that caused the lethal ventricular dysrhythmias.[41,42] In spite of these procedures, VT and VF recurred in the majority of the patients.[43,44] The purpose of direct surgical intervention is to remove or inactivate the irritable ventricular focus identified through epicardial and endocardial mapping. Mapping techniques pinpoint the ventricular dysrhythmia origin. Identification of the ventricular focus and dysrhythmia mechanism directs specific surgical therapy to remove only the necessary tissue and preserve cardiac structure and physiology.

The indicators of surgical intervention for the patient with refractory ventricular dysrhythmias include two or more episodes of VT or VF, which indicate a risk of recurrence; mapped sustained VT; anatomically correctable dysrhythmias; failed response to available pharmacologic treatment; inability to tolerate drug side effects; healed MI; possibility of improved LV function with coronary artery bypass grafting (CABG) or aneurysm resection; physiologic status; and age.[45-47] The patient, cardiologist, and cardiac surgeon must carefully analyze the risk-to-benefit ratio before making the decision to intervene surgically.

Preoperative Preparation

The diagnostic preparation of the patient for surgery is similar in many ways to all patients facing open heart procedures. Each body system is evaluated to identify problem areas. Coronary arteriography and left ventriculography are done preoperatively to identify cardiac function and determine if additional surgical procedures (e.g., CABG, aneurysm resection) are needed. Endocardial mapping is done to document the ventricular dysrhythmia morphology.

Preoperative cardiac patients with ventricular dysrhythmias have many special needs. They have failed repeated antidysrhythmic drug trials. Most likely, they have endured a long, discouraging hospitalization immediately before surgery.

Compromised nutritional status attributable to the hospital environment, modified diet, frequent NPO status before invasive procedures, side effects from medications, and anxiety are all of concern. These patients have an increased risk of infection from bacterial colonization in the hospital and frequent invasive testing. It is not unusual that they and their families are discouraged and frightened.

Generally, the preoperative hospitalized period is longer for the patient preparing for surgical treatment of ventricular dysrhythmias. This time provides an excellent opportunity for the critical care nurse to teach and support the patient and family. The purpose and goal of surgical intervention and familiarization with preoperative, intensive care unit (ICU), and postoperative environments and care routines should be discussed with the patient and family. They will benefit from an understanding of the postoperative goals of pain management, nutritional progression, and activity progression. Patients' ability to demonstrate coughing and deep breathing, incentive spirometry, and thoracic and arm exercise will enhance their ability to perform these procedures postoperatively.

The patient and family facing surgical intervention for ventricular dysrhythmias are anxious to have the risk of further dysrhythmias reduced, but they may fear the surgical procedure itself. It is important that accurate, consistent information be shared. Support provided by the family, health care professionals, and spiritual advisors will assist the patient to deal with the situation more effectively. Enhancing patient control through information sharing, mutual goal setting, and shared decision making will encourage patient and family participation.

Surgical Procedures

To facilitate induction of ventricular dysrhythmias, patients who have intraoperative mapping during surgical ablation procedures must stop taking their antidysrhythmic medications five half-lives before surgery. Use of antidysrhythmic medications is also avoided during anesthesia. A Class I drug, such as procainamide, may be infused during surgery after VT is induced to slow the rate so that the dysrhythmia can be mapped.

The surgery begins like most other adult cardiac surgeries. A median sternotomy incision is made for full cardiac access. Standard cardiopulmonary bypass is established. However, normothermic cardiopulmonary bypass is used to enhance inducibility of the ventricular dysrhythmias.

Intraoperative mapping is done during cardiopulmonary bypass. Intraoperative epicardial and endocardial mapping, together with preoperative endocardial electrophysiology studies, best influence the success of surgical treatment of the ventricular dysrhythmia and limit unnecessary surgical destruction.[48–50]

Intraoperative recording involves mapping the entire epicardial and endocardial surfaces to identify any possible origin sites of the dysrhythmias (Figure 5-4). The ventricular dysrhythmia focus or foci are delineated in the diseased myo-

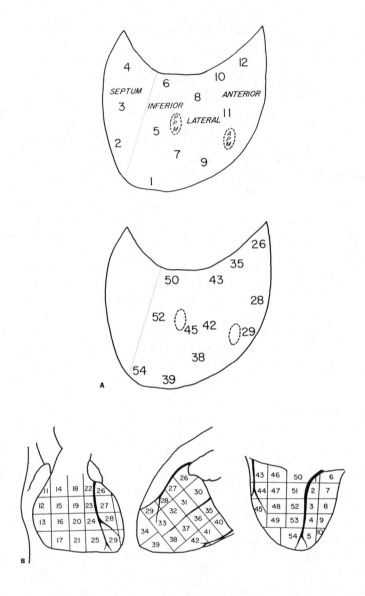

Figure 5-4 (A) Catheter endocardial mapping sites in the left ventricle are displayed on top. Site 1 = apex. Sites 2, 3, 4 = apical, mid, and basal septum. Site 5 = inferior. Site 6 = inferoposterior. Site 7 = apical low lateral. Site 8 = inferoposterolateral. Site 9 = anterolateral. Site 10 = lateral basal. Site 11 = midanterior. Site 12 = superior basal. In the bottom panel, corresponding epicardial sites are displayed. (B) Standard epicardial mapping sites in anterior (left), lateral (middle) and posterior (right) views. *Source*: Reprinted from *Circulation*, Vol. 61, No. 2, p. 397, with permission of the American Heart Association, Inc., © 1980.

cardial tissue.[51] After completion of intraoperative epicardial mapping, an incision is made in the ventricular aneurysm or infarct scar. Then, a hand-held or finger-ring (Figure 5-5) movable electrode is systematically placed on predetermined endocardial mapping sites and at the edges of the infarction scar.[52] Reentry origin sites exist most often in the mixture of healthy myocardial cells and fibrosis along the border of a healed MI scar.[53] Each ventricular dysrhythmia morphology is individually mapped and identified.

The delineation of the endocardial focus is essential because this is the site of earliest activation.[54] Endocardial activation occurs before epicardial activation. The site of epicardial activation is not reflected in endocardial activation. Therefore, endocardial focus identification is necessary to resect or ablate the ectopic focus accurately. Generally, this focus is located on the endocardium, at the edge of the normal and scarred myocardium.

Once the focus is identified, the surgeon's priority becomes destroying the irritable focus and the re-entrant circuit without injuring adjacent healthy myocardium.[55,56] The techniques of focus resection or ablation are EEV, endocardial resection, and cryoablation (Figure 5-6).

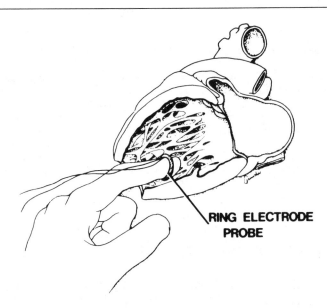

RING ELECTRODE PROBE

Figure 5-5 "Mapping" ventricular tachycardia. The ventricle has been entered through the aneurysm or infarcted tissue, and the earliest activation during induced ventricular tachycardia is identified by using a ring electrode and recording circumferentially and at 1-cm levels from the aneurysmal edge.
Source: Reprinted from *Surgical Clinics of North America*, Vol. 65, No. 3, p. 580, with permission of W.B. Saunders Company, © 1985.

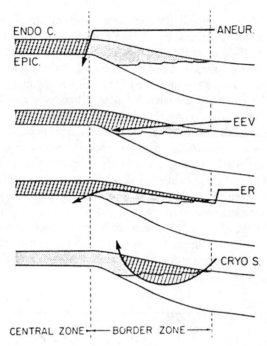

Figure 5-6 Schematic representation of surgical techniques to address VT associated with an infarct scar or aneurysm. The normal zone is clear, and the infarcted zone is hatched in this hypothetical cross-section of ventricular wall. Standard aneurysectomy (top) leaves behind the border zone, which may be arrhythmogenic. The endocardial ventriculotomy (second from top) follows the plane between normal muscle and scar and "excludes" the arrhythmogenic zone. Endocardial resection (third from top) also follows the scar plane, but the arrhythmogenic tissue is removed. Cryosurgery (bottom) destroys myocardium within the range of the probe and replaces it with homogeneous fibrous tissue. ANEUR = aneurysectomy, CRYOS = cryosurgery, EEV = encircling endocardial ventriculotomy, ENDOC = endocardium, EPIC = epicardium, and ER = endocardial resection. *Source*: Reprinted from *Cardiology Clinics*, Vol. 1, No. 2, p. 337, with permission of W.B. Saunders Company, © 1983.

Encircling Endocardial Ventriculotomy

EEV was the first surgery used to interrupt the arrhythmogenic tissue at the border of an infarction. In EEV, a perpendicular incision is made through the endocardium to the level of the subepicardium. The incision is made to just beyond the edges of the infarction or aneurysm (Figure 5-7). The epicardial surface and the coronary arteries are left intact.[57] EEV disrupts the re-entrant circuit of the ventricular dysrhythmia.[58,59]

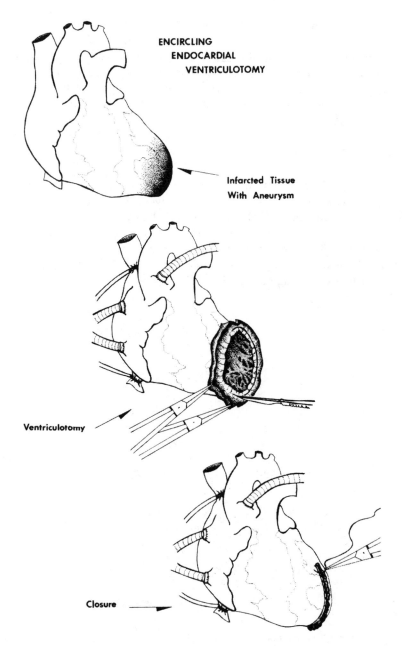

ENCIRCLING
ENDOCARDIAL
VENTRICULOTOMY

Infarcted Tissue
With Aneurysm

Ventriculotomy

Closure

Figure 5-7 Encircling endocardial ventriculotomy. *Source*: Reprinted from "Surgical Management of Ventricular Tachycardia" by P.J. Markmann, in *Heart and Lung*, Vol. 13, No. 6, p. 628, with permission of The C.V. Mosby Company, © November 1984.

Intraoperative mapping is not always used with EEV because the incision follows the outline of the infarction or aneurysm. Because of the size of the myocardial incision, LV function can be significantly impaired. Wetstein et al.[60] reported that the postoperative recurrence of VT, ventricular dysfunction caused by the procedure, and 13% operative mortality necessitate a delineation of the clinical advantages of this procedure.

Endocardial Resection

Endocardial resection removes the endocardium that contains arrhythmogenic tissue. This procedure is guided by intraoperative mapping. Using sharp dissection, a 2- to 3-cm endocardial margin is peeled away (Figure 5-8). In a well-defined, single focus ventricular dysrhythmia, this is the procedure of choice.[61]

Harkin et al.,[62] in a study of 107 patients treated with endocardial resection, found a 9% mortality in the first 30 days after surgery. They also found that the 18% of patients who had postoperative VT responded to antidysrhythmic medication therapy.

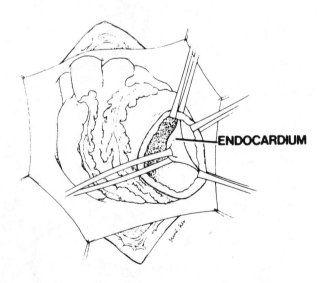

Figure 5-8 The endocardial resection procedure. The left ventricle has been entered through the aneurysm or previously infarcted tissue. The endocardium at the earliest site of activation is removed, encompassing a 2- to 3-cm margin. *Source*: Reprinted from *Surgical Clinics of North America*, Vol. 65, No. 3, p. 582, with permission of W.B. Saunders Company, © 1985.

Cryoablation

Cryoablation is a map-guided technique used alone or combined with other surgical techniques to ablate ventricular dysrhythmias.[63] Once the ventricular dysrhythmia is induced, a probe maps out potential endocardial dysrhythmia foci. A probe is then used to cool temporarily the endocardial tissue to 0°C (Figure 5-9). If the sustained dysrhythmia ceases after the temporary cooling, the focus of the ventricular dysrhythmia will have been identified.[64] The area is then permanently ablated with a nitrous oxide probe application of −60°C to −70°C.[65,66] Miller[67] reported that 60% of 50 patients were free of VT with or without postoperative antidysrhythmic medications when cryoablation was used as a primary method to ablate VT. This therapy provides a unique means to test its effectiveness before permanent endocardial change.

The precision of this method permits destruction of difficult-to-reach re-entrant circuits in conductive tissue and the papillary muscle of the mitral valve.[68] Before cryoablation, resection of the dysrhythmia focus in these areas led to heart block or mitral valve placement.[69]

Encircling endocardial cryoablation outlines the aneurysm or infarction edge with overlapping cryolesions.[70] The re-entrant circuit is thereby interrupted.

Future Ablation Therapies

Under investigation are transvenous electrical catheters and laser-powered ablation devices. Similar to cryosurgery, these instruments attempt to remove the focus of the ventricular dysrhythmia.

The technique of transvenous catheter electrocoagulation ablates an endocardial-mapped dysrhythmic focus by delivering 200 to 400 joules through a catheter electrode.[71] Ideally, this percutaneous procedure would limit myocardial disruption of nonarrhythmogenic tissue while eliminating the need for cardiac surgery. The technique of ablation of ventricular dysrhythmias is difficult. There is also a high occurrence of serious complications such as shock-induced dysrhythmias, LV dysfunction, and return of the dysrhythmias after the procedure.[72] Experience with transvenous catheter ablation has been limited, and it is considered an experimental therapy.

Laser ablation of ventricular dysrhythmias is done while the patient is on normothermic cardiopulmonary bypass after intraoperative mapping has identified the dysrhythmic foci. Pulsed laser energy is then directed at the foci to destroy them.[73] Selle et al.[74] reported successful laser ablation in 13 out of 15 post-MI patients who had recurrent ventricular dysrhythmias. One patient in the series died in surgery and another patient had postoperative VT at electrophysiology study that was responsive to medication. Isner et al.[75] reported that laser

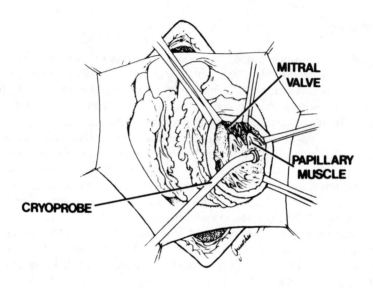

Figure 5-9 An example of cryosurgery. After the left ventricle is entered and the endocardium "mapped," the cryoprobe is applied to the endocardium. In this case, the earliest site of activation was the base of the papillary muscle. *Source*: Reprinted from *Surgical Clinics of North America*, Vol. 65, No. 3, p. 584, with permission of W.B. Saunders Company, © 1985.

ablation offered increased speed and precision to the surgical management of VT. Technical aspects of laser ablation are in early development, and patient experience is limited.

NURSING CARE OF THE PATIENT UNDERGOING SURGICAL INTERVENTION

Many care issues for the patient who has undergone surgical intervention for ventricular dysrhythmias are similar to those for patients who have had open heart surgery.

Table 5-9 identifies postoperative complications of cardiovascular origin. Prolonged cardiopulmonary bypass, used during the mapping procedure, can lead to neurologic, renal, hematologic, metabolic, and cardiovascular complications. The critical care nurse must closely monitor for and intervene to prevent these complications. It is imperative that the critical care nurse and physician establish early in the immediate postoperative period an assessment and treatment protocol for ventricular ectopy.[76]

Table 5-9 Cardiac Complications of Immediate Postoperative Phase

Complications	Indicators
Pericardial tamponade	Rising or elevated central venous pressure (CVP) Neck vein distension Narrowed pulse pressure (↓ systolic, ↑ diastolic) Pulses paradoxus Restlessness, clammy skin Muffled heart tones
Septal rupture	Murmur Progressive heart failure
Cardiac rupture	Bright red chest tube drainage Hypovolemic shock Hemothorax Cardiac arrest Exsanguination
Decreased cardiac output	Low mean arterial pressure Vasoconstriction Right and/or left ventricular failure
Heart blocks	First degree AV block Second degree AV block Third degree AV block Bundle branch block
Aneursymectomy suture line leakage	Excessive chest tube drainage Low cardiac output, pericardial tamponade

Alteration in Comfort: Pain

This patient population may have greater pain management needs because of extensive and prolonged surgery, fear of return of the dysrhythmia, limited or stressed support systems, and compromised preoperative preparation. They are also at increased risk for anxiety and depression because they may not have had the opportunity to ''settle their affairs'' at home preoperatively, or they may view this surgery as a last resort. Perception of pain is highly influenced by the patient's emotional state.

The critical care nurse can help to reduce a patient's and/or family member's anxiety by ensuring that they have an accurate perception of the situation, adequate situational support, an understanding of the care direction, and realistic short-term goals. McCauley and Polomano[77] also recommended minimizing feelings of powerlessness, encouraging rest, teaching patients about analgesia, and promoting activity.

Impaired Physical Mobility

The postoperative goal of early and progressive ambulation and thoracic exercise is very different than the preoperative self-restricted activity level this patient was accustomed to. The patient must be taught the rationale for the new activity regime, have meals and activity periods interspersed with rest, and be monitored during activity for orthostatic hypotension and dysrhythmias. The frequency of activity should be maintained while modifying activity duration and intensity to suit the patient's tolerance.

Knowledge Deficit

The patient and family should be instructed in the purpose of surgery, the expected outcome of surgery, self care, medications, and the plan and goals of care. The patient and family should be aware of the predischarge testing, which may include a postoperative electrophysiology study, a submaximal stress test, and/or a gated blood pool scan. The purpose of the electrophysiology study is to test for inducible ventricular dysrhythmias after surgical removal or destruction of the dysrhythmia focus.[78,79] The other tests may be done to evaluate LV function after surgery.

ADJUNCTIVE THERAPIES TO TREAT RECURRENT VENTRICULAR DYSRHYTHMIAS

Implantable Electrical Devices

In addition to a number of antidysrhythmic pharmacologic and surgical therapies, new electrical devices are being developed. The only FDA-approved device at the time of this writing is the automatic implantable cardioverter defibrillator (AICD), which can detect and terminate life-threatening VT and/or VF.

The AICD has two major components: a generator and a lead system. The pulse generator is approximately $3'' \times 4'' \times 3/4''$, weighs a half pound, is encased in titanium, is hermetically sealed, and is placed in the left upper quadrant of the abdomen. The lithium battery provides power to monitor a heart rhythm for approximately 18 months and can deliver 100 to 150 discharges.

Two different lead systems are used. In the first, a transvenous rate-sensing lead is placed in the right ventricle to be used with a low-resistance defibrillating spring electrode in the superior vena cava near the high right atrium and a flexible, rectangular patch electrode (27 cm^2 × 13.5 cm^2) is sutured to the apex of the heart (Figure 5-10). The second lead system is composed of two rectangular patch electrodes sutured to the anterior and posterior walls of the heart. Two standard epicardial screw-in leads are attached to the LV to serve as rate-sensing leads. The electrodes and leads for both systems are attached subcutaneously to the generator, which is placed in the left upper abdominal pocket.

The AICD can recognize the morphology and/or the rate of the patient's ventricular complexes. Each AICD unit has a predetermined rate cut-off. When the AICD senses a ventricular rhythm and determines that it exceeds the rate cut-off, it charges and defibrillates.

The AICD can deliver a four-pulse or defibrillation sequence. The initial pulse is delivered at approximately 24 joules (as opposed to 400 joules for external defibrillation) since less energy is required to defibrillate the heart with the patches sewn directly onto the myocardium. If the dysrhythmia continues, three more pulses of approximately 30 joules will be delivered (see Figure 5-11).

Candidates for AICD implantation have had one or more episodes of sustained VT with hemodynamic collapse and have failed to respond to antidysrhythmic pharmacologic therapy as evaluated by electrophysiologic testing.

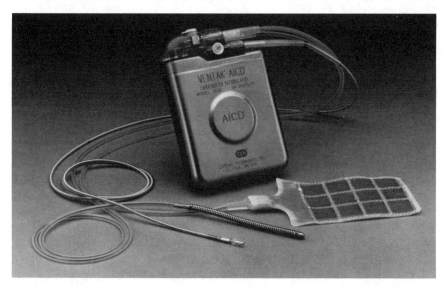

Figure 5-10 AICD pulse generator and leads. *Source*: Used with permission of Cardiac Pacemakers, Inc., St. Paul, Minnesota, © 1987.

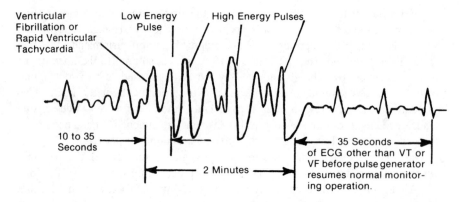

Figure 5-11 Output sequence of AICD. *Source*: Reprinted from *Physician's Manual*, p. 2, with permission of Cardiac Pacemakers, Inc., St. Paul, Minnesota, © 1986.

The survival rate of patients with recurrent VT treated with antidysrhythmic and/or surgical intervention but without an AICD is 34% to 73%. One-year survival rates of patients treated with the AICD alone and/or in combination with antidysrhythmic drug therapy and surgery is 97%.[80,81]

As with any implantable electrical device, patients often want to know what it looks like, how it works, what they will feel as it works, and how to care for themselves after it is implanted. Cardiac Pacemakers, Inc., the manufacturer of the AICD, has developed a patient resource manual that explains the device and its functioning in simple terms.[82] Discharge care instructions should be reviewed with patients and families (Exhibit 5-2).[83–86]

Research is underway to test a nonthoracotomy approach for implantation of the AICD. Wetherbee et al.[87] determined that effective defibrillation could be achieved in anesthetized dogs by transvenously placing a defibrillating catheter with the distal 5-cm^2 shocking electrode located near the right ventricular apex and the proximal 10-cm^2 electrode in the superior vena cava.

Two studies have reviewed the impact of the AICD on the patient's quality of life. Cooper et al.[88] surveyed 13 patients over a 10-month period of follow-up. They found persistent fear in 85% of the patients, sexual abstinence in 41%, fear of premature battery failure in 47%, significant daily awareness of AICD in 35%, reduced physical activity either from fear of AICD shock or limitations of heart disease in 65%, and decreased social interactions in 41%.

Vlay[89] reported, in anecdotal form, on the social impact of the AICD on eight patients followed for approximately 10 months. Four returned to work, full or part time, and were socially active. The other four were retired, but remained active socially. Vlay noted that the sample size was small and the follow-up period short, but commented that the dysrhythmias, when treated with AICD,

Exhibit 5-2 Discharge Instructions for Patients with an AICD

Before discharge, the patient and family are able to state:
- The purpose of the AICD: It is implanted to control VT or VF.
- How it works: continuously monitors heart rate and rhythm; delivers one to four internal shocks per episode of VT/VF.
- How AICD firing feels:
  —To the patient: like a hard thump on the chest or back
  —To others touching the patient: like a tingling sensation, which is harmless.
- What to do when it fires (Emergency Action Plan):
  —Patient lies down.
  —If possible, one person stays with patient, while another contacts the electrophysiologist.
  —If patient remains conscious, describe to electrophysiologist any prodromal symptoms, number of AICD shocks, compliance with antidysrhythmic therapy, and activity level associated with firing.
  —If patient loses conciousness, summon an ambulance and observe patient. Begin CPR after four AICD firings or if AICD fails to fire after 30 seconds.
- Where to take CPR training.
- How to care for surgical incision sites.
- How to observe for signs and symptoms of generalized and local infection.
- When and how to take prophylactic antibiotics before surgery or dental work.
- How to identify close contact with a strong magnetic field:
  —Strong magnetic fields may be caused by arc welding, large permanent magnets, diathermy, or electrocautery.
  —Notify electrophysiologist if beeping tones come from the AICD.
- How to return to activities of daily living.
- How to obtain "Medic Alert" identification.
- When to return for periodic battery checks:
  —Battery charge time and number of patient pulses are checked with each visit.
  —AICD is checked 1 month after implantation, then every 2 months for first 12 months, and then every month.

---

had not altered any of the patients' social outcomes, thus offering better results than the percentage of patients returning to work full time after coronary artery bypass graft surgery.

Several other electrical devices to terminate VT are in the development and clinical testing stages. They offer a variety of features including antibradycardia pacing, overdrive (burst) pacing, and internal cardioversion. The devices may be physician or patient activated or automatic.

Use of any electrical device poses several problems. First, inappropriate sensing may cause it to either not recognize the dysrhythmia (undersense) and not appropriately treat the patient; or inappropriately recognize supraventricular dysrhythmias (oversense) and inappropriately treat these dysrhythmias. Component failure may also occur, which may cause over- or undersensing.

Dysrhythmia acceleration is the most hazardous complication of antitachycardia pacing or cardioverter-defibrillation. Currently, antitachycardia pacemakers cannot terminate VF. The AICD can deliver transcardiac shocks of 25 to 30 joules in a four-pulse sequence, thereby providing greater ability to terminate accelerated ventricular dysrhythmias.

Localized and distant myocardial tissue damage may occur with the AICD, because of electrical defibrillation. Animal pathologic studies examining the myocardial tissue consequences of direct DC current discharge revealed myocardial necrosis and dehiscence of intercalated disks between myocytes. Also, adhesions, thrombi, endocardial fibrosis, and penetration of the myocardium can occur whenever a lead is chronically implanted in the heart as with the antitachycardia pacemakers, cardioverters, and certain lead configurations of the AICD.[90]

Because of these problems, the ideal implantable automatic electrical device for termination of recurrent VTs does not exist. If it did, it would have the following features:

- built-in tachycardia detection and recognition algorithms
- discrete pacing delivered in a preprogrammed sequence
- low-energy cardioversion
- back-up defibrillation
- back-up bradycardia pacing
- programmable rate and energy levels.

The development of implantable electrical devices for the treatment of VTs does offer additional therapeutic choices for patients with recurrent VTs. As electrical and engineering technology improves, critical care nurses can expect an increased number of new devices, responsive to individual patient needs.

Use of Automatic External Defibrillators and/or Lay Person Cardiopulmonary Resuscitation (CPR)

Automatic external defibrillators provide an adjunct to CPR in the acute treatment of sustained ventricular dysrhythmias. If advanced cardiac life support (including defibrillation) is given to a person in VF within 5 minutes of onset, 40% of the victims are successfully resuscitated. When it takes longer than 5 minutes, only 15% survive. Therefore, an easy to use, lightweight, portable defibrillator has been developed and is sometimes used by emergency medical technicians or lay rescuers to revive VT/VF victims. The device has a battery-operated power supply. The rescuer places a plastic airway in the victim's mouth, places an adhesive pad over the subxiphoid area, and turns on the device. The automatic external defibrillator begins to operate, assessing the patient's rhythm, giving appropriate treatment, and issuing voice commands to the rescuer to insure its proper use.

Lay person CPR is basic cardiopulmonary resuscitation, provided by nonmedical personnel. Certification courses are offered by the American Heart Association and the American Red Cross; approximately 10% to 40% of the American population have been certified. The actual CPR techniques taught are researched carefully, and technique changes are made periodically as research identifies more efficient and effective ways to circulate blood throughout the body artificially during an episode of VT or VF.

Mandel and Cobb[91] surveyed 1,271 citizens in Seattle, Washington, to determine the number of trained basic cardiac life support providers in the community. They found that trained providers tended to be younger, male, and unrelated to persons with known heart disease. They suggested that citizen CPR programs should concentrate on the more likely rescuers: middle-aged women or the families of cardiac patients.

Guzy et al.[92] assessed the effects of CPR training for families of high-risk cardiac patients. No adverse psychologic effects for family members were documented. However, patients whose family members had been trained in CPR were more anxious and depressed at 3- and 6-month follow-up compared with before the training or with patients whose families received no instruction on cardiac risk factors. The authors suggested that CPR training for family members may have adverse psychologic effects on high-risk cardiac patients.

In contrast, Chadda and Kammerer[93] provided CPR instruction and instruction on the use of an automatic external defibrillator to 12 high-risk patients and their families. They reported that all 12 patients and their families claimed a reduction in anxiety because of immediate access to ECG monitoring facilities, knowledge of CPR, and availability of lifesaving equipment.

Weaver et al.[94] also offered CPR training and instruction in the use of an automatic external defibrillator to families of 84 survivors of out-of-hospital cardiac arrest. Twenty-two patients enrolled, and all completed the training program. Seven were retested at 1 month. Five performed satisfactorily; two had difficulty with CPR. One had difficulty applying the automatic external defibrillator. No significant difference was found in patient or family depression indices before and after training. Interestingly, the reasons cited for nonparticipation by the 52 patient/family groups included death before enrollment (8); family member or patient had major comorbidity (8); no family to be instructed (12); refused (16); and other (18). The authors noted that a sizable percentage (81%) of cardiac survivors cannot take advantage of early defibrillation by household members for a variety of reasons. They also recommended that these training programs be aimed at older women and that periodic retraining be offered.

Exhibit 5-3 Needs of Patients Learning To Live with Controlled Ventricular Tachycardia

---

Information on:
—A treatment plan to prevent or control ventricular dysrhythmias
—Guidelines to return to activities of daily living, including sexual activity, return to
   work, driving
—Recognizing and managing signs and symptoms of VT/VF
—How to obtain medical alert jewelry
—How to obtain Social Security disability benefits
—CPR training for family

Problem-solving skills to determine:
—How to take medication(s)
—Methods to alleviate persistent fatigue, insomnia
—How to modify travel plans
—How to acquire financial capabilities to support family costs during diagnostic and
   treatment phases
—Spouse's ability to re-enter work force
—Access to adequate transportation
—An emergency plan of action

Emotional support to:
—Place fear of dying into realistic perspective
—Identify family fears related to future sudden death
—Continue social contacts with family
—Clarify values regarding prior roles and activities with family
—Continue responsibility for decision making in family matters
—Be reassured that the illness is not interfering with other family member's lives

---

NURSING CARE OF THE PATIENT WITH ADJUNCTIVE THERAPIES

Patients treated with adjunctive therapies have special problems. They have survived sudden death. They have faced failure of standard and/or possibly investigational drug trials. They must now learn to adapt their life style to incorporate living with an adjunctive therapy, either internal or external. These patients require a great deal of education as well as guidance and support. Exhibit 5-3 lists patient needs as they learn to live with controlled VTs.

Knowledge Deficit

Patients with a knowledge deficit verbalize either inadequate recall of information, inadequate understanding of information, or simply inadequate knowledge. Careful assessment of these patients is important to determine their baseline understanding of the heart's conduction system, the pathophysiology of the dysrhythmia, attempted treatments and reasons for their failure, and their expectations for the functioning and success of the adjunctive therapy. Provide information where deficits exist. Correct misunderstandings when detected. Clearly instruct the patient and family on how the adjunctive therapy works or how to work the device; realistic patient capabilities; physical limitations; name, purpose, and potential side effects of medications; when to call the physician; and what to do in an emergency.

Ineffective Coping (Individual)

Ineffective individual coping is the impairment of adaptive behaviors and problem-solving abilities of a person in meeting life's roles and demands. Patients may display a variety of behaviors including an inability to learn, giving up hope, apathy, or hypervigilance. (See also Chapter 8.)

Explore with patients their perception of the events surrounding their concern. Encourage them to describe their fears. Provide factual information when requested.

Help patients identify the behaviors they are exhibiting to validate your perceptions as to why they are behaving in the observed manner. Discuss other possible coping responses. Teach the patient problem-solving, decision-making, assertive, goal-setting, evaluation, and/or relaxation skills. Encourage the patient to maintain socialization and social support systems. Discuss past situations in which the patient used good coping skills and plan how they can be repeated in the future. Help the patient identify realistic daily (short-term) goals to regain emotional control.

Anticipatory Grieving

Despite the variety of treatments available for recurrent ventricular dysrhythmias, all patients, at some point in time, go through anticipatory grieving. Anticipatory grieving can be described as the beginning of an actual process of grieving that occurs when a significant loss is expected, before it actually takes place.

Although patients have now achieved control of their dysrhythmias to the best of medicine's and technology's ability, they continue to face potential future sudden death episodes.

To support anticipatory grieving, foster an environment in which the effects of the patient's death can be explored. Support patients' decisions to "set their affairs in order, just in case." Often, patients and families reset life goals. Reassure them that this is normal. Offer realistic hope about their prognosis.

SUMMARY

In recent years, there have been several new advances in the diagnosis and treatment developed for the patient with recurrent ventricular dysrhythmias. Critical care nurses have the potential to improve the patient's quality of life through nursing care, psychologic support, and patient education.

NOTES

1. J.J. Rozanski, A. Castellanos, and R.J. Myerburg, "Ventricular Ectopy and Sudden Death," *Cardiovascular Clinics* 11(1980):127.

2. P.R. Reid, "Ventricular Premature Beats, Ventricular Tachycardia, and Sudden Death: Identification of Patients and Drug Treatment," *Annals of the New York Academy of Sciences* 432(1984):286.

3. B. Lown and M. Wolf, "Approaches to Sudden Death from Coronary Heart Disease," *Circulation* 44(1971):130.

4. J.T. Bigger, Jr. and F.M. Weld, "Analysis of Prognostic Significance of Ventricular Arrhythmias after Myocardial Infarction: Shortcomings of the Lown Grading System," *British Heart Journal* 45(1981):717.

5. R.J. Myerburg et al., "Classification of Ventricular Arrhythmias based on Parallel Hierarchies of Frequency and Form (Editorial)," *American Journal of Cardiology* 54(1984):1355.

6. R.N. Fogoros, "Management of Ventricular Arrhythmias," *American Family Physician* 33(1986):236.

7. A.J. Moss, "Detection, Significance and Management of VPB's in Ambulatory Patients," *Cardiovascular Clinics* 11(1980):143.

8. H.L. Kennedy et al., "Five to Ten Year Follow-up of Apparently Healthy Subjects with Frequent and Complex Ventricular Ectopy," *Circulation* 68, Suppl. 3 (1983):107.

9. R.N. Fogoros, "Management of Ventricular Arrhythmias," *American Family Physician* 33(1986):236.

10. W.B. Kannel and D.L. McGee, "Epidemiology of Sudden Death: Insights from the Framingham Study," *Cardiovascular Clinics* 15(1985):93.

11. American Heart Association, *Heart Facts* (Dallas: American Heart Association, 1985).

12. C. Summers, "Sudden Cardiac Death," *Critical Care Quarterly* 7(1984):1.

13. J.M. Miller, J.A. Vassallo, and M.E. Josephson, "The Evaluation and Prevention of Sudden Cardiac Death," *Hospital Formulary* 19(1984):904.

14. I.P. Panidis and J. Morganroth, "Initiating Events of Sudden Cardiac Death," *Cardiovascular Clinics* 15(1985):81.

15. G. Nikolic, R.L. Bishop, and J.B. Singh, "Sudden Death Recorded during Holter Monitoring," *Circulation* 66(1982):218.

16. P.G. Milner et al., "Holter Monitoring at the Time of Sudden Cardiac Death," *Circulation* 68, Suppl. 3 (1983):106.

17. L.N. Horowitz, "Invasive Cardiac Electrophysiologic Testing," *Cardiology Clinics* 3(1985):101.

18. H.J. Wellens, P. Brugada, and W.G. Stevenson, "Programmed Electrical Stimulation of the Heart in Patients with Life-threatening Ventricular Arrhythmias: What is the Significance of Induced Arrhythmias and What is the Correct Stimulation Protocol?," *Circulation* 72(1985):1.

19. R. Slama, J.F. Leclera, and P. Coumel, "Paroxysmal Ventricular Tachycardia in Patients with Apparently Normal Hearts," in D.P. Zipes and J. Jalife, eds., *Cardiac Electrophysiology and Arrhythmias* (Orlando: Grune & Stratton, 1985).

20. Fogoros, "Ventricular Arrhythmias."

21. Miller, Vassallo, and Josephson, "Sudden Cardiac Death."

22. Rozanski, Castellanos, and Myerburg, "Ventricular Ectopy."

23. J.E. Dalen, and R.J. Goldberg, "Sudden Coronary Death: Current Odds Favor Prevention," *Consultant* 23(1983):219.

24. Kannel and McGee, "Epidemiology of Sudden Death."

25. P.R. Reid, "Management of Ventricular Arrhythmias," *Cardiovascular Clinics* 15(1985):279.

26. J.J. Haggerty, M.B. Burkett, and J.R. Foster, "Psychological Dysfunction in Patients Surviving Ventricular Tachycardia or Fibrillation," *Circulation* 68, Suppl. 3 (1983):429.

27. C. Summers et al., "The Psychological Profile of Survivors of Sudden Cardiac Death," *Circulation* 70, Suppl. 2 (1984):1543.

28. L. Rossi, "Nursing Care for Survivors of Sudden Cardiac Death," *Nursing Clinics of North America* 19(1984):411.

29. Ibid.

30. Ibid.

31. B.M. Dlin, A. Stern, and S.J. Poliakoff, "Survivors of Cardiac Arrest: The First Few Days," *Psychosomatics* 15(1974):61.

32. J. Morganroth, "Ventricular Premature Complexes: Newer Approaches to Therapy," *Practical Cardiology* 10(1984):122.

33. M.G. Kienzle et al., "Antiarrhythmic Drug Therapy for Sustained Ventricular Tachycardia," *Heart and Lung* 13(1984):614.

34. M. Dunn, "Clinical Use of Amiodarone," *Heart and Lung* 14(1985):407.

35. B. Belhassen, H.H. Rotmensch, and S. Laniado, "Response of Recurrent Sustained Ventricular Tachycardia to Verapamil," *British Heart Journal* 46(1981):679.

36. J.W. Mason, C.D. Swerdlow, and L.B. Mitchell, "Efficacy of Verapamil in Chronic, Recurrent Ventricular Tachycardia," *American Journal of Cardiology* 51(1983):1614.

37. P.F. Nestico et al., "Bepridil Hydrochloride for Treatment of Benign or Potentially Lethal Ventricular Arrhythmias," *American Journal of Cardiology* 58(1986):1001.

38. A. Squires et al., "Long-term Antiarrhythmic Therapy: Problem of Low Drug Levels and Patient Noncompliance," *American Journal of Medicine* 77(1984):1035.

39. L. Harris et al., "Effects of Prolonged Use of Amiodarone Therapy," *American Heart Journal* 106(1983):916.

40. L.K. Jackson, "Sustained and Nonsustained Ventricular Tachycardia: Genesis, Significance and Management," *Cardiovascular Clinics* 16(1986):83.

41. L. Wetstein, R.W. Landymore, and J.M. Herre, "Current Status of Surgery for Ventricular Tachyarrhythmias," *Surgical Clinics of North America* 65(1985):571.

42. P.J. Markmann and J. Chellemi, "Surgical Management of Ventricular Tachycardia," *Heart and Lung* 13(1984):622.

43. Wetstein, Landymore, and Herre, "Status of Surgery."

44. H. Garan et al., "Electrophysiologic Studies before and after Myocardial Revascularization in Patients with Life-threatening Ventricular Arrhythmias," *American Journal of Cardiology* 51(1983):519.

45. Wetstein, Landymore, and Herre, "Status of Surgery."

46. J.M. Miller, "Surgery for Ventricular Tachycardia," *Cardio* 3(1986):34.

47. C.D. Swerdlow et al., "Results of Operations for Ventricular Tachycardia in 105 Patients," *Journal of Thoracic and Cardiovascular Surgery* 92(1986):105.

48. Markmann and Chellemi, "Surgical Management."

49. M.K. Douglas, "The Use of Electrophysiologic Studies in the Management of Recurrent Ventricular Tachyarrhythmias," in M.K. Douglas and J.A. Shinn, eds., *Advances in Cardiovascular Nursing* (Rockville, Md.: Aspen Publishers, Inc., 1985).

50. J.A. Salerno et al., "Ventricular Tachycardia in Post-Myocardial Infarction Patients: Preoperative and Intraoperative Mapping," *European Heart Journal* 7(1986):157.

51. C. Summers and S.R. O'Mara, "Assessment and Treatment of Life-threatening Ventricular Arrhythmias: The Role of Programmed Electrical Stimulation, Intraoperative Mapping, and Endocardial Resection," *Heart and Lung* 14(1985):130.

52. Douglas, "Electrophysiologic Studies."

53. Salerno et al., "Ventricular Tachycardia."

54. T.D. Ivey et al., "Surgical Management of Refractory Ventricular Arrhythmias in Patients with Prior Inferior Myocardial Infarction," *Journal of Thoracic and Cardiovascular Surgery* 89(1985):369.

55. Miller, "Surgery for Tachycardia."

56. G.J. Klein and G.M. Guiraudon, "Surgical Therapy of Cardiac Arrhythmias," *Cardiology Clinics* 1(1983):323.

57. Wetstein, Landymore, and Herre, "Current Status of Surgery."

58. Ibid.

59. Klein and Guiraudon, "Surgical Therapy for Arrhythmias."

60. Wetstein, Landymore, and Herre, "Status of Surgery."

61. Ivey et al., "Surgical Management."

62. A.H. Harkin, L.N. Horowitz, and M.E. Josephson, "The Surgical Management of Ventricular Tachycardia," *Annals of Thoracic Surgery* 30(1980):499.

63. D.A. Ott et al., "Cryoablative Techniques in the Treatment of Cardiac Tachyarrhythmias," *Annals of Thoracic Surgery* 43(1987):138.

64. Wetstein, Landymore, and Herre, "Status of Surgery."

65. Jackson, "Sustained and Nonsustained Tachycardia."

66. Miller, "Surgery for Tachycardia."

67. Ibid.

68. Wetstein, Landymore, and Herre, "Status of Surgery."

69. Ibid.

70. Miller, "Surgery for Tachycardia."

71. M.M. Scheinman and J.C. Davis, "Catheter Ablation for Treatment of Tachyarrhythmias: Present Role and Potential Promise," *Circulation* 73(1986):10.

72. Ibid.

73. J.G. Selle et al., "Successful Clinical Laser Ablation of Ventricular Tachycardia: A Promising New Therapeutic Method," *Annals of Thoracic Surgery* 42(1986):380.

74. Ibid.

75. J.M. Isner et al., "Laser Photoablation of Pathological Endocardium: In Vitro Findings Suggesting a New Approach to the Surgical Treatment of Refractory Arrhythmias and Restrictive Cardiomyopathy," *Annals of Thoracic Surgery* 39(1985):201.

76. Summers and O'Mara, "Life-threatening Arrhythmias."

77. K. McCauley and R.C. Polomano, "Acute Pain: A Nursing Perspective with Cardiac Surgical Patients," *Topics in Clinical Nursing* 2(1980):45.

78. Wetstein, Landymore, and Herre, "Status of Surgery."

79. Douglas, "Electrophysiologic Studies."

80. D.S. Echt et al., "Clinical Experience, Complications, and Survival in 70 Patients with the Automatic Implantable Cardioverter-Defibrillator," *Circulation* 71(1985):289.

81. M. Mirowski et al., "Clinical Performance of the Implantable Cardioverter-Defibrillator," *PACE* 7(1984):1345.

82. Cardiac Pacemakers, Inc., *Patient Manual for the CPI Automatic Implantable Cardioverter Defibrillator (AICD System)* (St. Paul: Cardiac Pacemakers, Inc., 1985).

83. St. Luke's Samaritan Health Care, Inc., *Living with an Automatic Implantable Cardioverter Defibrillator (AICD) Unit* (Milwaukee: St. Luke's Samaritan Health Care, Inc., 1986).

84. D.K. Noel et al., "Challenging Concerns for Patients with Automatic Implantable Cardioverter Defibrillators," *Focus on Critical Care* 13(1986):50.

85. S.S. Crocetti et al., "Some Lifesaving Advice," *American Journal of Nursing* 86(1986):1006.

86. J.M. Bryant, P. Pardoe, and B.J. Riegel, "Care of the Patient with an Automatic Implantable Cardioverter-Defibrillator," in B.J. Riegel and L.W. Dreifus, eds., *Dreifus's Pacemaker Therapy: An Interprofessional Approach* (Philadelphia: F.A. Davis Company, 1986).

87. J.N. Wetherbee et al., "Subcutaneous Patch Electrode: A Means to Obviate Thoracotomy for Implantation of the Automatic Implantable Cardioverter Defibrillator System? " *Circulation* 72, Suppl. 3 (1985):384.

88. D.K. Cooper et al., "The Impact of the Automatic Implantable Defibrillator on Quality of Life," *Clinical Progress in Electrophysiology and Pacing* 4(1986):306.

89. S.C. Vlay, "The Automatic Internal Cardioverter-Defibrillator: Comprehensive Clinical Follow-up, Economic and Social Impact: The Stony Brook Experience," *American Heart Journal* 112(1986):189.

90. D.S. Echt, "Potential Hazards of Implanted Devices for the Electrical Control of Tachyarrhythmias," *PACE* 7(1984):580.

91. L.P. Mandel and L.A. Cobb, "A Survey of CPR Training in the Community," *Circulation* 68, Suppl. 3 (1983):284.

92. P.M. Guzy et al., "Psychological Consequences of CPR Training for Families of High Risk Cardiac Patients," *Circulation* 68, Suppl. 3 (1983):284.

93. K. Chadda and R. Kammerer, "Patient and Family Acceptance of Home Defibrillation and CPR Program," *Circulation* Suppl. 2 (1984):463.

94. W.D. Weaver et al., "Training Family of Victims at Risk for Cardiac Arrest in the Use of an Automatic External Defibrillator," *Circulation* Suppl. 3 (1985):9.

Chapter 6

Understanding Pacemaker Therapy

Patricia Wolff, RN, MSN, CCRN

Sophistication in microcircuitry has led to complex multiprogrammable (three or more programmable functions) single- and dual-chamber pacemakers to preserve atrioventricular (AV) synchrony.[1] The tremendous technologic growth and development in programmable (ability to alter a function noninvasively) functions and types of pacemaker systems make understanding, diagnosis, and troubleshooting increasingly complicated. It is imperative that nurses who care for recipients of physiologic (atrioventricular synchronous) pacers become familiar with the new generation of pulse generators. Without this understanding, the ability to differentiate normal pacemaker function from malfunction is severely limited.

The emphasis of this chapter is dual-chamber (atrial and ventricular) pacemakers. Since the advanced clinician has understanding and experience with basic ventricular demand pacemakers, discussion related to basic pacing and troubleshooting is not included. Concepts, functions, and causes of malfunctions are focused on physiologic pacing.

INTER-SOCIETY COMMISSION FOR HEART DISEASE CODE

As the complexity in pacemaker technology increased in the 1970s, confusion and misunderstanding grew from the lack of clearly defined terminology. Various terms were used by different people in different ways. In 1974, a three-letter code was established by the *Inter-Society Commission for Heart Disease Resources (ICHD)* to provide uniformity in pacemaker mode identification.[2,3] The development of multiprogrammable systems and special functions necessitated the addition of two letters in 1980. Table 6-1 shows the modes currently available.

For most purposes and convenience, the first three letters of the ICHD code are sufficient to describe pacemakers. The first letter refers to the chamber(s)

Table 6-1 Five-Position Pacemaker Code (ICHD)

Position Category	I Chamber(s) Paced	II Chamber(s) Sensed	III Mode of Response	IV Programmable Functions	V Special Tachyarrhythmia Functions
Letters/interpretation	A-atrium	A-atrium	I-inhibited	P-programmable (rate and/or output)	B-bursts
	V-ventricle	V-ventricle	T-triggered	M-multiprogrammable (3 or more functions)	N-normal rate competition
	D-dual	D-dual	D-dual†	C-multiprogrammable with telemetry	
	S-single chamber*	O-none S-single chamber	O-none R-reverse	O-none	S-scanning E-external

†Atrial triggered, ventricular inhibited.
*May be used for atrial or ventricular pacing.

Source: Adapted from "A Revised Code for Pacemaker Identification" by V. Parsonnet, *Circulation*, Vol. 64, No. 1, p. 61A, with permission of the American Heart Association, Inc., © 1981.

that is paced. The second letter indicates the chamber(s) where electrical activity is sensed. Examples are shown in Figure 6-1. The mode of response, the third letter, refers to how the pacemaker responds to sensed impulses. If the response is "inhibited" by a sensed signal, the pacemaker does not deliver a pacing signal. When sensed signals cause "triggering," a pacing signal is delivered. "Dual" indicates that a sensed signal inhibits an atrial signal while triggering a ventricular signal. "Reverse" indicates the pacer is inhibited at lower rates but paces at faster rates.[4]

The fourth letter identifies the programmable functions, also listed in Table 6-1. The letter "C" refers to multiprogrammable functions with telemetry, which allows noninvasive interrogation of the pacemaker functions. The fifth letter defines the special functions available for treatment of tachydysrhythmias.

Since the ICHD code describes a pacemaker in terms of how it functions, it is basic to understanding advanced pacemaker modalities and assessing functions and malfunctions.

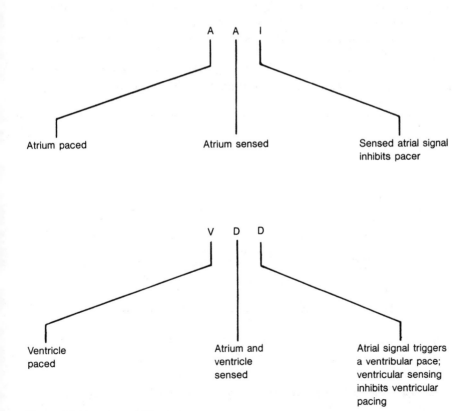

Figure 6-1 Three-Letter ICHD Code

PHYSIOLOGIC TIMING CYCLES

When discussing pacemaker functions and intervals, terminology can cause confusion because numerous terms are applied to identical functions.

The *pacing interval* is the interval between two consecutive ventricular pacer spikes (Figure 6-2). It is also called the *automatic interval, pulse repetition rate, pacemaker rate, lower rate limit, minimum rate,* and *V-V interval.* Pacing intervals are measured in milliseconds (msec) and determine the number of pacing pulses that may be elicited per minute (ppm). In physiologic pacing, the pacing rate is commonly communicated in milliseconds. For example, a pacing rate of 80 ppm produces a pacing interval of 750 msec.

The *AV delay interval* is the time between an intrinsic or a paced atrial event and the ventricular pacer spike (see Figure 6-2). It is an artificial "P-R interval" that determines when synchronous ventricular pacing occurs. The AV delay interval is also known as the *AV sequential interval.* In programming the AV interval, the patient's AV conduction time, or *P-R interval,* is considered. When the programmed AV interval and intrinsic P-R interval are closely approximate, competition for ventricular capture is created, and fusion beats frequently occur. This benign but unnecessary pacing is wasteful since it drains the battery and reduces the life of the pacemaker.

The *ventricular escape interval (VEI)* is the time between an intrinsic R wave and a consecutively paced ventricular beat. The VEI is also known as the *V-V*

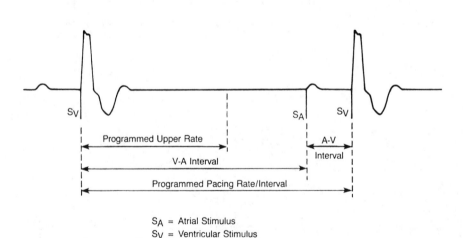

S_A = Atrial Stimulus
S_V = Ventricular Stimulus

Figure 6-2 Physiologic Timing Cycles. Programmed pacing is also called the V-V interval. *Source:* Reprinted from *Symbiotics Series: Selecting the DDD Patient,* p. 6, with permission of Medtronics, Inc., © 1984.

interval. It is the interval or rate below which the patient's intrinsic ventricular rate must fall to activate pacing. Frequently, it is the same as the pacing interval. However, when hysteresis is used, the VEI is programmed longer than the pacing interval. Nurses must be cognizant of the difference when interpreting physiologic pacing rhythms.

The time between the paced or intrinsic R wave and consecutively paced P wave is the *atrial escape interval (AEI).* After each sensed or paced R wave, the pacer's atrial timing cycle is activated. Some manufacturers refer to the AEI as the *ventriculoatrial (V-A) interval.* The V-A interval equals the difference between the AV delay interval and the VEI, as illustrated in Figure 6-2. If an intrinsic P wave or R wave is not sensed during the AEI, an atrial stimulus is emitted.

MODES OF CARDIAC PACING

The *modes* of cardiac pacing refer to the different methods of pacing the heart and the interface between the patient's cardiac rhythm and the pacemaker. Many patients require only a simple mode of pacing, ventricular demand. However, a significant number of patients need the additional contribution to cardiac output provided by AV synchrony, which is achieved with physiologic pacing.

For practical reasons, the emphasis in this chapter is placed on physiologic pacemaker modes, particularly those commonly used in clinical practice. Pacemaker modes are presented by their ICHD code. Although important, pacemakers used in the treatment of tachydysrhythmias are not discussed.

Atrial Demand Pacing: AAI

In *atrial demand (or atrial inhibited) pacing, AAI* means that the atrium is paced, atrial activity is sensed, and sensed signals inhibit the pacer. Sensing of electrical impulses occurs in the atrium to avoid competition between the intrinsic rhythm and the pacemaker. When a P wave is sensed, the atrial pacing signal is inhibited. Atrial pacing occurs if a spontaneous P wave is not sensed during the escape interval. Since ventricular events cannot be sensed (unless retrograde conduction occurs), the atrial pacer "ignores" ventricular ectopy, shown in Figure 6-3.

For effective atrial pacing, AV conduction must be intact. Many patients may benefit hemodynamically from atrial pacing because of the contribution of atrial systole to cardiac output. Although useful, it is a less frequently used mode, except after cardiac surgery, due to the frequency of lead difficulties and malfunction.[5-7] As atrial leads become more reliable, the prevalence of permanent AAI pacing is expected to grow.

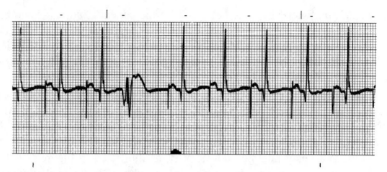

Figure 6-3 AAI pacing. The atrial pacing rate is 94/min (640 msec). Without R wave sensing, the ventricular ectopic beat is ignored and the atrial spike is delivered into the R wave.

Ventricular Demand Pacing: VVI

This is the most common mode of pacing, temporary or permanent. *Ventricular demand pacing* is also known as *ventricular-inhibited, R wave inhibited, standby, R suppressed*, and *noncompetitive inhibited pacing*.[8] The ICHD code for this pacing mode (VVI) has helped clarify that all these terms describe the same mode.

With VVI pacemakers, the ventricle is paced, ventricular activity is sensed, and sensed signals inhibit the pacer. When an intrinsic R wave is sensed, the pacemaker is inhibited. If an intrinsic R wave does not occur, the subsequent beat is paced (Figure 6-4). Advantages of VVI pacing include its simplicity, increased longevity, small size, low cost, and low complication rate.[9] The disadvantages are related primarily to hemodynamic changes. However, patients who do not require frequent pacing or the contribution of atrial kick tolerate ventricular demand pacing well.

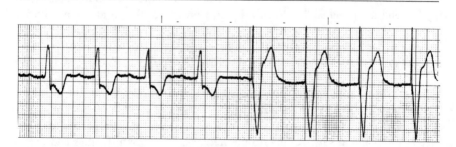

Figure 6-4 VVI pacing. The sinus rhythm gradually slows until ventricular pacing is initiated at a rate of 62/min (960 msec).

Atrial Synchronous Ventricular Inhibited Pacing: VDD

This pacing mode is also known as *P wave synchronous ventricular inhibited (ASVIP)*, *atrial tracking*, *atrial synchronous*, and *atrial sensing ventricular inhibited pacing*. A VAT device was known as *atrial synchronous pacing* in previous years. The ICHD code *VAT* indicates that the ventricle is paced, sensing occurs only in the atrium, and a P wave sensed in the atrium triggers (initiates) synchronous ventricular pacing. The VDD system has essentially replaced the VAT mode, which, without R wave sensing, permitted ventricular competition with life-threatening ventricular dysrhythmias.

In the VDD mode, the ventricle is paced, and the atrium and ventricle are sensed. A sensed P wave results in ventricular triggering after a programmed AV interval. If a P wave and R wave are sensed, the pacer will be inhibited, and there will be no pacing. When a P wave, but no R wave, is sensed, the ventricle is paced (see Figure 6-5a). Thus, the pacemaker "tracks" the P waves and paces the ventricle synchronously. When neither the P wave nor the R wave is sensed, the VDD pacer reverts to VVI pacing at a programmed rate (Figure 6-5b). Physiologic pacing occurs so long as the SA node functions normally or faster than the ventricular escape interval. Should the SA node fail or fall below the lower rate limit, VVI pacing will be initiated.

During VVI pacing, the atrial electrode is alert (detecting) for P waves. If the SA node regains function, VDD pacing ensues. As in any tracking (atrial sensing, which triggers synchronous ventricular pacing) mode in which the ventricles are paced 1:1 with a sinus or atrial rhythm, undesirable atrial tachydysrhythmias are possible. Upper rate limits and responses, which have been programmed, are often activated to avoid this problem. To summarize, the VDD mode responds in four ways: normal intrinsic rhythm sensed with no pacing, atrial tracking with ventricular pacing, absent intrinsic rhythm with ventricular demand pacing, and upper rate pacing.

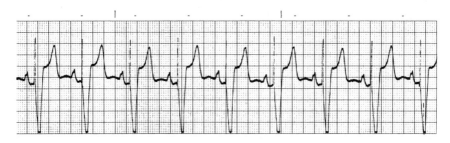

Figure 6-5a VDD pacing. Atrial synchronous ventricular pacing is shown. P waves are sensed and followed by ventricular pacing since AV conduction fails to occur.

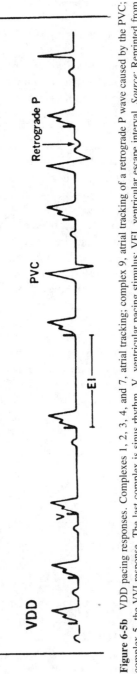

Figure 6-5b VDD pacing responses. Complexes 1, 2, 3, 4, and 7, atrial tracking; complex 9, atrial tracking of a retrograde P wave caused by the PVC; complex 5, the VVI response. The last complex is sinus rhythm. V, ventricular pacing stimulus; VEI, ventricular escape interval. *Source:* Reprinted from *New England Journal of Medicine*, Vol. 311, No. 26, p. 1676, with permission of the Massachusetts Medical Society, © 1984.

Asynchronous Atrioventricular Sequential Pacing: DOO

As with fixed-rate ventricular pacing, this fixed-rate pacing mode is now obsolete except when a magnet is used to evaluate dual-chamber pacers. A magnet placed over the pacemaker closes its reed switch and prevents sensing. Thus, the pacemaker AV sequentially paces asynchronously. As a permanent pacer, DOO pacing is hazardous because it paces irrespective of the patient's underlying rhythm and results in competition.

In the *DOO mode*, the atrium is paced. At the end of the programmed AV delay interval, the ventricle is paced. There is no sensing function. Thus, DOO pacing is used only for brief periods during follow-up clinic visits.

Atrioventricular Sequential Pacing: DVI

The AV sequential pacemaker is the most commonly used temporary dual-chamber pacer since it offers many benefits of physiologic pacing. In the *DVI mode*, the atrium and ventricle are paced, sensing occurs only in the ventricle, and a sensed R wave inhibits atrial and/or ventricular pacing. A concept basic to understanding and analyzing DVI functions is that only ventricular events can be sensed. P waves are not sensed.

An atrioventricular-inhibited response (no pacing) occurs when an R wave is sensed within the V-A interval (atrial escape interval) as illustrated in A, Figure 6-6. On electrocardiogram (ECG), the patient's intrinsic rhythm is observed. Atrial pacing occurs when an R wave is not sensed during the V-A interval but is sensed during the programmed AV delay interval (B, Figure 6-6). AV sequential pacing results when R waves are not sensed during the V-A or AV intervals, as seen in C, Figure 6-6. Atrial synchronous ventricular pacing (VDD) is not possible since there is no atrial sensing in the DVI mode. The major difficulty experienced by clinicians in rhythm interpretation is realizing that there is no P wave sensing.

Without atrial sensing, pacing in a DVI mode can result in competition between the intrinsic atrial rhythm and the atrial pacing stimulus (Figure 6-7). When atrial competition occurs, an atrial stimulus can fall into the atrial "vulnerable" period and cause atrial fibrillation.[10] Furman and Cooper[11] reported that atrial fibrillation results in 15% of patients with DVI devices.

In patients with AV block, physiologic pacing in a DVI mode is achieved only when the pacing rate exceeds the patient's intrinsic rate. Faster atrial rhythms cause loss of AV synchrony, and the hemodynamic benefits of dual-chamber pacing are lost. In temporary pacing, this problem is simply remedied by increasing the pacing rate to override the intrinsic rate.

Along with dual-chamber pacing, a new generation of pacemaker complications emerged, followed by a proliferation of alternative versions of pacemaker

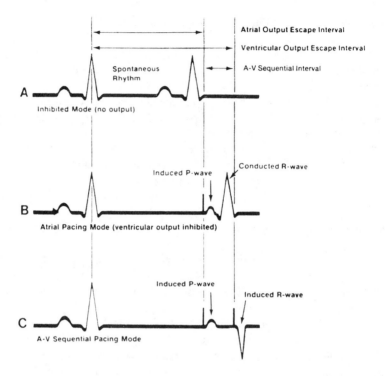

Figure 6-6 AV sequential (DVI) pacing responses. *Source*: Reprinted from *AV Sequential Demand Pulse Generator Manual* p. 3, with permission of Medtronics, Inc., © 1978.

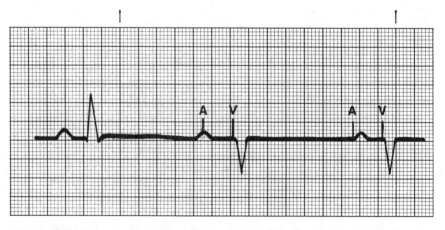

Figure 6-7 DVI pacing with atrial competition. In the DVI mode, atrial activity is not sensed. Competition between the intrinsic rhythm and the atrial pacing rate commonly occurs. *A*, atrial spike; *V*, ventricular spike.

modes. One hazardous complication is a type of *crosstalk* (i.e., ventricular electrode sensing of atrial pacing stimuli). Atrial stimulation commonly requires high output currents, which may be concurrently sensed by the ventricular electrode. When sensed by the ventricular electrode, the atrial signal is interpreted as an R wave, inhibits ventricular pacing, and results in ventricular asystole. This sequence of events can occur in the *"uncommitted" DVI mode* (Figure 6-8). *Uncommitted* means that an atrial stimulus is delivered and may or may not be followed by a ventricular spike, depending on the circumstances. To obviate the problem of crosstalk, permanent *"committed" DVI* (despite the need, a ventricular stimulus follows each atrial spike) systems were developed and automatically elicit a ventricular spike, whether or not an intrinsic R wave occurs. There is no ventricular sensing during the AV delay interval after an atrial spike.

The "committed" version (Figure 6-8) created another problem: failure to sense R waves, especially PVCs during the AV interval. Thus, ventricular spikes may be noted to occur in the T wave, risking ventricular tachycardia or fibrillation.[12]

"Semi-committed" (modified committed) versions have essentially replaced the other permanent DVI pacing systems (Figure 6-9). This device provides a short ventricular refractory period or "blanking" period during and immediately after the atrial pacing signal to prevent crosstalk. Ventricular safety pacing is an added feature to prevent inhibition by false signals, such as electromagnetic interference. These two functions are not available on temporary AV sequential pacemakers.

Atrioventricular Universal Pacing: DDD

The DDD pacemaker is the most advanced permanent pacemaker currently available. As designated by the ICHD code, both chambers are paced, both chambers are sensed, and triggering and inhibition responses are activated. The *DDD mode* is also referred to as *fully automatic* or *dual-chamber demand pacing*.

There are basically four ways the DDD pacemaker may respond (Figure 6-10):

1. No pacing occurs if the intrinsic rhythm (P-QRS) exceeds the pacing interval, in beat 5.
2. Atrial pacing (AAI) is initiated if a P-QRS complex is not sensed during the atrial escape interval. If AV conduction is intact, and the P-R interval is shorter than the AV delay interval, ventricular pacing is inhibited, in beat 2.
3. Atrial synchronous pacing (VDD) occurs when P waves but no R waves are sensed, in beat 6. Ventricular pacing results after the programmed AV delay interval is in 1:1 synchrony with the atrial rate. Atrial tracking with synchronous ventricular pacing is maintained, up to the upper rate limit.

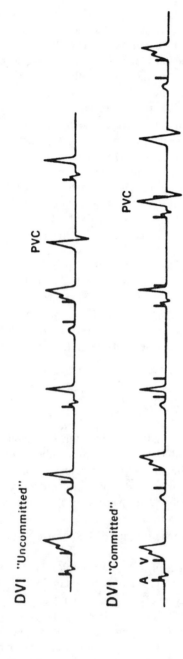

Figure 6-8 DVI pacing modes. The "uncommitted" mode shows ventricular sensing. In the "committed" mode, the pacer is committed (obliged) to deliver a ventricular spike following the atrial spike, irrespective of R waves. *V*, ventricular pacing stimulus; *A*, atrial pacing stimulus; *PVC*, premature ventricular complex. *Source:* Reprinted from *New England Journal of Medicine*, Vol. 311, No. 26, p. 1676, with permission of the Massachusetts Medical Society, © 1984.

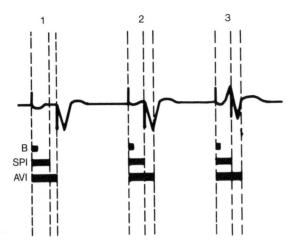

Figure 6-9 The safety pacing function. Complex 1, no activity is sensed by the ventricular circuit during the safety pacing interval (SPI). Therefore, the triggered ventricular response occurs at the end of the AV interval (AVI). Complexes 2 and 3, delivery of the ventricular pulse output at the end of the SPI in response to ventricular sensing of the atrial pacing stimulus and a premature ventricular contraction, respectively; *B*, blanking interval. *Source*: Reprinted from *Critical Care Nurse*, Vol. 6, No. 5, p. 23, with permission of Hospital Publications Inc., © 1986.

4. Universal AV (DDD) pacing is initiated when no intrinsic activity is sensed, in beats 1 and 4. At the end of the atrial escape interval, an atrial stimulus is delivered. After the AV delay interval, a ventricular spike is emitted. The DDD pacer can also function in other modes. VVI, VDD, DOO, DVI, and DDT modes may be programmed in many DDD pacemaker models to meet patients' needs.

Due to the complexity of DDD pacing, several problems related to programming may arise. To avoid problems, most DDD pacers have multiprogrammable functions.

A temporary DDD pacing mode is available to test for retrograde conduction. This DDD mode permits P wave triggered atrial pacing, P wave synchronized, and R wave inhibited ventricular pacing.[13] Since pacemakers cannot recognize the difference between retrograde and antegrade P waves, retrograde P waves can be detected. With P wave triggered atrial pacing, the pacemaker is triggered to send out a pacing signal into each sensed P wave. Thus, sensed P waves are marked by pacer spikes, as illustrated in Figure 6-11. During VVI pacing, retrograde (or V-A) conduction occurs. Retrograde P waves, which are frequently concealed in the T wave, may be diagnosed since the temporary DDD mode detects and marks them. In addition, V-A conduction time can be measured from

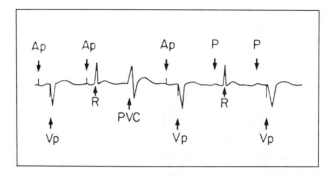

Figure 6-10 Simulated drawing shows the various responses of the DDD pacing mode. From left to right, AV sequential pacing (Ap-Vp); atrial pacing with intrinsic AV conduction resulting in inhibition of ventricular output (Ap-R); premature ventricular complex (PVC) with resetting of escape interval; AV sequential pacing (Ap-Vp); normal sinus complex (P-R) resulting in inhibition of both atrial and ventricular outputs; sinus depolarization that fails to conduct intrinsically to the ventricles, producing a triggered ventricular response (P-Vp). *Source*: Reprinted from *Critical Care Nurse*, Vol. 6, No. 5, p. 19, with permission of Hospital Publications Inc., © 1986.

the preceding R wave to the marked P wave. As a result, appropriate atrial refractory periods may be determined to prevent the complication of pacemaker-mediated tachycardia (PMT).

Another programmable but temporary mode of some DDD pacers is the DDT mode. The DDT mode for P wave triggered atrial pacing, P wave synchronized, and R wave triggered ventricular pacing has diagnostic and therapeutic uses.[14]

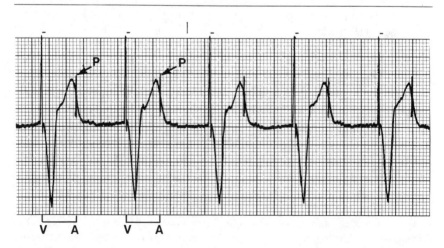

Figure 6-11 P wave triggered atrial pacing. Sensed P waves, hidden in the T waves, are "marked" by a pacer spike which permits recognition and measurement of V-A (retrograde) conduction.

Its noninvasive clinical uses include evaluation of atrial and ventricular lead sensing, determination of false electrical signal sensing, and facilitation of overdrive pacing therapy. Evaluation of both atrial and ventricular lead sensing is possible because all sensed impulses trigger a pacing signal. The pacing spikes, therefore, mark all sensed beats. Thus, if all P waves and QRS complexes are marked, then lead sensing will be confirmed. When a P-QRS complex appears without a spike, faulty lead sensing may be detected. False electrical signals cause pacer spikes to appear independent of P-QRS complexes. This diagnosis assists in identifying electromagnetic interference. The DDT mode is a temporary but useful diagnostic tool.

THE PACEMAKER SYNDROME

Permanent ventricular demand pacing has been used for 30 years in the treatment of sinus node and AV conduction disturbances and in fascicular blocks. Although some patients did not tolerate pacing well, the causes were attributed to progressive cardiac pathology and myocardial decompensation. In 1969, Mitsui and colleagues[15] reported the first patients who complained of low cardiac output symptoms unrelated to pacemaker failure. However, it was not until the past decade that *pacemaker syndrome* was recognized by the symptoms, listed in Exhibit 6-1, of low cardiac output and congestive heart failure.

Four major factors causing adverse hemodynamic effects precipitate pacemaker syndrome: loss of atrial contribution to cardiac output, retrograde or ventriculoatrial conduction, reciprocal beats, and fixed-rate pacing.[16] These factors may also be considered the major hemodynamic disadvantages of ventricular pacing.

Exhibit 6-1 Signs and Symptoms of Pacemaker Syndrome

Dizziness
Confusion
Syncope
Hypotension
Orthostasis
Easy fatigability
Dyspnea
Orthopnea
Hacky cough
Edema
Palpitations
Chest pain

Loss of Atrial Contribution

Normally, atrial kick contributes 15% to 35% of ventricular filling to stroke volume.[17,18] However, atrial contribution may exceed 35% in patients with cardiac deterioration. During ventricular pacing, atrial kick is lost, and cardiac output is reduced. From clinical observation, patients with poor left ventricular function after cardiac surgery exemplify this effect dramatically when paced in a VVI mode. In a VVI mode at a rate of 70 ppm, some patients show an immediate fall in mean arterial pressure below 65 mmHg and a precipitous drop in cardiac index below 2.0 L/min/m^2. In patients with atrial leads, nurses should immediately initiate atrial or dual-chamber pacing.

Another problem with loss of atrial systole immediately preceding ventricular contraction is the delay in tricuspid and mitral valve closure. Without atrial systole, mitral and tricuspid regurgitation occurs when the valves close during ventricular contraction. Effective stroke volume is reduced, by 30% in some patients, because of mitral regurgitation during right ventricular pacing.[19]

Ventriculoatrial (V-A) Conduction

Retrograde, or V-A, conduction commonly occurs during ventricular pacing. After depolarizing the ventricles, the pacemaker-initiated impulse can travel retrograde through the AV node, backwards into the atria, and depolarize the atria (Figure 6-12). Patients may retain 1:1 V-A conduction despite complete antegrade AV node block.[20] V-A conduction causes recurrent atrial activation at a time when the AV valves are closed during the ventricular ejection phase. As the atria contract against closed AV valves, the "negative atrial kick" produces backflow and increases pressures in the systemic and pulmonary veins.[21] Negative atrial kick adversely affects cardiac output. Intact V-A conduction can be identified during implantation and is an important factor in identifying patients at risk for pacemaker syndrome.[22]

Reciprocal Beats

Another consequence of retrograde conduction is *reciprocal,* or *echo, beats.* Following retrograde activation of the atria, the impulse may circle the atria, re-enter the AV node, and conduct antegrade through the ventricles immediately after the paced beat.[23] Due to limited diastolic filling time, echo beats may not be hemodynamically effective and may further compromise cardiac output.

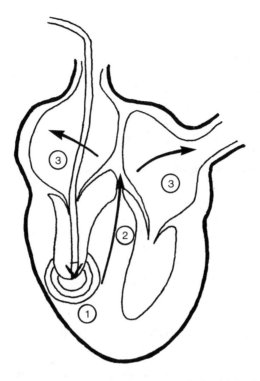

Figure 6-12 Retrograde conduction. The diagram shows ventriculoatrial depolarization. *1*, pacemaker impulse; *2*, impulse conduction backwards through the AV node; *3*, retrograde depolarization of the atria.

Fixed-Rate Pacing

A simple ventricular demand pacemaker can pace only at a programmed or fixed rate. It cannot increase heart rate to meet increased metabolic demands of activity. Therefore, many patients' activities are significantly restricted. Patients may develop weakness, fatigue, and shortness of breath with only mild exertion. These patients commonly respond favorably to the atrial kick provided by DDD pacemaker therapy.

INDICATIONS FOR PACING

In recent years, the number of permanent pacemakers implanted has risen dramatically. Studies[24,25] reflect on overzealous use of this therapeutic modality. A Joint American College of Cardiology/American Heart Association (AHA)

Task Force published a special report in 1984 on guidelines for permanent pacemaker implantation.[26] One objective of the AHA Task Force was to make recommendations on the indications and contraindications in the use of cardiac pacing. Table 6-2 is a summary of the Task Force's recommendations.

The Task Force defined conditions appropriate for the selection of each pacing mode. The category *undecided* lists conditions in which there is a lack of agreement regarding the appropriateness of a specific pacing mode. Generally, physiologic pacing modes are indicated in patients who may benefit from or require AV synchrony to improve cardiac output. Persistent atrial tachydysrhythmias that cannot be pharmacologically controlled preclude the implantation of dual-chamber pacemakers.

The indications for pacing approved by Medicare were explored and compiled to assist clinicians.[27] In general, pacemaker syndrome (pacemaker-related heart failure) is a common condition warranting the use of a dual-chamber pacer. Medicare approval depends on documentation of assessments reflecting pacemaker syndrome. Nurses share the responsibility for accurate and complete documentation of the signs and symptoms in these patients.

PROGRAMMABLE FUNCTIONS OF CARDIAC PACEMAKERS

Programmable pacemakers are those in which various electronically controlled functions can be reprogrammed noninvasively (Exhibit 6-2). In addition, different pacing modes can be programmed to best meet the patient's needs. Nurses must keep abreast of the rapidly developing technology to interpret and differentiate pacer functions from malfunctions accurately. Approximately 15% to 20% of reoperations are unnecessary if proper programming is provided.[28] Discussion focuses on the programmable functions not available with simple pacemakers.

Atrioventricular Delay Interval

In the event that AV conduction is intermittently or completely blocked (or prolonged), the *AV delay interval* (Figure 6-2) allows for ventricular pacing within a hemodynamically beneficial time period. When an atrial signal is elicited or an intrinsic P wave is sensed, the AV timing cycle is activated. During this time, the ventricular sensor is alert or responsive to incoming signals. If an R wave is sensed, the ventricular pacing signal is inhibited. If an R wave is not sensed, the ventricle is paced. The AV delay should be programmed at an interval that does not compete with normal AV conduction to prevent pseudomalfunction rhythms.

Table 6-2 Indications for Permanent Pacemakers

Mode	Appropriate	Undecided	Inappropriate
AAI	Symptomatic SA node dysfunction w/intact AV conduction	Overdrive SVT or ventricular dysrhythmias Symptomatic bradycardia	Pre-existing AV delay or block Atrial flutter, fibrillation, or asystole
VVI	Symptomatic bradycardia w/o pacemaker syndrome	Bradycardia w/senility, terminal illness, intact V-A conduction	Pacemaker syndrome Congestive failure, need for rate responsiveness
VDD	AV block w/intact atrial rate and need for AV synchrony	Normal sinus rhythm w/AV conduction	Frequent SVT, atrial fib, flutter, inadequate atrial complexes
DVI	Symptomatic atrial bradycardia w/need for AV synchrony Documented pacemaker syndrome	Overdrive pacing SVT w/drug SSS w/ or w/o drug	Frequent SVT, atrial fib, atrial flutter
DDD	Requirement of AV synchrony	AV block or SSS and stable atrial rate Tachydysrhythmias inhibited by controlled atrial and ventricular rates	SVT, atrial fib, atrial flutter Inadequate atrial complexes

SSS = Sick sinus syndrome; SVT = Supraventricular tachycardia.

Exhibit 6-2 Multiprogrammable Functions

Rate
Output
Sensitivity
Mode of pacing operation
AV delay
Hysteresis
Conversion from bipolar to unipolar pacing
Ventricular safety pacing
Ventricular blanking period
Refractory periods
Lead polarity
Upper rate limits
Mode of upper rate response

Refractory Periods

A *refractory period* is a programmable interval during which the pacemaker is unresponsive to an electrical stimulus. The refractory period follows a sensed R wave or paced impulse and prevents sensing or pacing during the programmed interval. Refractory periods are necessary to prevent the undesirable sensing of afterpotentials or T waves. Dual-chamber pacemakers require programmable atrial and ventricular refractory periods to avoid the numerous potential pacer-induced dysrhythmias.

The *atrial refractory period (ARP)* or *total ARP* is the period of time when the pacer's atrial sensing is unreceptive to electrical signals. As illustrated in Figure 6-13, the total ARP is the sum of the AV delay interval plus the post-ventricular atrial refractory period (PVARP). A pacer's PVARP extends throughout the ventricular event. R wave sensing by the atrial electrode (crosstalk) and retrograde P wave sensing are avoided by the PVARP.

The *ventricular refractory period* is the period of time after a sensed or paced R wave when ventricular sensing is unresponsive to electrical signals. It is usually programmed to extend past the T wave (Figure 6-13) to prevent oversensing (T wave sensing).

Hysteresis

Hysteresis refers to an escape interval or rate below which the patient's intrinsic rate must fall to activate pacing. When the hysteresis mode is programmed, it provides an escape interval that is longer than the programmed automatic or pacing interval. The design maximizes the opportunity for intrinsic cardiac ac-

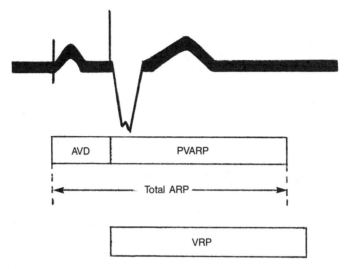

Figure 6-13 Refractory periods in dual-chamber pacing. *AVD*, atrioventricular delay period; *PVARP*, postventricular atrial refractory period; *ARP*, atrial refractory period; *VRP*, ventricular refractory period.

tivity to control the rhythm.[29] In pacemakers without hysteresis, the escape interval equals the pacing interval. Hysteresis offers a broader range for sinus nodal rates while maintaining AV synchrony, which offers hemodynamic benefits over a paced rhythm. In Figure 6-14, the prolonged interval between beats 4 and 5 illustrates hysteresis. Note that the prolonged interval is followed by a regularly paced rhythm at a faster rate, the pacing rate. To prevent the misdiagnosis of "end of life" or pacemaker failure, nurses must be knowledgeable of the hysteresis function.

Hysteresis may be contraindicated in patients with frequent ventricular ectopy since it prolongs the compensatory pause. This may perpetuate the ventricular dysrhythmia and lead to symptoms of low cardiac output. When low cardiac output from ectopy is coupled with a prolonged compensatory pause, the effective cardiac output is significantly reduced. If this problem occurs at any time, hysteresis will be simply programmed off.

Triggered Mode

In some pacemakers, there is a temporary programmable mode, the triggered mode. A *triggered (synchronous) mode* emits, rather than inhibits, a pacer stimulus when a signal is sensed. In triggered modes, such as VVT and ATT, the pacemaker is programmed to deliver a pacing spike immediately upon sensing

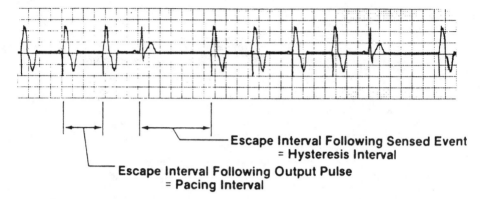

Figure 6-14 Hysteresis. A prolonged interval (hysteresis escape interval) following a sensed event is characteristic of the hysteresis function. This interval is sometimes mistaken for pacemaker malfunction. *Source:* Reprinted from *The Applications of Programmable Pacing Systems*, p. 9, with permission of Medtronics, Inc., © 1984.

an R wave in the ventricle (or P wave in the atrium). A spike is delivered into the QRS (or P wave) during the absolute refractory period, when it should be ineffective. This identifies the sensed event and denotes pacemaker discharge ("marks" the R or P wave). When an R wave is not sensed during the escape interval, pacing ensues at the programmed rate.

Permanent triggered devices were developed to prevent asystole caused by electromagnetic interference, or EMI (power lines, microwave).[30] Pacemakers, particularly with unipolar electrodes, may sense extraneous electrical signals, which results in inappropriate inhibition. This mode prevents inappropriate inhibition, but is seldom used for that purpose.[31,32] It is primarily used in two ways for temporary purposes: (1) diagnostically, for "marking" sensed signals to evaluate malfunctions (V-A conduction, crosstalk, EMI), and (2) therapeutically, for overdrive pacing of tachydysrhythmias.

Upper Rate Limit

In DDD pacing, the atria and ventricles are synchronously paced in response to sensed activity when AV conduction is delayed or blocked. The pacemaker tracks the atrial rate and rhythm. Therefore, the paced ventricular rate is directly related to and synchronous with the intrinsic atrial rate and is physiologically beneficial at rates below approximately 120 to 140 beats per minute. Potential problems occur with 1:1 tracking at higher rates. Cardiac output may be compromised by atrial tachydysrhythmias and rate-dependent angina.

To prevent ventricular tracking of rapid atrial rhythms, current DDD pacemakers have a programmable function known as the *upper rate limit* (atrial rate tracking limit, maximum tracking rate, or ventricular tracking limit). This limit protects the patient from undesirable hemodynamic consequences of excessively high ventricular pacing rates. The programmed upper rate limit (Figure 6-2) causes the pacemaker to respond to higher rates by selectively reducing the pacemaker response rate. Basically, there are three types of upper rate limit responses: Wenckebach, fixed-ratio block, and fallback.[33] Different manufacturers determine the type of response available in their products. The most common responses are the Wenckebach and block responses.

An *electronic Wenckebach*-like behavior is observed by progressive prolongation of the AV interval until a P wave occurs in the postventricular atrial refractory period, when it cannot be sensed. A ventricular response is dropped and results in an average reduction in the ventricular rate (Figure 6-15). As the atrial rate increases, more paced ventricular beats are dropped. Ventricular pacing with a Wenckebach response sustains the rate at the programmed upper rate limit. The Wenckebach response is preferred, particularly in active individuals, because of the gradual reduction in rate. An additional advantage over the 2:1 block is the gradual reduction in rate and a gradual return to a 1:1 atrial tracking rate.

The *fixed-ratio block* (Figure 6-16) results in a block response similar to a Mobitz II type 2° AV block. When the atrial rate exceeds the upper rate limit

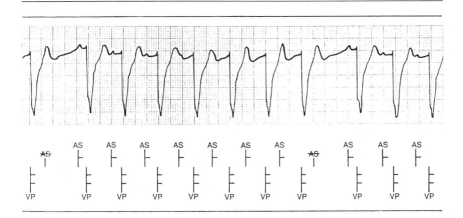

Figure 6-15 This simulated ECG illustrates a pacemaker's Wenckebach behavior when the atrial rate exceeds the programmed upper rate of 100 ppm. Note that each ventricular output that is synchronized to an atrial sensed event (AS) occurs at the rate of 100 ppm. The AV interval, however, grows progressively longer until the unused atrial sense event takes place, indicating that it occurred in the atrial refractory period. *VP*, ventricular pacing. *Source*: Reprinted from *Symbiotics Series: Managing the DDD Patient*, p. 29, with permission of Medtronics, Inc., © 1984.

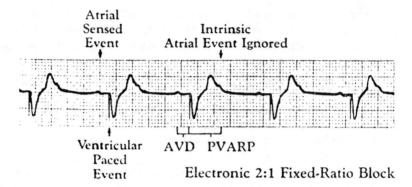

Figure 6-16 Fixed-ratio block response. In 2:1 block, every other P wave is in the atrial refractory period and is therefore ignored. At higher atrial rates, every third or fourth P wave may fall in the atrial refractory period and cause 3:1 or 4:1 block. *Source*: Reprinted from *Pacemaker Sustained Tachycardia* with permission of Intermedics, Inc., © 1984.

(URL), QRSs are dropped or blocked. Initially, the pacer drops to a 2:1 block, which abruptly reduces the effective heart rate and cardiac output by half. For example, if the upper rate limit is 150 ppm (400 msec), then the pacer will suddenly drop to a rate of 75 ppm. The AV interval remains constant so that AV synchrony is maintained. As the atrial rate increases, the degree of block increases to maintain a limited upper pacing rate. The ratio of sensed P waves to dropped QRSs increases (3:1, 4:1, etc.).

Fixed-ratio blocking is the simplest type of URL response, but the sudden drop in ventricular pacing may cause patient discomfort. Active or exercising patients do not tolerate the sudden hemodynamic alteration well.

Fallback is the third response. When the atrial rate exceeds the upper rate limit, the paced ventricular rate gradually decreases to a programmed fallback rate. The fallback rate may be set lower than the upper rate limit. It is most beneficial to patients who cannot hemodynamically tolerate sustained upper rate pacing.

Two types of fallback response may occur. A fallback response without AV synchrony results in VVI pacing at a programmed rate lower than the upper rate limit. The ventricle is paced irrespective of atrial activity. With AV synchronous pacing, a second type of fallback response produces a Wenckebach-type decrease in rate, an attempt to maintain AV synchrony.[34] This fallback response is easily distinguished from the Wenckebach response, which sustains the pacing rate at the upper rate limit.

Upper rate limit pacing is maintained in all three URL responses until the atrial rate drops below the upper rate level. DDD pacing then ensues. To evaluate an upper rate limit response, the manufacturer, model, and programmed functions of the pacer must be known.

Ventricular Blanking Period

To minimize the problem of crosstalk, many dual-chamber pacemakers have a programmable function called a *ventricular blanking period*. A blanking period is a type of ventricular refractory period during which the ventricle is unresponsive to an electrical stimulus. A ventricular blanking period is programmed for a very short interval during and after an atrial output signal (Figure 6-17). This prevents ventricular sensing of the atrial event, or crosstalk. Ventricular blanking periods range from 10 to 75 msec. Long ventricular blanking periods may cause failure to sense PVCs and allow the ventricular pacing spike to occur in the T wave.

Ventricular Safety Pacing

Ventricular safety pacing (VSP) is a function that assists in preventing inhibition of ventricular pacing caused by false electrical signals or interference. The sensing circuit in the pulse generator is responsible for recognizing true

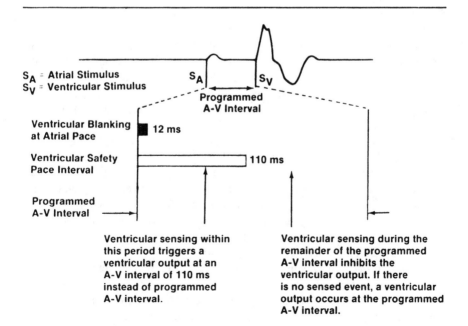

Figure 6-17 Ventricular Blanking Period and Ventricular Safety Pacing. *Source*: Reprinted from *Symbiotics Series: Managing the DDD Patient*, p. 33, with permission of Medtronics, Inc., © 1984.

intracardiac signals; however, false signals may be recognized and sensed as a spontaneous impulse or R wave. Thus, inappropriate inhibition of ventricular pacing occurs, and ventricular asystole is a possible complication. Frequent sources of false signals include electromagnetic interference (e.g., radio or microwave), crosstalk, afterpotentials (charge developed at the electrode-tissue interface, which dissipates into the myocardial tissue), skeletal myopotentials (electrical signals from skeletal muscle), electrocautery, and diathermy.

To prevent inappropriate inhibition of pacing, a ventricular signal is emitted from the pacemaker at the AV interval (VSP interval, nonphysiologic AV delay interval) of 110 msec, for example, whenever an electrical event is sensed by the ventricular lead within 110 msec after an atrial pacing signal (Figure 6-17). Ventricular safety pacing normally occurs after an atrial pacing signal. (Various pacemaker companies use different AV intervals.) If the sensed signal is a false signal, a VSP spike is delivered and triggers a ventricular event to prevent ventricular asystole. If the sensed signal is an R wave, such as a PVC, then the VSP pulse occurs safely within the ventricular refractory period before the T wave, when the ventricles cannot respond. This protects against the possibility of initiating ventricular tachycardia.

Overdrive Pacing

Overdrive pacing is used to suppress tachydysrhythmias. Rapid atrial stimulation (RAS) is one method effective in treating supraventricular tachycardias (SVT) as well as ventricular tachycardias. In this type of overdrive pacing, the pacemaker rate is gradually increased to a rate greater than the tachycardia rate. When pacemaker capture occurs, it suppresses the tachycardia. The pacer rate is then gradually decreased.

Atrial overdrive pacing requires a pacemaker capable of delivering rates of 400 to 600 ppm, and occasionally up to 1,200 ppm. Short bursts of RAS have been most successful. Although successful in treating atrial flutter and SVT, particularly with drug toxicity and postcardiac surgery, overdrive pacing is an adjunctive therapy.[35] Nurses should be prepared for potential complications. Adverse hemodynamic consequences (i.e., low cardiac output) or atrial fibrillation may develop. If the atrial lead should become displaced into the ventricle, ventricular fibrillation may result.

Ventricular overdrive pacing is used to suppress ventricular tachycardias. The success of overdrive pacing has led to the development of permanent implantable devices, such as burst and scanning pacemakers. These, too, are adjuncts to therapy and carry risks. The presence of the catheter in the ventricle alone is potentially dysrhythmogenic.

Overdrive pacing may be employed with temporary or programmable permanent pacemakers. With temporary atrial overdrive pacing, a special pacer capable of high rates is required. Ventricular overdrive pacing can be initiated using a temporary VVI pulse generator since rates over 150 ppm are not usually needed.[36] With some permanent dual-chamber pacers, the programmer is used to convert the pacer into a DDT mode for overdriving atrial or ventricular tachycardias.

IMPLICATIONS FOR NURSING PRACTICE

Assessment of Dual-Chamber Pacemaker Function

The primary implication for nursing practice is the ability to assess the function of dual-chamber pacemakers. There are seven basic steps in assessing pacer functions.

1. Know the pacer model and programmed mode.
2. Know the most recent programmed intervals and functions.
3. Identify the underlying heart rhythm, if present. Is the rate within the programmed lower/upper rate limits?
   a. if yes, pacer function may be normal
   b. if no, consider hysteresis, malfunction, or upper rate limit pacing
4. Determine whether every atrial pacing stimulus (APS) is followed by a P wave.
   a. if yes, atrial pacing may be normal
   b. if no, consider the pacer's capability for atrial sensing or atrial pacing problems
      (1) if APSs are present without P waves, consider loss of capture
      (2) if APSs are independent of P waves, consider failure to sense
      (3) if no APSs are present, consider loss of pacing
5. Determine whether atrial tracking (every APS or P wave is followed by a ventricular pacing spike [VPS] or R wave) within the AV delay interval is present:
   a. if yes, ventricular outputs may be normal
   b. if no R waves or VPS, consider loss of pacing or upper rate limit pacing
   c. if VPS occurs but AV interval is shorter than the programmed AV interval, consider ventricular safety pacing.
6. Determine whether every VPS is followed by an R wave.
   a. if yes, ventricular pacing may be normal
   b. if no, consider ventricular pacing problems
      (1) if VPSs are present without R waves, consider loss of capture
      (2) if VPSs are independent or superimposed on R waves, consider failure to sense or pseudomalfunctions.

7. Determine pacing interval. Is the interval within the lower and upper rate limits?
   a. if yes, pacemaker function may be normal
   b. if higher, consider pacemaker-mediated tachycardia
   c. if lower, consider hysteresis or pacemaker malfunction.

To interpret paced rhythms accurately, the clinician should adopt a system for analyzing pacemaker function.

Pseudomalfunctions in Dual-Chamber Pacemakers

As pacemakers advance technologically, there are numerous opportunities for diagnosing pseudomalfunctions (misinterpretations of normal functions). *Pseudomalfunctions* describe a group of human or technical errors in diagnosing paced rhythms. They are common, particularly with dual-chamber pacemakers, and usually result from misinterpretation, lack of adequate or accurate knowledge, faulty equipment, or errors in documentation of test data.[37] It is important to be cognizant of pseudomalfunctions because they occur frequently and can lead to unnecessary surgical intervention, pacemaker replacement, patient anxiety and discomfort, and undue expense.

Hysteresis

The prolonged escape interval in hysteresis may be mistaken as a malfunction or as oversensing.[38] Although the concept is easily understood, interpretation of the ECG in clinical practice leads to confusion and misdiagnosis by inexperienced staff, particularly when ventricular ectopy is observed. Misinterpretations may also include intermittent failure to pace.

On ECG, the patient's rhythm is followed by what appears to be an inappropriate delay (Figure 6-18). The subsequent rhythm is usually paced with a shorter interval, making the delay appear to be a malfunction.

Sensing and Failure to Sense

Of the pseudomalfunctions related to sensing, only two warrant discussion. First, oversensing attributable to crosstalk may be erroneously identified when the QRS size is small on the monitor, or the patient has low voltage on ECG. In either case, the QRSs may be misinterpreted as P waves. When QRSs are not observed, ventricular lead sensing of the P waves should be suspected.

Second, it is not uncommon for inexperienced staff to mistakenly diagnose a failure to sense P waves during DVI pacing. The same error occurs when temporary ventricular pacemakers are used for atrial pacing. P waves cannot be sensed in either mode, so when they fall in the V-A interval, the malfunction

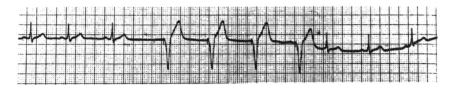

Figure 6-18 Rate hysteresis. Slowing of spontaneous heart rate below hysteresis interval is followed by onset of pacing. Note difference between hysteresis interval and automatic interval. These interval differences should not be misdiagnosed as pacemaker malfunction until it is known whether hysteresis was programmed. *Source*: Reprinted from *Journal of the American Medical Association*, Vol. 254, No. 10, p. 1350, with permission of The American Medical Association, © 1985.

of failure to sense is mimicked. Figure 6-19 illustrates this pseudomalfunction, attributable to a PAC. Figure 6-20 shows nonconducted PACs, which the DVI pacer cannot sense.

Capture and Failure to Capture

Several types of pseudomalfunction exist in relation to ventricular capture: pseudofailure, pseudocapture, and loss of capture.

Pseudofailure is identified by a large pacemaker stimulus that conceals the subsequent ventricular response.[39] Because of the voltage decay of unipolar spikes, the QRS is distorted or appears absent. The nurse can confirm ventricular capture by checking the patient's pulse and identifying T waves (Figure 6-21A) after each pacer spike.

Occasionally, a pacer spike precedes a QRS complex, but a slight delay between them is observed. The sequence may be misinterpreted as a paced beat

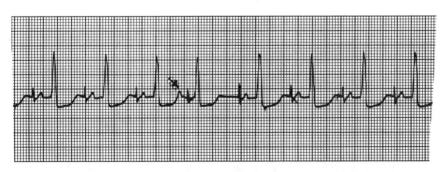

Figure 6-19 Psuedomalfunction: failure to sense. In the DVI mode, P waves are not sensed. The arrow shows a premature atrial complex that was not sensed but may be misdiagnosed as failure in atrial sensing.

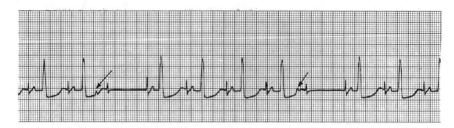

Figure 6-20 Pseudomalfunction: failure to sense. In the DVI mode, P waves cannot be sensed. The arrows show nonconducted premature atrial complexes. The following atrial pacing spikes occur in the refractory period and therefore elicit no response.

with an incomplete exit block caused by mild fibrosis at the electrode tip. However, the QRS is independent of the spike. This represents *pseudocapture* (Figure 6-21B). During VVI pacing, pseudocapture is observed when the pacing interval closely approximates the underlying ventricular rate. During physiologic pacing, the AV delay interval may coincide with the patient's AV conduction time. At the slower heart rates, the patient's AV node may conduct normally. As the heart rate increases, a diseased AV node may fail to conduct. Implications for nursing in diagnosing pseudocapture are to increase the patient's activity slightly, which increases the heart rate. As the patient's conduction slows or blocks, the pacemaker will capture. Typically, the QRS morphology changes, and the interval widens.

Pseudocapture is also observed when a tall, unipolar spike mimics an R wave because of the large overshoot and wide voltage-decay curve (Figure 6-21C).[40] The spike is falsely interpreted as a capture beat. Nursing assessment reveals

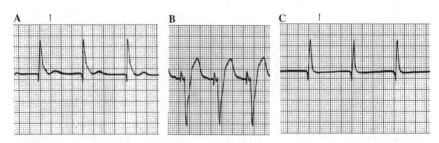

Figure 6-21 Pseudomalfunctions. A. Pseudofailure. The high voltage decay distorts the QRS so that it appears to be absent. T waves verify pacing with capture. B. Pseudocapture. Although the pacer spike appears to capture the ventricles after a slight delay, the QRS is independent of the spike. C. The wide voltage decay curve mimics a QRS; however, absence of a pulse and T waves show failure to capture.

the absence of a pulse with these pseudocapture complexes, and ECG shows absence of a T wave.

During temporary atrial or AV sequential pacing, DVI and VVI pacemakers are usually employed. A common misinterpretation is sporadic *loss of atrial capture*. The error is in assuming that atrial tracking is present. Since DVI pacers ignore P waves, nonconducted PACs, which are often hidden in the T wave, leave the atria refractory at the time of the atrial signal. Thus, the atrial spike without a P wave can lead to misdiagnosis of loss of atrial capture (Figure 6-22). Although common, this pseudomalfunction is not an important problem, and no intervention is required.

Committed DVI Pacing

Diagnosis of pseudomalfunctions in DVI pacing is simplified by first determining whether the pacing mode is "committed" or "non-committed." Committed DVI pacing indicates that there is no ventricular sensing during the AV delay interval. Consequently, a ventricular pacing stimulus will follow every atrial signal at the programmed AV interval, despite the presence of an intrinsic R wave (Figure 6-23). Pseudopseudofusion beats can occur. Committed DVI pacers respond in two ways: (1) no pacing, attributable to inhibition by an underlying rhythm, or (2) atrioventricular sequential pacing. The AV sequential pacing response can compete with the intrinsic rhythm.

Various types of extraneous electrical signals (myopotentials, crosstalk, electromagnetic) can be falsely sensed (Figure 6-24) and cause inappropriate ventricular inhibition. Since a committed ventricular stimulus prevents ventricular

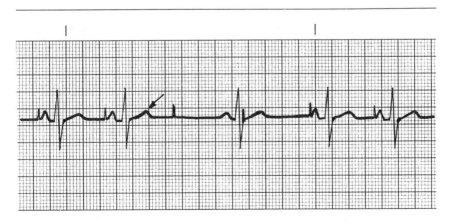

Figure 6-22 Pseudomalfunction: loss of atrial capture. The arrow points to a nonconducted PAC hidden in the T wave. In this DVI mode, the PAC cannot be sensed. An atrial spike occurring in the atrial refractory period can lead to misdiagnosis of loss of atrial capture.

COMMITTED

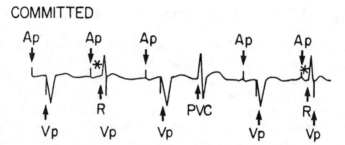

Figure 6-23 Committed DVI pacing mode. Nonpaced ventricular depolarizations (*R*) that occur during the programmed AV interval of the second and last beats (*) do not inhibit delivery of ventricular pacing stimuli (*Vp*). *Source*: Reprinted from *Critical Care Nurse*, Vol. 6, No. 5, p. 16, with permission of Hospital Publications Inc., © 1986.

asystole, patients who are pacemaker-dependent benefit from committed DVI pacing.

Unless nurses are familiar with committed DVI pacing, failure to sense is a common misdiagnosis when competition is observed between the pacemaker and the intrinsic rhythm. The first step in assessing the function of any pacemaker is to know which device was implanted.[41]

Fusion Beats

A *fusion beat*, particularly common in dual-chamber pacing, is the simultaneous depolarization of the ventricles (or atria) by a spontaneous impulse and a paced one.[42] The two impulses independently begin to conduct, then fuse to-

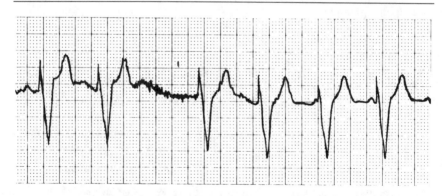

Figure 6-24 Myopotentials (skeletal muscle sensing) causing inappropriate ventricular inhibition of complex 3.

gether, to produce the QRS. Fusion beats are occasionally misinterpreted as failure to sense. The paced and spontaneous impulses occur simultaneously, so there is no time for the pacer to sense the spontaneous beat and to be inhibited. Ventricular fusion beats (Figure 6-25) may occur with all pacemaker modes. Atrial fusion beats (Figure 6-26) occur but are not frequently recognized. Clinical experience shows that ventricular fusion beats are common in DVI, VDD, and DDD pacing when the spontaneous AV conduction closely approximates the programmed AV delay interval.

Depending on the initiation time of each impulse, both foci may contribute equally to ventricular activation, or one may contribute more. The resulting complex shows a pacer spike preceding a QRS that has morphologic characteristics of both a paced beat and a normal QRS. Occasionally, a fusion beat is isoelectric and, therefore, easily mistaken as a failure to capture.[43] Fusion beats are also characterized by a QRS that is narrower than the pacer beat but wider than the intrinsic QRS.

Fusion beats do not cause discernible hemodynamic effects; consequently, they do not require intervention. If competition in AV conduction produces frequent ventricular fusion beats, the AV delay interval can be lengthened.

Pseudofusion Beats

Pseudofusion is more difficult to recognize as a normal pacemaker phenomenon. Pseudofusion (sandwich beats) results when the inscription of the surface ECG slightly precedes intracardiac events recorded by the pacemaker. The pacemaker does not sense the R wave until late in the QRS complex during the absolute refractory period.[44] When the latter peak or terminal portion of the QRS is sensed, the pacemaker is not inhibited until late in the QRS complex. Therefore, a pacer signal may occur early in the QRS before the intrinsic R wave is sensed (Figure 6-27). Thus, the spike occurs too late to cause fusion. Pseudofusion is encountered more often in patients with delayed intraventricular con-

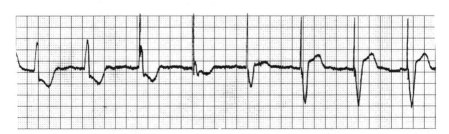

Figure 6-25 Ventricular fusion beats. Complexes 3, 4, and 5 show various QRS configurations of ventricular fusion beats as the intrinsic and pacer stimuli simultaneously depolarize the ventricle.

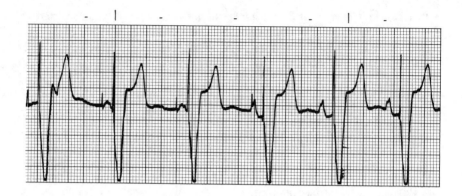

Figure 6-26 Atrial fusion beats. Complex 4 shows AAI pacing with an atrial pacing spike super-imposed on a P wave (atrial fusion beat). This occurs when the intrinsic sinus rate closely approximates the atrial pacing rate. Atrial fusion beats can be mistaken as failure to sense.

duction or conditions that delay conduction such as electrolyte imbalances, hypoxia, antidysrhythmic drugs, and acidosis.[45,46]

Several characteristics assist in differentiating pseudofusion beats from fusion beats or from failure to sense:

- The ventricular spike is superimposed on the QRS.
- It is the ventricular, not atrial, spike that is buried in the R wave (Figure 6-28).
- Pseudofusion beats resemble the intrinsic beat.
- The T wave is identical with the intrinsic beat.
- Both sensing and pacing occur from the ventricles.

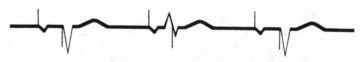

Figure 6-27 Pseudofusion or sandwich beats. Complex 2 shows a pseudofusion beat, which results when the pacer is not inhibited because of sensing of the latter peak of the QRS. Thus, the pacer delivers a stimulus, but the spike is too late to contribute to ventricular depolarization. *Source*: Reprinted from *DDD Pacing ERA of Cosmos: IV—Crosstalk Inhibition*, p. 7, with permission of Intermedics, Inc., © 1983.

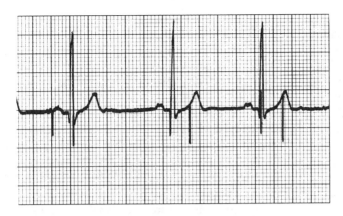

Figure 6-28 Pseudofusion and Pseudopseudofusion beats. Complex 1, pseudofusion beat; complex 2 and 3, different types of pseudopseudofusion beats. *P*, P wave; *R*, R wave; *A*, atrial spike; *V*, ventricular spike.

Although the spike appears in or is superimposed on the QRS complex, it does not contribute to ventricular activation.

Since pseudofusion beats are normal in demand pacing, they may occur in ventricular or in dual-chamber pacing. No intervention is indicated. The major nursing implication is in differentiating these beats from failure to sense. For diagnostic purposes, the most helpful criterion is determining whether the spike falls outside the QRS complex.

Pseudopseudofusion Beats

Clinically, *pseudopseudofusion* tends to cause confusion. These beats may normally occur during DVI pacing, in which there is no P wave sensing, only R wave sensing. At the end of the V-A interval, an atrial signal will be elicited if an R wave is not sensed. Again, when intracardiac sensing is delayed until the terminal portion of the R wave, an atrial signal is delivered into the ensuing QRS complex.[47,48] Characteristics that are helpful in differentiating a pseudopseudofusion beat from pseudofusion or failure to sense include:

- The atrial spike is superimposed or just precedes the QRS complex.
- It is the atrial, not ventricular, spike encroaching on the QRS complex.[49]
- Pseudopseudofusion beats resemble the intrinsic QRS and T wave.
- It is normal in some pacing modes, particularly the DVI mode.
- The atrial spike does not fall outside the QRS complex.

Since pacing is from the atrium and sensing is from the ventricles,[50] the atrial spike cannot contribute to ventricular depolarization.

Committed DVI pacing adds more confusion. Once an atrial signal is delivered into the QRS, a ventricular spike is committed to occur at the preset AV interval. As seen in Figure 6-28, the ventricular spike may occur in the R wave or in the ST segment. The result is an atrial and a ventricular spike superimposed on the QRS complex or T wave. A ventricular spike on the T wave can have deleterious effects, such as lethal ventricular dysrhythmias.

Pseudopseudofusion beats are not normal in DDD pacing during sinus or atrial rhythms. P waves should be sensed. PPF beats in sinus rhythm indicate failure to sense by the atrial electrodes. Other underlying cardiac rhythms, such as accelerated junctional or ventricular rhythms, may allow PPF beats to occur normally. However, only atrial spikes should be present in demand pacing. Experience shows that PPF beats are not common in DDD pacing.

Newer pacemakers with ventricular blanking and safety pacing functions may be replacing committed DVI pacing. A benefit should be fewer pseudopseudofusion beats. However, unless nurses recognize these beats in the different pacing modes, failure to sense may be diagnosed and result in unnecessary pacemaker replacement.

Malfunctions

During the past several decades, pacemaker therapy has offered a variety of malfunctions that have strengthened nurses' diagnostic skills. However, the newer physiologic pacing modalities present a new meaning to the word "challenge." In many instances, the task of simply differentiating normal pacemaker performance is a challenge.

In discussing malfunctions, emphasis is placed on how to diagnose the problems specific to physiologic pacemakers. Recommendations for resolving the malfunctions are explored. The malfunctions and the causes of malfunctions that are not unique to dual-chamber pacemakers are not discussed since there is ample information in the literature.

Crosstalk

Crosstalk is the sensing of a pacing (or electrical) signal by an electrode located in a separate cardiac chamber. It occurs in dual-chamber pacing. Simply, it is undesirable communication between the atrial and ventricular electrodes resulting in self-inhibition of the pacemaker. One form of crosstalk occurs when an atrial lead senses ventricular pacing outputs. Once the atrial lead senses the ventricular signal (interpreting the signal as the patient's intrinsic P wave), then the AV delay interval begins. During the AV interval, a QRS is not sensed by the ventricular electrode. Thus, the pacemaker produces inappropriate triggering of a sequentially paced ventricular response. This problem is also known as atrial oversensing or *"far field sensing."*

A more serious form of crosstalk is the sensing of atrial pacing signals by the ventricular lead (ventricular oversensing). When the signal is sensed by the ventricular lead, inappropriate inhibition results and can lead to syncopal episodes. Crosstalk resulting in ventricular asystole is shown in Figure 6-29 as a possible complication in DVI and DDD pacing.

A less common form of crosstalk is R wave sensing by the atrial electrode. When an intrinsic R wave is elicited, the atrial electrode senses it and inhibits an atrial output stimulus. Thus, in dual-chamber pacing, this form of crosstalk results in no atrial pacing.

Factors that increase the potential for crosstalk, a type of oversensing, include:

- high output setting
- high sensitivity settings
- short refractory periods
- lead dislodgement
- close proximity of the atrial and ventricular electrode locations.

In *atrial oversensing*, reduction in the atrial sensitivity or ventricular output may eliminate crosstalk. If not, an increase in the atrial refractory period may be helpful. When reprogramming is unsuccessful, pacer lead repositioning must be considered.

Troubleshooting for crosstalk due to *ventricular oversensing* is similar. Reduction in the ventricular sensitivity or atrial output frequently eliminates cross-

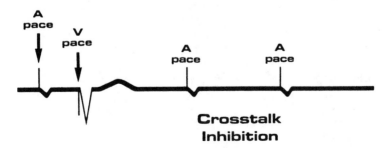

Figure 6-29 Crosstalk. Complex 1, dual-chamber pacing. Complexes 2 and 3, inappropriate inhibition of ventricular pacing results from crosstalk when the ventricular electrode senses the atrial pacer stimulus and interprets it as an R wave. Ventricular asystole can result. *Source*: Reprinted from *DDD Pacing Era of Cosmos: IV—Crosstalk Inhibition*, p. 2, with permission of Intermedics, Inc., © 1983.

talk. Two programmable features may be activated to preclude crosstalk (Figure 6-30): ventricular safety pacing and a ventricular blanking period. With safety pacing, if a ventricular lead senses a signal during the nonphysiologic AV delay or first 100 to 110 msec (depending on the mode), then a ventricular pacing signal occurs to prevent pacemaker inhibition. With a short ventricular blanking period, ventricular lead sensing is disabled; therefore, crosstalk is prevented.

Pacemaker-Mediated Tachycardia

With the advent of atrial tracking pacemakers, the VAT, VDD, and DDD modes, retrograde conduction from the ventricles to the atria has become a major concern. Retrograde (V-A) conduction frequently precipitates *pacemaker-mediated tachycardia (PMT)*. PMT results when a retrograde P wave is sensed and followed by a ventricular-paced impulse (Figure 6-31A). Pacemaker-mediated tachycardia is also known as *endless loop, pacemaker sustained,* and *pacemaker-induced tachycardia* and occurs in 50% of patients with VDD or DDD pacemakers.[51] It may be difficult for clinicians to recognize PMT since retrograde P waves are not always discernible (Figure 6-31B). To understand clearly and prevent PMT, it is necessary to review retrograde conduction and its causes.

Retrograde Conduction. Studies show that one-half[52,53] of patients receiving DDD pacers and two-thirds[54] of patients with normal AV conduction have intact *retrograde conduction.* V-A conduction is common when AV synchrony is lost, and retrograde conduction is not blocked at the AV node. Rubin and colleagues[55] reported that 90% of retrograde conduction is precipitated by premature ventricular complexes (PVC), which cause loss of AV synchrony. A PVC occurs before atrial depolarization. When the impulse from the PVC conducts through

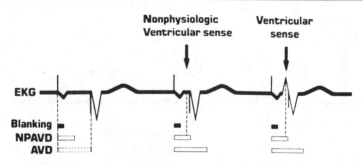

Figure 6-30 Prevention of crosstalk with a ventricular blanking period and ventricular safety pacing. Complex 2, crosstalk (nonphysiologic ventricular sense) that causes a ventricular safety spike to be delivered to prevent inappropriate inhibition. A PVC in Complex 3 occurs during the nonphysiologic AV delay (NPAVD) and also causes ventricular safety pacing. *Source*: Reprinted from *DDD Pacing Era of Cosmos: IV—Crosstalk Inhibition*, p. 11, with permission of Intermedics, Inc., © 1983.

A

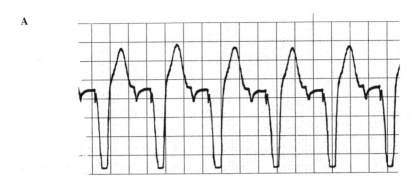

B

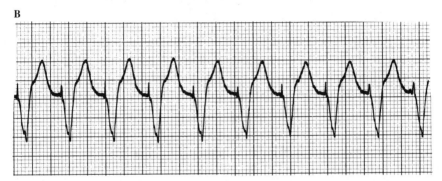

Figure 6-31 Pacemaker-mediated tachycardia (PMT). A. P waves (arrows) from retrograde conduction are sensed and result in PMT at a rate of 97/min (620 msec). B. PMT results from atrial tracking of retrograde P waves (P), which are hidden in the T waves. PMT rate is 125/min (480 msec).

the ventricles and AV node into the atria, a retrograde P wave results. The pacemaker, unable to differentiate a normal from an abnormal P wave, senses it as normal and responds by sequentially pacing the ventricles as shown in Figure 6-32.

Depending on the status of the AV node, V-A conduction time may range from 90 to 400 msec or more, generally averaging 240 msec. At the time of implantation, the patient's V-A conduction time is measured; however, it may vary with the patient's physiologic condition, age, and drug effects. To test for retrograde conduction, many DDD pacemakers can be programmed to a DDT/I mode: P wave triggered atrial pacing, P wave synchronized, and R wave inhibited ventricular pacing. When a retrograde P wave is sensed, an atrial signal is triggered. The atrial spike marks the P wave, which is often difficult to detect in the T wave. The V-A conduction time can easily be measured.

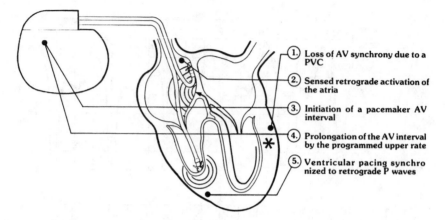

Figure 6-32 Sequences leading to pacemaker-mediated tachycardia. *Source*: Reprinted from *Symbiotics Series: Managing Retrograde Conduction*, p. 7, with permission of Medtronics, Inc., © 1984.

Electrophysiologic Sequence of PMT. The most common precipitating factor of PMT is a PVC, which causes loss of AV synchrony. If the atrial refractory period is programmed longer than V-A conduction time, the retrograde P wave is not sensed. However, when the atrial refractory period is shorter than V-A conduction, a retrograde P wave is sensed and initiates the AV delay interval. Ventricular pacing sequentially follows and results in repeated retrograde conduction or PMT (Figure 6-33).

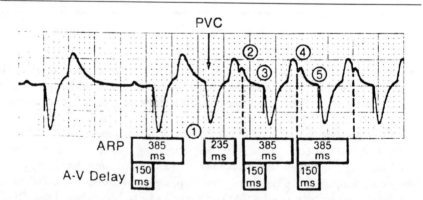

Figure 6-33 Electrophysiologic sequence of PMT: 1, atrial refractory period (ARP) initiated by sensed PVC; 2, retrograde P wave falls outside the ARP and is sensed; 3, ventricular tracking interval times out, and the ventricular pulse is delivered; 4, another retrograde P wave occurs; 5, cycle repeats, causing PMT. *Source*: Reprinted from *Upper Rate Limit Response* with permission of Intermedics, Inc., © 1984.

Mechanisms Precipitating PMT. In addition to PVCs, four other mechanisms[56] cause loss of AV synchrony and may precipitate PMT. Loss of atrial capture may occur because of a low output (MA) setting. The ventricular-paced impulse after the failure in atrial capture can lead to retrograde conduction. Loss of atrial sensing is a second mechanism permitting retrograde conduction. At low sensitivity settings, the pacemaker may fail to sense a P wave during the V-A interval. Retrograde conduction can occur with the subsequent QRS. A third cause is atrial oversensing from myopotentials or electromagnetic interference. The false signals can be sensed as P waves. Nonconducted atrial ectopy, particularly a premature atrial complex, is problematic when it occurs immediately after the atrial refractory period. The upper rate limit prolongs the AV interval and causes the ventricular stimulus to conduct after atrial repolarization. Consequently, PMT may ensue.

Management of PMT. With the rapid improvement in pacemaker technology and programmable options, the vast majority of DDD patients are unaffected by PMT. Retrograde conduction may be controlled by one or a combination of options.[57,58]

- Failure to capture is averted by using an appropriate output setting.
- Failure to sense is corrected by increasing the sensitivity and, in some instances, repositioning a dislodged lead.
- Oversensing may be corrected by adjusting the sensitivity or by placing a bipolar pacing lead and pulse generator.
- Retrograde conduction can be controlled in many cases by programming a longer atrial refractory period with a 50-msec safety margin.
- Slow retrograde conduction after a PVC is prevented by the automatic atrial refractory period extension function on new DDD pacers. The refractory period is extended to approximately 40 msec immediately after a PVC.
- AV synchrony may be restored by reprogramming the AV delay interval and the upper rate interval.
- When the above programmable options are not available, the DVI mode may be beneficial.

Defibrillation and Cardioversion

Nurses must keep abreast of the external factors that may alter pacemaker performance. Defibrillation and cardioversion can alter or destroy a pacemaker, a lead, and/or adjacent heart muscle by the electrical surge.[59] Even when paddles are correctly placed away from the pulse generator, damage and malfunction can occur.[60,61] The protective circuits incorporated into the most current pacemakers do not guarantee protection. Damage may be temporary or permanent. Pacemaker damages have included:[62,63]

- failure of sensing circuit
- changes in pacing mode
- failure to pace
- hemorrhagic myocardial burning and necrosis
- pacemaker turned to "off "
- change in pacemaker's model number (results in inability to reprogram the pacer)
- failure to allow reprogramming or interrogation
- elevation in pacing thresholds
- change in pacing rate.

Nurses must anticipate these potential life-threatening complications after cardioversion to be prepared for intervention. First, the pacemaker model and functions must be documented on admission. During cardioversion, nurses should take several precautionary measures. Paddles should be placed at least 10 cm away from the pacemaker and electrodes.[64,65] Anterioposterior paddles are preferred to avoid electrical discharge over the pacer.

The risk of damage is minimized by decreasing the electrical current during cardioversion to 50 to 100 joules or to the lowest possible setting with the fewest countershocks required.[66,67] A programmer may be helpful for interrogating the system or adjusting for changes in rate, output, mode, and sensitivity. An external or transcutaneous pacemaker can provide temporary intervention until the malfunction can be identified. The patient should be monitored closely for 24 hours to evaluate pacemaker function.

Nuclear Magnetic Resonance

Nuclear magnetic resonance (NMR) imaging is a new diagnostic modality. Due to the exposure of patients to radiofrequency radiation and time-varying magnetic fields, researchers[68-70] have explored the effects that NMR may have on health and on implanted metallic devices. Concerns specific to cardiac pacing include the effect of the magnetic field in reverting the pacemaker to an asynchronous mode, electromagnetic interference, and the force of attraction between the pacemaker and the magnet.

Pavlicek and associates[71] reported several important findings that have implications for clinical practice. First, magnetic fields may disrupt operation in many pacemaker components. NMR can also generate electrical signals that are sensed by the pacer as cardiac activity and cause inappropriate inhibition. Severe bradycardia, or even asystole, are potential outcomes. The magnetic attraction is sufficient to move the pacemaker inside the chest wall significantly. Closure of the reed switch, converting the pacer to an asynchronous mode (Figure 6-34), presents a potential problem. Erlebacher and associates[72] studied different DDD pacemakers and found that all units showed serious malfunctions during NMR scanning, including total inhibition of atrial and ventricular outputs and atrial triggering at rates up to 800 beats per minute. Malfunctions were found to be related to the high-power pulsed radio frequency field. The pacer's memory of the programmed functions can be erased and result in bizarre functions. For these reasons, under no circumstances should NMR imaging ever be used in patients with pacemakers.

Nurses and other health professionals should be cognizant of this hazard to ensure patient safety. Standards of practice should include assessing all patients for subclavicular or upper abdominal incision sites, which may indicate pacemaker implantation. Patients should be informed in pacemaker education sessions that they cannot be exposed to NMR imaging because of potential risks, even if they only have a pacing electrode without a generator. The electrode alone can be paced by induction at the rate of the pulsed radio frequency field (300 beats per minute or higher). They must also be informed about the various terms and acronyms used, such as NMR, magnetic resonance imaging, and MRI. Wrist bracelets identifying patients as having pacemakers are very helpful in screening NMR candidates.

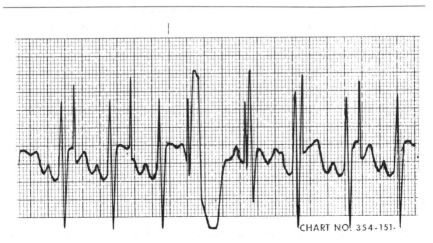

CHART NO. 354-151-

Figure 6-34 AAI pacing mode converted to atrial asynchronous pacing (AOO) by NMR scanning. *A*, atrial pacing spike; *P*, P wave; *R*, R wave; complex 4, a PVC.

Hyperbaric Conditions

Hyperbaric therapy has resulted in sudden and complete pacemaker failure. Tomatis and associates[73] first reported the complication after three temporary pacemakers were tested under hyperbaric conditions and failed. In 1983, Kratz and colleagues[74] investigated the effect of hyperbaric conditions on permanent and temporary cardiac pacing. Various models from different manufacturers were tested. Findings suggested that hermetically sealed permanent pacemakers within titanium cases may be resistant to the effects of hyperbaric conditions. However, temporary pacemakers performed inconsistently. Several showed sudden and complete failure during pressurization.

Although infrequent, patients with temporary pacing may be treated with hyperbaric therapy. In clinical practice, nurses who are cognizant of this complication can anticipate pacemaker failure and ensure effective intervention. Since permanent pacemakers hermetically sealed in titanium cases are dependable, they may be substituted for external pacing during the treatment.

NURSING DIAGNOSES

Knowledge Deficit: Twiddler's Syndrome

An uncommon yet preventable complication after implantation of a permanent pacemaker is the *pacemaker twiddler's syndrome*. In 1968, Bayliss and colleagues[75] first described failure to pace, secondary to lead dislodgement, which is caused by the flipping of the pulse generator over and over in the subcutaneous pocket. As the generator is flipped over, the lead coils around the generator, retracting it from its ventricular position. Lead fracture may also occur. Twiddler's syndrome may be readily diagnosed on x-ray. Depending on the degree of retraction, the continuous electrical stimulation may pace the brachial plexus or the phrenic nerve and produce unilateral diaphragmatic contractions.[76,77]

Prevention is the goal in educating patients about twiddler's syndrome; prevention simply entails advising the patient against pulse generator manipulation and about the potential consequences. Educating the patient about this complication can avert unnecessary reoperation for lead replacement, and in some cases, severe bradycardia, syncope, or sudden death.

Knowledge Deficit: Oral Contraceptive Therapy

Young women in their child-bearing years are not common recipients of permanent pacemakers. Deep vein thrombosis in the upper extremity is a risk for women with permanent venous pacemakers who are on oral contraceptives.[78]

Although case reports are limited, this may be a previously unrecognized complication related to pacemakers. Upper extremity thrombosis is reported to occur at the pacemaker insertion site.

Patient education requires minimal, but valuable, information to prevent deep vein thrombosis. Women should be instructed about the potential complication of upper extremity thrombosis and advised to choose an alternative method of birth control. Should the patient decide to continue use of oral contraceptives, then she must know the signs and symptoms that prompt urgent medical attention. These include nonpitting edema, aching pain, and mottled cyanosis of the extremity.[79]

Potential For Decreased Cardiac Output: Related to Pacemaker Syndrome

As previously discussed, pacemaker syndrome results from inadequate cardiac output during ventricular demand pacing. Patients cannot maintain their previous level of activity because of adverse hemodynamic effects or the inability to increase heart rate in response to metabolic demands. Pacemaker syndrome is estimated to cause serious effects in 7% of pacemaker recipients;[80,81] an estimated 21% are thought to suffer mild to moderate symptoms.[82] However, in the geriatric population, 20% of patients may develop pacemaker syndrome.[83]

The goals of nursing intervention are (1) cardiac tolerance to increased activity, and (2) early identification of pacemaker syndrome. Nurses are in a prime position to evaluate the hemodynamic consequences of pacemaker therapy and to educate patients regarding symptoms. Postimplantation, patients should be assessed (blood pressure, respirations, mentation, etc.) for tolerance during activity progression. When intolerance or poor tolerance is observed, low cardiac output should be evaluated as a potential cause. Abnormal physical findings should then be shared with the cardiologist to determine the presence of pacemaker syndrome. Exhibit 6-1 lists the symptoms that may occur. For patients who progress well postoperatively, these symptoms should be included in patient education. The need to inform the physician about the occurrence of symptoms is stressed.

Disturbance in Self-Concept Related to Altered Body Image

It is not unusual for patients to experience a change in self-concept, particularly related to physical appearance. These changes in body image can lead to anxiety and depression. Nurses should carefully assess patients to determine the specific cause. Middle-aged patients may perceive the need for a pacemaker as a sign of rapid aging or physical deterioration. Some patients are distressed by imagining that the pacemaker will noticeably bulge or that the incision may be unsightly. Men commonly fear the bulge may resemble a breast.[84] Others begin to view themselves as older or more fragile. However, most patients adjust well psychologically in the convalescence period.

The goal of intervention is to prevent psychologic disturbance or to promote healthy adaptation to the changed body image. Nurses can be helpful. First, many patients benefit from seeing an actual pacemaker, especially since advancing technology has produced smaller devices. Simple, factual information assists patients in gaining a realistic idea of the physical changes. As with all psychologic side effects of pacemaker implantation, therapeutic listening and reassurance are often beneficial. Postoperatively, patients who remain self-conscious about the visibility of the pacemaker may appreciate suggestions in choosing clothing that conceals the pacemaker bulge.

Anxiety

Anxiety is an uneasy feeling virtually all patients suffer before pacemaker implantation. It does not usually focus on one but encompasses a multitude of factors: death, pain of surgery, dependency, permanent disability, loss of control, irreversible heart disease, financial loss, and the unknown. Concerns about pacemaker failure, battery depletion, resumption of normal activities, and the possibility of repeated surgeries often cause anxiety postimplantation. A significant amount of the anxiety is related to knowledge deficits. The type of pacemaker, simple or dual-chamber, seems to make little difference in patients' responses.

The goal of care is to increase the psychologic comfort of the patient. Nursing intervention first entails listening as a means for identifying the source of the anxiety. Encouraging patients to explore and express their feelings to a supportive listener is frequently therapeutic.[85,86] Acknowledging anxieties as a normal response provides relief to many. Specific information, simple explanations, answers to questions, and reassurance are frequently curative.[87] An important skill is the ability to assess how much information the patient truly wants. Some cope best by maintaining denial and hearing very little information. Others require detailed explanations provided by a clinical expert who can confidently and completely answer questions.[88] Nurses must empower patients by encouraging them to make decisions, educating them about their pacemaker, and supporting their normal coping skills.

When appropriate, nurses should intervene to reduce sensory overload induced by the environment or other stressors. Misconceptions causing undue anxiety should be identified and clarified. A social service consult may be initiated when financial assistance is required. Flexible visitation may benefit patients experiencing fears and isolation. Uninterrupted sleep should be planned, particularly for patients suffering from sleep pattern disturbances. Appropriate and timely nursing intervention is a key factor in achieving positive patient outcomes.

Potential for Spiritual Distress

Judging by nursing experience with patients requiring pacemakers or cardiac surgery, patients consider the heart to be the most vital organ. A device implanted in the body to make the heart continue to beat can understandably cause spiritual distress. The pacemaker is perceived as unnatural. Patients experience feelings of dependency and fear over the need for this lifelong, life-sustaining artificial part. Complaints, such as feeling like a robot or not being a real person,[89] are clues to the nursing diagnosis: spiritual distress related to conflict between spiritual beliefs and prescribed health regimen. Others question whether they can die with a pacemaker or if the pacemaker will keep their heart beating after their brain is dead.[90]

The goal in planning care is the absence of or reduction in spiritual distress. Nurses are in ideal positions to assist these patients. Patients' beliefs and misunderstandings must be explored to correct misconceptions. Compassion, explanations, and reassurance are often sufficient. For some, a chaplain may help.

Potential for Injury

Ventricular fibrillation can result from microshock (small amounts of stray electrical current), produced from improperly grounded equipment or static electricity. This preventable hazard may occur when pacemaker electrodes are not insulated and are therefore exposed to stray current. This electrically induced and potentially fatal dysrhythmia may be averted by insulating or covering the pacemaker electrodes in a rubber glove or in finger cots. Nurses must wear rubber gloves when handling the electrodes or any pacing wire connected to the patient. All equipment on or near the patient's bed must be properly grounded.

In postcardiac surgical units, the practice of using a ventricular epicardial electrode as the ground lead during temporary atrial epicardial pacing presents a serious potential for injury. Atrial pacing is commonly required. It is not unusual for one of the two atrial leads to become dysfunctional. In some instances, the pacer is grounded by connecting the positive terminal to a ventricular epicardial wire. This situation enables the electrical current from the pacemaker to follow the path of least resistance to the myocardium through either the atrial or ventricular electrode. A ground wire carries away any leakage or stray current. So, in this case, the stray current may be conducted to the ventricle. The effects of stray current, as shown in Figure 6-35, can cause alternating atrial and ventricular pacing, a hazard resulting from this practice. In addition, this practice

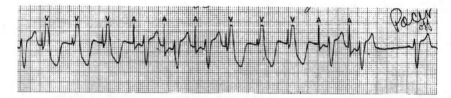

Figure 6-35 Atrial epicardial pacing (A) alternating with ventricular epicardial pacing (V) caused by grounding from a ventricular electrode. Ventricular pacing results from conduction of current leakage through the positive pacer terminal.

permits ventricular pacing without R wave sensing and leaves the patient vulnerable to life-threatening ventricular dysrhythmias.

Nurses can prevent injury by using indifferent (ground) skin electrodes. Many surgeons suture a surgical steel wire into the subcutaneous tissue on the chest. In urgent situations, the pacer can be grounded by attaching the alligator clip to a sterile needle, which is inserted subcutaneously.

FUTURE TRENDS

Transcutaneous Pacing

Historically, transcutaneous (or noninvasive external, temporary) pacemakers were introduced in the early 1950s. Although effective in many bradydysrhythmias, they were replaced by internal pacemakers later that decade to eliminate the problems of pain, skin burns, and local skeletal muscle contractions associated with external pacing. However, until a few years ago, quick reliable pacemaker intervention was a problem in emergencies and in anticipated emergency situations.

Recent modifications have been made in the transcutaneous pacemaker. It is safe, simple, noninvasive, easily applied, and well tolerated in emergency settings.[91] External pacing does seem to be successful early in a cardiac arrest and in hemodynamically compromising bradydysrhythmias. A recent study[92] indicated that transcutaneous pacing is highly successful in producing electrical capture, but mechanical activity is rare, particularly when initiated late in a cardiac arrest. Thus, long-term survival rates are similar to those achieved with transvenous and transthoracic pacing.

Although the nursing diagnosis remains the same, a few differences in patient education and technique should be explored. Technical differences include:

- a skin prep with soap and water
- hair clipping, not shaving
- a wide, negative pacing artifact (see Figure 6-36)
- distortion in the left arm pressure caused by the external pacer
- a propensity for skin breakdown at the electrode site.[93]

Conscious patients should be educated about the potential for chest wall twitching and discomfort.

Activity Responsive Pacemakers

Currently under investigation are several types of rate responsive pacemakers. Rate responsive pacing is a pacing mode in which the heart rate is determined by physiologic parameters other than the SA node. One type is activated by physical activity. Other types will have sensors for acid-base changes, PO_2, PCO_2, respirations, temperature, and intracardiac pressures.[94]

An activity responsive pacemaker is currently under clinical investigation. It is designed to provide changes in the pacing rate in response to changes in physical activity by sensing skeletal muscle activity (Figure 6-37). Based on a programmed activity threshold, it will increase in response as the patient's physical activity increases. Minimum and maximum rates of pacing are programmable. The activity responsive pacemaker offers patients with atrial fibrillation and SA node dysfunction the possibility of increased cardiac output during exercise.

SUMMARY

Nurses are faced with a tremendous challenge as pacemaker technology continues to advance rapidly. Understanding the multiprogrammable functions is

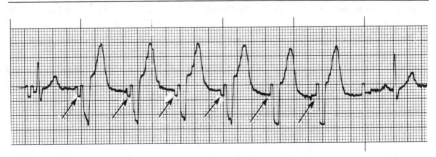

Figure 6-36 External temporary cardiac pacing. Effective pacing stimuli (*arrows*) result in ventricular pacing.

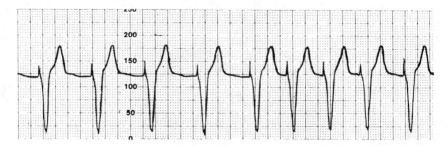

Figure 6-37 Activity responsive pacing. This rhythm shows an increasing pacemaker rate in response to physical activity.

essential in differentiating pacer functions from malfunctions. The nurse's role in analyzing and interpreting pacemaker function is crucial in the prevention and recognition of complications, as well as in the management of patient care. Nurses can also avert problems by educating patients about potential complications and by integrating standards of practice into patient care.

ACKNOWLEDGMENT

The author sincerely thanks Susan Crissman and Connie Shea for their confidence and support; Janet Howard, Brenda Cherry, Phil Faraci, Peter Guzy, and Joel Wachs for their helpful suggestions and contributions; Linda Poyser and Dawn Bettin for their long tedious hours of typing; and Charlie Wolff for his patience and understanding.

NOTES

1. P.L. Ludmer and N. Goldschlager, "Cardiac Pacing in the 1980s," *New England Journal of Medicine* 311(1984):1671.

2. N.T. Evans, "Clinical Assessment of Pacemaker Function: The ICHD Code," *Dimensions of Critical Care Nursing* 4(1985):140.

3. J.W. Harthorne, "Programmable Pacemakers: Technical Features and Clinical Applications," in B. Riegel et al., eds., *Dreifus' Pacemaker Therapy: An Interprofessional Approach* (Philadelphia: F.A. Davis Company, 1986).

4. H.G. Mond, *The Cardiac Pacemaker: Function and Malfunction* (New York: Grune & Stratton, 1983).

5. S.I. Cohen and H.A. Frank, "Preservation of Active Atrial Transport: An Important Clinical Consideration in Cardiac Pacing," *Chest* 81(1982):51.

6. J.J. Curtis et al., "Clinical Experience with Permanent Atrioventricular Sequential Pacing," *Annals of Thoracic Surgery* 32(1981):179.

7. Mond, *Cardiac Pacemaker*.

8. Ibid.

9. B. Shively and N. Goldschlager, "Progress in Cardiac Pacing: Part II," *Archives of Internal Medicine* 145(1985):2238.

10. Ibid.

11. S. Furman and J.A. Cooper, "Atrial Fibrillation during AV Sequential Pacing," *PACE* 5(1982):133.

12. Shively and Goldschlager, "Progress in Pacing."

13. *Cordis Model 415A Gemini: Automatic Universal (DDD) Cardiac Pacer* (Miami: Cordis Corp., 1985).

14. Ibid.

15. T. Mitsui et al., "The Pacemaker Syndrome," in J.E. Jacobs, ed., *Proceedings of the Eighth Annual International Conference on Medical and Biological Engineering* (Chicago: Association for the Advancement of Medical Instrumentation, 1969), pp. 29–33.

16. I. Panidis et al., "Hemodynamic Effects of Cardiac Pacing," in B. Riegel et al., eds., *Dreifus' Pacemaker Therapy: An Interprofessional Approach* (Philadelphia: F.A. Davis Company, 1986).

17. Mond, *Cardiac Pacemaker*.

18. P. Samet, C. Castillo, and W.H. Berstein, "Hemodynamic Sequelae of Atrial, Ventricular and Sequential Atrioventricular Pacing in Cardiac Patients," *American Heart Journal* 72(1966):725.

19. J.M. Haas and G.B. Strait, "Pacemaker-Induced Cardiovascular Failure," *American Journal of Cardiology* 33(1974):295.

20. S. Levy et al., "Retrograde (Ventriculoatrial) Conduction," *PACE* 6(1983):364.

21. Panidis et al., "Hemodynamic Effects."

22. K. Ausubel and S. Furman, "The Pacemaker Syndrome," *Annals of Internal Medicine* 103(1985):420.

23. Panidis et al., "Hemodynamic Effects."

24. R.L. Frye et al., "Guidelines for Permanent Cardiac Pacemaker Implantation: May, 1984," *Circulation* 70(1984):331A.

25. V. Parsonnet, "The Proliferation of Cardiac Pacing: Medical, Technical and Socioeconomic Dilemmas," *Circulation* 5(1982):841.

26. Frye et al., "Guidelines for Implantation."

27. *Pacing Indications and Peer Review* (Minneapolis: Medtronics, Inc., 1985).

28. Parsonnet, "Proliferation of Pacing."

29. Ludmer and Goldschlager, "Cardiac Pacing."

30. E.G. Duffin and D.P. Zipes, "Artificial Cardiac Pacemaker," in K.G. Andreoli et al., eds., *Comprehensive Cardiac Care* (St. Louis: C.V. Mosby Company, 1983), p. 404.

31. Mond, *Cardiac Pacemaker*.

32. B. Riegel, "Patient Responses to Pacemaker Therapy," in B. Riegel et al., eds., *Dreifus' Pacemaker Therapy: An Interprofessional Approach* (Philadelphia: F.A. Davis Company, 1986).

33. L. Tomatis et al., "Massive Arterial Air Embolism due to Rupture of Pulsatile Assist Device: Successful Treatment in the Hyperbaric Chamber," *Annals of Thoracic Surgery* 32(1981):604.

34. Ibid.

35. Mond, *Cardiac Pacemaker*.

36. J.W. Hurst et al., *The Heart*, 5th ed. (New York: McGraw-Hill Book Company, 1982).

37. Mond, *Cardiac Pacemaker*.

38. S.S. Barold et al., "Electrocardiographic Analysis of Normal and Abnormal Pacemaker Function," in B. Riegel et al., eds., *Dreifus' Pacemaker Therapy: An Interprofessional Approach* (Philadelphia: F.A. Davis Company, 1986).

39. Ibid.

40. Ibid.

248   CARDIAC CRITICAL CARE NURSING

41. R.C. Mace and J. Florio, "AV Sequential Demand (CVI) Pacing, Committed and Non-committed," *Technical Journal* 1(1982):1.

42. Mond, *Cardiac Pacemaker*.

43. Barold et al., "Electrocardiographic Analysis."

44. Mond, *Cardiac Pacemaker*.

45. Barold et al., "Electrocardiographic Analysis."

46. D. Shirley and K. Littrell, "Troubleshooting Malfunctions of the Dual-Chamber Pacemaker," *Dimensions of Critical Care Nursing* 4(1985):146.

47. S.S. Barold et al., "Characterization of Pacemaker Arrhythmias due to Normally Functioning AV Demand (DVI) Pulse Generators," *PACE* 3(1980):712.

48. S.S. Barold et al., "Interpretation of Electrograms Produced by a New Unipolar Multiprogrammable Committed AV Sequential (DVI) Pulse Generator," *PACE* 4(1981):692.

49. Shirley and Littrell, "Troubleshooting."

50. Barold et al., "Cardiographic Analysis."

51. Ausubel and Furman, "Pacemaker Syndrome."

52. S. Furman and D. Hayes, "Implantation of Atrioventricular Synchronous and Atrioventricular Universal Pacemakers," *Journal of Thoracic and Cardiovascular Surgery* 85(1983):839.

53. P. Littleford et al., "Pacemaker-Mediated Tachycardia: A Rapid Bedside Technique for Induction and Observation," *American Journal of Cardiology* 52(1983):287.

54. M. Akhtar, "Retrograde Conduction in Man," *PACE* 4(1981):548.

55. J.W. Rubin et al., "Current Physiologic Pacemakers: A Serious Problem with a New Device," *American Journal of Cardiology* 52(1983):88.

56. S.R. Spielman and B.L. Segal, "Pacemakers in the Elderly: New Knowledge, New Choices," *Geriatrics* 41(1986):13.

57. *Pacemaker Sustained Tachycardia* (Freeport, Texas: Intermedics, Inc., 1984).

58. Spielman and Segal, "Pacemakers in the Elderly."

59. M.K. Mathewson and J. Dusek, "Fact or Myth: DC Countershock Does Not Harm Today's Internal Pacemaker," *Critical Care Nurse* 4(1984):48.

60. G. Das and J. Eaton, "Pacemaker Malfunction following Transthoracic Countershock," *PACE* 4(1981):487.

61. L. Gould et al., "Pacemaker Failure Following External Defibrillation," *PACE* 4(1981):575.

62. Mathewson and Dusek, "Fact or Myth."

63. Mond, *Cardiac Pacemakers*.

64. *Automatic Universal Pacemaker*.

65. Gould et al., "Pacemaker Failure."

66. *Automatic Universal Pacemaker*.

67. K.M. McIntyre and A.J. Lewis, eds., *Textbook of Advanced Cardiac Life Support* (Dallas: American Heart Association, 1983).

68. T.F. Budinger, "Nuclear Magnetic Resonance (NMR) In Vivo Studies: Known Thresholds for Health Effects," *Journal CAT* 5(1981):800.

69. P.L. Davis et al., "Potential Hazards in NMR Imaging: Heating Effects of Changing Magnetic Fields and RF Fields on Small Metallic Implants," *American Journal of Radiology* 137(1981):857.

70. P.F.J. New et al., "Potential Hazards and Artifacts of Ferromagnetic and Nonferromagnetic Surgical and Dental Materials and Devices in Nuclear Magnetic Resonance Imaging," *Radiology* 147(1983):139.

71. W. Pavlicek et al., "The Effects of Nuclear Magnetic Resonance on Patients with Cardiac Pacemakers," *Radiology* 147(1983):149.

72. J.A. Erlebacher et al., "Effect of Magnetic Resonance Imaging on DDD Pacemakers," *American Journal of Cardiology* 57(1986):437.

73. Tomatis et al., "Massive Air Embolism."

74. J.M. Kratz et al., "Cardiac Pacing under Hyperbaric Conditions," *Annals of Thoracic Surgery* 36(1983):66.

75. C.E. Bayliss, D.S. Beanlands, and R.J. Baird, "The Pacemaker Twiddler's Syndrome: A New Complication of Implantable Transvenous Pacemakers," *Canadian Medical Association Journal* 99(1968):371.

76. A. Kumar, C.R. McKay, and S.H. Rahimtoola, "Pacemaker Twiddler's Syndrome: An Important Cause of Diaphragmatic Pacing," *American Journal of Cardiology* 56(1985):797.

77. Mond, *Cardiac Pacemakers.*

78. M.F. Halub, G. Robie, and L.F. Deere, "Thrombosis due to Permanent Pacemaker and Oral Contraceptives," *American Journal of Obstetrics and Gynecology* 153(1985):571.

79. Ibid.

80. Ausubel and Furman, "Pacemaker Syndrome."

81. Cohen and Frank, "Preservation of Transport."

82. Ausubel and Furman, "Pacemaker Syndrome."

83. S.M. Slusarczyk and F.D. Hicks, "Helping Your Patient to Live with a Permanent Pacemaker," *Nursing* 13(1983):58.

84. Riegel, "Patient Responses."

85. Ibid.

86. Shively and Goldschlager, "Progress in Pacing."

87. Mond, *Cardiac Pacemakers.*

88. Riegel, "Patient Responses."

89. Mond, *Cardiac Pacemakers.*

90. Riegel, "Patient Responses."

91. *Upper Rate Limit Response* (Freeport, Texas: Intermedics, Inc., 1984).

92. J.R. Hedges, A.S. Scott, and W.C. Dalsey, "Developments in Transcutaneous and Transthoracic Pacing During Bradyasystolic Arrest," *Annals of Emergency Medicine* 13(1984):822.

93. D. Mickus, K.J. Monahan, and C. Brown, "External Pacemakers," *American Journal of Nursing* 86(1986):403.

94. Mond, *Cardiac Pacemakers.*

Chapter 7

The Nurse's Role in Education of the Cardiac Patient

Carolyn Murdaugh, RN, PhD, CCRN

The goal of cardiovascular patient education is to assist patients to maximize their quality of life by understanding and adhering to the prescribed medical regimen, and reducing or eliminating the major modifiable cardiovascular risk factors. This chapter focuses on the nurse's role in educating patients to meet both components of this goal.

RISK FACTORS AND CORONARY HEART DISEASE (CHD)

Cardiovascular disease still accounts for the greatest number of deaths in the United States in spite of the decline in cardiovascular mortality observed since 1968.[1] Epidemiologic studies have established characteristics that aid in predicting the likelihood for developing cardiovascular disease. The major modifiable risk factors are serum lipid level, blood pressure, and smoking.[2] Others include sedentary life style, obesity, and stress. Risk factors that cannot be altered are gender (male), family history (genetics), and increasing age. The positive relation between all these risk factors and the development of atherosclerosis and its endpoint, cardiovascular disease, is now almost universally accepted.

Serum Lipids

The contribution of serum lipids as an independent risk factor for CHD has long been established.[3] The incidence of CHD increases linearly with total serum cholesterol levels. The risk also varies with the levels of low-density lipoprotein (LDL) and high-density lipoprotein (HDL) cholesterol. A high level of LDL is atherogenic; a high level of HDL is protective. The HDL component reflects the process of cholesterol removal from the peripheral tissues to the liver for degradation. The LDLs are the major cholesterol-carrying lipoproteins, transporting 60% to 75% of total plasma cholesterol and are considered responsible for the positive association between high total serum cholesterol and incidence of CHD.

Optimum serum cholesterol values for middle-aged American adults should not exceed 200 mg/dl.[4] A good rule of thumb is that a cholesterol level should not be greater than 170 mg/dl plus a person's age.[5] An optimum ratio of total cholesterol (which reflects LDL) to HDL cholesterol is 3.5. Total cholesterol levels above 200 mg/dl and ratios greater than 5 are causes for concern.

Diets high in saturated fatty acids and cholesterol increase levels of plasma LDL, and dietary restrictions of these components decrease LDL. Plasma HDL levels are higher in women, and higher levels are associated with moderate alcohol intake, exercise, and body leanness. In contrast, cigarette smoking, sedentary living, and obesity have been associated with lower HDL levels. The association of serum cholesterol with other risk factors substantiates the need to avoid a single risk factor reduction approach to lower LDL or raise HDL cholesterol levels.

Human and animal studies clearly indicate that cholesterol is involved in the development of atherosclerosis. The cholesterol found in the atherosclerotic plaque is not manufactured in the vessel wall; it is derived from circulating lipoproteins. Evidence consistently indicates that the type of diet eaten is the chief determinant of levels of serum cholesterol. In turn, the plasma cholesterol level, specifically LDL, is directly related to the clinical endpoint of atherosclerosis, namely CHD.

If elevated cholesterol levels are associated with an increased coronary mortality, lowering serum cholesterol should be associated with a lower coronary mortality. The Lipid Research Clinics' Coronary Primary Prevention Trial, a randomized, placebo, double-blind study, followed 3,806 patients in 12 lipid research clinics for 7 years.[6] The experimental group received a bile acid-binding resin, cholestyramine. The drug binds bile acids in the intestine and prevents their reabsorption. The depletion of the bile acids stimulates the liver to convert more cholesterol to bile acids, and this in turn causes the liver to produce a larger number of LDL receptors. The group who received the drug had a statistically significant 19% reduction in heart attacks and a 24% reduction in cardiac deaths. For every 1% reduction in cholesterol, a 2% reduction in heart attack and heart death was observed. The National Heart, Lung and Blood Institute designed a Type II Coronary Intervention Trial similar to that of the Lipid Research Clinics, except that subjects had diagnosed CHD.[7] Cholesterol reduction was associated with decreased atherosclerotic plaque progression as demonstrated by comparative angiography.

More recently, a class of drugs called *fungal metabolites* offer a new approach for the treatment of hyperlipidemia.[8,9] These drugs, mevinolin and compactin, competitively inhibit the activity of a rate controlling enzyme, 3-hydroxy-3-methyglutaryl-Co A reductase (HGM-Co A reductase), in cholesterol synthesis.

The resulting decrease in cholesterol synthesis lowers liver concentrations of cholesterol and triggers an increase in LDL receptor activity. Therefore cellular uptake of cholesterol increases, and the plasma level of LDL declines. The drugs have been shown to lower LDL markedly in patients with minimum side effects. However, long-term effects on morbidity and mortality are not yet available.

Recent research has also investigated the hypolipidemic effect of fish oils on the development of atherosclerosis. The investigations were stimulated by epidemiologic studies that suggested a low incidence of CHD in Greenland Eskimos may be related to their consumption of seal, whale, and fish.[10] Eicosapentaenoic acid, a polyunsaturated fatty acid of the omega-3 series, is believed to be an important factor in protecting the Eskimos against CHD. In comparison, highly polyunsaturated vegetable oils contain large amounts of the omega-6 fatty acid, linoleic acid.

Eicosapentaenoic acid may interfere with the normal metabolism and function of platelets. Eskimos have prolonged bleeding times; this has been attributed to a diminished response to agonists that stimulate the release of arachidonic acid. Arachidonic acid is rapidly converted to thromboxane A_2, a potent inducer of platelet aggregation. Eicosapentaenoic acid content in platelet membranes is increased in diets high in fish oil. Thus the omega-3 fatty acid is thought to inhibit the metabolism of arachidonic acid as well as to inhibit platelet function. Since platelets have a key role in thrombosis and promote the proliferation of smooth muscle cells in atherogenesis, the effects of eicosapentaenoic acid may retard the development of atherosclerosis.[11]

Dietary fish oils may also block the synthesis of very-low-density lipoproteins (VLDL) in the liver, or increase the removal of VLDL, and lower the rate of synthesis of LDL. The effects of a fish oil diet on cholesterol and triglycerides were examined over 4 weeks in 20 subjects.[12] In comparison to a vegetable oil diet and a control low-fat diet, the fish oil diet produced a 27% drop in serum cholesterol and a 64% decrease in triglycerides. Using a swine model, Weiner et al.[13] studied the effect of cod-liver oil on the development and progression of CHD in 7 pigs given cod-liver oil supplement and 11 controls. Significantly less coronary disease was observed in the vessels of animals fed cod-liver oil; in addition, platelet arachidonate was reduced, platelet eicosapentaenoic acid was increased and serum thromboxane was decreased.

Omega-3 capsules are currently available without a prescription. No research evidence currently warrants their consumption in addition to regular dietary consumption of fish, and vitamin A and D toxicity is a likely side effect.

Based on the animal studies and clinical trials a consensus panel convened by the National Institutes of Health developed recommendations to achieve a low-cholesterol, less than 300 mg, low-fat, less than 30% of calories, diet for all Americans. The recommendations are directed toward industry to develop and market leaner foods and provide detailed food labeling; and toward restaurants, government, and school food programs to serve meals consistent with dietary recommendations.

Strategies for Cholesterol Reduction. Diet changes, even modest ones, require motivation and continued adherence by patients. Lifelong habits are difficult to change. In contrast to other life style habits, such as smoking, abstinence is not an option, so new eating behaviors must be learned. Successful change requires active patient involvement. Racial, cultural, and individual food preferences; socioeconomic factors such as education; economic issues; environmental elements; and life styles must all be considered.

The American Heart Association (AHA) provides valuable guidelines for counseling the patient with hyperlipidemia.[14] The following guidelines are detailed in the booklet, *Counseling the Patient with Hyperlipidemia*, which is available at any local office of the AHA.

An initial dietary and behavioral assessment is necessary to determine how to tailor the changes to the patient's life style. Diet histories need to include previous dietary modifications, food preparation practices, eating-out habits, and food seasoning habits. A 1- to 3-day food record or information concerning the frequency that certain foods are eaten will enable the nurse to estimate calories, cholesterol, sodium, and alcohol intake. Physical activity level will also need to be assessed if obesity is a problem. Available support systems for the patient need to be elicited. Last, patient motivation and understanding of the need for the change need to be known. The assessment phase allows one to identify problem areas and establish rapport with the patient.

Each problem area identified needs to be assigned a priority by the nurse and the patient after the patient has evaluated the importance of each in the risk factor modification plan. Priorities provide the patient with the sequence of interventions to be implemented. If patients do not agree with the nurse's sequence, the priorities will need to be reordered to allow patient control over the steps to change their dietary habits. Otherwise, motivation may be decreased.

After an agreement on the priorities is reached, appropriate interventions are implemented. The patient's performance needs to be monitored to assess adherence throughout the implementation phase. Monitoring needs to be done by both the nurse and the patient. Self-monitoring enables patients to be actively involved in measuring their changes, and monitoring by nurses enables them to ascertain patient progress and to tailor the intervention accordingly.

Both short-term and long-term follow-up will be necessary. During every visit, the patient's progress needs to be reviewed, and any success needs to be emphasized. Always begin with positive feedback before discussing difficulties. When reviewing negative aspects, provide new strategies for change. If after a period of time decided by both parties the patient is not motivated to change and refuses to meet the mutually developed dietary goals, the dietary program can be terminated after consultation with the physician. However, patients should be encouraged to change their dietary habits and return to the educational program when ready to receive assistance.

Drug therapy is normally not instituted until a 2-month trial of diet alone is attempted.[15] Dietary restrictions should be emphasized even after drug therapy is implemented. Patients must not be allowed to believe the pill will enable them to forego previous dietary restrictions. Instead, drug therapy is a supplement to long-term diet therapy. The patient must be monitored for side effects of the drugs. For example, the bile-sequestering agents may cause constipation, bloating, or diarrhea. Such effects may decrease adherence in taking the drugs. As with other medications, patients need to be taught to report all side effects to the nurse or physician.

Smoking

Cigarette smoking is one of the major risk factors for atherosclerosis. Smoking has other negative effects on the cardiovascular system and other body systems as well. The negative effects are thought to be mediated through nicotine and carbon monoxide. Nicotine stimulates catecholamine release, increases myocardial irritability, raises heart rate, causes vascular constriction, and increases platelet adherence. Carbon monoxide buildup reduces the oxygen available to the myocardium, induces a chronic hypoxia in the endothelium of blood vessels, and alters platelet function.

Since most survivors of myocardial infarction (MI) have extensive underlying coronary atherosclerosis, it is reasonable to expect that smoking cessation will improve prognosis. Although randomized clinical trials have not been conducted because of ethical issues, evidence exists that smoking habits after an MI influence subsequent morbidity and mortality. In fact, all studies show negative effects on mortality.[16] Examination of the data from several studies designed to test the effect of subsequent smoking on mortality after an MI suggests the mortality rate is twice as high in smokers as in nonsmokers.[17,18] A significant reduction in the recurrence of nonfatal MIs also has been noted in patients who stopped smoking.

The adverse effects of cigarette smoking may be related to the number of cigarettes smoked per day rather than the duration of the habit.[19] In an early study by Mulcahy,[20] no difference in mortality was noted between patients who stopped smoking and those who reduced their smoking volume by half. Arteriography evidence also indicates a dose-related effect.[21] The evidence suggests that even if patients are unable to quit smoking cigarettes, a reduction in the number smoked has a potentially positive effect.

Cigarette smoking is the largest single preventable health problem, and one of the most difficult personal habits to break. Long-term success rates in formal programs rarely exceed 30%.[22] Schacter's[23] work showed that 64% of patients interviewed quit smoking on their own. Maybe only those persons who cannot stop on their own enter a smoking cessation program. This information is important to keep in mind when designing programs for patients, as most are probably those who have been unable to quit on their own.

Factors that differentiate smokers from ex-smokers have been identified. In a study of hospitalized cardiovascular patients, the variable explaining the greatest difference between smokers and ex-smokers was social support.[24] Those who had stopped smoking for at least 6 months had more encouragement from their immediate support persons than smokers. Ex-smokers also perceived a greater relation between smoking and heart disease than smokers and more benefits than barriers to smoking cessation.

Katz and Singh[25] found that willpower, self-confidence, and a sense of feeling healthier were the three most important factors in being able to quit and remain a nonsmoker. Feelings of self-confidence and social support lessened the difficulty of quitting. As expected, subjects who had been heavier smokers were bothered most by urges to resume smoking, were more troubled by withdrawal symptoms and loss of pleasure from not smoking, and made more initial attempts at quitting. The major reasons for relapse cited were loss of pleasure from smoking and lack of will power.

Predictors of success at quitting cigarette smoking were investigated as part of a community-wide stop-smoking contest conducted by the Minnesota Heart Health Program.[26] Perceived stress was the major predictor of short-term success. Subjects who reported high stress levels were less likely to succeed in quitting. The use of self-reward was one of the most distinguishing characteristics of successful subjects. Subjects who used self-rewards and fewer self-punishments were more successful at quitting.

Strategies for Smoking Cessation. Cigarette smoking behavior is extremely complex; a smoker's career can be described by four stages in which multiple psychosocial and physiologic factors intervene: initiation, maintenance, cessation, and resumption or relapse.[27] Psychologic factors such as curiosity, rebelliousness, and social pressures influence the initiation of smoking behavior. Continuation is enhanced by the pharmacologic effects of nicotine. The decision to stop is often related to health, i.e., cardiovascular disease, expense, social support, and will power. Relapse is associated with withdrawal symptoms, stress, social pressure, weight gain, and alcohol consumption. Identification of those factors operating at each stage in patients who smoke is necessary before initiating intervention strategies.

Smoking cessation counseling begins by assessing the smoking habits of your patients: how much do they smoke, when did they start, have they ever tried to quit? In addition, the psychosocial factors mentioned above need to be assessed such as the desire to quit (will power), social support, perceived barriers and benefits to quitting, and perceived stress. The assessment will enable the nurse to understand the role of smoking for patients, ascertain their knowledge level of smoking risks, and establish rapport before implementing interventions. Next, agree on a quit date.[28] Before the agreement, make certain the benefits of quitting as well as the consequences of smoking have been discussed with the patient. Also be sure that all patient concerns about quitting have been addressed.

Patients may decide to quit on their own or request professional help in a smoking cessation program. Regardless of the option, the patient's progress must be monitored. Support and positive reinforcement need to be provided during each visit. If patients are not able to quit completely, encourage them to decrease the amount smoked using various strategies. For example, implementing environmental restrictions, such as not smoking in one's car or certain rooms in the house, may be an initial step in cutting down on the amount smoked. In addition, self-help books, kits, and cassettes should be made available. Other tips for helping the patient quit are listed in Exhibit 7-1.

Almost all smokers are able to quit initially. However the majority will resume smoking within a few months. Thus, attention to maintenance strategies is extremely important. The major factor for successful maintenance, as stated earlier, is social support. If the patient does not have a supportive partner or friends, a group needs to be made available that can help sustain the motivation and decrease the stress of quitting. Partner support has been found to be extremely helpful in successful maintenance. Second, the patient needs to be taught self-control skills to manage the discomfort of withdrawal and loss of pleasure from smoking. They need to learn to recognize and modify cues that previously triggered smoking, and to develop substitute responses to replace smoking.[29] Last, cognitive restructuring approaches can also be undertaken to facilitate maintenance. These approaches assume that some change first occurs in the patients' attitudes toward smoking or their perception of their ability to maintain smoking cessation. In

---

Exhibit 7-1 Tips for Quitting Smoking

Write down all reasons for wanting to quit.
Use oral substitutes for cigarettes: toothpicks, sugarless gum, sugarless candy.
Immediately leave the table after a meal.
Initially avoid alcohol, coffee, etc. that are associated with smoking.
Wear a rubberband on one wrist and stretch and release it for a zap whenever there is a desire to smoke.
Inform family and friends of the decision to quit.
If possible, quit with a friend.
Write down all positive effects noted after quitting.
Avoid smokers.
Take 5 to 10 deep breaths whenever there is an urge to smoke.

other words patients are able to resist smoking because of perceived self-efficacy, or conviction that they can successfully maintain smoking cessation.[30]

Nicotine chewing gum shows promising results in combination with behavioral strategies because nicotine is a powerful physiologic reinforcer for cigarette smokers. Smoking is thought to be reinforced because nicotine stimulates specific reward-inducing centers of the nervous system, thereby generating dependency. Smoking regulates the level of nicotine circulating in the body. When the nicotine drops below a certain "set point" the patient smokes.[31] Thus the nicotine-regulation hypothesis is currently a popular area of investigation and may provide valuable insight for smoking cessation.

Hypertension

Hypertension is a powerful independent risk factor for cardiovascular disease (CVD), including stroke, CHD, congestive heart failure, intermittent claudication, and renal disease.[32] A chronically elevated blood pressure (BP) is associated with a tripling of cardiovascular mortality. Almost any elevation in BP seems to carry with it an increased risk for CVD, so hypertension can be defined as that level of intra-arterial pressure at which the earliest adverse effects on the structure or functional integrity of an individual's vessels occur.[33] In the Hypertension Detection and Follow-Up Program, hypertensive persons aged 60 to 69 had almost twice the mortality rate as normotensive subjects.[34] Each millimeter of increase in systolic pressure was associated with a 1% increase in mortality.

Individuals are classified as normotensive if the arterial blood pressure is less than 140/85. The Report of the Joint National Committee on Detection, Evaluation, and Treatment of High Blood Pressure[35] also defines mild hypertension as a diastolic pressure of 90 to 104 mmHg; moderate hypertension as a diastolic pressure of 105 to 114 mmHg; and severe hypertension as a diastolic pressure greater than 115 mmHg. Systolic pressure is also an important determinant of cardiovascular mortality. Borderline isolated systolic hypertension, 140 to 159 mmHg, and isolated systolic hypertension, greater than 160 mmHg, warrant medical evaluation.

The diagnosis of hypertension is not made on a single elevated reading. A single elevated reading, however, warrants follow-up. The diagnosis is confirmed when the average of two or more diastolic measurements on two different occasions is 90 mmHg or higher, or when the average of two or more systolic measurements is consistently higher than 140 mmHg. Therapy should begin as soon as the diagnosis is confirmed.

Risk factors for the development of primary or essential hypertension include a positive family history, a high salt intake in "salt-sensitive" persons, obesity, lack of exercise, chronic heavy alcohol consumption, and personality type. Psychosocial risk factors are lack of support systems, cultural food practices, economic status, and emotional stress. The precise etiology of hypertension is still unknown. Other possible etiologic factors under investigation include renin-angiotension-aldosterone system abnormalities, fluid and electrolyte alterations, and sympathetic nervous system effects.[36]

Treatment for Hypertension

Nonpharmacologic treatment of hypertension begins with reduction of risk factors. In patients with hypertension, these approaches may reduce BP to normal. In patients with severe hypertension, nonpharmacologic treatment is adjunctive to drug therapy. Moderate sodium and alcohol consumption, 2 to 5 g of sodium and less than 2 oz of alcohol per day, are recommended. Weight reduction by caloric restriction should be an integral part of treatment for obese patients. Yoga and muscle relaxation exercises have also been shown to reduce BP.

Pharmacologic treatment of hypertension decreases cardiovascular mortality and morbidity in both moderate and severe hypertension.[37] However, controversy continues about the drug treatment of mild hypertension. The controversy is based on the lack of evidence for reduced morbidity and mortality rates after treatment of mild hypertension. The potential harmful side effects may even negate the short-term effects of lowering BP. Hypokalemia, hyperuricemia caused by diuretic therapy, and hyperglycemia and hyperlipidemia produced by beta blockers are commonly occurring problems. Thus drug treatment of patients with mild hypertension needs to be limited to those who are at highest risk for cardiovascular complications.[38] Patients who do not receive drug therapy should be monitored closely over subsequent years.

A "step care" approach has been suggested as a guide for the treatment of hypertension. Implicit in the approach is the requirement that nonpharmacologic treatment has been tried without adequate success. The program advocates initiating therapy with small doses of an antihypertensive agent, increasing as necessary for optimum use, and adding or substituting drugs in steps as needed to reduce diastolic pressure to 90 mmHg or lower. Before proceeding to another step, possible reasons for a lack of responsiveness are assessed including poor adherence, insufficient dose of current drugs, excessive sodium intake, weight gain, and concurrent use of competing drugs such as oral contraceptives, vasopressor decongestants, or appetite suppressants. The approach has been criticized as an unscientific, rigid, cookbook approach. Such is not the case, as the approach leaves room for individualization and flexibility, has been proven valid in clinical trials, and is based on sound pharmacologic principles. The steps recommended by the 1984 Report of the Joint National Committee on the Detection, Evaluation and Treatment of High Blood Pressure are outlined in Exhibit 7-2.

Exhibit 7-2 The Step Care Approach to Hypertension Management

Step 1	Diuretics or beta blocker
Step 2	Sympatholytic drugs
	Beta-adrenergic blockers
	Central alpha-adrenergic stimulators
	Peripheral alpha-adrenergic blockers
Step 3	Vasodilators
Step 4	More potent agents
	Angiotension-converting enzyme*
	Calcium-entry blockers*
	Catecholamine depleters
	Direct vasodilators

*May be used as step 2 and step 3 drugs.

Strategies in Hypertension Management

Four steps are involved in the management of hypertension: detection, diagnosis, treatment, and adherence or compliance. Low patient adherence is the most important therapy-limiting factor in spite of the improvement in patient care. Patients often fail to keep appointments, take prescribed medications, and reduce weight and salt intake.[39] Patients with hypertension are asymptomatic and do not regard themselves as patients. Management of hypertension may make a patient feel worse after diagnosis, as antihypertensive medications have many unpleasant side effects. In addition, medications can be expensive, which may further contribute to the adherence problem.

Investigators have accounted for adherence failures in three ways: patient characteristics, structural or situational barriers, and functional factors.[40,41] Male sex, young age, low socioeconomic status, obesity, and cigarette smoking are associated with patient dropout. In contrast, well-adjusted, well-controlled hypertensive patients report greater satisfaction with health care; are less likely to smoke, eat, or use drugs to handle tension; and are less pessimistic than patients with uncontrolled hypertension.[42]

Situational or structural barriers to adherence refer to the environment or context in which adherence is to occur. Situational barriers include the high cost of treatment, poor access to care, and inadequate follow-up. Patients who are not satisfied with their physicians show less adherence than satisfied patients. If the patient's expectations are not met, the language of the health professional is not understood, or warmth is missing in the relationship, adherence will be poor.

Lack of motivation is another major barrier to adherence. Patients may not be motivated because they lack knowledge. If patients do not understand the disease and its consequences or the treatment regimen, they may believe the treatments are ineffective and fail to use them. Education provides patients with the information needed to understand their diagnosis, the consequences of inadequate treatment, the rationale for management regimens, and the effects of the regimens on morbidity and mortality. Patients need to become actively involved in the treatment, share responsibility for changing their life style, and monitor treatment outcomes. The patient-provider interaction must reflect a sensitivity to both individual and cultural differences.[43]

Several practical suggestions have been made to enhance adherence.[44] The patient needs to receive information. Patient satisfaction with providers needs to be maximized. Patients need to be involved in the management of their disease. Adherence must be continuously monitored by the health care team. Support systems need to be organized to assist the patient: either family, friends, or support groups. Each health care provider needs to be actively involved with the patient. Allow the patient as much control as possible in managing BP by providing choices, focusing attention on attainable goals, and providing positive feedback.[45]

Physical Activity

Epidemiologic studies now provide strong evidence for the protective effect of physical activity against cardiovascular disease. The Framingham data showed improved cardiovascular and CHD mortality with increased physical activity at all ages including the elderly.[46] The benefits apply to all persons. Paffenbarger et al.[47] examined the physical activity of Harvard alumni and showed that exercise was inversely related to cardiovascular mortality. A consistent trend toward a lower death rate was seen as physical activity increased.

Numerous randomized trials have studied the effect of cardiac rehabilitation, i.e., exercise training, on recurrent fatal and nonfatal MI.[48] In spite of the high dropout rates (40% to 50% in the first year) and other methodologic limitations, all trials showed a lower cardiovascular mortality but no significant difference in nonfatal recurrent MI. Since outcome was shown to be positively affected by adherence, efforts to increase patient adherence in cardiac rehabilitation should be undertaken.

The protective effects of physical activity may be attributable to several factors: HDL cholesterol is increased, and plasma triglyceride and LDL are reduced; stroke volume and oxygen use are increased; BP may be reduced; body weight is lowered; and fibrinolytic activity and platelet adhesiveness may be decreased.[49] The protective effect is seen at all ages. In patients with CHD, preanginal exercise and stress tolerance is increased even with low-intensity exercise. Improved self-care and emotional status were also reported. Early mobilization after an MI has been associated with shorter hospitalization and more complete return to work.

Characteristics of Exercise Nonadherence. Exercise programs for persons at risk for CHD and for patients with documented heart disease report the highest dropout in the first 3 months, and attrition leveling off between 50% and 70% after 12 to 24 months. The first 8 weeks are the critical period for dropout. In a review of primary and secondary prevention exercise programs of at least a 6-month duration, common factors associated with entering, maintaining, and dropping out of exercise programs were summarized.[50,51] Subjects who did not comply were usually smokers, exhibited type A behavior, were inactive in their leisure time, and had a partner who was unsupportive or neutral toward their participation. Reasons for dropout included program inconvenience, transportation problems, medical problems, and psychosocial factors such as lack of motivation or disinterest. Persons who remained in an exercise program cited reasons such as partner encouragement, health benefits, and social aspects. Positive reinforcement during the exercise program is also related to adherence. These factors provide information about the types of strategies needed to increase adherence to exercise programs in persons less likely to comply.

Additional data indicate few persons over age 35 will begin vigorous activities, but they will increase moderate activities such as walking.[52] Lower dropout rates (25% to 35%) were noted for moderate activities than for vigorous activity (50%) for men and women. Results point to the need to develop walking programs for middle-aged and elderly persons, as they may meet with greater success. As in previous research, Sallis et al.[53] supported the importance of self-efficacy and self-control in the maintenance of physical activity.

Stress: Type A Behavior Pattern (TABP)

TABP is another independent risk factor for CHD.[54] It is characterized by excessive competitive drive, intense ambition, time urgency, hostility, and vigorous speech. The contrasting behavior pattern, Type B, is characterized by the relative absence of these characteristics and a different coping style.

Research indicates individuals who exhibit TABP may make their environment more challenging and demanding and therefore more physiologically taxing.[55] They perceive situations as more challenging and demanding; they are more likely to choose participation in demanding and challenging situations; and their coping style may prolong exposure to stressors. Type A persons tend to elicit responses that are cues for further Type A behavior. They evaluate their performance in such a way as to motivate further aggressive striving. The cumulative effects of these behaviors are an increased exposure to stressors and physiologic reactivity. The pronounced reactivity is believed to play a role in the development of atherosclerosis and CHD.

Evidence suggests the hostility component of type A behaviors may be the major characteristic associated with the development of CHD. Several investigations support the link between hostility scores and coronary disease severity evidenced by coronary angiography,[56,57] and point to the need for additional work to understand the physiologic-pathologic components of Type A behavior.[58]

Strategies for Altering Type A. In spite of lack of knowledge of the mechanisms involved in the development of CHD, interventions have been developed and tested to alter TABP in both healthy persons and patients who have sustained an MI. Healthy subjects received both stress management and relaxation training, including EMG biofeedback, meditation, and progressive relaxation. However, all the studies suffer from methodologic flaws. In spite of the limitations, reductions have been noted in the hard driving/competitive and speed/impatience factors.[59]

Studies involving subjects with cardiovascular disease have attempted to alter TABP with both psychotherapy and behavior therapy. Inconsistencies in design make conclusions difficult. For example, most of the studies did not assess Type A with a standardized instrument, differing selection methods were used to obtain subjects, and various short-term interventions were offered.[60]

The Recurrent Coronary Prevention Project,[61] a 5-year clinical trial begun in 1977, is the only controlled prospective study to date to show that alterations in TABP are associated with significant reductions of recurrent MI. Treatment consisted of behavioral group counseling and cardiologic group counseling. The cardiologic or control groups met with a cardiologist for 90-minute sessions biweekly for 3 months, monthly for 3 months, and bimonthly for the remainder of the study. The control group focused on risk factor modification except TABP. Subjects in the experimental groups received the cardiologic counseling plus behavioral counseling to learn to recognize and control TABP. An expanded social learning model was used that views ongoing human experience as a function of cognitive, physiologic, behavioral, and environmental factors. Treatment methods were based on behavioral self-management and cognitive behavioral strategies. A behavior practice manual was provided to provide new behaviors to focus on each day. Three-year results indicate an almost 50% lower MI recurrence rate for subjects who received behavioral counseling when compared with subjects in the cardiologic group only. Reduction in scores on the TABP questionnaire were significantly greater in the treatment group during the third year.

Several helpful suggestions for altering TABP are offered by Recurrent Coronary Prevention Project. Small groups are highly effective to learn behavior change. A comprehensive treatment protocol can teach patients to identify overt TABP behaviors and characteristics that need to be modified. Cognitive behavior modification can be used successfully to alter beliefs about oneself and others. Behavioral self-management strategies that are practical can also decrease TABP. In summary, TABP can be altered, but the treatment is complex, long-term, and requires a major time commitment. More controlled studies are needed to learn to assess clearly and modify the behaviors.

Pharmacologic approaches are also being studied. The rationale is based on observations that suggest TABP may reflect an underlying sympathetic responsivity.[62] This would suggest that TABP might be suppressed by beta-adrenergic blockade. Two studies provide support for this hypothesis.[63,64] Patients receiving chronic beta-blockade therapy showed a greater decrease in intensity of TABP than controls. The data are descriptive, and neither study contained a placebo control group, so further investigations are needed. However, the data provide evidence for further studies on the role of drugs in modifying TABP.

THE TEACHING-LEARNING PROCESS

To be effective as a teacher, the cardiovascular nurse needs an appreciation of how adults learn and the elements necessary to provide a creative learning environment. Knowledge of content needed to teach patients to change their life styles or adhere to their regimens is vital, but such knowledge is only one of the elements of an effective teaching-learning situation. To illustrate, how often do we hear: "They really know their material, too bad they can't teach it." Knowing content and teaching are distinctly different. Thus other elements of the teaching-learning process need to be integrated into the teaching style of the nurse to provide effective patient education.

The teaching-learning process begins when the nurse identifies a patient need for knowledge or the patient expresses a desire to make a change. Entering into a teaching relationship requires a commitment to seeing that the patient is taught until the goals are reached or teaching is no longer profitable. The relationship should be interpreted to patients in terms of how teaching will assist them to meet the learning goals, when the nurse will be available as a resource person, and how long the teaching relationship will last. The nurse involves patients in formulating the teaching plan by listening and assessing the experiences they bring to the teaching process.

Theories of teaching prescribe ways to influence individuals to learn. Teaching principles provide the framework for developing and implementing the plan and evaluating the results. Thus, the teaching framework guides the process by providing the learning stiuation with the essential ingredients to facilitate learning. Guidelines to increase teaching effectiveness have been formulated, based on the works of Rogers, Watson, and other learning theorists. These guidelines are principles of learning that are relevant to cardiovascular teaching and are described later in the chapter.

Knowles[65] established a series of principles concerning the role of the teacher in relation to specific conditions of learning as shown in Table 7-1. They emphasize the need to individualize the process. Effective teachers have the ability to improve learning through planned activities based on each learner's abilities, perceived needs, and input.

Table 7-1 Role of the Teacher

Conditions of Learning	Principles of Teaching
Patient feels need to learn.	Nurse helps patients clarify their goals for improved health. Nurse diagnoses gap between goals and present knowledge.
Characteristics of learning environment: physical comfort, mutual trust and respect, freedom of expression, acceptance of differences.	Nurse provides comfortable physical environment. Nurse accepts and respects patient's feelings and ideas. Nurse builds mutual trust.
Learning goals are perceived to be patient's goals.	Nurse involves patient in formulating objectives.
Patient shares in planning learning experiences.	Nurse shares options available and involves patient in selection.
Patient actively participates in learning process.	Nurse helps patient share responsibility.
Learning process makes use of patient's experiences.	Nurse helps patient use experiences as resources. Nurse helps patient apply new learning to experience.
Patient has a sense of progress toward goals.	Nurse involves patient in developing criteria to measure progress. Nurse encourages self-evaluation.

Source: *The Adult Learner: A Neglected Species* by M. Knowles, pp. 70–72, Gulf Publishing Company, © 1973.

Adult Learning Theory

Whether or not they can verbalize it, nurse teachers also operate in a framework of learning. Otherwise the teaching activity would be purposeless. Knowles' andragogical theory of learning is perhaps the best known framework for adult learners. The adult learning theory differentiates adult learners from child learners.

Andragogy theory states that as a person matures, the need and capacity to be self-directing, to use experiences in learning, to identify one's own readiness to learn, and to organize learning around life's problems increase steadily. Adult learning theory is based on four assumptions.[66] First, as people mature, their self-concept moves from dependency to increasing self-directedness. Adults can make their own decisions and take responsibility for managing their life. Second, as individuals mature, they accumulate an expanding reservoir of experiences that provides a base on which to relate new learning. Third, as one matures, readiness to learn is increasingly based on developmental tasks required to perform evolving roles. These roles include spouse, parent, worker, and friend. Last, adults tend to have a problem-centered rather than a subject-centered orientation to learning. Adults enter learning situations because of some inadequacy in coping with current life problems. Thus immediate application of new knowledge is needed. Most patients with cardiovascular disease are independent, self-directed people who bring a lifetime of experience to the learning situation. They have endured a life-threatening illness and need to learn to adjust to the current problem as well as prevent further complications by making life style changes.

The andragogical model is a process model in contrast to a pedagogical content model. In other words, instead of deciding in advance what content is to be presented and how to present the content, the teacher prepares a set of procedures. The procedures establish a climate conducive to learning, create a mechanism for mutual planning, diagnose learning needs, formulate objectives to meet learning needs, design learning experiences, and evaluate learning outcomes and rediagnose learning needs. A content model focuses on transmitting information and skills; the process model provides procedures and resources for helping learners acquire the information and skills needed to live with their disease.

Widely accepted principles of adult learning have been summarized.[67] These principles represent a broad range of learning theories and are supported by the research of reputable educational psychologists. The major principles, which are summarized in Exhibit 7-3, provide valuable information about how people learn.

Barriers to Teaching-Learning

Although nurses now have a legitimate role in education of the cardiac patient, evidence indicates efforts have not been extremely successful. Factors that hinder

---

Exhibit 7-3 Accepted Principles of Learning

Motivation for learning is increased by personal involvement.
Learning under the control of reward is more effective than learning under the control of punishment.
Meaningful material is learned more readily than irrelevant material.
Behaviors that are reinforced are more likely to recur.
Reinforcement should follow the desired behavior immediately.
Practice alone is not adequate. Feedback on one's efforts is necessary.
Learning thrives on success. Continuous failure discourages learning.
Learning is more effective if spaced over a period of time with frequent review periods.
Information concerning progress toward goals facilitates learning.
Learning is more effective if the material is presented in multiple ways.

teaching and learning efforts have been identified.[68] Lack of time was identified in studies in the 1960s and has escalated as a major problem for nurses in today's cost-cutting health care environment. As nurses take on more technical responsibilities and staffing decreases, teaching is assigned a lower priority. Thus lack of time intensifies the decreased emphasis assigned to patient education.

Another major barrier is inadequate preparation of nurses to teach.[69] Although the teaching-learning process is now included in undergraduate curricula, the amount of time devoted to the subject is minimal, and clinical supervision for teaching is limited. In addition, nurses who did not have the basic content in their nursing program may not have ever had the opportunity to learn teaching-learning theory.

Barriers to learning in cardiac patients have also been identified. Four types of obstacles have been proposed: physiologic, psychologic, environmental, and iatrogenic. Physiologic barriers include the magnitude of the illness event, pain, restlessness, the age of the patient, and prognosis. Maslow's hierarchy of needs indicates that an individual's basic needs must be met before higher order needs, i.e., learning, can be attended.[70] Thus, teaching efforts are limited to explaining interventions and answering questions during the acute phase of the illness, as the nurse must focus on the patient's physiologic needs.

Psychologic barriers to learning in cardiac patients include anxiety, denial, and depression. Anxiety is highest on admission, upon transfer from an intensive care unit, and before discharge. Teaching during periods of high anxiety is limited by patients' inability to concentrate and retain information. The nurse needs to provide consistent, frequent explanations during these high-anxiety periods. During episodes of denial, teaching is limited to explanations oriented to the immediate situation. Depression is not uncommon in the cardiac patient after an MI or coronary artery bypass surgery. The nurse's role is to listen and provide support without fostering dependence. Psychologic manifestations must be decreased before teaching can be attempted.

Obstacles in patients' environments contribute to psychologic disturbances and limit learning. Loss of privacy, unfamiliar noises, bright lights, separation from loved ones, and observation of procedures on other patients are some factors that may contribute to the patient's cognitive impairment during hospitalization. Explanations provided in terminology understood by the patient need to begin on admission to alleviate anxiety caused by the strange environment.

Iatrogenic barriers or obstacles to learning because of attitudes and behaviors of the health care team are all too common. Talking down to patients, teaching too hurriedly, or teaching in a fragmented manner triggers obstacles to learning. Nonverbal cutoffs, i.e., breaking eye contact or glancing at one's watch, also deter learning. Nurses must keep in mind that what they do and how they do it has as much impact as what they say.

In summary, before the nurse begins to teach patients, barriers that may inhibit either teaching or learning must be identified. Thus the process begins with a thorough assessment of potential or actual barriers in the nurse (teacher) and patient (learner). Then, the objectives of the process can be formulated to take into account those obstacles identified. Interventions based on the objectives are implemented. Evaluation of the degree of success of the interventions completes the process.

ENHANCING LIFE STYLE CHANGE

The CHD epidemic is a result of a Western life style in which people eat too much of a too rich diet, grow fat, smoke too much, and exercise too little.[71] The powerful contribution of these life style habits to the etiology of atherosclerosis is now scientifically established. The good news is that the risk factors can be detected, and CHD may be prevented. The bad news is that life style change is not easy, especially in the absence of symptoms. This section discusses four nursing diagnoses relevant to enhancing life style change: knowledge deficit, nonadherence, powerlessness, and inadequate social support. All four are related to cardiovascular risk factor modification.

Cardiovascular mortality has declined since 1968.[72] The decrease has been attributed to medical interventions, preventive measures, and changes in life style. Improved medical and emergency care, earlier hospital admissions to coronary care units, and coronary artery bypass surgery have all had a role. The decline also coincided with advocated changes in life style to reduce cardiovascular risk factors. Cholesterol values have decreased along with per capita consumption of butter, eggs, milk, and animal fat. Physical activity has become a national pastime. Widespread detection and better treatment and control of hypertension have occurred. Smoking has decreased, especially in middle-aged men.

Although the contribution of life style change to the reduction of cardiovascular mortality has not been precisely quantified, over one-half of the decline is attributed to reduction of serum cholesterol levels and cigarette smoking, and control of hypertension. All these major risk factors have behavioral components. One's risk for cardiovascular disease can be decreased by changing one's life style. Habits can be altered. The nurse plays a vital role in risk factor modification for both primary and secondary prevention and improving adherence to medical regimens.

A major obstacle to life style modification is that the benefits of adopting preventive behaviors are delayed and may seem remote compared with the immediate pleasures of indulgence and the effort and inconvenience involved in risk factor reduction. The barrier is less of a problem after a patient experiences a cardiac insult, as the effects of the risk factors may become more obvious. Second, forces in our environment serve as barriers to life style change. Economic pressures perpetuate cigarette and unhealthy food commercials on television and in other media. Fast food chains serving high cholesterol foods continue to expand. Healthier foods are often less available and more expensive, producing an economic barrier for many. Most work sites do not provide opportunities for exercise. These two major barriers must be kept in mind when working with patients to assist with life style change.

Evaluation of the need to change life style habits begins with a physiologic assessment, which includes a serum lipid profile, exercise stress testing, skinfold measurements, BP measurements, etc. Next, current behavior patterns are obtained including usual dietary intake, stress management, type/frequency of exercise, smoking habits, patients' perceived barriers and benefits to changing their life style, and feasibility of the needed changes. The patient's willingness to commit to life style change can be influenced by many factors. Four nursing diagnoses address the main factors or problems encountered when patients attempt life style change.

Nursing Diagnoses

Knowledge Deficit Related to Cardiovascular Risk Factor Reduction

This diagnosis in a patient with CHD indicates a deficiency in either cognitive information or psychomotor skills to the extent the deficiency interferes with risk factor modification. The diagnosis is based on the initial assessment of baseline knowledge. The nurse asks, what does the patient know about the disease, its treatment, and expected outcomes? Barriers to the teaching-learning process will help identify factors that may be interfering with learning the necessary content about risk factors. Patients should also be asked to perform a self-assessment so they know what they need to learn and want to learn. If possible their partner should be involved.

Objectives are then formulated based on the assessment. Stated objectives let the patient know what is expected and what needs to be done to reach goals. The nurse's role in teaching is also clarified when objectives are defined. Content to be taught is then delineated. The content needed to provide an adequate knowledge must be determined; an appropriate level needs to be chosen based on educational level, prior experiences with the health care system, age, occupation, and reading level. It is also important to give correct and relevant information; thus nurses should review any information unclear in their own mind before teaching the patient.

Teaching to alleviate knowledge deficit may be implemented individually or in a group. Group teaching is economical, and patients learn from each other. Audiovisual aids, at the appropriate content level, should be used, as multiple variations increase learning. Principles of learning outlined in Exhibit 7-1 need to be kept in mind when implementing the teaching plan.

After the teaching intervention, an evaluation of learning is necessary. Was the teaching successful? Success can be defined in terms of increased knowledge, or an attitude or behavior change. Evaluation provides information for a follow-up assessment. Methods of evaluation include direct observation, written tests, or patient and family reports of a gain in knowledge. Future teaching will be based on the results of the evaluation.

Research on patient education is abundant, and evidence suggests that an increase in knowledge does not necessarily mean a change in behavior will occur. Recent research reports indicate other factors, such as social support, stress reduction, and feeling of control, have a greater role in successful life style change than knowledge about one's disease.[73,74] However, knowledge remains the first step, and an essential one, in the teaching-learning process.

Nonadherence to Cardiovascular Risk Factor Reduction

When a patient is said to be nonadherent, he is not conforming to some set standard. Demographic, psychologic, environmental, and social factors must all be taken into consideration in assessing reasons for nonadherence. Once the factors are identified, nursing interventions can be appropriately planned.

Young[75] stated that strategies to improve adherence can be broken down into organizational, educational, and behavioral factors. Organizational strategies focus on the structure for delivery of care: arranging convenient appointment times, decreasing time spent in waiting rooms, keeping the treatment plan as simple as possible. Educational strategies are related to the transmission of information. Behavioral strategies include interventions that attempt to modify behaviors. The relationship between the patient and the person involved in the intervention is a critical component in behavioral strategies. A positive relation increases adherence.

Achieving adherence begins when the patients agree that a problem increasing their risk for extension of their disease exists. Once the problem is acknowledged, potential solutions can be proposed and an acceptable plan formulated. Written contracts might be negotiated at this time.

Continuous personal contact is necessary throughout the life style intervention phase. The patient needs continuous feedback on progress from a credible source. In addition to feedback and reinforcement, the personal contact allows questions to be answered. Family and peer involvement should also be encouraged by including them in the intervention sessions.

Ongoing monitoring of the patient's level of adherence facilitates the early diagnosis of relapse and enables the nurse to plan, with the patient, new strategies. Patients should be encouraged to discuss their adherence problems. When problems are detected, factors that may be operating again need to be diagnosed. Thus evaluation returns both the patient and nurse to the assessment phase.

Powerlessness

This nursing diagnosis describes a subjective state in which patients perceive a lack of personal control over their situation. Powerlessness inhibits motivation to engage in life style change. Patients feel they have no control and therefore do not participate in self-care behaviors to reduce risk factors. The present health care system creates patient dependency beginning in the hospital. Control is relinquished to powerful others (i.e., physician, nurse) by the "good" patient. Privacy is often limited; personal territory is reduced; social isolation is allowed; explanations may be omitted or inadequate; and patients are rarely consulted regarding decisions about their care.[76]

Perceived control has a significant role in life style change. Subjects who believe they have control of their health are more likely to engage in preventive behaviors than subjects who perceive others controlling their health or fate or luck being responsible. Recent studies indicate patients with chronic CHD believe health care professionals control their health.[77] The effect of this finding on life style changes warrants further investigation.

Once the diagnosis of powerlessness is made, interventions that enable patients to increase control over their care need to be implemented. If lack of knowledge contributes, teaching can be undertaken. Keep patients informed and ensure their participation in decision making. Focusing attention on attainable goals, providing choices, and providing positive feedback enhance patient perception of personal control. A measure of success that patients are developing control is their degree of self-care. Thus interventions need to be directed toward establishing a nurse-patient relationship that allows self-care.

Inadequate Social Support

Social support refers to the emotional and material resources available to the patient through relationships with others. Social support includes the provision of money, information, and emotional support. Positive social support has consistently been related to increased adherence in cardiac programs. Inadequate support has been observed in patients who drop out of exercise and other life style change programs.[78] Spousal support has been linked to adherence in patients with cardiovascular disease.[79] The Framingham study[80] reported higher rates of CHD in men who were married to working women with higher educational levels than in men married to nonworking women or to those with a lower level of education. Being employed may have decreased the amount of spousal support provided by these women.

Social support may be beneficial in two ways.[81] First, it may directly influence behavior in helping the patient sustain motivation. Or it may have an indirect role by modifying or buffering other factors that influence behaviors. For example, a spouse may create a more calm environment in which to alleviate hassles or stress. The second factor points to the need to assess other support resources in addition to those directly related to the behavior change.

Although the research on social support suffers from several methodologic concerns, as with other psychosocial variables, the consistency of findings suggests that it is an important factor in enhancing life style change. Thus, the nursing assessment must identify significant persons in the patient's social network, the type of support provided, patient satisfaction with the support, and the actual quality of the support. Once the assessment is complete, interventions to ensure provision of adequate support are implemented. Family members or partners need to participate fully in the treatment plan. Partner support needs to be continuously monitored and nurtured by the health care providers. If the patient does not have a social network, appropriate groups need to be identified. As with the other nursing diagnoses, the adequacy of the support needs to be monitored and evaluated at intervals, and new strategies implemented to provide needed support as necessary.

Behavioral Management Strategies

Methods of behavior change derived from behavior psychology, in combination with traditional education techniques, can be applied to assist in establishing habits beneficial to cardiovascular health and in eliminating the harmful ones. Habits are maintained through practice and repetition. Thus strategies that interfere with or discourage unhealthful habits should assist in their elimination. Techniques to promote healthy habits and discourage negative ones include shaping, reinforcement, stimulus control, and contracting.

Shaping

Shaping is the process by which behavior is broken down into a series of successive approximations that are gradually progressed until the desired end behavior is reached. One begins with simple, easily performed behaviors and provides positive reinforcement. In other words, start low and build to more complex behavior changes. For example, a sedentary patient should begin an exercise program at an easily mastered walking exercise frequency and intensity. The exercise can be progressively increased until the long-term goal of aerobic exercise is achieved. During the early stages of shaping, the primary goal is to establish the habit; therefore the change must not be too challenging or uncomfortable to the patient. Frequent positive reinforcements and rewards are critical during the early phase.

Reinforcement

Reinforcement is the process by which behaviors are strengthened by positive environmental effects.[82] Reinforcers are stimuli presented during or after the behavior that increase the future probability of the behavior. Reinforcement is most effective when it is delivered during or shortly after the behavior. Reinforcement contingencies, such as a lottery at the end of the program, gift certificates, and achievement awards, increase motivation to change. As with shaping, regular feedback on one's progress is crucial.

Stimulus Control

Stimulus control is the process of identifying antecedent conditions, cues, and prompts that trigger certain behaviors. The technique can involve removing things from the environment that promote unhealthy habits to prevent the behavior from occurring, or providing environmental cues to stimulate a positive behavior. For example, tempting foods can be removed from the kitchen. If patients are trying to stop smoking, they should sit in nonsmoking sections of airplanes and restaurants. Avoiding situations in which the negative response normally occurs is particularly beneficial for compulsive behaviors. To promote positive behaviors, environmental prompts can be used. For example, laying out one's exercise clothes the night before can stimulate the desired response of exercise. Spending time with friends who exercise frequently and wearing exercise clothes around the house are other examples.

Contracting

Behavioral contracting is a formal agreement to work toward a specific goal. Contracts help the patient commit to specific actions and establish clear-cut criteria for achievement of the goal. They provide a mechanism for specifying consequences of engaging or not engaging in the behavior. Progress can be evaluated against the terms of the contract. Contracts need to include a clear description of the proposed change, rewards for adherence, consequences of failure to adhere, and time limitations. Good contracts have short-term goals. Both the patient and the involved party (nurse, family member, etc.) sign the agreement and receive copies.

Exhibit 7-4 is a summary of these four behavioral management strategies. Textbooks are available for detailed methods.

Stress Management Strategies

Efforts to minimize psychologic stress emphasize techniques to decrease levels of general arousal. The rationale for the use of these techniques is based on the cardiovascular effects of the stress response. Psychologic perceptions and evaluations are translated into physiologic changes that produce increased glucocorticoid and catecholamine release. Release of these hormones results in increased heart rate, BP, blood glucose, free fatty acid production, and enhanced platelet

Exhibit 7-4 Steps in the Use of Behavioral Management Strategies*

Shaping
1. Establish criterion for first approximation.
2. Arrange environment to achieve success.
3. Reinforce desired behavioral response.
4. Shift criterion toward goal behavior.
5. Reinforce achievement of goal.

Reinforcement
1. Identify reinforcers that are functional for patient.
2. Deliver reinforcers immediately after behavior.
3. Reinforce behavior frequently initially.
4. Use social reinforcement (behavior of others) whenever feasible.

Stimulus Control
1. Identify link between antecedent cues and behavior.
2. Identify cues for negative behavior.
3. Remove cues for negative behavior.
4. Make cues for positive behavior obvious.

Contracting
1. Clearly describe desired change.
2. Set criterion for time or frequency limits.
3. Specify positive reinforcement.
4. Make provisions for negative consequences.
5. Provide bonus clause if demands exceeded.
6. Describe procedure for providing feedback to patient.

*Note: For details, see *Helping People Change: A Textbook of Methods* by F. Kanfer and A. Goldstein, Pergamon Press, Ltd., © 1980.

aggregation. These effects may further compromise the already damaged myocardium of the cardiac patient. Four strategies that affect the stress response are relaxation, biofeedback, anxiety management training, and anger management training.

Relaxation

Relaxation techniques have been used effectively in controlling the cardiovascular response to stress by producing a response that seems to be a parasympathetically mediated counterpart of the fight or flight response.[83] Some effects of the relaxation response are decreased oxygen consumption and blood lactate levels, decreased heart rate, and lowered BP.

Relaxation techniques include four important components.[84] First, the patient must be able to achieve muscle relaxation. Second, the patient must be able to control mental activity by focusing attention on the relaxation techniques. Third, regular practice is necessary; and last, patients must believe they will be successful in using the technique.

Progressive muscle relaxation (PMR) assists patients to achieve conscious control over skeletal muscles.[85] Patients are taught how to tense and relax separate skeletal muscle groups, progressing through the body. The muscle group is tensed for 5 to 7 seconds and then relaxed in an exercise sequence. The entire procedure lasts approximately 20 minutes and is performed in a quiet, softly lit room. The patient should be seated in a recliner chair or lying down. Tapes and detailed instructions are available for those interested in learning to instruct or perform the technique.

Similar relaxation techniques include transcendental meditation, yoga, hypnosis, and autogenic training. In these methods, patients focus on a constant mental stimulus, such as a number or phrase. A passive attitude, decreased muscle focus, and a quiet setting are needed. For example, Benson's[86] relaxation response instructs patients to focus on the number one as they exhale. Patients are told to sit quietly, focus on their breathing, maintain a passive attitude, and ignore distractions. They are instructed to practice the exercise twice a day for 20 minutes.

Adverse side effects have been reported in persons who practice relaxation techniques more than 30 minutes twice a day. Psychiatric disturbances, including hallucinations, may result. No negative physiologic effects have been reported.

Biofeedback

Biofeedback involves the use of noninvasive instrumentation that provides physiologic information continuously to the patient. It includes the measurement, quantification, and feedback of responses of the nervous system. For example, heart rate, BP, and skin temperature feedback involve the assessment and quantification of responses mediated by the autonomic nervous system. Electromyelogram biofeedback represents the assessment and quantification responses mediated by the somatic nervous system. Hypertension and cardiac arrhythmias have been treated with biofeedback.

Biofeedback training takes place in a controlled setting. As physiologic responses are measured, continuous feedback is provided. Reinforcers are presented whenever the physiologic response changes in the desired direction. The patient learns to control the physiologic response through the feedback and reinforcers. Shaping is also used. Once some degree of control is achieved, larger physiologic changes are necessary to receive reinforcement.

Anxiety Management Training

Anxiety management training (AMT) is a conditioning procedure designed to reduce anxiety reactions.[87] The training consists of three stages. First, patients are taught relaxation techniques. Then, they are instructed to visualize a situation that produces an anxiety reaction, to recognize the sensations of anxiety, and then to shift to the relaxation exercise until relaxation is achieved. The technique has been used successfully in controlling the stress response in patients who exhibit TABP and hypertension.

Anger Management Training

Anger management training focuses on reducing the hostility component of TABP.[88] The three phases of training are cognitive preparation, skill acquisition, and application training. First, patients are educated about anger arousal. They are taught self-monitoring to identify circumstances that trigger anger and are introduced to anger management techniques. They then learn to recognize the determinants of their anger. Alternate coping strategies are then practiced under supervision in predetermined provocative situations. After role-playing and practice, the skills are applied to real-life situations. Patients learn not to take things personally, to delay their responses to provocation, and to use nonaggressive communication.

SUMMARY

This chapter reviewed the major modifiable risk factors for cardiovascular disease and attempted to apply principles of the teaching-learning process and current research in the discussion of strategies to reduce or eliminate them. The nurse has both an independent and collaborative role in enhancing life style change in patients. Formulating appropriate diagnoses, designing effective interventions, and evaluating outcomes on which to reformulate diagnoses are all within the nurse's role. Modifying unhealthy life styles is complex and offers a challenge both to cardiovascular nursing practice and research.

NOTES

1. L. Goldman and F. Cook, "The Decline in Ischemic Heart Disease Mortality Rates," *Annals of Internal Medicine* 101(1984):825.

2. American Heart Association, *Heart Facts, 1986* (Dallas: American Heart Association, 1986).

3. W. Kannel and G. Ward, "Overview of Cardiovascular Risk Factors," *Practical Cardiology* 12(1986):63.

4. W. Kannel and A. Schatzkin, "Risk Factor Analysis," *Progress in Cardiovascular Diseases* 26(1986):309.

5. R. Levy, "Changing Perspectives in the Prevention of Coronary Artery Disease," *American Journal of Cardiology* 57(1986):17G.

6. Lipid Research Clinics Program, "The Relationship of Reduction in Incidence of Coronary Heart Disease to Cholesterol Lowering," *Journal of the American Medical Association* 251(1984):365.

7. J. Brensike, R. Levy, and S. Kelsey, "Effects of Therapy with Cholestyramine on Progression of Coronary Artery Disease: Results of the MHLBI Type II Coronary Intervention Study," *Circulation* 69(1984):313.

8. S. Grundy, G. Vega, and D. Bilheimer, "Influence of Combined Therapy with Mevinotin and Interruption of Urle Acid Reabsorption on Low Density Lipoproteins in Heterozygous Familial Hypercholesteremia," *Annals of Internal Medicine* 103(1985):339.

9. D. Bilheimer et al., "Mevinolin and Colestipol Stimulate Receptor-Mediated Clearance of Low Density Lipoprotein from Plasma in Familial Hypercholesteremia Heterozygotes," *Proceedings of the National Academy of Sciences* 80(1983):4124.

10. J. Dyerberg et al., "Eicosapentaenoic Acid and Prevention of Thrombosis and Atherosclerosis," *Lancet* 2(1978):117.

11. J. Glomset, "Fish, Fatty Acids and Human Health," *New England Journal of Medicine* 312(1985):1253.

12. B. Phillipson et al., "Reduction of Plasma Lipids, Lipoproteins and Apoproteins by Dietary Fish Oils in Patients with Hypertriglyceridemia," *New England Journal of Medicine* 312(1984):1210.

13. D. Weiner et al., "Inhibition of Atherosclerosis by Cod Liver Oil in a Hyperlipidemic Swine Model," *New England Journal of Medicine* 315(1986):841.

14. American Heart Association, *Counseling the Patient with Hyperlipidemia* (Dallas: American Heart Association, 1984).

15. W. Castelli, "The Triglyceride Issue: A View from Framingham," *American Heart Journal* 112(1986):432.

16. R. Mulcahy, "Influence of Cigarette Smoking on Morbidity and Mortality after Myocardial Infarction," *British Heart Journal* 49(1983):410.

17. A. Aberg, R. Bergstrand, and S. Johansson, "Cessation of Smoking after Myocardial Infarction: Effect on Mortality after 10 Years," *British Heart Journal* 49(1983):416.

18. G. Cutter et al., "The Natural History of Smoking Cessation among Patients Undergoing Coronary Arteriography," *Journal of Cardiopulmonary Rehabilitation* 5(1985):332.

19. J. Salonen, "Stopping Smoking and Long Term Mortality after Acute Myocardial Infarction," *British Heart Journal* 43(1980):463.

20. Mulcahy, "Cigarette Smoking."

21. Cutter et al., "Smoking Cessation."

22. K. Brownell, "Obesity: Understanding and Treating a Serious Prevalent and Refractory Disorder," *Journal of Consulting and Clinical Psychology* 50(1982):820.

23. S. Schacter, "Recidivism and Self Care of Smoking and Obesity," *American Psychologist* 37(1982):436.

24. V. Gianetti, J. Reynolds, and T. Rehn, "Factors Which Differentiate Smokers from Ex-smokers Among Cardiovascular Patients: A Discriminant Analysis," *Social Science and Medicine* 20(1985):241.

25. R. Katz and N. Singh, "Reflections of the Ex-smoker: Some Findings on Successful Quitters," *Journal of Behavioral Medicine* 9(1986):191.

26. R. Glasglow et al., "Quitting Smoking: Strategies Used and Variables Associated with Success in a Stop Smoking Program," *Journal of Consulting and Clinical Psychology* 53(1985):905.

27. E. Lichenstein and R. Brown, "Social Learning, Smoking and Substance Abuse," in N.A. Krasnegar, ed., *Behavioral Analysis and Treatment of Substance Abuse*. NIDA Research Monograph 25, DHEW Publication No. 79-839 (Washington: Government Printing Office, 1980).

28. U.S. Department of Health and Human Services, *The Physician's Guide: How to Help Your Hypertensive Patients to Stop Smoking*, NIH Publication No. 83-1271 (Washington: Government Printing Office, 1983).

29. E. Lichenstein, "The Smoking Problem: A Behavioral Perspective," *Journal of Consulting and Clinical Psychology* 50(1982):804.

30. A. Bandura, *Social Learning Theory* (Englewood Cliffs, NJ: Prentice Hall, 1977).

31. H. Leventhal and P. Cleary, "The Smoking Problem: A Review of the Research and Theory in Behavioral Risk Modification," *Psychological Bulletin* 88(1980):370.

32. J. Abramson, "Prevention of Cardiovascular Disease in the Elderly," *Public Health Reviews* 13(1980):166.

33. A. Marks, *Essential Hypertension: Modern Concepts and Current Practice* (East Hanover, NJ: Sandoz, Inc., 1984).

34. J. Curb et al., "Isolated Systolic Hypertension in 14 Communities," *American Journal of Epidemiology* 121(1985):371.

35. U.S. Department of Health and Human Services, *The 1984 Report of the Joint National Committee on Detection, Evaluation and Treatment of High Blood Pressure*, NIH Publication No. 894-1088 (Washington: Government Printing Office, 1984).

36. Marks, "Essential Hypertension."

37. Hypertension Detection and Follow-Up Program (HDFP) Cooperative Group, "The Effect of Treatment on Mortality in 'Mild' Hypertension," *New England Journal of Medicine* 307(1982):976.

38. Hypertension Detection and Follow-Up Program (HDFP) Cooperative Group, "Implications of the Hypertension Detection and Follow-up Program," *Progress in Cardiovascular Diseases* 29, Suppl. 1 (1986):3.

39. T. Luscher et al., "Compliance in Hypertension: Facts and Concepts," *Journal of Hypertension* 3, Suppl. 1 (1985):3.

40. Leventhal and Cleary, "Smoking Problem."

41. I. Barofsky, "Therapeutic Compliance and the Cancer Patient," *Health Education Quarterly* 11(1983):43.

42. M. Powers and A. Jaloweic, "Profile of the Well-controlled, Well-adjusted Hypertensive Patient," *Nursing Research* 36(1987):106.

43. J. Kuh, "Ethnicity: An Important Factor for Nurses to Consider in Caring for Hypertensive Patients," *Western Journal of Nursing Research* 8(1986):445.

44. Barofsky, "Therapeutic Compliance."

45. R. Lindquist, "Providing Patient Opportunities to Increase Control," *Dimensions of Critical Care Nursing* 5(1986):304.

46. W. Kannel et al., "Physical Activity and Physical Demand on the Job and Risk of Cardiovascular Disease and Death: The Framingham Study," *American Heart Journal* 112(1986):820.

47. R. Paffenbarger et al., "Physical Activity, All Cause Mortality, and Longevity of College Alumni," *New England Journal of Medicine* 314(1986):605.

48. M. Pollock and L.K. Smith, *Cardiac Rehabilitation Services: A Scientific Evaluation* (New York: American Association of Cardiovascular and Pulmonary Rehabilitation, 1986).

49. Abramson, "Prevention of Disease."

50. N. Oldridge, "Compliance and Exercise in Primary and Secondary Prevention of Coronary Heart Disease: A Review," *Preventive Medicine* 11(1982):56.

51. N. Oldridge and J. Spencer, "Exercise Habits and Perceptions Before and After Graduation or Drop-out from Supervised Cardiac Exercise Rehabilitation," *Journal of Cardiopulmonary Rehabilitation* 5(1985):313.

52. J. Sallis et al., "Predictors of Adoption and Maintenance of Physical Activity in a Community Sample," *Preventive Medicine* 15(1986):331.

53. Ibid.

54. Kannal and Ward, "Overview of Risk Factors."

55. T. Smith and N. Anderson, "Model of Personality and Disease: An Interactional Approach to Type A Behavior and Cardiovascular Risk," *Journal of Personality and Social Psychology* 6(1986):1166.

56. J. Barefoot, W. Dahlstrom, and W. Williams, "Hostility, CHD Incidence and Total Mortality: A 25 Year Follow-up of 255 Physicians," *Psychosomatic Medicine* 45(1983):59.

57. J. McDougall et al., "Components of Type A, Hostility and Anger: Further Relationships to Angiographic Findings," *Health Psychology* 4(1985):137.

58. R. McLellain, P. Bornstein, and T. Carmody, "A Methodological Critique of the Structured Interview Assessment of Type A Behavior," *Journal of Cardiopulmonary Rehabilitation* 6(1986):21.

59. R. Suinn, "Intervention with Type A Behaviors," *Journal of Consulting and Clinical Psychology* 50(1982):933.

60. Ibid.

61. C. Thoreson et al., "Altering the Type A Behavior Pattern in Postinfarction Patients," *Journal of Cardiopulmonary Rehabilitation* 5(1985):258.

62. H. Moos and W. Procci, "Sexual Dysfunction Associated with Oral Hypertensive Medication," *General Hospital Psychiatry* 4(1982):121.

63. D. Krantz, L. Durel, and J. Davia, "Propanolol Medication Among Coronary Patients: Relation to Type A Behavior and Cardiovascular Response," *Journal of Human Stress* 8(1982):4.

64. R. Schnieder, G. Friedrich, and H. Neus, "The Influence of Beta Blockers on Cardiovascular Reactivity and Type A Behavior Pattern in Hypertensives," *Psychosomatic Medicine* 45(1983):45.

65. M. Knowles, *The Adult Learner: A Neglected Species* (Houston: Gulf Publishing Co., 1973).

66. Ibid.

67. M. Bigge, *Learning Theories for Teachers* (New York: Harper & Row, 1976).

68. C. Murdaugh, "Barriers to Patient Education in the Coronary Care Unit," *Journal of Cardiovascular Nursing* 18(1982):31.

69. C. Murdaugh, "Effects of Nurse's Knowledge of Teaching-Learning Principles on Knowledge of CCU Patients," *Heart and Lung* 9(1980):1072.

70. A. Maslow, *Motivation and Personality* (New York: Harper & Row, 1970).

71. Kannel et al., "Physical Activity."

72. Goldman and Cook, "Decline in Mortality."

73. A. Steinbinder, *Instrument Development to Assess Knowledge of Life-style Change*, Masters thesis (Tucson: University of Arizona, 1987).

74. R. Friis and G. Taft, "Social Support and Social Networks, and CHD and Rehabilitation," *Journal of Cardiopulmonary Rehabilitation* 6(1986):132.

75. M. Young, "Strategies for Improving Compliance," *Topics in Clinical Nursing* 7(1986):65.

76. L. Carpenito, *Nursing Diagnosis: Application to Clinical Practice* (Philadelphia: J.B. Lippincott, 1983), pp. 332–337.

77. C. Murdaugh and J. Verran, "Theoretical Modeling to Predict Physiological Indicants of Cardiac Preventive Behaviors," *Nursing Research*, in press.

78. Gianetti, Reynolds, and Rehn, "Factors Which Differentiate Smokers."

79. J. Hibbard, "Social Ties and Health Status: An Examination of Moderating Factors," *Health Education Quarterly* 12(1985):23.

80. S. Haynes, E. Eaker, and M. Feinleib, "Spouse Behavior and CHD in Men: Prospective Results from the Framingham Heart Study," *American Journal of Epidemiology* 118(1983):1.

81. R. Mermelstein et al., "Social Support and Smoking Cessation and Maintenance," *Journal of Consulting and Clinical Psychology* 54(1986):447.

82. J. Elder et al., "Application of Behavior Modification to Community Health Education: The Case of Heart Disease Prevention," *Health Education Quarterly* 13(1985):151.

83. S. Melvile, "Relaxation Techniques in Acute Myocardial Infarction: The Theoretical Rationale," *Focus on Critical Care* 14(1987):9.

84. M. Chesney and M. Ward, "Biobehavioral Treatment Approaches to Cardiovascular Disease," *Journal of Cardiopulmonary Rehabilitation* 5(1985):226.

85. E. Jacobson, *Progressive Relaxation* (Chicago: University of Chicago Press, 1983).

86. H. Benson, *The Relaxation Response* (New York: Avon Books, 1975).

87. R. Suinn and F. Richardson, "Anxiety Management Training: A Nonspecific Behavior Therapy Program for Anxiety Control," *Behavioral Therapy* 2(1971):498.

88. J. Moon and R. Eisler, "Anger Control: An Experimental Comparison of Three Behavioral Treatments," *Behavioral Therapy* 14(1983):493.

Chapter 8

Ineffective Coping: Patient and Family

Suzanne Clark, RN, MSN, MA

A patient admitted to a critical care unit with a cardiac-related illness experiences a life-threatening event. Without warning, patients and families confront a situation that not only presents the possibility of death but also raises fears regarding changes in role, self-esteem, appearance, and body function. Disequilibrium is created in an otherwise steady state, and adaptation must occur to re-establish a sense of balance. These efforts to regain a feeling of control in the face of stressful circumstances are referred to as *coping*. Although every patient's and family's experience is unique, and coping behaviors will vary, caregivers can identify similar patterns and develop a systematic approach to help patients and families cope.[1]

For some, hospitalization constitutes a crisis, a situation so unfamiliar that usual successful coping mechanisms are no longer effective. People in crisis feel helpless to meet the demands of the situation and may experience feelings of disorganization, anxiety, and fear, which further add to the already existing feelings of helplessness. Their usual responses are not adequate to maintain a state of equilibrium.[2] However, many patients and families continue to function in a reasonable manner.

Why do some people weather the crises of critical illness and hospitalization? What kind of coping skills do they use to maintain an equilibrium? What effect does ineffective coping have on recovery? How can nurses identify patients and families who cope ineffectively? What nursing interventions can be employed to maintain effective coping in patients and families who are coping well? What interventions should be used to assist those coping ineffectively to feel more in control?

The answers to these questions can be found by first identifying a model that describes coping behaviors and distinguishes between responses that are effective from those that are not. A model provides a framework for understanding interactions among related phenomena.[3] Once the interrelationship of the model's components are understood, a basis for interventions can be built. Once we understand the coping process and the variables that lead to effective coping, we can plan interventions that help patients and families adapt positively to a critical cardiac event.

The framework advanced by Richard Lazarus is useful for helping nurses understand the process of coping with psychologic stress.[4]

COPING MODEL

Threat

Coping is an attempt to gain mastery over conditions of threat.[5] In general, people try to maintain psychologic equilibrium, a feeling of well-being, a feeling of being in control. When a stimulus from an internal or external source arouses feelings that one's important goals are not going to be met, a threat exists. Threat is the *anticipation of harm*. Anticipation of pain, loss of body function, loss of self-esteem, and loss of a loved one can produce feelings of impending harm. The amount of harm can vary and is related to both its imminence and probability of occurring. In summary, a threat is anticipation that one's goals will be thwarted. Threats vary according to their qualitative and quantitative aspects.

Cognitive Appraisal

Appraisal is the process by which the quality or worth of something is judged. In Lazarus' coping model, cognitive appraisal *must* be present for a stimulus to be identified as a threat. It is the intervening variable between the stimulus and the emotional response. Appraisal is influenced by past experience. A previous experience with pain that remained severe and unrelieved makes it likely that future experiences involving pain or the *possibility* of pain will be perceived as threatening.

The feeling of threat in human beings is often symbolic rather than tangible. For example, power rankings that give individuals authority to distribute rewards and punishments are symbolic stimuli. If people have had negative experiences with authority figures, all individuals representing authority may be perceived as threatening. The stimulus need not really be capable of harm to qualify as a source of threat. These two important concepts, past experiences and symbolic meanings, help explain why we see so many different responses to similar situations. Threat exists only when it is *perceived and interpreted*. Lazarus refers to this process as *primary appraisal*.

To this point, then, our model for coping can be represented by the following sequence of events:

$$\text{Stimulus} \longrightarrow \text{Cognitive appraisal} \longrightarrow \text{Feelings of anticipated}$$
$$\text{of threat} \qquad \text{harm}$$
$$\text{(emotional response).}$$

Stimulus Characteristics That Influence Threat Appraisal

Factors inherent in the stimulus can influence an individual's perception of threat. One has already been mentioned: the imminence of the threat. The closer in time it is to the anticipated confrontation, the greater the threat.

A second factor relates to the balance between the strength of the stimulus and individuals' beliefs in the power of their own resources to combat the threat.[6,7] On the strength of the stimulus side of this relation, some situations seem to carry with them an *objective* danger that all individuals would perceive and react to as threatening: a fire blazing out of control, a dam breaking, an admission to an emergency room with crushing chest pain. However, even in these circumstances, some individuals do not interpret them as harm-producing. In some cases, the seriousness of the situation may not be understood because people have not received needed information. In other cases, patients may be using protective mechanisms to shield themselves from the full impact of the threat. Finally, patients may call on past experiences of successful coping to help them through unfamiliar events. It is better to think about peoples' reactions to situations in terms of the amount of information they have available and the coping style being used rather than anticipate a reaction based on the caretaker's perception of the situation.

On the strength of the resources side of the ratio, if individuals believe they can control the danger, the feelings of threat can often disappear. This belief in one's own resources can come from past experiences with similar threats or from a strong belief in one's own inner abilities. Another important component on the resource side of the equation is environmental resources. The support of powerful people or economic security can bolster a person's feeling that harm can be resisted.

Finally, stimulus ambiguity can influence perception of threat. In general, the more uncertain the cues are concerning the nature of the threat or what actions will best combat the threat, the more likely a stimulus will be seen as dangerous.

Factors in the Individual That Influence Appraisal of Threat

Individual differences in biopsychologic make-up also account for differences in coping responses. These are deeply rooted personality traits that are not usually amenable to change in the relatively brief interactions critical care nurses have with patients. Cues will be appraised as potentially harmful depending on the goals, belief system, intellectual resources, and sophistication of the individual. If situations interfere with important life goals, they will be perceived as threatening. A person who is mistrustful of others will certainly perceive more situations as potentially harmful than someone who has a basic belief in the trustworthiness of his fellow man. People who have decreased intellectual resources or sophistication have an increased chance of misinterpreting the reality of a situation. In summary, personality factors are difficult to influence but are important in understanding individual reactions to similar stimuli.

Metabolic and neurologic influences on perception can also influence threat appraisal and are particularly important in the critical care setting. Hypoxia, electrolyte imbalances, changes in cerebral blood flow, and drugs are but a few of the factors that can alter an individual's ability to perceive internal and external stimuli accurately.

We can now expand the conceptual framework, adding the components just discussed:

Stimulus   ⟶ *Cognitive appraisal*   ⟶ *Feelings of anticipated*
Imminence   *of threat*   *harm*
Threat:resource ratio   Personality factors:
Ambiguity   goals
                           belief systems
                           intellectual
                               capacity/
                               sophistication
                          Metabolic/
                               neurologic
                               factors.

Feelings of Anticipated Harm

The reactions that occur in response to threat appraisal are varied. We can observe disturbance in affect, behavioral responses, and physiologic reactions. The response is unpleasant and serves as a trigger, activating coping behaviors to reduce the feelings of threat.[8,9] Just as cognitive appraisal serves as an intervening variable between the stimulus and the response, so does the response serve as the intervening variable between threat appraisal and coping behaviors. The coping model can now be expanded:

Stimulus⟶Cognitive appraisal⟶Anticipation of harm
                                            ↓
                                 Coping behaviors.

Coping Behaviors[10–12]

There are two general types of coping responses: action-oriented behaviors and cognitive maneuvers called *defense mechanisms*. Examples of action-oriented coping are problem-solving behavior, attack, and avoidance.

Problem-solving behaviors are based on the assumption that an individual can take steps to reduce a threat by either influencing the conditions of the stimulus or by activating resources. The person looks for ways to influence the threat:resource ratio.

Attack is a primitive form of coping designed to injure, destroy, and remove the agent of harm. The affect most seen with attack behavior is anger.

Avoidance is one of the most basic and universal coping behaviors. The goal is to prevent contact with the threat-producing stimulus. The affect most seen with avoidance is fear.

Defense mechanisms are psychologic activities in which people deceive themselves about the actual conditions of threat; they are normal responses to life events and should be viewed on a continuum from healthy to unhealthy. Examples of healthy, mature defenses are sublimation, suppression, and humor. Sublimation is the modification of a human impulse into an action that is more socially acceptable. Participation in competitive activities is one way to express aggression. Suppression is a conscious decision not to deal with a given situation or response at a particular time. Humor is the ability to laugh at oneself and one's circumstances.

Less healthy coping responses are neurotic defenses, which have a high energy cost but can be understood in terms of an individual's life history. Examples of neurotic defenses are manipulation, intellectualization, and displacement. Manipulation is an excessive attempt to control the environment to reduce feelings of internal threat. Intellectualization is the exclusion of emotional reactions to situations. Displacement is focusing on the less threatening aspects of a situation.

Immature defenses are another step down the continuum of defenses. They are used by children or adults who have regressed to an earlier pattern of behavior. They are used when more mature coping mechanisms are failing. Examples of immature defenses are acting-out behavior, passive-aggressive behavior, and projection. *Acting-out* is the expression of impulses directly. *Passive-aggressive behavior*, however, is the inability to express feelings, especially angry feelings, directly. *Projection* is the externalization of internal feelings to the environment.

Psychotic defenses are the result of a total breakdown of previously used coping mechanisms and are the result of a series of breakdowns. Distortion is an example of a psychotic defense mechanism in which hallucinations and delusions reshape reality to suit internal needs. If psychotic defenses are called into play, we have not intervened soon enough.

Coping mechanisms are *successful* if, upon reappraisal of the stimulus, the threat is absent. The resulting emotional response should be positive. Both direct action tendencies and defense mechanisms can, in this sense, be successful. A person successfully using intellectualization to cope with stress may feel just as relaxed as a person who is directly confronting the threat through problem solving and direct action. But successful coping does not necessarily mean *effective* coping.

Janis[13] identified five coping patterns among patients with life-threatening diseases. He labeled the effective, or adaptive, pattern as *vigilance*. When this coping pattern is used, effective problem-solving behavior is the result. There is a search for information, a laying out of alternatives, and a choice made after the information has been assimilated in an unbiased manner.

On the other hand, Janis identifies four patterns of maladaptive coping patterns seen in people struggling with a life-threatening illness. The first is *unconflicted inertia*. The person using this pattern ignores the threat and sees no need to take protective action. Often, this behavior is seen in patients who do not receive sufficient information regarding their illness. Once the information is available, this pattern is easily corrected.

The second ineffective pattern is *defensive avoidance*. People using this pattern avoid unpleasant feelings by selectively ignoring threat cues. Usually, the underlying feelings are those of hopelessness regarding an acceptable solution to the problem. It is well documented that a common response to chest pain is denial of the implications of the pain and a delay in seeking treatment.[14]

A third pattern is *unconflicted change*. People using this pattern are so fearful of their current situation that they are willing to jump to a solution without really weighing the problems that could accompany the new direction.

The fourth maladaptive pattern is *hypervigilance*. People using this pattern are in or close to a state of panic. They are overwhelmed by any information, every option seems undesirable, and they are unable to integrate information in any meaningful way.

It is important for nurses to distinguish between successful coping behavior and effective behavior. Coping behavior that is successful may indicate that the patient and family do not present difficulties for the nurse because they do not experience feelings of threat in response to the original stimuli. However, coping that is successful for the patient and family may create a terrible disturbance for the staff if the patient's usual style is that of attack. People who use avoidance may feel more comfortable when they refuse a treatment because of their fear of the consequences, but the staff may feel in conflict because they cannot deliver an intervention they feel will be helpful. Nurses are quite familiar with the negative effects of a manipulative patient and family. Patients who use immature defense mechanisms may have reduced their own anxiety but have certainly raised the anxiety of the staff.

Effective coping, then, includes behaviors oriented toward the reality of the situation: information seeking and informed choice. With the understanding that all people respond in an individual manner to stressful stimuli, and that certain conditions can lead to maladaptive responses, it is still important that nurses direct their interventions toward this type of coping behavior.

THE IMPORTANCE OF HELPING CRITICALLY ILL CARDIOVASCULAR PATIENTS COPE EFFECTIVELY

Coronary care units and cardiac surgical units, the places where most critically ill cardiovascular patients are found, can be hectic. With the increased use of technology to monitor vital signs and sustain life, nurses often have all they can do just to keep up with the patient's physiologic status. Attending to the patient's reactions to illness and hospitalization can be a source of stress for intensive care unit (ICU) nurses.[15] Often this becomes the last thing a nurse is able to do. Families, too, can be a source of increased tension for nurses. Their presence can interfere with care, and their expectations for cure can add to nurses' stress.[16] Given these barriers, why should nurses direct their often limited energies toward helping patients and families cope effectively?

The Mind-Body Relationship

A 31-year-old man had just suffered a major heart attack and was admitted to a coronary care unit. His monitor showed frequent runs of ventricular tachycardia (VT), which deteriorated into ventricular fibrillation (VF). He lost consciousness and was successfully defibrillated. When he opened his eyes he saw the typical postarrest scene: a room full of people all talking at once. He looked panic-stricken. His eyes were bulging; his body was shaking; he could not control his tremors. His monitor continued to show intermittent bursts of VT. He had received the maximum safe dose of lidocaine possible. The house staff was conferring over the bed as to what step to take next. At this point, a nurse walked to the head of the bed, took the patient's hand, established eye contact, and began doing relaxation exercises with him. His eyes riveted to the nurse's face, he followed her instructions, and visibly relaxed. Meanwhile, the residents had decided to hang bretylium, and another nurse had mixed and hung the medication. After several minutes, the monitor showed regular sinus rhythm and the residents congratulated themselves on a correct intervention.

It would be difficult to measure the effect the relaxation exercise had on the outcome, but most nurses are familiar with the idea that emotional reactions can trigger the physiologic flight or fight response described by Selye (Figure 8-1).

The effect that this response has on a failing myocardium can contribute to a cardiac patient's illness in several important ways:

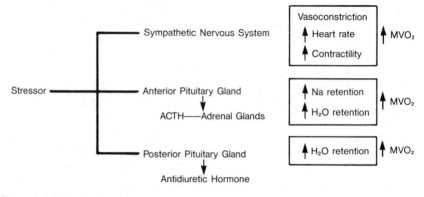

Figure 8-1 Major Cardiovascular Effects of Stress

- Increased heart rate increases myocardial oxygen consumption, decreases diastolic filling time, and decreases the time for coronary artery filling.
- Increased contractility increases myocardial oxygen consumption.
- Increased vasoconstriction increases the afterload, increasing myocardial oxygen consumption and decreasing cardiac output.
- Increased water retention increases preload, increasing myocardial oxygen consumption and possibly contributing to pulmonary edema.

Other studies have shown the influence of psychosocial factors on the recovery from heart disease. Emotional responses and their connection with heart rate and rhythm changes, including ventricular dysrhythmias, have been identified by several researchers.[19,20] Lown et al. reported on the animal studies that support the increased risk for VF attributable to psychophysiologic factors.[21] They also stated that factors that may seem to be innocuous stimuli to the nurse can unduly arouse the nervous system and elicit a dysrhythmia because of the symbolic nature of the stimulus. Mumford et al.[22] summarized research studying the effects of psychologic intervention on recovery from surgery and heart attacks. In one study, mortality from open-heart surgery was highest among patients who had been identified as depressed before surgery, although, as a group, they were not at greater risk based on their cardiovascular status. Other studies showed that patients with low morale or depression had higher mortality rates. Kimball[23] reported that patients with considerable amounts of preoperative anxiety and depression have a greater chance of not surviving the surgery and a greater chance of morbidity after surgery than other patients with less reported anxiety and depression.

Other physiologic systems react to emotional and environmental stimuli. DeVillier[24] reported that stress prolongs the surgical recovery process, and that wound healing can be inhibited by the cortisol production that occurs with stress (Exhibit 8-1).

Locke[25] reviewed a number of studies looking at the link between stress, adaptation, and the immune response. He concluded that when a state of arousal is prolonged, depression of the immune system can result. The effect is moderated by both the magnitude of the stressor and the individual's ability to cope with the stressor. This supports the idea of the threat:resource ratio. He emphasized that it is not the threat itself that can lead to immunosuppression, but rather the person's ability to cope with the threat. Poor coping can be a long-standing trait or a situational response to a threat so large that normally adequate mechanisms are overwhelmed. He also summarized that factors such as social support can enhance psychobiologic adaptation and the immune response in the face of severe stress.

We can now expand our coping model:

Stimuli⟶Cognitive appraisal⟶Anticipation of harm
↓
Coping behaviors
↙   ↘
Fight/flight response   Adaptation.

Nurses have always been seen as "care" givers, providing the humanistic element in the health care setting. They have always been concerned with how people are responding to illness and hospitalization. This model, however, shows how "cure" can be the potential outcome of nursing care.[26] In the critically ill cardiovascular patient, the health problem interacts with the patient's response to the problem. If psychologic responses can influence the course of the disease, then nursing interventions directed toward these phenomena are imperative.

THE CARDIOVASCULAR PATIENT IN THE CRITICAL CARE SETTING: DISEASE TRAJECTORIES

When people are confronted with a life-threatening illness, they can respond in varied ways. When admission to a critical care unit is part of the illness,

Exhibit 8-1 Major Effects of Cortisol on the Immune System

Suppression of acute and chronic inflammatory responses
Decreased neutrophil accumulation at site of inflammation
Decreased monocyte accumulation at site of inflammation
Decreased clearing of foreign particles from blood
Lymphocytopenia with decreased cellular immunity and decreased antibody production

patients and families must adapt to an environment that carries unique stressors. How does a cardiovascular illness differ from other life-threatening illnesses? The heart is a symbol of life and longevity. A cardiac illness forces individuals and families to confront the possibility of death and initiates a grieving process in response to the loss of health and the real possibility of death.[27,28] Will cardiac patients and their families respond in unique ways that set them apart from patients and families coping with trauma or respiratory illnesses? Probably not. A life-threatening illness, no matter what the underlying pathophysiology, will evoke similar feelings and require similar adaptations. Nurses can apply the coping model described above in all situations perceived as threatening by an individual, regardless of the initiating event.

A more useful way of viewing the patient and family trying to cope with cardiovascular illness is to identify the illness trajectories created by the disease processes. It is the progression of the disease that directs the uniqueness of response. That is, an acute event will evoke one set of responses, and a chronic illness with a slow progression will evoke another. A chronic illness with periods of acute crises will require still another. Viewed in this manner, nurses can use the coping theory in a wide variety of situations. The knowledge nurses have related to the specific cardiac illness and the expected progression and outcome will determine which aspects of the theory and which interventions are applicable to a given patient at a given time.

When confronted with a life-threatening illness, patients must face the reality of death. This event, regardless of how people cope, places an individual in a period of time between the initial knowledge of death and death itself. Wright[29] discussed three phases of this time period:

The *acute phase* begins with the knowledge that death is a real possibility. Intense anxiety is the feeling most characteristic during this period. Emotional responses will vary depending on the type of death trajectory the disease process creates. Glaser and Straus[30] identified four possible trajectories:

1. *Certain death at a known time* relates to acute and fatal illness. The patient in severe cardiogenic shock with multisystem failure is in this category. Defense mechanisms such as denial are common during this period; frequently, patients and families use a mixture of denial and hope. The task for nurses is to live with the intensity of response alternating with the use of mechanisms to reduce anxiety.

2. *Certain death at an unknown time* can apply to patients with newly diagnosed cardiomyopathy who are not candidates for cardiac transplantation. Again, patients and families experience intense anxiety that can interfere with the learning necessary to help them manage their illness after discharge.

3. *Uncertain death but a known time when the question will be resolved* would apply to patients with crescendo angina who are waiting to hear the results of their angiogram to determine if their condition is correctable. Patients with end-stage cardiomyopathy who are waiting to hear if they are acceptable transplant candidates might also be in this category. Patients who are "high-risk" cardiac surgical candidates may feel their life-death question is resolved when they leave the ICU. Patients with life-threatening dysrhythmias may feel safe when the correct pharmacologic agent is found. Patients waiting for the results of echocardiography, nuclear imaging, or treadmill testing may also fit into this category. Patients and families facing this trajectory use a variety of mechanisms to control their anxiety. Some are able to cope effectively, and others use coping mechanisms detrimental to themselves or to those trying to assist them. Interventions need to be based on the presenting behavior and the needs expressed.

4. *Uncertain death at an unknown time* applies to many acutely ill cardiovascular patients who expect to return to a previous level of well being: the patient with an uncomplicated myocardial infarction (MI); the "low-risk" cardiac surgery patient; the patient having an angioplasty. During this phase, the rehabilitative aspects of interventions are usually emphasized. Patients, families, and staff use knowledge regarding postdischarge life style changes to cope with the uncertainty of the prognosis.

The *chronic phase* of an illness is punctuated by increasing physical limitations and increasing dependency. During this time, there may be periods of improved functioning and well-being, but the general course is downhill. Such cardiovascular patients have end-stage pump failure from a variety of causes such as ischemic disease and idiopathic myopathy. Patients during this phase experience specific fears related to their decreased functioning: loss of independence; loneliness; loss of control. Interventions are directed toward supporting the function that remains and helping patients and families cope with increasing losses.

The *terminal phase* patients are experiencing their last hospitalization. There are no surgical or medical interventions that would be useful. Nursing interventions during this phase are directed toward the acceptance of death.

The concept of illness trajectories can be useful in several ways. First, the commonality of human experience and the universality of nursing interventions can be better understood. Descriptive studies can be applied to a variety of patient populations to identify the usual course of the disease process and coping styles used. In this way, patients, families, and caregivers can be prepared for usual outcomes, and interventions can be planned. Independent nursing interventions can be identified and applied to a variety of patient populations to document the role of these activities in influencing the course of an illness and hospitalization.

PLANNING CARE

Because of the nature of critical care units, it is sometimes difficult for nurses to meet patients' and families' psychosocial needs. The patient's unstable condition may require all the attention of the nurse. Rapidly changing orders and the need for astute assessment of patient response often do not leave time for attention to patients' reactions to their condition or environment. Concerned family members can add to the nurse's burden in several ways: crowding the work space; setting unrealistic goals of care; needing emotional support. The nurse is often torn between meeting the need for expert and constant physical care and the intensified need for emotional support.[31]

A case example can illustrate this point. The incident involves the family of a patient who had had surgery for cancer and was in a surgical ICU. This was a recurrence of cancer that had been treated successfully a number of years previously. The wife had a need to spend a great deal of time at the bedside with the patient, and when she wasn't at the bedside, she sat in a chair outside the unit. She began to be a problem for the staff, not because of her behavior, i.e., complaining or crying, but just because she was there. Some nurses had difficulty providing care for the patient when she was at the bedside; others did not. The staff asked a mental health consultant to talk with the wife. The results of the assessment were not unexpected: anxiety that was relieved by being close to her husband. The nurse caring for the patient on that particular day had done quite a good job of working with the wife. She had not been disturbed by her presence and the wife had felt comfortable enough to leave for part of the day. When talking to the nurse regarding her interventions, the consultant suggested they identify specifically what she had done that had been successful, and write it down on the plan of care so that nurses on the next shift could implement the interventions. The nurse responded that she couldn't do that because one couldn't expect other nurses to practice nursing the way she did. She didn't mind working with the patient while family members were present, but other nurses did, and no one could expect them to implement a plan that included this intervention.

This response raises questions about professional nursing practice:

1. What is the basis for problem identification in nursing? Do we identify something as a problem if we are uncomfortable or if the smooth running of a unit is disrupted? Or do we identify a problem if the response of patient or family is not adaptive to the situation?

2. Can we develop a nursing approach to patients that is research-based so that we feel assured that our interventions will achieve a desirable result?

3. Can we hold other nurses accountable for interactions that require them to change their usual way of interacting with patients and families?

These issues are particularly relevant to psychosocial nursing diagnoses because interventions in this area are often difficult to quantify and replicate. Also, nurses work with patients in a highly personal way that involves their own emotions and reactions. Implementing psychosocial research findings would often necessitate changing our innate and automatic ways of responding. This is a difficult endeavor. However, if we are to continue to grow as an independent profession, we must begin to identify effective interventions that affect patient outcomes. With these issues and questions in mind, let us begin an exploration of interventions that are appropriate for the nursing diagnosis *ineffective coping*.

Assessment and correct diagnosis of the problem are the first steps in the scientific process. Refer to the information reprinted from the proceedings of the third and fourth national conferences on nursing diagnosis for the defining characteristics of diagnoses related to ineffective coping (Appendix 8-A). Although these diagnostic categories still need to be refined, they provide nurses with a common perspective with which to identify patients and families who are not coping effectively.

A COPING MODEL AS A FRAMEWORK FOR NURSING INTERVENTIONS

When planning interventions for patients and families with the diagnosis of ineffective, compromised, or disabling coping, the stress-coping model developed earlier provides direction. Let us first return to the coping framework developed by Lazarus. By understanding the relations between the framework's components, we can identify how nurses can influence them to promote (or interfere with) adaptive coping.

Stimuli⟶Cognitive appraisal⟶Anticipation of harm
↓
Coping behaviors
↙ ↘
Fight/flight response   Adaptation.

Nurses can plan interventions based on the relations between the stimuli, its cognitive appraisal, the resulting feelings once a stimuli is perceived as threatening, the coping behaviors used, and the fight or flight response that can result if coping is unsuccessful earlier in the cycle.

Interventions Affecting Stimuli

A stimulus is the beginning of the stress-coping cycle. Factors that influence the stimulus have been discussed: the imminence of the threat; its perceived strength in relation to the perceived strength of resources; the ambiguity of the stimulus. Nurses can influence these factors in several ways.

First, nurses can eliminate known stressors. For example, in a review article, Hansell[32] described the relation between noise in the ICU and behavioral alterations in critically ill patients. She pointed out that noise can create a startle response that will stimulate the sympathetic nervous system (SNS), increasing catecholamine secretion. This initiates the deleterious cardiovascular responses described above. Noise also can frequently decrease the patient's quantity and quality of sleep. When this occurs, changes in behavior and perception can occur: Patients are less able to cope with situational demands. Their perception of events may be altered by delusions and hallucinations so that stimuli that ordinarily would be accepted become a source of threat and anxiety. The author reported data from a study that suggests that the noise levels produced by nursing and medical personnel were more intrusive than those produced by mechanical devices and nursing interventions. The communications among nurses and between nurses and other patients seemed to be the single greatest source of disturbance for patients.

Hansell made several recommendations. Decreasing the amount of personnel communications over a patient's bedside and limiting unnecessary interactions with other staff and patients are two interventions that do not increase nursing time yet could make an impact on the stimulus–ineffective coping cycle.

Other researchers have identified sources of stress for critically ill patients and their families. One stimulus for the patient with an MI is the transfer from the critical care unit (CCU) to another unit for the remainder of the hospital stay.[33] This was related to emotional responses and subsequent cardiovascular complications including reinfarction and fatal dysrhythmias.[34] Two nurses studied this reaction and found they could reduce patient stress through nursing interventions.[35] Patients in the experimental groups scored lower for stress as reported by patient, family, and nurse; they had fewer cardiovascular complications within 24 hours of transfer and within 24 to 72 hours after transfer. One of the interventions used can be incorporated into care to support effective coping to this source of stress: identify the admitting nurse from the unit to which the patient will be sent; the nurse will visit the patient in the CCU before transfer to answer questions and tell the patient what to expect in terms of physical layout, nursing routine, visiting hours, etc. It is sometimes difficult to coordinate the schedules of patient transfer and nurse activity, but if this intervention promotes more effective coping to this stressful stimulus, are nurses not obligated to incorporate it into nursing practice?

Other stimuli have been identified as possible sources of stress for the critically ill patient. Several authors[36–38] have delineated adaptive or coping tasks that critically ill patients face. In the context of our coping model, these "tasks" can be viewed as stimuli to which the patient must adapt. The following stimuli confront critically ill cardiovascular patients: pain; feelings of hopelessness; loss of control; unknown caregivers; potential for dying. Nurses can view these stimuli in the framework of the strength of stimulus:strength of resources ratio to plan interventions. Which interventions will decrease the magnitude of the stimulus and which will increase the perception of strength of resources?

Pain

Pain control can be seen as a strategy to decrease the strength of a stimulus that can lead to ineffective coping. Important interventions that can be easily incorporated into routine care include identifying pain relief as a mutual goal for patient and nurse.[39] This allows patients the confidence to know they are not the only ones who are concerned about their pain. The patient should be included in identifying measures that are helpful in reducing pain and those that increase pain. Assure them that around-the-clock analgesia and other pain-relief measures shown to be very helpful will be available as needed. This paves the way to using nonpharmacologic pain-relief measures such as relaxation and distraction. Analgesics offered before activities reinforce the concern the nurse has about the patient's pain and will improve compliance with needed interventions. Again, these interventions can be incorporated in the usual interactions nurses have with patients and do not increase nursing time.

Hopelessness

Helping patients combat feelings of hopelessness and maintain a sense of future is one way nurses can influence the strength of the resources side of the stimulus:resource ratio. Nurses can assist patients by helping them draw on their personal resources.[40] Nurses can tap these resources in several ways: Telling patients that the loss of control they are experiencing is temporary is one way to decrease feelings of hopelessness in patients who find loss of control a threat. Providing factual information concerning diagnosis, treatment, and prognosis also gives people a sense of control and a feeling that things are being done to help them get well. Cardiovascular patients in the acute phase of their illness usually have many treatment options that offer hope for recovery. Even the critically ill patient in cardiogenic shock can hold out hope for the success of drugs, mechanical devices, or surgery.

Another approach to enhance patients' perceptions of the strength of their resources and thus maintain hope is to provide environmental support. If patients believe that powerful resources are on their side, their sense of power in the face of threatening stimuli will be enhanced and the degree of threat reduced. Effective coping is promoted. Two environmental sources are available to the patient: the family and the nursing staff.

Maintaining Family Relationships to Sustain Hope. Even though caring for families as well as patients can, at times, seem to be an overwhelming task, some studies have shown that families can make a difference in the patient's recovery. Chatham[41] showed that postcardiotomy patients who experienced structured involvement by their significant family members had fewer manifestations of postcardiotomy psychosis. Schwartz and Brenner[42] showed that family involvement in the transfer from the CCU reduced stress levels of patients and reduced post-transfer cardiovascular complications. So it is important from both a psychologic and a physiologic standpoint to have families involved with their critically ill loved ones.

To maintain effective relationships with patients, family members must be helped to cope effectively with the patient's illness. The same framework used to understand and plan interventions for patients can be used for family members. Several nursing studies have identified the needs of families of critically ill patients,[43,44] families of cardiac surgery patients,[45] and spouses of patients with MI.[46,47] These needs reflect what the families see as potentially threatening stimuli. The most frequently identified threats are lack of knowledge regarding the patient's condition, hopelessness regarding the condition, fear of loss of a spouse, and fear of the patient being treated in a depersonalized manner. By attending to the families' concerns in these areas, nurses help family members cope more effectively. They can then be more available to patients and provide the invaluable support patients need to strengthen their own coping resources. Specific interventions for spouses of critically ill patients in a CCU were studied by Breu and Dracup.[48] The care plan they developed included orienting the spouse to the CCU environment, arranging for one telephone call at home to give an update on the patient's condition, talking with the spouse for 15 minutes away from the bedside, and identifying one or two nurses per shift who would be the primary caregivers for the patient. They observed fewer symptoms of crisis in these families.

Families who are coping effectively can be useful in helping to care for and support critically ill patients. Preventive intervention can be effective in avoiding time-consuming maladaptive coping later on.

The Nurse as a Source of Hope. Although families are the most powerful influence on sustaining a patient's hope, the relationship a patient has with the nursing staff can also be an important source of support. Nursing interventions can be based on a life-promoting rather than a life-succumbing framework.[49]

In a study by Drew,[50] the relationship between nurses and patients was explored in terms of depersonalization and confirmation. The purpose of the study was to explore patients' perceptions of caregivers and to identify the meaning patients gave to the interaction. This study provides some direction in how a nurse can develop interactions perceived as caring and avoid behaviors felt to be dehumanizing. Some caregivers were described as lacking emotional warmth. The adjectives they used are telling: starchy, mechanical, bored, impatient, irritated, flip, superior, preoccupied. The tone of voice contributed to feelings of depersonalization. When imitating these caregivers, they usually lowered their voices and spoke rapidly, without expression. They described a flat facial expression, a lack of eye contact, and too casual an attitude. The patients interpreted this behavior as an indication of the caregiver's negative attitude toward them. They experienced fear, shame, and anger in response.

Caregivers perceived as confirming or enhancing were described as caring about what happens, liking their work, and having personality. Eye contact, lack of haste, and a low, modulated but expressive tone of voice were extremely important. The reactions of patients experiencing this type of interaction were hope, comfort, confidence, assurance, and a sense of ease and relaxation.

The patients were asked what they thought the effects of dehumanizing interactions were, and their responses are important in light of our coping framework. Some thought these types of interactions could slow recovery and leave a patient feeling hopeless. Others felt the feelings they experienced used up energy they could have put into the healing process. On the other side, patients who experienced confirming interactions felt they were stronger, more in control. They felt that some sort of energy was passed from the caretaker to the patient that helped in the healing process.

Clearly, nurses have the potential for powerful influence in the stimulus-coping framework. Nurses can, unfortunately, become a threatening stimulus themselves. However, the relationship the nurse develops with the patients can also add to patients' perception that they have the resources to cope with the threatening stimuli presented by a critical illness. This is a powerful tool to sustain hope.

Loss of Control

A critical illness carries with it the implication that one has lost control over one's body, one's routine of daily living, and one's destiny. Patients struggle to regain a sense of power in their lives. Incorporating interventions that enhance a sense of control influences the strength of the resources side of the stress: resources ratio. The patient maintains a sense of identity and power in the face of impending doom. Many nurses incorporate this into their routine interactions with patients by providing information about condition, treatment plans, and expected results, and by encouraging questions. Provide the patient with realistic choices about certain aspects of care. If the nursing unit can adapt to nursing measures such as bathing being offered according to patient preference rather than hospital routine, then this choice can be offered to the patient and incorporated into the plan of care.

In summary, there is a reality to the feelings of loss of control that patients experience when they are ill and hospitalized in a critical care unit. Two interventions that increase feelings of control are providing information and encouraging input into decision making about care. Again, these interventions require more from a nurse in terms of the general approach to patients than in terms of the amount of time required.

Unknown Caregivers

As discussed previously, caregivers can be a source of hope and consequently a source of strength against the threat of illness and hospitalization. However, in the critical care setting, patients come in contact with many caregivers in a single day. The laboratory technician, ECG technician, physician, interns and residents if a teaching hospital, the patient care representative, social worker, dietician, the nurse giving care for the shift, the nurse relieving for break, and the nurse relieving for lunch are all potential contacts for the patient feeling sick and frightened. It takes a great deal of interpersonal skill to relate positively to this number of people who have access to one's body and private reactions.

One helpful intervention is to provide the patient and family with a primary caregiver who can be seen as "theirs."[51,52] This person can become a trusted source of information and comfort.

Potential for Dying

All cardiac patients confront the issue of their own death to some degree. This is a major threat to most people, which demands adaptation. The interventions already discussed are appropriate to assist the patient to adapt to this threat as well: information, a sense of hope, the ability to maintain relationships with family and staff. The type of intervention and support needed depends on the particular illness trajectory of the patient. The acutely ill patient admitted to the CCU with a first MI, for whom death is uncertain, will respond best to information and increased control. Because the situation is ambiguous, the emphasis is usually on maximizing rehabilitation. The patient with end-stage cardiac disease admitted for another, and perhaps final, episode of congestive heart failure has a different illness trajectory. This patient may need help talking more directly about feelings regarding the loss of strength and function. Rethinking and talking about alternatives can reduce anxiety and support effective coping.

Interventions Affecting Cognitive Appraisal

The factors that influence what will be perceived as threatening are rooted in the personality characteristics and the personal goals of the individual. How can nurses use this information to plan interventions for care? First, it is important to accept the patient's perception of the threat. At this point, nurses' skills as listeners are more important than their ability to impart knowledge and advice. Only after nurses understand patients' fears from their perspective can they offer appropriate help. It is during this listening phase that misconceptions can be identified and gently corrected. It is sometimes difficult for critical care nurses to realize that listening is a powerful intervention because they are used to being actively involved in the myriad of tasks that need to be done. Just listening doesn't feel like doing much. But if listening to identify the patient's cognitive appraisal of threat can be put into the context of the stress-coping model, we can see that it is a vital link in understanding a patient's response to illness.

Critically ill patients' cognitive appraisal of threat can be influenced by organic and environmental factors as well as personality factors. Alterations in perception can be mild illusions, such as the patient hearing the hissing of the oxygen wall unit as whispering. Patients could accept this as part of their environment or could become quite fearful. At the more extreme end of the spectrum, patients can become convinced that caregivers are trying to kill them, or they can see or hear things that are, in reality, not present.

The organic factors that can cause altered perception are metabolic states such as hypoxia, hypercapnia, electrolyte imbalance, drugs, and changes in pH. Sensory deprivation, sensory overload, and sleep deprivation are environmental factors that can alter perception. There is a tendency when caring for these patients who, unfortunately, do not respond to reason, to use sedation and restraints. This approach can contribute further to ineffective adaptive responses. Sedation can increase confusion, hypotension, cardiac toxicity, and decreased ventilation. Restraints can cause hostility, uncooperativeness, and extreme exertion.[53] When caring for patients whose perceptions are altered by these factors it is particularly important to reduce stimuli in the environment that could be misinterpreted as threatening. The most important intervention is to correct misconceptions. However, these corrections must be made repeatedly since the hallmarks of organic brain syndrome are short attention span and impaired recent memory. This can be time-consuming and drain the energy of the most patient nurse. If appropriate, selected family members can share this responsibility with guidance from the nurse.

Interventions in Response to Coping Behaviors

A relevant example of interventions geared to personality factors was described by Gentry et al.[54] when discussing the Type A/B differences in coping with acute MI. Type A individuals have an unusual sense of time urgency, excessive job involvement, and angry and competitive interactions. Type B individuals are more relaxed. In response to an MI, Type A patients were more likely to use denial as a coping mechanism to the implications of a heart attack. Type A individuals were more likely to be discharged sooner because they engaged in self-care activities sooner. The implications for intervention that Gentry suggested included developing a "therapeutic alliance" with these patients and using their defense mechanism to work with them rather than try to confront the denial.

For example, urging patients to change their behavior to decrease the spouse's anxiety might be more effective with this patient population.[55] Type A patients should be encouraged in self-monitoring activities, such as taking their own BP and becoming actively involved in setting goals for returning to work, sex, and recreational activities. This is an example of interventions geared to a particular perceptual style.

The Type A patient's coping style is often appreciated by caregivers. These patients appear friendly and alert and become involved in their care. They are what many caregivers think of as "ideal" patients. Unfortunately, not all coping responses are so adaptive and most require more from caregivers.

The response of patients to an acute MI is well documented.[56–60] Two common responses are anxiety and depression. Patients cope with these uncomfortable feelings in ways that are not always comfortable for the nurses caring for them. Some patients become hyperactive and are unable to comply with aspects of the treatment plan that require rest and inactivity. Others become sexually provocative with behaviors ranging from mild flirtatiousness to blatant exhibitionism.[61]

Patients whose coping behaviors interfere with getting appropriate treatment and support are using ineffective adaptation measures. Behaviors that lead to effective problem-solving behavior that reduces the threat are effective coping mechanisms.[62] It is important to be able to identify the difference between effective and ineffective coping strategies. Patients who use denial to control their anxiety but still participate in care are coping effectively. They are using a defense mechanism as opposed to a direct action mechanism, but they are still able to deal with the reality of their situation. Patients whose denial prevents them from seeking treatment or accepting recommendations are coping ineffectively. Patients who are angry but can talk about their feelings with caregivers are coping effectively. They are using support to cope with their emotions and eventually move toward acceptance. Patients who act out their anger by taking off their monitoring equipment, pulling out their intravascular lines, and throwing things are coping ineffectively. Patients who translate their feelings into behaviors that alienate potential support people are coping ineffectively. Patients who are sad after acknowledging their cardiac condition are responding within the expected norm. Patients who have a prolonged depression with loss of appetite, sleep disturbance, and withdrawal from usual activities are coping ineffectively.

When patients are coping ineffectively they require a different type of support from their caregivers. Support can be defined in several ways.[63] The most common use of the term *support* in relation to a critical illness is *to offer comfort*. Sharing another person's burden, the feelings of loss and anxiety that can result from an acute or chronic cardiac illness, is the type of support to which most patients who are coping ineffectively can respond.

Another way to convey support is to bolster one's ability to function effectively. Specific understanding of an individual's motivations and concerns provides a guide to planning interventions. By helping patients identify the concerns behind their behavior, the concerns can be dealt with more directly and the ineffective coping can be replaced by mechanisms that are more helpful.

A patient with a recent heart attack was making sexual innuendos to all the nurses who came in contact with him. A supportive intervention in this situation might be saying: "You are making a lot of sexual remarks. Some men who have had a heart attack worry about sexual functioning afterward. I wonder if that's something that is on your mind, too?" This type of support requires two things from nurses: They must remain in a therapeutic relationship in which their own reactions do not interfere with effective functioning. They must be able to confront the patient gently in a way that can be heard. These two skills often take the help of someone outside the situation, either peers who are objective about the situation or, in the case of patients who engage the reactions of the entire nursing staff, a mental health consultant. An outsider can help nurses understand the patient's motivations and their own reactions to the behavior. Once nurses understand the cycle of communication breakdown, they have a better chance of offering appropriate support.

Interventions in Reponse to the Fight or Flight Response

When patients are not able to cope with stress through direct action mechanisms or defenses, the flight or fight response is activated (see Figure 8-1).

One intervention that deals directly with the physiologic arousal of the flight or fight response is relaxation training to achieve the relaxation response. The relaxation response is an involuntary response that is opposite to the fight or flight response and reduces SNS activity.[64] Many techniques have been used to achieve this state of relaxation with decreased oxygen consumption, decreased heart rate, decreased respiratory rate, and decreased muscle tone. Transcendental meditation, biofeedback, and progressive muscle relaxation achieve the same results. The four critical components of the relaxation response are a quiet environment; a mental device, such as a repetitive word or concentration on one's breathing, that provides a way to shift from externally oriented thought; a passive attitude; and a comfortable position. The critical care unit does not always provide the ideal setting for helping patients achieve a relaxed state, but recall the example given earlier of the patient in the postarrest situation. The nurse intervened successfully despite the circumstances. Two nursing studies are of interest in the area of relaxation training. One involves heart surgery patients, and the other, a variety of postoperative patients.

Aiken and Hendricks[65] taught prospective open-heart surgical patients progressive relaxation by having them listen to a relaxation tape and practice with the help of a nurse specialist. The researchers were interested in the effect this technique would have on the psychiatric complications that can occur after open-heart surgery. Although statistical significance was not achieved, the findings were in the predicted direction, and the incidence of postoperative reactions was significantly lower than had been expected based on research findings.

Flaherty and Fitzpatrick[66] taught preoperative patients a simple relaxation technique of letting the lower jaw drop slightly and keeping the tongue quiet. This procedure was intended to reduce muscle tension and to keep the patient from being preoccupied with thoughts of pain. These patients reported less pain during their first attempt to get out of bed postoperatively and used less narcotics in the first postoperative 24 hours than did those who did not use the technique. The results were statistically significant.

Both studies indicate the usefulness of relaxation techniques to decrease anxiety and effect a positive patient care outcome. Relaxation techniques and how to teach them to patients need to be components of nursing practice. This technique can help patients cope effectively with the variety of physical, environmental, and psychologic stimuli that confront them in the critical care setting.

BARRIERS TO HELPING PATIENTS AND THEIR FAMILIES COPE

Lack of Information

Knowledge of how people cope and the ability to distinguish between ineffective and effective behaviors help nurses intervene appropriately. If nurses can see the sexually provocative patient as a person who is coping ineffectively with feelings of anxiety, they have a better chance of using a problem-solving approach to identify appropriate nursing interventions. Knowledge gives people a chance to react rationally rather than emotionally. Just as information about the disease process and treatment outcomes gives patients more control and opportunities to plan future actions, information regarding patient responses provides nurses with more control in situations that can create feelings of powerlessness.

Coping with Nursing

Helping patients and families cope effectively also requires the ability to provide comfort and support, instill hope and confidence, and convey understanding and empathy. That is a tall order in the face of the stresses that critical care nurses work with.

Studies have identified the sources of stress that impinge on the critical care nurse. Inadequate staffing patterns, caring for dying patients, inadequate support from unresponsive nursing leadership, and interpersonal conflict are the major sources of stress for the nurse.[67,68] One coping strategy that nurses use is detachment from or the depersonalization of patients for whom they are caring.[69,70] This coping mechanism does not promote a confirming relationship; rather, it promotes the exclusionary type of relationship that patients felt was detrimental to the healing process. If nurses are to maintain the type of relationships that patients view as healing, they must learn how to cope effectively with the stresses that are part of their working environment.

Nursing administrators can find direction for staffing patterns and management styles in the studies that identify these as major sources of stress for ICU nurses.[71] In this way, the strength of the stress side of the stress:resource ratio is affected. Adequate staffing reduces the amount of stress and increases the ability to cope with a variety of other stresses.

Nurses providing direct care need to devise a personal stress-management program, which could include exercise, good nutrition, enough sleep, laughter, and fun. The message here is that nurses need to accept the stresses that will always be present in the job and actively work to find a solution.

Nurses can also work together to develop meaningful support in the work setting. Support groups are one way for nurses to deal with the anxiety produced by the daily interactions with sick and dying patients and their families. It is also a way for nurses to learn more mature coping styles through talking through their reactions and observing how others effectively adapt to the day-to-day strain.[72] Developing individual and group coping strategies is a way to influence the strength of the resource side of the stimulus:resource ratio.

Helping patients cope effectively is a prime responsibility of the nurses caring for them. Not only is the caring nurse–patient relationship important from a humanitarian perspective but, as we have seen, from the perspective of improved patient morbidity and mortality.

NOTES

1. Andrew E. Slaby and Arvin S. Glicksman, *Adapting to Life-threatening Illness* (New York: Praeger, 1985).

2. Rudolph H. Moos and Vivien D. Tsu, "The Crisis of Physical Illness: An Overview," in Rudolph Moos, ed., *Coping with Physical Illness* (New York: Plenum Medical Book Co., 1977).

3. Joan P. Riehl and Callista, Roy, *Conceptual Models for Nursing Practice* (New York: Appleton-Century-Crofts, 1974).

4. Richard S. Lazarus, *Psychological Stress and the Coping Process* (New York: McGraw-Hill Book Co., 1966).

5. Geraldine M. Goosen and Helen A. Bush, "Adaptation: A Feedback Process," *Advances in Nursing Science* 1, no. 4 (1979):15.

6. Lazarus, *Psychological Stress*, p. 93.

7. Margaret Clarke, "The Constructs 'Stress' and 'Coping' as a Rationale for Nursing Activities," *Journal of Advanced Nursing* 9(1984):267.

8. Lazarus, *Psychological Stress*, p. 93.

9. Charles Spielberger, *Understanding Stress and Anxiety* (New York: Harper & Row, 1979).

10. Lazarus, *Psychological Stress*, pp. 258–315.

11. Spielberger, *Understanding Stress*, pp. 90–94.

12. Robert Pasnau, "Coping Responses and Defense Mechanisms," lecture presented at seminar, Psychosocial Aspects of Cancer, Los Angeles, 1986.

13. Irving L. Janis, "Coping Patterns among Patients with Life-threatening Diseases," *Issues in Mental Health Nursing* 7(1985):461.

14. Ned H. Cassem and Thomas P. Hackett, "Psychological Aspects of Myocardial Infarction," *Medical Clinics of North America* 61(1977):711.

15. Nathan M. Simon and Suzanne Whiteley, "Psychiatric Consultation with MICU Nurses: The Consultation Conference as a Working Group," *Heart and Lung* 6(1977):497.

16. J. Dunkel and S. Eisendrath, "Families in the Intensive Care Unit: Their Effect on Staff," *Heart and Lung* 12(1983):258.

17. Maryann F. Pranulis, "Loss: A Factor Affecting the Welfare of the Coronary Patient," *Nursing Clinics of North America* 7(1972):445.

18. J. Tache and Hans Selye, "On Stress and Coping Mechanisms," *Issues in Mental Health Nursing* 7(1985):3.

19. Sue A. Thomas, James J. Lynch, and Mary E. Mills, "Psychosocial Influences on Heart Rhythm in the Coronary Care Unit," *Heart and Lung* 4(1975):746.

20. Patrick T. Donlon, Arnold Meadow, and Ezra Amsterdam, "Emotional Stress as a Factor in Ventricular Arrhythmias," *Psychosomatics* 20(1979):233.

21. Bernard Lown et al., "Psychophysiologic Factors in Sudden Cardiac Death," *American Journal of Psychiatry* 137(1980):1325.

22. Emily Mumford et al., "The Effects of Psychological Intervention on Recovery from Surgery and Heart Attacks: An Analysis of the Literature," *American Journal of Public Health* 72(1982):141.

23. Chase P. Kimball, "Psychological Responses to the Experience of Open-heart Surgery," in Rudolph Moos, ed., *Coping with Physical Illness* (New York: Plenum Medical Book Co., 1977).

24. Becky DeVellier, "Physiology of Stress: Cellular Healing," *Critical Care Quarterly* 6(1984):15.

25. Steven E. Locke, "Stress, Adaptation and Immunity: Studies in Humans," *General Hospital Psychiatry* 4(1982):49.

26. Maxine E. Loomis and Delores J. Wood, "Cure: The Potential Outcome of Nursing Care," *Image* 15(1983):4.

27. Mary Delaney-Naumoff, "Loss of Heart," in Jean Werner-Beland, ed., *Grief Responses to Long-term Illness and Disability* (Reston, VA: Reston Publishing Company, 1980).

28. Pranulus, "Loss."

29. Lore K. Wright, "Life Threatening Illness," *Journal of Psychosocial Nursing* 23, no. 9 (1985):7.

30. B.G. Glaser and A.L. Straus, *Time for Dying* (Chicago: Aldine, 1968).

31. Dunkel and Eisendrath, "Families in Intensive Care Unit."

32. Heidi N. Hansell, "The Behavioral Effects of Noise on Man: The Patient with Intensive Care Unit Psychosis," *Heart and Lung* 13(1984):59.

33. Linda P. Schwartz and Zara R. Brenner, "Critical Care Unit Transfer: Reducing Patient Stress through Nursing Interventions," *Heart and Lung* 8(1979):540.

34. Robert F. Klein et al., "Transfer from a Coronary Care Unit: Some Adverse Responses," *Archives of Internal Medicine* 122(1968):104.

35. Schwartz and Brenner, "Critical Care Unit Transfer."

36. Moos and Tsu, "Crisis of Physical Illness."

37. Margaret Hoffman, Susan Donckers, and Martha Hauser, "The Effect of Nursing Intervention on Stress Factors Perceived by Patients in a Coronary Care Unit," *Heart and Lung* 7(1978):804.

38. Joan E. Beglinger, "Coping Tasks in Critical Care," *Dimensions of Critical Care Nursing* 2, no. 2 (1983):80.

39. Ibid.

40. Judith F. Miller, "Inspiring Hope," *American Journal of Nursing* 85(1985):22.

41. Margaret A. Chatham, "The Effect of Family Involvement on Patients' Manifestation of Postcardiotomy Psychosis," *Heart and Lung* 7(1978):995.

42. Schwartz and Brenner, "Critical Care Unit Transfer."

43. Nancy C. Molter, "Needs of Relatives of Critically Ill Patients: A Descriptive Study," *Heart and Lung* 8(1979):332.

44. Jane S. Leake, "Needs of Relatives of Critically Ill Patients: A Follow-up," *Heart and Lung* 15(1986):189.

45. Cathy D. Rodgers, "Needs of Relatives of Cardiac Surgery Patients during the Critical Care Phase," *Focus on Critical Care*. 10, no. 5 (1983):50.

46. Joyce A. Bedsworth and Marilyn T. Molen, "Psychological Stress in Spouses of Patients with Myocardial Infarction," *Heart and Lung* 11(1982):450.

47. Adeline Nyamathi, "An Exploration of the Coping Processes of the Spouses of Myocardial Infarction Patients," Ph.D. dissertation, Case-Western Reserve University, 1983.

48. Christine Breu and Kathleen Dracup, "Helping Spouses of Critically Ill Patients," *American Journal of Nursing* 78(1978):50.

49. Miller, "Inspiring Hope."

50. Nancy Drew, "Exclusion and Confirmation: A Phenomenology of Patient's Experience with Caregivers," *Image* 18, no. 2 (1986):39.

51. Beglinger, "Coping Tasks."

52. Breu and Dracup, "Helping Spouses."

53. Samuel Perry and Milton Viederman, "Management of Emotional Reactions to Acute Medical Illness," *Medical Clinics of North America* 65(1981):3.

54. W. Doyle Gentry et al., "Type A/B Differences in Coping with Acute Myocardial Infarction: Further Considerations," *Heart and Lung* 12(1983):212.

55. Ibid.

56. Thomas P. Hackett, Ned H. Cassem, and Howard A. Wishnie, "The Coronary Care Unit: An Appraisal of its Psychologic Hazards," *New England Journal of Medicine* 279(1968):1365.

57. Ibid.

58. Howard A. Wishnie, Thomas P. Hackett, and Ned H. Cassem, "Psychological Hazards of Convalescence Following Myocardial Infarction," *Journal of the American Medical Association* 215(1971):1292.

59. Ibid.

60. Cynthia C. Scalzi, "Nursing Management of Behavioral Responses Following an Acute Myocardial Infarction," *Heart and Lung* 2(1973):62.

61. Thomas P. Hackett, "Management of the Disruptive Patient in the Intensive Care Setting," *Cardiovascular Nursing* 11, no. 6 (1975):45.

62. Janis, "Coping Patterns."

63. John R. Peteet, "A Closer Look at the Concept of Support: Some Applications to the Care of Patients with Cancer," *General Hospital Psychiatry* 4(1982):19.

64. Herbert Benson, *The Relaxation Response* (New York: Avon Books, 1975).

65. L. Aiken and T. Hendricks, "Systematic Relaxation as a Nursing Intervention Technique with Open Heart Surgery Patients," *Nursing Research* 20(1971):212.

66. Geraldine G. Flaherty and Joyce J. Fitzpatrick, "Relaxation Technique to Increase Comfort Level in Postoperative Patients: A Preliminary Study," *Nursing Research* 27(1978):352.

67. W. Doyle Gentry and Katharine R. Parkes, "Psychologic Stress in Intensive Care Unit and Non-intensive Care Unit Nursing: A Review of the Past Decade," *Heart and Lung* 11(1982):43.

68. Ernest H. Friedman, "Stress and Intensive Care Nursing: A Ten Year Reappraisal," *Heart and Lung* 11(1982):26.

69. Gentry and Parkes, "Psychologic Stress."

70. Joseph P. Maloney and Claudia Bartz, "Stress Tolerant People: Intensive Care Nurses Compared with Non-intensive Care Nurses," *Heart and Lung* 12(1983):389.

71. Gentry and Parkes, "Psychologic Stress."

72. Simon and Whitely, "Psychiatric Consultation."

Appendix 8-A*

Coping, Ineffective Individual

Definition: Ineffective coping is the impairment of adaptive behaviors and problem-solving abilities of a person in meeting life's demands and roles.

Etiology	*Defining Characteristics*
Situational crises	*Verbalization of inability to cope or inability to ask for help
Maturational crises	Inability to meet role expectations
Personal	Inability to meet basic needs
vulnerability	Inability to problem-solve
	Alteration in societal participation
	Destructive behavior toward self or others
	Inappropriate use of defense mechanisms
	Change in usual communication patterns
	Verbal manipulation
	High illness rate
	High rate of accidents

*Critical defining characteristic.

Comments: Further development is needed in the defining characteristics and critical characteristics. Changed and refined from previous nursing diagnosis, Coping patterns; individual, maladaptive.

Coping, Ineffective Family: Disabling

Definition: The behavior of a significant person (family member or other primary person) disables his or her own capacities and the client's capacities to address tasks effectively essential to either person's adaptation to the health challenge.

Etiology	*Defining Characteristics*
Significant person with chronically unexpressed feelings of guilt, anxiety, hostility, despair, etc.	Neglectful care of the client in regard to basic human needs and/or illness treatment
Dissonant discrepancy of coping styles being used to deal with the adaptive tasks by the significant person and client or among significant people	Distortion of reality regarding the client's health problem, including extreme denial about its existence or severity
Highly ambivalent family relationships	Intolerance
	Rejection

Source: Reprinted from *Classification of Nursing Diagnoses: Proceedings of the Third and Fourth National Conferences* by M.J. Kim and D.A. Moritz, pp. 286–289, with permission of McGraw-Hill Book Company, © 1982.

Arbitrary handling of a family's resistance to treatment which tends to solidify defensiveness as it fails to deal adequately with underlying anxiety

Abandonment
Desertion
Carrying on usual routines, disregarding client's needs
Psychosomaticism
Taking on illness signs of client
Decisions and actions by family which are detrimental to economic or social well-being
Agitation, depression, aggression, hostility
Impaired restructuring of a meaningful life for self, impaired individualization, prolonged overconcern for client
Neglectful relationships with other family members
Client's development of helpless, inactive dependence

Degree of independent nursing therapy: Moderate to high.

Comments: Regarding the family member's disabling coping response to the client's health challenge, one can describe a family member's response as disabling if it involves short-term coping behaviors which are highly detrimental to the welfare of the client or the significant person. In addition, chronically disabling patterns by a primary person are described as continued use of selected coping skills which have interrupted the person's longer-term capacity to receive, store, or organize information or to react in regard to it. This diagnosis is changed and refined from previous nursing diagnosis, Coping patterns, ineffective family.

Coping, Family: Potential for Growth

Definition: The family member has effectively managed adaptive tasks involved with the client's health challenge and is exhibiting desire and readiness for enhanced health and growth in regard to self and in relation to the client.

Etiology	*Defining Characteristics*

The person's basic needs are sufficiently gratified and adaptive tasks effectively addressed to enable goals of self-actualization to surface

The family member attempts to describe growth impact of crisis on his or her own values, priorities, goals, or relationships
Family member is moving in direction of health-promoting and enriching life style which supports and monitors maturational processes, audits and negotiates treatment programs, and generally chooses experiences which optimize wellness
Individual expresses interest in making contact on a one-to-one basis or on a mutual-aid group basis with another person who has experienced a similar situation

Degrees of independent nursing therapy: High.
Comments: New diagnosis.

Coping, Ineffective Family: Compromised

Definition: A usually supportive primary person (family member or close friend) is providing insufficient, ineffective, or compromised support, comfort, assistance, or encouragement which may be needed by the client to manage or master adaptive tasks related to his or her health challenge.

| | *Defining Characteristics* | |
Etiology	*Subjective*	*Objective*
Inadequate or incorrect information or understanding by a primary person	Client expresses or confirms a concern or complaint about significant other's response to his or her health problem	Significant person attempts assistive or supportive behaviors with less than satisfactory results
Temporary preoccupation by a significant person who is trying to manage emotional conflicts and personal suffering and is unable to perceive or act effectively in regard to client's needs	Significant person describes preoccupation with personal reactions, (e.g., fear, anticipatory grief, guilt, anxiety) to client's illness, disability, or other situational or developmental crises	Significant person withdraws or enters into limited or temporary personal communication with the client at time of need.
Temporary family disorganization and role changes		Significant person displays protective behavior disproportionate (too little or too much) to the client's abilities or need for autonomy
Other situational or developmental crises or situations the significant person may be facing	Significant person describes or confirms an inadequate understanding or knowledge base which interferes with effective assistive or supportive behaviors	
The client providing little support in turn for the primary person		
Prolonged disease or disability progression that exhausts the supportive capacity of significant people		

Degree of independent nursing therapy: High.

Comments: Differential diagnosing: the coping strategies of family members addressed in this diagnosis are basically constructive in nature. The constructive but compromised response and intent fall short of their realistic potential for effective situation or crisis management. Changed and refined from previous nursing diagnosis, Coping patterns, ineffective family.

Chapter 9

Nursing Challenge: The Patient with End-Stage Heart Failure

Brigid Doyle, RN, MS

INTRODUCTION

The patient with end-stage heart failure presents a true challenge to the cardiac critical care nurse. New technology and pharmacologic agents have made longer-term survival of these patients a reality. This population of patients, primarily with dilated congestive heart failure (CHF), has a high rate of recidivism and comes to the critical care unit with complex medical and nursing problems, both acute and chronic. Each admission builds on the next, allowing the nurse to affect significantly patients' perceptions of and course of their disease.

This chapter explores how the nurse can face the challenges presented by this patient group. Medical treatment options are discussed within a nursing framework and the use of nursing diagnoses emphasizes what nurses can do about these real patient problems. The overall nursing goal in caring for patients with end-stage heart failure is to restore each person to the level of activity, physical and mental, compatible with the functional capacity of the person's heart and the patient's personal wishes.

DEFINITION OF END-STAGE HEART FAILURE

Heart Failure

Heart failure is a general term used to describe the inability of the heart to pump an adequate amount of blood to meet the metabolic demands of the body. Heart failure can result from volume or pressure overload, myocardial dysfunction, filling disorders, or increased metabolic demands of the body.

Myocardial Failure

Myocardial failure is a more specific term and refers to a primary cardiac defect that decreases the intrinsic contractility of the myocardium. Myocardial failure can occur from a sustained overload with severe ventricular hypertrophy or from loss of myocardium, either segmental, as in coronary artery disease, or diffuse, with focal loss of myocardium, fibrosis, and resultant secondary hypertrophy as in cardiomyopathies.[1,2] Severe hypertrophy is then associated with depressed myocardial functioning and loss of the ability to develop adequate contractile tension. Ventricular dilatation occurs as pump function declines.

Congestive Heart Failure

CHF is a clinical syndrome that describes the systemic response to inadequate pump function or myocardial failure. In short, the circulation mounts a series of interrelated compensatory mechanisms designed to meet the metabolic demands of the body, increase cardiac output, and maintain an adequate perfusion pressure. Activation of the sympathetic nervous system (SNS) and the renin-angiotensin system leads to augmented peripheral vascular resistance and a maldistribution of peripheral blood flow. Systemic and/or pulmonary congestion and edema result. CHF can result from noncardiac causes such as high output states, which overstress the ventricular reserve, and once the underlying cause is corrected the congested state and circulatory derangements can resolve. See Exhibits 9-1 through 9-4 for more information.

Exhibit 9-1 Pathophysiology of CHF: General Features

Pressure overload
Volume overload
Loss of muscle
Decreased contractility
Restricted filling

Source: Reprinted from *American Journal of Cardiology*, Vol. 55, p. 10A, with permission of Yorke Medical Group, © January 1985.

Exhibit 9-2 Common Causes of CHF

Coronary artery disease
Systemic hypertension
Valvular heart disease
Cardiomyopathy
Congenital heart disease

Source: Reprinted from *American Journal of Cardiology*, Vol. 55, p. 10A, with permission of Yorke Medical Group, © January 1985.

Exhibit 9-3 High Output Failure

Hyperthyroidism
Anemia
Paget's disease
Polyostotic fibrous dysplasia (Albright's syndrome)
Hypernephroma with bone metastases
Arteriovenous fistula
Dermatologic disorders
Acute glomerulonephritis
Hepatic cirrhosis

Source: Reprinted from *American Journal of Cardiology*, Vol. 55, p. 10A, with permission of Yorke Medical Group, © January 1985.

Exhibit 9-4 Pathophysiology of CHF in Coronary Artery Disease

Loss of muscle
Ischemia
Aneurysm—paradoxical expansion, increased wall stress
Increased wall stress of remaining normal muscle
Decreased ventricular compliance

Source: Reprinted from *American Journal of Cardiology*, Vol. 55, p. 10A, with permission of Yorke Medical Group, © January 1985.

End-Stage Congestive Heart Failure

There may be a prolonged interval from the onset of myocardial injury to the development of clinically apparent myocardial failure and CHF. The correlation of myocardial dysfunction and myocardial loss is relatively close and consistent. Once 35% to 40% of the left ventricular (LV) myocardium is destroyed in an acute myocardial infarction (AMI), CHF and cardiogenic shock are manifested.[3] A smaller volume of myocardial loss may produce no congestive symptoms, and the patient may be well compensated with hypertrophy of the remaining heart muscle. In the clinical entity of end-stage chronic heart failure, both myocardial failure and CHF are essentially irreversible.

A chronic derangement of the circulation occurs with organ dysfunction as a result of excessive compensatory peripheral vasoconstriction and redistribution of peripheral blood flow. A vicious cycle begins with the depressed myocardium failing to respond and, in fact, worsening from the body's attempt to move toward homeostasis. Aggressive measures must be taken to augment the failing heart and curtail the negative vascular changes.

Several forms of CHF are irreversible or without effective forms of treatment and lead to end-stage heart failure. The long-term prognosis is poor. According to the Framingham study,[4] the probability of dying within 5 years from the onset of CHF was 62% for men and 42% for women. The annual incidence of CHF is approximated at 2.3 per 1,000 men and 1.4 per 1,000 women. It is thought that there are at least 10 million patients with CHF in the United States today. New therapies have improved the morbidity, but little has changed overall mortality.

The aim of treatment of end-stage heart disease is essentially twofold: ameliorate symptoms and, with new agents or new combination of conventional agents, attempt to prolong survival.

PATHOPHYSIOLOGY OF END-STAGE HEART FAILURE

Mechanisms of Cardiac Contraction

Since end-stage heart failure is usually caused by an impairment of ventricular systolic performance, it is necessary to understand the basic mechanics and biochemistry of contraction. This forms the basis for a later discussion on the use of inotropic agents used to augment contractility in the failing heart.

Biochemistry of Cardiac Bioenergetics

Along with oxygen, the principal substrates used in myocardial metabolism are fatty acids, glucose, pyruvate, and lactate. Breakdown of these fuels through the Krebs cycle liberates free energy, which is transferred via hydrogen to the phosphate bonds of adenosine diphosphate (ADP) and creatinine. These go on to form the high-energy compounds of adenosine triphosphate (ATP) and creatine phosphate. Energy is stored in ATP for later use in chemical reactions in the cell that require energy, one of these being the contractile process. ATPase is the calcium-dependent enzyme that breaks down the ATP to the simpler form, ADP, liberating energy.

Energy Release and Mechanical Coupling

Myofibrils are the contractile elements of the myocardial cell and are composed of bundles of myofilaments. When viewed with an electron micrograph, myofibrils exhibit a periodic pattern of dark and light areas that are formed by components of a repeating morphologic and functional unit, the sarcomere (see Figure 9-1).

The sarcomere varies in length, 1.5 to 2.2 micrometers, relative to the degree of relaxation or contraction of the myofibril.[5] Interdigitating thick and thin protein filaments dominate the myofibril. Actin molecules are arranged in thin filaments

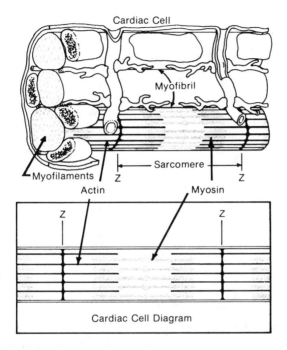

Figure 9-1 The Cardiac Cell. *Source*: Reprinted from *Calcium in Cardiac Metabolism* with permission of Knoll Pharmaceuticals, © 1980.

and together with tropomyosin (another contractile protein) optically represent "light zones." Dark zones, thick bands, are made up of myosin filaments and are arranged in the central part of the sarcomere. The myocardium develops force by forming cross-bridges between actin and myosin myofilaments. The amount of force depends on the number of cross-bridges formed.

During contraction, the length of the filaments does not change, only the relation between these two sets of filaments changes. Huxley and Hanson[6] first simplified this theory of muscle contraction when they introduced the "sliding filament hypothesis." The myocardial muscle unit shortens when actin filaments slide toward the center of the sarcomere and attach to myosin binding sites. Energy contained in ATP is necessary for this interaction to occur.

This filament interaction is stimulated by calcium and regulated by troponin and tropomyosin, two proteins intertwined on the actin filament. Troponin has three subunits, I, T, and C, which in the absence of calcium inhibit contraction by occupying the myosin binding sites. Once the cell is electrically depolarized, and calcium enters the cell, it triggers the release of more calcium from intracellular stores (see Figure 9-2). Free calcium binds with troponin C. The calcium-troponin C complex abolishes the inhibitory action of troponin I. Troponin T

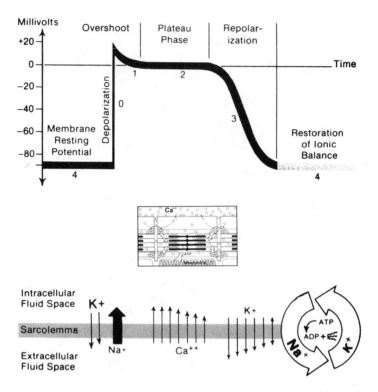

Figure 9-2 Excitation of cardiac or skeletal muscle cell prompts rapid inflow of both calcium and sodium across the cell membrane and release of calcium sequestered in intracellular binding sites, chiefly in the sarcoplasmic reticulum, for delivery to the contractile apparatus. *Source*: Reprinted from *Calcium in Cardiac Metabolism* with permission of Knoll Pharmaceuticals, © 1980.

binds all the subunits to tropomyosin, freeing the myosin binding sites, and contraction takes place (see Figure 9-3). Development of force depends on the number of troponin C units and the intracellular calcium concentration. Both attachment and disengagement of the myosin and actin filaments require ATP.

Intracellular calcium is stored mainly in the sarcoplasmic reticulum and mitochondria, or bound to intracellular buffers.[7] Calcium can enter the cell through "gated" voltage-dependent and time-dependent channels during electrical depolarization,[8] through nongated ionic channels, or through the sodium-calcium exchange mechanism.[9] Intracellular calcium is altered by the intracellular second messenger cyclic AMP (cAMP). cAMP is produced by the enzyme adenylate cyclase,[10] which interacts with many surface cell receptors such as that of the beta-adrenergic system. An increased level of cAMP favors intracellular phosphorylation of numerous proteins,[11] resulting in a transmembrane calcium influx, an increase in intracellular calcium, calcium from gated pathways,[12] and an

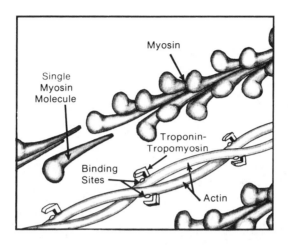

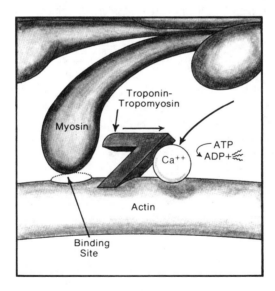

Figure 9-3 Actin Myosin Binding. *Source*: Reprinted from *Calcium in Cardiac Metabolism* with permission of Knoll Pharmaceuticals, © 1980.

increased storage of calcium in the sarcoplasmic reticulum.[13] The complete impact of cAMP on cardiac cellular physiology is still unknown. Evidence thus far favorably correlates its presence with mechanisms to increase and transport intracellular calcium through stimulation of beta-adrenergic receptors.

cAMP is degraded by a number of cyclic nucleotide phosphodiesterases. Inhibition of phosphodiesterase, especially phosphodiesterase III enzymes in the heart, results in an elevated cAMP level and may effect changes resembling adenylate cyclase stimulation,[14] increasing availability of calcium for contraction.

Compensatory Mechanisms in Congestive Heart Failure

Activaton of Sympathetic Nervous System

An augmentation of SNS activity is the most immediate response to a decreased cardiac output. An increase in impulse traffic in the sympathetic signals to the heart leads to release of the neurotransmitter norepinephrine from terminal sympathetic neurons and release of its synthetic enzyme, dopamine-beta-hydroxylase. Epinephrine, a circulating catecholamine from the adrenal medulla, and norepinephrine from peripheral nerve endings are also released.

Release of catecholamines stimulates adrenergic alpha and beta receptors located on the surface of cells throughout the body. In the heart, this receptor stimulation increases both the force and frequency of cardiac contraction[15] and can also produce the extracardiac manifestations of arterial and venous constriction.

Beta-adrenergic stimulation is particularly important in supporting cardiac function in heart failure. Beta$_1$ receptors dominate the myocardium where stimulation increases inotropic and chronotropic activity. Beta$_2$ receptors are found predominantly in respiratory and vascular smooth muscle where they regulate bronchodilation and vasodilation, respectively. There is evidence that some beta$_2$ receptors are located on the myocardial surface, but their function is not yet clearly understood.[16]

Alpha receptors can also be divided into two types: alpha$_1$ are postsynaptic and mediate vascular smooth muscle contraction; alpha$_2$ are presynaptic, and their functional response is still under study.[17] Little information is available regarding the newly identified alpha receptors on the myocardial surface.[18]

Reflecting this compensatory response, it was shown that patients with CHF have high levels of plasma and urinary norepinephrine both at rest and during exercise.[19] Data by Thomas et al.[20] suggest that the level of plasma norepinephrine correlates with the degree of clinical decompensation.

Modulation of the adrenergic response is not completely understood. It is known that the number and reactivity of the adrenergic receptors themselves are important in determining the dominant response, especially when dual stimulation leads to opposing interactions (as in alpha$_1$ and beta$_2$ response).

Figure 9-4 illustrates the vicious cycle that begins when the adrenergic and hormonal mechanisms combine to compensate for a low cardiac output. Beta stimulation is viewed as a beneficial response, maximizing the inotropic potential of the failing heart. But, since functional myocardium is the primary deficit, the

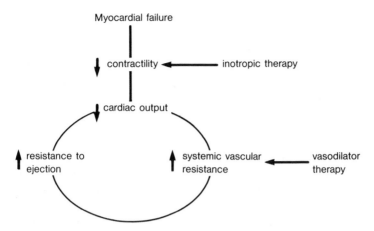

Figure 9-4 The vicious cycle in heart failure. Myocardial failure is associated with decreased contractile function and reduced cardiac output. Systemic vascular resistance rises in an attempt to maintain arterial pressure. Increased systemic vascular resistance, however, further decreases cardiac output by increasing the resistance to ventricular ejection. *Source*: Reprinted from "Congestive Cardiomyopathy: Therapeutic Approach" by K. Chatterjee, in *Comprehensive Therapy*, Vol. 8, No. 7, pp. 25–34, with permission of The Laux Company, Inc., Maynard, Mass., © 1982.

response, no matter how strong, is diminutive compared with the additional vascular changes triggered by alpha$_1$ stimulation augmented by the humoral response of the angiotensin-renin-aldosterone and arginine-vasopressin systems. The end point is vascular constriction, increasing the pressure against which the failing heart must pump. This further reduces the ejection by the heart, and ultimately the cardiac output falls even further.

Desensitization of Myocardial Beta-Adrenergic Receptors. Thomas and Mach[21] put forth the hypothesis that, over time, there was decreased beta-adrenergic responsiveness in the failing human heart. This theory is supported by the research of Bristow and Ginsburg, et al.[22,23] who showed that in patients with chronic heart failure there were both reduced myocardial beta-adrenergic receptor density and reduced myocardial responsiveness to beta-adrenergic stimulation. The mechanism for these changes is not clear, but seems to be related to prolonged exposure to increased levels of catecholamines. In failing hearts, the decreased beta-receptor density was transmitted to distal events in the contractile process, namely a reduction in adenylate cyclase activity. So, over time, the adrenergic compensatory mechanism fails to maximize contractility, and the patient begins to decompensate.

Clinical evidence supports this theory: (1) The resting heart rate and mean arterial blood pressure (BP) of patients with end-stage cardiac heart failure is not proportional to increased levels of sympathetic stimulation; (2) exercise- or stress-induced activation of the sympathetic system is inappropriately blunted and results in increased symptoms of heart failure and performance abnormalities;[24] this is reflected in a decreased cardiac reserve; (3) intravenous (IV) sympathomimetic amines improve cardiac performance only for short periods of time, losing their hemodynamic effectiveness when administered during continuous long-term infusions.[25]

Activation of the Renin-Angiotensin-Aldosterone System

Two powerful renal mechanisms are activated by a decrease in cardiac output and a reduction in perfusion pressure. Corrective measures combine to expand the effective blood volume and reduce the potential arterial space (vasoconstriction). Intravascular fluid expansion is accomplished by renal retention of sodium and water. In heart failure this is achieved by (1) a reduction in the glomerular filtration rate (GFR), and (2) activation of the renin-angiotensin-aldosterone system.

Decreased arterial blood flow to the kidneys causes a release of renin from the juxtaglomerular apparatus. Renin cleaves angiotensinogen to angiotensin I. Angiotensin-converting enzyme (ACE) cleaves angiotensin I to angiotensin II. (This conversion takes place during circulation through the lungs.) Angiotensin II, a potent vasoconstrictor, is an important stimulus for the release of aldosterone from the adrenal gland, facilitates noradrenergic transmission in the autonomic nervous system,[26] and is a stimulus for the release of arginin vasopressin,[27] (antidiuretic hormone [ADH]). The net result of this cascade of endocrine interactions is vasoconstriction caused by angiotensin II and sodium and water retention mediated by aldosterone. In patients with severe heart failure, aldosterone levels may be increased to 4 to 5 mg daily in contrast to a secretion of 50 to 200 µg/day in normal people.[28]

ADH release is stimulated by extracellular hyperosmolality and decreased extracellular fluid volume. Though it plays a small part in the renal response to heart failure, its contribution is to increase absorption of free water. In long-standing heart failure, this can become problematic if there is inappropriate ADH secretion in response to dilutional hyponatremia. The result is an inability of patients to excrete an ingested water load. This can also occur if there is appropriate ADH but an inadequate delivery of sodium and water to the distal nephron of the kidney.

An additional factor that contributes to the regulation of sodium and water is the atrial natriuretic factor (ANF). Currently under investigation, this peptide seems to be released from atrial and possibly ventricular tissue. Investigators have found that ANF promotes sodium excretion by the kidneys, blocks the adrenal gland's production of aldosterone, and inhibits the action of endogenous vasoconstrictors. Plasma concentration of ANF is increased in patients with CHF.[29] The exact role of this counter-regulatory hormone has yet to be elucidated, but it seems to be important in the myocardial compensatory response to high filling pressures.

The result of these renal compensatory mechanisms is to increase the circulating blood volume, increasing the amount of blood delivered to the heart for ejection. This translates into an increased end-diastolic volume, preload for the failing heart. According to the Frank-Starling mechanism (see Chapter 3), this increased preload would increase the wall stress, stretch the myofibrils, and increase the force of contraction. In end-stage heart failure, this mechanism is exhausted. The myocardial fibers can no longer appropriately respond to an increased stretch. The reserve funtion is gone when the pulmonary capillary wedge pressure (PCWP) chronically remains in a range of 15 to 20 torr.[30] Further increase in preload cannot improve cardiac output and perfusion and, in some cases, will decrease cardiac performance and worsen the signs and symptoms of congestion and heart failure. Increased vascular tone mediated by angiotensin further restricts the arteriolar vascular bed and increases the impedance to ejection (the afterload), further contributing to the vicious cycle of cardiac decompensation.

Myocardial Hypertrophy and Dilation

For the heart to maintain the ability to increase its pressure development in response to an increased work load, the heart must increase muscle mass. Protein synthesis is stimulated by excessive intramyocardial tension[31] and results in an increased number of myocardial contractile units and an increase in the size of existing cells. Changes occur in the ventricles to maintain a relatively constant wall tension. Ventricles respond to pressure loads such as aortic stenosis or hypertension by increasing wall thickness in a concentric manner with little or no change in chamber size. This results in decreased ventricular compliance.

The response to volume loads is quite different. Conditions that chronically increase the preload, as in regurgitant valvular lesions or weakened, damaged myocardium resulting from an MI, change the myocardium by producing chamber dilation with an increase in ventricular wall thickness, which is initially proportional to the dilation. The net result is a decrease in compliance, a marked decrease in the force of contractions, and an increase in heart size.

As long as wall stress (in accord with the LaPlace relation) remains relatively normal, the heart can remain compensated for the additional pressure load placed on it. Once wall stress becomes greater than normal, the heart begins to fail and irreversible changes occur in calcium activation sequence and thus in the contractile ability of the muscle.[32] The result is reduced systolic emptying despite an increased diastolic volume. This usually translates into a decreased ejection fraction (EF) and a limited cardiac output associated with effort.

$$EF = Systolic\ volume/End\text{-}diastolic\ volume.$$

Some patients with heart failure can have a normal cardiac output despite a low EF by dilating even further and increasing the end-diastolic volume (EDV) such that forward stroke volume (SV) is maintained (SV = EDV × EF).

Increased Tissue Oxygen Extraction

A modest compensatory reaction operative in end-stage heart failure is the ability of peripheral tissues to increase the extraction of oxygen from hemoglobin. A low cardiac output state increases the level of lactic acid as a byproduct of cellular metabolism. This leads to a decrease in overall body pH. An increase in erythrocyte levels of 2,3,diphosphoglycerate (DPG) results, and there is a shift in the oxygen-hemoglobin dissociation curve, which favors release of more oxygen from the blood at any given P_{O_2} (the Bohr effect). This enhances the ability of peripheral tissues to increase their extraction of oxygen from the circulating blood.

Presence of this compensatory mechanism can be detected clinically in two measurable ways. The first is to measure the percent of oxygen saturation of the venous blood. A true mixed venous blood sample can be obtained from the distal port of a Swan-Ganz catheter in the pulmonary artery. Continuous monitoring of mixed venous oxygen saturation can be obtained by fiberoptic reflectometry, which is incorporated into certain pulmonary artery catheters. Normal mixed venous oxygen saturation is in the range of 33 to 36 torr. A lower value reflects increased oxygen extraction at the tissue level; less than 25 torr indicates severe cardiovascular compromise, and less than 20 torr indicates severe shock.

A second way to quantify the use of oxygen in the peripheral tissues is to compare the arteriovenous oxygen content difference (AV_{O_2}). The normal AV_{O_2} is 4 to 6 mL O_2/dL and represents an average oxygen extraction from body tissues in the basal state. The greater the difference in the AV_{O_2}, the "slower" the circulation time and the greater the oxygen extraction; hence the lower cardiac output. In most instances, there is an inverse relation between the value obtained from the AV_{O_2} and the cardiac output measurement.

Effect of End-Stage Heart Failure on Major Body Organs

Compensatory mechanisms activated in response to a diminished cardiac output and perfusion pressure alter the normal distribution of cardiac output, patterns of perfusion, and resultant organ function. Changes are often manifest in the signs and symptoms of CHF. Others are detected only through a complete diagnostic workup including invasive and noninvasive testing procedures. A systems approach assists in detecting target organ damage. It may be helpful to categorize organ alterations as resulting from underperfusion, congestion, or a combination of the two.

Signs and symptoms resulting from CHF are listed in Table 9-1. See Chapter 1 for an in-depth description of cardiovascular physical assessment findings.

Table 9-1 Clinical Indicators of Right and Left Ventricular Failure

Left Ventricular Failure	*Right Ventricular Failure*
Subjective indicators (behaviors reported by patient)	
Weakness	Weight gain
Fatigue	Transient ankle swelling and pigmentation
Memory loss and confusion	Abdominal distension
Breathlessness	Subcostal pain
Cough	Gastric distress
Insomnia	Anorexia, nausea
Anorexia	
Palpitations	
Diaphoresis	
Objective indicators (findings observed by clinician)	
Tachycardia	Edema
Decreased S_1	Ascites
S_3 and S_4	Left parasternal lift
Moist rales	Increased jugular venous pressure
Pleural effusion	Hepatomegaly
Diaphoresis	Neck vein pulsations and distension
Pulsus alternans	Positive hepatojugular reflux

Source: Reproduced by permission from *Congestive Heart Failure* by C.R. Michaelson (Ed.), p. 46, St. Louis, © 1983, The C.V. Mosby Company.

Integumentary

The skin normally receives approximately 4% to 9% of the cardiac output. With activation of the SNS, blood flow is shunted away from nonvital organs such as the skin. Depending on the level of sympathetic stimulation, skin may have generalized pallor and decreased temperature or be cyanotic (central or peripheral) or diaphoretic. Cutaneous vasoconstriction occurs when patients with heart failure are stressed. It is thought that strong afferent stimulation contributes to the patient's inability to tolerate thermal stress. This occurs by way of hypothalamic inhibition caused by increased body temperature.[33]

Another major change noted in the skin is edema. Skin overlying edematous areas may become reddened, pigmented, indented, and shiny. Cardiac edema is usually soft, pitting, and symmetric in dependent parts of the body during early failure. In patients with end-stage heart failure and limited activity, edema can progress to presacral and genital regions. Circulatory impairment and congestion can lead to an accumulation of fluid in the abdominal cavity (ascites), fluid in the pleural space (hydrothorax), or total body edema (anasarca).

Kidney

Renal perfusion pressure remains depressed in end-stage heart failure and leads to even further changes in the kidney that promote electrolyte and biochemical disorders and edema formation. GFR is reduced, decreasing the kidney's ability to metabolize waste and manage fluid or sodium loads. As a result, (1) blood urea nitrogen (BUN) rises disproportionally to a rise in serum creatinine (BUN/creatinine ratio of 20:1 or greater), indicating prerenal azotemia; (2) urine analysis reveals a very low sodium content and concentration frequency less than 5 mEq/L; (3) urine volume diminishes to oliguric levels; (4) small amounts of sodium lead to volume overload; and (5) kidneys become refractory to diuretic therapy.[34]

Lungs

When the left side of the heart fails, the LV end-diastolic pressure increases. This increase in pressure is transmitted to the pulmonary circulation where the pulmonary capillary pressure (hydrostatic pressure) may exceed the oncotic pressure of plasma proteins. In the later stages of heart failure, transudation of fluid occurs from pulmonary vessels into surrounding lung fields. Fluid in the alveolar spaces inhibits gas exchange, decreases lung compliance, and increases the work of breathing. Hypoxia and hypercapnia result. The patient experiences the subjective feeling of dyspnea. Rales, wheezing, and pleural effusions can be detected on physical examination.

Liver

Hepatic congestion occurs as a result of a right-sided failure as a late consequence of left-sided failure. On physical examination, the hepatojugular reflex can indicate hepatic congestion and is viewed as an early sign of circulatory overload and venous congestion from right ventricular (RV) dysfunction. Pain and tenderness can often be present in early heart failure but is sometimes absent in chronic stages, even though enlargement persists. Laboratory values can indicate organ dysfunction secondary to this passive congestion. Serum glutamic oxaloacitic transaminase (SGOT) is mildly to moderately elevated in end-stage heart failure (normal 5 to 40 IU/L). Prothrombin time may also be prolonged (normal 12 to 14 seconds), making anticoagulation in these patients a careful exercise. Reduced dosages of any drug metabolized in the liver must be considered in patients with end-stage heart failure.

Gastrointestinal (GI)

Most abnormalities associated with heart failure are the result of venous congestion. Interstitial edema results in a relative cellular hypoxia.[35] Hypoxia is thought to interfere with nitrogen and fat absorption across the intestinal villous membrane.[36] GI hypomotility with delayed gastric emptying are present in end-stage heart failure. The stomach may be compressed by an enlarged liver or by ascites. Vague abdominal pain and distension are common in CHF and are often intensified by the digestion of food or oral medications. Cardiac cachexia is often present.

Brain

If cerebral perfusion decreases, the patient's mental status will be altered. Early manifestations are insomnia, restlessness, decreased attention span, feelings of anxiety, and memory loss. When perfusion falls below a critical level, disorientation occurs.[37] In the end, unresponsiveness and obtundation harbinger death.

THE CHALLENGE: NURSING DIAGNOSES AND INTERVENTIONS FOR THE PATIENT WITH END-STAGE HEART FAILURE

It is not uncommon for patients with heart failure to progressively decompensate and deteriorate on subsequent admissions to the CCU. A change in the patient's condition can indicate worsening of the heart failure or may be a manifestation of an event that precipitates a state of decompensation. The most common precipitating events are (1) poor patient compliance with the therapeutic regimen as occurs with dietary indiscretion (increased salt intake) or discontinuance or manipulation of drug therapy; (2) physical, emotional, or environmental stress; (3) excessive diuresis; (4) onset of arrhythmias; (5) development of an unrelated illness.

A critical care nurse can view these events in the framework of nursing diagnoses (Table 9-2). This perspective can assist the nurse in the assessment process (Chapter 1) and subsequent care planning.

This section does not outline every possible nursing action to be taken on behalf of the patient with heart failure. It presents principles and rationales to guide nursing diagnosis and major nursing and medical interventions for this very special group of patients with end-stage heart failure. Exhibit 9-5 lists the

Table 9-2 Precipitating Events of CHF and Possible Nursing Diagnoses

Event	Possible Nursing Diagnoses
Poor compliance with medical treatment plans	Noncompliance Knowledge deficit
Physical, emotional, environmental stress	Activity intolerance Knowledge deficit Anxiety/fear
Excessive diuresis	Fluid volume deficit
Arrhythmias	Alteration in cardiac output, decreased

Exhibit 9-5 Nursing Diagnoses to Consider for the Patient with End-Stage CHF

Alterations in cardiac output
Activity intolerance
Impaired gas exchange
Alteration in fluid volume: excess
Potential for injury
Alteration in nutritional status: less than body requirements
Knowledge deficit
Ineffective coping: family and individual
Noncompliance

major nursing diagnoses that must be considered in the patient with end-stage heart failure.

ALTERATION IN CARDIAC OUTPUT: DECREASED, RELATED TO DIMINISHED LV PERFORMANCE

This nursing diagnosis is the particular domain of the critical care nurse. Through independent, interdependent, and dependent role functions, the nurse aggressively moves toward maximizing the cardiac output of the patient by addressing the four major factors that determine ventricular performance: preload, afterload, contractility, and heart rate. In the clinical setting it is difficult to isolate the effective change produced by altering one of these factors. Through the use of hemodynamic monitoring with the Swan-Ganz catheter, evaluation is made easier. Useful bedside indicators of these factors are described thoroughly in Chapter 3. In brief they are as follows.

Preload, the volume of blood in the ventricles at the end of diastole immediately before contraction, is indirectly measured by the PCWP.

Afterload, the resistance against which the LV must pump, is best reflected in the systemic vascular resistance (SVR). This is a value calculated to reflect the resistance to blood flow by the force of friction between the blood and the blood vessels. It is related to the diameter of the arterioles and therefore reflects the vasoactive state of the smallest perfusion unit in the vascular system. The formula to calculate SVR is:

$$SVR = [(\text{Mean arterial BP} - \text{Right atrial pressure})/\text{Cardiac output}] \times 80.$$

Normal values are 800 to 1,200 dynes/sec/cm^{-5}.

Contractility, perhaps the most interrelated factor, reflects the inotropic state of the ventricle but relies on both the preload for optimal muscle stretch and afterload as a measure of resistance to ejection. Ultimately, contractility is tied to the number and functional state of the myocardial contractile units. At the bedside, the overall performance is reflected in the cardiac output, which also takes into consideration heart rate. (Cardiac output is a product of heart rate and stroke volume.)

Heart rate, the number of times per minute the heart beats, is a determinant of myocardial oxygen consumption (MV_{O_2}). The faster the heart rate, the more oxygen the muscle will require. It reflects the metabolic and adrenergic states of the body. The critical care nurse must monitor for both the rate and regularity to optimize cardiac output.

Nursing Goal

Optimize cardiac output by careful monitoring and manipulation of the indicators of contractility.

Nursing Interventions

1. *Allow for periods of physical and emotional rest.* Physical and emotional rest decreases the body's demands for oxygen and can provide for a redistribution of blood flow to nonvital organs, especially the kidneys. Bed rest alone can often produce a diuresis, reducing congestion. Bed rest must be maintained until overt heart failure is under control. Progressive activity and ambulation should begin as soon as the patient stabilizes and can tolerate the workload. Complications of bed rest must be considered, especially in the patient with heart failure. Of special importance is the nursing management of skin, circulation, bowel regularity, and prevention of thromboemboli. Patients who require long periods of bed rest or inactivity may require anticoagulation with subcutaneous heparin 5,000 units twice a day. Nursing measures must then also include monitoring for signs of internal bleeding.
2. *Administer prescribed agents to augment contractility.* Calcium seems to be the final pathway of all drugs that increase contractility. Currently there are three classifications of inotropic agents available to augment the amount of calcium available to the myocardium with each beat: (1) digitalis glycosides, (2) sympathomimetic amines, and (3) phosphodiesterase inhibitors. Drugs to increase contractility are often given in combination with vasodilators to maximize the performance of the LV.

Drugs

Digitalis Glycosides

The primary conventional oral agent used to improve cardiac contractile function is digitalis. The mechanism of action of this inotropic agent is thought to be by way of the inhibition of the sodium potassium–ATPase interface (see Figure 9-3). Intracellular sodium concentrations are increased, creating an intracellular environment conducive to a calcium-sodium exchange. More calcium is allowed into the cell, maximizing the actin myosin coupling of the contractile process. The result is increased force and velocity of contraction. Digitalis also exerts a vagal effect, assisting in the rate control of patients with supraventricular arrhythmias (especially atrial fibrillation).

It is important to ascertain whether the patient is taking digitalis. Digitalis toxicity is not uncommon, and its incidence is increased by concomitant administration of several other cardiac drugs: quinidine, verapamil, amiodarone, and spironolactone. Other factors that influence an individual's sensitivity to digitalis include serum potassium imbalances, acid-base balance, thyroid status, renal function, autonomic nervous system tone, and respiratory disease.

Although cardiac glycosides such as digitalis are the mainstay of chronic inotropic support, their role in management of pump failure is controversial in some circles where it is thought that sympathetic stimulation is so dominant that the effects of digoxin are negligible at best. This controversy exists despite a 1982 double-blind study conducted by Lee et al.,[38] which showed the beneficial effects of oral digitalis in patients with severe chronic heart failure. Administration of the drug is nonetheless hindered by its limited dosage response, long duration of action, and possibility of toxicity.[39] Exhibit 9-6 lists the primary treatment modalities used in digoxin toxicity.

Exhibit 9-6 Treatment of Digitalis Toxicity

1. Discontinue digoxin. Obtain digoxin serum level.
2. Place patient on bed rest to avoid sympathetic stimulation.
3. Monitor heart rhythm to identify arrhythmias associated with digitalis toxicity.
4. Treat arrhythmias with appropriate pharmacologic agents.
   - Administer potassium chloride (avoid with renal failure, hyperkalemia, and depressed AV conduction).
   - Administer antiarrhythmic agents, i.e., phenytoin/lidocaine.
5. Treat hyperkalemia if present.
   - potassium exchange resins
   - glucose and insulin
   - sodium bicarbonate
   - hemodialysis.
6. Assist with insertion of a temporary pacemaker for hemodynamically significant bradycardias refractory to atropine. (Atrial placement is preferred to avoid ventricular irritability.)
7. Administer activated charcoal (PO or NG) to decrease the half-life of digoxin.
8. Consider administration of digoxin-specific FAB antibody fragments. (Available at certain regional medical centers.)

Sympathomimetic Agents

These drugs are designed to stimulate the alpha- and beta-adrenergic and dopaminergic receptors in the myocardium and vascular tree. Beta$_1$ agents augment myocardial contractility through activation of the adenylcyclase, ATP, cAMP sequence previously described. It also stimulates the breakdown of glycogen to increase the substrate energy supply to the myocardial cells.

Beta$_2$ and alpha agents regulate vasomotor tone and are administered to achieve a specific desired effect.

Sympathomimetic Amines

Dobutamine. Dobutamine is a beta-adrenergic sympathomimetic agent particularly beneficial for the acute management of CHF. Dobutamine through its beta$_1$ properties provides inotropic support independent of the patient's adrenergic reserves. The drug has beta$_2$ properties, which decrease afterload through mild peripheral vasodilation. These two properties combine to maximize ventricular systolic function while reducing impedance of ejection, making the work of the failing heart easier.

The critical care nurse titrates the drug to achieve the desired hemodynamic outcome. As with any of the parenteral vasoactives, the nurse follows the principles outlined in Exhibit 9-7. The desired effect with dobutamine is to increase cardiac output, decrease SVR, and maintain or increase BP without increasing PCWP or heart rate. It is less likely to cause tachycardia than other sympathomimetics.

Exhibit 9-7 Nursing Guidelines for the Administration/Titration of a Parenteral Vasoactive Agent for Patients with CHF

1. Determine initial hemodynamics for selection of agent (HR, BP, RA, PA, PCW, cardiac output, SVR).
2. Start the therapy with low initial dose using an infusion device for increased control and safety.
3. Gradually increase the infusion rate every 5 to 15 minutes, monitoring changes.
4. Monitor changes in BP, HR, PCW, CO, SVR.
5. If CO increases with a decrease in SVR and PCWP and little change in BP, maintain or increase the infusion rate.
6. If BP decreases without change in CO or PCW, discontinue vasodilator and add an inotropic agent.
7. Evaluate the hemodynamic response when oral agents are substituted for parenteral drugs.

Source: Adapted from *Critical Care Quarterly*, Vol. 4, No. 3, pp. 20–21, Aspen Publishers, Inc., © December 1981.

Dobutamine exerts its maximal hemodynamic effect within 72 hours of administration. There is evidence that suggests a 43% reduction in efficacy after 96 hours of continuous infusion.[40] This change is thought to be attributable to the previously described down regulation of beta receptors because of the continuous high level of sympathetic tone at the heart failure. This principle has been applied in a new therapeutic approach: Short-term (72-hour) infusions of dobutamine are being administered to heart failure patients on a weekly or biweekly basis. Improvements in exercise performance and functional class have been reported.[41,42] This method can provide the patient with IV drug therapy at home under the supervision of a visiting nurse. Subcutaneous dobutamine pumps are currently in clinical trial. This is another method of providing more independence to the patient.

Dopamine. Dopamine is a precursor of norepinephrine. With alpha and beta properties, it acts on the peripheral vasculature and the myocardium. The positive inotropic effects are attributable to stimulation of the beta-adrenergic receptor sites. This effect dominates at a dosage of 5 to 10 μg/kg. Above this range, the alpha stimulation may cause an unwanted increase in SVR, necessitating the concomitant administration of a vasodilator such as sodium nitroprusside or nitroglycerine (NTG). Dopamine alone or in combination with dobutamine may also be used to augment contractility. The dose response of dopamine is somewhat dependent on the adrenergic state of the patient, so dose-response curves may vary from patient to patient. As with any agent that increases inotropy, it must be recognized that MVo_2 may increase. Arrhythmias and tachycardia may also follow dopamine administration.

Low-dose dopamine (3 to 5 μg/kg) may be administered to produce a "renal effect." In this dosage range, dopamine acts on the renal and mesenteric vascular beds to increase renal cortical blood flow. This dopamanergic effect blunts the renal compensatory mechanisms brought into play by the failing heart and low cardiac output, increasing GFR and concomitant urine output.

Isuprel. Isuprel is a beta-adrenergic sympathomimetic amine that stimulates both $beta_1$ and $beta_2$ receptors. Low dosages of this agent IV have successfully been given in some centers to provide inotropic support and peripheral vasodilation. Careful monitoring of BP, cardiac output, and heart rate are imperative when administering this agent. It is necessary to determine early if the $beta_1$ receptors can generate enough contractile force to provide adequate perfusion volume to the dilated vasculature mediated by $beta_2$ receptors.

Levodopa. Levodopa is a precursor of dopamine and, in the presence of pyridoxine (50 mg/day), is converted to dopamine after oral ingestion. A dosage of 1.0 to 1.5 g has been shown to produce a hemodynamic effect in heart failure patients similar to that of a 2 to 4 μg/kg infusion of dopamine. At present, the limiting use of this agent is the nausea and vomiting experienced by a large number of patients. This effect is attenuated with a gradual dosage schedule. Other oral agents that seem to mimic the salutary effects of dopamine and are currently in clinical trials include ibopamine and propylbutyl dopamine.

Butopamine. This is an oral agent with properties similar to those of dobutamine. The beneficial positive inotropic effects, however, are often overshadowed by a notable increase in heart rate and ectopy.

Prenalterol. Selective beta$_1$ agonist properties with little beta$_2$ effects are noticed with administration of this oral agent. Patients who received this drug first IV and then orally for up to 1 month showed functional improvement at first. Then later, in a double-blind crossover trial, no improvement was discernible, either hemodynamically or from exercise tolerance.[43]

Pirbuterol. Structurally similar to isuprel, this oral agent is prescribed to provide inotropic support with peripheral vasodilation. Unfortunately, clinical trials of 1 month failed to show any sustained improvement in cardiac performance.[44]

Like the IV agents, these newer oral sympathomimetics fail to show long-term beneficial effects for patients with end-stage heart failure. The "down regulation" phenomenon is thought to be the limiting factor in long-term responsiveness to this entire class of drugs.

Phosphodiesterase Inhibitors

Several new agents fall into this broad category of drugs. Though structurally dissimilar, they all seem to increase myocardial cAMP concentrations, presumably because of relatively selective inhibition of cyclic nucleotide phosphodiesterase F-111.[45] An increased inward calcium flux as a result of the increased cAMP seems to be the major mediator of the physiologic actions. This results in an increased contractile state of the myocardium. Drugs in the category include amrinone, milrinone, MDL 17,043 (enoximone), sulmazole, and RO13. Several of these agents are still under investigation.

Amrinone. This was the first to undergo extensive clinical trials. Oral and IV administration were studied in patients with heart failure and showed a marked increase in cardiac output, a substantial reduction in PCWP, and a drop in systemic vascular resistance. Heart rate and systolic BP response were variable, but at high doses a substantial fall in systolic BP was predictable.[46,47] The mechanism of action of the vasodilating properties of the drug are not yet elucidated.

Because of substantial adverse side effects from oral amrinone administration, the drug is approved only for IV therapy. An initial IV dose is usually 0.5 to 1.5 mg/kg infused over 2 to 3 minutes. This is followed by an infusion of 5 to 10 μg/kg/min titrated to desired hemodynamic response. The drug should not be diluted in a dextrose solution. Total daily dose should not exceed 10 mg/kg. Careful monitoring of arterial BP is mandatory during initiation of therapy because of the potent venodilator action, which can result in profound hypotension.

Milrinone. Closely related to amrinone, this agent is well tolerated in oral and IV forms. It is 15 times more potent than amrinone on a per-milligram basis.[48] The overall hemodynamic effects are attributable to myocardial and vascular actions, which have been described as intermediate between those of dobutamine and nitroprusside. Observed in patients with heart failure is an increase in rate of rise of ventricular systolic pressure (dP/dt) and a substantial reduction in systemic vascular resistance.[49] Long-term oral administration shows marked increase in exercise tolerance[50] and does not seem to increase the propensity of these patients for arrhythmias.[51] This medication is not yet available commercially.

MDL 17,043 (Enoximone). This experimental drug is active when given IV or orally. Unlike amrinone and milrinone, which are bipyridines in structure, MDL 17,043 is an imidazol derivative that not only acts to inhibit phosphodiesterase F-111, but also acts to inhibit the sodium potassium–ATPase mechanism.[52] When administered to patients with moderate or severe CHF, there is an increase in cardiac output and LV stroke work, a fall in systemic vascular resistance and PCWP, and a rise in peak dP/dt.[53]

When given orally, MDL 17,043 is metabolized to form the active compound MDL 19,438.[54] Both agents produce the previously described hemodynamic effects, but no studies have yet shown an increased exercise tolerance for patients receiving the drug. Patients who can tolerate the drug, however, report symptomatic improvement.[55]

A high incidence of side effects has limited the usefulness of MDL 17,043. GI side effects are common to all phosphodiesterase inhibitors and include nausea, anorexia, vomiting, abdominal pain, and diarrhea. Thrombocytopenia seems to be uncommon with milrinone and MDL, but is prevalent with amrinone. Headaches, light-headedness, and paresthesias have also been reported with oral administration of phosphodiesterase inhibitors. Despite the limitations, these drugs promise to be useful adjuncts in the treatment of patients with end-stage heart failure.

ALTERATION IN CARDIAC OUTPUT: DECREASED, RELATED TO INCREASED AFTERLOAD

When low cardiac output accompanies CHF, SVR increases to maintain perfusion pressure (BP = cardiac output × systemic vascular resistance). This increased SVR increases resistance to LV ejection, further reducing cardiac output, and the vicious cycle begins. Reduction of the resistance to LV ejection forms the basis for vasodilator therapy for heart failure.[56] The hemodynamic mechanism of vasodilators seems to be largely determined by their principal site of action on the peripheral vascular bed. They are classified as arterial dilators, venous dilators, or combined arterial and venodilators. Only agents that reduce the SVR (arterial or combined agents) are discussed in this section. Venous dilators do affect cardiac performance through the Frank-Starling mechanism, but their primary role in treatment of heart failure is to reduce pulmonary venous congestion.

Nursing Goal

Optimize cardiac output by careful manipulation and monitoring of SVR and systolic BP.

Nursing Interventions

1. Administer parenteral vasodilators as prescribed. Monitor effects closely, watching especially for hypotension and cardiac arrhythmias. Follow guidelines outlined in Exhibit 9-7.
2. Monitor patient's hemodynamic response as continuous IV agents are weaned off and oral vasodilators are added. Major direct arterial dilators found to be of long-term benefit for patients with heart failure are hydralazine, endralazine, and minoxidil. Prazosin, once thought beneficial, is no longer recommended for long-term afterload reduction because of tachyphylaxis. ACE inhibitors, captopril and enalapril, are new vasodilators with combined arterial and venous effects.

Drugs

Parenteral Vasodilators

Sodium Nitroprusside. IV sodium nitroprusside produces a potent and balanced arteriolar and venous effect. It reduces pulmonary congestion by increasing venous capitance and reducing LV end-diastolic pressure or PCWP. It reduces impedance to ejection by directly reducing arteriolar tone. Because of this effect, a profound reduction in SVR occurs.

It must be emphasized that unless a concomitant increase in cardiac output occurs, arterial BP may fall. For this reason it is imperative that not only arterial BP but also intracardiac pressures and cardiac output measurements be taken and evaluated. Dosage must be initially very low, 10 to 15 μg/min, and increased every 10 to 15 minutes until adequate response is achieved. Because of its quick onset of action (5 to 10 minutes) and balanced effect even at low doses, nitroprusside is often a drug of choice in the end-stage heart failure patient. As systemic and pulmonary vascular resistance falls, there is usually a concomitant increase in stroke volume, stroke work index, and cardiac output.

Of note, however, is a ventilation perfusion mismatch that can be worsened by nitroprusside. Several investigators have hypothesized that nitroprusside worsens intrapulmonary shunting by inhibiting the normal hypoxic vasoconstriction in the lung. This inhibition results in perfusion to poorly ventilated regions of the lung.[57]

Once reconstituted and diluted, the solution must be protected from light and used within 24 hours. Prolonged usage is limited in a very small number of patients who develop cyanide toxicity as a result of nitroprusside metabolism.

Nitroglycerine. Aqueous NTG has a potent effect on venous tone even in low doses and can markedly reduce LV end-diastolic pressure. As dosage approaches 200 μg/min, arterial dilatation becomes evident.[58] The vasodilating action of this drug is preferential to the larger arteries and veins, whereas sodium nitroprusside affects the smaller sites in the vascular bed (arteriole/venule). Therefore its effect on SVR is less than that of sodium nitroprusside. NTG has a more favorable effect on the arteriolar-alveolar oxygen gradient and intrapulmonary shunting than does nitroprusside. It was also shown that in the presence of ischemia NTG increases flow through collateral coronary beds to a greater magnitude than nitroprusside.[59]

Initial dosage of NTG must also be low, 10 μg/min, and titrated up every 10 to 15 minutes to achieve the clinical hemodynamic effect. Nonporous tubing must be used to administer NTG, otherwise the active nitrate component migrates into conventional IV tubings and alters in a nonlinear way the dosage actually delivered to the patient.

Oral Vasodilators

Hydralazine. Vasodilation of the arterial vascular bed is a direct result of this smooth muscle relaxant. This action can increase cardiac output by lowering BP and SVR. It usually has no effect on systemic venous congestion. Oral dose is 50 to 100 mg every 6 hours. Side effects are usually dose related and include headache, palpitations, and postural hypotension. Long-term therapy has produced drug fever, lupus syndrome, and peripheral neuropathy. Data suggest that a treatment regimen of hydralazine, combined with isosorbide dinitrate, digoxin, and diuretics can improve LV performance and mortality in patients with CHF.[60]

Endralazine. Endralazine is a structured analogue of hydralazine currently under investigation. Its primary advantage is that it does not require acetylation for metabolism and therefore avoids the lupus syndrome side effect.

Minoxidil. Similar to hydralazine in effect, minoxidil also reduces SVR with little or no change in PCWP. Dosage for heart failure is 10 to 20 mg given twice a day. Consistent fluid retention and weight gain limit its long-term usefulness.

Captopril. The first of the oral ACE inhibitors, it lowers systemic and pulmonary venous congestion and SVR. The mechanism of action is not fully understood, but a major effect is competitive inhibition of the ACE. Therefore it blocks the renin-angiotensin-aldosterone compensatory mechanism, which stimulates vasoconstriction and sodium and water retention. Hemodynamic improvements are reflected in decreased (or no change) heart rate, SVR, and PCWP. Chatterjee and co-workers[61] showed an improvement in pump efficiency by a reduction in MV_{O_2}.

Patients with high circulating renin levels might more consistently respond to therapy with an ACE inhibitor. This hypothesis has not been fully evaluated but seems valid. There is an inverse relation between plasma renin levels and serum sodium concentration in patients with CHF. Since serum sodium levels are readily available in the critical care setting, they are a useful indicator to predict responders to ACE inhibitors. Patients with serum sodium less than 130 mg/L are more than 30 times more likely to develop symptomatic hypotension during initiation of captopril therapy.[62] This is a serious side effect, which must be assessed in any patient begun on an ACE inhibitor.

Other observations of the drug effects include the fact that the effect of the medication persists longer than the measurable inhibition of ACE and that local and central sympatholytic activity may be present.[63]

Dosage of captopril for heart failure is 6.25 to 25 mg given three times a day. Patient response to a first dose of 6.25 mg must be carefully evaluated before therapeutic dosage is determined. As much as 95% of the dose is excreted in the urine. Elimination of the drug directly correlates with creatinine clearance, and therefore the dose must be reduced in patients with renal insufficiency.

Because of interference with aldosterone, the amount of potassium supplementation must be adjusted if diuretic therapy is administered. Other side effects include a bad taste, skin rash, and proteinuria.

Enalapril. This ACE inhibitor is closely related to captopril but is active only after metabolism to enaloprilic acid. A single or divided dose of 5 to 40 mg is used for patients with heart failure. Side effects and hemodynamic benefits are the same as with captopril. When combined with conventional treatment for heart failure, including vasodilators, enalapril was shown to reduce mortality and improve symptoms in patients with severe heart failure (NYHA functional class IV).[64]

ALTERATION IN CARDIAC OUTPUT: DECREASED, RELATED TO ARRHYTHMIAS

The pathogenesis of ventricular arrhythmias in patients with CHF is poorly understood. Underlying ischemic heart disease, wall motion abnormalities, electrolyte imbalances (hypokalemia/hypomagnesemia), and inotropic therapy may contribute to the high prevalence of premature ventricular contractions (PVCs) and ventricular tachycardia (VT) in these patients. A causal link between high circulating catecholamines is not firmly established, but may also be a factor. Data from eight studies, including 701 patients with heart failure, showed a prevalence of ventricular couplets, multiform PVCs, or both, of 71% to 95%, and a 28% to 80% prevalence of nonsustained VT.[65–72] The link between these complex arrhythmias and actual survival in these patients is unclear. Most,[72–75] but not all,[76] studies have shown that repetitive forms of ventricular arrhythmias are associated with increased risk for sudden death (see Chapter 5).

Further complicating the issue is the fact that little information is available on the efficacy and safety of antiarrhythmic therapy in patients with CHF. Of concern is the known potential for antiarrhythmic agents to depress the inotropic state of the LV and the possibility of a proarrhythmic effect in certain patients. Changes in pharmacokinetics of antiarrhythmic agents should be expected in patients with CHF. The direction of the change is not always predictable. The volume distribution is often decreased by as much as 40%.[77] Drug clearance may also be diminished by decreased blood flow to the kidneys and liver and decreased hepatic drug-metabolizing activity.

While the decision to treat patients long-term with antiarrhythmic therapy prophylactically has not been adequately addressed in the research arena, it is straightforward that in the critical care unit, patients with CHF who are symptomatic or hemodynamically compromised should be treated.

Nursing Goal

Optimized cardiac output will be achieved by careful detection and treatment of arrhythmias.

Nursing Interventions

1. Monitor patient's ECG for baseline and response to antiarrhythmic agents or overdrive pacing. Follow guidelines described in Chapter 5.
2. Adjust loading dose and total daily dose to accommodate for slow drug clearance from liver. Follow serum blood levels of the drug as a guide for dosage.
3. If the patient is receiving concomitant digitalis preparation, monitor serum digoxin levels, which may increase if the antiarrhythmic agent displaces digoxin from noncardiac tissue stores.
4. Carefully monitor serum potassium levels as patients with underlying cardiac dysfunction may be even more prone to dysrhythmic effects of low potassium.

IMPAIRED GAS EXCHANGE RELATED TO INCREASED PRELOAD/ALTERATIONS IN FLUID VOLUME: EXCESS

The most common, bothersome, and often earliest symptom of heart failure or decompensation of a controlled state is the patient's complaint of the subjective feeling of dyspnea. With end-stage heart failure, the range of shortness of breath may be from a compensated state with shortness of breath only upon exertion, to shortness of breath at rest, to frank pulmonary edema. The underlying mechanism of the more objective impairment of gas exchange is a result of alterations in pulmonary capillary hydrostatic pressures. When hydrostatic pressure exceeds the oncotic pressure (usually 25 torr) at the alveolar-capillary membrane, fluid and protein move into the lung tissue. Congestion results, which interferes with the alveolar-capillary diffusion of oxygen. Elasticity of the lung tissue decreases. Arterial blood gases reflect hypoxemia and hypercapnea. Acidemia is a common finding related both to diminished ventilation and tissue perfusion. The patient is air hungry, anxious, and afraid. It is important to realize, however, that much of dyspnea is because of stimulation of lung reflexes by interstitial lung fluid, which may occur without hypoxia.

Nursing Goal

Reduce patient anxiety, increase ventilation, and reduce venous return to the heart.

Nursing Interventions

1. Assist patient into a high Fowler's position to decrease work of breathing and enhance gas exchange.
2. Place legs in a dependent position to encourage venous pooling in the extremities.
3. Administer oxygen. Depending on the degree of hypoxemia and presence of hypercapnea, supplemental oxygen should be administered to raise the arterial oxygen tension to a PO_2 above 60 torr. (Refer to Table 9-3 for the available modes of delivering oxygen and the expected oxygen concentrations.) Monitor therapeutic results with arterial blood gas measurements. Mechanical ventilation may be necessary if hypoxemia and hypercapnea cannot be corrected by the above measures.
4. Administer preload reducing agents.

Preload Reducing Agents

Morphine

IV morphine works to relieve anxiety and causes transient arterial and venous dilation. Reduced anxiety decreases sympathetic tone and the resultant vascular

Table 9-3 Guidelines for Oxygen and Aerosol Therapy

Type of Equipment	Flow Rate	Approximate Concentration	Comments	Precautions
Nasal cannula	Rough estimate; assumes normal breathing: 1 LPM 2 LPM 3 LPM 4 LPM 5 LPM 6 LPM	24% 28% 32% 36% 40% 44%	Usually comfortable and convenient. Patient can eat and speak w/o removing. Irritation of nasal mucosa frequent at flow rates >5 LPM; at 1–4 LPM, humidifier not required but may be added if patient complains of nasal irritation, burning, or dryness. Concentration not precise: increases w/slow and shallow breathing, decreases w/rapid breathing.	Mouth breathing does not appreciably change inspired O_2 concentration unless nose totally obstructed.
All oxygen masks			May be uncomfortable and irritate skin. Must be removed for eating, speaking, etc.	Risk of vomiting and aspiration in patients w/decreased sensorium.
Simple mask	Rough estimate; assumes normal breathing: 6 LPM 8 LPM 10 LPM	35–40% 40–45% 45–50%	Potential for rebreathing exhaled air (CO_2) if liter flow inadequate to flush mask. Concentration not precise: increases w/slow and shallow breathing, decreases w/ deep and rapid breathing (dilution with room air pulled in around mask and through ports).	Always use liter flow of at least 6 LPM. Use w/caution in patients w/ compensated respiratory acidosis (example: pH 7.44, P_{CO_2} 62, P_{O_2} 50, HCO_3 42); O_2 may cause respiratory depression.

Partial rebreathing mask	6–12 LPM, at least enough to prevent complete deflation of reservoir bag	35–65%	Intermediate to high oxygen concentration; not precise: increases w/slow and shallow breathing, decreases w/deep and rapid breathing (dilution with room air pulled in around mask and through ports). Patient rebreathes gas in upper airway, high in O_2, low in CO_2. No significant rebreathing of CO_2.	Use w/caution in patients w/ compensated respiratory acidosis (example: pH 7.44, P_{CO_2} 62, P_{O_2} 50, HCO_3 42); O_2 may cause respiratory depression .
Nonrebreathing mask	6–12 LPM, at least enough to prevent complete deflation of reservoir bag	60–90%	Highest O_2 concentration possible w/a mask. Suffocation possible if O_2 supply inadvertently obstructed or disconnected and patient cannot remove mask. Concentration not precise; dependent on breathing pattern.	Always remove one valve from side of face mask. Use w/caution in patients w/ compensated respiratory acidosis (example: pH 7.44, P_{CO_2} 62, P_{O_2} 50, HCO_3 42); (O_2 may cause respiratory depression).
Venturi or air-entrainment mask	4 LPM 6 LPM 8 LPM 10 LPM 12 LPM 12 LPM	24% 28% 31% 35% 40% 50%	High flow system; low to intermediate O_2 concentration; concentration less affected by changes in breathing pattern than low-flow devices. Actual concentration provided with a venturi mask when 31%–50% adapters used is frequently not constant or predictable because of inadequate total flow rates. Does not require humidifier (O_2 mixes w/a large volume of room air).	Use 'high flow' settings. See package insert. Connect mask directly to O_2 flow meter with nipple adapter. Aerosol must be driven by compressed air, not O_2. Always attach aerosol cup (even if additional humidity not required), to prevent accidental occlusion of entrainment ports by bed linen. Do not attach O_2 extension tubing.

continues

Table 9-3 continued

Type of Equipment	Flow Rate	Approximate Concentration	Comments	Precautions
			Additional humidity can be provided by aerosol hose connected to cup around jet. Air-entrainment device will not operate correctly if ports occluded or if too much resistance to flow in tubing.	
Aerosol mask	At least 10 LPM or high enough so that mist is visible during entire inspiratory phase	Venturi-type device with variable O_2 concentration (35–90%).	Less dilution of O_2 with room air than with face tent due to enclosed design. O_2 concentration may be increased by attaching 6-in section of aerosol tubing to ports on each side of mask.	Risk of vomiting and aspiration in patients w/decreased sensorium.
Face tent			Less risk of vomiting and aspiration due to open design.	O_2 concentration somewhat less than nebulizer setting due to dilution with room air.
All aerosols			Frequently increase bronchospasm in patients w/hyper-reactive airways (e.g., asthma). Questionable therapeutic benefit when goal is to thin secretions (very little aerosol reaches lower airway).	If patient has increased dyspnea or wheezing, or paroxysms of coughing, disconnect aerosol and call MD to re-evaluate mode of therapy. Double nebulizers in tandem may be required for patients requiring high

Flow rate decreases as O_2 concentration increases.

Collection of water in aerosol tubing or nebulizer loosely connected to flowmeter will obstruct flow of gas.

Maximum humidification of inspired gas possible by heating water in nebulizer to body temp. Heated aerosols most suitable for patients w/artificial airways. Insufficient water in nebulizer, low flow rates, or malfunctioning heater may produce hot aerosol capable of injuring patient's airway.

Increased risk for nosocomial pneumonia from contamination of water in nebulizer.

Handling electrical equipment, such as immersion heater, while standing in water on floor is hazardous to patient and nurse.

O_2 concentrations (over 60%).

Always place water collection bag in aerosol tubing for patients w/ heated aerosol or T-piece.

Always place thermometer in aerosol tubing to monitor inspired gas temperature of patients receiving heated aerosol. If gas temperature exceeds 35° C, unplug the heater.

Change delivery device, all tubing, and nebulizer q 24 hours; label with date. Always use sterile, distilled H_2O in nebulizer. Do not empty water collecting in aerosol tubing back into nebulizer.

Use water collection bag, container, or towel to keep water from draining onto floor.

Source: Data from *Clinical Application of Respiratory Care*, 3rd ed., by Barry A. Shapiro et al. Copyright © 1985 by Year Book Medical Publishers, Inc., Chicago. Reproduced with permission.

changes. Respiratory status must be carefully evaluated because of potential respiratory suppression.

Diuretics

Potent, fast-acting IV diuretics may be prescribed to reduce the circulating blood volume. Furosemide and ethacrynic acid are loop diuretics that reduce sodium reabsorption from the loop of Henle and have a direct effect on arterial and venous dilation. Potassium supplementation is necessary with these agents. Long-term management of heart failure almost always includes oral furosemide. Dosage is 20 to 200 mg daily, usually divided.

Thiazide diuretics do not frequently benefit patients with end-stage heart failure. A potent diuretic, close in structure to the thiazide group, is metolozone. It is rarely prescribed as a single agent, but is used as an effective adjunctive agent for patients already taking loop diuretics. Usual daily dose is 2.5 to 20 mg.

Spironolactone, a weak diuretic alone, may also be used with a loop diuretic. Daily dose is usually 75 to 200 mg in divided doses. Because of its potassium-sparing effect (it is an aldosterone antagonist), potassium supplementation is often unnecessary. Serum potassium levels must be followed carefully in patients who receive spironolactone in combination with an ACE inhibitor. Both agents retain potassium and may precipitate a hyperkalemic state.

Nitrates

These drugs provide smooth muscle relaxation. Dilation is pronounced, especially in the large veins (capitance vessels) and in the coronary arteries. Peripheral arterial vasodilation is minimal primarily because of reflex sympathetic activity. Nitrates are now considered mainstream agents in acute and long-term management of heart failure. They consistently reduce LV workload by reducing venous return to the heart, lowering PCWP, and optimizing the Frank-Starling relation between fiber stretch and contractility. The result is overall increased LV performance and reduced signs and symptoms of systemic and pulmonary venous congestion.

Organic nitrates can be administered in several ways. (IV NTG has been discussed.) Sublingual and oral forms are well absorbed from mucosal and GI tracts. Oral nitrate therapy in the form of isosorbid dinitrate is often combined with hydralazine to provide both pre- and afterload reduction and, as previously mentioned, has a favorable effect on LV performance and mortality in patients with chronic CHF. Dosage of isosorbide dinitrate for heart failure can be as high as 120 mg QID.

Topical nitrates are well absorbed from the skin and come in a variety of preparations from ointment to prepared transdermal patches. Ointment dosage varies from 1 to 4 inches of drug. It should be spread over a nonhirsute area and changed every 4 to 6 hours. To gain a dosage to treat heart failure, the transdermal patches usually need to be changed more frequently than the every-24-hours recommended by the manufacturer.

Side effects include, most commonly, tolerance to the drug, headache, dizziness, weakness, postural hypotension, and skin rash.

ACTIVITY INTOLERANCE RELATED TO DECREASED CARDIAC OUTPUT/IMPAIRED GAS EXCHANGE/ KNOWLEDGE DEFICIT

Fatigue from a diminished cardiac output is the second most common complaint of patients with heart failure. It is rare in the end stages that this symptom occurs without the symptoms of congestion. Together these symptoms greatly limit the lives of patients with heart failure.

The ability of the heart to respond to the increased demands of the activities of life is called the *cardiac reserve*. Theoretically, cardiac reserve may be looked upon as the difference between the length of cardiac fibers at rest when their limit is reached. Because of the compensatory changes of hypertrophy and dilatation with CHF, this difference may be very small. The normal response to increased activity is to increase the cardiac output by increasing heart rate and stroke volume. Patients with heart failure have a deficit in this ability. The result is tachycardia, exertional hypotension, fatigue, and dyspnea.

The severity of heart failure has been quantified by classifying patients into four groups based on the patient's report and the practitioner's evaluation of symptoms in response to activity. Considerable skill is required in making this evaluation. The New York Heart Association classifies patients with heart failure as follows:

Class I: patients with heart disease with no symptoms
Class II: patients who are comfortable at rest but have symptoms with ordinary activity
Class III: those who are comfortable at rest but have symptoms with less than ordinary activity
Class IV: those who have symptoms at rest.

Nursing Goal

The patient will progress to highest level of activity compatible with the limits of the cardiac reserve.

Nursing Interventions

1. Administer prescribed cardiac drugs to optimize cardiac performance.
2. Assess heart rate and BP at rest and in response to activity. Determine pulse parameters, which reflect the cardiac reserve. Assist patient as needed so as not to exceed this reserve.
3. Instruct patient and family regarding activity and environmental factors that minimize exertion. Follow guidelines outlined in Appendix 9-A.
4. Discuss adaptations to activity intolerance with patient and family so they can take control of the limitations.

ALTERATION IN FLUID VOLUME: EXCESS, RELATED TO ALTERATION IN CARDIAC OUTPUT

This diagnosis has two distinct components. The first relates directly to the pulmonary venous congestion that results from excess fluid volume. The second relates to the electrolyte abnormalities that result from the body's compensatory response to low cardiac output.

One of the most familiar and difficult problems for patients with end-stage heart failure is hyponatremia. Hyponatremia needs to be viewed as a further impairment in cardiac function as well as a metabolic alteration. The finding of a low serum sodium concentration (<130 mg) presents as either (1) the water-intoxicated state or (2) the sodium-depleted state. Recent studies[78] indicate hyponatremia as a poor prognostic indicator and show a significant correlation with markedly elevated levels of plasma renin. Studies by Dzau et al.[79] show that patients with low serum sodium concentrations react inappropriately to circulatory stress and proceed to a decompensated state of heart failure more quickly. It is hypothesized that the expansion of extracellular fluid volume is inadequate to sustain systemic perfusion, and that greater than normal reliance is placed on the renin-angiotensin system.

Sodium depletion may occur as a result of vigorous diuretic therapy and enforcement of a sodium-restricted diet. Patients present with a high blood urea nitrogen:creatinine ratio indicative of prerenal azotemia (20:1). Pulse pressure is narrow, often with marked hypotension. The patients are weak, with anorexia and complaints of continuous thirst. Edema is not usually present.

In the water-intoxicated state, edema is present, venous pressure is high, and overt signs of decompensated heart failure are evident. An adult may retain 4 to 7 L of fluid before pitting edema occurs. Hyponatremia is a result of excessive water overload, producing a dilutional low serum sodium value. (Urinary sodium values are also low.) Most patients do not become symptomatic as a result of the electrolyte imbalance, but instead from the effect of heart failure. Careful free water restriction is necessary to prevent further hyponatremia. Administration of salt solutions is contraindicated in most patients and may worsen CHF and result in onset of pulmonary edema.

Weakness, lethargy, and nausea are early signs of the water-intoxicated state of hyponatremia. (At this point, a nursing diagnosis of "Potential for Injury" must be entertained and appropriate protective and corrective measures initiated.) These signs can progress to headache and stupor and can lead to obtundation and death from hyponatremic encephalopathy. Hyponatremia generally develops slowly in patients with end-stage heart failure. The morbidity and mortality rates associated with chronic hyponatremia are much less than with an acute drop in serum sodium concentration. Correction of hyponatremia must be approached with caution. If normonatremia is achieved too rapidly, brain cells cannot restore the lost solute, and the brain continues to distend, compressed by the cranial vault.

No prospective studies in humans have addressed the therapy of symptomatic hyponatremia. Based on retrospective studies in humans and anecdotal experience, Narins[80] recommends for symptomatic patients (usually serum sodium <120 mmol/L) an infusion of 2 mmol/L/hr to bring a serum sodium concentration to 120 to 130 mmol/L.

Nursing Goal

Fluid volume is monitored so that maximal fluid balance will be achieved for the patient's condition.

Nursing Interventions

1. Monitor intake and output. Evaluate trends and report to physician consistent imbalances of greater than 500 mL/day. Report urine outputs of less than 30 mL/hr if it persists for 2 hours.
2. Evaluate weight change in light of intake and output. One kilogram of body weight reflects approximately 1 L of fluid. Daily weight fluctuations (0.25 kg or more) in a patient with end-stage heart failure are most likely attributable to water loss or gain. A gain of 1 to 2 kg in a few days would indicate the need for additional diuretics.
   - Instruct patients in the importance of daily or every other day weights at home.
   - Provide parameters of concern and specific actions the patient should take if weight gain occurs.
3. Monitor trends in serum sodium values as an indicator of hemodilution or concentration. Normal serum sodium is 136 to 142 mEq/L. Alert the phy-

sician of trends and evaluate in light of the patient's hemodynamic status and medication and diet regimen to determine if the low serum is because of sodium depletion or water intoxication.

- Sodium depletion: Interrupt or reduce diuretic therapy; liberalize dietary ingestion of salt; carefully monitor serum sodium values.
- Water intoxication: Restrict free water; replace insensible loss (400 to 600 mL/day).
- Severe water intoxication: Provide safety measures for patients with altered mental status; carefully monitor hypertonic saline infusion; restrict free water.

4. Discuss fluid limitations with the patient and family. Arrange for form and frequency of fluids based on patient preference.
5. Discuss sodium restriction with patient and family. Patients with advanced heart failure may require a 1- to 2-g sodium diet. This requires the total elimination of salt in food preparation and the elimination of many foods high in salt. Refer the patient and family to a dietician to assist in meal planning at home.
6. Monitor serum potassium. Potassium is lost with loop diuretics, especially lasix and ethacrinic acid, and with metolazone. Replace potassium to keep a serum potassium level of 3.5 to 4.5 mEq/L.
7. Instruct the patient on the concomitant administration of potassium supplementation with diuretics.
8. Observe for and monitor changes in edema. Inspect dependent parts of the body first. If ascites are present, measure abdominal girth daily. Institute measures to maintain skin integrity. Instruct patient in these interventions.

ALTERATION IN NUTRITION: LESS THAN BODY REQUIREMENTS RELATED TO A VOLUNTARY REDUCTION IN FOOD INTAKE/UNPALATABLE PRESCRIBED DIET/CONSTANT SUBJECTIVE FEELING OF FULLNESS[81]

Patients with end-stage heart failure often have mild to moderately severe cardiac cachexia.[82] Cardiac cachexia is a state in which there is wasting and eventual exhaustion of nutrient stores. This process is thought to be mediated by several factors.

Anorexia, defined as a decreased hunger and food intake, is the hallmark of cardiac cachexia. GI hypomotility, delayed gastric emptying, stomach compression by an enlarged liver or ascites, and GI atony all may contribute to a premature sensation of fullness.[83] Fatigue often results in decreased food intake because the patient is "too tired" to eat.

Nutrient loss in the urine or stool increases in the cachetic state. It is thought that cellular hypoxia of the GI tract causes edema, which impairs the normal physiologic digestive and absorptive process. More nutrients, especially fat and protein, are lost in the urine and stool.

A hypermetabolic state results from the overactive SNS in heart failure and from increased thyroid activity triggered by thyroxin (secreted during cachetic states).[84] This results in a higher basal energy expenditure, one that is not met in patients with a limited cardiac reserve.

Impaired delivery of cellular nutrients and removal of waste was hypothesized by Pittman and Cohen[85] as a fourth factor in cardiac cachexia. They argued that a low cardiac output state with decreased capillary blood flow leads to incomplete conversion of substrate nutrients to ATP. This hypothesis is supported by the high lactate levels in patients with heart failure, which may symbolize the presence of anaerobic metabolic activity in the body.

Nursing Goal

Provide patients the opportunity for optimal nutrition while in the hospital, and educate them regarding nutrition before discharge.

Nursing Interventions

1. Include a nutritional assessment on admission; determine usual weight, appetite, and eating patterns.
2. Weigh patient to establish baseline weight. Consider using anthropometric assessment tools such as triceps, skin folds, and mid-arm circumference as a more accurate measure of nutrition. (Fluid status influence on weight makes it an unreliable measurement of nutritional status.)
3. Examine and evaluate laboratory data that may indicate nutritional status. Albumin levels less than 3.5 mg/dL and lymphocyte counts less than 20% of the total white blood count or an absolute number of 2,000 suggest protein depletion. Fluid overload can falsely represent low values in these parameters.
4. Assist the dietician in determining the patient's caloric goal. Basal caloric requirement of healthy men and women can be calculated from the Harris-Benedict equation.[86]

Men: $665 + (13.7 \times \text{wt in kg}) + (5 \times \text{ht in cm}) - (6.8 \times \text{age})$
Women: $665 + (9.6 \times \text{wt in kg}) + (1.7 \times \text{ht in cm}) - (4.7 \times \text{age})$.

This value can be increased by 30% to 50% in severe heart failure because of the increased cardiac and pulmonary energy expenditure.[87,88] Heymsfeld and associates[89] recommended additions to these base caloric requirements: 15% to 25% for minimal physical activity of patients with severe heart failure, and another 10% to 20% for the hypermetabolism of the disease.

5. Discuss nutritional status with patients to enlist their assistance in reaching nutritional goals. Do a calorie count for 2 to 3 days. Find out food preferences, patterns of eating while in the hospital. Offer six small feedings if patient prefers. Offer options of favorite foods.
6. Minimize fatigue. Organize care to allow periods of 1-hour rest before and after meals.
7. Control the environment to enhance appetite.
8. Offer food supplements that agree with the patient and the treatment plan.

KNOWLEDGE DEFICIT RELATED TO COMPLEX PATHOPHYSIOLOGY AND COMPLICATED TREATMENT REGIMENS/INEFFECTIVE COPING

To best assist the patient with management of the medical regimen, it is the responsibility of the nurse to understand that the medical plans and treatment do not stand alone: they are just one element in the complex pattern of a person's life. Teaching the patient and family the rationale for treatment, fluid and diet changes, and activity restrictions can assist understanding but may also increase anxiety when the impact on personal identity and freedom is realized. The effort, energy, and sometimes discomfort of compliance should be explored with the patient so the risk/benefit analysis takes place in an environment where accurate information and support are available. Denial of the severity of disease and the reliance on medications may contribute to the patient's refusal to submit to the medical regimen or lack of interest in learning more about CHF. Comprehension of the seriousness of the condition, the state of acceptance, and the patient's personal choice all contribute to the patient's compliance in the management of the medical regimen. In the end, it is the patient's decision. The nurse is there to educate and support.

Strauss and Glaser[90] explored the quality of life in patients with chronic illness. Two main areas of patient concern surfaced in their research, which the nurse can address. Teaching can be organized around Strauss' focus areas: (1) preventing and managing the medical crises and (2) managing medical regimens. Both areas must be thoroughly explored with the patient and family.

Preventing and managing medical crises involves reading the signs and symptoms of heart failure the patient manifests. It means looking at a sign or symptom with the total picture of heart failure, not assuming that a recurrent sign is attributed to "something else." Patients must be taught to have confidence in their own perceptions and to take action on the early warning signals of heart failure.

Organizing for a medical crisis enables the patient and family to respond to an exacerbation of heart failure. Teaching the family to be prepared for further hospitalization allows them to cope in a planned manner. When the family is aware of the facts, they can be guided toward identifying people and other resources that might be at their disposal in an emergency situation.

Nursing Goal

The patient and family will verbalize understanding of treatment regimen, signs and symptoms of heart failure decompensation, and will establish a plan of action when decompensation occurs.

Nursing Interventions

1. Individualize teaching plan for patient, taking into account the patient's and family's readiness to learn, pre-existing knowledge, phase of illness, and patient's major concerns.
2. Develop scope of content to be discussed. Consider:
   - normal anatomy and physiology of the heart and circulation
   - definition of heart failure
   - reasons for signs and symptoms of worsening CHF
   - concept of cardiac reserve*
   - pulse taking*
   - activity conservation/progression*
   - when to phone physician*
   - emergency plans
   - dietary restrictions (sodium, fluids, calories)
   - weight management
   - medications rationale
   - psychologic aspects of chronic illness
   - importance of compliance
   - community resources
   - follow-up care.

---

*See Appendix 9-A.

3. Use instructional aids to facilitate learning.
4. Collaborate with other health team members to reinforce teaching content and assure consistency of information

INEFFECTIVE COPING: INDIVIDUAL AND FAMILY, RELATED TO DISTURBANCE IN SELF-CONCEPT, ROLE PERFORMANCE, POWERLESSNESS, SELF-ESTEEM

Lazarus[91] developed a framework in which stress is viewed in the context of the person (patient) and the environment that exists when a situation is relevant and resources are taxed. The effort to manage stressful demands, regardless of outcome, is the process of coping. This implies that no one strategy is inherently better than any other. The effort, the process, is individual. The efficacy and appropriateness of a coping strategy are determined by the effectiveness in a given encounter and the long-term effects. Coping can be contrasted with adaptive changes that are routine long-term alterations incorporated into a patient's life.[92] Coping is a process that incorporates the patient's appraisal and reaction to a stressful event or situation, such as a hospitalization or an episode of cardiac decompensation.

Factors that contribute to the coping process in this group of patients may include the adaptive changes the patient has made already in response to the chronicity of end-stage heart failure. The patient's self-esteem and self-concept may reflect negative feelings because of a loss of significant role function, decreased socialization, or perceived powerlessness. Decreased independence, changes in body image from weight loss, weakness, malaise, or dyspnea can contribute to an altered sense of personal identity. Cognitive functioning and thought processes may also be altered if the cardiac output falls so low as to impair cerebral perfusion, or if serum sodium levels fall below 130 mEq/L. Emotional states, triggered by the hospitalization, influence the ability of the patient and family to appraise the situation and also affect their reactions to it. They include anxiety, fear, and reactive depression. The complexities of the psychosocial aspect of the patient and family must be assessed and evaluated in light of the present hospitalization and long-term trajectory (see Chapter 8).

Nursing Goal

Assist the patient and family in mobilizing coping strategies consistent with their values and beliefs and beneficial to the patient's long-term goal. Reduce the effects of stress on the cardiovascular system.

Nursing Interventions

1. Provide opportunities for the patient and family to express their feelings. Determine their health-related long-term goal.
2. Assess the psychosocial status of the patient in relation to factors previously described.
3. Engage the patient and family in problem solving to identify measures that will help them cope with the current situation.
4. Engage the patient and family in discussions to explore changes in life style, dealing with loss of physical integrity and role performance, social interaction/isolation, and facing death. Assist them with developing adaptive changes to maintain as much normalcy as feasible in their life.
5. Organize care to allow the patient as much control as possible.
6. Provide information when knowledge deficit is contributing to the inability to cope.
7. Assist the patient and family with setting realistic goals and maintaining a positive self-image despite limitations and changes in life style.
8. Provide care in a helpful, hopeful manner.

NONCOMPLIANCE RELATED TO KNOWLEDGE DEFICIT/INEFFECTIVE COPING

Adherence to a therapeutic plan requires active participation by patients, who assume responsibility for their life and the results of behaviors that lead to health or illness. Whether or not a patient is compliant is a complex issue. Personal factors centering on the patient's personal values, beliefs, perception of illness, presence and degree of denial, age, attribution of causality, perceived control of illness or symptoms, and satisfaction with caregivers are related to compliance.[93,94]

Treatment-related factors also affect compliance. They include the risk-benefit ratio for the treatments, the side effects, the time necessary to execute the plan, the effort involved, the perceived discomfort, and the expense of medication or other therapies. Of utmost importance is that the patient and family have an accurate view of the sequelae of not following the treatment plan. Both the knowledge base and the coping mechanisms of the patient must be addressed, as described in this chapter and in Chapter 7.

Nursing Goal

The nurse addresses factors that will enhance the patient's adherence to the treatment plan.

Nursing Interventions

1. Establish a caring, consistent relationship with the patient and family.
2. Assess personal and treatment factors that relate to compliance.
3. Minimize factors that can be altered to enhance compliance.
4. Set realistic goals with the patient, allowing the patient as much control as possible. Consider a contractual agreement for behavior modification strategies.
5. Direct the patient's thoughts beyond the present state to the future.
6. Explore the use of a support group to assist the patient with compliance.

SUMMARY

The patient with end-stage heart failure presents a new type of challenge for the cardiac critical care nurse. During periods of acute failure, the nurse plays a major role in monitoring the patient's response to drug therapies. Once optimal medical treatment is achieved, the nurse teaches the patient how to live within the limits of his/her functional capacity. Nurses afford a unique opportunity to utilize their holistic skills in caring for this growing and special patient population.

NOTES

1. L.A. Scoloff, "Coronary Artery Disease and the Concept of Cardiac Failure," *American Journal of Cardiology* 22(1968):43.

2. E.H. Sonnenblich, et al., "The Pathophysiology of Heart Failure: The Primary Role of Micro-vascular Hyper-reactivity and Spasm in the Development of Congestive Cardiomyopathies," in E. Braunwald, M.B. Mock, and J. Watson, eds., *Congestive Heart Failure: Current Research and Clinical Applications* (New York: Grune & Stratton, 1982), pp. 291–302.

3. D.L. Page, et al., "Myocardial Changes Associated with Cardiogenic Shock," *New England Journal of Medicine* 285(1971):133.

4. P.A. McKee, et al., "The Natural History of Congestive Heart Failure: The Framingham Study," *New England Journal of Medicine* 285(1971):1441.

5. E. Braunwald, J. Ross, and E.H. Sonnenblich, "Mechanisms of Contraction in the Normal and Failing Heart," *New England Journal of Medicine* 277(1967):794.

6. H.E. Huxley and J. Hanson, "Changes in the Cross-striations of Muscle during Contraction and Stretch and Their Structural Interpretation," *Nature* 173(1954):973.

7. R.A. Chapman, "Control of Cardiac Contractility on the Cellular Level," *American Journal of Physiology* 245(1983):H532.

8. T. McDonald, "The Slow Inward Calcium Current in the Heart," *Annual Review of Physiology* 44(1982):425.

9. G.A. Langer, "Sodium-Calcium Exchange in the Heart," *Annual Review of Physiology* 44(1982):435.

10. A.M. Katz, "Adenosine Monophosphate Effects on the Myocardium: A Man Who Blows Hot and Cold with One Breath," *Journal of the American College of Cardiology* 2(1983):143.

11. M. Tada, and A. Katz, "Phosphorylization of the Sarcoplasmic Reticulum and Sarcolemma," *Annual Review of Physiology* 44(1982):401.

12. N. Sperelakis, "Cyclic AMP and Phosphorylization in the Regulation of Ca^{++} Influx into Myocardial Cells and Blockade by Calcium Antagonistic Drugs," *American Heart Journal* 107(1984):347.

13. E.L. Kraniss and J. Solaro, "Coordination of Cardiac Sarcoplasmic Reticulum and Myofibrillar Function by Protein Phosphorylization," *Federal Proceedings* 42(1983):33.

14. W.S. Colucci, R.F. Wright, and E. Braunwald, "New Positive Inotropic Agents in the Treatment of Congestive Heart Failure," *New England Journal of Medicine* 314(1986):290.

15. E.H. Sonnenblich, "Implication of Muscle Mechanics of the Heart," *Federal Proceedings* 21(1962):975.

16. R.J. Lefkowitz, J.M. Stadel, and M.A. Caron, "Adenylate Cyclose-Coupled Beta Adrenergic Receptors: Structure and Mechanism of Activation and Desensitization," *Annual Review of Biochemistry* 52(1983):159.

17. S.Z. Langer, "Presynaptic Regulation of Catecholamine Release," *Biochemistry and Pharmacology* 23(1974):1793.

18. W.S. Collucci, "Alpha-Adrenergic Receptors in Cardiovascular Medicine," in J.S. Karliner and I.J. Half, eds., *Receptor Science in Cardiology* (Mt. Kisco, NY: Futura, 1984), pp. 43–87.

19. J.A. Thomas and B.H. Marks, "Plasma Norepinephrine in Congestive Heart Failure," *American Journal of Cardiology* 41(1978):233.

20. Ibid.

21. Ibid.

22. M.R. Bristow, et al., "Decreased Catecholamine Sensitivity and β-Adrenergic Receptor Density in Failing Human Hearts," *New England Journal of Medicine* 307(1982):205.

23. R. Ginsburg, et al., "Study of Normal and Failing Isolated Human Hearts: Decreased Response of Failing Hearts to Isoproterenol," *American Heart Journal* 106(1983):535.

24. J.O. Parker, R.O. West, and J.R. Ledwick, "The Effects of Acute Digitalization on the Hemodynamic Response to Exercise in Coronary Artery Disease," *Circulation* 40(1969):453.

25. D.V. Unverferth, et al., "Tolerance to Dobutamine after 72 Hours Continuous Infusion," *American Journal of Medicine* 69(1980):262.

26. B.A. Zimmerman, "Actions of Angiotensin on Adrenergic Nerve Endings," *Federal Proceedings* 37(1976):199.

27. L. Share, "Interrelations Between Vasopressin and the Renin Angiotensin System," *Federal Proceedings* 38(1979):2267.

28. O.J. Davis, "The Role of the Adrenal Cortex and Kidney in the Pathogenesis of Cardiac Edema," *Yale Journal of Biological Medicine* 35(1963):402.

29. J.C. Burnett, Jr., et al., "Atrial Natriuretic Peptide Elevation in Congestive Heart Failure in Humans," *Science* 231(1986):1145.

30. W.W. Parmley, "Cardiac Failure," in M.R. Rosen and B.F. Hoffman, eds., *Cardiac Therapy* (The Hague: Martinus Niijoff Publishers, 1983), pp. 21–44.

31. H.T. Dodge, and W.A. Baxley, "Left Ventricular Volume and Mass and Their Significance in Heart Disease," *American Journal of Cardiology* 23(1969):528.

32. W. Grossman, D. Jones, and L.P. McLaurin, "Wall Stress and Patterns of Hypertrophy in the Human Left Ventricle," *Journal of Clinical Investigation* 56(1975):56.

33. R. Zelis, et al., "Peripheral Circulatory Control Mechanisms in Congestive Heart Failure," in D.T. Mason, ed., *Congestive Heart Failure Mechanisms: Evaluation and Treatment* (New York: Yorke Medical Books, 1976), p. 129.

34. J.S. Agus, and M. Goldberg, "Renal Function in Congestive Heart Failure," in H.J. Levine, ed., *Clinical Cardiovascular Physiology* (New York: Grune & Stratton, 1976), pp. 403–444.

35. J.A. Pittman, and P. Cohen, "The Pathogenesis of Cardiac Cachexia," *New England Journal of Medicine* 217(1964):453.

36. S.E. Heymsfeld, "Nutritional Support in Cardiac Cachexia," *Surgical Clinics of North America* 61(1981):635.

37. M. Harvey, "Physical Assessment: A Tailored Approach for Patients in Heart Failure," in C.R. Michaelson, ed., *Congestive Heart Failure* (St. Louis: The C.V. Mosby Company, 1983), pp. 123–178.

38. D.C.S. Lee, et al., "Heart Failure in Outpatients: A Randomized Trail of Digoxin Versus Placebo," *New England Journal of Medicine* 306(1982):699.

39. T.W. Smith, and E. Braunwald, "The Management of Heart Failure," in E. Braunwald, ed., *Heart Disease: A Textbook of Cardiovascular Medicine*, ed. 2 (Philadelphia: W.B. Saunders Co., 1984), pp. 503–559.

40. Unverferth, et al., "Tolerance to Dobutamine."

41. D.V. Unverferth, et al., "Long-term Benefit of Dobutamine in Patients with Congestive Cardiomyopathy," *American Heart Journal* 100(1980):622.

42. C.V. Leier, et al., "Drug-induced Conditioning in Congestive Heart Failure," *Circulation* 65(1982):1382.

43. K. Fitzpatrick, et al., "Hemodynamic, Humoral and Electrolyte Response to Prenalterol Infusion in Heart Failure," *Circulation* 67(1983):613.

44. V. Andrews, and J.S. Janicki, "Pirbuterol in the Long-term Treatment of Congestive Heart Failure," *Circulation* 64 Suppl. 4 (1981):307.

45. T. Kariya, L.T. Willis, and R.C. Doge, "Biochemical Studies on the Mechanism of Cardiotonic Activity of MDL 17,043," *Journal of Cardiovascular Pharmacology* 4(1982):509.

46. J.R. Benotti, et al., "Hemodynamic Assessment of Amirinone: A New Inotropic Agent," *New England Journal of Medicine* 299(1978):1373.

47. T.H. Le Jemtel, K. Keung, and E.H. Sonnenblich, "Amirinone: A New Non-glycosidic, Non-adrenergic Cardiotonic Agent Effective in the Treatment of Intractable Myocardial Failure in Man," *Circulation* 59(1979):1098.

48. A.A. Alousi, et al., "Characterization of the Cardiotonic Effects of Milrinone, a New Potent Cardiac Bipyridine on Isolated Tissue from Several Species," *Journal of Cardiovascular Pharmacology* 5(1983):804.

49. W.S. Colluci, R.F. Wright, and E. Braunwald, "The Newer Positive Inotropic Agents in the Treatment of Congestive Heart Failure," *New England Journal of Medicine* 314(1986):349.

50. H.D. White, et al., "Immediate Effects of Milrinone on Metabolic and Sympathetic Response to Exercise in Severe Congestive Heart Failure," *American Journal of Cardiology* 56(1985):93.

51. D.S. Baim, et al., "Survival of Congestive Heart Failure Patients Treated with Oral Milrinone, Abstract," *Journal of the American College of Cardiology* 5(1985):441.

52. T. Kariya, L.J. Willis, and R.C. Doge, "Biochemical Studies on the Mechanism of Cardiotonic Activity of MDL 17,043," *Journal of Cardiovascular Pharmacology* 4(1982):509.

53. B.F. Uretsky, et al., "The Acute Hemodynamic Effects of a New Agent MDL 17,043 in the Treatment of Congestive Heart Failure," *Circulation* 67(1983):823.

54. R. Arbogast, et al., "Hemodynamic Effects of MDL 17,043, a New Cardiotonic Agent, in Patients with Congestive Heart Failure: Comparison with Sodium Nitroprusside," *Journal of Cardiovascular Pharmacology* 5(1983):998.

55. D. Keriakas, et al., "Intravenous and Oral MDL 17,043 (a New Inotro-vasodilator Agent) in Congestive Heart Failure: Hemodynamic and Clinical Evaluation in 38 Patients," *Journal of the American College of Cardiology* 4(1984):884.

56. K. Chatterjee, "Congestive Cardiomyopathy: Therapeutic Approach," *Comprehensive Therapy* 8(1982):25.

57. P.S. Colley, F.W. Cheney, and M.P. Hlastala, "Ventilation-Perfusion and Gas Exchange Effects of Sodium Nitroprusside in Dogs with Normal and Edematous Lungs," *Anesthesiology* 50(1979):489.

58. J.T. Flaherty, et al., "Comparison of Intravenous Nitroglycerine and Sodium Nitroprusside for Treatment of Acute Hypertension Developing after Coronary Artery Bypass Surgery," *Circulation* 65(1982):1072.

59. M. Chiarello, et al., "Comparison Between the Effects of Nitroprusside and Nitroglycerine on Ischemic Injury during Acute Myocardial Infarction," *Circulation* 54(1976):766.

60. J.N. Cohn, et al., "Effect of Vasodilator Therapy on Mortality in Chronic Congestive Heart Failure," *New England Journal of Medicine* 314(1986):1547.

61. K. Chatterjee, J.L. Rouleau, and W.W. Parmley, "Captopril in Congestive Heart Failure: Improved Left Ventricular Function with Decreased Metabolic Cost," *American Heart Journal* 104(1982):1137.

62. M. Packer, N. Medina, and M. Yushak, "Relation Between Serum Sodium Concentration and Hemodynamic and Clinical Response to Converting Enzyme Inhibition with Captopril in Severe Heart Failure," *Journal of the American College of Cardiology* 3(1984):1035.

63. D.P. Clough, et al., "Interaction of Angiotensin-Converting Enzyme Inhibitors with the Function of the Sympathetic Nervous System," *American Journal of Cardiology* 49(1982):1410.

64. Consensus Trial Study Group, "Effects of Enalapril on Mortality in Severe Congestive Heart Failure," *New England Journal of Medicine* 316(1987):1429.

65. S.K. Huang, J.V. Messer, and P. Denes, "Significance of Ventricular Tachycardia in Idiopathic Dilated Cardiomyopathy: Observations in 35 Patients," *American Journal of Cardiology* 51(1983):507.

66. J.R. Wilson, et al., "Prognosis in Severe Heart Failure: Relation to Hemodynamic Measurements and Ventricular Ectopic Activity," *Journal of the American College of Cardiology* 2(1983):403.

67. T. Meinertz, et al., "Significance of Ventricular Arrhythmias in Idiopathic Dilated Cardiomyopathy," *American Journal of Cardiology* 53(1984):902.

68. C.S. Maskin, S.J. Siskind, and T.H. Lejemtel, "High Prevalence of Nonsustained Ventricular Tachycardia in Severe Congestive Heart Failure," *American Heart Journal* 107(1984):896.

69. K. Von Olshausen, et al., "Ventricular Arrhythmias in Idiopathic Dilated Cardiomyopathy," *British Heart Journal* 51(1984):195.

70. J. Holmes, et al., "Arrhythmias in Ischemic and Nonischemic Dilated Cardiomyopathy: Prediction of Mortality by Ambulatory Electrocardiography," *American Journal of Cardiology* 55(1985):146.

71. C.S. Chakko, and M. Gheorghiade, "Ventricular Arrhythmias in Severe Heart Failure: Incidence, Significance, and Effectiveness of Antiarrhythmic Therapy," *American Heart Journal* 109(1985):497.

72. D.A. Archibald, "Intra-group Report on Holter Tape Data," Cooperative studies program 153 (V-HEFT), April 11, 1985.

73. J.A. Franciosa, et al., "Survival in Men with Severe Chronic Left Ventricular Failure due to Either Coronary Heart Disease or Idiopathic Dilated Cardiomyopathy," *American Journal of Cardiology* 51(1983):831.

74. W.P. Follansbee, E.L. Michelson, and J. Morganroth, "Nonsustained Ventricular Tachycardia in Ambulatory Patients: Characteristics and Association with Sudden Cardiac Death," *Annals of Internal Medicine* 92(1980):741.

75. J. Holmes, et al., "Arrhythmias in Ischemic and Nonischemic Dilated Cardiomyopathy: Prediction of Mortality by Ambulatory Electrocardiography," *American Journal of Cardiology* 55(1985):146.

76. Huang, Messer, and Denes, "Significance of Ventricular Tachycardia in Idiopathic Dilated Cardiomyopathy."

77. R.L. Woosley, D.S. Echt, and O.M. Roden, "Effects of Congestive Heart Failure on the Pharmacokinetics and Pharmacodynamics of Antiarrhythmic Agents," *American Journal of Cardiology* 57(1986):25B.

78. W.H. Lee, and M. Packer, "Prognostic Importance of Serum Sodium Concentration and its Modification by Converting Enzyme Inhibition in Patients with Severe Heart Failure," *Circulation* 73(1986):257.

79. V.J. Dzau, et al., "Prostaglandins in Severe Congestive Heart Failure: Relation to Activation of the Renin-Angiotensin System and Hyponatremia," *New England Journal of Medicine* 310(1984):347.

80. R.A. Narins, "Therapy of Hyponatremia," *New England Journal of Medicine* 314(1986):1573.

81. J.M. Georges, and N.A. Stotts, "Reducing Cardiac Cachexia before Cardiac Valve Replacement," *Dimensions of Critical Care Nursing* 4(1985):349.

82. S.B. Heymsfield, et al., "Detection of Protein-Calorie Undernutrition in Advanced Heart Disease," *Circulation* 56, Suppl. 2 (1977):10.

83. J.G. Pittman and P. Cohen, "The Pathogenesis of Cardiac Cachexia (Concluded)," *New England Journal of Medicine* 271(1964):453.

84. Pittman, and Cohen, "Pathogenesis of Cardiac Cachexia."

85. Ibid.

86. G.L. Blackburn, et al., "Nutritional and Metabolic Assessment of the Hospitalized Patient," *Journal of Parenteral and Enteral Nutrition* 1(1977):11.

87. Pittman, and Cohen, "Pathogenesis of Cardiac Cachexia."

88. Ibid.

89. Heymsfield, "Nutritional Support in Cardiac Cachexia."

90. A. Strauss, and B. Glaser, *Chronic Illness and the Quality of Life* (St. Louis: C.V. Mosby Co., 1975).

91. R.S. Lazarus, and S. Folkman, *Stress, Appraisal and Coping* (New York: Springer Publishing Company, 1984).

92. V. Carrieri, and S. Janson-Bjerklie, "Strategies Patients Use to Manage the Sensation of Dyspnea," *Western Journal of Nursing Research* 8(1986):284.

93. I.L. Janis, and J. Rodin, "Attribution, Control and Decision Making: Social Psychology and Health Care," in G. Stone, F. Cohen, and N.E. Adler, eds., *Health Psychology* (San Francisco: Jossey-Bass, 1979).

94. J.J. Sampson, and C.L. Arbona, "Causes and Effects of Noncompliance in Cardiac Patients," *Clinical Cardiology* 3(1980):207.

Appendix 9-A

Activity Teaching Guidelines

PULSE TEACHING

Pulse represents the heart rate per minute as it is transmitted through the arteries. At rest, the heart beats more slowly, ___ times a minute. With exercise or stress, the heart works harder to pump blood to the working muscles. The harder the heart works, the faster the pulse rate. By careful observation it can be determined at what heart rate the heart is working so fast that symptoms of heart failure develop, especially shortness of breath. Shortness of breath can be avoided by pacing activities so that the pulse rate stays below the rate at which symptoms develop.

CONCEPT OF CARDIAC RESERVE

If the heart beats ___ times a minute at rest, and symptoms develop at a heart rate of ___ beats a minute, the cardiac reserve is symptom heart rate minus resting heart rate = ___ beats a minute. This means a reserve of ___ beats within which activity can be increased. Certain things can change (increase) the heart rate even when one is sitting quietly.

Environmental Factors

Heat. Hot weather will make the heart beat faster to pump more blood to the skin so it can evaporate perspiration and heat.

Cold. When it is very cold out, especially if it is windy and cold, BP goes up. This is because the blood is shunted away from the skin to avoid heat loss, which results in a relative increase in blood volume and more peripheral resistance for the heart to pump against.

Humidity. When it is muggy outside, there is more water vapor in the air. It is harder to evaporate perspiration, so heat builds up in the body. This makes the heart rate go up.

Altitude. The higher above sea level, the lower the amount of oxygen in the air; the air is "thinner." Therefore the heart has to pump faster to circulate the same relative amount of oxygen.

Air pollution. With increasing amounts of pollutants or smoke in the air, there is less oxygen per volume. So, similar to altitude, the heart must beat faster to circulate the same amount of oxygen.

Note: When showering or bathing, the heart is affected by both heat and humidity (steam). Do not take *hot* showers/baths because they result in too much stress on the heart. Comfortable water is fine. Avoid finishing with a cold rinse. This is a sudden shock to the system, which the heart may not be able to handle.

Emotions. Emotional tension raises the resting heart rate.

Activity After Meals

Heart rate is higher for an hour or so after eating because the heart must pump more blood to the stomach and digestive system. Therefore, relax for 1 to 1½ hours after meals.

Breath Control with Activity

It is important to avoid breath holding with activities such as bending over to tie shoes or lifting heavy objects. Even more important, avoid breath holding while straining, as in having a bowel movement. This causes significant increases in both heart rate and BP. (Most patients take stool softeners in the hospital and should continue to take them at home as long as they are ordered by the physician.)

Upper Extremity Activities

For unknown reasons, working with the arms, especially above shoulder height, causes the heart to pump faster than working with the legs. Monitor heart rate more closely when pushing, pulling, or lifting heavy objects. If fatigue or shortness of breath occurs while performing work, the body is signaling that the work is too hard. Frequent rest is needed so the heart and body can revive.

Cramped Positions

Working in cramped positions raises the heart rate. This includes such simple tasks as tying shoes or weeding the garden. Instead of bending down to tie shoes, place the foot up on a chair or stool.

Pacing Activities

When planning a daily schedule, be careful to allow rest periods between bouts of activity to avoid becoming overly fatigued. Do not cram all chores into the morning or into one day of the week. Pace yourself! Do a little at a time, spread tasks over the entire day and the entire week. Rest when tired or a little winded, even if only for 5 minutes.

Smoking (If Applicable)

Smoking cigarettes causes faster heart rate, higher BP, and sometimes spasms of the coronary artery: a triple blow to the heart. The most important change one can make to ease the burden on the heart is to quit smoking.

Sexual Relations

Research indicates that sexual activity raises the heart rate about as high as climbing 60 stairs a minute, but is usually sustained for 15 to 20 minutes. Therefore sex is a fairly vigorous activity. However, effects on the heart can be minimized by considering many of the factors already discussed:

Room temperature. This should be neither too hot nor too cold since these extremes raise the resting heart rate.

Meals. Wait at least 2 hours after a heavy meal or more than two drinks.

Cigarette smoking. Wait an hour after smoking even one cigarette.

Timing. It is best to wait until relaxed and well rested, not at the end of a long or tense day, not after having an argument, etc. First thing in the morning may be the best time.

Positions. Most research has shown little difference in energy requirements using one position rather than another. (Discourage positions in which patients support themselves on their arms.) Lying on the back or side may be the most relaxing.

Nitroglycerine. Many patients find that taking one nitroglycerine before becoming involved prevents chest pain or tightness. Discuss prescription with physician.

Unusual partners (extramarital affairs, etc.). Research has shown that the heart rate goes much higher when a person is involved with someone other than his or her usual partner.

This may seem like a lot of information, but the idea is to teach patients what circumstances require more caution and increased attention to how they are feeling. The rest is common sense.

THINGS TO REMEMBER

1. Wait at least 1 hour after eating before activities.
2. Dress according to the weather.
3. Pace your activities.
4. Use common sense!
   - Rest if you feel tired or any discomfort.
   - Slow down or decrease your walking time if you feel a little "blah" on a particular day. We all have days when we just don't feel so great. Sometimes you may find that you actually feel better once you get out and go for a walk; if so, fine. If not, and you still feel a little tired, slow down and take it a little easier that day.
   - Do not do any extra activities/walking program on a day when you have a bad cold, flu, etc.

SIGNS AND SYMPTOMS OF HEART FAILURE

1. Shortness of breath with minimal exertion or at rest, as a result of the increased fluid in the lungs.
2. Cough, sometimes with blood streaking in the mucus.
3. Inability to lie flat in bed (or as flat as normal) without feeling more short of breath.
4. The need to sleep on more pillows than usual or to sleep sitting up in a chair to feel comfortable.
5. Significant increase in weight over 1 to 3 days, as a result of the accumulation of fluid.
6. Swelling of feet and ankles.
7. Increased urinary frequency at night.
8. Generalized malaise, increased fatigue.

ACTIONS TO BE TAKEN

1. The first thing you should do is to learn to pay attention to how you feel, to the signals just discussed.
2. If you note any of these symptoms, or if you have any questions, you should call your physician within 24 hours. Remember, the quicker you receive treatment, the faster your heart failure will be brought back into control.
3. Of course, it is best to call your physician during normal working hours since you will be more likely to reach him or her and benefit from the

care. So, if you suspect problems, call. Don't wait until things become worse.

4. On the other hand, if you do develop real problems in the middle of the night, do not wait until morning. If you cannot reach your own physician, you may always call the Coronary Care Unit. The number is _____.

5. If you begin to develop serious problems with shortness of breath, chest pain, dizziness or fainting, weakness, palpitations, or nausea and vomiting, seek help right away:

   • Call the physician.
   • Call the Emergency Ambulance Service. The number is _____.

HOME PROGRAM

For the heart to continue to grow stronger and more efficient, it is important to keep up activity after discharge from the hospital. Do the warmup exercises practiced in the hospital, just before walking. Walk at least once a day. The day after discharge, walk as long as you did the last day you were in the hospital, ___ minutes. Increase the amount of time by 1 minute every day or two. Once walking 30 minutes nonstop without any problems, increase the pace. Do this by starting out at a normal pace for 5 minutes; then pick up the pace a little bit for the next 5 minutes. If tired, short of breath, if there is a little chest pain or discomfort, or if the heart rate is up to the maximum limit, slow down to regular speed. If no symptoms occur, continue walking at the faster pace for 5 more minutes, then slow down. Continue to increase the amount of time at the faster pace, up to 30 minutes. Then repeat the entire process again, if you like.

Take your pulse before doing warmup exercises, after the exercises and before beginning the walk, in the middle of the walk, and just after finishing. Record the walking time, pulse, and any symptoms noted (tiredness, shortness of breath, dizziness, chest pain or discomfort, leg pain, etc.). Bring this data sheet when you next see your physician.

Chapter 10

Current Trends in Heart Transplantation

Diane Dressler, RN, MSN

Recent advances have made cardiac transplantation an accepted mode of therapy for selected patients with end-stage heart failure. The use of air transportation has facilitated organ retrieval. The mechanism of allograft rejection is better understood, and rejection can be monitored more accurately with techniques such as the endomyocardial biopsy. Surgical techniques and organ preservation methods have improved.[1] Most importantly, immunosuppressive drug therapy now includes cyclosporine, a drug that inhibits T-lymphocytes selectively without suppressing the entire immune system. This new drug therapy has simplified the postoperative course of most transplant recipients and allowed for earlier discharge from the hospital.[2]

As a result of these advances, survival after cardiac transplantation has improved with 1 year survival approaching 80% in some centers.[3,4] As an increasing number of transplants are being carried out in an increased number of centers, critical care nurses have become involved in all areas of transplantation from donor recognition and management to the clinical care of transplant recipients.

Several emerging trends related to cardiac transplantation directly affect critical care nurses. At one time, transplants were performed only at university-based hospitals. Now, some community-based hospitals with adequate preparation and commitment are beginning transplant programs.[5] Patient selection is also changing, and has expanded to include more pediatric patients and patients into their 60s. New cardiac assist devices and the total artificial heart are being used as a bridge to transplantation in some heart centers. There are also constant changes in immunosuppressive drug therapy regimens and in the drugs used to treat the side effects of immunosuppressive drug therapy.

These trends have nursing implications that have resulted in the increasing involvement of critical care nurses as procurement coordinators, clinical (recipient) coordinators, and primary caregivers for patients undergoing transplant surgery.

Patients considered to be transplant candidates proceed through five phases of transplantation:

1. evaluation
2. the waiting period
3. the surgery
4. acute care and recovery
5. rehabilitation and long-term follow-up.

Nurses are involved with patients and families during all these phases, and need to be aware of common patient problems, research related to these problems, and nursing strategies that meet the unique needs of transplant patients.

EVALUATION OF RECIPIENTS

Referred candidates are screened as soon as possible by members of the cardiac transplant team to determine whether they meet the criteria for transplantation, and whether major contraindications to transplantation are present. Exhibit 10-1 lists the cardiac recipient criteria. In general, recipients have end-stage heart failure from idiopathic cardiomyopathy or ischemic heart disease. They are expected to survive less than 6 months to 1 year, and have no other medical or surgical options. Age limits were recently expanded to include infants and patients over 55 years of age.

A number of physiological and psychological variables may be considered contraindications or relative contraindications. Irreversibly elevated pulmonary vascular resistance above 6 to 8 Wood units can result in acute failure of the donor heart. Some patients with fixed high pulmonary vascular resistance may be candidates for heart and lung transplantation.[6] The immunosuppressive drug therapy used postoperatively may exacerbate insulin dependent diabetes mellitus, active peptic ulcer disease, cancer, infection, and irreversible liver and kidney dysfunction. Other conditions that limit survival post-transplantation include recent pulmonary embolism, cerebrovascular disease, and chronic obstructive

---

Exhibit 10-1 Cardiac Recipient Criteria

Untreatable cardiomyopathy
Less than 6 months to live
Under 60 years of age
PVR <6–8 Wood units
No systemic infection
No cancer or other diseases that would limit survival post-transplantation
No recent pulmonary embolism
No history of drug or alcohol abuse
Compliant, well motivated

pulmonary disease. Relative contraindications include psychosocial instability and a history of drug or alcohol abuse because of potential compliance problems.[7]

Patients proceed through an extensive evaluation that begins with a cardiac catheterization and that may include endomyocardial biopsy to rule out active myocarditis. After the cardiologist and cardiac surgeon evaluate these results, the patient is evaluated by the transplant team, which may include an infectious disease specialist, a psychiatrist, a dentist, a social worker, a clinical dietician, and a hospital financial counselor. A second opinion from an independent cardiologist may also be sought. The evaluation is often coordinated by the clinical transplant coordinator.

Blood is drawn for viral and fungal serology to obtain baseline values and to determine whether the patient has been exposed to an infectious agent that could pose a problem after the transplant. Kidney and liver functions are carefully assessed to determine whether problems would be reversible with improved cardiac function.

Another blood sample is sent for tissue typing, which includes determination of ABO blood type, human leukocyte antigen (HLA) typing, and screening for cytotoxic antibodies. The antibody screen involves exposing the recipient's serum to a panel of random cells from multiple donors. If minimal or no antigen-antibody reactivity is observed, the screen is considered negative. A transplant can then be performed without a lymphocyte crossmatch with the prospective donor.[8,9] In long-distance procurement, the need for a lymphocyte crossmatch causes delays and increases cost as blood samples must be rapidly transported and undergo the 4-hour crossmatch procedure before the decision is made to proceed with the transplant.

The psychological stability of the patient and the availability of a supportive family are important considerations because of the commitment required from both the patient and health care team. Patients must understand and accept the follow-up care and medical regimen essential to maintaining health after transplantation. The nurses caring for patients who are being evaluated are often able to provide important information regarding the patient's and family's responses to the evaluation process and the option of transplantation. Nurses who provide direct care and interact with patients 24 hours a day may see evidence of ineffective coping responses or noncompliant behavior that might be important considerations. They may also learn of strengths and appropriate coping behaviors not obvious to the transplant team. Nurses' observations complement the medical evaluation and often provide valuable information that is useful in planning for an individual's care post-transplantation.

During the evaluation, patients and their families receive an overwhelming amount of information. Some patients have known of the possibility of transplantation for months and have had the opportunity to obtain at least some information. Others have only learned recently of their condition and may still be in a state of shock and disbelief that their condition requires a treatment so radical. Nurses have an important role in assisting the patient through review and clarification of the information when they are ready to discuss it, as often patients are too anxious to understand what they have been told by physicians. Collaboration between physicians and nurses is extremely important when the results of the evaluation are presented to the patient, who may then be requested to make the decision whether or not to proceed.

THE WAITING PERIOD

The waiting period begins when a patient is found to be a transplant candidate, and ends when a donor is available and procurement is arranged. Patients are often listed as potential recipients with one or more organ procurement agency. There may be a formal or informal network with the state. In addition, patients are placed on the national computerized network. In compliance with the rec-ommendations of the Federal Task Force on Organ Transplantation to provide a unified national network, the Organ Procurement and Transplantation Network (OPTN) was established in 1986. The network maintains computerized lists of patients in need of a vital organ transplant and provides a nationwide system to match donated organs and individuals in need. A 24-hour telephone service facilitates access to the system by transplant centers and organ procurement programs.[10]

The growing shortage of suitable organs for transplantation has meant that patients may wait for days, months, or even years. Patients are listed on the computerized networks according to their medical status as shown in Exhibit 10-2. Efforts are made to give priority to candidates in critical condition.

Cardiac donor criteria are listed in Exhibit 10-3. Patients are matched with prospective donors according to ABO blood type and body weight. Body size of the donor and recipient should be matched so the donor weighs no more than 20% less than the recipient since the heart will have to function immediately to

---

Exhibit 10-2 Status of Transplant Candidates: North American Transplant Coordinators
Organization Criteria

Status 0 (Status 9): Imminent danger of loss of life within 24 to 48 hours.
Status 1: In hospital critical care area, in unstable condition. Continually hospitalized with
no prognosis of discharge.
Status 2: Hospitalized in stable condition. With medical therapy there is a prognosis of
discharge before transplant.
Status 3: Awaiting transplant but not hospitalized.

Source: Organ Recovery Manual, St. Luke's Organ Sharing Network, St. Luke's Hospital, Milwaukee, Wisconsin.

Exhibit 10-3 Cardiac Donor Criteria

Brain death declared
ABO compatible
Under 40 years of age
Size and weight match
Minimal inotropic support
No cardiac arrest
No prolonged periods of hypotension
No cardiac contusion
No abnormal wall motion on echocardiogram
No systemic infection

support the recipient's circulation. In patients with increased pulmonary vascular resistance, a donor larger than the recipient may be preferred as the increased afterload might compromise a smaller heart. The donor may be 30% to 40% larger than the recipient since the pericardial cavity has already accommodated a hypertrophied and enlarged heart.[11] ABO compatibility is essential because an incompatible transplant will result in rejection because of antibodies directed against incompatible antigens on the vascular endothelium of the graft.[12] As important as ABO compatibility is, Rh antigens are weak immunogens with regard to organ transplantation and are not considered important.[13] In addition to size and ABO matching, a lymphocyte crossmatch is carried out when indicated.

Prospective HLA matching is important in kidney graft survival, and donor kidneys are often placed with recipients who have the closest HLA match. However, in heart and other extrarenal organs, it is questionable whether HLA matching improves survival.[14] Heart recipients generally receive donor hearts according to priority rather than HLA matching since the process would prolong the ischemic time. Most cardiac transplants are done across an HLA mismatch, with the matching done retrospectively.

The donor heart is obtained during a multiple-organ recovery from a heart-beating donor with a diagnosis of brain death who has been maintained on organ support systems. Potential cardiac donors must meet strict criteria since the transplanted heart must function immediately. Ideal donors must be younger than 35 years of age for men and 40 years of age for women because of the increasing incidence of coronary artery disease beyond this age.[15,16] If an older donor is considered, coronary angiography may be performed as part of the donor evaluation.

A cardiologist usually evaluates the prospective donor to determine that electrocardiogram (ECG), echocardiogram, cardiac enzymes, chest x-ray, and other indices of cardiac function are normal. Contraindications to cardiac donation include hemodynamic instability, prolonged hypotension, cardiac arrest, significant inotropic support, a history of cardiac disease, or cardiac trauma. In addition, evidence of sepsis, a history of diabetes mellitus, or cancer other than a primary brain tumor will exclude a donor.

While arrangements for the transplant surgery are taking place, care of the potential organ donor is aimed at maintaining all transplantable organs in optimal condition. Fluid resuscitation is regulated to prevent hypovolemia and subsequent hypotension. Diabetes insipidus is common in potential donors and is treated with pitressin to minimize fluid volume depletion. Since brain death may lead to decreased vasomotor tone, vasopressors (most commonly dopamine 5 to 10 μg/kg/min) may be necessary to avoid hypotension. High doses of vasopressors can decrease organ perfusion. When an acceptable blood pressure (BP) (usually above 90 mmHg systolic) cannot be maintained without high-dose vasopressors, a decision not to use the heart for transplantation may be made.[17]

Arterial blood gases and mechanical ventilation are monitored to ensure adequate oxygenation of vital organs. Episodes of hypoxia can damage organs before the transplant surgery.

Body temperature is monitored closely after brain death. Hypothermia and hyperthermia are treated with warming and cooling blankets when autoregulation of body temperature is disturbed.

Care is taken to maintain sterile conditions during suctioning and other procedures to prevent infection in the donor. Prophylactic antibiotics are routinely ordered.

Efficient arrangements for organ recovery can avoid increasing instability in the donor as prolonged maintenance of brain-dead donors is associated with functional deterioration of all vital organs.[18] An established nursing procedure for obtaining consent, maintaining the donor in optimal condition, and contacting the local organ procurement agency can facilitate organ donation.

For the potential cardiac recipient, the waiting period is a time of physical and emotional stress. Common nursing diagnoses during the period include (1) alteration in cardiac output, (2) potential for thromboembolism, (3) potential for infection, (4) anxiety related to future surgery, and (5) lack of knowledge.

Alteration in Cardiac Output

Patients may suffer repeated episodes of congestive heart failure, life-threatening arrhythmias, and progressive deterioration of cardiac function while awaiting transplantation.[19] Controlling symptoms may require increasing medical and nursing intervention. High doses of diuretics are often necessary, along with digoxin, other inotropic drugs, and drugs that decrease afterload.

Patients who are stable enough to wait at home are seen frequently by their physician to monitor their condition. They are assigned a pager so they can be reached if a donor becomes available. Some patients are able to remain out of the hospital for a few months during the waiting period with close medical supervision. However, when signs and symptoms can no longer be controlled at home, they are admitted to the hospital and listed at a more urgent status on the computerized network. After admission to the hospital, some patients may seem to be improved with strict dietary control, professional administration of medications, and bed rest. For these patients, an increase in activity or change in environment will again cause them to become unstable. They are then advised to wait in the hospital until a donor is located.

Potential for Thromboembolism

Patients with cardiomyopathy tend to develop thrombi in the cardiac chambers of their enlarged and poorly contracting hearts and in the deep veins of the lower extremities. Often, transplant candidates will have a history of a stroke or other embolic event. These patients must be encouraged to be as active as their condition permits to discourage the formation of deep venous thrombi and subsequent pulmonary emboli. To prevent mural thrombi from forming on hypokinetic areas of the endocardium, many are placed on anticoagulants including warfarin and/ or platelet inhibitors.[20] A therapeutic balance is maintained between the patient's need for anticoagulation and the prospective surgery. In patients awaiting surgery, the prothrombin time is maintained at no higher than one and one half times the control value. Some patients may receive heparin instead of warfarin since its anticoagulant effects are more easily reversed, and there is less risk of surgical bleeding.

Potential for Infection

As patients' conditions deteriorate while they are waiting for a donor, some require admission to an intensive care setting, hemodynamic monitoring, and occasionally mechanical ventilation and cardiac assist devices. Sepsis from invasive lines is a particular threat. Poor nutritional status predisposes these patients to infection and makes it difficult to treat. Active infection is a contraindication to transplantation because of the need for immunosuppressive drug therapy, and a patient with an infection may be unable to have the surgery until the infection is resolved.

Nursing care is aimed toward preventing infection. A nutritional evaluation is carried out to identify patients with cardiac cachexia, anorexia, and impaired digestion and absorption because of their high risk of infection.[21] Nutrition is enhanced with nutritional supplements, vitamins, and favorite foods from home. Strict adherence to sterile technique is followed related to invasive lines, tubes, and devices. Any sign of infection such as fever or inflammation is investigated so that threatening infection can be treated promptly.

Anxiety Related to Future Surgery

Anxiety is an expected reaction to cardiac surgery, but its degree increases when a surgery this extensive is planned, and when the operative date is unknown. Patients describe ambivalent feelings—wishing to "get it over with" but fearing the surgery. Transplant candidates have often gone through a gradual and painful adjustment to their deteriorating health. Along with this they have had to cope with social changes including inability to work, loss of earnings, loss of status, and reversal of roles in the family.[22] The option of transplantation provides the hope of a meaningful future, and for these patients is their only option for survival.

The presentation of factual information related to transplantation may be helpful in relieving anxiety. However, at times it may increase uncomfortable feelings as candidates deal with emotions pertaining to organ donation, the postoperative course, and postoperative life style recommendations.

Patients may verbalize fears about personality changes or physical changes that may occur after receiving the heart of someone else. Although intellectually they know the heart is a muscular pump, emotions and personality are still associated with the heart in literature, music, and conversation. Positive nursing intervention includes discussion of these feelings. Factual information can be presented comparing organ donation to blood transfusions; i.e., a donor's sex, race, and personality characteristics are not relevant to transfusion or transplantation.

Other patients fear they will acquire disease through the transplanted organ. Reassurance regarding the testing of donors for hepatitis, acquired immune deficiency syndrome, and other transmissible diseases must be provided.

Anxiety that a donor will not be found in time is expressed by both patients and families. The family may find themselves searching the daily news for accidents that might result in a donor.[23] Their feelings regarding this search may need to be dealt with.

It is particularly important to maintain a sense of hope during the waiting period. Both patients and staff can become discouraged at the realization that the majority of the hospitalization is often spent waiting. The patient and family need to hear success stories of how others have waited and eventually were transplanted. A visit from a previously transplanted patient to offer encouragement can be helpful at this time.

Specific nursing strategies can also assist patients to maintain some semblance of normalcy during this period of extreme stress. Patients should be encouraged to be active and participate in usual activities as their condition permits. For the hospitalized patient, occasional passes to leave the hospital or nursing unit are therapeutic. Occupational therapy can be helpful in encouraging hobbies and projects that promote a positive self-image. Conferences involving the patient, family, and caregivers can be productive in modifying stressors and meeting individual patient needs.

Knowledge Deficit

Teaching assumes great importance with cardiac transplant patients, as the quality and length of life after transplantation depend on the patient's ability to understand rejection, infection, immunosuppressive drug therapy, and life style modifications.[24]

Patients with end-stage cardiac disease are often quite knowledgeable about their condition and medical options. However, newly diagnosed patients may know very little, and their anxiety over the option of transplantation may interfere with their ability to learn. Another consideration is that their low cardiac output state can interfere with brain perfusion and their ability to learn. Because of this, the patient's family is included in the preoperative teaching sessions. The patient's cardiologist and surgeon often present the information on transplantation to the patient initially. The nurse devises a teaching plan to complement and enhance this information. The expected outcomes of these sessions are outlined in Exhibit 10-4. Teaching the transplant candidate is a collaborative effort involving physicians, staff nurses, and the clinical transplant coordinator. Frequent review and clarification from various sources is necessary before patients can demonstrate a good understanding of the information.

THE SURGERY

When a donor is identified, much needs to be accomplished in a short period of time. The patient is contacted and admitted to the hospital if not already an inpatient. Loading doses of immunosuppressive drugs are administered. If the patient has been taking warfarin, anticoagulation is reversed with the administration of vitamin K. Admission laboratory work is completed or updated. During this time the patient welcomes any available information regarding the location and suitability of the possible donor.

Travel arrangements are made if the organ recovery is to take place at another hospital. These arrangements may involve jet, airplane, helicopter, and/or ambulance to accomplish the 4-hour ischemic time limit usually adhered to in cardiac transplantation. The surgeons and transplant coordinators discuss the time frame for organ recovery and surgery on the recipient. Timing is critical and can determine the success of the transplant. In addition to the location of the donor, other considerations may include the flying conditions, which other organs are being recovered, and whether the recipient has had cardiac surgery previously. In patients who are being reoperated, dense adhesions slow the surgery as the chest is opened and the patient is prepared to be placed on cardiopulmonary bypass.

Two surgical teams are arranged. The procurement team often includes a cardiovascular surgeon, surgical assistants, and the organ procurement coordinator. The recipient team includes a second cardiovascular surgeon, an anes-

Exhibit 10-4 Preoperative Heart Transplant Teaching Plan

Before surgery, it is expected that the patient/family will:
1. Describe the clinical condition requiring transplantation
2. Verbalize information related to transplant surgery
   a. average waiting time
   b. listing according to status
   c. notification of patient and family when donor becomes available
   d. administration of preoperative medication
   e. orthotopic versus heterotopic transplantation
3. Demonstrate knowledge of the organ donation system
   a. evaluation of potential donor
   b. long-distance procurement
   c. definition of brain death
   d. conditions that result in brain death
   e. consent from donor family
   f. possibility of canceling surgery during donor evaluation
4. Verbalize knowledge of postoperative care
   a. intensive care setting, hemodynamic monitoring
   b. basic understanding of rejection process, how it is monitored and treated
      (1) role of the immune system in rejection
      (2) endomyocardial biopsy procedure
      (3) immunosuppressive drugs—actions and common side effects (cyclosporine, prednisone, azathioprine (Imuran), antithymocyte globulin)
   c. awareness of risk of infection postoperatively
      (1) due to immunosuppressive drugs
      (2) basic precautions taken by patient, family, and staff
      (3) hospital procedure for protective isolation
   d. awareness of late complications that may occur
      (1) graft atherosclerosis
      (2) increased risk of cancer
5. Demonstrate knowledge of life style recommendations after transplantation
   a. cessation of smoking
   b. low-cholesterol, no-added-salt diet
   c. exercise regimen
   d. lifelong medication
   e. follow-up biopsies and clinic visits.

thesiologist, surgical assistants, a perfusionist, and the clinical transplant coordinator. Frequent communication between the teams is necessary to plan and update a timetable of events that will minimize ischemic time.

Surgery is started on the recipient when the donor heart is found to be satisfactory by the procurement surgeon. It is possible to cancel the surgery at any time before this if an unexpected problem arises (cardiac arrest of the donor, unsuspected congenital defect of the donor heart, etc.).

The donor heart is arrested with cardioplegia solution. After excision and inspection, it is rapidly cooled in iced saline and sterilely stored in a cooler for transport. The ischemic time begins when the crossclamp is placed on the donor aorta and ends when the crossclamp is removed from the recipient aorta and coronary perfusion is re-established.[25]

The recipient is placed on cardiopulmonary bypass, and the diseased heart is excised when the procurement team returns to the operating room with the donor organ. As seen in Figure 10-1, the donor heart is implanted through four anastamoses that connect the left atria, right atria, pulmonary artery, and aorta in a procedure called *orthotopic transplantation.* Occasionally, the original heart is left in place and a *heterotopic* or "piggyback" transplant is performed. Indications for this procedure would include high pulmonary vascular resistance or a recipient too large for a weight match with a donor. Although transplant centers in other countries have reported success with heterotopic transplantation, most centers in the United States perform only the orthotopic procedure.[26] Patients receiving orthotopic transplants have better survival expectancy than those receiving heterotopic transplants.[27]

Before the surgery is completed, a right ventricular (RV) biopsy may be taken from the donor endocardium to serve as a control for future biopsies. As the

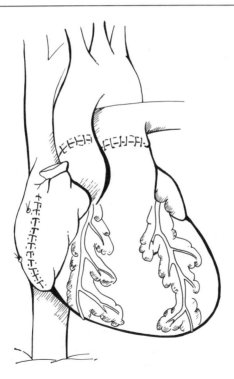

Figure 10-1 Orthotopic cardiac transplantation. The completed transplantation shows the anastamoses between the right atria, aorta, and pulmonary arteries.

anastamoses are completed, the transplanted heart is rewarmed and recovers from the cold ischemia. Pacing wires are placed on the RV and possibly on the right atrium. Temporary pacing and inotropic support may be necessary to achieve an adequate heart rate and stroke volume. Failure of the transplanted heart is an emergency situation, as cardiopulmonary bypass can only be used for a limited number of hours. If the donor heart fails, and does not respond to the usual supportive measures such as pharmacologic therapy and the intra-aortic balloon pump, another donor will be searched for through a nationwide alert. In some centers a ventricular assist device or total artificial heart may be an option until another donor is located. (For detailed discussion see Chapter 11.) The shortage of donors has resulted in increased use of heart assist devices and the artificial heart as a bridge to cardiac transplantation.[28] These options can be considered when a patient is critically ill and no cardiac donor is available, or when a transplanted heart fails.

Fortunately most transplanted hearts recover well from the ischemia. When the transplanted heart is ejecting vigorously, the patient is weaned from cardiopulmonary bypass and the sternum is closed. The patient is then transported to the cardiovascular surgery intensive care unit.

ACUTE CARE AND RECOVERY

Nursing care of these patients is in many ways similar to the care of other patients who have undergone open heart surgery. After rewarming and recovery of the transplanted heart there may be a period of hemodynamic instability. The transplanted heart lacks the benefit of neural feedback to help it cope with hemodynamic stresses, and is dependent on adequate preload and circulating catecholamines to increase heart rate and contractility.[29] Because of this, careful hemodynamic monitoring is particularly important in the immediate postoperative period.

Patients are closely observed for bradyarrhythmias. Both inotropic drugs and temporary pacing may be required. Isoproterinol may be routinely begun in the operating room and continued for a number of days to prevent bradycardia and low cardiac output. The use of atropine, frequently a first-line intervention in bradycardia, is ineffective since the vagus nerve is severed during the surgery, resulting in denervation of the transplanted heart.

The BP may be labile, and treatment with volume replacement and inotropic support may be necessary. In general, the arterial BP is maintained between 90 and 140 mmHg systolic. Central venous pressure is measured, and fluid is administered to maintain adequate preload. Hemodynamic monitoring may also include a Swan-Ganz catheter to monitor pulmonary artery pressures, but surgeons may prefer to minimize invasive monitoring because of the risk for infection. As an alternative to thermodilution cardiac output measurements, the venous oxygen saturation drawn from the central venous catheter may be observed as an indicator of cardiac output.

Hemodynamic parameters are correlated with clinical assessment, chest x-ray results, and other studies to monitor the patient for cardiac failure, which is most likely to occur during the first 2 days postoperatively. RV failure can occur because of pre-existing elevated pulmonary vascular resistance. Patients are closely observed for increased central venous pressure and decreased cardiac output caused by increased RV afterload. Biventricular failure is also possible because of prolonged ischemia. Isoproterinol is often the drug of choice for inotropic and chronotropic support because it is a pure beta-adrenergic stimulator and can dilate the pulmonary artery, decreasing pulmonary vascular resistance. Alternatively, dobutamine, epinephrine, and norepinephrine may be used. Nitroprusside is also commonly used for afterload reduction, and occasionally the intra-aortic balloon pump may be required.[30]

During the immediate postoperative period, patients are also observed for evidence of postoperative hemorrhage, which can occur because of preoperative anticoagulation, liver dysfunction, or surgical bleeding from the vascular anastamosis sites or chest wall. In patients whose blood tested negative for cytomegalovirus (CMV) exposure, CMV negative blood transfusions are given.

Another problem that commonly occurs in the acute period is transient renal failure. Renal function is often compromised preoperatively by the patient's low cardiac output, and the use of the cyclosporine in the perioperative period can contribute to early renal toxicity in some patients. Occasionally, hemodialysis is necessary to restore fluid and electrolyte balance. Further refinement of immunosuppressive drug therapy is aimed at minimizing this problem.[31] The urine output, blood urea nitrogen (BUN), and serum creatinine are monitored closely after surgery. The administration of nephrotoxic drugs is avoided when possible, and the cyclosporine dose is carefully adjusted according to the patient's renal function.

After the immediate postoperative period, the major priorities of care specifically related to the transplant are the recognition of rejection, the administration and monitoring of immunosuppressive drug therapy, and the recognition and prevention of infection. The standardized nursing care plan in Table 10-1 outlines nursing diagnoses, nursing orders, and expected outcomes related to these priorities.

Rejection in Cardiac Transplantation

To understand the body's response to a transplanted organ, it is necessary to review the immune system. The immune system determines how an organism will react when confronted with anitgens (or "immunogens"), substances capable of evoking an immune response. In addition to defense against microor-

Table 10-1 Standard Care Plan: The Patient with a Cardiac Transplant

Nursing Diagnosis	Expected Outcome	Nursing Interventions
Potential for injury related to acute rejection	Patient will show minimal signs of rejection on biopsy. Patient will have no signs/symptoms of acute rejection.	1. Monitor vital signs for hypotension, unexplained fever. 2. Assess for decreased energy level. 3. Monitor for atrial, ventricular dysrhythmias. 4. Observe for signs of congestive heart failure: hypotension, decreased cardiac output/cardiac index, decreased peripheral perfusion, chest x-ray changes. 5. Administer immunosuppressive therapy per physician.
Potential for injury related to endomyocardial biopsy (EMB)	Patient will have no complications from EMB (bleeding, cardiac tamponade, dysrhythmia, pneumothorax, hemothorax).	1. Hold anticoagulant therapy before procedure per physician. 2. Activity limitation as ordered; often bed rest for 4 to 6 hr postprocedure. 3. Observe dressing site for bleeding, hematoma. 4. Apply pressure dressing to jugular site prn. 5. Apply sandbag to femoral site prn. 6. Perform cardiovascular assessment every 15 min × 4, then every hour × 4, observing BP, apical pulse, peripheral perfusion. 7. Perform respiratory assessment every 15 min × 4, then every hour × 4, observing respiratory rate, depth, pattern, symmetry of breath sounds.

Potential for injury to kidney and liver function related to immunosuppressive drugs	Patient will have adequate urine output, normal kidney and liver function tests, BP >90/60 and <140/90, therapeutic cyclosporine trough level (serum RIA: 100–150 μg/mg).	1. Monitor BUN, serum creatinine, urine output. 2. Monitor liver function tests. 3. Monitor BP; administer antihypertensives to maintain systolic <140 and diastolic <100. 4. Teach BP monitoring to patient/family for postdischarge monitoring. 5. Draw cyclosporine trough level on schedule; report results to physician for dose adjustment.
Potential for fluid, electrolyte, and glucose imbalance related to immunosuppressive drugs	Patient will have normal electrolyte panel, balanced output, normoglycemia.	1. Monitor electrolytes; notify physician of abnormalities. 2. Measure daily weight, intake, output. 3. Assess for edema. 4. Adjust IV fluids, diet restrictions per physician. 5. Monitor blood sugar; report consistent elevation for evaluation. 6. Instruct patient and family on importance of fluid and sodium restriction.
Potential for injury related to antithymocyte globulin (ATG)	Patient will have no signs/symptoms of anaphylaxis, febrile reaction, serum sickness. Patient will have minimal pain from injections.	1. Follow hospital ATG administration protocol. When experimental ATG (such as rabbit) used, patient must sign permit. 2. Observe for anaphylactic reaction during and after administration; difficulty breathing, wheezing, hypotension, peripheral vasodilation. Resuscitative measures as necessary.

continues

Table 10-1 continued

Nursing Diagnosis	Expected Outcome	Nursing Interventions
		3. When ATG given IM: Administer analgesics and acetaminophen pre- and postinjection to minimize discomfort and fever Use Z-track injection and divided doses to minimize discomfort Assist patient with leg exercise prn Apply warm packs prn Assess injection sites for inflammation each shift. 4. For 2 or 3 wk after ATG administration, observe for signs/symptoms of serum sickness: fever, arthralgia, rash, thrombocytopenia, leukopenia.
Potential for infection	Patient will have no signs/symptoms of infection: temperature <37°C; no chills; normal WBC; no cough; negative blood, sputum, urine cultures; normal wound healing.	1. Meticulous handwashing. 2. Modified protective isolation. 3. Prohibit patient contact with persons having cold, diarrhea, open skin, skin infection, cold sore. 4. Observe incisions, IV sites, pacemaker wire sites, skin and mucous membranes. 5. Discontinue indwelling lines and tubes as soon as possible. 6. Routine respiratory care, assessment. 7. Report fever, abnormal WBC and differential (prednisone may alter values), culture results to physician.

| Potential for disturbance in self-concept | Patient will verbalize and demonstrate sense of well-being and responsibility for self-care. | 1. Encourage verbalization of feelings related to mood swings, changes in body image, rejection, life style changes.
2. Encourage independence in self-care: medication and vital sign measurement, etc.
3. Consult clinical specialist, clinical transplant coordinator, chaplain, social worker as appropriate.
4. Dietary consult to minimize effects of steroid therapy.
5. Introduce patient to other heart transplant recipients.
6. Invite patient to a support group. |
| Potential for ineffective family coping | Family will verbalize understanding of physical and psychological changes associated with transplantation. Family will effectively serve as a source of patient support. | 1. Establish physician and primary nurse spokesperson with family representative to promote consistent communication and serve as a support person.
2. Encourage family verbalization of feelings and concerns.
3. Provide private, comfortable visiting.
4. Encourage family involvement in patient care.
5. Include family in education. |

Source: Adapted with permission of St. Luke's Samaritan Health Care, Inc., Milwaukee, Wisconsin.

ganisms, the immune system has a surveillance function that recognizes foreign or mutant cells. Immune surveillance is responsible for the recognition of malignant cells, and it has a key role in the recognition of a transplanted organ.[32]

When the body is confronted with a foreign substance, two types of immune response occur: nonspecific and specific. The nonspecific responses include phagocytosis by nonlymphoid white blood cells (WBCs) such as neutrophils and macrophages. The inflammatory response assists in bringing the WBCs to the area where they are needed. Two types of specific immunity also enable the body to develop a defense against specific invading organisms, toxins, or cells. Humoral immunity involves the production of specific antibodies toward these substances. Cellular immunity enables the body to form small, sensitized lymphocytes that can bind to and destroy the foreign substance.[33]

These two types of specific immunity result from different processing sites of the lymphocytes released from the bone marrow (Figure 10-2). Lymphocytes processed in the thymus are *T-lymphocytes*. Those processed in the bone marrow are *B-lymphocytes*. Both the T- and B-cells eventually become trapped in the lymph nodes where they await stimulation by an antigen.

When an antigen binds to a B-cell receptor, the cell differentiates into clones of plasma cells. These plasma cells then begin the production of antibodies, which are released into the circulation.

When an antigen binds to a T-cell receptor, small sensitized lymphocytes are produced. These T-lymphocytes are then released into the circulation where they can recognize and bind to invading cells, and destroy them along with other types of WBCs.[34]

Three basic types of T-cells are recognized: Cytotoxic (or effector) T-cells hunt and destroy cancer and other abnormal cells, including those of a transplanted organ. Helper T-cells enhance B and T responses through the release of mediators such as interleukin 2. Suppressor T-cells act to inhibit B responses.

T-cell cytotoxicity is thought to be the most important mechanism in the destruction of a transplanted organ (Figure 10-3). In addition, antibody-dependent cell-mediated cytotoxicity, activated macrophages, and complement-dependent antibodies can have a role in the cellular damage.[35]

Transplant rejection can occur in three ways: hyperacute, acute, and chronic. The immune system is responsible for all types of rejection, but each type is carried out through a different mechanism.

Hyperacute Rejection

Hyperacute rejection can occur immediately after transplantation, resulting in rapid graft failure. It is thought to be caused by an acute antigen-antibody reaction. Pre-existing antibodies circulate to the donor organ where they begin an antigen-antibody reaction on the vascular endothelium. This is followed by endothelial cell damage, platelet aggregation, and fibrin formation. The ischemic

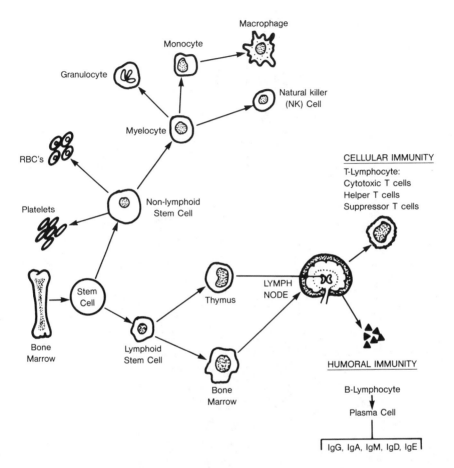

Figure 10-2 The differentiation of cells destined to perform specific and nonspecific immune responses. Cellular components of blood begin as stem cells, which differentiate into nonlymphoid and lymphoid stem cells. Two different pathways are then followed: The nonlymphoid blood cells develop into platelets, RBCs, and nonlymphoid WBCs including granulocytes, monocytes (macrophages), and natural killer cells. The lymphoid stem cells follow a different pathway. Influenced by the thymus, the T-lymphocytes become a population of small lymphocytes responsible for cell-mediated immunity. The B-lymphocytes, thought to be influenced by bone marrow, can then become plasma cells capable of humoral immunity or antibody synthesis. *Source*: Adapted from *Immunology: Basic Processes*, 2nd ed., by J.A. Bellanti, p. 48, with permission of W.B. Saunders Company, © 1985.

damage that results leads to inevitable loss of the graft.[36] This reaction can occur so rapidly that graft survival can be measured in minutes. Careful ABO typing and screening for preformed donor specific antibodies is important in the prevention of hyperacute rejection.

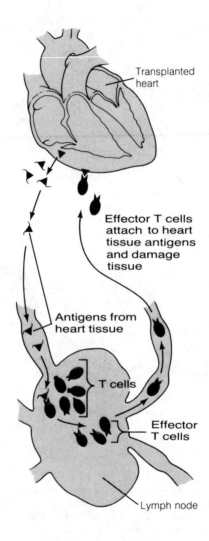

Figure 10-3 Role of cell-mediated immunity in transplant rejection. When an organ is transplanted into another person who is not an identical twin, the HLA antigens on the donor tissue cells are recognized as foreign, and T-lymphocytes of the recipient become sensitized to them. This sensitization is initiated by antigenic stimulation of T-cells in the lymph nodes, and results in the formation of effector T-cells that circulate to the transplanted heart, where they attach to the antigens on the donor cells and attempt to destroy the cells through cell-mediated immunity. The ability of T-cells to respond in this fashion is weakened by immunosuppressive drug therapy. *Source*: Reprinted from *Human Anatomy and Physiology*, 2nd ed., by A.P. Spence and E.B. Mason, p. 565, with permission of Addison-Wesley Publishing Company, Inc., © 1983.

Acute Rejection

Episodes of acute rejection occur sporadically, with the incidence decreasing over time. Cellular mediated immunity is thought to be most responsible for acute rejection, although other cells such as macrophages and killer cells (K-cells) are involved. The cellular response is mobilized within hours post-transplantation, and is followed by a humoral reponse from B-cells, which occurs over a few weeks.[37]

It is thought that T-cells can kill transplanted cells directly, and this is why they are considered the most important mechanism of rejection. The effector T-cells, while traveling throughout the body, will come upon foreign antigens and combine with them. Some effector T-cells can lyse and destroy cells that have antigen on their surfaces. Others secrete lymphokines, which destroy incompatible cells and recruit macrophages.[38] The macrophages and K-cells, which are thought to be another T-cell subset, require antibodies, so their effort is delayed. However, when the B-cells have produced antibodies to the transplanted organ, the antibodies plus complement and other WBCs also have a part in the destruction of the organ.

It is difficult to predict which recipients will experience acute rejection episodes and how often. Some never do, while others have frequent occurrences.

There are usually no early signs and symptoms of rejection. The patient may feel fine until heart failure occurs. Signs and symptoms during moderate to severe rejection may include fever, lethargy, atrial or ventricular arrhythmias, pericardial rub, and signs of heart failure such as hypotension, decreased cardiac output, and an enlarged heart on chest x-ray.[39]

The introduction of the transjugular endomyocardial biopsy (EMB) by Caves in 1973 enabled transplant physicians to diagnose rejection in the early stages when it can be successfully managed. The bioptome is advanced through the right jugular vein into the RV (Figure 10-4).Three to five tissue samples are obtained from the ventricular septum and sent to the pathology department. The tissue samples are rated on a scale from no rejection to mild, moderate, and severe rejection. The changes vary from occasional WBCs to extensive perivascular infiltration of lymphocytes, interstitial edema, and myocyte necrosis.

Preparing the patient for EMB is similar to preparation for other invasive vascular procedures. Generally, a sedative is ordered and other medications, food, and fluids are held until after the procedure. A preprocedure scrub to the right neck or right groin may be ordered. Patients rarely complain of discomfort during or after the procedure, but they often are anxious during the hours they await biopsy results.

Routine nursing care after the procedure includes site observation, activity limitation for 4 to 6 hours, and frequent vital sign measurement. Cardiac and respiratory assessment is performed to observe for the rare complications of cardiac tamponade, hemothorax, and pneumothorax.

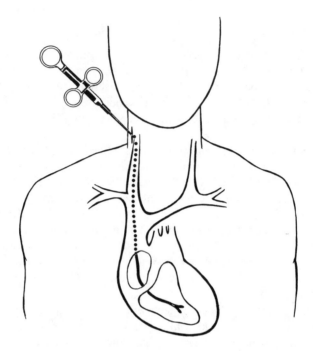

Figure 10-4 Technique for transjugular EMB to detect acute rejection.

The immunosuppressive regimen is adjusted according to the results of the biopsy. Moderate rejection is commonly treated with "pulse" doses of steroids. One gram of methylprednisolone may be given intravenously (IV) or 100 mg of prednisone may be given orally for a few successive days. More severe episodes of rejection may be treated with antithymocyte globulin (ATG). After treatment, the biopsy is generally repeated after a few days to a week. The frequency varies according to institutional protocol and the individual patient. Biopsies are usually done once a week for the first 6 weeks post-transplantation since acute rejection is most likely to occur during the first 60 days.[40] Biopsies are then done at progressively longer intervals provided the patient's condition is stable. In patients who develop scarring of the jugular vein or anatomy, which makes this approach difficult, the femoral vein is used as an alternative approach.

The first rejection episode may be emotionally traumatic to patients and their families. Reassurance by the nurse can help patients put it into a realistic perspective. Patients need to be reassured that rejection is common, and is almost always effectively treated with medication.

Chronic Rejection

Another type of rejection can occur over time as a result of immunologic injury to the endothelial membrane of the transplanted organ. This chronic form of rejection appears as a panvasculitis, which affects the proximal coronary arteries and the distal vessels as well. The intimal hyperplasia that occurs can narrow the coronary vessels dramatically.[41] Chronic rejection may not be related to the frequency of acute rejection episodes, and may not be modified by cyclosporine. It is detected through a full cardiac catheterization and coronary arteriogram that is done yearly after transplantation. Transplant recipients do not develop angina during cardiac ischemia because the heart is denervated. Because of its extremely diffuse nature, the only treatment for severe chronic rejection is retransplantation.[42] In addition to the low cholesterol diet, antiplatelet agents, usually aspirin and dipyridamole, are prescribed post-transplantation because they reduce the incidence of coronary atherosclerosis.[43]

Immunosuppressive Drug Therapy

There are many theories pertaining to which drugs and what doses constitute optimal immunosuppressive therapy post-transplantation. The four agents commonly used are azathioprine, prednisone, antithymocyte globulin, and cyclosporine.

Azathioprine (Imuran)

Azathioprine was introduced in 1961, and is a derivative of the antimetabolite 6-mercaptopurine. It interferes with DNA synthesis and affects rapidly replicating cells. After transplantation, the most actively dividing cells are those of the lymphoid system. Thus the drug acts as an immunosuppressive agent by inhibiting lymphocyte proliferation and activity, including that of T-cells. Azathioprine also inhibits myeloproliferative cells and can cause bone marrow depression, most commonly resulting in a decreased WBC count. Its effect on the mucosal cells of the gastrointestinal (GI) tract can also lead to GI problems in some patients.[44]

Since cyclosporine became available, some transplant programs have used azathioprine only in patients who cannot tolerate cyclosporine. It is common in other centers to use azathioprine in conjunction with cyclosporine and prednisone (''triple therapy'') so that lower doses of cyclosporine can be used, minimizing the toxic side effects.[45]

Prednisone

Prednisone was added to azathioprine immunosuppression in 1962. Its action as an immunosuppressive is not well defined. The drug's major action is anti-inflammatory, but it is also thought to have a lympholytic effect, which inhibits small sensitized lymphocytes. Steroids, usually 250 mg to 1 g of methylprednisone are given intraoperatively, and doses are then tapered to a maintenance dose. "Pulse therapy" with high doses of steroids given IV or orally may be administered to treat episodes of acute rejection.

There are multiple actual and potential side effects and complications associated with long-term steroid use. Cardiac transplant patients are monitored carefully for fluid and electrolyte disturbances, osteoporosis, loss of muscle mass, peptic ulcers, dermatologic problems, psychosis, steroid-induced diabetes, cataracts, and infection.[46,47]

Antithymocyte globulin

Introduced in 1967, ATG is an antisera containing antibodies that recognize T-lymphocytes and destroy them through complement-dependent lysis. It is produced by injecting human lymphocytes into a horse, rabbit, or other animal. The IgG antibodies the animal produces are then separated from the serum and processed so they will be tolerated.[48] The resultant globulin is given intramuscularly (IM) or IV along with diphenhydramine hydrochloride (Benadryl) to prevent anaphylaxis. Severe muscle pain and fever are commonly experienced after IM injection. Patients often require morphine or meperidine hydrochloride (Demerol) for pain relief and acetaminophen for relief of fever.

Some centers reserve the use of ATG as "rescue ATG," which is used only to treat acute rejection. Other centers routinely use ATG to prevent rejection. In additon to the potential complications of serum sickness and anaphylaxis, the use of ATG and cyclosporine together may be associated with an increased incidence of lymphoma in transplant recipients.[49]

A monoclonal antibody ATG has recently become available for use in transplant recipients. Orthoclone OKT3 is a monoclonal antibody of the IgG class that is generated from hybridoma technology. Mouse spleen cells immunized with human T-lymphocytes produce an antibody that can block the killing action of T-cells directed against the transplanted organ. Clinical studies are being conducted to determine the effectiveness and potential side effects of this more specific immunosuppressant.[50]

Cyclosporine (Sandimmune)

Cyclosporine, a fungus-derived metabolite, was first introduced as an immunosuppressant in 1978. It acts selectively to inhibit T-cells. It is thought to prevent the function of the early activation mediators of T-cells, such as the acquisition of receptors for interleukin 2 and interleukin 1 (IL-2 and IL-1).[51] Since cyclosporine interferes with the triggering of T-cells at an early stage of antigenic stimulation, it effectively suppresses the cell-mediated immunity responsible for allograft rejection (Figure 10-5).[52] Without the mediator substances, there can be no proliferation of T-cell clones, and no subsequent appearance of cytotoxic T-cells. The advantage that cyclosporine brings to immunosuppressive drug therapy is its ability to inhibit these T-cells without disarming the entire

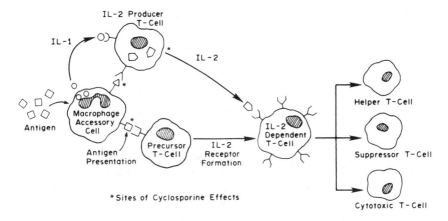

Figure 10-5 Cyclosporine is thought to inhibit the expression of IL-2 receptors by helper T-cells, preventing proliferation of cytotoxic T-cells. It also inhibits the synthesis of IL-1, preventing amplification of the T-cell response. *Source*: Reprinted from *Surgical Clinics of North America*, Vol. 65, No. 3, p. 639, with permission of W.B. Saunders Company, © 1985.

immune system. It has no direct effect on B-cells, macrophages, or polymorphonuclear leukocytes. Because of its preventative effects on the immune mechanism, cyclosporine is used to prevent rather than treat rejection.

Patients receiving cyclosporine have been reported to experience fewer rejection episodes, shorter hospitalization, and better survival when compared with patients receiving "conventional therapy" (azathioprine and steroids), although studies continue to explore immunosuppressive drug therapy with this relatively new agent.[53] It is not usually necessary to use as much prednisone when using cyclosporine, and this decreases the risk of infection.

Cyclosporine is usually administered orally twice a day to cardiac transplant patients. The dose is regulated according to its trough levels in the serum or whole blood. Methods of determining levels vary between transplant centers, and centers have varying therapeutic level goals. A loading dose may be given preoperatively, and oral doses are preferable since the IV form is very nephrotoxic. Patients receiving the drug are monitored closely for renal problems and hypertension. Other complications may include hepatotoxicity, neurotoxicity, gingival hyperplasia, hirsutism, vascular thrombosis, and lymphoma.[54]

Long-term evaluation has shown that nephrotoxicity is the most frequent and severe complication of the drug. Cardiac transplant patients also have a high incidence (60% to 90%) of persistent hypertension, which may require intensive and combined antihypertensive regimens.[55]

In order to prevent acute renal failure in the immediate postoperative period, some cardiac transplant patients are routinely given triple therapy. Other centers may use ATG and/or azathioprine instead of cyclosporine.[56] Patients with preoperative elevations in serum creatinine and liver function studies are most likely to receive less cyclosporine in the initial postoperative period. Their kidney and liver problems are generally reversible, but care must be taken to avoid the nephrotoxic and hepatotoxic effects of high-dose cyclosporine in the immediate postoperative period.

Patients who develop chronic renal failure and severe hypertension in the late postoperative period may be phased off cyclosporine completely, and placed on azathioprine and prednisone.[57] In these patients, the summation voltage of serial ECGs may be compared to monitor for rejection. Summation voltage is calculated by adding the height in millimeters of the peak deflections of the QRS complexes in leads I, II, III, V_1, and V_6. A 10% to 20% decrease in summation may indicate acute rejection in patients receiving conventional immunosuppressive therapy.[58]

The use of a flow sheet to monitor responses to immunosuppressive drugs can be helpful in recognizing dangerous trends in renal function, hepatic function, WBC count, body weight, and BP. A flow sheet that includes the most important parameters related to laboratory values, vital signs, and drug doses can be initiated the day of the transplant and continued as part of the patient's follow-up care after discharge. Many key indicators of problems will continue to be monitored for the rest of the patient's life.

Recognition and Prevention of Infection

Prevention of infection is another major goal of both medical and nursing care. Immunosuppressive drug therapy is maintained at effective levels to prevent unnecessary suppression of the immune system. Drugs with the least effect on normal defense mechanisms are preferred. Yet the possibility of a life-threatening infection is always present after transplantation.

Early mobilization in the immediate postoperative period is important in preventing pulmonary infections, which are common and can be life threatening.[59] Tubes and monitoring lines are discontinued as soon as possible to decrease access routes for infectious organisms. Meticulous care of IV sites and incisions is carried out. The number of people in contact with the patient is kept to a minimum.

There is a trend toward liberalizing the traditional reverse isolation. Many centers follow the Centers for Disease Control recommendations for the severely compromised patient: (1) a private room, (2) careful handwashing with an antiseptic agent, and (3) wearing of masks. Some centers recommend masks only for those who may have an upper respiratory tract infection. A study of cardiac transplant patients with and without complete isolation found no difference in infection rates.[60]

Infections are most common during the first few months after transplantation when the patient is most immunosuppressed. Bacterial infections occur most frequently in the beginning, followed by viruses, fungi, and protozoa.[61-64] Major organisms commonly seen in transplant recipients are listed in Exhibit 10-5. Since pulmonary infections can be very serious, any fever, rise in WBC count, or infiltrate on a chest x-ray is carefully investigated. Sputum is cultured and may involve transtracheal aspiration, percutaneous transpulmonary needle biopsy, or open lung biopsy.[65] If a respiratory tract infection is confirmed, appropriate antimicrobial agents are administered, and the patient is carefully monitored for respiratory insufficiency and septicemia.

Viral infections continue to be a threat as recovery progresses. Viral titres for common viruses are analyzed periodically and compared with preoperative titres to identify developing problems. After discharge, patients are expected to monitor themselves carefully for any sign or symptom of infection. If suspicious signs or symptoms develop, the patient will be readmitted to the hospital for careful monitoring and specific diagnosis.

In addition to the increased risk of infection, all transplanted patients receiving immunosuppressive drugs have an increased risk of cancer. This risk increases with time and seems to be highest in cardiac transplant recipients because of the high levels of immunosuppressive therapy.[66] It is thought that there is impairment of immunosurveillance for mutant cells arising from somatic mutation or viral

---

Exhibit 10-5 Common Infections in Transplant Recipients

Bacterial
  Escherichia coli
  Enterococcus
  Klebsiella
  Pseudomonas
  Serratia
  Staphylococcus
  Streptococcus
  Legionella
  Nocardia
Viral
  Cytomegalovirus
  Herpes simplex
  Herpes zoster
  Varicella zoster
  Epstein-Barr virus
Fungal
  Aspergillus
  Candida
  Cryptococcus
Protozoal
  Pneumocystis carinii
  Toxoplasma

infestation. The cardiac transplant recipient may be less able to resist oncogenic viruses such as Epstein-Barr virus and cytomegalovirus, which have been associated with lymphoma and skin cancer.

Because of the risk of cancer, patients are advised to avoid excessive ultraviolet radiation and to check their skin and mucous membranes for unusual growths. Patients are also instructed on palpation of cervical, axillary, and inguinal lymph nodes.

REHABILITATION AND LONG-TERM FOLLOW-UP

Exercise

Cardiac rehabilitation is an important part of the recovery from transplant surgery. Many patients are cachectic and debilitated with very low activity levels before surgery. Physical therapy is begun as soon as possible after the surgery. General strengthening exercises are combined with activities specific to the recovery from cardiac surgery. Most patients are ready to begin progressive activity within a day or two post-transplantation. Patients ambulate around the intensive care unit with appropriate assistance as soon as they are able. After transfer from the intensive care unit, patients may begin cardiac rehabilitation with a walking and/or biking program while they recover in the hospital.

The importance of a regular exercise program continues after recovery from the acute phase. An exercise regimen helps decrease the muscle wasting that can occur from long-term steroid therapy. In addition, a regular exercise program is part of the life style program that will slow the atherosclerotic process that can occur over time in the transplanted heart.

The patient's response to exercise differs from other cardiovascular surgical patients because the heart has been denervated. Since there is no autonomic control, the cardiovascular response to exercise depends mainly on the release of catecholamines. The pulse is generally faster at rest, and a slower response to exercise is observed as the patient's catecholamine level begins to rise. BP rises with exercise because of the increased peripheral vascular resistance. Cardiac output and ejection fraction increase with aerobic exercise, first because of the augmentation in preload, and later because of the increase in catecholamines. Drugs that block the central effects of catecholamines such as propanolol may limit exercise capacity in some recipients.[67]

Implications for nursing management of the patient's exercise program include providing instruction on forms of appropriate exercise and the best way to carry out the exercise program. Because of the delay in cardiovascular response, it is particularly important to include a warm-up and cool-down phase during exercise. Before strenuous activity, patients can be advised to carry out arm, thoracic, and lower extremity exercises such as marching in place and flexing ankles.

After strenuous exercise it is recommended that the pace be slowed for 5 to 10 minutes before the activity is stopped, and that a cool-down exercise such as seated stretching be used.

Nutritional Management

Before surgery many patients receive nutritional therapy aimed at reversing their compromised nutritional status and preventing postoperative complications. Anorexia and impaired digestion and absorption are common and may necessitate liquid nutritional supplements and total parenteral nutrition.

In the immediate postoperative period, nutritional support continues to meet the increased requirements of postoperative recovery plus the accelerated protein catabolism induced by corticosteroids. Postoperative renal dysfunction, liver dysfunction, steroid-induced diabetes, and fluid retention may require carefully planned dietary therapy.

Long-term goals include the maintenance of ideal body weight and a reduced intake of saturated fats to minimize graft atherosclerosis. A 2-g sodium diet is also advised because of the sodium and fluid retention caused by corticosteroid therapy.[68]

The same patients who were encouraged to eat preoperatively often have difficulty limiting their appetite postoperatively. After recovery from the surgery, excessive weight gain is common, and most patients require continuing dietary counseling to minimize it.

Long-Term Follow-Up Care

Close monitoring for rejection, complications of immunosuppressive drug therapy, and infection continues indefinitely. Patients are scheduled for routine biopsy procedures according to previous biopsy results and a protocol. After discharge, recipients do not require overnight hospitalization for a biopsy. Routine stress tests, radionuclide studies, and a yearly cardiac catheterization are scheduled. Routine clinic visits are necessary periodically between these procedures to monitor laboratory work, BP, and body weight, and to assess for other problems.

Psychological tasks continue to appear, and psychological problems are common after the surgery. Depression and mood alterations, increased family and marital stress, difficulties returning to work, body image alterations, chronic pain, impotence, and problems with compliance (especially overeating) have been reported.[69,70] These problems may be seen during the initial hospitalization and/or later on in the recovery. Counseling services are used by some centers in follow-up care. A support group for cardiac transplant patients and their families can effectively enhance both learning and psychological adjustment.[71] Sharing concerns related to health maintenance and life style modifications can be helpful to both patients and their families.

Despite the challenges faced by cardiac transplant patients, most report the quality of their lives to be good to excellent.[72] Nursing assessment and intervention regarding the patient's concerns and problems can do much to promote a positive adjustment. Patients' family members may also require individual or group counseling. Transplant recipients become very focused on themselves after months of constant attention from family members and health professionals. These families may need counseling as they move toward resuming normal relationships.

As patients return for clinic visits and follow-up procedures, the continuous relationships provided by nurses can be a source of psychological support. Nurse coordinators can also recognize subtle changes in health status, perform a focused assessment, and design a plan of intervention to minimize problems. In the follow-up care as well as in the initial evaluation, nurse coordinators assume a pivotal role in patient assessment and collaboration with the many other health professionals involved with these patients. The nurse's role in teaching, emotional support, coordination of care, identification of problems, and facilitation of medical intervention continues to be as important in long-term follow-up as it was during the critical phase surrounding the transplant surgery.

NOTES

1. Arnold G. Diethelm, "Transplantation," *Bulletin of the American College of Surgeons* 70, no. 1 (January 1985):57

2. Catherine Hoe Harwood and Christine V. Cooke, "Cyclosporine in Transplantation," *Heart and Lung* 14 (1985):529.

3. G. Arnaud Painvin et al., "Cardiac Transplantation: Indications, Procurement, Operation, and Management," *Heart and Lung* 14 (1985):484.

4. Kathleen L. Grady, "Development of a Cardiac Transplantation Program: Role of the Clinical Nurse Specialist," *Heart and Lung* 14 (1985):491.

5. Michael H. Schatzlein, "The Case for De-Centralization," *Journal of Heart Transplantation* 4, no.4 (July/August 1985):378.

6. William A. Baumgartner et al., "Heart and Heart-Lung Transplantation: Program, Development, Organization, and Initiation," *Journal of Heart Transplantation* 4, no. 2 (February 1985):199.

7. James M. Levett and Robert B. Karp, "Heart Transplantation," *Surgical Clinics of North America* 65 (1985):613.

8. R.M. Bolman, III, et al., "Cardiac Transplantation without a Prospective Crossmatch," *Transplantation Proceedings* 17, no. 1 (February 1985):209.

9. T.A.H. English et al., "Selection and Procurement of Hearts for Transplantation" *British Medical Journal* 228 (1984):1889.

10. "Matching Systems to be Unified under UNOS Contract with HHS," *North American Transplant Coordinators Organization Newsletter* 8, no. 2 (December 1986):6.

11. Levett and Karp, "Heart Transplantation."

12. Joseph A. Bellanti, *Immunology III* (Philadelphia: W.B.Saunders Co., 1985), p.399.

13. D.K.C. Cooper and R.P. Lanza, eds., *Heart Transplantation* (Boston: MTP Press Limited, 1984), p. 78.

14. Bellanti, *Immunology III*, p. 398.

15. Levett and Karp, "Heart Transplantation."

16. Painvin et al., "Cardiac Transplantation."

17. Jamie Goldsmith and Cheryl M. Montefusco, "Nursing Care of the Potential Organ Donor," *Critical Care Nurse* 5, no. 6 (November/December 1985):25.

18. Goldsmith and Montefusco, "Nursing Care."

19. Suzette Cardin and Suzanne Clark, "A Nursing Diagnosis Approach to the Patient Awaiting Cardiac Transplantation," *Heart and Lung* 14 (1985):500.

20. Paula Jarzemsky, "Nursing Care of the Patient with Dilated Cardiomyopathy," *Critical Care Nurse* 6, no. 2 (March/April 1986):14.

21. O.H. Frazier et al., "Nutritional Management of the Heart Transplant Recipient," *Journal of Heart Transplantation* 4, no. 4 (July/August 1985):450.

22. Virginia C. O'Brien, "Psychological and Social Aspects of Heart Transplantation," *Journal of Heart Transplantation* 4, no. 2 (February 1985):229.

23. Francois M. Mai and June Burley, "Psychosocial Aspects of Heart Transplantation," *Transplantation Today* 2, no. 1 (February 1985):21.

24. Laurel Gunderson, "Teaching the Transplant Recipient," *Journal of Heart Transplantation* 4, no. 2 (February 1985):226.

25. Levett and Karp, "Heart Transplantation."

26. Marjorie Funk, "Heart Transplantation: Postoperative Care during the Acute Period," *Critical Care Nurse* 6, no. 2 (March/April 1986):30.

27. Eduardo Solis and Michael P. Kaye, "The Registry of the International Society for Heart Transplantation: Third Official Report—June 1986," *Journal of Heart Transplantation* 5, no. 1 (January/February 1986):2.

28. Bartley P. Griffith et al., "Temporary Use of the Jarvik-7 Total Artificial Heart Before Transplantation," *New England Journal of Medicine* 316 (1987):130.

29. R. Rex Dietz et al., "Characteristics of the Transplanted Heart in the Radionuclide Ventriculogram," *Journal of Heart Transplantation* 5, no. 2 (March/April 1986):116.

30. Funk, "Heart Transplantation."

31. Robert L. Hardesty, "Sequential AZA/CSA Therapy with RATG and Low Dose Steroids for Cardiac Transplantation," *Transplantation & Immunology Letter* 3, no. 3 (October 1986):3.

32. Bellanti, *Immunology III*, p. 7.

33. Mary Frances Jett and Larry E. Lancaster, "The Inflammatory-Immune Response: The Body's Defense Against Invasion," *Critical Care Nurse* 3, no. 5 (September/October 1983):74.

34. Jett and Lancaster, "Inflammatory-Immune Response."

35. Cooper and Lanza, *Heart Transplantation*, pp. 88–89.

36. Bellanti, *Immunology III*, p. 399.

37. Cooper and Lanza, *Heart Transplantation*, pp. 88–89.

38. Calvin R. Stiller, Paul A. Keown, and F.N. McKenzie, "Heart Transplantation: Immunologic Considerations," *Transplantation Today* 2, no. 1 (February 1985):12.

39. Levett and Karp, "Heart Transplantation."

40. Mitchell H. Goldman et al., "Cyclosporine in Cardiac Transplantation," *Surgical Clinics of North America* 65 (1985):644.

41. Cooper and Lanza, *Heart Transplantation*, pp. 243–248.

42. Baumgartner et al., "Heart and Heart-Lung."

43. Painvin et al., "Cardiac Transplantation."

44. John S. Najarian, "Immunologic Aspects of Organ Transplantation," *Hospital Practice* 17, no. 10 (October 1982):65.

45. R. Morton Bolman, III, et al., "Improved Immunosuppression for Heart Transplantation," *Journal of Heart Transplantation* 4, no. 3 (May 1985):315.

46. Cooper and Lanza, *Heart Transplantation*, p. 275.

47. Najarian, "Immunologic Aspects."

48. Ibid.

49. Goldman et al., "Cyclosporine."

50. G. Goldstein et al., "Orthoclone OKT3 Treatment of Acute Renal Allograft Rejection," *Transplantation Proceedings* 17, no. 1 (February 1985):129.

51. Goldman et al., "Cyclosporine."

52. Harwood and Cook, "Cyclosporine."

53. Solis and Kaye, "Registry Report."

54. Goldman et al., "Cyclosporine."

55. J.Rottembourg et al., "Renal Function and Blood Pressure in Heart Transplant Recipients Treated with Cyclosporine," *Journal of Heart Transplantation* 4, no. 4 (July/August 1985):404.

56. David C. McGriffin, James K. Kirklin, and David G. Naftel, "Acute Renal Failure After Heart Transplantation and Cyclosporine Therapy," *Journal of Heart Transplantation* 4, no. 4 (July/August 1985):396.

57. Bartley P. Griffith et al., "Management of Cyclosporine Toxicity by Reduced Dosage and Azathioprine," *Journal of Heart Transplantation* 4, no. 4 (July/August 1985):410.

58. William A. Baumgartner et al., "Cardiac Homo-Transplantation," *Current Problems in Surgery* 16, no. 9 (September 1979):28.

59. Funk, "Heart Transplantation."

60. Norma Hess et al., "Complete Isolation: Is It Necessary? " *Journal of Heart Transplantation* 4, no. 4 (July/August 1985):458.

61. Cooper and Lanza, *Heart Transplantation*, pp. 198–200.

62. Robert W. Emery and Jack G. Copeland, "Heart Transplantation in Arizona," *Journal of Heart Transplantation* 4, no. 2 (February 1985):205.

63. Jack G. Copeland et al., "Heart Transplantation," *Journal of the American Medical Association* 251 (1984):1564.

64. Levett and Karp, "Heart Transplantation."

65. Emery and Copeland, "Heart Transplantation."

66. Colleen Duncan, "De Novo Cancer in Transplant Recipients," *Transplantation Today* 2, no. 1 (February 1985):32.

67. Levett and Karp, "Heart Transplantation."

68. Frazier et al., "Nutritional Management."

69. Mary Jean McAleer et al., "Psychological Aspects of Heart Transplantation," *Journal of Heart Transplantation* 4, no. 2 (February 1985):232.

70. Mary E. Lough et al., "Life Satisfaction Following Heart Transplantation," *Journal of Heart Transplantation* 4, no. 4 (July/August 1985):446.

71. Barbara J. Hyler, Mary C. Corley, and Dale McMahon, "The Role of Nursing in a Support Group for Heart Transplantation Recipients and Their Families," *Journal of Heart Transplantation* 4, no. 4 (July/August 1985):453.

72. Lough et al., "Life Satisfaction,"

REFERENCES

Baumgartner, William A.; Borkon A. Michael; Achuff, Stephen C.; Baughman, Kenneth L.; Traill, Thomas A.; and Reitz, Bruce A. "Heart and Heart-Lung Transplantation: Program, Development, Organization, and Initiation." *Journal of Heart Transplantation* 65 (1985):197–202.

Bellanti, Joseph A. *Immunology III*. Philadelphia: W.B. Saunders Co., 1985.

Cooper, D.K.C., and Lanza, R.P., eds. *Heart Transplantation*. Boston: MTP Press Limited, 1984.

Levett, James M., and Karp, Robert B. "Heart Transplantation." *Surgical Clinics of North America* 65 (1985):613–634.

Painvin, G. Arnaud. "Cardiac Transplantation: Indications, Procurement, Operation, and Management." *Heart and Lung* 14 (1985):484–489.

SUGGESTED READINGS

Cardin, Suzette, and Clark, Suzanne. "A Nursing Diagnosis Approach to the Patient Awaiting Cardiac Transplantation." *Heart and Lung* 14 (1985):499–504.

Funk, Marjorie. "Heart Transplantation: Postoperative Care During the Acute Period." *Critical Care Nurse* 6 (1986):27–45.

McAleer, Mary Jean. "Psychological Aspects of Heart Transplantation." *Journal of Heart Transplantation* 4 (1985):232–233.

Solis, Eduardo, and Kaye, Michael P. "The Registry of the International Society for Heart Transplantation: Third Official Report—June 1986." *Journal of Heart Transplantation* 5 (1986):2–5.

Chapter 11

Mechanical Treatment of the Failing Heart

Susan Quaal, RN, MS, CVS, CCRN

During the past three decades, considerable progress has been made in the development of mechanical devices that augment, supplement, and replace the native heart. The value of such an effort can best be appreciated from an estimation of patients who could benefit from cardiac assistance or replacement, which has been placed at 165,000 annually by the Heart Failure Study Group.[1] Designs of mechanical assistance devices are numerous; engineering complexity increases exponentially as their purpose expands from temporary support to permanent replacement of the native myocardium as a pump.

Recipients of mechanical assistance are heterogeneous with varying ages, etiologies, and severities of myocardial dysfunction. The spectrum of cardiac assist modalities under development permits the selection of the most appropriate, and perhaps most cost-effective, technique for each patient. Temporary mechanical assist devices allow natural healing or surgical procedures to reverse the ravages of a failing myocardial pump; these devices range from intra-aortic balloon counterpulsation (IABC) to left and right ventricular assist devices (VADs) and the total artificial heart (TAH) employed as a bridge to heart transplantation. Permanent support devices are designed to maintain lifelong cardiac circulation when the patient's heart disease is irreversible and death is imminent.

IABC is the most widely used modality of mechanical assistance. Pulsatile assist devices, percutaneous insertion techniques, modification of balloon designs and consoles for pediatric adaptation, and pulmonary artery counterpulsation (PAC) have greatly expanded clinical applications. Logical progression of mechanical assistance in the form of intravascular volume displacement has extended to true implantable extra- and intracorporeal blood pumps. Left and right VADs are now readily available to wean patients from cardiopulmonary bypass, to rest the myocardium during cardiogenic shock, and as a bridge to cardiac transplantation.

Nursing care of patients requiring cardiac mechanical assistance necessitates application of the principles of cardiac physiology used in caring for any critically ill cardiac patient. Special measures unique to each device employed also need to be implemented. Expanded nursing responsibilities, for example, include an understanding of the effect of IABC on the arterial pressure waveform, how to assess proper patient interfacement, understanding blood flow through a VAD with proper care of lines and monitoring for blood loss and trauma to red blood cells (RBC).[2] Implantation of the TAH demands expanded dimensions in nursing care such as learning to interpret compressed air waveforms as indicators of filling and emptying of the artificial ventricles. Certainly these patients have emotional and psychologic needs that require empathy, insight, and understanding from the cardiovascular nurse. Mechanical assistance therefore affords the nurse a most challenging opportunity for practicing nursing both as science and art.

MYOCARDIAL PUMP FAILURE: WHY THE NEED FOR MECHANICAL ASSISTANCE?

Devices and Indications

A major challenge facing cardiovascular researchers is to elucidate a molecular basis for heart failure. Primary pathophysiologic mechanisms of myocardial failure have been suggested and offer a link to understanding why drugs such as isoproteronol, dopamine, and dobutamine may prove ineffective in improving cardiac function. Thus far, research has not discovered a method for replacing or regenerating sarcomeres. Pharmacologic advancements are noteworthy, but not curative. Mechanical assistance is therefore an essential component of the armamentarium for advanced cardiac therapies. To understand fully the benefits of each progressive modality of mechanical assistance, the clinical picture of left ventricular (LV) failure necessitating mechanical assistance must be reviewed.

A self-perpetuating cycle of progressive LV dysfunction is characteristic of the cardiogenic shock syndrome. Goals of treatment are directed toward increasing cardiac output (CO), decreasing myocardial work and oxygen demands, increasing myocardial oxygen supply, and reducing myocardial ischemia.

However, despite the impressive cadre of pharmacologic interventions, limitations exist in their capacity to reduce myocardial oxygen demands and to improve myocardial contraction. Intra-aortic balloon pumping is the first line of cardiac assist devices that may further reduce oxygen demands and enhance circulation, but this counterpulsation device is contingent on a left ventricle that is able to contract and sustain some degree of cardiac output independent of balloon counterpulsation. If the left ventricle is severely depressed and needs to be totally but temporarily relieved of the workload associated with left ventricular contraction, a left ventricular assist device (LVAD) may be employed, thus allowing the left ventricle time to rest and recover.

A decision as to when to use pharmacologic therapy, IABC, or VAD can perhaps be better understood by reviewing Figure 11-1. Persistent LV failure after IABC support has been initiated is characterized as mean blood pressure (BP) <60 mmHg, cardiac index <1.8 L/min, pulmonary artery wedge pressure (PAWP) >20 mmHg.[3]

Persistent LV failure may necessitate advancement to a VAD or even a total artificial heart. Such a scenario could occur after acute myocardial infarction,

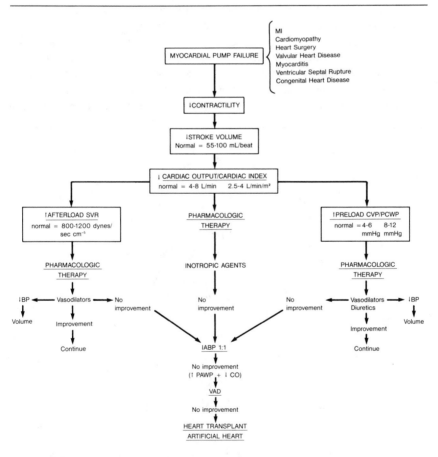

Figure 11-1 Schematic for classification of severity of pump failure and application of IABC. PAWP, pulmonary artery wedge pressure; BP, blood pressure; SVR, systemic vascular resistance; CO, cardiac output; IABC, intra-aortic balloon counterpulsation; VAD, ventricular assist device. *Source*: Adapted from *Critical Care Nurse*, Vol. 6, No. 2, p. 54, with permission of Hospital Publications, Inc., © March/April 1986.

as a bridge to heart transplantation, or for the patient who has undergone coronary artery bypass surgery. Improvements in materials, designs, fabrications, and prosthetics have brought about clinically acceptable cardiac assist devices. Each of these is presented.

INTRA-AORTIC BALLOON COUNTERPULSATION

Balloon Insertion Techniques

A distensible nonthrombogenic balloon mounted on a vascular catheter is inserted via the femoral artery and passed in a retrograde fashion into the descending thoracic aorta, just distal to the left subclavian artery. Insertion may be through a direct arteriotomy incision into the femoral artery (Figure 11-2) or percutaneously. With direct arteriotomy, a Dacron graft is sutured to the femoral artery, facilitating insertion and avoiding interruption of blood flow to the extremities.[4] Inability to insert the balloon catheter via a femoral arteriotomy has

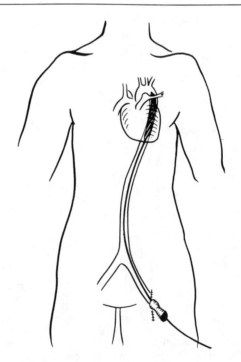

Figure 11-2 IAB is inserted via a femoral arteriotomy graft and positioned in the descending thoracic aorta. *Source*: Reproduced by permission from *Comprehensive Intra-Aortic Balloon Pumping* by S.J. Quaal, p. 79, St. Louis, © 1984, The C.V. Mosby Company.

occurred in 28% to 29% of attempted insertions.[5,6] In these cases, the percutaneous method is preferred; Figure 11-3 illustrates this technique.[7] This method allows for guidewire insertion and provides for injection of contrast medium through the inner percutaneous balloon catheter, which promotes insertion into a tortuous or obstructed femoral vessel.

The balloon catheter extends outside the insertion site and is attached to the balloon pump console equipped with R-wave detector triggering circuitry and helium or carbon dioxide driving gas, which phasically pulses the intra-aortic balloon (IAB) with the cardiac cycle. Figures 11-4 to 11-7 illustrate the various types of balloon pump consoles available for clinical use. Each manufacturer (Aries, Datascope, Kontron, and Mansfield) offers an abundance of instructional

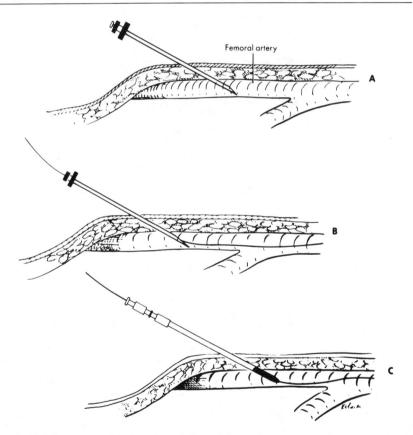

Figure 11-3 Percutaneous IAB insertion technique: *A*, femoral artery punctured percutaneously with 18-gauge angiographic needle; *B*, guidewire advanced, 18-gauge needle removed, and femoral artery dilated; *C*, dilator (12F) inserted over guidewire leaving only sheath in situ. Percutaneous balloon inserted through sheath. *Source*: Reproduced by permission from *Comprehensive Intra-Aortic Balloon Pumping* by S.J. Quaal, p. 123, St. Louis, © 1984, The C.V. Mosby Company.

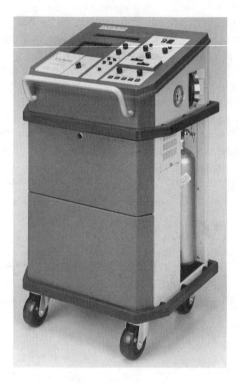

Figure 11-4 Aries Model 700 Control System Intra-Aortic Balloon Pump. *Source*: Courtesy of Aries Medical, Inc., Woburn, Massachusetts.

services. The operator should be thoroughly familiar with the features of the pump console in use before assuming responsibility for interfacing counterpulsation to the patient.

During insertion of the balloon, the nurse's role will vary depending on the organizational structure of the hospital. If a balloon pump team is in place, team members may be organized to handle necessary duties of organizing supplies, preparing the sterile fields, assembling a transducer and associated hemodynamic software, prepping the patient's groin, and moving the balloon pump console from storage to the patient's room, operating room, or catheterization laboratory. Such organization of a team, where resources are available, or alternatively functional statements for staff nursing roles is highly encouraged. Regardless of whether the patient's staff nurse assumes technical duties, it is imperative that the nurse monitor hemodynamic status before, during, and after insertion. The nurse must also have an in-depth understanding of counterpulsation and its resultant effect on the arterial pressure waveform as described below.

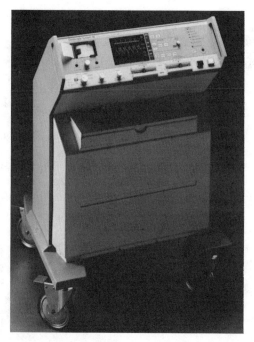

Figure 11-5 Datascope System 90 Intra-Aortic Balloon Pump. *Source*: Courtesy of Datascope Corp., Paramus, New Jersey.

Physiology of Intra-Aortic Counterpulsation

Inflation of the IAB during diastole and deflation during isovolumetric contraction is termed *counterpulsation* (Figure 11-8). Despite clinical evidence supporting the beneficial effects of IABC, the underlying mechanisms and basis for hemodynamic improvements are not clearly elucidated.[8] Inflation of the 40-60-cc adult balloon during diastole augments or elevates intra-aortic pressure; blood volume in the aorta is actively displaced proximally and distally. Hence the counterpulsation effect of balloon inflation-deflation is *volume displacement*. Aortic and systemic perfusion is potentially increased because the blood volume displaced by balloon inflation imparts momentum to the column of blood in the aorta. Normally, runoff into the peripheral tissues continues well into diastole under the head of pressure generated by systolic ejection; this process is termed *Windkessel Effect*.[9] Balloon inflation in diastole augments this intrinsic Windkessel effect.

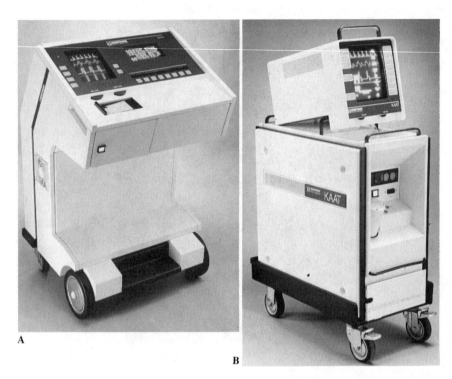

Figure 11-6 Kontron Intra-Aortic Balloon Pumps: **A**, System 2000; **B**, KAAT Transport Pump. *Source*: Courtesy of Kontron Cardiovascular, Inc., Everett, Massachusetts.

Is Coronary Artery Perfusion Improved by Balloon Inflation in Diastole?

Coronary perfusion is "potentially" increased with balloon inflation, but this now seems to be dependent on the degree of vasodilitation already present in the coronary artery beds. Myocardial ischemia is a potent stimulus for increasing blood flow and oxygen delivery to the myocardium through the autoregulated process of coronary vasodilatation. If the coronary arteries are already maximally dilated, little, if any, improvement in coronary flow will occur with balloon inflation in diastole.[10]

Autoregulatory vasodilatation of coronary vessels is, however, impaired by atherosclerosis. Augmentation of coronary perfusion pressure by balloon inflation in diastole may therefore afford some improvement in coronary perfusion through atherosclerotic coronary arteries and has been shown to facilitate collateral pathways of perfusion.[11]

Coletti and co-workers[12] observed the effect of balloon counterpulsation in improving coronary artery perfusion during the course of open chest cardiopul-

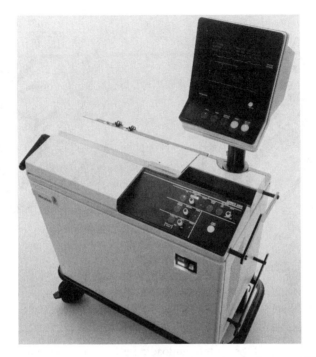

Figure 11-7 Mansfield Scientific Intra-Aortic Balloon Pump. *Source*: Courtesy of Mansfield Scientific, Mansfield, Massachusetts.

monary resuscitation (CPR). They measured the effect of balloon counterpulsation on coronary blood flow (CBF) during open resuscitation of five mongrel dogs, in which ventricular fibrillation (VF) had been induced. Manual cardiac compression was applied through a left lateral thoracotomy at 100 compressions per minute. CPR restored CBF to 30% of the prearrest CBF. Addition of IABC resulted in restoration of normal aortic pressure and nearly 60% of the prearrest CBF.

Physiologic Benefit of Intra-Aortic Balloon Deflation During Isovolumetric Contraction

By deflating the IAB during isovolumetric contraction, the intra-aortic end-diastole pressure is transiently lowered. This reduces the pressure the LV must generate to move its load of stroke volume out through the aortic valve. Thus, the resistance, or afterload, component of ventricular systole is reduced, and myocardial oxygen consumption is lowered. Research is ongoing to assess the potential benefits of deflation during various points of isovolumetric contraction and early systole.

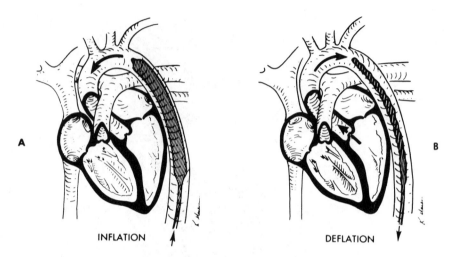

A   INFLATION   DEFLATION   B

Figure 11-8 The nonthrombogenic balloon is positioned in the descending aorta: *A*, inflated with helium or carbon dixoide during diastole; *B*, deflated during systole. *Source*: Reproduced by permission from *Comprehensive Intra-Aortic Balloon Pumping* by S.J. Quaal, p. 80, St. Louis, © 1984, The C.V. Mosby Company.

Akyurekli[13] studied the systolic unloading effects of balloon deflation during isovolumetric contraction, independent of diastolic augmentation. The coronary perfusion pressure was lowered to produce acute cardiac failure. When IABC was instituted, systolic unloading, as evidenced by decreased LV systolic pressure, was observed at normotensive states only. Employment of IABC in profound hypotensive states did not produce systolic unloading or reduce oxygen consumption.

A plausible explanation for this lack of systolic unloading in hypotensive states is that the aortic wall becomes compliant during hypotension. Balloon inflation into a compliant aorta does not effect the needed augmentation of aortic pressure. Rather, the aorta has been observed to move with balloon inflation. Consequently, unloading after deflation does not occur.[14] The combination of dobutamine and IABC, however, seems to offer a hemodynamic gain.[15] Dobutamine elevates BP, which affords the physiologic vascular integrity needed to augment aortic pressure in diastole and reduce afterload in isovolumetric contraction.

Interfacing Intra-Aortic Balloon Counterpulsation with Patient Hemodynamics: Conventional Timing

All balloon pump manufacturers employ safety mechanisms that prohibit inflation of the IAB during peak systole, which would deleteriously increase myocardial workload and oxygen consumption. "Conventional timing"[16] is first presented whereby the balloon console determines inflation for each cardiac cycle by assessing an average of the intervals of previous cycles.

Figure 11-9 illustrates the familiar arterial pressure waveform. Note the landmark of systole, dicrotic notch, which denotes closure of the aortic valve, diastole, and end-diastolic pressure. Contrast this to Figure 11-10, which illustrates the impact of balloon inflation and deflation on the native arterial pressure waveform. Diastolic pressure elevates above all other pressure during balloon inflation,

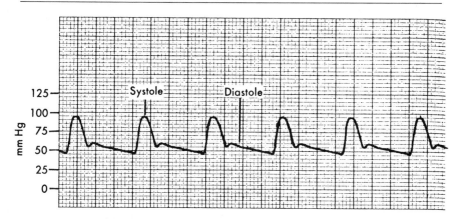

Figure 11-9 Normal arterial pressure waveform. *Source*: Reproduced by permission from *Comprehensive Intra-Aortic Balloon Pumping* by S.J. Quaal, p. 153, St. Louis, © 1984, The C.V. Mosby Company.

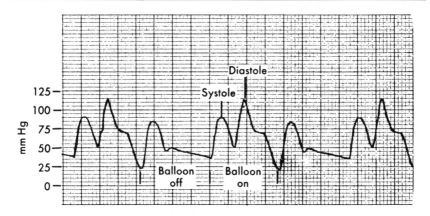

Figure 11-10 Comparison of arterial pressure waveform without balloon assistance (Balloon off) and with 2:1 counterpulsation (Balloon on). *Source*: Reproduced by permission from *Comprehensive Intra-Aortic Balloon Pumping* by S.J. Quaal, p. 153, St. Louis, © 1984, The C.V. Mosby Company.

hence the term "peak diastolic augmented pressure." Balloon inflation displaces blood in the aorta proximally and distally. With this displacement, pressure in the aorta falls. Therefore, upon deflation, the aortic end-diastolic pressure is lower than the native aortic end-diastolic pressure in which blood volume (and pressure) remains in the aorta. Note the difference in arterial pressure waveform morphologies when the balloon inflates and deflates with every other heartbeat (Fig 11-11). It is imperative that the augmented beat (heartbeat and resultant arterial pressure waveform impacted by balloon inflation) is compared with the patient's native beat to assure proper counterpulsation. The term "patient" precedes the components of the arterial pressure waveform not affected by balloon inflation-deflation and "assisted" is used before labeling the components of the waveform affected by counterpulsation.

The intent is for balloon inflation to occur during physiologic diastole, immediately after closure of the aortic valve. Physiologically, aortic valve closure actually occurs before the appearance of the dicrotic notch on the subclavian or radial arterial pressure waveform. This is because of the delay in transmission of aortic valve closure, as a mechanical event, through the fluid-filled, catheter-plumbing system to the transducer. Proper inflation, which allows for this delay, occurs when the dicrotic notch assumes a V-shaped configuration.

Proper deflation is recognized by two landmarks on the arterial pressure waveforms: assisted systole must be lower than patient systole; and assisted aortic end-diastolic pressure must be lower than patient aortic end-diastolic pressure.

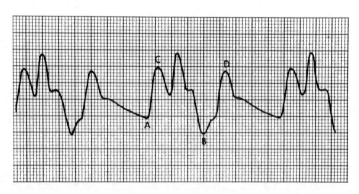

Figure 11-11 Proper balloon inflation-deflation on 2:1 assistance ratio: *D*, assisted systole is lower than *C*, patient systole, and *B*, assisted aortic end-diastolic pressure is lower than *A*, patient aortic end-diastolic pressure. *Source*: Reproduced by permission from *Comprehensive Intra-Aortic Balloon Pumping* by S.J. Quaal, p. 153, St. Louis, © 1984, The C.V. Mosby Company.

Examples of improper inflation-deflation are illustrated as follows:

Early Inflation (Figure 11-12)

Features. Early inflation seems to encroach on the previous systole. The dicrotic notch is no longer visible because of the early rise of the augmented pressure as the balloon inflates.

Potential for Hemodynamic Penalty. Early inflation can raise the pressure in the aorta, thus closing the aortic valve permanently, which impedes complete emptying of the ventricle. Regurgitation of blood may occur back into the LV. CO may decrease, and intraventricular volume (preload) and pressure may increase.

Late Inflation (Figure 11-13)

Features. Inflation occurs well after aortic valve closure. A plateau appears at the point of the dicrotic notch.

Potential for Hemodynamic Penalty. May lower diastolic augmentation pressure because balloon inflates later in diastole. Coronary perfusion pressure may be reduced.

Early Deflation (Figure 11-14)

Features. Assisted systole is now higher than patient systole. Assisted aortic end-diastolic pressure decreases with balloon deflation. However, this afterload reduction occurs too soon before the next systolic ejection to be of benefit in reducing the pressure that needs to be generated to open the aortic valve.

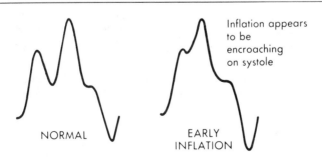

Figure 11-12 Early inflation. *Source*: Reproduced by permission from *Comprehensive Intra-Aortic Balloon Pumping* by S.J. Quaal, p. 148, St. Louis, © 1984, The C.V. Mosby Company.

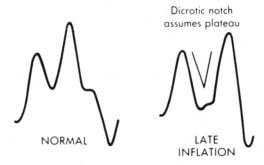

Figure 11-13 Late inflation. *Source*: Reproduced by permission from *Comprehensive Intra-Aortic Balloon Pumping* by S.J. Quaal, p. 148, St. Louis, © 1984, The C.V. Mosby Company.

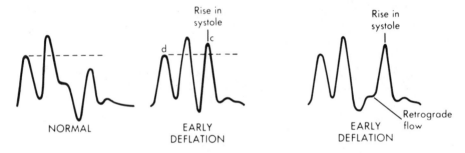

Figure 11-14 Early deflation. The decrease in aortic end-diastolic pressure occurs too soon to reduce work of next systole. Assisted systole may rise *c*, in comparison with patient systole, *d*. *Source*: Reproduced by permission from *Comprehensive Intra-Aortic Balloon Pumping* by S.J. Quaal, p. 148, St. Louis, © 1984, The C.V. Mosby Company.

Potential for Hemodynamic Penalty. Afterload may not be decreased. Myocardial oxygen consumption is not reduced. This premature drop in assisted aortic end-diastolic pressure is nonphysiologic. Because of the time delay before the next systolic ejection, retrograde flow may occur from the coronary, cerebral, or renal arteries in an attempt to restore the aortic end-diastolic pressure to its baseline. Retrograde perfusion can be identified by a plateau on the upstroke of the next assisted systole.

Late Deflation (Figure 11-15)

Features. Balloon deflation occurs in competition with the next systolic beat. There is no reduction in assisted aortic end-diastolic pressure (there is insufficient time for this to occur).

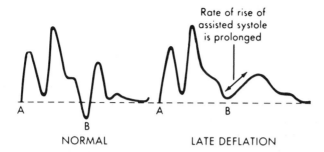

Rate of rise of
assisted systole
is prolonged

A
B
NORMAL

A
B
LATE DEFLATION

Figure 11-15 Late deflation. *Source*: Reproduced by permission from *Comprehensive Intra-Aortic Balloon Pumping* by S.J. Quaal, p. 149, St. Louis, © 1984, The C.V. Mosby Company.

Potential for Hemodynamic Penalty. The LV must eject against this resistance of a partially inflated IAB. Isovolumetric contraction is prolonged, and myocardial oxygen consumption is increased. The rate of rise of assisted systole may be prolonged because of the increase in resistance to pressure buildup in the LV.

Analysis of Electromechanical Data to Achieve Timing: An Alternative to Conventional Timing

Tyson and associates[17] at Duke University modified a Kontron Model 10 balloon pump to allow control by an external microprocessor. Temporary pacing wires were placed in the patient, and deflation was triggered by the ventricular pacing spike. Inflation was set to occur at a fixed interval after deflation. Thus deflation was timed rather than inflation, which is the format of conventional timing. Timing of deflation is based on the concept that the interval from QRS to the onset of ejection and duration of systolic ejection are relatively constant for all rhythms. With this method, the IAB is actively deflating as ejection begins and is fully inflated at aortic valve closure.

Triggering of deflation by a pacemaker signal was studied in eight post–coronary artery bypass grafting patients. Atrial fibrillation occurred in two, atrial or ventricular ectopy in three, and skeletal muscle shivering in one. During these electrocardiographic (ECG) disturbances, conventional timing was inaccurate and counterpulsation frequently was ineffective. Timing deflation with a pacemaker signal (ECG) provided correct diastolic deflation for 100% of cardiac cycles. Mean diastolic aortic pressure increased, cardiac output increased slightly, and LV stroke work decreased as ventricular unloading occurred. These researchers suggested that early systolic deflation assisted LV ejection through an active transfer of energy from the balloon to the ejecting column of blood.

Literature Synthesis on Experience with Intra-Aortic Balloon Counterpulsation

Most attention has been focused on counterpulsation for patients with refractory LV failure. Bregman[18] recently reviewed indications for balloon pumping in 196 patients: 71 were balloon pumped because of intraoperative low CO; 16 for postoperative low CO; 4 for postoperative cardiac arrest; 37 for unstable angina; 21 for postinfarction angina; 18 for anesthesia support; 13 for cardiogenic shock; 5 for cardiac arrest; 4 for acute ventricular septal defect complicating myocardial infarction (MI); 1 for recurrent ventricular tachycardia; and 6 for unsuccessful percutaneous transluminal coronary angioplasty.

Of the 105 patients in whom an IAB was successfully inserted for medical indications, 79 (75%) underwent a cardiac surgery procedure, and 26 (25%) were treated medically. Fifty-six of the 91 patients (62%) who required intraoperative or postoperative IAB support died. Only 13 of the 79 patients (16%) who underwent preoperative intra-aortic balloon pumping followed by surgery died.

Goldman[19] studied the effects of IAB pumping in patients who deteriorated into cardiogenic shock after the sudden onset of ventricular septal defect (VSD) as a complication of MI. Peak hemodynamic improvement occurred within the first 24 hours of counterpulsation. Counterpulsation reduced afterload so that stroke volume was more easily moved out of the aortic valve rather than shunting through the VSD. The level of hemodynamic stability gained permitted cineangiography and further assessment of the VSD.

Complications

Insertion and removal of the IAB, the period of balloon pumping, and post-removal all carry potential for complications:[20]

During balloon insertion:

- compromised circulation to lower extremities
- dissection of aorta
- dislodgment of plaque.

While balloon and catheter are in descending thoracic aorta and iliac-renal arterial system:

- emboli to head, upper or lower extremities, kidneys, gastrointestinal tract, spinal column

- thrombosis associated with prolonged immobilization
- thrombocytopenia
- infection
- rupture of aorta
- compromised circulation to leg
- compromised circulation because balloon positioned too high (into left sub-clavian artery) or too low (occluding mesenteric and/or renal arteries)
- gas emboli from balloon rupture
- bleeding from insertion site, intravenous and invasive monitoring sites, and stress ulcer
- inability to wean
- improper timing of inflation/deflation
- intensive care psychosis.

During removal of balloon:

- dislodgment of plaque or emboli
- bleeding at site of insertion.

After removal:

- recurrence of LV failure
- thrombosis
- emboli.

Complications do not seem to be related to duration of counterpulsation.[21] One patient is reported to have been balloon pumped for 327 days with a single balloon catheter implant. No complications were reported.[22] Vascular complications of IABC occur predominantly in patients with sclerotic peripheral arteries when peripheral circulation is further compromised by the indwelling balloon catheter. Limb ischemia secondary to balloon catheter placement was reported as a complication in 16% to 35% of all balloon-pumped patients.[23]

Of 45 patients who died after insertion of an IAB, 16 had one or more of the following complications: dissection of the aorta or its distal branches, arterial perforation, arterial thrombi, arterial emboli, and/or local wound infection.[24] A more recent study itemized complications after 637 cases pumped over 11 years as wound infections (0.2%), vascular complications (10.4%), and balloon failure (1.3%).[25] Assessment for potential complications is further reflected in the nursing care plan (Table 11-1).

Table 11-1 Nursing Care Plan for the Patient Requiring IABC

Nursing Diagnosis	Expected Patient Outcomes	Nursing Interventions
Potential for injury: hematologic abnormalities, anemia, and thrombocytopenia related to: 1. Mechanical trauma of inflation disrupts platelet integrity 2. Blood loss during balloon insertion/frequent blood sampling 3. Patients often heparinized to reduce threat of thrombus formation at insertion site.	No anemia, thrombocytopenia, hemorrhaging.	1. Guaiac all stools/N/G returns. Observe for bleeding mucous membranes/skin bruising. 2. Attempt to minimize lab work drawn. 3. Assure a unit of blood is on hand at all times. 4. Record all blood losses, including milliliters of blood samples drawn. 5. Monitor platelet count daily: hemoglobin, hematocrit, prothrombin time, partial thromboplastin time. 6. Replace platelets/RBCs as lab work indicates and per physician.
Potential for infection related to: 1. Number of indwelling catheters/invasive procedures 2. Patient debilitated/immunosuppressed.	No infection: patient afebrile; no leukocytosis; invasive catheter sites free from redness, swelling, tenderness, drainage; negative cultures.	1. Culture any drainage: blood cultures and antibiotics per physician. 2. Care of catheter insertion sites meticulously per hospital procedure.
Alteration in peripheral tissue perfusion related to: 1. Occlusion of femoral artery by catheter or thrombus 2. Peripheral embolization 3. Transient arterial spasm.	Adequate peripheral perfusion to leg where balloon catheter inserted as evidenced by: palpable pulses (or present by Doppler exam); warmth of peripheral extremity; normal color.	1. Record quality of peripheral pulses before insertion to establish baseline: record dorsalis pedalis and posterior tibial pulses. 2. After insertion, note pulses, color, temperature every 15 min, four times every 30 min. 3. If radial arterial line in place, perform Allen tests at least every 4 hr to assess perfusion through radial artery as follows: (1) have patient open hand; palpate ulnar artery; (2) compress ulnar artery; instruct patient to make closed fist; (3) maintain pressure on artery as patient opens fist; hand should flush and regain pink color if perfusion adequate through radial artery (around

Potential for impaired skin integrity related to:

1. Bed rest/immobility
2. Impaired circulation
3. Decreased nutritional intake
4. Sedation/anesthesia.

No dermal ulcers at sacrum; calcaneous/malleolus tuberosity.

indwelling catheter); (4) if patient unable to co-operate, manually close patient's hand into a fist and release while compressing ulnar artery w/ other hand.

1. Turn patient from side to side every 2 hr; straight alignment of leg where balloon inserted.
2. Position patient in protective mattress bed.
3. If skin over bony prominences reddened, apply occlusive opaque dressing according to manufacturer's directions.
4. Good skin care; proper cleaning after bowel movements.
5. Passive range-of-motion exercises.
6. Provide adequate calories/protein.

Alteration in CO: decreased, related to LV failure

1. Improved LV function: reduced SVR, pulmonary artery and PAWP; increased CO.
2. Adequate urine output.
3. Improved mixed venous P_{O_2}.
4. Skin warm and dry.
5. Patient alert and oriented.
6. No chest pain.
7. Decreased dosage of cardiotonic drugs needed.
8. Chest auscultation free of rales.
9. No cardiac dysrhythmias.

1. Monitor hemodynamic measurements every 30 min until patient stabilizes, then every hour, increasing to every 2–3 hr w/ improvement; measure urine output every hour.
2. Vital signs/ECG monitoring according to unit protocol.
3. Monitor blood gases/venous O_2 saturation at least every 8 hr, more frequently if abnormal.
4. Follow physician's orders for medications.

Potential for sleep disturbance related to:

1. Sleep latency
2. Noise level of ICU
3. Unfamiliar environment

Patients have 4 hr uninterrupted sleep; will say they feel rested.

1. Organize nursing care to allow for blocks of time for "sleep therapy."
2. At night, turn down bright lights.
3. Provide for comfort measures.

continues

Table 11-1 continued

Nursing Diagnosis	Expected Patient Outcomes	Nursing Interventions
4. Necessity for performing nursing procedures 24 hr day 5. Immobility/lack of privacy.		4. Allow patient to participate in decisions of care when possible. 5. Frequently reorient patient to surroundings, date, time. 6. Discuss sleeping patterns with patient before admission.
Potential for ineffective family member coping; compromised, related to: 1. Fear of patient not recovering 2. Frightening environment 3. Seeing loved one strapped w/ tubes/lines 4. Disruption of life/schedule 5. Financial burden imposed by patient's hospitalization; often family needs to stay close to hospital (away from home), which causes added financial burden 6. Feeling of helplessness in aiding patient's recovery.	1. Family acknowledges concerns/anxieties. 2. Family conveys they understand meaning/goals of patient's care plan (including balloon counterpulsation). 3. Family able to cope effectively w/ patient's illness and demonstrates adaptive, goal-directed behaviors.	1. Afford thorough explanations to family regarding patient's treatment/care. 2. Prepare family before first visit to bedside so they understand tubes/lines in patient (pictures are helpful). 3. Assure family that tubes/lines are normal part of patient's comprehensive critical care. 4. Encourage family to communicate questions/express feelings. 5. Keep family apprised of changes in patient's condition. 6. At change of shift, oncoming nurses should introduce themselves to family.

Source: Adapted by permission from *Comprehensive Intra-Aortic Balloon Pumping* by S.J. Quaal, pp. 235–240, St. Louis, © 1984, The C.V. Mosby Company.

PULMONARY ARTERY COUNTERPULSATION

Right ventricular (RV) failure secondary to RV infarction and after implementation of IAB pumping has been documented.[26] After LV decompression by an IAB pump or (with severe failure) a LVAD, RV filling pressures may elevate, thus unmasking RV failure.[27] RV infarction, pulmonary hypertension, cardiopulmonary bypass, and implantation of an IAB or LVAD may all be followed by RV failure. When RV failure occurs, left-sided CO will also decrease, as the two ventricles are in a series circuit arrangement. Volume loading and inotropic drug infusions may improve RV output, but if these measures fail, mechanical support must be implemented. Although IABC has been employed for many years, research and clinical trials with PACs have been performed in patients in whom right-sided heart failure developed after cardiac surgery.[28]

The pulmonary balloon is placed within a tubular graft, which functions as a reservoir, anastomosed to the main pulmonary artery. The tip of the balloon must extend slightly beyond the pulmonary artery graft suture line to avoid tearing of the friable anastomosis by the vibrations created by counterpulsation.[29] Pulmonary artery balloon placement by an open chest technique is illustrated in Figure 11-16. Figure 11-17 illustrates pulmonary artery pressures before and during counterpulsation. The average augmentation of pulmonary artery pressure during diastole is 5 mmHg, with a presystolic unloading pressure of 4 to 5 mmHg. Placement of the pulmonary artery balloon via percutaneous technique has also been successfully accomplished; research continues on the designing of balloons specifically for pulmonary artery insertion and improvement of placement technique.

Interfacing PAC to the patient's hemodynamics can easily be accomplished by transferring principles of intra-aortic counterpulsation to that of the pulmonary artery. The pulmonary artery tracing replaces the arterial line for assessing proper inflation and deflation. The patient who requires PAC may already have IABC support. Thus, two balloon pump consoles will be required to maintain PAC concomitantly.

The efficacy of PAC has been evaluated in a pig model.[30] Right ventricular CO increased from 519 ± 76 to $1,117 \pm 110$ mL/min. Right atrial pressure decreased from 15.5 ± 0.9 to 10.7 ± 1.00 mmHg. During VF, PAC did not improve RV output. These findings suggest that PAC is effective in the management of RV failure. However, this approach is indeed limited by the need to perform a sternotomy to anastomose a graft into the pulmonary artery. Thus research is ongoing to design and evaluate a percutaneously inserted pulmonary artery balloon.

VENTRICULAR ASSIST DEVICES

Physiology

Mechanical left or right VADs replace the work of the failing ventricle by mimicking the action of the native, contracting ventricle. Oxygenated blood is

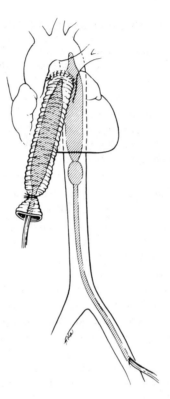

Figure 11-16 Schematic of balloon positioned in aorta and pulmonary artery. *Source*: Reprinted from "Pulmonary Artery Balloon Counterpulsation for Acute Right Ventricular Failure" by C.D. Miller et al. in *Journal of Thoracic and Cardiovascular Surgery*, Vol. 80, No. 5, p. 760, with permission of The C.V. Mosby Company, © 1980.

diverted from either the left atrium or LV to the artificial pump and is then reperfused back into the arterial circulation through a cannula placed in the aorta. The VAD can capture the entire CO with the biologic heart remaining in situ and can be activated either synchronously or asynchronously and therefore is not dependent on native heart function.

The effectiveness of VAD is primarily the result of the pump's ability to reduce ventricular ejection impedance during biologic systole and to eject blood during biologic diastole. VAD function therefore can best be appreciated as an integrated combination of a biologic and a prosthetic pump system. During biologic systole, blood is diverted from the natural ventricle into the VAD. In biologic diastole, the VAD pumps blood back into the circulation through a cannula placed into the aorta (Figure 11-18). Hence, counterpulsation occurs: the VAD is in diastole while the native ventricle contracts and vice versa.

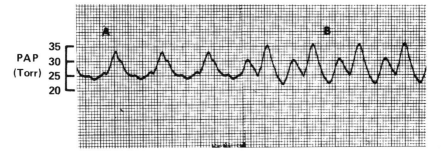

Figure 11-17 *A*, pulmonary artery pressure. *B*, pulmonary artery pressure reflecting counterpulsation and augmentation of pulmonary artery pressure in diastole. *Source*: Reprinted from "Pulmonary Artery Balloon Counterpulsation for Acute Right Ventricular Failure" by C.D. Miller et al. in *Journal of Thoracic and Cardiovascular Surgery*, Vol. 80, No. 5, p. 760, with permission of The C.V. Mosby Company, © 1980.

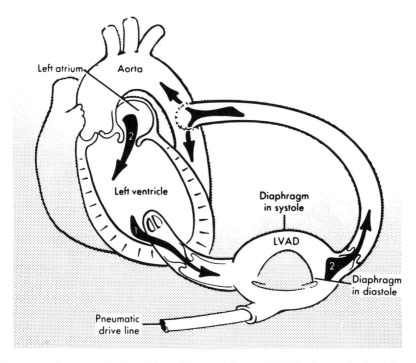

Figure 11-18 Synchronized blood flow with natural heart and LVAD. *Source*: Reprinted by permission from *Comprehensive Intra-Aortic Balloon Pumping* by S.J. Quaal, p. 335, St. Louis, © 1984, The C.V. Mosby Company.

Indications

Patients who cannot be weaned from cardiopulmonary bypass despite volume loading, inotropic support, and IABC may be candidates for VAD. Gaines and Pierce[31] suggested that patients with a cardiac index less than 1.8 L/min/m², systolic BP below 90 mmHg, and left atrial pressure greater than 25 mmHg are candidates for VAD. LVADs have also been used as interim support for patients awaiting cardiac transplantation. Future applications include percutaneous insertion, which may allow support of other patients in cardiogenic shock.

Types

Several designs have been developed through intensive animal research at centers such as Texas Heart Institute, Cleveland Clinic, University of Utah, and Boston Children's Hospital in conjunction with Harvard University, Pennsylvania Medical Center at Hershey, and Stanford University.

Ventricular assist pumps are of three principle designs: roller pumps, centrifugal pumps, and pneumatic (air-driven). Roller pumps are occlusive, propelling blood forward by compressing the tubes containing the circulating blood. Centrifugal pumps consist of two magnetic cones, which rotate to propel the blood forward in a circular motion, generating centrifugal force, pressure, and flow. Pneumatic pumps consist of a bladder- or saclike device that houses the blood diverted from the patient's left atrium or left ventricle. Pulsatile air compresses the bladder, which moves the blood forward. A representation of various models of VAD is presented but is not intended to be inclusive or to indicate a preference for one device over the other.

Roller Pump

The Litwak device[32] (Figure 11-19), from Mt. Sinai Hospital in New York, is a nonpulsatile pump that consists of atrial and ascending aorta silicone elastomer cannulas and polyester suturing skirts. One skirt is sutured into the left atrium, and the second is inserted into the lateral aspect of the ascending aorta. One important feature of this device is that the left atrial cannulation is performed from the right side of the aorta. The distal ends of both cannulas are positioned subcutaneously in the upper abdominal wall and are connected to a simple extracorporeal circuit since the blood returning from the left atrium has already been oxygenated.

A roller pump is interposed between the left atrium and the ascending aorta, which steadily returns diverted blood into the ascending aorta. Maximum flow capacity is approximately 6 L/min. Ventricular preload is reduced as blood volume is diverted from the left atrium into the Litwak device. An integral

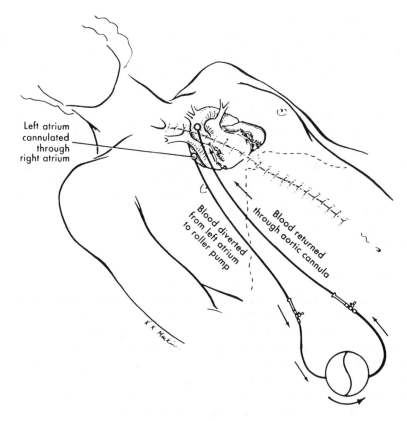

Left atrium
cannulated
through
right atrium

Blood diverted
from left atrium
to roller pump

Blood returned
through aortic cannula

Figure 11-19 Litwak VAD. *Source*: Reprinted with permission from *New England Journal of Medicine*, Vol. 291, p. 1342, © 1974, Massachusetts Medical Society.

component of this device is that the procedure can be discontinued without reopening the chest. The cannulas are simply obturated and the abdominal wound closed. Infections of these obturators have occurred and have required reoperation for removal.

Litwak et al.[33] recently reported their clinical experiences with this VAD in 27 patients with life-threatening LV dysfunction who could not be separated from conventional coronary bypass. IABC had first been tried in 21 patients but could not sustain circulatory support. Flow rates of 1.5 to 6.0 L/min achieved immediate hemodynamic stability in 26 patients. One third remained VAD dependent and died. Two-thirds were weaned from the VAD, but 50% of these patients also died of recurrent low CO. Nine of the 27 patients were discharged, but 2 in this group later died: 1 from mediastinitis several weeks postoperatively, and the other from recurrent MI 10 weeks postoperatively. The duration of VAD support in the weaned patients who ultimately died was from 68 to 501 hours (mean 166.3 hours); of the 9 patients discharged, the duration ranged from 43 to 114 hours (mean 57.8 hours). Heparinization was minimal to keep the activated clotting time in the range of 110 to 140 seconds, but if chest tube drainage was excessive, anticoagulation was halted, and the activated clotting time fell to normal levels.

The Litwak pump carries the potential of tubing laceration, through wear and tear in the pump housing and chipping of the plastic microparticles of polyvinyl chloride or polyethylene from the inner surface of the roller pump. Microair embolus orginating from the pump is also possible.

Factors generating blood trauma with roller pumps have been examined.[34] Experiments were performed using various tubing diameters, roller diameters, and degrees of roller occlusion. Results suggest that when roller pumps are used for long-term cardiac support, the diameter of the rollers should be as large as possible, the tubing diameter should be as large as practical, and the occlusion setting should be as open as possible, while still maintaining required flow rates.

Centrifugal Pumps

Kinetic, or centrifugal, pumps are a more recent development.[35] Kinetic energy may be added to a fluid either by rotating it at high speed or by providing an impulse in the direction of flow. This transfer of energy requires a rapidly rotating impeller. Such a design allows for high volumes of blood to be circulated at relatively low pressure, and the pump does not continue to generate pressure when operated against a closed discharge, thus avoiding high line pressure generation, which might disrupt the connectors. If air enters the centrifugal system, it remains with the vortex of the pump and is not expelled into the arterial circulation. The drive console is approximately one-third the size of an IAB pump. Two to three hundred milliliters of blood are housed in the VAD pump and tubing. Flow rate is adjusted on the pump console by increasing the revolutions per minute of the magnet until satisfactory flow rates are achieved.

Golding Centrifugal Pump. Golding[36] and researchers at the Cleveland Clinic modified a technique developed by Zwart that allows rapid, easy access to the ventricle. A single bifurcated synthetic graft is anastomosed to the ascending aorta (Figure 11-20). Two cannulas are then inserted through this graft: one is positioned across the aortic valve into the LV, and the second returns blood into the ascending aorta. The limbs of this graft are brought out to the subcutaneous tissue, which allows for easy removal under local anesthesia once the procedure is terminated. Blood is therefore removed from the centrifugal pump, which provides nonpulsatile flow of blood out through the first cannula into the pump, which reinfuses the blood into the ascending aortic cannula.

Golding and associates[37] have supported 21 patients with this device for a profound, low-output state; 10 were weaned from support, and there were 5 long-term survivors (24%). Characteristics of the survivors were pump support

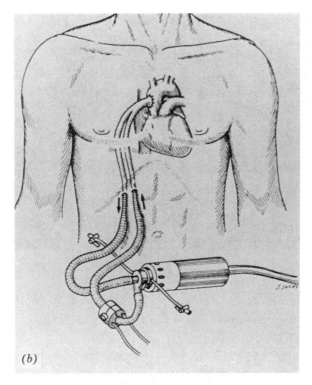

(b)

Figure 11-20 Golding LVAD. *Source*: Reprinted from *Artificial Organs*, Vol. 2, p. 318, with permission of International Society for Artificial Organs, © 1978.

less than 75 hours, RV failure mild or absent, some recovery of LV function within 24 hours, and no evidence of postoperative MI.

Biomedicus Centrifugal Pump. The Biomedicus LVAD works on the same principle as a cyclone. The pumping part of the device is a small, clear, plastic, cone-shaped centrifugal pump that contains rotary blades (Figure 11-21). The valveless rotor cones are made from nonthrombogenic acrylics and impart a circular motion to the blood, generating centrifugal force, pressure, and flow. This hydrodynamically designed flow path of the pump eliminates turbulence, which contributes to air embolism formation and insult to blood elements.

A cannula is placed in the right superior pulmonary vein and advanced to the LV for emptying of the heart. Blood flows into the pump where the blades whir like a fan and spin the blood into the cannula that returns the blood to the ascending aorta. Return blood flow can also be accomplished through a cannula placed in the femoral artery. The console is depicted in Figure 11-22. Various modalities for synchronous or asynchronous assistance are described below.

Figure 11-21 Biomedicus centrifugal LVAD. *Source*: Courtesy of Biomedicus Corp., Eden Prairie, Minnesota.

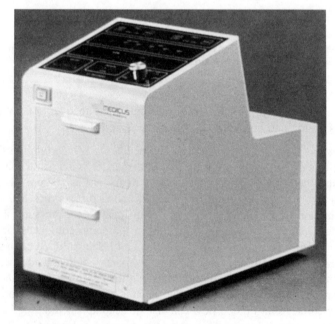

Figure 11-22 Console for Biomedicus. *Source*: Courtesy of Biomedicus Corp., Eden Prairie, Minnesota.

McGovern et al.[38] employed the Biomedicus pump in 21 patients after IAB pumping failed to provide satisfactory support: 5 survived, and 16 did not. Duration of pumping for the survival group averaged 35 hours. All patients were placed on VAD support after unsuccessful attempts to wean off bypass. The survival group averaged one and one half attempts to wean off bypass; the nonsurviving group averaged four. The platelet count for both groups dropped, which required infusion of supplements to maintain the count above 70,000. Serum potassium showed a progressive climb in the nonsurvival group, believed to be the result of multiple organ system failures.

Park[39] reported using this design in 50 patients from July 1980 to July 1986 with a 40% long-term survival rate. Easy application, low cost, minimal damage to blood cells, and satisfactory engineering features provided a very effective means of temporary mechanical assist for patients unweanable from bypass and as a bridge to heart transplantation.

Sactype Pumps

Pierce and associates[40] at Pennsylvania State University, Hershey, designed a sactype blood pump (Figure 11-23), which is a one-piece, seam-free sac made from segmented polyester polyurethane that employs Bjork-Shiley tilting inlet and outlet valves (Figure 11-24). A separate diaphragm is positioned between the side of the housing that receives the air and the blood sac, which thus isolates

Figure 11-23 Thoratec Pierce Donachy Pump. *Source:* Courtesy of Thoratec Corp., Berkeley, California.

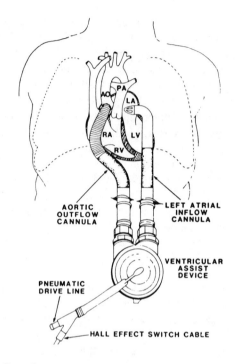

Figure 11-24 Pierce-Donachy sactype pump.

---

the blood sac from the driving air. A pneumatic power unit (Figure 11-25) provides the compressed air driving pressure needed to expand the blood-containing sac and to apply vacuum to allow the sac or blood bladder to collapse during filling. Blood is diverted into the pump from a LV apex or left atrial cannula and is returned into the ascending aorta through a cannula of a woven Dacron graft. Maximum output is 6.5 L/min.

Hill[41] reported his experience with the Pierce-Donachy pump from 1984 to 1986. This device was used in three patients as a bridge to transplantation. Duration of pumping was from 1.6 to 3.6 days. All patients were on IAB assistance. After transplantation, these three patients were discharged at 71, 16, and 15 days.

Results of use at the developing institution were published in conjunction with two case studies from 1976 to 1985.[42] In all instances, the device was employed for patients unweanable from bypass. The survival rate was 14%: 11 received LVAD, 1 RVAD, and 3 biventricular assistance (between 1980 and 1983). Of the nonsurvivors, two died from diffuse bleeding, two from VAD dependence, one from a patent foramen ovale causing cyanotic right-to-left shunt, one from recurrent VSD, one from late mitral insufficiency, and one from subsequent low CO postweaning.

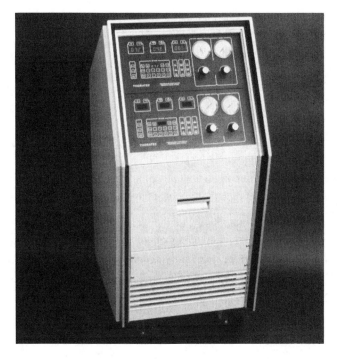

Figure 11-25 Thoratec Pierce Donachy Pump Console. *Source*: Courtesy of Thoratec Corp., Berkeley, California.

Control Modes of Ventricular Assist Devices

The VAD can be operated under three control modes: (1) fixed rate, asynchronous to the heart rate; (2) full-to-empty, and (3) synchronous R-wave. Each of these is discussed in greater detail.[43]

Fixed Rate Asynchronous

This variable stroke volume method is the simplest of the control modes. Only the duration of the cycle is specified but is not synchronized to the ECG. This mode is useful for initiating support and for weaning patients from the device when less than maximal flow rates are desired. It is also used as a backup mode in case other synchronization signals are lost.

Full-to-Empty Asynchronous

This method is offered in response to the blood flow needs of the body and, at the same time, provides a consistent washing of all blood-contacting surfaces in the blood pump to minimize the possibility of thrombus formation. A magnet

(Hall switch) is used to determine when the blood pump is full, which signals the driving console to initiate the ejection phase. Ejection then proceeds for a preset time. After completing ejection, the drive system switches back to the filling cycle to wait for the signal from the Hall switch to indicate that the blood pump is again ready for ejection.

R-wave Synchronous

R-wave counterpulsation synchronizes the VAD to the intrinsic heart rate, resulting in a variable rate and stroke volume control mode. The R-wave of the ECG signals the drive console to end ejection. Pump filling occurs to coincide with biologic systole. Ejection then follows with biologic diastole (counterpulsation), which ends with the next R-wave. The advantage of this mode is that a greater reduction in LV pressure and volume is achieved as well as reduction in myocardial oxygen consumption.[44] Disadvantages include difficulty in controlling filling and ejection with irregular heart rhythms. Also, a complete VAD stroke volume may not be achieved, which inhibits complete washing of the blood-contacting surfaces of the blood pump. A predilection for thrombus formation therefore exists.

Patient Management

It has been our experience that the perfusionist monitors the VAD function and control for flow rate, which, on the average, is between 2 to 4 L/min. Too high flow rates can cause poor VAD filling and collapse of the atrium around the cannula. Assessing for adequate flow rates (evidenced by satisfactory vital signs, hemodynamic pressures, and peripheral perfusion) is most certainly a nursing responsibility as is reflected in the nursing care plan (Table 11-2).[45]

VADs have most frequently been employed for support of LV failure, but bioventricular support has also been used.[46] When this has been required, both biventricular assistance devices and a TAH such as the Akutsu III, Berlin, Jarvik, Liotta/Hall, Pennsylvania State, and Phoenix devices have been employed.[47] The superiority of one technique is unknown. Multiple-center trials with established protocols have not been tried. Therefore, clinical research on both VAD and TAH needs to be ongoing. Accordingly, the American Society of Artificial Internal Organs has established a registry for such evaluation.[48]

A great resurgence in cardiac transplantation exists. Temporary support of a severely depressed heart can be maintained by biventricular VAD or a TAH. Thus these devices seem to have a role in staged transplantation, that is, as a bridge to transplantation. An overview of one clinically used TAH, the Jarvik-7, is presented to conclude this chapter on methods of mechanical assistance.

Table 11-2 Nursing Care Plan for a Patient with a VAD

Nursing Diagnosis	Expected Patient Outcomes	Nursing Interventions
Potential for injury: excessive bleeding related to: 1. Mechanical coagulopathy 2. Need for anticoagulation 3. Cardiopulmonary bypass effects on blood.	Control of bleeding, prevention of coagulopathy	1. Coagulation profiles every 4 hr. 2. Measure/record chest tube loss hourly. 3. Assess stools, urine, N/G suction plan, endotracheal suction for bleeding. Observe for bleeding of mucous membranes/skin bruising. 4. Attempt to minimize lab work drawn.
Potential for infection related to patient's debilitated state, multiple invasive lines, complexity of procedure	No infection: patient afebrile; no leukocytosis; cultures negative; invasive catheter sites free from redness, swelling, tenderness, drainage.	1. Meticulous hand washing. 2. Monitor temperature/WBC count. 3. Clean VAD tubing at exit sites with H_2O_2; apply betadine every 8 hr. 4. Meticulous care to catheter insertion sites per hospital procedures.
Alteration in CO: decreased, due to myocardial depression	Patient able to sustain independent myocardial function, without VAD.	1. Calculate total systemic blood flow every 4 hr by subtracting VAD flow rate from total CO. Thermal dilution CO can be used for LV assistance but is inaccurate with RVAD. 2. Check peripheral pulses, skin, temperature, capillary refill every 1 hr; record vital signs as indicated. 3. Measure direct hemodynamic parameters; calculate indirect parameters of stroke work index systemic and pulmonary vascular resistance as indicated. 4. Monitor hourly intake/output.

continues

Table 11-2 continued

Nursing Diagnosis	Expected Patient Outcomes	Nursing Interventions
		5. Monitor arterial/mixed venous blood gases minimally every 4 hr.
		6. Anticipate inotropic drug support.
Impaired physical mobility due to confinement imposed by severity of illness and VAD	Patient maintained in stable pulmonary function with healthy skin integrity free of dermal ulcers.	1. Since patient may be intubated, follow hospital procedure for pulmonary toilet/maintenance of ventilator. If extubated, no vigorous pulmonary toilet (due to hemodynamic instability of patient). Gentle vibration of chest to mobilize secretions.
		2. If patient not able to be turned completely from side to side, gently rotate patient to provide skin care.
Potential for injury: blood may pool in native ventricle and cause thrombus	No signs of thrombus formation in ventricle; no emboli to other body organs or peripheral circulation.	1. Follow manufacturer's recommendations; anticipate procedure for turning off VAD for 10–20 sec every 20 min to allow native ventricle to contract, thus decreasing stagnation of blood flow/potential for thrombus formation.
		2. Observe tubing to prevent kinks/tension on tubing/cannulas.
Alteration in nutrition due to limited calorie intake	Patient maintained in positive nitrogen balance with normal electrolytes.	1. Monitor weight, electrolytes, intake/output.
		2. Follow orders for parenteral nutrition and/or tube feedings.
		3. Monitor elimination patterns; prevent stool impaction.

Anxiety/alteration in family processes related to disruption of family life, fear of outcome, stressful ICU environment	1. Anxiety lessened. 2. Patient/family understand care given/purpose of LVAD/ICU procedures.	1. Keep patient/family informed, offering kindness and empathy. Allow for questions; offer reinforced learning. 2. Instruct patient/family about purpose of LVAD and how it assists the failing ventricle. 3. Answer family questions honestly about prognosis and treatment options if heart function does not recover. Discuss indications, procedure, and lifestyle changes for heart transplantation, if indicated.

THE TOTAL ARTIFICIAL HEART

Improvements in biomaterials, pump and energy systems, and prosthetic valves and years of observation and animal experiments followed by human implantations have advanced the development of the artificial heart.[49-53] The Jarvik-7 has received FDA approval and has been used for permanent replacement and as a bridge to transplantation in more than 18 patients.

Description

Pneumatically driven, this model was designed in components consisting of right and left hemispherical ventricles; Dacron connections to the remnant atria, pulmonary artery, and aorta called "quick connects;" and four mechanical tilting disk prosthetic valves, which assure laminar flow. Inflow and outflow tracts are angled so as to provide correct alignment with the native vascular structure and to maintain good laminar flow without turbulence or stagnation (Figure 11-26).

Because of the confines of the adult mediastinum, that is, the anatomic position of the atria and the great vessels, the artificial heart is manufactured in two components of the right and left artificial ventricle. The base of each is molded from aluminum or plastic, and the outer housing is molded from polyurethane, reinforced with Dacron mesh. The interior surfaces are formed from segmented polyurethane, which is thromboresistant when adhered to an ultrasmooth surface.

Four layers of polyurethane, each 0.004 inches thick, are used to mold a flexible blood-containing bladderlike chamber, called the diaphragm, which is fitted inside each artificial ventricle (Figure 11-27). This diaphragm separates the blood-occupying space from the compressed-air-occupying space. During systole, compressed air is pulsed into the artificial ventricle, which expands the ventricle and thus pushes the blood forward into the pulmonary artery and aorta. During diastole, the diaphragm collapses as it fills with blood from the atria; the compressed air is exhausted out of the silastic tubing. A gentle vacuum is applied to aid in collapse and filling of the diaphragms.

The right and left ventricular diaphragms are extremely flexible, offering minimal resistance to inflowing blood, yet this polyurethane material (Biomer) is also extremely durable. When maximally expanded, the diaphragm never touches the outer housing, thus preventing hemolysis of RBCs.

With each heartbeat, the diaphragm is expected to attain maximum flexion in end-systole, which is achieved through precise adjustment of the driving pressure of compressed air. This pressure must be of sufficient force to evacuate the end-systolic stroke volume through the higher-than-normal resistances of the artificial valves and the afterload resistances of the systemic and pulmonary arterial circuits.

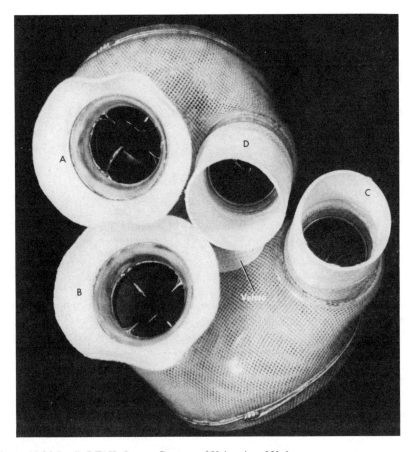

Figure 11-26 Jarvik-7 TAH. *Source*: Courtesy of University of Utah.

Control of the Artificial Heart

Figure 11-28 depicts the electropneumatic control unit called the *Utah Heart Driver*. Eight-foot silastic driveline tubings connect it to an exit port at the base of each artificial ventricle. The tubing is channeled out through the patient's subcutaneous tissue to an exit point at about the level of the umbilicus (Figure 11-29). Control of compressed air through the artificial ventricles is governed by the Utah Heart Driver, achieving expansion of the diaphragm in systole and exhaust of compressed air via the vacuum during diastole. Driveline compressed air pressures range from 145 to 160 mmHg on the left and approximately 50 to 55 mmHg on the right prosthetic ventricle.

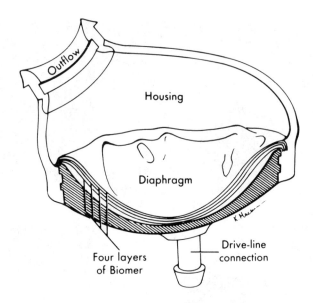

Figure 11-27 Schematic of TAH diaphragm. *Source*: Reproduced by permission from *Comprehensive Intra-Aortic Balloon Pumping* by S.J. Quaal, p. 355, St. Louis, © 1984, The C.V. Mosby Company.

Driveline compressed air pressures are recorded graphically in Figure 11-30. Console pressure transducers generate driveline pressure waveforms for each ventricle, which allows for monitoring proper ejection and filling. Characteristic landmarks the nurse must learn to recognize in the artificial heart recipient are (1) end of diastole; (2) time during which air pressure increases to equal diastolic pressure; (3) ventricular ejection and aortic blood flow; (4) end of ventricular ejection; (5) peak driving pressure (ejection point), which is total emptying of the ventricle and full bladder distension; and (6) complete filling of the ventricle. Driving pressure of compressed air is set at the lowest value that completely empties the ventricle.

If complete emptying of end-diastolic blood volume does not occur, the ventricle is *underdriven*. The driveline pressure curve then lacks the usual peak representative of complete emptying. Clinical signs of underdriving include those of systemic venous overload and/or pulmonary vascular overload attributable to a large end-systolic volume that causes heart failure. Underdriving can be observed with a rise in afterload and outflow obstruction, such as a crack or break in a prosthetic valve, thrombus formation on the valve, and stiffening of the diaphragm from calcification or rupture. Temporary and random driveline pressure curve changes, representative of underdriving, are the result of variations in physiologic changes of the host. For example, exercising, which increases

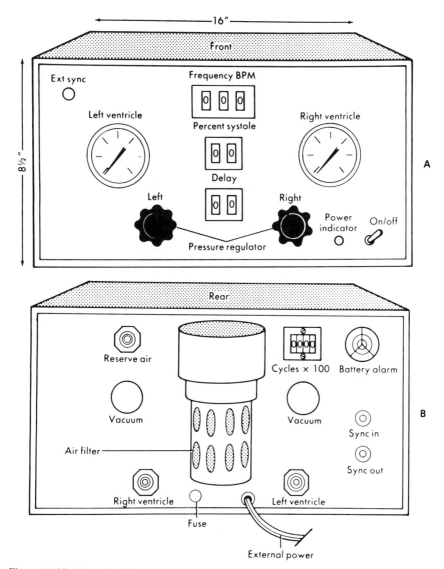

Figure 11-28 Schematic of Utah Heart Driver. *A*, front view; *B*, rear view. *Source*: Reproduced by permission from *Comprehensive Intra-Aortic Balloon Pumping* by S.J. Quaal, p. 361, St. Louis, © 1984, The C.V. Mosby Company.

venous return to the TAH, necessitates a temporary need for increasing the driving pressure to assure complete emptying of the ventricle in systole. Any sudden and progressive underdriving problems should serve as a warning that a potentially catastrophic alteration has occurred.

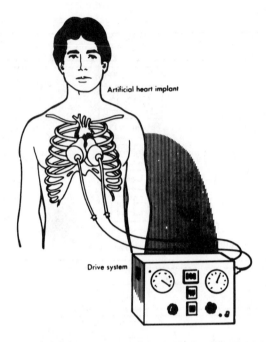

Figure 11-29 Schematic of human implantation of the Jarvik-7 total artificial heart; drivelines are attached to the Utah Heart Driver. *Source*: Reproduced by permission from *Comprehensive Intra-Aortic Balloon Pumping* by S.J. Quaal, St. Louis, © 1984, The C.V. Mosby Company.

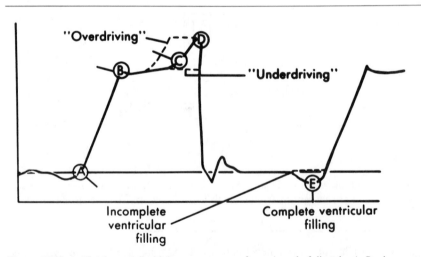

Figure 11-30 Artificial ventricle driving pressure waveform: *A*, end of diastole; *A–B*, air pressure increases to equal diastolic pressure; *B*, ventricular ejection and aortic blood flow; *C*, end of ventricular ejection; *D*, peak driving pressure (ejection point: full emptying of ventricle: bladder fully distended); *E*, full filling of ventricle. *Source*: Reproduced by permission from *Comprehensive Intra-Aortic Balloon Pumping* by S.J. Quaal, p. 362, St. Louis, © 1984, The C.V. Mosby Company.

In contrast, *overdriving*, or excessive drive pressures, appears as a plateau on the end-systolic portion of the driveline waveform. Overdriving is *not* desirable, because this is a nonproductive time of neither emptying nor filling of the ventricles. Systemic hypovolemia, inadequate delivery of the blood to the affected ventricle, or a change in vascular pressure and resistance can contribute to overdriving.

Controlling Heart Rate and Percentage of Systole on the Utah Heart Driver

Control of the Utah Heart Driver is usually maintained by a specially trained technician. Staff nurses are beginning to assume more of this responsibility (see Nursing Care Plan, Table 11-3). Compressed air pressure, heart rate, and the percentage of the cardiac cycle devoted to systole must be adjusted manually. With higher heart rates, systolic ejection duration requires a greater percentage of the cardiac cycle because of the relative inefficiency of the artificial ventricle. This inefficiency has been attributed to: (1) the artificial heart lacking coordinated atrial contraction, which results in loss of the 20% to 30% atrial components of ventricular filling; and (2) the decreased orifice size of the prosthetic valves (as compared with the native heart valves) increasing resistance to ejection.

Approximately 40% of each cardiac cycle in the native myocardium is usurped by systole. Setting the Utah Heart Driver for a percentage of systole of 50% to 54% is effective for heart rates between 75 and 100. If the heart rate is increased beyond 100 to 110 in an effort to increase CO, the percentage of systole needs to be concomitantly increased, again owing to the inefficiency of the artificial ventricle.

Maximum stroke volume of either ventricle is approximately 100 cc, which is sensitive to the inflow pressure. Atrial pressures of 5 to 7 mmHg generate a CO output of 4 to 5 L/min. Increased atrial pressures of 10 to 15 mmHg can increase the cardiac output to 12 to 13 L/min without an increase in heart rate. In effect, a Frank-Starling–like effect is intrinsic in the artificial ventricle. When the host's need for CO increases beyond the limitations of the stroke volume capacity, heart rate must be manually increased on the Utah Heart Driver.

Measurement of CO is very useful in assessing TAH performance. The Cardiac Output Monitoring Diagnostic Unit (COMDU) has allowed for continuous and reliable calculation of the stroke volume and further calculation of the CO. A pneumotach (airflow transducer) and a computer are used to sense the amount and rate of air exhausting from the right and left ventricles during diastole. Integration of this airflow signal with time yields the rate of air displaced during diastole, which equals the volume of blood filling the diaphragm during the same period.

A portable computer analyzes this exhausting air, and the airflow signal is displayed on the screen of the computer, which indicates the filling and emptying

Table 11-3 Care Plan of the Patient with a TAH

Nursing Diagnosis	Expected Patient Outcomes	Nursing Interventions
Mechanical dysfunction: potential alteration in CO	Patient maintained with satisfactory CO perfusion by the artificial ventricle.	1. Observe pressure waveforms of driver/COMDU (no ECG to interpret): note right/left emptying/filling points, percentage systole, CO measurements. 2. Ensure secure unobstructed drive lines. 3. Know troubleshooting techniques for equipment. 4. Be familiar w/emergency procedure/backup systems; know how to switch drivers, how to use emergency power/air sources. 5. Observe/record standard parameters for hemodynamic monitoring of postoperative cardiac patients; frequently calibrate all monitoring equipment for accuracy. 6. Administer vasoactive drugs per physician.
Potential for injury: bleeding		1. Observe chest tube drainage for excessive amount. 2. Observe driver waveforms for signals of hypovolemia. 3. Observe for external sources of bleeding. 4. Check for occult blood in stools, nasogastric aspirate, urine. 5. Observe/record hemodynamic pressures (aortic root, pulmonary artery, atria). 6. Assess circulatory system (no physiologic heart sounds w/auscultation); alternate nursing

assessments include observation of chest movement, presence/nature of peripheral pulses, BP, skin temperature/moisture.

7. Follow lab values: hematocrit, hemoglobin, platelets, PT, PTT, DIC workups.

8. Administer anticoagulant drugs (heparin, Coumadin, ASA, dipyridamide) per physician.

9. Check for external bruising/petechiae.

10. Administer blood, FFP, platelets, aquamephyton, protamine sulfate as prescribed.

11. Protect patient from sources of trauma.

12. Check neurologic signs for intracerebral bleeding every 1–2 hr.

Potentially ineffective airway management/gas exchange

Patient dyspnea-free, adequate CO_2 and O_2 exchange.

Maintain airway patency, ventilation, oxygenation:

1. Breath sounds difficult to auscultate because of TAH noise; alternate nursing observations: frequent observation of respiratory rate/pattern, symmetry of chest excursions w/ respiration, general skin coloring, check nail beds for capillary refill/cyanosis, ABGs prn, observe for subcutaneous air.

2. Prevent atelectasis: turn, cough, deep breathe every 2 hr; suction prn; incentive spirometry; administer narcotics as prescribed to prevent atelectasis from pain w/resulting hypoventilation.

Potential infection

Patient afebrile, maintaining normal white count, no local signs of infection.

1. Protective isolation: good handwashing technique.

2. Limit personnel/visitor contact w/ patient.

continues

Table 11-3 continued

Nursing Diagnosis	Expected Patient Outcomes	Nursing Interventions
		3. Remove all invasive lines/catheters as soon as clinical conditions warrant; culture tips.
		4. Sterile dressing changes to invasive lines per hospital protocol.
		5. Sterile dressing change (gown, gloves, mask) to drive lines qid. Cleanse exit sites w/ half strength H_2O_2; apply half strength providone-iodine–soaked gauze dressings around drive lines at skin exit site; cover w/ dry outer dressing making it as occlusive as possible.
		6. Check rectal temperature every 2 hr.
		7. Observe wounds for swelling, heat, redness, drainage.
		8. Initially, daily cultures of sputum, urine, blood, rectum, axilla, groin, drive lines, any open skin lesions.
		9. After initial daily cultures discontinued, culture specific sites as clinical conditions indicate.
Alterations in fluid balance	Patient maintains balanced intake/output.	1. Observe driver waveforms/COMDU for signs of hypo- or hypervolemia.
		2. Intake/output every 1 hr.
		3. Observe/record urinary output as adjustments made in heart driver.
		4. Urine checks for sugar, acetone, specific gravity every 4 hr.
		5. Collect urine, test for serum electrolytes/osmolarity as prescribed.

Alterations in tissue perfusion: cerebral

Patient alert and oriented; no neurologic deficit.

6. Collect daily urine for cytology/urinalysis.
7. Daily weights.
8. Observe/describe body edema.
9. Administer IV fluids/diuretics as prescribed.

1. Neurologic checks with vital signs every 1–4 hr; particularly note deficits that might indicate embolism/bleeding.
2. Frequently orient patient to person, place, time.
3. Carefully observe for seizure activity.
4. Follow metabolic/biochemical parameters (lab values).
5. Correlate drive pressures/COs to change in neurologic status.

Impaired physical mobility

Patient free from skin breakdown/muscle atrophy.

Prevent complications from bed rest:
1. Maintain skin integrity: sheepskin, air mattress, or low pressure mattress (e.g., Mediscus bed, Kin-Air bed); frequent turning after initial 24 hr prone; meticulous cleansing/dressing to areas of skin breakdown; protective coverings to bony or prominent areas to prevent shearing effect.
2. Prevent contractures; maintain muscle mass: ROM program, passive/active, initiated early; up walking/sitting in chair as soon as possible after initial 24 hr; use of stationary exercicle.

Alteration in nutrition

Patient maintained in adequate nutrition.

Maintain positive nitrogen balance:
1. Assist in acid-base calculations/oxygen consumption studies.

continues

Table 11-3 continued

Nursing Diagnosis	Expected Patient Outcomes	Nursing Interventions
		2. Administer oral, enteral, parenteral feedings.
		3. Provide patient food choices to avoid anorexia.
		4. Encourage family to help w/ feeding, especially favorite foods.
		5. Calorie counts.
		6. 24-hr urine collection for urine urea nitrogen (UUN).
Disturbance in self-concept	Patient maintains levels of control.	1. Preoperatively inform patient what may be involved in daily living w/ TAH; discuss being "tethered" to compressed air source.
		2. Realize patient may have altered body image and may feel like a "freak."
		3. Encourage patient to verbalize fears/grief; convey empathy and understanding.
Fear	Patient's anxieties alleviated.	1. Spend time w/ patient other than to meet physical needs; listen actively.
		2. Be calm/reassuring but not unrealistic.
		3. Explain procedures, answer patient's questions on patient's level.
Powerlessness:	1. Patient maintains external control.	1. Allow patient to make decisions when possible and respect them.
1. Loss of environmental control	2. Patients feel they have right to privacy.	2. Solicit opinions/comments from patient.
2. Loss of privacy.		3. Begin patient/family teaching preoperatively to help them realize expectations.
		4. Provide privacy w/curtains/covers when appropriate.

		5. Keep extraneous personnel out of area.
Potential ineffective coping:	Patient verbalizes techniques of coping as exhibited by behavior.	1. Have patient interact w/ familiar people/objects.
1. Patient: depression, withdrawal		2. Use primary nursing care if possible.
2. Family: fear of death of loved one; loss of privacy.		3. Hold health care conferences away from bedside.
		4. Keep family informed; be supportive, hopeful, realistic.
		5. Allow family frequent physical/emotional contact w/ patient.
		6. Provide diversional activities (walks/rides outside hospital, occupational therapy).
Sleep pattern disturbances; sleep deprivation	Patient maintains adequate sleep.	1. Cluster nursing activities to provide rest periods.
		2. Coordinate patient's required general daily activities w/ other health care team members to allow uninterrupted sleep.
		3. Maintain day/night routines.
		4. Provide calm, therapeutic environment.
		5. Frequently orient patient to time.

Source: Adapted by permission from "The Initial Surgical Intensive Care Unit Nursing Experience with the Permanent Total Artificial Heart" by J. Stetich, D. Empey, and M. Sasmor, *Heart & Lung*, Vol. 15, No. 5, pp. 480–482, St. Louis, Mo., © September 1986, The C.V. Mosby Company.

pattern of the ventricles. A calibration constant is used to convert the area under the exhaust air curve to volume in milliliters, or CO, by multiplying the calculated stroke volume by the heart rate. Eight diastolic periods are sampled over a 30-second period, and the average is displayed on the COMDU. High exhaust air flow rates accompany high atrial pressure, which rapidly displace the compressed air in diastole. Low flow rates may be the result of hypovolemia and/or inflow valvular obstruction.

Monitoring Responsibilities: Technical Staff and Nursing

Anticipation of fluctuation of fluid volume status and SVR during the first 2 to 4 days post implantation necessitates constant monitoring of the driveline and COMDU pressures. Experienced personnel at Humana Heart Institute have described their protocols, which consist of the technician remaining in the patient's room for the first 24 to 36 hours postoperatively. Thereafter, the recording console is moved to an adjacent monitoring room, which diminishes noise and activity, and frees up more space in the patient's room. All signals from the COMDU, Utah Heart Driver, and bedside monitor are wired directly to an adjacent monitoring room, which facilitates comprehensive patient evaluation and training of staff.

After 3 to 5 days, when stability is achieved, nurses monitor and interpret the alarms of the Utah Heart Driver and COMDU. Members of the technical team are readily available on call. Nursing and technical staff together must train to recognize potential physiologic and mechanical emergencies, which have been described by the Humana Group in Louisville:[54]

- Hypervolemia recognized by low COs and low filling rates displayed on the COMDU.
- Hypervolemia recognized by high COs, and the drive pressure waveform may show incomplete ejection.
- Severe compromise to CO by inability to eject either ventricle sufficiently (underdriving) because of increased resistance to ejection that may be caused by a fractured valve; outflow obstruction, which may be attributable to a thrombus; and calcification or rupture of the diaphragm.
- Kinking of driveline tubes, which now seems to have been corrected by the development of kink-resistant material for the drivelines.

Research continues to determine proper interpretation of the information displayed by the computer and the most effective clinical contribution rendered by measurement of these compressed air exhaust flow rates. With further research and experience, COMDU flow rate analysis will, no doubt, provide information that will guide more precise adjustments of the artificial heart.

Complications

None of the nonanticoagulated calves or sheep that have received TAHs has experienced strokes. However, human recipients have experienced thromboembolic stroke, embolic and cerebral hemorrhage, and hemorrhagic stroke. Further investigation is needed to establish the appropriate anticoagulation regime and the efficacy of platelet-modifying agents such as dipyridamole, aspirin, and low-molecular-weight dextran.[55,56]

Dr. Donald Olsen,[57] Director of Artificial Heart Research Laboratories at the University of Utah, concluded the following with regard to observations of human coagulation systems and anticoagulation regimes in artificial heart recipients:

1. The coagulation and platelet response to polymers exposed to blood is far different among humans than calves and sheep.
2. Anticoagulants, platelet-modifying agents, and dosages that have been successful in the calf experiments appear to be too severe in the management of the coagulation system of humans, possibly resulting in hemorrhagic strokes.
3. Coagulation-anticoagulation studies in animals have been conducted on healthy animals, whereas the sick and compromised human recipient of the artificial heart may have far different responses.
4. Rapid recovery of the liver in one patient after implantation of the total artificial heart, with markedly lowered venous pressure and increased liver perfusion, resulted in a hypercoagulable state.
5. It would appear that to date there are no experimental models that can be used to predict the outcome in humans. Therefore, it behooves the various investigators to pay careful attention to coagulation and anticoagulation in the clinical recipient of the total artificial heart and to publish the observations to establish guidelines for others to follow.

Patient Selection

Two types of patients qualify under FDA approval: patients who cannot be weaned from the cardiopulmonary bypass machine at the conclusion of a cardiac surgical procedure if traditional pharmacologic support and/or IAB pumping failed to restore adequate function to the heart; and patients suffering from severe cardiopulmonary myopathy who meet the criteria for Class IV of the New York Heart Association's clinical classification scheme. These are patients who are symptomatic at rest in spite of an aggressive pharmacologic regime and whose cardiac problem is not amenable to surgical correction. Class IV patients considered for artificial heart implantation must also undergo a myocardial biopsy to confirm that no active inflammatory disease is present, thus ruling out heart failure from which the patient may recover. Any chronic or terminal disease that may threaten the successful performance of the artificial heart also disqualifies the potential recipient.

Once selected, patients and their families must undergo a thorough evaluation by a panel of physicians and ancillary personnel to assess their ability to cope with the great stress that accompanies implantation. If this evaluation determines that the potential recipient is intelligent, has an understanding of the surgical procedure and postoperative function of the TAH, is motivated, and has a stable family nucleus who can offer support and share the burden of stress and the postoperative care demands, the individual qualifies as a candidate.

Several implantations have occurred on an emergency basis for patients who were evaluated to be candidates for transplantation, but a donor was not readily available. Interim organ support while awaiting a suitable donor does not carry the family responsibilities that accompany permanent implantation.

The Surgical Procedure[58]

Preoperative preparation is almost identical with all open heart surgery patients, including intraoperative preparation, careful anesthesia induction, and hemodynamic monitoring. A medial sternotomy incision is made, which allows for removal of the natural ventricles and valves and anastomosis of the prosthetic ventricles. The atria are left in situ, and it is to these remnant atria that the artificial ventricles are anastomosed. Manufacturing of the artificial ventricles in components allows for ease in joining the right and left ventricles to the remaining atria, pulmonary artery, and aorta. Suturing of the TAH, as one unit, directly to the native vascular structure would be impossible because of the confines of the adult mediastinum, which limits anatomical exposure.

Arterial bypass cannulation is via the thoracic aorta or femoral artery; venous cannulation is via the superior and inferior vena cava through the right atrium. Total body hypothermia is employed to decrease the metabolic rate of all organs during full cardiac arrest. Once adequate flow rates are achieved, the aorta is cross-clamped, and the vena cava occluded with tourniquets. Both ventricles are excised at the atrioventricular groove after cardiac arrest. Mitral and tricuspid valves are also excised, but the atria are left in situ. The pulmonic and aortic valves are also excised (Figure 11-31).

Connection of the prosthetic ventricles to the native atria, pulmonary artery, and aorta is made by fabric pieces called "quick connects." The atria quick connect is actually a felt cuff that serves to attach the artificial ventricle securely and to maintain the volume of the natural atria. A short segment of Dacron woven graft serves as the "quick connect" from the prosthetic ventricle to the aorta and pulmonary artery remnants. The graft position is precisely measured

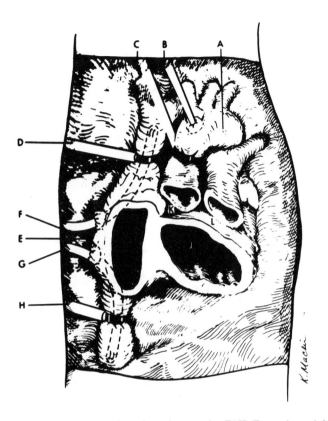

Figure 11-31 Remnant of the natural heart is ready to receive TAH. Two atria are left intact with dissection carefully performed so that all portions of mitral and tricuspid valves are removed. Aortic and pulmonic valve leaflets are excised, and aorta and pulmonary artery are separated a short distance. *A*, aorta; *B*, aortic cannula; *C*, aortic tourniquet; *D*, superior vena cava tourniquet; *E*, right atrium; *F*, superior vena cava cannula; *G*, inferior vena cava cannula; *H*, inferior vena cava tourniquet; *I*, right atrium; *J*, left atrium; *K*, aorta; *L*, pulmonary artery. *Source*: Reproduced by permission from *Comprehensive Intra-Aortic Balloon Pumping* by S.J. Quaal, p. 374, St. Louis, © 1984, The C.V. Mosby Company.

for each recipient. Graft material that is too long will cause kinks, and any acute angle or tension on the graft could reduce the hemodynamic action of the prosthetic ventricles. Attached to the quick connect cuffs are rigid rings made of plastic that contain an internal ledge that corresponds to a lip on the inflow port of the Jarvik-7 ventricle. The artificial ventricles are then snapped into the quick connect, which is analogous to fitting a plastic lid into a Tupperware bowl.

Silastic drivelines are then attached to ports on each ventricle, brought out between the ribs, and tunneled for a short distance subcutaneously before emerging through the skin. At the exit from the skin and the intercostal space, the drivelines are covered with Dacron velour, which allows the patient's tissue to grow into this material and provides for stability and a barrier to bacterial contamination. This velour covering over the drivelines at the skin level is termed the "skin button" (Figure 11-32).

Each ventricle is then aspirated via a venting port to remove all air. Once the ventricles are primed with blood, the clamps and tourniquets on the aorta and vena cava are released, and the pumping of the TAH commences. Rate and driving pressures of each ventricle are gradually increased, and the patient is weaned off cardiopulmonary bypass.

Figure 11-33 is a schematic arrangement of the TAH in a human recipient. Drivelines exit from the skin at the level of the umbilicus and are attached to the Utah Heart Driver.

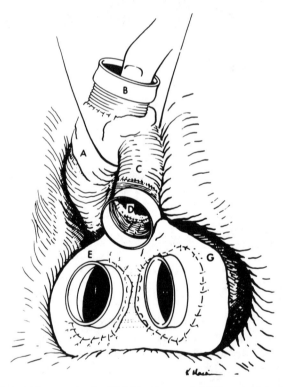

Figure 11-32 Four quick connects of artificial heart are sequentially sewn into place. *A*, aorta; *B*, aortic quick connect; *C*, pulmonary artery; *D*, pulmonary artery quick connect; *E*, right atrium; *F*, right atrial cuff and quick connect; *G*, left atrium; *H*, left atrial cuff and quick connect. *Source*: Reproduced by permission from *Comprehensive Intra-Aortic Balloon Pumping* by S.J. Quaal, p. 375, St. Louis, © 1984, The C.V. Mosby Company.

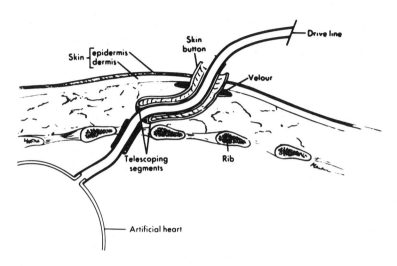

Figure 11-33 Drivelines are exited between ribs and tunneled for short distances subcutaneously before exiting skin. At the exit site from the skin and intercostal space, the drivelines are covered with velour. *Source*: Reproduced by permission from *Comprehensive Intra-Aortic Balloon Pumping* by S.J. Quaal, p. 377, St. Louis, © 1984, The C.V. Mosby Company.

Postoperative Care

The usual care plan required for all post–open heart surgical patients is applicable (Table 11-3). This patient will not require monitoring for and treatment of arrhythmias, cardiopulmonary resuscitation, a Swan-Ganz catheter, or inotropic drugs. Additional modalities of postoperative monitoring that will require special training are monitoring of the drivelines and COMDU.

SUMMARY

The magnificence of the natural myocardium has been underscored by the difficulty encountered in attempting to duplicate its performance mechanically. VADs, albeit temporary, are not intended to substitute for the native myocardium, but rather to support or replace myocardial function until the myocardium can heal and regain its strength or until the severely diseased myocardium can be replaced by heart transplantation.

The clinical genesis of left and right VADs and the TAH does not indicate they are perfect. Scientific investigations continue to improve existing devices, based on observations learned about polymer chemistry and circulatory physiology after human implantation.

Many ethical issues now exist as a result of implantation of the artificial heart. Our society must again confront such issues as defining death, considering health care as a right, and deciding who is to receive a scarce therapy. Quality of life becomes an issue of great concern but is somewhat relative for the patient with an artificial heart. For artificial heart patients, their quality of life may never be like "typical" persons of their age, yet better than states of coma, certainly.[59] What, therefore, is the moderate interpretation that applies to this patient group?

A balancing of scientific purpose and human purpose is necessary. Human values and scientific methods must be brought into a relation that does not damage the vital structure of either. Mechanical assist devices, and namely the TAH, are innovations that provide an important test of our ability to create such a balance.[60]

NOTES

1. J. Smith, "Epidemiology of Congestive Heart Failure," *American Journal of Cardiology* 55(1985):33A.

2. *Guide to the Physiology and Operation of the Intra Aortic Balloon Pump* (Everett, Ma.: AVCO Medical Products).

3. G.J. McGovern, S.B. Park, and T.D. Maher, "Use of a Centrifugal Pump Without Anticoagulants for Postoperative Left Ventricular Assist," *World Journal of Surgery* 9(1985):25.

4. A. Kantrowitz, "Clinical Experience with Cardiac Assistance by Means of Intra Aortic Place-Shift Balloon Pumping," *Transactions of the American Society of Artificial Internal Organs* 14(1968):334.

5. D. Bregman, "Percutaneous Intra Aortic Balloon Pumping: A Time for Reflection," *Chest* 82(1981):397.

6. D.C. Lundell, "Randomized Comparison of the Modified Wireguided and Standard Intra Aortic Balloon Catheters," *Journal of Thoracic and Cardiovascular Surgery* 81(1981):297.

7. V.A. Subramanian, "Percutaneous Intra Aortic Balloon Pumping," *Annals of Thoracic Surgery* 29(1980):102.

8. S. Chatterjee and J. Rosenweig, "Evaluation of Intra Aortic Balloon Counterpulsation," *Journal of Thoracic and Cardiovascular Surgery* 61(1971):405.

9. R.M. Berne and M.N. Levy, *Cardiovascular Physiology*, ed.4, Chapter 5 (St. Louis, Missouri: C.V. Mosby Co., 1981).

10. W.M. Chilian and M.L. Marcus, "Phasic Coronary Blood Flow Velocity in Intramural and Epicardial Coronary Arteries," *Circulation Research* 50(1982):775.

11. W.J. Powell, Jr, "Effects of Intra Aortic Balloon Counterpulsation on Cardiac Performance, Oxygen Consumption, and Coronary Blood Flow in Dogs," *Circulation Research* 26(1970):753.

12. R.H. Coletti, P.S. Kaskel, and D. Bregman, "Coronary Blood Flow Augmentation by Intra Aortic Balloon Pumping during Open Chest Cardiopulmonary Resuscitation," *Transactions of the American Society of Artificial Internal Organs* 24(1983):93.

13. M.D. Akyurekli, "Effectiveness of Intra Aortic Balloon Counterpulsation on Systolic Unloading," *Canadian Journal of Surgery* 23(1980):122.

14. G.B. Brown, "Diastolic Augmentation by Intra Aortic Balloon: Circulatory Hemodynamics and Treatment of Severe, Acute Left Ventricular Failure in Dogs," *Journal of Thoracic and Cardiovascular Surgery* 53(1967):798.

15. B. Reichart, "Treatment of Acute Left Heart Failure using Dobutamine and Intra Aortic Counterpulsation," *Intensive Care Medicine* 7(1981):135.

16. S.J. Quaal, *Comprehensive Intra-Aortic Balloon Pumping* (St. Louis: C.V. Mosby Co., 1984).

17. G.S. Tyson, J.W. Davis, and J.S. Rankin, "Improved Performance of the Intra Aortic Balloon Pump in Man," *Surgical Forum* 37(1986):214.

18. D. Bregman, "Intra Aortic Balloon: New Development Techniques, Complications and Results," in S. Attar, ed., *New Developments in Cardiac Assist Devices*, Surgical Science Series, Vol.6 (New York: Praeger Scientific Publishers, 1985).

19. B.W.L. Goldman, "Increasing Operability and Survival with Intra Aortic Balloon Pump Assist," *Canadian Journal of Surgery* 19(1976):69.

20. Quaal, "Comprehensive Balloon Pumping."

21. J. Alpert, "Limb Ischemia During Intra Aortic Counterpulsation," *Journal of Thoracic and Cardiovascular Surgery* 79(1980):729.

22. B. Aschar, and L.R. Turcohg, "Analysis of Longest IAB Implant in Human Patient (327 Days)," *Transactions of the American Society of Artificial Internal Organs* 27 (1981):372.

23. M.T. McEnany et al., "Clinical Experience with Intra Aortic Balloon Pump Support in 728 Patients," *Circulation* 58, Suppl.(1978):124.

24. J.M. Isner et al, "Complications of the Intra Aortic Balloon Counterpulsation Device: Clinical and Morphologic Observations in 45 Neuropsy Patients," *American Journal of Cardiology* 45(1980):260.

25. P.M. Sanfelippo et al., "Experience with Intra Aortic Balloon Counterpulsation," *Annals of Thoracic Surgery* 41(1986):36.

26. J.M. Isner, and W.C.P. Roberts, "Right Ventricular Infarction Complicating Left Ventricular Infarction Secondary to Coronary Artery Disease," *American Journal of Cardiology* 42(1978):885.

27. Ibid.

28. D.C. Miller et al., "Pulmonary Artery Balloon Counterpulsation for Acute Right Ventricular Failure," *Journal of Thoracic and Cardiovascular Surgery* 80(1980):760.

29. S.J. Phillips, "Percutaneous Cardiopulmonary Bypass and Innovations in Clinical Counterpulsation," *Critical Care Clinics* 2(1986):297.

30. P.A. Spence, et al., "The Hemodynamic Effects and Mechanisms of Action of Pulmonary Artery Balloon Counterpulsation in the Treatment of Right Ventricular Failure during Left Heart Bypass," *Annals of Thoracic Surgery* 39(1985):329.

31. W.E. Gaines and W.S. Pierce, "Left and Right Ventricular Assistance for Postoperative Cardiogenic Shock," in S. Attar, ed., *New Developments in Cardiac Assist Devices*, Surgical Science Series, Vol.6. (New York: Praeger Scientific Publishers, 1985).

32. R.S. Litwak et al., "Use of a Left Heart Assist Device after Intracardiac Surgery: Technique and Clinical Experiences," *Annals of Thoracic Surgery* 21(1976):191.

33. R.S. Litwak et al., "A Decade of Experiences with Left Heart Assist Devices in Patients Undergoing Open Intracardiac Operation," in S. Attar, ed., *New Developments in Cardiac Assist Devices*, Surgical Science Series, Vol.6 (New York: Praeger Scientific Publishers, 1985).

34. G.P. Noon et al., "Reduction of Blood Trauma in Roller Pumps for Long-term Perfusion," *World Journal of Surgery* 9(1985):65.

35. M.F. Lynch, D. Peterson, and V. Baker, "Centrifugal Blood Pumping for Open Heart Surgery," *Minnesota Med* 61(1978):536.

36. L.R. Golding, "Mechanical Assist of the Failing heart," in D.G. Vidt, ed., *Cardiovascular Therapy* (Philadelphia: F.A. Davis Co., 1984), p.536.

37. L.A. Golding, F.D. Loop, and Yukihiko Nose, "Clinical and Experimental Use of the Centrifugal Pump," in S. Attar, ed., *New Developments in Cardiac Assist Devices*, Surgical Science Series, Vol.6 (New York: Praeger Scientific Publishers, 1985).

38. G.J. McGovern, S.B. Park, and T.R. Maher, "Use of Centrifugal Pump without Anticoagulants for Postoperative Left Ventricular Assist," in S. Attar, ed., *New Developments in Cardiac Assist Devices*, Surgical Science Series, Vol. 6 (New York: Praeger Scientific Publishers, 1985).

39. S.B. Park, "Mechanical Ventricular Assist Using Vortex Centrifugal Pump," in S. Attar, ed., *Proceedings from Heart Assist Devices: Heart Replacement* (New York: Futura Publishers, in press).

40. W.S. Pierce and J.L. Myers, "Frontiers of Therapy: Left Ventricular Assist Pumps and the Artificial Heart," *Journal of Cardiovascular Medicine* 42(1981):667.

41. D. Hill, "Experience with the Pierce-Donachy VAD," in S. Attar, ed., *Proceedings from Heart Assist Devices: Heart Replacement* (New York: Futura Publishers, in press).

42. Gaines and Pierce, "Ventricular Assistance."

43. D.J. Farrar et al., "Control Modes of a Clinical Ventricular Assist Device," *IEEE Engineering in Medicine and Biology* 19 (March 1986).

44. J. Laaas et al., "Oxygen Consumption of the Left Ventricle during Transapical Left Ventricular Bypass," *Journal of Thoracic and Cardiovascular Surgery* 80(1980):280.

45. C.M. Doughery, "Decreased Cardiac Output: Validation of a Nursing Diagnosis," *Dimensions of Critical Care Nursing* 5(1986):1982.

46. Park, "Mechanical Ventricular Assist."

47. O.H. Frazier et al., "Replacement of the Left Ventricle with a Single-Chambered Artificial Pump," *Journal of Heart Transplantation* 5(1986):286.

48. W.F. Pae, and W.S. Pierce, "Combined Registry for the Clinical Use of Mechanical Ventricular Assist Pumps and the Fatal Artificial Heart," *Journal of Heart Transplantation* 5(1986):6.

49. W.C. DeVries et al., "Clinical Use of the Total Artificial Heart," *New England Journal of Medicine* 310(1984):273.

50. J. Stetich, D. Empey, and M. Sasmor, "The Initial Surgical Intensive Care Unit Nursing Experience with the Permanent Artificial Heart," *Heart and Lung* 15(1986):475.

51. J.B. Mays et al., "Diagnostic Monitoring and Drive Systems Management of Patients with Total Artificial Heart," *Heart and Lung* 15(1986):466.

52. S.J. Quaal, "The Artificial Heart," *Heart and Lung* 14(1985):317.

53. R.K. Jarvik, "The Total Artificial Heart," *Scientific American* 244(1981):74.

54. Mays et al., "Diagnostic Monitoring."

55. D.B. Olsen, "The Total Artificial Heart in a Transition to the Clinical Arena," *Proceedings of the International Society of Artificial Organs* 5(1981):40.

56. D.B. Olsen, and Y. Taenaka, "State-of-the-Art and Clinically Applied Pneumatic Artifical Hearts," *Critical Care Clinics* 2(1986):195.

57. K. Murray and D. Olsen, "Design and Functional Characteristics of Blood Pumps," in S. Ahar, ed., *New Developments in Cardiac Assist Devices* (New York: Praeger Scientific Publishers, 1985).

58 Quaal, "Artificial Heart."

59. F.R. Woolley, "Ethical Issues in the Implantation of the Total Artificial Heart," *New England Journal of Medicine* 310(1984):292.

60. S.J. Reiser, "The Machines as Means and End: The Clinical Introduction of the Artificial Heart, in M. Shaw, ed., *After Barney Clark: Reflection on the Utah Artificial Heart Program* (Austin: University of Texas Press, 1984).

Chapter 12

Clinical Nursing Research in Cardiac Care

Debra Laurent-Bopp, RN, MN
Polly E. Gardner, RN, MN

As critical care nursing pratice in the coronary care unit (CCU) grows in complexity, and as nurses assume more responsibility and accountability for patient care, it is increasingly evident that research is vital to nursing practice. Kinney[1] states that "research is the avenue by which one learns what data are crucial for diagnosis, what actions are preventative, and how nursing interventions relate to patient outcomes." Nursing practice must be influenced and directed by empirical findings rather than by practice, intuition, and beliefs.[2]

In 1980, the American Association of Critical-Care Nurses (AACN) commissioned and funded a nationwide study, which used the Delphi technique to determine research priorities for critical care nursing.[3,4] The results were a compilation of the 15 top research priorities in critical care nursing (Exhibit 12-1).

Studies that can be placed under the questions identified as the top 15 AACN research priorities are addressed in this chapter. Selection of nursing research for discussion was based on identifying studies by nurse investigators in which physiologic phenomena and variables were examined in human subjects and had the most relevance to cardiovascular nursing. This chapter includes an in-depth review of the research literature for priority questions numbers 10 and 13 (Exhibit 12-1). Four additional ranked research questions are briefly addressed as to their potential impact on the welfare of the critically ill patient (Exhibit 12-2).

To highlight relevant research studies, the studies were categorized into three areas: (1) hemodynamic monitoring, (2) suctioning techniques, and (3) cardiac rehabilitation. As cardiac rehabilitation encompasses a wide variety of studies, the focus of this review is limited to select studies in which effects of activity were investigated. Other chapters in this book, including Chapters 3, 7, and 8, review other nursing practices common to the CCU setting that could be categorized under cardiac rehabilitation. The Delphi technique is addressed.

Exhibit 12-1 Top 15 Research Priorities for Critical Care Nursing from the AACN Delphi Study

1. What are the most effective ways of promoting optimum sleep-rest patterns in the critically ill and preventing sleep deprivation?
2. In light of the nursing shortage, especially in critical care nursing, what measures can be taken to prevent or lessen burnout among critical care nurses?
3. What type of orientation program for critical care nurses is most effective in terms of cost, safety, and long-term retention?
4. What effects do verbal and environmental stimuli have on intracranial pressure in the head injured patient?
5. What are the most effective, least anxiety-producing techniques for weaning various types of patients from ventilators?
6. What types of patient classification systems are the most valid, reliable, and sensitive in determining staffing ratios in critical care areas?
7. What types of incentives (e.g., wage scales, recognition programs, clinical ladders, etc.) will retain nurses in critical care units?
8. What are effective ways of reducing staff stress in critical care areas?
9. What are effective nursing interventions in patients with impaired communication (e.g., intubated patients, aphasic patients) to minimize anxiety, helplessness, and pain?
10. What are the effects of patient positioning on cardiovascular and pulmonary functioning of various types of critically ill patients?
11. What are the most effective staffing patterns (e.g., 12-hour shifts, rotating nurses to non–critical care areas) to reduce burnout and provide continuity of patient care?
12. What nursing measures (e.g., frequency of IV tubing or dressing changes, use of antibiotic ointment) are most effective in preventing infections in patients with invasive lines and/or undergoing invasive procedures?
13. What is the maximum time a patient on a mechanical ventilator with PEEP can be off the ventilator during suctioning without significantly lowering the PaO_2?
14. What are the effective methods of encouraging the incorporation of research findings into critical care nursing practice?
15. What nursing measures singly or in combination are most effective in assessing and relieving pain in various types of critically ill patients (e.g., infants, children, burn patients, neuro patients, etc.)?

Source: Reproduced by permission from *Heart and Lung*, Vol. 12, No. 1, pp. 35–44, St. Louis, © January 1983, The C.V. Mosby Company.

DELPHI TECHNIQUE AND APPLICATION IN AACN RESEARCH PRIORITIES FOR CRITICAL CARE NURSING

The Delphi technique is a process of formulating group consensus. The Delphi method is a way of systematically soliciting, collecting, tabulating, and evaluating opinions of experts without bringing them together.[5] According to Dalkey,[6] the Delphi technique has three essential features: (1) anonymity, (2) controlled feedback, and (3) statistical group response.

The purpose of the study by AACN was to answer the question: ''What are the most significant problems or questions affecting the welfare of critically ill

Exhibit 12-2 Selected Rank Ordered Questions from AACN Delphi Study

35. What are conditions during monitoring (e.g., duration, effect of positioning, blood sampling method) which influence pulmonary artery pressure and cardiac output determination?

38. What are the effects of different approaches to nursing procedures (e.g., chest tube milking, endotracheal tube, cuff deflation, suctioning) on the respiratory status of patients requiring ventilatory assistance?

56. What is the effect of selected nursing therapies (e.g., initiation of activity programs, visiting policies) on the rate of recovery of MI patients?

72. What are the most effective methods for storing and cooling cardiac output injectate solutions?

Source: Reproduced by permission from *Heart and Lung*, Vol. 12, No. 1, pp. 35–44, St. Louis, © January 1983, The C.V. Mosby Company.

patients that can be solved or answered through nursing research?"[7] Seventy-four research questions were rated by a cross-section of critical care nurses throughout the United States as to their potential impact on the care of the critically ill patient.[8] The top 15 ranked questions (Exhibit 12-1) provide direction for critical care nursing research efforts.

HEMODYNAMIC MONITORING

The AACN specified research priority question 10 asks, "What are the effects of patient positioning on cardiovascular and pulmonary functioning of various types of critically ill patients?" Question 35 asks, "What are the conditions during monitoring (e.g., duration, effect of positioning, blood sampling method) which influence pulmonary artery pressure and cardiac output determination?"[9,10] Hemodynamic monitoring by means of a pulmonary artery catheter has become a valuable tool for cardiovascular assessment. Nurse researchers have investigated mechanical factors such as patient position and mode of ventilation to determine the effects on the measurement of pulmonary artery pressure (PAP), pulmonary artery wedge pressure (PAWP), and left atrial pressure (LAP) (Table 12-1) and cardiac output (CO) determinations (Table12-2).

Measurement of Pulmonary Artery, Pulmonary Artery Wedge, and Left Atrial Pressures

Patient Position

PAPs are frequently monitored with the patient in the supine position. Many times, nurses flatten the backrest position or turn the patient to a supine position

Table 12-1 Summary of Research on Pulmonary Artery, Pulmonary Artery Wedge, and Left Atrial Pressures

Year Published	Nurse Researcher(s)	Sample (n)	Methodology	Results	Limitations	Nursing Implications
1976	Woods and Mansfield[11]	10 pts with normal hemodynamics; 40–68 years of age (x = 53.4 yrs)	Backrest angles 0°, 20°, 45°, 90°, and dangling at bedside Protractor Equipment calibrated before/after measurements Phlebostatic axis/level Carpenter's level Analog data read through one representative respiratory cycle	PA pressures fluctuated: PAS ↓ 3.4 mm Hg ($p < 0.05$) PAD ↓ 1.1 mm Hg ($p > 0.05$) PAM ↓ 1.6 mm Hg ($p > 0.05$) PAW ↓ 1.2 mm Hg ($p > 0.05$) Individual differences: 0°, 20°, 45° PAS ↓ 2.5 mm Hg PAD ↓ 1.1 mm Hg PAM ↓ 1.6 mm Hg PAW ↓ 0.7 mm Hg	Small sample size Time after position change not controlled Subjects had normal hemodynamics Sequence of position change not varied Sample was selective including only outpatients who were pre- and post-coronary artery bypass	Findings cannot be generalized Well-defined methodology
1979	Shinn et al.[12]	18, 30–81 years of age (x = 62 yr)	Protractor Phlebostatic axis/level Carpenter's level Equipment calibrated 5-min stabilization after position change 5 sec after ventilator disconnected Analog data read through one	PA pressures fluctuated: PAS ↓ 1.1 mm Hg off ($p < 0.05$) PAD ↓ 1.6 mm Hg off ($p < 0.001$) PAM ↓ 1.5 mm Hg off ($p < 0.001$) PAW ↓ 0.3 mm Hg off ($p > 0.05$)	Sample did not include subjects on PEEP One position (flat supine) was studied Data read through full respiratory cycle	PA pressures should be checked on/off ventilator to determine if differences exist

Year	Author	Sample	Methods	Findings	Limitations	Recommendations
				representative respiratory cycle Flat supine position	4 of 12 pts had pressure differences more than 4 mm Hg	PA pressures should be checked on/off ventilator to determine if differences exist
1981	Grose and Woods[13]	60, 18–88 years of age ($\bar{x}$ = 61 yr)	Equipment calibrated 5-min stabilization after position change Protractor Analog data read through one representative respiratory cycle Group A sequence: 0°, 20°, 0°; on-off, on-off ventilator Group B sequence: 20°, 0°, 20°; on-off, on-off ventilator Repeated measurements done to confirm clinically significant differences	PA pressures fluctuated: PAS 1 mm Hg ($p < 0.01$) PAD 2 mm Hg ($p < 0.01$) PAM 1 mm Hg ($p < 0.01$) PAW 1 mm Hg ($p < 0.01$) 13/60 pts had differences on/off ventilator that exceeded 4 mm Hg	Sample did not include subjects on PEEP One position (flat supine) studied Data read through full respiratory cycle	
1982	Woods et al.[14]	126, 18–88 years of age ($\bar{x}$ = 61 yr)	(n = 63) Group A sequence: 0°, 0° (n = 63) Group B sequence: 20°, 0°, 20°	Group A (0°–20°): PA pressures fluctuated 0.5–2.4 mm Hg ($p < 0.01$) Group B (20°–0°): PA pressures fluctuated	Sample did not include subjects on PEEP	Individual differences in Group B, thus recommended differences be determined in position of comfort

continues

Table 12-1 continued

Year Published	Nurse Researcher(s)	Sample (n)	Methodology	Results	Limitations	Nursing Implications
			Protractor Phlebostatic axis/level Carpenter's level Analog data read through one representative respiratory cycle Equipment calibrated Stopwatch	0.5–1.6 mm Hg ($p \leq 0.01$); PAW pressure fluctuated 0.3–0.6 mm Hg		and flat supine position. Otherwise, reliable pressures can be obtained at backrest elevation of 20° or less
1982	Laulive[15]	30	Backrest angles 0°, 20°, 45°, 60°, 0°	PA pressures fluctuated: PAS 0.28 mm Hg PAD 1.03 mm Hg PAW 0.57 mm Hg Individual variations fluctuated from 0 to 2 mm Hg	Pressures read off digital display Second investigator to verify reading was random	Reliable pressures can be obtained in most pts with backrest elevations up to 60°
1982	Nemens and Woods[16]	26, 25–88 years of age ($x = 56$ yr)	Assumed backrest position of 0°–20° Phlebostatic level Equipment calibrated Stopwatch Analog data read through one representative respiratory cycle	PA pressures fluctuated: PAS 2–7 mm Hg (4) PAD 1–6 mm Hg (3) PAM 1–5 mm Hg (3) PAW 0–7 mm Hg (3)	Depicts fluctuations in PA pressures only in 30-min period	Provided baseline data of normal fluctuations of PA pressures

Year	Author	N	Variables/Methods	Results	Limitations	Conclusions/Recommendations
1982	Van Sciver[17]	14, 11 on 5 cm PEEP		↑ PA/PAW pressures off ventilator ($p < 0.05$)	Individual variations not discussed / Mean data not provided	PA pressures should be measured at end-expiration on ventilator
1982	Whitman et al.[18]	50	Backrest elevation of 20°, 20° right and left lateral positions / Six sequences of position change / Phlebostatic axis/level	PA pressures fluctuated: PAS 0–2 mm Hg (4) PAD 0–11 mm Hg (3) PAW 0–9 mm Hg (2)	Data collection occurred over a 65–75-minute time period during which PAPs could have varied / Measurements were not evaluated for deviation from mean / Each sequence had less than 10 subjects	Differences may be due to hemodynamic changes over time / Pressures must be measured with patient in the flat, supine position and in the selected lateral position to determine if differences exist
1983	Cengiz et al.[19]	40	PA/PAW measurements obtained using 3 methods: 1. manual interpretation at end-expiration using analog data 2. automated interpretation by computing area under curve (digital display) 3. automated interpretation by computer algorithms	Significant differences ($p < 0.01$) in PA pressures among 3 methods / Least variation w/ manual		Recommended reading PA pressures at end-expiration using analog data

Table 12-1 continued

Year Published	Nurse Researcher(s)	Sample (n)	Methodology	Results	Limitations	Nursing Implications
1983	Gershan[20]	30, all on various levels of PEEP		Significant differences ($p < 0.01$) in wedge pressures on/off ventilator	Individual variations not discussed Only PAW measured	Compare digital display pressure w/analog pressure recording
1984	Chulay and Miller[21]	32, x = 54 yr; age range not given	Backrest angles 0°, 20°, 45°, 0° Phlebostatic axis/level Equipment calibrated Digital data read at end-expiration	PA pressures fluctuated less than 1.4 mm Hg difference from control pressures ($p > 0.05$)	Individual variations not indicated	Difficult to make recommendations without discussion of individual changes
1984	Clochesy et al.[22] 17		Backrest angles 0°, 20°, 45°, 60°	PA pressures fluctuated: PAS ↓ 0.3– 0.9 mm Hg ($p < 0.05$) PAD ↑ 0.4– 1.1 mm Hg ($p < 0.05$) PAW ↑ 0.4– 2 mm Hg ($p < 0.05$)	Individual variations not indicated	Difficult to make recommendations without discussion of individual changes
1984	Kennedy et al.[23] 25		Flat supine position and in 90° right and left lateral positions	PA pressures fluctuated: PAS ↑ 0.2– ↑ 0.3	Study selective of medical patients No repeated measures	Reliable reproducible PA pressures can be obtained in the 90°

Year	Author	Sample	Method	Results		
			Midsternum used as zero reference level	mm Hg ($p > 0.05$) PAD ↑0.1–↓0.1 mm Hg ($p > 0.05$) PAM ↓0.2–↑0.1 mm Hg ($p > 0.05$) PAW ↑0.3–↑0.7 mm Hg ($p > 0.05$) Individual variations 0–2 mm Hg	at end of data collection in initial position	right and left lateral positions
1984	Wild and Woods[24]	30	(n = 15) Group A sequence: 0°–30° left lateral, 30° right lateral, 0° (n = 15) Group B sequence: 0°–30° right lateral, 30° left lateral, 0° Phlebostatic axis/level for supine 4th intercostal space at midsternal line for lateral 3-min stabilization after each position change	PA pressures fluctuated: PAS 3.6–3.8 mm Hg ($p < 0.01$) PAD 3.2–4.4 mm Hg ($p < 0.01$) PAM 3.6–4.4 mm Hg ($p < 0.01$) PAW 4.3–4.9 mm Hg ($p < 0.01$) 93% showed clinically significant changes (> 4 mm Hg)		Further study needed to define atrial reference level in pts positioned w/ various degrees of lateral recumbency
1985	Retalliau et al.[25]	26, 42–79 years of age, x = 62 yr	Group A sequence: 0°, 30°, 0° Group B sequence: 30°, 0°, 30° Analog data read	Left atrial pressures fluctuated 0 to 3 mm Hg (T)	Only left atrial pressure measured Depicts fluctuations in left atrial only in 30-min period	Provided baseline data of normal fluctuations of left atrial pressures

continues

Table 12-1 continued

Year Published	Nurse Researcher(s)	Sample (n)	Methodology	Results	Limitations	Nursing Implications
			through one representative respiratory cycle			
			3-min stabilization after each position change			
			Equipment calibrated before/after measurement			
			Phlebostatic axis/level			
			Carpenter's level			

Note: PA, pulmonary artery; PAS, pulmonary artery systolic; PAM, pulmonary artery mean; PAW, pulmonary artery wedge.

Table 12-2 Summary of Research on the Measurement of Thermodilution Cardiac Output

Year Published	Nurse Researcher(s)	Sample (n)	Methodology	Results	Limitations	Nursing Implications
Injectate Volume and Temperature						
1981	Killpack et al.[26]	30	5 mL iced and 10 mL room compared w/ 10 mL iced PA catheter thermistor Triplicate measurements using automatic injector gun at end-expiration	CO 5 mL iced compared w/ CO 10 mL iced (r = 0.964) CO 10 mL injectate compared w/ CO 10 mL iced (r = 0.973)	Discussion of methodology limited in abstract Strip chart recorder not used	5 mL iced/10 mL room produce accurate CO measurements w/ automatic injector gun
1982	Davidson et al.[27]	30	5 and 10 mL compared w/ 10 mL room Group A sequence (n = 15): 5 mL, 10 mL Group B sequence (n = 15): 10 mL, 5 mL PA catheter thermistor 3–5 measurements (within 10%) at end-expiration 90-sec stabilization between measurements	CO iced compared w/ CO room (r = 0.973) CO 5 mL iced compared w/ 10 mL iced (r = 0.964) Mean difference 0.3 L/min	Strip chart recorder not functioning for 24/30 pts	Both volumes should be checked to determine if differences exist

continues

Table 12-2 continued

Year Published	Nurse Researcher(s)	Sample (n)	Methodology	Results	Limitations	Nursing Implications
1982	Larson and Woods[28]	30, 24 on ventilators	5 mL room compared w/ 10 mL iced Group A sequence (n = 15): 5 mL, 10 mL Group B sequence (n = 15): 10 mL, 5 mL CO computer 3–5 measurements (within 10%) at end-expiration PA catheter thermistor	CO room compared w/ CO iced (r = 0.963) CO 5 mL room within 10% of CO 10 mL iced in 83% 5 subjects had clinically significant effects due to sequence or type differences (>10%) injectate nonsignificant (p > 0.05)	Strip chart recorder broke during study	5 mL room temperature reliable for measuring normal CO Researchers recommend comparing room w/ iced to determine if differences exist
1983	Hruby and Woods[29]	30, on ventilators	10 mL room compared w/ 10 mL iced Group A sequence (n = 15): iced, room Group B sequence (n = 15): room, iced 3–5 measurements (within 10%) obtained at end-expiration within hours after cardiac surgery	CO room compared w/ CO iced (r = 0.972; p < 0.01) Mean cardiac range 2.08–8.84 L/min	Sample selective of hypothermic cardiac surgery pts (postop) PA temperature fluctuations not monitored in all pts	

Year	Sample	Methods	Results	Comments	Conclusions
1983	Shellock and Riedinger[30] 45, 15 on ventilators	PA catheter thermistor Strip chart recorder CO computer 10 mL compared w/ 10 mL iced (alternated) Manual injection PA catheter thermistor Strip chart recorder Resting supine position	CO iced compared w/ CO room (r = 0.972) Percent variation in readings: iced = 5.5%, room = 5.3%	Phase of respiratory cycle used for injection not specified Individual variations not discussed Sequence not varied	CO 10 mL iced compares well w/ CO 10 mL room
1983	Shellock et al.[31] 26, on ventilators	5 and 10 mL room compared w/ 10 mL iced Manual injection at end-expiration PA catheter thermistor Strip chart recorder Resting supine position on PEEP of 7 ± 44 cm H_2O 4 CO measurements for each volume/ temperature 2 values averaged	CO 5 mL room compared w/ CO 10 mL iced (r = 0.925) CO 10 mL room compared w/ CO 10 mL iced (r = 0.951) Range of CO 1.82– 5.34 L/min	Sample selective to hypothermic cardiac surgery pts Overestimation of CO w/ 5 mL	CO 5 and 10 mL room can be used to obtain CO measurements CO 10 mL room produces more comparable results; should be used unless limited by fluid restriction
1984	Vennix et al.[32] 27, on ventilators	10 mL room compared w/ 10 mL iced Manually injected within 4 sec or less 3 measurements	CO room compared w/ CO iced (r = 0.989) Range CO 2.2–15.7 L/min Average difference	Use of strip chart recorder not indicated Individual variations not described	CO room and iced compare favorably

continues

Table 12-2 continued

Year Published	Nurse Researcher(s)	Sample (n)	Methodology	Results	Limitations	Nursing Implications
			obtained w/ each method as quickly as possible. Measurements within 0.5 L/min of each other averaged to obtain CO. If measurements exceeded 0.5 L/min of each other, at least 2 more measurements were obtained (high/low readings were discarded) PA thermistor catheter	between the 2 methods 5 ± 4.8%	Injectate temperature not measured directly. Pts reported to be receiving vasoactive medications	
1985	Nelson and Anderson[33]	42, on ventilators	10 mL room compared w/ 10 mL iced (order varied). Automatic injection at 1 min intervals after deliberate mandatory ventilation. Sample subdivided into 3 subgroups according to mean arterial pressure: low	CO room compared w/ CO iced (r = 0.97). Insignificant differences (p > 0.05) in subgroups of mean arterial pressure, body temperature, and CO w/ room and iced	Sample selective of surgical intensive care pts. Some subgroups studied have less than 10 subjects. Individual variations not described. Fluctuations of PA temperature w/ room injectate	CO room compares well w/ iced. Larger subgroup sizes needed to make findings generalizable

(<70 mm Hg)
$n = 6$, moderate
(70–100 mm Hg)
$n = 26$, high
(>100 mm Hg)
$n = 9$
Sample subdivided
based on PA
temperature (°F): low
(<90° F) $n = 8$,
moderate (98–
100° F) $n = 19$, high
(>100° F) $n = 14$
Sample subdivided
based on CO
measurement: low
(<5 L/min) $n = 9$,
moderate (5–10 L/
min) $n = 21$, high
(>10 L/min) $n = 12$
4 measurements
obtained (1st
measurement
discarded) with 3
measurements
averaged
Total data collection
time 12–15 min

10 mL room compared
w/ 10 mL iced

CO iced prefilled
syringes compared

Small sample size
Comparison of all 3

Further study needed
using larger, more

continues

Open vs Closed Systems
1985 Barcelona et
al.[34]

21

Table 12-2 continued

Year Published	Nurse Researcher(s)	Sample (n)	Methodology	Results	Limitations	Nursing Implications
			Pts randomly assigned to 1 of 2 groups: Group 1: (n = 10) iced prefilled syringes vs room temperature prefilled syringes Group 2: (n = 11) iced prefilled syringes vs room temperature using COSet™ 3 measurements averaged 3–5 min between 2 consecutive sets of measurements	w/ room prefilled syringes (r = 0.93) CO iced prefilled syringes compared w/ CO room COSet™ system (r = 0.71)	methods not done in all pts Use of strip recorder not specified Phase of respiratory cycle used for injection not specified	diverse population Small sample limits generalizability of findings
1987	Gardner et al.[35]	57	10 mL iced compared w/ 10 mL iced and room COSet Pts randomly assigned to 1 of 3 sequences: Sequence A: Room COSet Open Iced-Iced COSet Sequence B: Open Iced-Iced COSet-	Statistically significant differences (p < 0.01) in CO between Room COSet Open Iced Statistically significant differences (p < 0.01) in CO between Iced COSet	Data collection over 30–45 min during which CO could have varied Differences in CO may have been due to individual variations rather than particular injectate system	COSet produced reliable results w/ room or iced injectate Differences in CO values using 2 temperatures should be checked to determine if differences exist

	Sample	Methods	Findings	Comments
		and Open Iced Room COSet Sequence C: Iced COSet-Room COSet-Open Iced Strip chart recorder 3–5 measurements injected at end-expiration within 4 sec 60 sec between measurements Data collection period lasted 30–45 min	Insignificant differences ($p > 0.05$) between Room COSet Iced COSet CO COSet Systems compared w/ CO Open Iced ($r = 0.96$, $p < 0.001$)	Pts on PEEP excluded Hissing sound of automatic injection device noted Use of strip chart recorder not indicated	CO measurements comparable at backrest elevation of 0° and 20° Comparison of CO should be made between the 2 positions to determine if differences exist
Patient Position 1981 Grose et al.[36]	30, 8 on ventilators	10 mL iced automatically injected at end-expiration Protractor PA catheter thermistor Pts randomly assigned to one of two sequences: Sequence A: 20°, 0°, 20° Sequence B: 0°, 20°, 0° 7-min stabilization after each position change	CO at 0° compared w/ CO at 20° ($r = 0.981$) Range of CO between 2 positions 0.01–1.35 L/min 7/30 pts had clinically significant ($> 10\%$) differences	

continues

Table 12-2 continued

Year Published	Nurse Researcher(s)	Sample (n)	Methodology	Results	Limitations	Nursing Implications
			Data collection time: < 28 min each subject			
1982	Whitman et al.[37]	50	10 mL iced manually injected by 1 investigator Pts randomly assigned to 1 of 6 sequences of 3 positions (20° supine, 20° right, and left lateral recumbent) 15-min stabilization after each patient change Mean of 2 measurements determined CO	Statistically significant differences ($p < 0.05$) in CO in left lateral position only Individual differences when moved from one position to another (0.0–3.9 L/min)	Sample selective of postop surgical pts Data collection: 60–75 min; CO could have varied	Differences in CO may be due to hemodynamics changing over time
1984	Kleven[38]	30, all on ventilators	10 mL iced manually injected at end-expiration Pts randomly assigned to 1 of 2 sequences: Sequence A: 0°, 20°, 0°	CO at 0° compared w/ CO at 20° ($r = 0.98$; $p < 0.0001$) Individual variations in 8 (> 10% difference in CO w/ position change)		Comparison of CO should be made between selected backrest position and flat supine to determine if differences exist

Year	Author	n	Methods	Results	Limitations	Implications
			Sequence B: 20°, 0°, 20°			Differences in CO may be due to hemodynamic changes over time
			3–5 measurements (within 10%); 3 values averaged			Measurement of CO using consistent position to control for physiologic changes may be indicated
			Protractor			
			PA catheter thermistor			
1986	Doering and Dracup[39]	51	10 mL iced manually injected at end-expiration	Statistically significant differences (p < 0.05) in CO in left lateral position	Sample of postop surgical pts	
			Pts randomly assigned to sequences of 3 positions: 20° supine, 20° right, left lateral)	45% pts had > 10% difference in CO in the 3 positions	Data collection over 60 min during which CO could have varied	
			Mean of 2 measurements within 10% determined CO		Analysis of CO thermodilution curves not reported	

Manual and Automatic Injections

Year	Author	n	Methods	Results	Limitations	Implications
1984	Manifold[40]	19	10 mL manually and automatically injected sequentially	Mean CO higher w/ automatic injection	Use of strip chart recorder not indicated	Replication needed using strip chart recorder to analyze CO curves
			Sequence varied			
			3 measurements w/ both methods			
			PA catheter thermistor			

continues

Table 12-2 continued

Year Published	Nurse Researcher(s)	Sample (n)	Methodology	Results	Limitations	Nursing Implications
Sterility of Open System						
1981	Grose et al.[41]	In vitro; 37 baths cultured	Broth cultures obtained from open system bath surrounding injectate syringes Cultures obtained at time of preparation and at 8-hr intervals	33% baths contaminated 58% baths contaminated within 8 hr All cultures obtained at time of preparation showed no growth of organisms	Syringe caps not airtight as indicated by investigators	Replication is needed to include syringe cultures
1985	Riedinger et al.[42]	In vitro: 11 beakers cultured	A number of syringes, 10 mL each, aseptically prepared/ placed in 18 beakers (iced or room temperature baths) Exposed to typical ICU environment for 36 hr 25 syringes randomly selected from 11 beakers and sent for culture	No growth of organisms in 7 days	Water bath not cultured	Syringes are sterile up to 36 hr Further study with larger sample

to maintain consistency in obtaining PAPs. It was also thought that head elevation would decrease hemodynamic measurements. However, research studies have been conducted to evaluate the effects of backrest elevations on these hemodynamic measurements.

Nurses have long recognized the complications of prolonged immobility and have turned and moved patients to varying positions to prevent pressure sores. Nursing researchers have wondered if reproducible PAPs, PAWPs, and LAPs can be obtained with patients in varying positions (backrest elevated or lateral recumbent) to alleviate disturbing the patients during periods of sleep.

Twelve studies were conducted to examine the effects of backrest elevation on PAP, PAWP, and LAP: seven were conducted by nurses. Woods and Mansfield[43] studied ten cardiac outpatients with normal hemodynamics in conjunction with an exercise tolerance study that necessitated the insertion of a pulmonary artery catheter. Small differences in PAPs were found with changes in backrest positions. Although the sample size was small ($n = 10$) and was drawn from a group of patients with normal hemodynamics, the well-defined methods were used in a later study using a larger, more diverse population of patients. This study also emphasized use of the phlebostatic axis and levels as standard reference levels when measuring PAPs, PAWPs, and LAPs. The phlebostatic axis is the junction between a transverse plane of the body passing through the fourth intercostal space at the lateral margin of the sternum and a frontal plane of the body passing through the midpoint of a line from the outermost point of the sternum to the outermost point of the posterior chest. The phlebostatic level is a plane that rotates about the axis as the patient moves from a flat to an upright position.[44]

Woods and associates[45] refined the methods of Woods and Mansfield[46] by controlling the time after position change and varying the sequence of position change (0°-20°-0° or 20°-0°-20°). They studied 126 critically ill patients, excluding patients on positive end-expiratory pressure (PEEP). They found that with the air-fluid interface of the transducer maintained at the zero-reference level (phlebostatic level), PAP could be reliably obtained at backrest positions of 20° or less without disturbing the patient.

Laulive[47] also researched the effects of varying backrest elevations on PAPs and PAWPs. Reliable results were reported in most patients with backrest elevations up to 60°.

In 1982, Nemens and Woods[48] studied 26 critically ill patients to assess pressure fluctuations over 30 minutes. Patients were studied in their assumed position. PAPs fluctuated 4 mmHg or less with the greatest fluctuation with pulmonary artery systolic pressure. This study provided baseline information heretofore not considered in measuring PAPs. This information now provides the researcher with the expected fluctuations of PAPs. Without this information, the validity of studies that measure changes in PAPs would be limited.

Retalliau and associates[49] also described expected fluctuations in LAPs in 32 cardiac surgery patients. LAP did not fluctuate more than 3 mmHg. They also studied the effect of backrest elevation (0°-30°-0° or 30°-0°-30°) on measurement of LAP. Although most patients had small changes in LAP (<3 mmHg) with changes in backrest elevation, they recommended that LAPs be measured in the different backrest positions in each patient before measurement in the selected position. Determination of differences needs to be established before assuming there is no difference from one position to another.

Thirty-two cardiac surgery patients were studied by Chulay and Miller[50] to determine if varying backrest elevations (0°, 20°, 45°, and 60°) had any effect on the measurement of PAPs and PAWPs. When patients were moved to a different position, PAPs did not fluctuate more than a mean of 1.4 mmHg from baseline pressures. Unfortunately, individual differences were not reported and, therefore, it is difficult to make recommendations.

To determine if backrest elevations of 0°, 20°, 45°, and 60° had any effect on the measurement of PAP and PAWP, 17 critically ill patients on PEEP were studied. Clochesy et al.[51] found small mean differences in PAPs and PAWPs with changes in backrest position. Recommendations are limited because individual differences were not described.

Lateral positioning was also researched in three published studies of its effects on the measurement of PAPs and PAWPs. In 1982, Whitman[52] studied PAPs in 50 cardiac surgery patients with backrest elevations of 20° supine and 20° right and left lateral positions. Each of the three changes was varied in six sequences. The effect of positioning showed a statistically significant difference ($p<0.05$) in the measurement of pulmonary artery diastolic pressures. Insignificant differences ($p>0.05$) in pulmonary artery systolic and wedge pressures were found.

Kennedy and co-workers[53] studied the effects of lateral positioning in 25 cardiac patients. Patients were positioned in the flat supine, and 90° right and left lateral positions. Using the zero-reference level at the midsternum, these investigators found small differences in PAP and PAWP measurements between the flat supine and the 90° lateral positions. Therefore, reproducible PAPs and PAWPs can be reliably obtained in the right and left lateral positions of 90°.

Wild and Woods[54] also studied the effect of lateral positioning on PAP and PAWP measurements. Patients were positioned in the flat supine and 30° right and left lateral positions, and returned to the flat supine position. Using the fourth intercostal space at the midsternal level as the zero-reference level, statistically significant differences ($p<0.01$) in PAPs and PAWPs were found between the supine and lateral positions. These investigators suggested that further study was needed to define the reference level for the left atrium for patients in the 30° right and left lateral recumbent positions.

Ventilation

Mechanical ventilation imposes changes in intrathoracic pressure, thereby affecting pressure measurements. Various researchers have investigated its effects on PAPs and PAWPs. To date, no study has investigated the effect of mechanical ventilation on the measurement of LAP.

Shinn and associates[55] studied the effects of mechanical ventilation on the measurement of the PAPs and PAWPs in 18 critically ill patients. Patients on PEEP were excluded. Pressure recordings were read throughout a full respiratory cycle on and off the ventilator in the flat supine position. Statistically significant differences ($p<0.01$) in PAPs were found with removal from the ventilator.

Statistically significant differences ($p<0.01$) in PAPs and PAWPs were also found when patients were removed from the ventilator in a study done by Grose and Woods.[56] They studied the effects of mechanical ventilation (on and off) in 60 critically ill patients. Patients were also studied in varied backrest positions (0° to 20°). The sequencing of both were varied for study. Patients on PEEP were excluded. Pressure recordings were read through one full respiratory cycle.

Another study looking at the effects of mechanical ventilation on PAPs and PAWPs included patients on PEEP. Van Sciver[57] studied 14 critically ill patients, 11 of whom were receiving 5 cm H_2O of PEEP. Statistically significant ($p<0.05$) increases in PAPs and PAWPs were found when patients were removed from the ventilator. This study advocated measuring pressures at end-exhalation on the ventilator.

Gershan[58] studied 30 mechanically ventilated patients with various levels of PEEP. Statistically significant differences ($p<0.01$) in PAWPs were found when patients were removed from the ventilator. Digital display data were compared with analog data for agreement.

Some investigators have studied various methods of measuring PAPs and PAWPs to determine which phase of the respiratory cycle has the least variation in intrathoracic pressure. These methods include obtaining the pressure at end-expiration, averaging the analog pressure waveforms through one representative respiratory cycle, and reading the mean pressure on the digital display ([systolic-diastolic]/3) + diastolic. Riedinger et al.[59] concluded that end-expiration caused least variation in intrathoracic pressure and could easily be identified in the clinical setting. Similarly, Wild and Woods[60] and Cengiz et al.[61] recommended that pressure measurements be obtained at end-expiration. Both researchers advocated that digital and analog data be compared. If feasible, PAPs should be obtained from analog waveforms.

Nursing Implications

Based on these studies, several nursing implications can be derived. Using the phlebostatic axis as the zero-reference level, reproducible PAP and PAWP measurements can be obtained in most patients with normal hemodynamics in the supine position with backrest elevations up to 45°. In critically ill patients with unstable hemodynamics, reproducible PAPs and PAWPs can be obtained with backrest elevations of 20° or less. Some individuals, however, may have changes in PAP with backrest elevation because of numerous clinical factors (e.g., rapid volume infusion, vasoactive medications). Thus, before measuring pressures in varied backrest positions, it is necessary to determine if differences exist by comparing the elevated position with the flat supine position.

In patients undergoing cardiac surgery, reproducible LAP measurements can be obtained at backrest elevations up to 30°. LAPs should also be obtained in the assumed and in the flat supine positions to determine if differences exist. Further studies are needed to define specific patient populations in which differences exist. Ongoing studies are needed to replicate existing studies.

In most patients, reproducible PAP and PAWP measurements can be obtained in the right and left lateral position of 90° using the midsternum as the reference level. Further study is needed to define the reference level for lateral recumbency of less than 90°.

PAPs and PAWPs should be measured at end-expiration. For patients receiving mechanical ventilation who do not require PEEP, investigators recommend checking PAPs and PAWPs on and off the ventilator to determine if differences exist. Physiologic studies indicate that if patients receiving PEEP therapy are removed from the ventilator, an "autotransfusion effect" can occur from the instant reduction of intrathoracic pressure, resulting in a rebound increase in venous return to the right side of the heart.[62] It is also believed that pressures obtained off the ventilator will not accurately reflect the patient's actual hemodynamic state.[63] Further studies are needed in this area.

Digital display recording should be checked with analog data for agreement. Analog data provides more accurate interpretation of pressure measurements.

MEASUREMENT OF THERMODILUTION CARDIAC OUTPUT

CO is a hemodynamic parameter affected by a wide range of physiologic and pathophysiologic conditions. It is easily measured at the bedside. Data derived from serial CO measurements are used by clinicians to guide and evaluate therapy. Addressed in the AACN study, question 35 asks, "What are conditions during monitoring (e.g., duration, effect of positioning, blood sampling method) which influence pulmonary artery pressure and cardiac output determination?"[64,65] The literature is replete with research studies that have evaluated various conditions that can alter the validity of the CO measurement. Question 72 asks, "What are the most effective methods for storing and cooling cardiac output injectate solutions?" The selected studies are described in Table 12-2.

Injectate Volume and Temperature

Investigators have compared CO with various volumes of room and iced temperature injectates.[66-73] Ten milliliters of room and iced temperature injectate were compared by eight nurse researchers in critically ill patients and were found to have high intercorrelation ($r>0.90$).[63-73] Five milliliters of room and iced temperature injectate were compared and found to have high intercorrelation ($r>0.90$).[66-73] Studies evaluating the use of 5 to 10 mL of injectate in critically ill patients showed comparable results.[66-73] Five milliliters injectate can be used in critically ill patients who may be at risk for volume overload. Killpack,[74] Davidson et al.[75] and Larson and Woods[76] advocated that CO be compared using both volumes of 5 and 10 mL to determine if differences exist, as some individuals in their studies had variation in the measurement of CO.

Automatic versus Manual Injection

Injection techniques using the manual and automatic methods have been evaluated by one nurse investigator. Manifold[77] studied 19 patients and found individual variations in CO curves associated with manual injections, although resultant CO measurements were comparable. Increased grip strengths were associated with the least variation in CO. Further studies evaluating the efficacy of automatic injection are needed before recommendation of its use in the clinical setting over manual injection can be made. Further studies are also warranted evaluating the effects of various grip strengths (force of manual injection) on CO. The advantages of the automatic injection device are that it allows minimal handling and rapid injection, and therefore decreases injectate rewarming before its exit from the pulmonary artery catheter.

Patient Position

Themodilution CO measurements, along with other hemodynamic measurements, are routinely performed with the patient in the flat supine position. However, reproducible CO measurements have been obtained in patients with 20° of backrest position.[78-80] Grose and associates[81] evaluated CO measurements in 30 critically ill patients in the flat supine position and 20° backrest elevation. They found CO measurements comparable at backrest positions of 0° and 20°. The investigators did recommend CO should be compared between the two positions to determine if differences exist. Kleven[82] studied 30 patients on ventilatory support with PEEP therapy. CO measurements in the flat supine position were compared with CO measurements in the 20° backrest position. Although a high correlation ($r = 0.98$) was found between the two positions, this study did have eight patients with clinically significant differences (>10%). Recommendation was made to compare CO in the two positions to determine if differences exist. Mechanically ventilated patients on PEEP are appropriate candidates for thermodilution CO measurement. High levels of PEEP, however, may decrease CO because of increases in intrathoracic pressure. Further study is needed to evaluate various levels of PEEP therapy on thermodilution CO.

Thermodilution CO measurements in patients in the lateral recumbent position are more variable. Whitman and associates[83] evaluated CO measurements in patients in 20° supine and left lateral positions. Statistically significant differences ($p < 0.05$) in CO measurements were found in the left lateral position. Data collection took between 60 and 75 minutes, which meant that CO values could have changed over time. Further study is needed to evaluate the effects of lateral positioning on thermodilution CO.

Doering and Dracup[84] recently studied 51 patients in various positions of 20° supine and 20° right and left lateral. Forty-five percent of the patients studied had a greater than 10 percent difference in CO in the three positions. The duration of data collection (60 minutes) meant that CO values may have changed; however, measurements were not repeated.

These findings do allow clinicians some flexibility in determining the backrest position for CO measurements in selected patient populations who may not tolerate flat supine positions, including patients with respiratory dysfunction or with increased intracranial pressures. It may also be unnecessary to awaken or disturb a sleeping patient. Because some patients are more susceptible to position changes, as indicated by studies showing individual differences, CO measurements should be compared between the assumed position and the flat supine position. These comparisons are necessary to determine if differences exist and if the CO measurements are reproducible.

Infection Control of Injectate

A research study examining the contamination of open system preparations showed that prefilled syringes lack a water-tight seal, and the ice bath surrounding the syringes become contaminated with microorganisms after 8 to 24 hours.[85] Nurses need to ensure a water-tight seal on the syringe cap and enclose syringes in a waterproof plastic bag before placing them in the bath preparation. It is also recommended that syringes be discarded at the end of each shift. Another in vitro study[86] examined the cultures of 25 syringes selected at random from 18 beakers of room and iced temperature baths. No growth was found in 7 days. Further study is needed to examine for culture growth in room and iced temperature bath preparations and samples of prefilled syringes. Effective methods for storing injectate syringes need further exploration.

Closed System of Injectate

The disadvantages of the open system (e.g., time preparation, contamination of prefilled syringes) led to the development of closed injectate delivery systems. The obvious advantages are that they preclude preparation of individual syringes and reduce entries into a sterile system. Several closed systems have been designed, but only one has been marketed, the COSet™ closed system by American Edwards Laboratories.[87] A study done by Barcelona and associates[88] evaluated 21 patients in two groups. CO measurements with 10 mL room temperature injectate in prefilled syringes were compared with CO measurements with 10 mL iced injectate in prefilled syringes in the first group of 10 patients. CO measurements in the second group of 11 patients were compared using 10 mL iced injectate in prefilled syringes and 10 mL room temperature injectate with the COSet™ system. Regression analysis showed a moderate correlation ($r = 0.71$) between CO measurements obtained using the standard method of iced prefilled syringes and the COSet system with room temperature injectate. Gardner and associates[89] compared CO measurements using 10 mL iced injectate in prefilled syringes, the COSet with room temperature injectate, and the COSet with iced injectate. Fifty-seven critically ill patients were studied with a wide range of CO measurements. High correlations ($r = 0.827$ to 0.901) were found, and six individuals had clinically significant differences ($>10\%$) attributable to various clinical factors. The investigators recommended comparing CO measurements between the two systems in individual patients. Nurses depend on the reliable system of obtaining CO measurements; thus, further study is needed to evaluate the validity of closed systems of injectate.

Nursing Implications

Based on these studies, several nursing implications can be described. Five to ten milliliters of room temperature injectate allows accurate measurements of thermodilution CO in most critically ill patients including those who are hypothermic or on mechanical ventilators with PEEP. Most nurse researchers advocate comparing CO measurements using both volumes and temperatures to determine if differences exist. Reliable CO measurements can be obtained in patients with 20° of backrest position. However, CO measurements have been variable in the lateral recumbent positions. CO measurements should be compared in the flat supine position and the position of comfort before assuming measurements are reproducible.

With minimal handling of the syringe barrel, CO measurements are comparable with automatic or manual injections. If iced injectate is manually injected, care should be taken in removing the syringe from the bath reservoir, and injection should be made within 30 seconds. If possible, thermodilution curves should be run concurrently with each injection to ensure reliability of the digital value. Injections should be made at end-expiration of the respiratory cycle and within a 4-second period.

Care must also be used with the open system of injectate. Syringe caps must be secured to ensure a water-tight seal. Leftover syringes should be discarded at the end of each shift. Reliable CO measurements can be obtained in most patients using the COSet system. The calibration constant of the CO computer should be adjusted based on volume and temperature of injectate, type of catheter, and type of system selected.

SUCTIONING TECHNIQUES

Endotracheal suctioning is associated with a number of serious complications, including cardiac arrhythmias, hypoxia, laryngospasm, microatelectasis, and trauma. Hypoxemia, which frequently occurs with suctioning, can lead to these life-threatening effects.

Cardiac arrhythmias refractory to antiarrhythmic drugs can occur with ventilatory mismanagement that leads to hypoxia or hypocarbia.[90] Although PEEP has several advantages, there are specific implications for the cardiac patient. The constant positive intrathoracic pressure decreases CO and venous return to the heart. The decreased CO is most pronounced in the hypovolemic patient but also seriously threatens the cardiac patient who may already exhibit a compromised CO.

The studies selected for this review were grouped in a classification system and are shown in Table 12-3. Although some studies could be classified in more than one category, the studies are included in the category that seemed most appropriate.

Maintaining Positive End-Expiratory Pressure

One of the 15 AACN research priorities specifies suctioning as a phenomenon of interest. Question 13 asks "What is the maximum time a patient on a mechanical ventilator with PEEP can be off the ventilator during suctioning without significantly lowering the PaO_2?"[101,102] None of the studies reviewed specifically addressed this question but evaluated the effect of maintaining PEEP during suctioning when subjects were intubated and received PEEP as part of the respiratory support.

St. Ogne and co-workers[103] examined whether maintenance of PEEP during preoxygenation would minimize suction-induced hypoxemia. No significant differences ($p>0.01$) in PaO_2 values were found among the 12 critically ill patients studied who were removed from PEEP during suctioning and those for whom

Table 12-3 Summary of Research on Suctioning Techniques

Year Published	Nurse Researcher(s)	Sample (n)	Methodology	Results	Limitations	Nursing Implications
Maintaining PEEP Pressure						
1982	St. Ogne et al.[91]	12 (x = 53 yr); intubated, mechanically ventilated PEEP = 5 cm H_2O (n = 8) PEEP = 10 cm H_2O (n = 4) FIO_2 = 0.3–0.8 ($\bar{x}$ = .45)	Treatment 1: Preoxygenation w/ out PEEP; manually bagged w/ FIO_2 1.0 × 4 breaths at ventilator rate Treatment 2: Same except for preoxygenation w/ PEEP via a PEEP valve Suctioning duration 15 sec ABGs checked 1 min before disconnecting ventilator, immediately after reconnecting ventilator, at 60, 180 sec after suctioning	No significant differences ($p < 0.05$) between treatments postsuctioning	Small sample size Limited to pts receiving < 10 cm H_2O PEEP Sequence not varied No repeated measures	Maintenance of PEEP may not be required during oxygenation if pt receives PEEP of 10 cm H_2O or less Unconditional recommendation not possible. Further study involving larger sample size and varied levels of PEEP needed.
1983	Baker et al.[92]	6 hypoxemic pts (required at least	Sequence randomly assigned Method I: pre- and postsuctioning	Ventilator methods (I and II) more effective than bag technique (III and IV)	Small sample size V_T delivered by the methods varied (III and IV provided	Hypoxemic pts may maintain high PaO_2 levels and receive larger tidal volumes

continues

Table 12-3 continued

Year Published	Nurse Researcher(s)	Sample (n)	Methodology	Results	Limitations	Nursing Implications
		FIO_2 of 0.4 to maintain PaO_2 of > 60 mm Hg) PEEP = 10 cm H_2O (n = 2) PEEP = 12.6 cm H_2O (n = 1) PEEP = 15 cm H_2O (n = 3) FIO_2 = 0.40–0.55	hyperoxygenation via ventilator; suction catheter inserted through uncapped swivel adapter Method II: same as Method I except hyperinflation added during hyperoxygenation Method III: same as Method I except hyperoxygenation done via hand-operated bag resuscitator Method IV: same as Method III except resuscitator removed from airway for suctioning period; suction catheter inserted directly into airway Suction duration 15 sec 14F suction catheter	in terms of PaO_2 levels before, during, and after suctioning ($p < 0.05$) Ventilator technique more effective than bag w/ tidal volumes ($p < 0.02$)	hypoinflation rather than hyperinflation)	w/ endotracheal suctioning methods using ventilator rather than bag. Due to the varied V_T no recommendations can be made

Year	Author	N	Settings	Procedure	Results	Comments	Conclusions
			Suction at 120 mm Hg Indwelling arterial catheter ABGs drawn preprocedure; last 10 sec of hyperoxygenation period; immediately postsuctioning; last 10 sec of postsuction hyperoxygenation period; 5 and 10 min postsuctioning				
1985	Schumann and Parsons[93]	15	PEEP = 5–18 cm H_2O FIO_2 = 0.35–0.60	Procedure 1: ventilator tubing change w/out PEEP; manually ventilated w/ PMR bag w/ FIO_2 1.00. V_T 1 1/2 × ventilator V_T Procedure 2: ventilator tubing change w/ Carden PEEP valve. Identical w/ Procedure 1 except for Carden PEEP valve inserted, maintaining PEEP identical w/ mechanically ventilated PEEP	Procedure 1 and 2 showed similar results: PaO_2 increased 1 min after procedure, returned to baseline at 5, 15, and 30 min after procedure During procedure 3, no significant increase in PaO_2 1 min after ventilator reattached ($p > 0.05$); decreases in PaO_2 in 5 pts Procedure 4 performed w/ PEEP significantly	Small sample size Hypoxemia did not occur after any procedure No report of varying sequence of procedure Very small differences between procedures	Use of Carden PEEP valve during bagging allowed PEEP to be maintained during tubing change procedure, before, and after suctioning. Cannot recommend use of Carden PEEP valve for all pts, but may benefit pts at greatest risk for hypoxemia and who require the greatest levels of PEEP

continues

Table 12-3 continued

Year Published	Nurse Researcher(s)	Sample (n)	Methodology	Results	Limitations	Nursing Implications
			Procedure 3: suctioning w/out PEEP; respirator disconnected, 5 manual presuction ventilations w/ PMR w/ FIO_2 1.00, V_T 1 1/2 ventilator V_T, and 5 manual breaths postsuction Procedure 4: suctioning w/ Carden PEEP valve; identical w/ procedure 3 except Carden PEEP valve adjusted to ventilator PEEP used Suction duration 10–15 sec 14F suction catheter Puritan manual resuscitation bag Carden PEEP valve In line Wright respirometer Tubing change 60–90 sec	increased PaO_2 at 1 min ($p < 0.005$) 1 pt paralyzed w/ pancuronium bromide on 18 cm H_2O PEEP had decrease in PaO_2 at 1 min of 114–74 mm Hg, returning to 111 mm Hg at 5 min		

Year	Investigators	Sample/Procedures	Procedures	Results	Limitations	Recommendations
1985	Douglas and Larson[94]	12 (x = 60 yr); intubated, mechanically ventilated PEEP = 5–18 cm H_2O PEEP < 10 cm H_2O PEEP > 10 cm H_2O For both treatments, ABGs checked before/after treatment Preoxygenation 1 min pre- and postsuction Suction duration 15 sec Experimental: identical w/ control except suctioning done with PEEP adapter Sequence 1: control, experimental Control: suctioning w/out PEEP adapter; manual resuscitation via bag delivering 100% oxygen; 4 hyperinflations presuction; 4 postsuction	Procedures performed over 24 hr Indwelling arterial catheter ABGs: before ventilator disconnected, 1, 5, 15, and 30 min after reconnected	Mean SaO_2 and PaO_2 fell slightly after suctioning in both samples at 1 min. PaO_2 remained below baseline at 5 and 10 min SaO_2 elevated at 5 and 10 min postsuctioning w/ control group; SaO_2 below baseline even at 10 min	Small sample size No variance of sequence	PEEP adapter valve added expense; may not be warranted except for severely hypoxic pts

continues

Table 12-3 continued

Year Published	Nurse Researcher(s)	Sample (n)	Methodology	Results	Limitations	Nursing Implications
			Sequence 2: experimental, control 14F suction catheter PMR II bag Pre- and postoxygenation 1 min duration 2–4 hr between data collections ABGs immediately pre- and postsuction			Preoxygenation should precede suctioning in all pts
Preoxygenation 1978	Adlkofer and Powaser[95]	64 ICU "stable" critical pts intubated, mechanically ventilated FIO₂ unspecified	Treatment 1: no preoxygenation; pts reconnected to ventilator between suction trials Treatment 2: preoxygenation via "sighing" delivered by ventilator w/out increasing FIO_2 or delivery of unspecified FIO_2 by resuscitation bag	Treatment 1: significant drop in PaO_2 ($p < 0.05$) at all testing times Treatment 2: no significant change ($p > 0.05$) in PaO_2 after 1st and 2nd suction pass. At 60 sec after 2nd suction $PAO_2 <$ baseline levels ($p < 0.05$)	Methods of preoxygenation diverse (unspecified duration, unspecified FIO_2 Suction duration varied Time elapsed between protocols not specified No analysis of data of the two methods of preoxygenation	

1980	Belknap et al.[96]	13 post-CABG, normal respiratory function; intubated, mechanically ventilated FIO_2 not stated	Treatment 1: preoxygenation w/ "sigh" control of ventilator w/out FIO_2 Treatment 2: preoxygenation by manual inflation w/ FIO_2 at 100%	PaO_2 differences between Treatment 1 and 2 statistically significant ($p < 0.05$) Treatment 1 PaO_2 mean 155.6 mm Hg Treatment 2 PaO_2 mean 187.9 mm Hg pH, $PaCO_2$, HCO_3 no difference	Small sample size Preoxygenation FIO_2 for "sigh" control not reported No repeated measures	Findings not generalizable
1980	Skelley et al.[97]	11 post–cardiac surgery (<12 hr); intubated, respiratory support $FIO_2 = 0.33–0.70$	Three protocols done in random order I. Suctioning w/out preoxygenation II. One hyperinflation (150% V_T) breath w/ 100% oxygen before suctioning III. 3 hyperinflations (150% V_T) breaths w/ 100% oxygen before suctioning Suction duration 15 sec Suction flow 18 L/min Time between procedures 1 hr Second volume ventilator used to deliver preset volume and O_2 level	Protocol I: Mean fall 33 mm Hg PaO_2 ($p < 0.001$) 30 sec after suctioning Protocol II: Mean rise 12 mm Hg PaO_2 Protocol III: Mean rise 49 mm Hg PaO_2 Considerable variation among pts in magnitude of fall in PaO_2	Small sample size Pts had no respiratory disease Short-term respiratory support Effects of hyperinflation not separated from effects of 100% oxygen	Well-defined methodology Preoxygenation by hyperinflation and hyperoxygenation with 1 or 3 breaths results in increased PaO_2

continues

Table 12-3 continued

Year Published	Nurse Researcher(s)	Sample (n)	Methodology	Results	Limitations	Nursing Implications
			Indwelling arterial line ABGs drawn at 0, 30, 60, 90, 120, 180, and 300 sec for protocol I, immediately after hyperinflation, and times 0, 90, and 180 for protocols II and III			
1982	Conforti[98]	33 post–cardiac surgery (< 18 hr); intubated, mechanically ventilated FIO_2 not stated	Randomly determined treatments Treatment I: hyperinflation 3 × in 15 sec w/ ventilator "sigh"; $FIO_2 = 1.0$ Treatment II: hyperinflation 3 × in 15 sec w/ manual resuscitation bag; $FIO_2 = 1.0$ Suctioning duration 15 sec 14F suction catheter Suction pressure 120 mm Hg	Both treatment PaO_2 above control levels ($p = 0.001$) 30% increase in PaO_2 w/ ventilator "sigh" as compared w/ ventilation bag ($p < 0.001$) No significant differences in pH, $PaCO_2$ HCO_3 ($p < 0.05$)	Small sample size Pts had no respiratory disease Short-term respiratory support No control of V_T	No recommendations can be made

Oxygen Insufflation

Year / Study	Sample	Methods	Results	Limitations	Conclusions
1981 Langrehr et al.[99]	10; intubated, respiratory support $FIO_2 = X$ 0.42	1 hr elapsed between data collections Four protocols tested in random order Protocol 1: preoxygenation w/ 1 hyperinflation w/ 100% oxygen at 1 1/2 × V_T Protocol 2: preoxygenation w/ 3 hyperinflations w/ 100% O_2 at 1 1/2 × V_T Protocol 3: oxygen insufflation at 10 L/min Protocol 4: oxygen insufflation at 15 L/min Suctioning duration 15 sec 14F suction catheter Suction flow rate 18 L/min Indwelling arterial catheter ABGs checked at times 0, 30, 90, 180, 300 seconds	Protocol 1: rise in PaO_2 immediately after suctioning ($p < 0.01$); PaO_2 below control values at 30 and 300 sec Protocol 2: rise in PaO_2 immediately after suctioning ($p < 0.01$); PaO_2 below control level at 30 sec, returning to control level at 300 sec Protocols 3 and 4: oxygen insufflation at 10 or 15 L/min prevented significant change at all times of sampling ($p < 0.01$) in mean PaO_2 Fall in PaO_2 at 30 sec after suctioning; not uncovered by prior studies	Small sample size No repeated measures	Well-defined methodology Oxygen insufflation most effective when insufflation flow rates approximated suction flow rate, when pulmonary function less impaired, and when subjects made spontaneous efforts during insufflation and suctioning Further study needed to make findings more generalized. Additional research to develop a catheter to provide insufflation w/out impairing suctioning efficiency needed

continues

Table 12-3 continued

Year Published	Nurse Researcher(s)	Sample (n)	Methodology	Results	Limitations	Nursing Implications
Hyperinflation/Hyperoxygenation						
1985	Goodnough[100]	28 post-cardiac surgery (4–6 hr postop); intubated, mechanically ventilated	Procedure 1: ↑ FIO$_2$ 1.0 before suctioning; hyperinflation at pt baseline FIO$_2$ after suctioning Procedure 2: ↑ FIO$_2$ 1.0 before/after suctioning Procedure 3: hyperinflation before/after suctioning at pt baseline FIO$_2$ Procedure 4: hyperinflation/FIO$_2$ to 1.0 before/after suctioning All ↑ FIO$_2$ and/or hyperinflation interventions lasted 1 min Suction duration 15 sec 14F suction catheter Suction flow rate 140 mm Hg	Presuctioning interventions: Hyperinflation did not protect 75% of pts from PaO$_2$ ($p < 0.001$) Preoxygenation protected 75% of pts from PaO$_2$ ($p < 0.01$) Preoxygenation w/ hyperinflation protected 96% pts from PaO$_2$ ($p < 0.0001$) Postsuctioning interventions: all successful in preventing decrease in PaO$_2$ or in restoring decreased PaO$_2$ to control levels	No PEEP Sampling of ABGs at 5 and 10 min intervals (more frequent sampling might show progressive PaO$_2$)	Hyperinflation w/ 100% oxygen 1 min before/after endotracheal suctioning may protect cardiac surgery pts not requiring PEEP from a fall in PaO$_2$. Hyperinflation may cause decrease in arterial BP, so BP and HR should be visually monitored

Laerdal resuscitator
bags
Hyperinflation 150% of
pt baseline V_T
Indwelling arterial
catheter
ABGs obtained
immediately and 5
and 10 min
postsuctioning

Note: ABGs, arterial blood gas; FIO_2, fractional inspired oxygen; V_T, tidal volume; PaO_2, arterial oxygen tension.

EP was maintained via a PEEP valve. Only patients receiving PEEP at 10 n H_2O were studied.

Results reported by Douglas and Larson[104] on a group of 12 medical and surgical intensive care patients agreed with those of St. Ogne et al.[105] in that there were no significant differences between the PaO_2 during suctioning of the "experimental" treatment (suctioning with a PEEP adapter on the manual resuscitation bag) and the "control" treatment (suctioning without a PEEP adapter). The investigators included five patients in their study with PEEP values greater than 10 cm H_2O.

Fifteen critically ill adults with adult respiratory distress syndrome (ARDS) on PEEP of 5 to 18 cm H_2O were studied by Schumann and Parsons[106] using a Carden PEEP valve. When hyperinflation via bagging was performed with the Carden PEEP valve (procedure 4), there was a significant increase in PaO_2 ($p<0.005$) 1 minute postsuctioning compared with patients who had hyperinflation via bagging and suctioning without maintaining PEEP. However, there was no significant difference in PaO_2 between the two methods at 5, 10, and 30 minutes postsuctioning ($p<0.01$). They also looked at ventilator tubing change without PEEP compared with the use of the Carden PEEP valve during tubing changes. The results of an initial rise in PaO_2 at 1 minute and return toward baseline at 5, 15, and 30 minutes after the tubing change procedure were similar with and without maintenance of PEEP. The most profound decrease in PaO_2 without PEEP occurred in one patient who was on the highest level of PEEP (18 cm H_2O) and was paralyzed with pancuronium bromide. The decrease in PaO_2 in this patient led the authors to speculate that patients who could benefit most with the Carden PEEP valve are those who are most hypoxic initially, require the highest levels of PEEP, and are phamacologically paralyzed.

In a study of six hypoxemic patients on PEEP greater than 5 cm H_2O, Baker et al.[107] reported that endotracheal suctioning methods using hyperoxygenation with a ventilator are more effective in maintaining higher PaO_2 levels and in delivering larger tidal volumes than are techniques using a resuscitator. They also reported a beneficial effect of inserting the suction catheter through a swivel adaptor cap, also used by Belling et al.[108] Suctioning through the swivel adapter produced a much smaller decrease in PaO_2 than did suctioning with the gas-delivery tubing disconnected from the airway, although no statistical data to support this finding were noted.

Preoxygenation

The 38th ranked question asks, "What are the effects of different approaches to nursing procedures (e.g., chest tube milking, endotracheal tube, cuff deflation, suctioning) on the respiratory status of the patients requiring ventilatory assistance?"[109] (Exhibit 12-2). The research studies including preoxygenation, insufflation, and hyperinflation can be clustered under the 38th ranked question or under question number 13 (Exhibit 12-1).

Preoxygenation is the administration of oxygen before suctioning and may include one or a combination of 1) hyperoxygenation, 2) hyperinflation, and 3) hyperventilation. The techniques of preoxygenation include manual bagging, a change in ventilator rate, or a mechanical "sigh."

Adlkofer and Powaser[110] examined preoxygenation versus no preoxygenation in the control of suction-induced hypoxemia. Since the authors surveyed the practices of others rather than designing their own experimental model, preoxygenation methods were diverse. Despite the limitations of the study, the significant fall in PaO_2 ($p<0.05$) in the patients without preoxygenation led the authors to recommend preoxygenation precede suctioning in all patients, and further to suggest that hyperinflation after suctioning may be beneficial in preventing hypoxemia. The initial groundwork was established for further studies to examine preoxygenation variables.

As the method in which to preoxygenate patients in preventing or minimizing suction-induced hypoxemia was not made clear, two further studies compared the use of ventilator "sigh" with the use of the resuscitation bag. The conclusions of these two studies, however, differed. In one study, Belknap and co-workers[111] found differences between the techniques of mechanical "sigh" versus manual bag inflation for the PaO_2 levels ($p<0.053$). The authors concluded that preoxygenation by ventilating bag was the preferred method because it raises the PaO_2 level higher before suctioning. The FIO_2 concentration used with the "sigh" method was not reported, nor were the tidal volumes, making it difficult to make any recommendations. In a similar study, Conforti[112] found that the ventilator "sigh" method with 100% oxygen caused significantly higher PaO_2 levels than did manual hyperinflation with 100% oxygen. This study, although controlling for the FIO_2 levels, had a limitation in that the subjects studied had no respiratory disease and required short-term respiratory support, making it difficult to generalize the results to a larger population.

In a well-defined study, Skelley et al.[113] investigated the effectiveness of two methods of preoxygenation, utilizing three protocols. Both preoxygenation methods used resulted in an increase in PaO_2 before suctioning and minimized the fall in PaO_2 as compared to no preoxygenation prior to suctioning. These authors concluded that even though initial PaO_2 levels may equal or exceed normal levels, preoxygenation with even modest hyperinflation volumes using 100% oxygen minimizes or prevents a mean fall in PaO_2 because of endotracheal suctioning.

Insufflation

Insufflation describes the delivery of oxygen through the double lumen of a suction catheter or the sidearm of an endotracheal tube adapter, allowing oxygen be administered simultaneously without suctioning. Langrehr et al.[114] evaluted the ability of oxygen insufflation with hyperinflation to maintain arterial vygen tension during suctioning. Two protocols used one or three lung hyperiflations similar to the study by Skelley and co-workers.[115] Two other protocols used oxygen insufflation at 10 or 15 L/min during suctioning. The authors noted a fall in PaO_2 30 seconds after suctioning with the hyperinflation technique, suggesting an adverse hemodynamic effect of hyperinflation may have influenced the fall in PaO_2. They suggested that oxygen insufflation may be the preferred route to prevent hypoxemia by minimizing or preventing varying levels of PaO_2 during suctioning.

Hyperinflation/Hyperoxygenation

Hyperinflation implies lung inflation by means of a resuscitation bag or ventilator. The volume delivered can be equivalent to the ventilator setting or as much as one and one half times the ventilator setting. The technique of hyperinflation can be accomplished by either bagging or "sighing."

The effects of hyperinflation and increasing the FIO_2 to 1.0 on PaO_2 after endotracheal suctioning were examined by Goodnough[116] in 28 patients after cardiac surgery. The author concluded that 100% oxygen administered by hyperinflation for 1 minute before and after endotracheal suctioning protects patients after cardiac surgery from a fall in PaO_2. As 29% of the patients responded to hyperinflation with transient decreases in arterial blood pressure (BP), both BP and heart rate were recommended to be visually monitored during endotracheal suctioning procedures.

Nursing Implications

Methods of maintaining PEEP during endotracheal suctioning need further study, as results are inconclusive. A preliminary recommendation may be that maintenance of PEEP during oxygenation and/or suctioning is necessary when the patient requires high levels (>10 cm H_2O) of PEEP for ventilatory support.

From the data of Adlkofer and Powaser,[117] it is clear that some method of preoxygenation for endotracheal suctioning is necessary. However, the preferred method remains controversial. Supplemental oxygen may be provided by increasing the FIO_2, hyperinflation, hyperventilation, or insufflation. The ultimate goal of nursing practice is to minimize or prevent hypoxemia associated with endotracheal suctioning through use of appropriate preoxygenation methods. Based on the studies reviewed, the technique of hyperinflation with hyperoxygenation is recommended. Although studies have substantiated the positive effects of hyperinflation, responses in particular patient populations should be considered. Patients with limited cardiac reserve may develop a decrease in CO, hypotension, or bradycardia. The patient with severe lung disease who requires respiratory support with high positive pressure is at risk for decreased CO and barotrauma.

Oxygen delivery can be increased by a volume-controlled ventilator or a reservoir bag. The nurse should consider the advantages and disadvantages of each. Questions still remain regarding the timing at which oxygen should be provided; e.g., before suctioning, after suctioning, or continuously through the procedure (insufflation). Two well-documented studies by Skelley et al.[118] and Langrehr et al.[119] indicated that three breaths of 100% oxygen at 150% tidal volume before suctioning was adequate to prevent hypoxemia.

Most authors advocated the administration of 100% oxygen before suctioning. One concern that has not been addressed by investigators is: Can a high PaO_2 resulting from hyperoxygenation be dangerous? Absorption atelectasis resulting in a decrease in the ventilation perfusion or an increase in interpulmonary shunt has been found in patients receiving 100% oxygen.[120]

The research protocols reviewed advocated limiting suctioning to 15 seconds, but further studies are needed that would indicate the influence of suction duration on hypoxemia. Use of an adapter has also been advocated to avoid disconnection from the oxygen source during suctioning; but again, the studies were too limited in scope to allow a generalized recommendation.

Many questions remain unanswered in the pursuit of a research-based procedure for endotracheal suctioning. It is evident that no single procedure will benefit every patient because of the wide variation in cardiovascular and pulmonary dysfunction encountered in the critically ill patient.

CARDIAC REHABILITATION

Arteriosclerotic narrowing of the coronary arteries is currently responsible for approximately 80% of all cardiac-related deaths.[121] The management of the progression of this pathologic condition necessitates changes in the patient's life style. The success of the treatment for any individual is dependent, in part, on the patient's degree of adherence to the prescribed dietary, exercise, and medication regimen.

One of the 74 ranked questions, number 56, asks "What is the effect of selected nursing therapies (e.g., initiation of activity programs, visiting policies) on the rate of recovery of myocardial infarction (MI) patients?"[122] A number of nursing practices common to the cardiac intensive care unit setting have been tested and replaced by nurse researchers. Activity after MI has been the focus of several researchers.[123–136] Selected clinical nursing research in this area is presented in this section. Other studies of cardiac rehabilitation are in this book. For example, the validity of coronary precautions is in Chapter 3; patient teaching

Chapter 7, and patient transfer and the patient stress of visiting with staff family is in Chapter 8.

Exercise has been linked to improvements in cardiovascular efficiency as well as to a sense of psychologic well-being. Nurses have an important role in the study of low-level treadmill testing for assessing the functional status of patients after MI or coronary artery bypass grafting.[124–126] Sivarajan et al.[127] studied treadmill responses of patients 7 to 17 days after an acute myocardial infarction (AMI). They found that low-level treadmill testing was safe as early as 11 days after infarction when appropriately supervised and when the test was halted at the threshold of symptoms. As part of a study identifying medical problems and physiologic response during supervised inpatient cardiac rehabilitation, Dion and co-workers[128] found that treadmill exercise began 7.6 ± 4.3 days after coronary artery bypass surgery. Of the 521 patients studied, 50% started exercises within 6 days. They concluded that a low-level exercise program may begin as soon as 12 to 24 hours after surgery.

In a randomized controlled study to determine the effects of early exercise and of teaching and counseling after AMI, Sivarajan and co-workers[129] studied 258 patients for 2 years. Patients in the control group received conventional medical and nursing care; patients in the experimental group followed an exercise protocol. The final component of the study was performance of a low-level treadmill test by each study participant. Results showed no significant differences ($p<0.05$) between the groups in their ability to finish the low-level treadmill test and their hemodynamic response to exercise.

In viewing in-hospital progressive activity of MI patients, Beeby and Cowan[130] undertook a 2-year study to compare the in-hospital activity progression of a group of patients with AMI without complication (AMI patients) and a group of patients with AMI with out-of-hospital ventricular fibrillation (AMI/VF). The AMI/VF patients were consistently later than the uncomplicated AMI patients in initiating four activities ($p=0.003$): AMI/VF patients got up to go to the bathroom significantly later (mean 6.3 ± 2.1 days after admission) than AMI patients (mean 4.7 ± 1.6) ($p=0.012$). A mean of 8.9 ± 2.3 days after admission to ambulate in the hallways was found in the AMI/VF compared with a mean of 6.7 ± 1.9 days in AMI patients ($p=0.027$). However, activities of sitting in a chair at the bedside or getting up to go to the commode were not significantly different.

With the advent of new procedures such as percutaneous transluminal angioplasty (PTCA), treadmill responses could be studied. One study by Gentry and Leimgruber[131] investigated the safety of discharging patients 1 day after an uncomplicated PTCA. Of the 115 patients studied, 82 (76%) had an exercise tolerance test 1 day post-PTCA. The data indicated that the majority of patients with uncomplicated PTCA could safely be exercised and discharged the day after PTCA, which results in a shorter hospital stay and cost savings to the patient.

Of continued interest has been the cardiac and hemodynamic response to routine hospital activities and to sexual activity. Of interest is Kirchoff's[132] review of the literature in which she examined the physiologic basis for coronary precautions, such as restriction of very hot or cold and stimulant beverages, avoidance of rectal temperatures, and avoidance of vigorous backrubs. Her review reported that many of the widely accepted coronary precautions that follow an MI have little or no scientific rationale. Only the avoidance of stimulant beverages was well supported by research.

Oxygen consumption, hemodynamic, and ECG responses to bathing by patients 3 to 5 days post-MI were studied by Johnston et al.[133] Oxygen consumption was higher during showering than during either tub or bed bathing. The pressure-rate product was greater for showering than for bed bath. The premature ventricular contractions noted occurred regardless of the type of bathing done. Winslow and Lane[134] also studied oxygen consumption and cardiovascular responses. Eighty-seven patients were divided into four groups: normals, cardiac inpatients, medical inpatients, and AMI inpatients. Very small differences between methods of toileting (bedpan versus bedside commode for women, and urinal versus standing urinal for men) were noted. The investigators concluded that out-of-bed toileting is not a major cardiac stress and that early bed-toileting could potentially eliminate orthostatic intolerance common to the AMI patient in early recovery. The investigators did cite a limitation to their study in that the MI patients were studied 5 to 28 days postinfarction, and results could not be generalized directly to the immediate postinfarction patient.

Johnston et al.[135] studied the coital activities of cardiac patients participating in an outpatient exercise program. Patients who had experienced an AMI reported a decrease in frequency of sexual intercourse; surgically revascularized patients reported no difference in frequency. More than 20% in each patient group reported angina with sexual intercourse.

McNaughton et al.[136] and other investigators[137,138] sought to determine if response to sexual activity could be predicted by a response to stair climbing. They found stair climbing to be a useful test of readiness for resuming sexual activity after an AMI.

Nursing Implications

Several investigators have shown the ability of uncomplicated MI patients to engage in activities requiring low levels of energy expenditure. Selected patients can be exercised at low levels on the treadmill and discharged with an appropriate exercise prescription. This information is useful for in-hospital management.

The well-conducted experimental study by Sivarajan and co-workers[139] has important implications for nursing practice. The commonly held belief that in-hospital exercise programs minimize or prevent the deleterious effects of bed rest was not supported by their study. Further research is needed to test the scientific rationale of these nursing activities.

A valuable description of which practices prevail regarding activity progression in subgroups of patients with AMI and VF should also direct future inquiry into the basis of nursing practice in hospital rehabilitation programs.[140]

Kirchoff's[141] literature review strongly points out the need to examine cardiovascular nursing practice for scientific validity and to incorporate existing research findings into practice.

RESEARCH FOR THE FUTURE

Nursing science is only in the early stages of building sufficient empirical findings on which to base nursing practice. Many questions remain to be answered relative to the aspects of physiologic phenomena as they relate to cardiovascular nursing.

Most nursing research studies reviewed in this chapter were single investigations or one-of-a-kind studies. The few exceptions are research studies by Woods et al.[142–153] (hemodynamic monitoring); Powaser et al.[154–156] (endotracheal suctioning, oxygenation); Johnston et al.[157–159]; and Sivarajan et al.[160–164] (cardiac rehabilitation).

As found by other authors,[165–168] replication of research is of particular concern. A necessary step is verification of findings in different populations and settings, and under varying conditions, before conclusions can be generalized and viewed as a basis for nursing practice.[169]

To incorporate scientific findings into cardiovascular nursing practice, nurse researchers must find topics relevant to practice. The AACN identification of research priorities can provide for this deliberative approach to critical care nursing practice. Clustering of studies relevant to cardiovascular nursing under the top 15 ranked questions can provide a basis for nurse investigators to work with the same research priority, and also to develop research questions and protocols that address similar and different questions about the same priority.[170]

Acknowledgment

The authors acknowledge Susan L. Woods, our mentor and friend, who has been a constant source of encouragement and assistance. Our special thanks to our husbands, Jerry and Todd, without whose support and patience this chapter could not have been completed.

NOTES

1. Marguerite R. Kinney, "The Scientific Basis for Critical Care Nursing Practice: 1972 to 1982," *Heart and Lung* 13(1984):116.

2. Ada M. Lindsey, "Research for Clinical Practice," *Heart and Lung* 13(1984):496.

3. Linda A. Lewandowski and Ann M. Kositsky, "Research Priorities for Critical Care Nursing: A Study by the American Association of Critical-Care Nurses," *Heart and Lung* 12(1983):35.

4. AACN Research Committee, "Five Year Plan for AACN Research Activities," *Focus on Critical Care* 10(1983):61.

5. R.M. Fuller, "Forecasting the Future," *Managerial Planning* 21(1972):1.

6. N.C. Dalkey, "Studies in the Quality of Life." *Delphi and Decision-Making* (Lexington, MA: 1972), p. 13.

7. Lewandowski and Kositsky, "Research Priorities."

8. Ibid.

9. Ibid.

10. AACN Research Committee: "Five Year Plan."

11. Susan L. Woods and Louise Mansfield, "Effect of Patient Position upon the Pulmonary Artery and Pulmonary Capillary Wedge Pressure in Non-Acutely Ill Patients," *Heart and Lung* 5(1976):89.

12. Julie A. Shinn, Susan L. Woods, and John Huseby, "The Effect of IPPV on Pulmonary Artery and Pulmonary Capillary Wedge Pressures in Acutely Ill Patients," *Heart and Lung* 8(1979):322.

13. B. Lynn Grose and Susan L. Woods, "Effects of Mechanical Ventilation and Backrest upon Pulmonary Artery and Pulmonary Artery Capillary Wedge Pressure Measurements," *American Review of Respiratory Diseases* 123, no. 4 (April 1981):120.

14. Susan L. Woods, B. Lynn Grose, and Debra Laurent-Bopp, "Effect of Backrest Position on Pulmonary Artery Pressures in Critically Ill Patients," *Cardiovascular Nursing* 18, no. 4 (July-August 1982):19.

15. J. Laulive, "Pulmonary Artery Pressures and Position Changes in the Critically Ill Adult," *Dimensions of Critical Care Nursing* 1, no. (1982):28.

16. Ellen J. Nemens and Susan L. Woods, "Normal Fluctuations in Pulmonary Artery and Pulmonary Capillary Wedge Pressures in Acutely Ill Patients," *Heart and Lung* 11(1982):393.

17. T. Van Sciver, "Effect of Positive Pressure Ventilation and Static Effective Compliance upon Pulmonary Artery and Wedge Pressures," in *Proceedings of the AACN International Intensive Care Nursing Conference* (London: American Association of Critical-Care Nurses, 1982).

18. Gayle R. Whitman, Dianna L. Howaniak, and Tanya S. Verga, "Comparison of Cardiac Output Measurements in 20° Supine and 20° Right and Left Lateral Recumbent Positions," *Heart and Lung* 11(1982):256.

19. M. Cengiz, R.O. Crapo, and R.M. Gardner, "The Effect of Ventilation on the Accuracy of Pulmonary Artery and Wedge Pressure Measurement," *Critical Care Medicine* 11(1983):502.

20. J.A. Gershan, "Effect of Positive End-Expiratory Pressures on Pulmonary Capillary Wedge Pressure," *Heart and Lung* 12(1983):143.

21. Marianne Chulay and Therese Miller, "The Effect of Backrest Elevation on Pulmonary Artery and Pulmonary Capillary Wedge Pressures in Patients after Cardiac Surgery," *Heart and Lung* 13(1984):138.

22. J.M. Clochesy, A.S. Hinshaw, and C.W. Oho, "Effects of Change in Position on Pulmonary Artery and Pulmonary Capillary Wedge Pressures in Mechanically Ventilated Patients," *NITA* 7(1984):138.

23. Gemma T. Kennedy, Azerlea Bryant, and Michael H. Crawford, "The Effects of Lateral Body Positioning on Measurements of Pulmonary Artery and Pulmonary Artery Wedge Pressures," *Heart and Lung* 13(1984):155.

24. Lorie Wild and Susan L. Woods, "Effect of Lateral Recumbent Positions on the Measurement of Pulmonary Artery and Pulmonary Artery Wedge Pressures in Critically Ill Adults." *Heart and Lung* 13(1984):305.

25. Mary A. Retalliau, Mary M. Leding, and Susan L. Woods, "The Effect of Backrest Position on the Measurement of Left Atrial Pressure in Patients after Cardiac Surgery," *Heart and Lung* 10(1985)447.

26. Ann K. Killpack et al., "Effect of Injectate Volume and Temperature on Measurement of Thermodilution Cardiac Output in Acutely Ill Patients," *Circulation* 64(1981):IV–165.

27. Linda Davidson et al., "Effect of Injectate Variables on Cardiac Output," *Western Journal of Nursing Research* 4(1982):66.

28. Christine Larson and Susan L. Woods, "Effect of Injectate Volume and Temperature on Thermodilution Cardiac Output Measurement in Critically Ill Patients," *Circulation* 66(1982):II–98.

29. Ilene Hruby and Susan L. Woods, "Effect of Injectate Temperature on Measurement of Thermodilution Cardiac Output in Cardiac Surgical Patients," *Circulation* 68(1983):III–223.

30. Frank G. Shellock and Mary S. Riedinger, "Reproducibility and Accuracy of Using Room Temperature Versus Ice Temperature Injectate for Thermodilution Cardiac Output Determination," *Heart and Lung* 12(1983):175.

31. Frank G. Shellock et al., "Thermodilution Cardiac Output in Hypothermic Cardiac Surgery Patients: Comparison of Ice Versus Room Temperature Injectate," *Circulation* 66(1983):II–98.

32. Clarice V. Vennix, Donna H. Nelson, and Gordon L. Pierpont, "Thermodilution Cardiac Output in Critically Ill Patients: Comparison of Room-Temperature and Iced Injectate," *Heart and Lung* 13(1984):574.

33. L.D. Nelson and H.B. Anderson, "Patient Selection for Iced Versus Room Temperature Injectate for Thermodilution Cardiac Output Determinations," *Critical Care Medicine* 13(1985):182.

34. Marlene Barcelona et al., "Cardiac Output Determination by the Thermodilution Method: Comparison of Ice Temperature Injectate Versus Room Temperature Injectate Contained in Prefilled Syringes or a Closed Injectate Delivery System," *Heart and Lung* 14(1985):232.

35. Polly E. Gardner, Lise Monat, and Susan L. Woods, "Accuracy of the COSet™ System on Measurement of Thermodilution Cardiac Output," pending publication in Heart and Lung (Sept/Oct, 1987).

36. B. Lynn Grose, Susan L. Woods, and Debra Laurent, "Effect of Backrest Position on Cardiac Output Measured by the Thermodilution Method in Acutely Ill Patients," *Heart and Lung* 10(1981):661.

37. Whitman, Howaniak, and Verga, "Comparison of Measurements."

38. M. Kleven, "Effect of Backrest Position on Thermodilution Cardiac Output in Critically Ill Patients Receiving Mechanical Ventilation with Positive End-Expiratory Pressure," *Heart and Lung* 13(1984):303.

39. Lynn Doering and Kathleen Dracup, "Comparison of Cardiac Output in Supine and Lateral Positions in Adult Post-Cardiac Surgical Patients," *Proceedings from the 10th World Congress of Cardiology* (1986):307.

40. Susan Manifold, "A Comparison of Two Alternative Methods for the Determination of Cardiac Output by Thermodilution: Automatic Versus Manual Injection," *Heart and Lung* 13(1984):304.

41. B. Lynn Grose, Marilyn Adair, and Mary Reim, "Incidence of Contamination of Thermodilution Cardiac Output Bath," *Circulation* 64(1981):IV–179.

42. Mary Riedinger et al., "Sterility of Prefilled Thermodilution Cardiac Output Syringes Maintained at Room Temperature and Ice Temperatures," *Heart and Lung* 14(1985):8.

43. Woods and Mansfield, "Effect of Patient Position."

44. T. Winsor and G.E. Burch, "Phlebostatic Axis and Phlebostatic Level: Reference Levels for Venous Pressure Measurement in Man," *Proceedings of the Society of Experimental Biologic Medicine* 58(1945):165.

45. Woods, Grose, and Laurent-Bopp "Effect of Backrest Position."

46. Woods and Mansfield, "Effect of Patient Position."

47. Laulive, "Pulmonary Pressures."

48. Nemens and Woods, "Normal Fluctuations."

49. Retalliau, Leding, and Woods, "Effect of Backrest Position."

50. Chulay and Miller, "Effect of Elevation."

51. Clochesy, Hinshaw, and Oho, "Effects of Change."

52. Gayle R. Whitman, "Comparison of Pulmonary Artery Catheter Measurements in 20° Supine and 20° Right and Left Lateral Recumbent Positions," in *Proceedings of the AACN International Intensive Care Nursing Conference* (London: American Association of Critical-Care Nurses, 1982).

53. Kennedy, Bryant, and Crawford, "Effects of Lateral Positioning."

54. Wild and Woods, "Effect of Recumbent Positions."

55. Shinn, Woods, and Huseby, "Effect of IPPV."

56. Grose and Woods, "Effect of Mechanical Ventilation."

57. Van Sciver, "Effect of Positive Pressure Ventilation."

58. Gershan, "Effect of Positive End-Expiratory Pressures."

59. Mary S. Riedinger, Frank G. Shellock, and H.J.C. Swan, "Reading Pulmonary Artery and Pulmonary Capillary Wedge Pressure Waveforms with Respiratory Variations," *Heart and Lung* 10(1981):675.

60. Lorie Wild and Susan L. Woods, "Comparison of Three Methods for Interpreting Pulmonary Artery Wedge Pressure Waveforms with Respiratory Variation," *Heart and Lung* 14(1985):308.

61. Cengiz, Crapo, and Gardner, "Effect of Ventilation."

62. W. Kaye, "Invasive Monitoring Techniques: Arterial Cannulation, Bedside Pulmonary Artery Catheterization, and Arterial Puncture," *Heart and Lung* 12(1983):395.

64. Lewandowski and Kositsky, "Research Priorities."

65. AACN Research Committee, "Five Year Plan."

66. Killpack et al., "Effect of Injectate Volume."

67. Davidson et al., "Effect of Injectate Variables."

68. Larson and Woods, "Effect of Injectate Volume."

69. Hruby and Woods, "Effect of Injectate Temperature."

70. Shellock and Riedinger, "Reproducibility and Accuracy."

71. Shellock et al., "Thermodilution Cardiac Output."

72. Vennix, Nelson, and Pierpont, "Thermodilution Cardiac Output."

73. Nelson and Anderson, "Patient Selection."

74. Killpack et al., "Effect of Injectate Volume."

75. Davidson et al., "Effect of Injectate Variables."

76. Larson and Woods, "Effect of Injectate Volume."

77. Manifold, "Comparison of Two Methods."

78. Grose, Woods, and Laurent, "Effect of Backrest Position."

79. Kleven, "Effect of Position."

80. Whitman, Howaniak, and Verga "Comparison of Measurements."

81. Grose, Woods, and Laurent, "Effect of Backrest Position."

82. Kleven, "Effect of Position."

83. Whitman, Howaniak, and Verga, "Comparison of Measurements."

84. Doering and Dracup, "Comparison of Cardiac Output."

85. Grose, Adair, and Reim, "Incidence of Contamination."

86. Riedinger et al., "Sterility of Syringes."

87. *American Edwards Laboratories COSet*™ (Santa Ana, CA: American Edwards Laboratories, (1982).

88. Barcelona et al., "Cardiac Output."

89. Gardner, Monat, and Woods, "Accuracy of COSet."

90. S.M. Ayres and W.J. Grace, "Inappropriate Ventilation and Hypoxemia as Causes of Cardiac Arrhythmias," *American Journal of Medicine* 46(1969):495.

91. Donald St. Ogne, Leslie H. Kirilloff, and Thomas G. Zullo, "The Effect of Maintaining and Removing Positive End-Expiratory Pressure during Endotracheal Suctioning," in *Proceedings of the Ninth National Teaching Institute* (Newport Beach, CA: 1982), p. 307.

92. Pat O. Baker, James P. Baker, and Peter A. Koen, "Endotracheal Suctioning Techniques in Hypoxemic Patients," *Respiratory Care* 28(1983):1563.

93. Lorna Schumann and Gibbie H. Parsons, "Tracheal Suctioning and Ventilator Tubing Changes in Adult Respiratory Distress Syndrome: Use of a Positive End-Expiratory Pressure Valve," *Heart and Lung* 14(1985):362.

94. Sara Douglas and Elaine L. Larson, "The Effect of a Positive End-Expiratory Pressure Adapter on Oxygenation During Endotracheal Suctioning," *Heart and Lung* 14(1985):396.

95. R.M. Adlkofer and Mary M. Powaser, "The Effect of Endotracheal Suctioning on Arterial Blood Gases in Patients after Cardiac Surgery," *Heart and Lung* 7(1978):1011.

96. J.D. Belknap, Leslie H. Kirilloff, and Thomas G. Zullo, "The Effect of Preoxygenation Technique on Arterial Blood Gases in the Mechanically Ventilated Patient," *American Review of Respiratory Diseases* 121(1980):210.

97. Billie F. Holladay Skelley, Susan M. Deeren, and Mary M. Powaser, "The Effectiveness of Two Preoxygenation Methods to Prevent Endotracheal Suction-Induced Hypoxemia," *Heart and Lung* 9(1980):316.

98. Christina Conforti, "The Effect of Two Preoxygenation Techniques in Minimizing Hypoxemia during Endotracheal Suctioning," in *Proceedings of the Ninth National Teaching Institute* (Newport Beach, CA: 1982), p. 309.

99. Ellen A. Langrehr, Susan Campbell Washburn, and Mary Powaser Guthrie, "Oxygen Insufflation during Endotracheal Suctioning," *Heart and Lung* 10(1981):1028.

100. Sandra K. Crabtree Goodnough, "The Effects of Oxygen and Hyperinflation on Arterial Oxygen Tension after Endotracheal Suctioning," *Heart and Lung* 14(1985):11.

101. Lewandowski and Kositsky, "Research Priorities."

102. AACN Research Committee, "Five Year Plan."

103. St. Ogne, Kirilloff, and Zullo, "Effect of Positive End-Expiratory Pressure."

104. Douglas and Larson, "Effect of Adapter."

105. St. Ogne, Kirilloff, and Zullo, "Effect of Positive End-Expiratory Pressure."

106. Schumann and Parsons, "Use of Pressure Valve."

107. Baker, Baker, and Koen, "Endotracheal Suctioning."

108. Dorothy Belling, Robert R. Kelley, and Richard Simon, "Use of the Swivel Adapter Aperture During Suctioning to Prevent Hypoxemia in the Mechanically Ventilated Patient," *Heart and Lung* 7(1978):320.

109. Lewandowski and Kositsky, "Research Priorities."

110. Adlkofer and Powaser, "Effect of Suctioning."

111. Belknap, Kirilloff, and Zullo, "Effect of Preoxygenation."

112. Conforti, "Effect of Two Techniques."

113. Skelley, Deeren, and Powaser, "Effectiveness of Two Methods."

114. Langrehr, Washburn, and Guthrie, "Oxygen Insufflation."

115. Skelley, Deeren, and Powaser, "Effectiveness of Two Methods."

116. Goodnough, "Effects of Oxygen."

117. Adlkofer and Powaser, "Effect on Suctioning."

118. Skelley, Deeren, and Powaser, "Effectiveness of Two Methods."

119. Langrehr, Washburn, and Guthrie, "Oxygen Insufflation."

120. T.C. McAslan et al., "Influence of Inhalation of 100% Oxygen on Intrapulmonary Shunt in Severely Traumatized Patients," *Journal of Trauma* 13(1973):811.

121. *Heart Facts 1984* (Dallas: American Heart Association, 1984).

122. Lewandowski and Kositsky, "Research Priorities."

123. Karen T. Kirchoff, "An Examination of the Physiologic Basis for Coronary Precautions," *Heart and Lung* 10(1981):874.

124. Erika Sivarajan, A.V. Syndsman, and B. Smith, "Feasibility Study of Low Level Treadmill Testing for Assessing Acute Myocardial Infarction Patients before Discharge," *Circulation* 54(1976):II–94.

125. Diane J. Christopherson, Erika Sivarajan, and L.J. Clark, "Subjective and Hemodynamic Responses of Patients during Low-Level Treadmill Tests Before and After Coronary Artery Bypass Surgery," *Circulation* 60(1979):II–201.

126. Erika S. Sivarajan et al., "Low-level Treadmill Testing of 41 Patients with Acute Myocardial Infarction Prior to Discharge from the Hospital," *Heart and Lung* 6(1977):975.

127. Ibid.

128. Wendy Faraher Dion et al., "Medical Problems and Physiologic Responses During Supervised Inpatient Cardiac Rehabilitation: The Patient After Coronary Artery Bypass Grafting," *Heart and Lung* 11(1982):248.

129. Erika Sivarajan et al., "In-Hospital Exercise After Myocardial Infarction Does Not Improve Treadmill Performance," *New England Journal of Medicine* 305(1981):357.

130. Barbara J. Beeby and Marie Cowan, "In-Hospital Progressive Activity: Comparison Between Myocardial Infarction Occurring Without Complications and With Out-Of-Hospital Ventricular Fibrillation," *Heart and Lung* 13(1984):361.

131. Larry J. Gentry and Pierre P. Leimgruber, "Advisability of Stress Test and Discharge One Day After Uncomplicated Coronary Angioplasty," *Circulation* 72(1985):III–179.

132. Kirchoff, "Examination of Physiologic Basis."

133. B.L. Johnston, E.W. Watt, and G.F. Fletcher, "Oxygen Consumption and Hemodynamic and Electrocardiographic Response to Bathing in Recent Post-Myocardial Infarction Patients," *Heart and Lung* 10(1981):666.

134. Elizabeth Hahn Winslow and Linda Denton Lane, "Oxygen Consumption and Cardiovascular Response During Different Methods of Toileting," in *Proceedings of the Ninth Teaching Institute* (Newport Beach, CA: 1982) p. 301.

135. B.L. Johnston et al., "Sexual Activity in Exercising Patients After Myocardial Infarction and Revascularization," *Heart and Lung* 7(1978).

136. Michael McNaughton, J.L. Larson, and Louise Mansfield, "Heart Rate and Blood Pressure Response to Stair Climbing and Sexual Activity," *Circulation* 58(1978):II–215.

137. Johnston et al., "Sexual Activity."

138. E.D. Nemec and Louise Mansfield, "Blood Pressure and Heart Rate Responses During Sexual Activity in Normal Males," *Circulation* 50(1974):II–254.

139. Sivarajan et al., "In-Hospital Exercise."

140. Beeby and Cowan, "In-Hospital Activity."

141. Kirchoff, "Examination of Physiologic Basis."

142. Woods and Mansfield, "Effect of Patient Position."

143. Woods, Grose, and Laurent-Bopp, "Effect of Backrest Position."

144. Nemens and Woods, "Normal Fluctuations."

145. Retalliau, Leding, and Woods, "Effect of Backrest Position."

146. Wild and Woods, "Effect of Recumbent Positions."

147. Shinn, Woods, and Huseby, "Effect of IPPV."

148. Grose and Woods, "Effects of Mechanical Ventilation."

149. Wild and Woods, "Methods for Interpreting PAWP Wave Forms."

150. Killpack et al., "Effect of Injectate Volume."

151. Davidson et al., "Effect of Injectate Variables."

152. Larson and Woods, "Effect of Injectate Volume."

153. Hruby and Woods, "Effect of Injectate Temperature."

154. Adlkofer and Powaser, "Effect on Suctioning."

155. Skelley, Deeren, and Powaser, "Effectiveness of Two Methods."

156. Langrehr, Washburn, and Guthrie, "Oxygen Insufflation."

157. B.L. Johnston, J.D. Cantwell, and G.F. Fletcher, "Eight Steps to Cardiac Rehabilitation: The Team Effort: Methodology and Preliminary Results, *Heart and Lung* 5(1976):97.

158. Johnston, Watt, and Fletcher, "Oxygen Consumption."

159. Johnston et al., "Sexual Activity."

160. Erika Sivarajan, J. Lerman, and Louise Mansfield, "Hemodynamic and Polarcardiographic Responses of Acute Myocardial Infarction Patients During Three Selected Levels of Activity," *Circulation* 52(1975):II–264.

161. Sivarajan, Syndsman, and Smith, "Feasibility Study."

162. Christopherson, Sivarajan, and Clark, "Subjective and Hemodynamic Responses."

163. Sivarajan et al., "Treadmill Testing."

164. Sivarajan et al., "In-Hospital Exercise."

165. Lindsey, "Research."

166. Kirchoff, "Examination of Physiologic Basis."

167. Marguerite R. Kinney, "Trends in Cardiovascular Nursing Research: 1972–1983," *Cardiovascular Nursing* 21, no. 5 (September-October 1985):25.

168. Susan B. Foster, Judith Astie Kloner, and Susan Sumner Stengrevics, "Cardiovascular Nursing Research: Past, Present, and Future," *Heart and Lung* 13(1984):111.

169. Kinney, "Trends in Research."

170. Lindsey, "Research."

Index

AACN. *See* American Association of Critical-Care Nurses (AACN)

AAI. *See* Atrial demand pacing (AAI)

Ablation
cryosurgery techniques, 181, *182*
future therapies, 181–182

ACE. *See* Angiotensin-converting enzyme (ACE)

Acebutolol, pharmacologic properties of, *170*

Actin myosin binding, *317*

Acting-out, 285

Activity. *See also* Exercise
breath control with, 358
diversional, for patients undergoing diagnostic procedures, 162
effect on heart rate after meals, 358
energy cost of, *71*
and exercise regimen nonadherence, 262
intolerance. *See* Activity intolerance
pacemakers responsive to, 245
pacing of, 359
regulation in AMI. *See* Activity regulation, in AMI
research studies, 497
as risk factor in CHD, 261
teaching guidelines, 357–361
upper extremity, 358

Activity intolerance
decreased cardiac output/impaired gas

exchange/knowledge deficit related to, 343–344
defined, 68–69
in survivors of sudden cardiac death, 151–152

Activity regulation, in AMI, 70
and activity intolerance defined, 68–69
bed rest, 69–70
and exercise response, 70–72
nursing care plan after AMI, *77*
research on
bathing, 72–74, *75*
implications from, 76–77
metabolic and cardiac work, *73*
positioning and transfer, 76
toileting, 74–75

Acute myocardial infarction (AMI)
activity regulation in, 68–77
assessment and nursing diagnoses in, 1, *2*
cardiac arrhythmias in, 67–68
complications of, *21*
coping ability in, 77–86
echocardiography, indications for, 36–37
morbidity and mortality associated with, 59
myocardial imaging, indications for, 44
myocardial oxygen consumption (MVO$_2$), 60–61
stressors and, *64*

Note: Pages appearing in italics indicate entries found in artwork.